LOGIC IN TEACHING

LOGIC IN TEACHING

Robert H. Ennis
Cornell University

PRENTICE-HALL, INC., *Englewood Cliffs, N.J.*

13-540096-1

Library of Congress Catalog Card Number: 69-17479

Current printing (last digit):
10 9 8 7 6 5 4 3 2 1

Printed in the United States of America

PRENTICE-HALL, INTERNATIONAL, INC., *London*
PRENTICE-HALL OF AUSTRALIA, PTY. LTD., *Sydney*
PRENTICE-HALL OF CANADA, LTD., *Toronto*
PRENTICE-HALL OF INDIA PRIVATE LTD., *New Delhi*
PRENTICE-HALL OF JAPAN, INC., *Tokyo*

Dedication

I dedicate this book to the man who gave me my first lessons in the logical aspects of teaching, Wayne E. Koontz; to my students, colleagues, teachers, and friends who have supplemented these lessons, including Gene Agre, Frederich Bauck, Mark Beach, Max Black, Hiram Bleeker, Donald Burrill, John Canfield, Keith Donnellan, Charles Dwyer, Gail Ennis, Gail Erpenbeck, Gary Fenstermacher, Mark Finkelstein, Paul Grice, James C. Haba, Kenneth B. Henderson, Robert Holtzman, David Howrey, Mauritz Johnson, Robert Kaplan, B. Paul Komisar, Leonard Linsky, David Lyons, C. J. B. Macmillan, James B. McClellan, Glenn Olsen, Rayananda Ratnaike, B. Othanel Smith, Edward L. Smith, Michael Stocker, Leonard F. Swift, Alice Thomas, Margaret Unsworth, Bruce Warner, Frederick L. Will, and Manuel Zax; and especially to my wife, Helen.

R. H. E.

Contents

CHAPTER 1 **Introduction** 1

Logical Teaching 1
Organization 2
Reading This Book 3

Part One
DEDUCTIVE LOGIC

CHAPTER 2 **Basic Ideas** 7

Some Basic Terms 8
Truth and Validity 9
Emphasis on Criteria 10
Types of Deductive Reasoning 11
Chapter Summary 12
COMPREHENSION SELF-TEST, 12

CHAPTER 3 **Sentence Reasoning** 13

Conditional Reasoning 13
The antecedent and the consequent, 14 The four basic forms, 14
COMPREHENSION SELF-TEST, 16
Order of premises, 18 The converse, 19 The contrapositive, 19 Double negation, 20

COMPREHENSION SELF-TEST, 20
Putting an argument in shape, 22 Using symbols to represent sentences, 25
COMPREHENSION SELF-TEST, 28
Necessary and/or sufficient conditions, 30 Only if, 33 The biconditional: if, and only if, 35 A conditional chain, 37
COMPREHENSION SELF-TEST, 40
Other Major Types of Sentence Reasoning 42
Reasoning using the conjunction 'and', 42 Negajunction: 'not both' reasoning, 43 Alternation: 'either-or' reasoning, 44
COMPREHENSION SELF-TEST, 47
⁘Greater Complexities 48
⁘Step-by-step organization of arguments, 49
COMPREHENSION SELF-TEST, 51
⁘Complex sentences, 51 ⁘Indirect proof, 55 ⁘Proving a conditional, 56
COMPREHENSION SELF-TEST, 57
⁘Material implication, 59
Chapter Summary 62

CHAPTER 4 Class Reasoning 64

A Simple Euler Circle System 66
General strategy, 68
COMPREHENSION SELF-TEST, 69
Invalidity, 70
COMPREHENSION SELF-TEST, 71
Negatives, 71 Transformations among negatives and positives, 72
COMPREHENSION SELF-TEST, 75
Partial inclusion, 76 Ambiguity of 'some', 76 'At least some', 77 'Some but not all', 78 Partial exclusion, 79
COMPREHENSION SELF-TEST, 80
Multiple premises, 81
COMPREHENSION SELF-TEST, 83
Other interpretation problems, 83 Extent of the predicate class, 84
COMPREHENSION SELF-TEST, 87
Combination of Class and Sentence Reasoning 87
Part-by-part use of the two systems, 88 Instantiation, 89
COMPREHENSION SELF-TEST, 90
Chapter Summary 91

CHAPTER 5 Practical Application of Deductive Logic 93

Looseness of Reasoning 93
Step 1: the shift into idealized form, 94 Step 2: judgment of validity, 96 Step 3: the shift from the conclusion back to the world of reality, 96 Summary, 100

Other Types of Deduction 100
Mathematics, 100 Alethic logic, 101 Deontic logic, 101
Epistemic logic, 101 Spatial logic, 101 Other types, 101
Examples of Practical Reasoning in More Detail 102
An Aspect of the frontier thesis, 102 Supply and demand, 108 Neoclassical English writing, 111 A body immersed in a fluid, 113
Chapter Summary 116
COMPREHENSION SELF-TEST, 117
Suggested Further Reading in Logic 118

Part Two

DEFINITION

Section A: functions of definitions

CHAPTER 6 **An Introduction to the Functions of Definitions** 123

The Definition of 'Definition' 124
An Argument Over the Meaning of a Word 126
COMPREHENSION SELF-TEST, 127

CHAPTER 7 **Stipulating a Meaning** 129

The Basic Move 129
Purpose, 130 Arbitrariness of word meanings, 130
Adhering to the stipulation, 131
Stipulation Maneuvers 131
The invitation to suppose, 132 Instruction about the nature of symbols and stipulation, 133 Handling suspected shifts in meaning, 136
The Uses and Abuses of Stipulative Definition 140
Uses, 140 Dangers and abuses of stipulation, 144
Chapter Summary 150
COMPREHENSION SELF-TEST, 150

CHAPTER 8 **Reporting Usage** 153

Turning to a Dictionary 154
A source of conventions, 154 Problems with dictionaries, 155
Established Usage 161
Determining usage, 162 Establishing the usage, 170
Advantages and Disadvantages of Reported Definitions 172
Chapter Summary 173
COMPREHENSION SELF-TEST, 174

CHAPTER 9 **Shades of Definition** 176

Suggesting a Program 177
A Proposal, 179 The value question, 179
Interpreting Basic Terms: 'A Good X', 'The Same X', and 'Different X's' 180
Defining a good X, 180 Defining the same X and different X's, 183
Marking Limits 186
Identifying 187
Describing 187
Chapter Summary 188
COMPREHENSION SELF-TEST, 188

Section B: definition forms

CHAPTER 10 **Equivalence Forms: Synonym and Classification Definition** 191

Synonym Definition 193
Classification Definition 194
What can be done, 195 Problems in framing classification definitions, 199 ⁘Conceptually mistaken extra material, 209 An appraisal of classification definition, 211
Chapter Summary 213
COMPREHENSION SELF-TEST, 214

CHAPTER 11 **Equivalence Forms: Equivalent-Expression Definition and Range Definition** 217

Equivalent-Expression Definition 217
Defining particles, 218 Defining relational terms, 218 Convenience, 219 A spurious advantage of equivalent-expression definition, 220 The suggestion of a context, 220 Helping a student in search of a category, 221
Range Definition 221
Retaining looseness, 223 The looseness inherent in most terms, 225
Chapter Summary 225
COMPREHENSION SELF-TEST, 225

CHAPTER 12 **Concrete Interpretation Forms** 228

The Need for Concrete Interpretation 228
The logical problem, 229 The 'etc.' definition, 232 The meaning of 'concrete interpretation', 233
Examples (and Nonexamples) 234
⁘Conditional Definition 236
The initial condition, 236 The relationship between an

observation and the term being defined, 237 Other examples, showing variations, 238 Qualifiers, 239 The utility of conditional definitions, 240 Some common misconceptions, 241

Chapter Summary 243

COMPREHENSION SELF-TEST, 243

CHAPTER 13 **Definition: An Overview** 245

Function 246

Form 248

COMPREHENSION SELF-TEST, 250

Suggested Further Reading on the Topic, Definition 251

Part Three

EXPLANATION

CHAPTER 14 **Basic Kinds of Explanation** 255

Descriptive Explanation 255

Cues 257

Interpretive explanation, 258 Descriptive explanation, 258 Reason-giving explanation, 259

COMPREHENSION SELF-TEST, 260

Basic Features of a Reason-Giving Explanation 261

Completing explanations, 261 Applying evaluation criteria, 263

COMPREHENSION SELF-TEST, 264

Chapter Summary 265

CHAPTER 15 **Gap-Filling** 267

Reasons for Not Always Directly Securing Completion by the Explainer 269

Inferring the Gap-Filler 271

Rules of thumb, 271 Summary, 273

The Focus of an Explanation 273

Necessity 274

Chapter Summary 276

COMPREHENSION SELF-TEST, 277

CHAPTER 16 **Introductory Evaluation and Probing of Reason-Giving Explanations** 280

The Interdependence of Completion and Evaluation 281

Truth 281

Qualifications, 282 Probing, 283

COMPREHENSION SELF-TEST, 286

Proper Level of Sophistication 286
Noncircularity 288
The importance of context, 288 Probing: level and circularity, 291
COMPREHENSION SELF-TEST, 291
Proper Function and Type 292
Two functions of reason-giving explanations: accounting for and justifying, 292 Proper type of explanation, 296 Nondeductive justification explanation, 297 Summary, 297
COMPREHENSION SELF-TEST, 298
Chapter Summary 298

CHAPTER 17 ∴ **Types of Explanation** 300

Analytic and Synthetic Statements 300
Analytic statements, 300 Synthetic statements, 302 Applying the distinction between analytic and synthetic statements, 302 The categorization of explanations, 304
COMPREHENSION SELF-TEST, 304
Analytic Explanations 306
Empirical Explanations 308
Causal Explanation 309
Causal language, 310 Gap-filling and probing a causal explanation, 318 Asking for a causal explanation, 320 Fields in which causal explanation is used, 320
COMPREHENSION SELF-TEST, 321
Reason-for-Acting Explanation 322
Gap-filling, probing, and evaluating, 323 Requesting a reason-for-acting explanation, 326 Historical explanation, 326 Summary, 327
COMPREHENSION SELF-TEST, 328
Value and Obligation Explanation 328
Gap-filling, 329 Evaluation of value and obligation explanations, 330 Asking for value and obligation explanations, 331 Probing value and obligation explanations, 333 Summary, 333
COMPREHENSION SELF-TEST, 334
Loose Ends 335
Chapter Summary 336

CHAPTER 18 ∴ **Testability/Applicability** 339

Testability 339
Practical testability, 340 Conceptual testability, 340
Applicability 353
Chapter Summary 355
COMPREHENSION SELF-TEST, 356

CHAPTER 19 **Explanation: An Overview by Way of Application** 358

A Dialogue 358
Analysis 362
Chapter Summary 368
Suggested Further Reading About Explanation 369

Part Four
JUSTIFICATION

CHAPTER 20 **Early Stages of Justification Decisions** 375

Justification and Truth 375
What the Statement Is 376
Vagueness and ambiguity, 377 Types of statements, 379 Summary, 383
COMPREHENSION SELF-TEST, 383
The Reasons 384
Observation Statements 384
Observations and conclusions from observations, 384 Reliability of observation statements: criteria, 388 Summary, 390
COMPREHENSION SELF-TEST, 391
Statements by Alleged Authorities 392
Ambiguity of 'authority', 392 Criteria for authorities, 392 Nature of the statement, 395 Summary, 396
Assumptions 396
Explicit assumptions, 397 Implicit assumptions, 398 Summary, 401
COMPREHENSION SELF-TEST, 402
Chapter Summary 403

CHAPTER 21 **Value Statements** 405

Value Questions and Statements Delimited 407
Strategies 408
Obtain the reasons, 408 Check the facts, 408 Apply a general principle, 409 Examine the consequences in detail, 410 Take other general goals into account, 411 Summary, 412
Relativism 412
Cultural relativism, 412 Personal relativism, 416 Absolutism vs. relativism, 417 The zoning case, 418
Justification 419
Chapter Summary 420
COMPREHENSION SELF-TEST, 421

CHAPTER 22 **Material Inferences** 423

Generalizing 424

Types of generalizations, 424 Justification of generalizations, 426 Summary, 434

COMPREHENSION SELF-TEST, 435

Inferring to Explanations 435

Criteria, 436 Causation, 441 Summary, 445

COMPREHENSION SELF-TEST, 446

Chapter Summary 446

CHAPTER 23 **Justification: Two Cases** 448

Iago's Character 449

Brown vs. Board of Education (1954) 456

Chapter Summary 461

COMPREHENSION SELF-TEST, 461

Suggested Further Reading about Justification 465

APPENDIX A **Selected Reading about the Logical Aspects of Teaching** 469

APPENDIX B **Selected Texts from Which Students Might Study about Clear and Critical Thinking** 472

Answers 474

Index 506

LOGIC IN TEACHING

CHAPTER 1

Introduction

Although books dealing with the psychological aspects of teaching abound in the education market-place, there is none that deals other than superficially with the logical moves that continuously occur in the classroom. Almost totally neglected in pedagogical literature are definitions, explanations, and justifications, which form the basic structural units in any teaching area consisting of other than simple mechanical skills. But perhaps more important than their forming the basic structural units is the fact that definition, explanation, and justification make the difference between confusion and rigor in the classroom.

Logical Teaching

This book is concerned with rigor of instruction and learning at all levels and in all subject-matter areas where rigor is possible. Its treatment of definition, explanation, and justification ultimately reduces to a treatment of the broad logical aspects of how to talk and think in the classroom. Although psychological aspects, such as motivating and controlling students, are extremely important and should temper the application of principles of logical teaching, they are not the subject matter of this book. Please be absolutely clear that although I do not continuously say so, I believe that logical teaching can only be effective if the proper psychological moves are made also. All the rigor you can muster is of no value if no one is paying attention. On the other hand, having the attention and enthusiasm of students is to no avail if the result of your teaching is confusion and error.

Neglect of the logical aspects of teaching in the pedagogical literature is due partially to the heavy (though needed) emphasis this century on motivation, interest, growth, and readiness. But it is also due to the fact that much of the essential philosophical spade work has not been done until recently. Although much philosophical work remains to be done (requiring some important points in this book to remain unsettled), a great deal has been accomplished in the various phases of the analytic movement in this century, thereby enabling a teacher to do far more justice to the logical side of his teaching than ordinarily occurs.

Organization

Of the four major parts to this book, the first may be regarded as a prerequisite to the others, because it treats elementary deductive logic, which is used in the other three parts. Because deductive logic is a necessary tool for the rest, and because some readers will already know enough deductive logic, most of Part I is a concentrated treatment of deductive logic alone, neglecting for the time being the problems of teaching. I hope that those who do not know elementary deductive logic will bear with me in my attempt to explain it—without mentioning its relevance to teaching. However, Chapter 5 (the last one in Part I) does contain advice about a problem of teaching: the problem of evaluating practical deductive arguments.

Part II examines the problems of formulating, probing, and evaluating definitions which occur in various kinds of classroom situations, paying attention to both the form of the definition and the purpose it is supposed to serve in the context in which it is used. Two of the basic assumptions of this book are thus illustrated: one, that there are various legitimate approaches to defining, explaining, and justifying; and two, that the context is extremely important in judging which is the best approach. The actual application of these assumptions is sometimes difficult.

Part III treats explanation, with emphasis on those explanations that serve as answers to the question, "Why?" A third general assumption of this book is that the frequent use of the question, "Why?", is very helpful in probing, evaluating, and promoting understanding. Part III treats the problems that one faces in dealing with attempts to answer this question.

Justifications of observation statements, of inductive hypotheses, generalizations, and theories, and of value statements are the topics of Part IV. Teachers are continually faced with the problem of justifying their statements, and also with the problem of teaching their students to evaluate attempts at justification. The fourth general assumption is that ways exist to justify statements other than by deducing them from already justified statements.

Reading This Book

If you have prior knowledge of elementary deductive logic, you will be able to omit most of Part I. Chapter 5 should not be neglected even if you do know logic, because it treats a topic which you presumably have not studied, the practical application of deductive logic.

Chapters 2–4, those dealing formally with deductive logic, are practically self-teaching when used in conjunction with the answers to the deductive logic exercises, answers to which appear at the end of the book. It is essential that you do these and the other exercises in the book (labeled "Comprehension Self-Tests"). Exceptions are those exercises which are busy work to you, but even if most of the exercises in a series strike you as unnecessary practice, you should always do the last one or two, because these often contain a new twist or an especially difficult application. Advanced discussion questions which call for essays commenting on other published logical material are provided for those who find the topics interesting in themselves, but answering them is not essential to grasping the content of this book at the level at which it is written.

There is no specified formal prerequisite for reading this book, although an understanding and knowledge of the material you teach is necessary. More important than any specific formal prerequisite is a willingness to look at things in a new way and an interest in rigorous instruction. Furthermore you must be ready on occasion to put aside such problems as control and motivation, and to devote full attention to logical problems, because the logical ideas here are in many cases difficult.

The incorporation of these logical ideas in your spontaneous classroom behavior does not come immediately, but only with carefully considered practice. Some of this considered practice can be hypothetical: For example imagine yourself to be the teacher in the classroom dialogues and ask what you would do and why. Some longer dialogues are found in Chapters 6, 13, and 19. To get the flavor of the practical problems to which a teacher should be able to apply the principles of this book, you might look at those dialogues now. A second kind of helpful hypothetical practice is to try to imagine the application of each principle you find in this book to situations and content with which you are familiar. But actual classroom practice is necessary as well.

Throughout you will find sections that are labeled '⁘'. Generally this material is more difficult than material not so designated, and it can be omitted without destroying continuity. If the symbol '⁘' appears at the beginning of a paragraph, then that paragraph is ⁘ material; if it appears before the title to a chapter, the whole chapter is ⁘ material; and if it appears only at the beginning of a phrase, the phrase (but not necessarily the next phrase) is ⁘ material. Some will find this material the most interesting and challenging in the book, while others will find it a bit too difficult for the amount of time they have to spend on this enterprise. Anyone who wants to pursue some of the problems beyond the ⁘ material is referred to the suggested further reading at the end of each part and to the advanced discussion questions.

About every topic in this book, as in all books, there is more to be said. For the sake of simplification I have omitted many qualifications—an unavoidable practice. In addition, as I said before, some philosophical spade work is still to be done. The justification of value judgments and the nature and status of concepts are two examples of topics needing considerable further work. Fortunately, on most of the topics in this book the work has been done in broad outline at least, enabling us to secure considerable guidance. So let us proceed, content, as Aristotle suggests, "to indicate the truth roughly and in outline, and . . . to look for precision in each class just so far as the nature of the subject admits."*

* *Nicomachaen Ethics* (Ross translation), Book I, chap. iii.

Part One

DEDUCTIVE LOGIC

CHAPTER 2

Basic Ideas

This book first attempts to present a simple account of common forms of deductive reasoning by describing these forms and suggesting ways of judging whether the reasoning is satisfactory. We will not consider other types of reasoning, except as contrasts to deductive reasoning. But one should remember that there are other types of reasoning, and that the ways of judging deductive reasoning do not directly apply to these other types.

DEDUCTIVE REASONING is that sort of reasoning in which the conclusion is supposed to follow necessarily from what is given. It is this fact that distinguishes deductive reasoning from all other types of reasoning. If the conclusion is supposed to follow necessarily, then we apply the standards of deductive reasoning.

Should you be in doubt about the meaning of 'follows necessarily', then the following might help—if your doubt is an unsophisticated one. If, on the other hand, your doubt is a sophisticated one, then the following interpretation will not help; for purposes of your study of this book, you already understand well enough the concept, *necessarily follows*. Here is the interpretation:

> To say "A conclusion FOLLOWS NECESSARILY from what is given" is to say: "If you accept what is given, you are thereby automatically committed to accepting the conclusion; there is no way out." It is also to say: "You would be contradicting yourself to accept what is given and deny the conclusion."

Now to say that a conclusion follows necessarily does not mean that you **do** accept what is given, nor that you **do** accept this conclusion. It merely means that **IF** you accept what is given, you are committed inescapably to the conclusion.

Some Basic Terms

In order to make it easier to talk about deductive reasoning, we will use certain basic terms with which you may already be familiar, but which are somtimes confusing if not explained. These terms are 'premise', 'argument', and 'validity'.

The PREMISES are what is given. An ARGUMENT is a set of one or more premises and a conclusion such that the conclusion is supposed to follow from the premises. Here is an argument which contains two premises and a conclusion: the solid line separates the premises from the conclusion. The premises are above the line and the conclusion below.

Example 2-1
If Mike is a dog, then Mike is an animal.
Mike is a dog.
___
Mike is an animal.

The argument consists of all three statements. The premises (or what is given) are the first two statements, and the conclusion is the last one.

The word 'VALID' will here be used to apply to arguments in which the conclusion follows necessarily from the premises and the word 'INVALID' for those in which the conclusion does **not** necessarily follow. This is standard usage in the field of logic. However, there is a danger in this usage; often, perfectly good arguments (which are thus valid in the ordinary sense of 'valid') are invalid in our technical sense. Unfortunately some people have the inclination, after judging such an argument invalid in this technical sense, to then claim that the argument is invalid in the ordinary sense of the term 'invalid', which is to say that the argument is defective. Many arguments are invalid in this technical sense but ought to be judged by criteria other than those for deductive arguments.

If we apply the criteria for validity (in the technical sense) to such arguments, declare the argument invalid, and then interpret our declaration according to the ordinary sense of 'invalid', we find ourselves rejecting good arguments. In our technical sense of 'valid', most cases of reasoning to generalizations in science are invalid, because the conclusions do not follow necessarily from the evidence. But we must not thereby conclude that such reasoning is defective. It just is not deductive reasoning. So please keep in mind the fact that 'valid' is being used in a technical sense in deductive logic, and that the standards of validity that you will learn do not apply to non-deductive arguments.*

Truth and Validity

In this technical sense of 'validity', judgments about the truth of a conclusion are quite distinct from judgments about the validity of the argument. A valid argument can have a false conclusion and one or more false premises. Here is an example:

Example 2-2
If the piece of iron is in the beaker containing water, then it is floating on the water.
The piece of iron is in the beaker containing water.
____
It is floating on the water.

The first premise is false; the conclusion is false; but the argument **is valid**, because the conclusion follows necessarily from the premises.

Of course a valid argument can have true premises and a true conclusion. For example:

Example 2-3
If the piece of iron is in the beaker of water, it is at the bottom.
The piece of iron is in the beaker of water.
____
It is at the bottom.

Again the conclusion follows necessarily from the premises.

Perhaps you do not realize that an argument can be valid and the conclusions can be true, even though one or more of the premises are false. Here is an illustration:

Example 2-4
Bananas are magnets.
Magnets are fruit.
____
Bananas are fruit.

The argument is valid; both premises are false, but the conclusion is true. The moral to be learned from the preceding example is this: the fact that

* Valuable discussions of this point may be found in F. L. Will's "Generalization and Evidence," an essay in Max Black's *Philosophical Analysis* (Ithaca, N.Y.: Cornell University Press, 1950), pp. 384–413; and in J. O. Urmson's "Some Questions Concerning Validity," an essay in Antony Flew's *Essays in Conceptual Analysis* (London: Macmillan & Co. Ltd., 1956), pp. 120–133.

a premise is false, even though the argument be valid, does not by itself prove that the conclusion is false.

But if the premises are true and the argument is valid, then the conclusion must be true. It is this fact that we often exploit when using deduction in a proof. Generally, we show or assume the premises to be true; we show the argument to be valid; and thus we show that the conclusion must be true. Another way to use this fact is to show that an argument is valid and that the conclusion is false. From this we know that at least one of the premises is false. This second procedure is called indirect proof. This fact about validity can also be used to show an argument to be invalid; if we show the premises to be true and the conclusion to be false, then we have shown the argument to be invalid; for a valid argument cannot have true premises and a false conclusion.

The above discussion of the relationship between truth and validity can be summarized in the following charts. The first chart shows the possible combinations for valid arguments:

CHART 2-1 Combinations for Valid Arguments

	True premises	One or more false premises
True conclusion	Possible	Possible
False conclusion	Not possible	Possible

The second chart shows the possible combinations for invalid arguments:

CHART 2-2 Combinations for Invalid Arguments

	True premises	One or more false premises
True conclusion	Possible	Possible
False conclusion	Possible	Possible

Thus all combinations but one are possible. The impossible combination is seen in the first chart: a valid argument having true premises cannot have a false conclusion.

Emphasis on Criteria

This is not a book on psychology and does not attempt to describe what goes on in people's minds when they reason. Instead we shall concentrate on the results of such processes, whatever they might be. When speaking of reasoning, I shall be referring to that which can be produced in words and laid out in the form of an argument, and shall not be referring to the process of producing arguments.

I shall emphasize the **criteria** (standards of judgment) to be used in evaluating arguments, rather than the **process** of reasoning. This emphasis will be dominant, even though I shall try to give you some hints about how to go about discovering conclusions that do and do not follow necessarily, and shall give hints about how to make judgments more efficiently. I am assuming that guided practice in applying the proper criteria will result in higher quality and more efficient processes of producing arguments.

Types of Deductive Reasoning

No one has ever successfully categorized all types of deductive reasoning, so I cannot give you a total picture into which the material in this book fits. But I can say that the kinds of deductive reasoning that you will encounter here are very commonly found in all walks of life.

Roughly following a fairly traditional division in the field of logic, I have divided the deductive reasoning to be considered into two types: sentence reasoning and class reasoning, so named because of the basic units involved, the sentence and the class. In sentence reasoning, the basic sentence units appear and reappear in the argument, but they do not change in meaning (although they might be rephrased for stylistic purposes). Sentences thus are the building blocks of sentence reasoning.

Example 2-1 above is sentence reasoning. Each of these sentences appears twice in the argument:

Mike is a dog.
Mike is an animal.

In their first appearance they are connected using the words 'if' and 'then' and form a more complicated sentence. In the second appearance, each stands by itself. Here again is the complete argument:

If Mike is a dog, then Mike is an animal.
Mike is a dog.
____
Mike is an animal.

You can see that the two basic sentences are the units of that argument.

If the first premise (the 'if-then' premise) reads 'he is an animal' instead of 'Mike is an animal', this does not make any difference; the result is still sentence reasoning, even though one of the sentences is changed in wording for reasons of style:

Example 2-5
If Mike is a dog, then he is an animal.
Mike is a dog.

Mike is an animal.

In that argument, we treat 'he is an animal' and 'Mike is an animal' as the same sentence, so in effect the sentences do not change in meaning throughout.

Example 2-4 above is class reasoning. It contains no sentence which appears and reappears unchanged. It instead focuses on three classes and their relationships. The classes are *bananas, magnets,* and *fruit.* Here again is the complete argument, which, you will remember, is valid, though the premises are both false:

Bananas are magnets.
Magnets are fruit.

Bananas are fruit.

Chapter Summary

By now you should have at least a rough understanding of what a deductive argument is, and be familiar with the following terms: 'follows necessarily', 'premise', 'conclusion', 'argument', 'valid', and 'deductive reasoning'. The distinction between truth and validity should be clear to you. You should also know that if the argument is valid and the premises are true, then the conclusion must be true.

COMPREHENSION SELF-TEST

True or false? If the statement is false, change a crucial term (or terms) to make it true.

2–1. Deductive reasoning is that kind of reasoning in which the conclusion is supposed to follow necessarily from the premises.

2–2. If a conclusion follows necessarily, then it would be contradictory to deny the premises while asserting the conclusion.

2–3. To say that an argument is valid (in the ordinary sense of 'valid') is to say that the conclusion follows necessarily from the premises.

Answer the following:

2–4. What combination of truth and validity is impossible?

2–5. Define 'argument'.

CHAPTER 3

Sentence Reasoning

Conditional Reasoning

One very important kind of sentence reasoning is conditional reasoning, so named because it involves the use of conditions, which are often introduced by the word 'if'. This example, which you have seen before is conditional reasoning:

Example 3-1
If Mike is a dog, then Mike is an animal.
Mike is a dog.

Mike is an animal.

The first premise is a CONDITIONAL. It gives a condition (Mike's being a dog) which, according to that premise, would make Mike an animal. Since this reasoning makes use of a conditional, it is called CONDITIONAL REASONING.

Let us look very carefully at that first premise. Note what it tells us and what it does not tell us. Presumably you are agreed that it gives a condition (Mike's being a dog) which, according to the premise, would make Mike an animal. But it does **not** say that Mike's being an animal is a condition which would make Mike a dog. By substituting 'Mike is an animal' as the second premise,* it would not be established as the conclusion that Mike

* If Mike is a dog, then Mike is an animal.
Mike is an animal.

Mike is a dog.

is a dog. On the other hand, given the first premise and that Mike **is** a dog, it **would** thereby be established that Mike is an animal. The first premise enables us to go from Mike's being a dog to Mike's being an animal, but it does not enable us to go from Mike's being an animal to Mike's being a dog, because it does not say that Mike's being an animal is a **condition** which would necessarily make Mike a dog.

The antecedent and the consequent

Before we say more about what that first premise would enable us to do, two technical terms should be introduced, terms which are used to label the two sentences which make up a conditional statement. The sentence which follows the word 'if' is called the ANTECEDENT. In the above example, 'Mike is a dog' is the antecedent. The sentence which follows the word 'then' is called the CONSEQUENT. In the above example, 'Mike is an animal' is the consequent.

There are several different ways of writing the conditional statement, but the antecedent and the consequent do not change. For example, the word 'then' can often be omitted:

If Mike is a dog, Mike is an animal.

The order can be reversed (so long as the word 'if' stays with the antecedent):

Mike is an animal, if Mike is a dog.

In both examples 'Mike is a dog' is the antecedent, and 'Mike is an animal' is the consequent. Other ways of writing the conditional will be presented later when we deal with the expression 'only if'.

The four basic forms

In the language of antecedents and consequents, we can restate what was said about what that first premise enables us to do. Given a conditional statement (containing an antecedent and a consequent), establishment of the antecedent enables us to conclude the consequent; but establishment of the consequent does not thereby enable us to conclude the antecedent.

Example 3-1 then is a valid argument. It contains a conditional statement as a premise. Another premise consists of the affirmation of the antecedent. The conclusion consists of the consequent. This is a common form of valid deductive argument and is called AFFIRMING THE ANTECEDENT.

The following argument is somewhat different. Is it valid?

Example 3-2
If Mike is a dog, then Mike is an animal.
Mike is an animal.

Mike is a dog.

You will remember that, given the first premise as it stands, Mike's being an animal does not force us to conclude that Mike is a dog. This argument is a case of AFFIRMING THE CONSEQUENT. It is called this because the second premise affirms the consequent of the conditional statement of the first premise. It is an invalid form of argument; for establishing the consequent does not enable us to conclude the antecedent.

So far you have seen two different arguments making use of the same conditional first premise. The first, which proceeded by way of affirmation of the antecedent, is valid. The second, which affirmed the consequent, is invalid.

Consider now this argument, which exemplifies a third form:

Example 3-3
If Mike is a dog, then Mike is an animal.
Mike is not a dog.

Mike is not an animal.

This is not a valid argument for the conclusion does not necessarily follow. The first premise says that Mike's being a dog would make him an animal, but it does not say that his **not** being a dog would make him a nonanimal. He might be a fox. He thus might still be an animal, even though he is not a dog.

This third form of argument, as you might have already guessed, is called DENYING THE ANTECEDENT. It is an invalid form. Given a conditional statement, the denial of the antecedent does not by itself force us to conclude the denial of the consequent.

The following example (3-4) illustrates a fourth argument form. Many people are confused by this type of argument. As you read it over, see if you can tell intuitively whether the conclusion follows necessarily:

Example 3-4
If Mike is a dog, then Mike is an animal.
Mike is not an animal.

Mike is not a dog.

In this example the second premise is the denial of the consequent of the conditional premise. This form of argument is called DENYING THE CONSEQUENT. It is a valid form. Given the denial of the consequent, the appropriate conclusion is the denial of the antecedent. When faced with such arguments, some people do not immediately see that they are valid—that is, that the conclusion does necessarily follow. If you are such a person, then read this next passage carefully.

The first premise tells us that Mike's being a dog would make him an animal. But, if he is not an animal, then he could not possibly be a dog, because **if** he were a dog, then he **would** be an animal. Since the second premise tells us that he is not an animal, we are forced to conclude that he is not a dog. Thus the argument is valid.

If the explanation in the preceding paragraph does not satisfy you, then make up some simple examples of your own. These examples should consist of a conditional statement and a denial of its consequent. After thinking about these examples, you will see that you are forced by the denial of the consequent to deny the antecedent also. Keep thinking about them until you do see this.

Here is a chart which summarizes what has been said about the four basic forms of conditional reasoning. See that you **understand** and not merely memorize it.

CHART 3-1 Validity of the Four Basic Forms of Conditional Reasoning

	Antecedent	Consequent
Affirming	Valid	Invalid
Denying	Invalid	Valid

In summary, affirming the antecedent and denying the consequent are valid forms of argument. That is, an appropriate conclusion **follows necessarily** when the antecedent is affirmed, or when the consequent is denied. On the other hand, affirming the consequent and denying the antecedent are invalid forms.

COMPREHENSION SELF-TEST

For each of the following conditionals, decide which part is the antecedent and which is the consequent. Indicate this by underlining the antecedent once and the consequent twice. Do not allow your underlining to extend to the logical connectives, 'if' and 'then'. The first one is a sample.

3–1. If <u>Mike is a dog,</u> then <u>Mike is an animal.</u>

3–2. Mike is an animal, if Mike is a dog.

3–3. If Mary knows the rules of punctuation, then she did well on the test today.

3–4. If John is nearsighted, his eyes are defective.

3–5. John's eyes are defective, if he is nearsighted.

3–6. If in that sentence the word 'going' is a gerund, then it functions like a noun.

3–7. Mike, if he is a dog, is an animal.

3–8. The soil in your field is sweet, if Jones added the truckload of calcium carbonate to it.

3–9. If the President is not going to veto this bill, the Senate will not stand by him in his efforts to get his tax legislation passed.

3–10. Angles A and B, if they are alternate interior angles of parallel lines, are equal.

3–11. Joan's room has light-colored walls, if it is well lighted.

3–12. If the music room does not have light-colored walls, then it is not well lighted.

3–13. The livingroom, if Mrs. Smith likes it, is well lighted.

Here is a set of arguments. With each argument do two things. State the form of the argument and tell whether the argument is valid or invalid. The first is a sample. Remember that the premises are the sentences above the line, the conclusion the sentence below the line.

3–14. If Mary knows the rules of punctuation, then she did well on the test today.
Mary did not do well on the test today.

Mary does not know the rules of punctuation.
(Answer: Denying the Consequent. Valid.)

3–15. If John is nearsighted, then his eyes are defective.
His eyes are defective.

John is nearsighted.

3–16. John's eyes are defective, if he is nearsighted.
John is nearsighted.

John's eyes are defective.

3–17. If in that sentence the word 'going' is a gerund, then it functions like a noun.
It does not function like a noun (in that sentence).

In that sentence the word 'going' is not a gerund.

3–18. The soil in your field is sweet, if Jones added the truckload of calcium carbonate to it.
The soil in your field is sweet.

He added that truckload of calcium carbonate.

3–19. If the President is not going to veto this bill, then the Senate will not stand by him in his efforts to get his tax legislation passed.
The President is not going to veto this bill.

The Senate will not stand by him in his efforts to get his tax legislation passed.

3–20. Angles A and B, if they are alternate interior angles of parallel lines, are equal.
Angles A and B are not alternate interior angles of parallel lines.

They are not equal.

In this next set of problems you will be given two premises and you will be asked to supply the valid conclusion, if any. More specifically, do these two things:

a. If there is a valid conclusion other than the repetition of one of the premises, supply it. Otherwise write 'Nothing follows necessarily'.
b. State the form involved. You might well abbreviate.

Avoid doing these exercises mechanically. Make sure that you see and feel the answers that you give. The first two are samples.

3–21. Premises:
Joan's room has light-colored walls, if it is well lighted.
Joan's room is well lighted.
(Answer: Joan's room has light-colored walls. Affirming the antecedent.)

3–22. Premises:
If the sewing room is not well lighted, then it has dark-colored walls.
The sewing room is well lighted.
(Answer: Nothing necessarily follows. Denying the antecedent.)

3–23. Premises:
If the sewing room is well lighted, then it has light-colored walls.
The sewing room is well lighted.

3–24. Premises:
If the sewing room has light-colored walls, then it is well lighted.
The sewing room is not well lighted.

3–25. Premises:
The kitchen is not well lighted, if it has dark-colored walls.
The kitchen has dark-colored walls.

3–26. Premises:
If my new office has dark-colored walls, then it is not well lighted.
It is well lighted.

3–27. Premises:
If the music room does not have light-colored walls, then it is not well lighted.
The music room is well lighted.

3–28. Premises: (There are two forms combined here. Identify each. For your conclusion, make use of all of the premises.)
If the livingroom has dark-colored walls, then it is not well lighted.
The livingroom is well lighted, if Mrs. Smith likes it.
Mrs. Smith likes the livingroom.

Order of premises

Although the examples so far considered have presented the conditional statement as the first premise, the order of the premises can be changed without affecting the logical status of the argument. And you will remember that the order of the parts in the conditional statement can be changed, as long as the word 'if' remains attached to the same part. So the following example is logically the same as Example 3-1, even though the conditional statement appears second, and even though the antecedent of the conditional statement is the second half of that statement. Example 3-5 is thus in the valid form, affirming the antecedent:

Example 3-5
Mike is a dog.
Mike is an animal, if Mike is a dog.

Mike is an animal.

The converse

One change in particular is not automatically permissable, namely the **exchange** of the antecedent and consequent in a conditional statement. For instance, the following two conditional statements are different in meaning and you do not have the right to substitute one for the other:

If Mike is a dog, then Mike is an animal.
If Mike is an animal, then Mike is a dog.

The first says that Mike's being a dog would enable you to conclude that he is an animal, but it does **not** say that his being an animal would enable you to conclude that he is a dog. This last is just what the second sentence says, so the two are different in meaning.

These two sentences are called CONVERSES of each other. The converse of a conditional statement is the same statement with the antecedent and consequent exchanged. An important rule to remember, which should be obvious from an inspection of these two converses, is that the converse does not follow necessarily from a conditional statement.

The contrapositive

Consider this pair of conditionals:

If Mike is a dog, then Mike is an animal.
If Mike is not an animal, then Mike is not a dog.

Do they say the same thing? For our purposes in deductive logic, they do, but this is sometimes difficult to see.

Suppose we know that the first conditional is true. That is, suppose we know that if Mike is a dog, then he is an animal. From this we can tell that if he is not an animal, then he is not a dog. (The denial of the consequent requires the denial of the antecedent.) So the second conditional follows necessarily from the first.

Does the first follow necessarily from the second? Suppose we know that if Mike is not an animal, then Mike is not a dog. Suppose we also know that Mike is a dog. Then he would have to be an animal, for if he were not, then he would not be a dog. Thus from the second conditional the first also follows necessarily.

Since each of these follows necessarily from the other, for our purposes, they can be treated as meaning the same thing. We can substitute each for the other as a proper step in an argument.

In terms of antecedents and consequents, you should note that each of these can be formed by exchanging and denying the antecedent and consequent of the other. The antecedent of the second conditional is the denial of the consequent of the first, and the consequent of the second conditional is the denial of the antecedent of the first. Going the other way (from the second to the first) involves the principle of double negation, so a word about it is in order.

Double negation

The principle of double negation is this: Two negatives make a positive. (Actually you have already used this principle in doing Exercise 3-27.) Although there are difficulties with it, for purposes of elementary logic this principle is a good one. If you were to say that Mike is **not** a dog and someone else were to say, "That's false", then he in effect would be saying that Mike **is** a dog. His denial of your negative statement amounts to the positive statement, "Mike is a dog."

So a denial of the consequent of the second of the above pair of contrapositives amounts to the antecedent of the first of the pair. Similarly the denial of the antecedent of the second of the pair is the consequent of the first. So you can see that a contrapositive can be formed by denying and exchanging the antecedent and consequent of a conditional statement. Since contrapositives are essentially equivalent in meaning, this formation of contrapositives can be useful in deductive proofs, because they can be substituted for each other. This application of the principle of double negation to the formation of contrapositives is but one of its many uses.

COMPREHENSION SELF-TEST

True or false? If the statement is false, change a crucial term (or terms) to make it true.

3–29. A conditional statement is equivalent to its converse.

3–30. A conditional statement is equivalent to its contrapositive.

3–31. For purposes of elementary logic, two negatives make a positive.

3–32. For purposes of elementary logic the order of the premises with respect to each other sometimes affects the validity of the argument.

Short-answer Questions. **3–33** through **3–45.** Take each of the conditionals listed in 3–1 through 3–13 and write out the converse and contrapositive of each. As an example, 3–33 is done below:

SAMPLE: 3–33

a. Converse: If Mike is an animal, then Mike is a dog.
b. Contrapositive. If Mike is not an animal, then Mike is not a dog.

Here is a set of arguments. In each case judge the validity of the argument and indicate your reason. The first two are samples. Some of them serve to review earlier sections.

3–46. If the majority leader is against the bill, then Senator Jones is against it.

If Senator Jones is not against the bill, then the majority leader is not against it.
(Answer: Valid. Contraposition.)

3–47. Senator Jones is against the bill, if the majority leader is against it.

If Senator Jones is against the bill, then the majority leader is against it.
(Answer: Invalid. Conversion.)

3–48. If Senator Jones is against the bill, then the Commissioner testified vigorously in its favor.
It is false that Senator Jones is not against the bill.

The Commissioner testified vigorously in its favor.

3–49. If the object of the preposition is written correctly, then it is in the objective case.
The object of that preposition is in the objective case.

The object of that preposition is written correctly.

3–50. Emilia thinks Iago to be essentially good throughout most of *Othello.*
If Iago is really supposed to be a melodramatic villain, then Emilia would not think Iago to be essentially good throughout the play.

Iago is not really supposed to be a melodramatic villain.

3–51. The question mark is not inside the quotation marks.
The quoted material is not a question, if the question mark is not inside the quotation marks.

The quoted material is not a question.

3–52. There is no dot between the two numbers.
Those two numbers should be multiplied together, if there is a dot between them.

The numbers should not be multiplied together.

3–53. If the litmus did not turn red, then the liquid is not an acid.

If the liquid is an acid, the litmus turned red.

3–54. If there are no leaves on the tree, then it is dead.

If the tree is dead, then there are no leaves on it.

3–55. If the power was not increased, the plane did not gain altitude.

If the plane gained altitude, the power was increased.

3–56. Smith cannot lift the elephant, if the mechanical advantage is not over thirty.

If the mechanical advantage is over thirty, then Smith can lift the elephant.

Putting an argument in shape

Unfortunately, arguments that we meet while doing the work of the world do not come served up to us in the tidy form of those you have been considering. Here is an example of something that is in a form that you might meet:

Example 3-6

I am convinced that the lighting in the livingroom is satisfactory. There can be no doubt about this, for it follows from the following reasons: If the lighting in the livingroom is indirect, then Mrs. Smith will like it. And one thing is clear—Mrs. Smith is a fair judge. If she does not like it, then it is clearly unsatisfactory. This morning she said that the lighting in the livingroom is indirect. My conclusion is therefore obvious.

The above argument, when taken as a whole, is fairly complicated. Let us rearrange it so it is in a more workable form. The first thing to do is to locate the conclusion. In this case the conclusion is **indicated** by the first sentence, but it is not exactly the first sentence; for the speaker is not trying to prove that he is convinced of something, but rather that the thing of which he is convinced is so. What is the thing of which he is convinced? The following:

The lighting in the livingroom is satisfactory.

When the argument is put in form, this sentence, the conclusion, will appear last. We can leave the next sentence ("There can be no doubt about this, for it follows from the following reasons:") out of the completed argument.

This sentence merely shows that the first sentence is the conclusion and that the reasons (premises) come next. It does not contribute to the content of the argument.

The third sentence provides us with one of the premises. It is the first one to write down:

> If the lighting in the livingroom is indirect, then Mrs. Smith will like it.

The fourth sentence, which claims that Mrs. Smith is a fair judge, does not in this case play a clear role in the argument, although it adds to the flavor and might be treated as a vague statement of the next premise, which appears as the following sentence, the fifth:

> If she does not like it, then it is clearly unsatisfactory.

To return to the fourth sentence, a question might be raised about whether it implies the converse of the fifth sentence. That is, someone might suggest that it implies the following:

> If it is clearly unsatisfactory, then she will not like it.

This is a difficult but important matter to settle, because (to look ahead) adopting this interpretation of the fourth sentence will make the argument valid; the argument is invalid if we reject this converse as a legitimate interpretation. Must it be that a **fair** judge will not like unsatisfactory things? If you say yes, then you are committed to the converse as an interpretation.

The important thing to see here is that there is sometimes a choice to be made in the interpretation of the premises, and that the validity of an argument sometimes depends upon the decision. In this particular case I shall proceed as if this converse interpretation is incorrect, because I believe that fair judges can correctly judge things unsatisfactory, even if such judges do personally like the unsatisfactory things. Mrs. Smith, though a fair judge, might personally like the lighting in the livingroom, although by the accepted standards of lighting, she might properly judge it unsatisfactory. But this is a point that might be argued against by reasonable men, so a legitimate problem of interpretation exists.

In solving such problems of interpretation, one usually does well to err on the side of caution. Then you can say to the person offering the argument something like the following:

> Look, the conclusion does not follow necessarily if we interpret the premises strictly. Would you care to add this explicitly as a premise: "If it is unsatisfactory, then she will not like it"? If not, then the conclusion does not follow necessarily. If so, then you must be confident of the truth of this additional premise, and be able to back it up.

Having been cautious in the interpretation, you can force a person to choose between having: (1) an invalid argument, and (2) another premise that he must be able to defend.

The sixth sentence in the original argument gives us the third premise, although again we must make an adjustment, because the statement holds only that she **said** that the lighting was indirect, rather than explicitly stating, "the lighting in the livingroom is indirect." So we must adjust the premise (on the assumption that what she said is true) and write it as follows:

The lighting in the livingroom is indirect.

Again there is room for dispute about whether to adjust that sentence. In this case we will proceed as if this is a legitimate adjustment, but we do want to note the possibility of error of interpretation.

Given the above interpretations let us rewrite the argument in better form:

Example 3-7

If the lighting in the livingroom is indirect, then Mrs. Smith will like it.
If she does not like it, then it is clearly unsatisfactory.
The lighting in the livingroom is indirect.

The lighting in the livingroom is satisfactory.

Now what do you do? You inspect the premises to see if there is a valid way of going to the conclusion. Inspection shows that the first and third premises can be taken as a separate argument which will yield a subconclusion that is related to the first premise. This subargument is valid because the antecedent is affirmed. It looks as follows:

Example 3-8

If the lighting in the livingroom is indirect, then Mrs. Smith will like it.
The lighting in the livingroom is indirect.

Mrs. Smith will like it.

Does this subconclusion help in arriving at a valid argument yielding the main conclusion? Let us combine this subconclusion with the original second premise in a separate argument:

Example 3-9

If she does not like it, then it is clearly unsatisfactory.
She will like it (or she does like it).

It is satisfactory.

This second subargument (Example 3-9) is invalid because it makes use of the denial of the antecedent.

An inspection of the three premises shows that there is no other plausible way to combine the three premises, so we must judge the entire argument invalid. If one part of a complex argument is invalid, then the entire argument is invalid, since the conclusion does not follow necessarily from the premises.

In this section on putting an argument into shape, you have seen that the conclusion might very well not appear at the end of the argument; that the premises might not be in the most convenient order; that there is sometimes material that is not part of the substance of the argument; that decisions must often be made about the interpretation of the premises; and that these decisions should be made conservatively. The order in which to do these things is roughly that in which they were done for the example, but do not follow this advice rigidly. Sometimes a decision on an earlier step (for example, what the conclusion really is) might be affected by a decision on a later step (for example, the validity of the argument). We might decide that a particular person could not have been foolish enough to make the simple mistake about validity that we would have to attribute to him if the originally selected conclusion were the one he actually intended. So we might change our decision about what the conclusion of the argument really is on the basis of a judgment about validity.

Using symbols to represent sentences

Often it is convenient to use an arrow to represent the if-then relationship and to use single letters to stand for the sentences of sentence reasoning. The letters, 'p', 'q', 'r', etc., are conventional symbols.

Let 'p' stand for 'Mike is a dog', and let 'q' stand for 'Mike is an animal'. Then the conditional, 'If Mike is a dog, then Mike is an animal', can be represented as follows:

$$p \longrightarrow q$$

Note that this is quite different from the converse, 'If Mike is an animal, then Mike is a dog', which would be represented this way (assuming the same assignment of letters):

$$q \longrightarrow p$$

Thus '$q \longrightarrow p$' does not necessarily follow from '$p \longrightarrow q$'; and, of course, '$p \longrightarrow q$' does not necessarily follow from '$q \longrightarrow p$'.

The contrapositive of the original, 'If Mike is not an animal, then Mike is not a dog', would be symbolized as follows (assuming the same assignment of letters):

$$\text{not } q \longrightarrow \text{not } p$$

The conditional, 'not $q \longrightarrow$ not p', follows necessarily from '$p \longrightarrow q$', and vice versa, since contrapositives follow necessarily from each other. But be careful, because 'not $p \longrightarrow$ not q' does not necessarily follow from '$p \longrightarrow q$'; or, in other words, the falsity of the antecedent does not imply the falsity of the consequent. This fact is another way of stating the principle that denial of the antecedent is an invalid form.

In symbolized form the antecedent always appears first and the arrow always points to the right. This is so even if the antecedent appears last in the premise as written. Remember that the following two statements are the same:

If Mike is a dog, then Mike is an animal.
Mike is an animal, if Mike is a dog.

Assuming the previous assignment of letters, each of these two statements would be symbolized as follows:

$$p \longrightarrow q$$

They have the same antecedent and the same consequent. The order of appearance is antecedent, arrow, and consequent.

Let us consider the simple argument of Example 3-1 in order to see the procedures to follow in symbolizing an argument and judging its validity. That argument looked like this:

If Mike is a dog, then Mike is an animal.
Mike is a dog.

Mike is an animal.

The first thing to do is to assign the letters, making sure that no one letter is assigned to two different sentences, unless they differ only by virtue of the fact that one is the negation of the other, in which case you would assign the same letter. (If, for example, you had assigned the letter 'p' to represent the sentence 'Mike is a dog', then 'Mike is not a dog' would be symbolized as 'not p'.) Make sure that no extra letters are unnecessarily assigned. Write out your assignment of symbols to represent the different sentences in the argument:

Let 'p' = 'Mike is a dog'
Let 'q' = 'Mike is an animal'

Sometimes you can save time (but you must be careful) by simply writing the letters over the first appearance of each sentence involved, as shown here:

If $\overbrace{\text{Mike is a dog}}^{p}$, then $\overbrace{\text{Mike is an animal}}^{q}$.

The next step is to write out the entire argument in symbolic form, as follows:

Example 3-10

Premises:

$p \longrightarrow q$

p

Conclusion:

q

You should recognize that form as the valid form, **affirmation of the antecedent.**

Symbolization of the other three basic forms looks as follows:

Affirming the consequent	Denying the antecedent	Denying the consequent
$p \longrightarrow q$	$p \longrightarrow q$	$p \longrightarrow q$
q	not p	not q
p	not q	not p
(An invalid form)	(An invalid form)	(A valid form)

The argument that was discussed in the previous section, "Putting an Argument in Shape", would be symbolized as follows:

Example 3-11

Let 'p' = 'the lighting in the livingroom is indirect'
Let 'q' = 'Mrs. Smith will like it'
Let 'r' = 'the lighting in the livingroom is unsatisfactory'

$p \longrightarrow q$

not $q \longrightarrow r$

p

---

not r

An inspection of the symbolized argument shows that the third premise affirms the antecedent of the first premise, validly producing 'q'. But 'q' is the denial of the antecedent of the second premise, so the move to a denial of the consequent of the second premise, if that move is based upon 'q', is not a valid move.

Thinking of the argument as having two stages may be clearer. The first yields an intermediate conclusion:

Stage 1.

$p \longrightarrow q$

p

---

q

Valid. Affirming the Antecedent.

In the second stage the intermediate conclusion ('q') is used as one of the premises:

Stage 2.
not $q \longrightarrow r$
q
———
not r
Invalid. Denial of the Antecedent.

So the whole argument is judged invalid.

The reason for introducing the use of symbols should now be apparent to you. Symbols make the basic structure of arguments easier to see. With practice, a glance at the premises of a symbolized argument will reveal its validity or invalidity.

COMPREHENSION SELF-TEST

True or false? If the statement is false, change a crucial term (or terms) to make it true.

3–57. The order in which the premises appear does not affect the validity of the argument.

3–58. The last sentence of an argument in its natural state is always the conclusion.

3–59. An arrow pointing to the right is used to symbolize the conditional relationship.

3–60. '$q \longrightarrow p$' does not necessarily follow from '$p \longrightarrow q$'.

3–61. '$q \longrightarrow p$' does not necessarily follow from 'not $p \longrightarrow$ not q'.

Arguments to Judge. Here is a set of arguments. On a separate sheet of paper, symbolize them and put them in shape; then judge whether each is valid, explaining why you judge as you do. The first is done as a sample:

3–62. The two numbers obviously should not be multiplied together. Think of it this way. You realize that the two numbers should be multiplied together, if there is a dot between them. But there is no dot between those two numbers. So they should not be multiplied together.
Let 'p' = 'there is a dot between the two numbers'
Let 'q' = 'the two numbers should be multiplied together'
$p \longrightarrow q$
not p
———
not q
(Answer: The argument is invalid because the antecedent is denied.)

3–63. Jones must be at least thirty-five years of age. I know this because he is President; and if he is President, then he must be at least thirty-five years of age.

3–64. If this figure is an equilateral triangle, then it has all sides equal. I conclude that it cannot be an equilateral triangle, since not all sides are equal.

3–65. If these two plants are not closely related, then they cannot be crossed. However, they are closely related. Therefore they can be crossed.

3–66. No photosynthesis can be occurring in this plant. That this is so can be seen from the fact that it is not getting any light whatsoever. Photosynthesis cannot occur in this plant, if there is no light reaching it.

3–67. "Macbeth shall never vanquished be until
Great Birnam wood to high Dunsinane hill
Shall come against him."
"That will never be."
(You must state the conclusion yourself.)

3–68. You may fly now, because the beacon is not lit. If it were lit, then you would not be permitted to fly.

3–69. I know that Senator Franklin will oppose the tax legislation. Furthermore if he opposes it, then Senator Inkling will vote in favor of it. Senator Inkling and Senator Franklin do not get along well together. If Senator Inkling votes in favor of that legislation, my wife, a loyal member of the League of Women Voters, will be busy all next year trying to get her friends and acquaintances to help defeat him at the polls. And if she and her friends are occupied with the League all next year, we won't be eating very good dinners around here for a while. That figures, doesn't it? So now you know why I expect dinners that are less than the best next year.

3–70. If the Board of Education suspends young Brown from school, then it will be punishing him for refusing to salute the flag on religious grounds. And if it does that, it will be acting unconstitutionally. Since the Board will not act unconstitutionally, we can be sure that the Board will not suspend young Brown.

Argument Forms. Using 'p' to represent the antecedent and 'q' to represent the consequent, fill in the gaps in the following representation of the **four** basic forms of conditional argument:

The following argument form is an example of Affirming the . . . . (**3–71**)

Premises:

. . . . (**3–72**)

p

Conclusion:

. . . . (**3–73**)

Is the above a valid or invalid form? (**3–74**)

The following argument form is an example of Denying the . . . . (**3–75**)

Premises:

$p \longrightarrow q$

. . . . (**3–76**)

Conclusion:

. . . . (**3–77**)

The above is a valid form.

The following argument is an example of . . . . (**3–78**) the . . . . (**3–79**)

Premises:

$p \longrightarrow q$

q

Conclusion:

. . . . (**3–80**)

Is the above a valid or invalid form? (**3–81**)

The following argument is an example of . . . . (**3–82**) the . . . . (**3–83**)

Premises:

$p \longrightarrow q$

. . . . (**3–84**)

Conclusion:

. . . . (**3–85**)

Is the above a valid or invalid form? (**3–86**)

Necessary and/or sufficient conditions

You might find, as many do, that it is often convenient, when thinking about an argument, to think in terms of necessary and/or sufficient conditions. Consider the basic example:

If Mike is a dog, then Mike is an animal.

The proposition that Mike is a dog is claimed by this statement to be a sufficient condition for the truth of the proposition that Mike is an animal. In other words, Mike's being a dog is claimed to be a sufficient condition for Mike's being an animal. If we know that Mike is a dog, then, according to that conditional, we have sufficient evidence to justify saying that he is an animal.

On the other hand, his being a dog is not held by the conditional statement to be a necessary condition for his being an animal. The statement allows that he be a fox. Thus he might be an animal without being a dog. Thus being a dog is not held to be a necessary condition for his being an animal.

But his being an animal **is** held to be a necessary condition for his being a dog. He cannot be a dog without being an animal as well, according to the statement. The truth of the proposition that Mike is an animal is held to be a necessary condition for the truth of the proposition that he is a dog.

And, of course, his being an animal is not held to be a sufficient condition for his being a dog. It is only held to be a necessary condition.

Summarizing symbolically, given $p \longrightarrow q$, the truth of p is a sufficient, but not necessary, condition for the truth of q; and the truth of q is a necessary, but not sufficient, condition for the truth of p. If the truth of one statement is a sufficient condition for the truth of another, then the truth of the other is a necessary condition for the truth of the first, and vice versa.

Let us apply the language of necessary and sufficient conditions to one of the recent exercises, 3-64:

> If this figure is an equilateral triangle, then it has all sides equal. I conclude that it cannot be an equilateral triangle, since not all sides are equal.
>
> Let 'p' be 'this figure is an equilateral triangle'
> Let 'q' be 'it has all sides equal'

Symbolically the argument looks like this:

Example 3-12

$p \longrightarrow q$
not q

---

not p (valid; denying the consequent)

One might talk about the valid argument of the above example in the following manner:

> Having all sides equal is given as a necessary condition for the figure's being an equilateral triangle. Since that necessary condition does not hold, it is not an equilateral triangle.

Symbolically, the talk might go like this:

> q is a necessary condition for p. q is false. Hence p is false.

The language of necessary and sufficient conditions is an aid to quick insight into logical arguments, because of the conceptual economy that it effects. Look again at Exercise 3-69, which is reproduced below:

> I know that Senator Franklin will oppose the tax legislation. Furthermore if he opposes it, then Senator Inkling will vote in favor of it. Senator Inkling and Senator Franklin do not get along well together. If Senator Inkling votes in favor of that legislation, my wife, a loyal member of the League of Women Voters, will be busy all next year trying to get her friends and acquaintances to help defeat him at the polls. And if she and her friends are occupied with the League all next year, we won't be eating very good dinners around here for a while. That figures, doesn't it? So now you know why I expect dinners that are less than the best next year.

Thinking about this example in the language of necessary and sufficient conditions, one might come up with the following brief analysis, which is correct:

> Each condition given is a sufficient condition for the next. Since the first condition is affirmed (this occurs in the first sentence), each succeeding condition follows necessarily. Hence the conclusion, "Dinners will not be very good around here for a while", follows necessarily.

Although the use of the language of necessary and sufficient conditions is an aid to quick insight into the structure of an argument, two precautions should be noted: (1) the lack of precision of the language as often used, and (2) the distinction between the necessary and sufficient conditions of sentence reasoning and the necessary and sufficient conditions of causal relationships. For our purposes the second precaution is more important than the first, but we shall take them in order.

1. Note that a strict substitution into the statement, "q is a necessary condition for p" (one of the symbolic statements made earlier), does not make sense:

> This figure has all sides equal is a necessary condition for this figure is an equilateral triangle.

In order to be precise there are basically two alternatives: (a) incorporate the sentences into broader units, as in the following example:

> That this figure has all sides equal is a necessary condition for the truth of the proposition, 'This figure is an equilateral triangle'.

(b) alternatively and less awkwardly, use gerunds instead of sentences to indicate the conditions:

> Having all sides equal is a necessary condition for this figure's being an equilateral triangle.

The use of gerunds, however, results in the new problem of transition from one manner of speaking to the other, a problem that matters in rigorous treatments of logic.

The standards of rigor alluded to here can generally be ignored when the language of necessary and sufficient conditions is used as an aid to insight. If, however, one wants to state a rigorous proof using this language, of course the standards cannot be ignored.

2. The second precaution deals with the distinction between causal language and general necessary and sufficient condition language. CAUSALLY NECESSARY AND SUFFICIENT CONDITIONS are events (or states of being) such that, respectively, another event (or state of being) cannot occur without the condition, and another event (or state of being) must occur if the condition occurs.

Here is an expression of a causally necessary condition:

> The presence of oxygen was a necessary condition for the burning of the building.

Here is an expression of a causally sufficient condition:

> Knocking out that block of wood was a sufficient condition for the collapse of the building.

Causally necessary and sufficient conditions can often be expressed in 'if-then' language:

> If the building burned, then oxygen was present.
> If that block of wood was knocked out, then the building collapsed.

The point is that causally necessary and sufficient conditions are only one kind of necessary and sufficient conditions. Each type of such conditions requires a different kind of proof for its establishment and is applied in its own special ways. Hence it is important to know with which kind one is dealing.

Speaking of causally necessary and sufficient conditions makes sense only when the thing mentioned as a condition precedes or accompanies the thing for which it is a condition. Hence, if you tried to locate a necessary condition in the above example, "If that block of wood was knocked out, then the building collapsed", you probably had difficulty. It would seem odd to say that the collapse of the building was a necessary condition for the knocking out of the block of wood, as that would imply that the collapse of the building preceded the knocking out of the block of wood, since we are dealing with a causal relationship.

However, the truth of the statement that the building collapsed is a necessary condition for the truth of the statement that the block of wood was knocked out, according to the original conditional. For if the building did not collapse, then according to the original, the block of wood could not have been knocked out. Thus, as long as we speak strictly in terms of sentence-reasoning necessary and sufficient conditions, 'p' in '$p \longrightarrow q$' always is a sufficient condition and 'q' always is a necessary condition. But, if we start speaking in terms of events or states of affairs, then we sometimes end up with odd results if the two items are causally connected.

Only if

So far no examples have contained the words, 'only if', because this phrase is rather different from 'if' in meaning and a danger of confusion exists. But it is time to face the problem. Consider these two statements and decide whether they mean the same:

1. Mike is a dog, only if Mike is an animal.
2. If Mike is a dog, then Mike is an animal.

As you can see, there are differences and similarities. Superficially a difference is that the word 'if' is connected with different sentences in the two statements. It is connected with 'Mike is an animal' in the first (but remember that the word 'only' is there also), whereas it is connected with 'Mike is a dog' in the second.

An important difference, so far as the use of the total statements is concerned, is that the first seems to give us a test for telling whether Mike is a dog, while the second seems to give a test for telling whether Mike is an animal. Thus we would tend to use the first in contexts in which we are trying to determine whether he is a dog, and the second in contexts in which we are trying to tell whether he is an animal.

In spite of these differences, the two statements are essentially the same for purposes of deductive logic. In each case Mike's being an animal is held to be a necessary condition for his being a dog; and his being a dog is held to be a sufficient condition for his being an animal.

Each of the statements implies the other. Suppose we know the first to be true. Then if Mike is a dog, he must be an animal; for if he is not an animal, he could not be a dog. The first does say that he is a dog **only if** he is an animal.

Working the other way, suppose we know that the second of the two statements is true. By contraposition you know from this that if Mike is not an animal, then he cannot be a dog. Or in other words he is a dog **only if** he is an animal.

Thus for our purposes the following two forms are logically equivalent:

If p, then q.
p, only if q.

Furthermore the following ones, which simply change the order, are equivalent to the above two and to each other:

q, if p.
Only if q, p.

And all of these are represented by the following elementary symbol group:

$$p \longrightarrow q$$

The definition of 'conditional' should now be extended to cover statements containing the phrase 'only if', since for our purposes such statements can be treated by the rules of conditional reasoning.

The biconditional: if, and only if

Sometimes the relationship between two sentences is such that each implies the other. For example the following two sentences imply each other:

> Jones is a bachelor.
> Jones is a man who is not yet married.

Since the first implies the second, we might want to say the following:

> If Jones is a bachelor, then Jones is a man who is not yet married.

And we might want to say the converse, since it is also true:

> If Jones is a man who is not yet married, then Jones is a bachelor.

The relationship of mutual implication can be written in one statement, a BICONDITIONAL, which makes use of the phrase, 'if, and only if':

> Jones is a bachelor, if, and only if, Jones is a man who is not yet married.

The following is a longer, but logically equivalent, way to write this:

> If Jones is a bachelor, then Jones is a man who is not yet married; and if Jones is a man who is not yet married, then Jones is a bachelor.

The advantage of using the phrase, 'if, and only if', should be evident; it saves time and space.

That the biconditional does state the relationship of mutual implication can be seen from the following discussion, which makes use of symbols in order to save time and space:

> Let 'p' = 'Jones is a bachelor'
> Let 'q' = 'Jones is a man who is not yet married'

Then we are entitled to say that if p, then q, and this entitles us to say the following:

> p, only if q.

We are also entitled to say the converse, 'If q, then p'. And we are entitled to reverse the order, leaving the 'if' with the same sentence, 'q':

> p, if q.

So we have 'p, only if q' and 'p, if q'. Thus we have the biconditional:

p, if, and only if, q,

which means the same as:

p is a necessary and sufficient condition for q,

and also the same as:

q is a necessary and sufficient condition for p.

For convenience the biconditional is represented by a double arrow, as in the following:

$p \longleftrightarrow q$

Given a biconditional, '$p \longleftrightarrow q$', you are entitled to make use of either of the converse relationships between 'p' and 'q'. That is, you can derive each of the following from it:

$p \longrightarrow q$
$q \longrightarrow p$

And since each of these has a derivable contrapositive, the following can also be derived from the original biconditional:

not $q \longrightarrow$ not p
not $p \longrightarrow$ not q

Furthermore by an argument similar to the one that showed that '$p \longrightarrow q$' and '$q \longrightarrow p$' together give '$p \longleftrightarrow q$', we can show that the above two contrapositives give the following biconditional:

not $p \longleftrightarrow$ not q

This also follows from the original biconditional, since it follows from things that followed from the original biconditional.

In summary, given a biconditional and the affirmation of either part, the other part is implied. Furthermore, given the denial of either part, the denial of the other part is implied. Each part is a necessary and sufficient condition for the other part. Lastly, the phrase, 'if, and only if', is an accepted way of indicating the biconditional and is conveniently symbolized by a double arrow.

This treatment of biconditionals opens the door for a qualification to the earlier discussion of the rule that the antecedent does not necessarily follow from the affirmation of the consequent. Consider this argument:

Example 3-13
If Jones is a bachelor, then Jones is a man who is not yet married.
Jones is a man who is not yet married.

Jones is a bachelor.

This argument is in the invalid form, affirming the consequent. But the conclusion does follow necessarily from the premises. In fact, it follows necessarily from the second premise alone. This is so because of the definitional relationship between the second premise and the conclusion. To say that Jones is a man who is not yet married is to say that Jones is a bachelor, so each follows necessarily from the other. We have this problem whenever there is a biconditional relationship that is true by definition. Our rule can be restated, however:

> The antecedent does not necessarily follow from the affirmation of the consequent as a result of its being the consequent, although the antecedent might follow from the affirmation of the consequent for other reasons.

Similarly the rule about the denial of the antecedent might be revised to take care of a like difficulty:

> The denial of the consequent does not necessarily follow from the denial of the antecedent as a result of its being the antecedent, although the denial of the consequent might follow from the denial of the antecedent for other reasons.

These qualifications are made because people sometimes are confused by this problem. There is no point to your learning the above revised rules. Just understand them and the reason for them.

A conditional chain

Another basic form of conditional reasoning appears in the following example:

Example 3-14
If Mike barks, then Mike is a dog.
If Mike is a dog, then Mike is an animal.

If Mike barks, then Mike is an animal.

Note that in this example the conclusion itself is a conditional statement, and both premises are conditional statements. Note also that the argument is valid. One who accepts the premises is thereby committed to the conlusion. The form of the above argument can be shown as follows:

Example 3-15

Let 'p' = 'Mike barks'
Let 'q' = 'Mike is a dog'
Let 'r' = 'Mike is an animal'

$$\begin{array}{l} p \longrightarrow q \\ q \longrightarrow r \\ \hline p \longrightarrow r \end{array}$$

This is a valid form of argument. Call it a CONDITIONAL CHAIN.

Similarly, the following is also a conditional chain, and valid argument form.

$$\begin{array}{l} p \longrightarrow q \\ r \longrightarrow p \\ \hline r \longrightarrow q \end{array}$$

You may find it easier to recognize this as a conditional chain, if the order of the premises is reversed:

$$\begin{array}{l} r \longrightarrow p \\ p \longrightarrow q \\ \hline r \longrightarrow q \end{array}$$

Note carefully the relationship between the parts, because there are series of conditionals that are invalid. The two conditional premises have a part in common, which serves as the antecedent of one and the consequent of the other. The remaining antecedent and consequent are put together as antecedent and consequent **respectively** of the conclusion.

Now examine these invalid arguments and see how they depart from the above criteria:

Example 3-16

$$\begin{array}{l} p \longrightarrow q \\ q \longrightarrow r \\ \hline r \longrightarrow p \end{array}$$

Example 3-17

$$\begin{array}{l} p \longrightarrow q \\ r \longrightarrow q \\ \hline p \longrightarrow r \end{array}$$

Example 3-18

$$\begin{array}{l} p \longrightarrow q \\ \text{not } q \longrightarrow r \\ \hline p \longrightarrow r \text{ (or } p \longrightarrow \text{not } r) \end{array}$$

In Example 3-16 the conclusion is the converse of the conclusion in Example 3-15, which is the valid argument. The trouble with Example 3-16 is that the antecedent and consequent of the conclusion do not come from the right places in the premises. Example 3-16 would be valid if its conclusion were the converse of the presented conclusion.

In example 3-17 the common part is the consequent of both premises, so even if the converse of the given conclusion had been presented the argument would still be invalid. And of course the trouble with Example 3-18 is that no common part is shared by the two premises as antecedent in one and consequent in the other. The consequent of the first premise is 'q' while the antecedent of the second premise is different. It is 'not q'. Furthermore substituting contrapositives will not solve the problem. Try it and see what happens.

Sometimes, however, it is helpful to substitute contrapositives in order to establish the form of the conditional chain. Consider this argument:

Example 3-19

If the dish of sweet and sour pork contains sufficient meat, then it is expensive.
If the dish of sweet and sour pork contains several pieces of sweet pineapple, then it is not expensive.

If the dish of sweet and sour pork contains sufficient meat, then it does not contain several pieces of sweet pineapple.

First let us symbolize the argument.

Example 3-20

Let 'p' = 'the dish of sweet and sour pork contains sufficient meat'
Let 'q' = 'it is expensive'
Let 'r' = the dish of sweet and sour pork contains several pieces of sweet pineapple'

$p \longrightarrow q$
$r \longrightarrow \text{not } q$

$p \longrightarrow \text{not } r$

Now this argument is not in the form of the conditional chain. It could be, if the consequent of one premise were the antecedent of another. And by substituting the contrapositive of either premise, we do achieve that result. Substituting the contrapositive of the second premise ('$q \longrightarrow \text{not } r$') for the second premise that appears ('$r \longrightarrow \text{not } q$'), we have the following argument:

Example 3-21

$p \longrightarrow q$
$q \longrightarrow \text{not } r$

$p \longrightarrow \text{not } r$

Since 'q' is the consequent of the first premise and the antecedent of the next one, we can validly conclude '$p \longrightarrow \text{not } r$', which is the conclusion of the original argument.

Instead we could have substituted the contrapositive of the first premise—with this result, also valid:

Example 3-22

$\text{not } q \longrightarrow \text{not } p$
$r \longrightarrow \text{not } q$

$r \longrightarrow \text{not } p$

In this case the conclusion is the contrapositive of the original. But since we can substitute contrapositives for each other, we can substitute the original conclusion for the one that appears in Example 3-22.

Although conditional chains do not usually have many steps, they can be longer. The following is a valid argument:

Example 3-23

If the nail had not been lost, the shoe would not have been lost.
If the shoe had not been lost, the horse would not have been lost.
If the horse had not been lost, the man would not have been lost.
If the man had not been lost, the battle would not have been lost.
If the battle had not been lost, the kingdom would not have been lost.

If the nail had not been lost, the kingdom would not have been lost.

Glossing over the difference between 'had not been' and 'would not have been', symbols, assigned in the obvious way, give the following form:

Example 3-24

$p \longrightarrow q$
$q \longrightarrow r$
$r \longrightarrow s$
$s \longrightarrow t$
$t \longrightarrow v$

$p \longrightarrow v$

That this is valid can be seen by noting the following steps:

1. The first two premises give us '$p \longrightarrow r$'.
2. That result ('$p \longrightarrow r$') together with the third premise gives '$p \longrightarrow s$'.
3. That result ('$p \longrightarrow s$') together with the fourth premise gives '$p \longrightarrow t$'.
4. That result ('$p \longrightarrow t$') together with the fifth premise gives the conclusion, '$p \longrightarrow v$'.

To summarize, a basic valid form, the conditional chain, contains two conditional premises with a common part as antecedent in one and consequent in the other. The other parts of the premises form the conclusion in such a way that each of these parts preserves its original status—as antecedent or consequent. Secondly, in deciding whether an argument is equivalent to this form, it is sometimes helpful to substitute contrapositives for existing conditionals. And lastly longer conditional chains can be constructed out of the basic unit described above.

COMPREHENSION SELF-TEST

True or false? If the statement is false, change a crucial term (or terms) to make it true.

3–87. 'If p, then q' is symbolized the same way as 'p, only if q'.

3–88. 'If p, then q' is for the purposes of logic treated the same as 'p, only if q'.

3–89. 'q, if p' is symbolized in the same way as 'q, only if p'.

3–90. An arrow pointing in both directions is used to symbolize the biconditional relationship.

3–91. The following is a valid form of argument:

$$\begin{array}{l} q \rightarrow p \\ p \\ \hline q \end{array}$$

3–92. The denial of either side of a biconditional implies the denial of the other.

3–93. A pair of conditional premises and a conditional conclusion make a valid argument, if the premises share a common antecedent.

3–94. If q is a necessary condition for p, then p is a sufficient condition for q.

3–95. Given that p is a sufficient condition for q, the falsity of q implies the falsity of p.

Arguments to Judge. Here is a set of arguments. Symbolize them and put them in shape; then judge whether each is valid, explaining why you judge as you do.

3–96. Your report is satisfactory only if every word is spelled correctly. Since your report is unsatisfactory, the obvious conclusion is that not every word is spelled correctly.

3–97. Triangles A and B are congruent, if, and only if, they have two angles and the included side equal. But they are not congruent. Therefore, they do not have two angles and the included side equal.

3–98. If the lighting in the livingroom is not indirect, then it is not satisfactory. And if it is not satisfactory, then Mrs. Smith will not like it. So, if it is not indirect, then Mrs. Smith will not like it.

3–99. If Shakespeare had intended Polonius to be a comic figure, then he would not have made Polonius the father of two tragic characters. But Polonius was made the father of two tragic characters, Laertes and Ophelia. Hence Polonius was not supposed to be a comic figure.

3–100. If Governor Jones signed the letter, then serious damage to his chances for the Vice-presidency was permitted by his advisers. Such damage would have been permitted by them, only if they did not really want him to be the candidate for the Vice-presidency. Therefore, the Governor's advisors did not really want him to be such a candidate, if he actually signed the letter.

3–101. If the ceiling is not one thousand feet or above, you may not fly. If, and only if, the sequence report reads less than '10', the ceiling is below one thousand feet, since the last two zeros are always omitted. The sequence report, however, reads more than '10'. The conclusion is obvious: You may fly.

3–102. Evidently Joe is spelling words as they sound to him. I conclude this from the following facts: Only if he spells words as they sound to him will he spell 'trough' as 'troff'. If he spells words as they sound to him, he will spell 'didn't' as 'ding'. Now he never spells 'trough' as 'troff', but he always spells 'didn't' as 'ding'. See?

3–103. Plants X and Y can be crossed only if they are closely related. If their immediate parents have produced hybrids in the past, then X and Y cannot be crossed. Since their immediate parents have never produced hybrids, plants X and Y are closely related.

Necessary and Sufficient Conditions. **3–104 to 3–111.**

Take each conditional statement from each of the above arguments (3–96 to 3–103) and express it in the language of necessary and sufficient conditions. For convenience you may use the symbolization already assigned.

Other Major Types of Sentence Reasoning

Before examining some of the more difficult maneuvers in dealing with sentence reasoning, let us look at a few other basic types of statements that are made up of sentence units, and some elementary types of arguments in which they play a role. The words that are used to connect the unit sentences will be called 'LOGICAL OPERATORS'. 'If' and 'then', for example, are logical operators. Others are 'and', 'not both', 'either . . . , or'. It is these to which we now turn.

Reasoning using the conjunction 'and'

Very little needs to be said about conjunction. When we have a sentence of the form 'p and q', we can operate as if we had two sentences, one being 'p' and the other being 'q'. Each of these is called a conjunct, because they are joined by the conjunction 'and'. For example the following is a valid argument:

Example 3-25

If this object sinks in water, then it has a specific gravity greater than 1.
This object is made of brass and it sinks in water.

This object has a specific gravity greater than 1.

When we treat the two conjuncts of the second premise independently, we can isolate the second conjunct and treat it as affirming the antecedent.

Conversely two separate assertions can be conjoined at our convenience. Here is an example of a valid argument in which this is the case:

Example 3-26

If Jones is a man and Jones is not yet married, then Jones is a bachelor.
Jones is a man.
Jones is not yet married.

Jones is a bachelor.

In this case the antecedent consists of the conjunction of the last two premises, so we can treat the antecedent as having been affirmed when each of its conjuncts is separately affirmed. Incidentally, the antecedent would **not** have been affirmed had only one of the conjuncts been asserted.

Two conjuncts can be reordered without changing the meaning. In other words, '*p* and *q*' can be translated into '*q* and *p*'. This is in direct contrast to if-then sentences, where a reordering of sentences vitally affects the meaning.

Negajunction: 'not-both' reasoning

Sometimes one of the premises in an argument contains the words, 'not' and 'both'. Here is an example:

Example 3-27
It is not true that 'smearing' is both a noun and a verb in that sentence.
'Smearing' is a verb in that sentence.
———————————————
'Smearing' is not a noun in that sentence.

The first premise can be viewed as two sentences, each of which I shall call a NEGAJUNCT, joined by logical operators. Representing these sentences by '*p*' and '*q*' as follows:

Let '*p*' = '"Smearing" is a noun in that sentence'
Let '*q*' = '"Smearing" is a verb in that sentence'

the premise can be symbolized as follows:

Not both *p* and *q*,

which might be rewritten in English as follows:

Not both of these are true: (a) 'Smearing' is a noun in that sentence, and (b) 'Smearing' is a verb in that sentence.

In this last formulation, which is equivalent to the first premise—although a bit longer, the sentences under consideration appear explicitly. Whenever you can make such a translation to something of the form of this last formulation, you are involved in NEGAJUNCTION.

The following form, AFFIRMING THE NEGAJUNCT, is valid:

Not both *p* and *q*
p
———————
not *q*

The assertion of one of the negajuncts in 'not-both' reasoning requires the denial of the remaining negajunct. So, if the second premise were 'q', then the conclusion 'not p' could be validly drawn.

The following form, however, is **invalid**:

Not both p and q
Not p
―――――――――
q

It is an invalid form because the premise says that it is not the case that both sentences are **true**; but this leaves open the possibility that they are both false, and it leaves open the possibility that one is true and the other false. Only one thing is ruled out: their both being true.

As with conjunction, the two sentences in the not-both relationship are interchangeable. That is, 'not both p and q' means the same as 'not both q and p'.*

This form, negajunction, is not translatable into a conditional relationship, although a negajunction is implied by a conditional relationship. That is,

'$p \longrightarrow q$' does imply 'Not both p and not q.'

Why? Think of it this way. Suppose 'If p, then q' is true; then one thing which we cannot have is 'p' true and 'q' false, for we know that if 'p' is true, then 'q' must be also true.

The reason that the converse ('not both p and not q' implies '$p \longrightarrow q$') does not hold is a difficult topic. Those who are interested may read something about it later in this chapter under the topic, "⁘ Material Implication".

*Alternation: 'either–or' reasoning***

Sentences which are joined by the logical operators, 'either' and 'or', are called alternations. Here are two examples:

This phenolphthalein solution will be pink, or it will be colorless.
Either Mark Twain intended to satirize local customs, or he was a foolish man.

* A qualification might be added here, and it might well have been added in the discussion of the interchangeability of conjuncts: This interchangeability is ordinarily a safe assumption, but it does ignore the time sequence in accord with which conjuncts and disjuncts are often arranged.

** A common practice among logicians nowadays is to reserve the title 'disjunction' for 'either-or' sentences, to which I assign the word 'alternation'. The terminology that I have adopted, because I think it to be more clear, is that used by Morris Cohen and Ernest Nagel in *An Introduction to Logic and Scientific Method* (New York: Harcourt, Brace and Company, 1934), and by Peter Strawson, *Introduction to Logical Theory* (London: Methuen and Company, Ltd., 1952).

Taking the second sentence, let us construct an argument making use of it:

Example 3-28
Either Mark Twain intended to satirize local customs, or he was a foolish man.
Mark Twain clearly was not a foolish man.

Therefore, Mark Twain intended to satirize local customs.

This argument can be symbolized as follows:

Let 'p' = 'Mark Twain intended to satirize local customs'
Let 'q' = 'he was a foolish man'

p or q
not q

---

p

The argument is valid. If he was not a foolish man, then according to the first premise, he must have intended to satirize local customs. The above symbolization represents a valid form of argument using alternation.

Here is one way to see that the argument is valid: the alternation premise can be translated into either of the following conditional statements, which are contrapositives of each other:

If Mark Twain did not intend to satirize local customs, then he was a foolish man.
If Mark Twain was not a foolish man, then he intended to satirize local customs.

The addition of the second premise, "Mark Twain clearly was not a foolish man", to either of the conditional translations gives the conclusion, "Mark Twain intended to satirize local customs."

Unfortunately there is some controversy among logicians over whether such alternation statements also imply the converses of the above conditionals:

If Mark Twain was a foolish man, then he did not intend to satirize local customs.
If Mark Twain intended to satirize local customs, he was not a foolish man.

If the alternation also implies these conditionals, then it implies a biconditional and vice versa. The problem can be put symbolically: using the same symbols assigned for Example 3-28. Which of the following does 'p or q' mean, the conditional or the biconditional?

1. not $p \longrightarrow q$ (which is the same as 'not $q \longrightarrow p$'), or
2. not $p \longleftrightarrow q$ (which is the same as 'not $q \longleftrightarrow p$')

Another way to state the choices is to point out that according to the first interpretation, the affirmation of one alternant does not imply anything about the other, although the denial of either does imply the affirmation of the other. According to the second interpretation, the affirmation of either alternant implies the denial of the other, and the denial of either alternant implies the affirmation of the other. You can see that one's choice of these two interpretations of an alternation statement makes considerable difference in the judgment of alternation arguments.

The first interpretation, which is endorsed here, is called the WEAK 'OR' interpretation; the second the STRONG 'OR'. Many contemporary logicians endorse the weak 'or' interpretation, but with a qualification. They have a special definition of the conditional, which I will mention later on under the topic, "⁘Material Implication". Another qualification holds for complex sentences. See that topic for this qualification.

An additional qualification exists which everyone should recognize—that sometimes when using the word 'or' people do intend that the affirmation of one alternant imply the negation of the other. This is often done by emphasizing the word 'or', which emphasis takes the place of the phrase 'but not both'. Consider this statement:

Either Frank put hydrochloric acid in that beaker, **or** he put in sulphuric acid.

The speaker seems to preclude Frank's having put both acids in the beaker.

Furthermore, features of the situation sometimes make clear that both alternants cannot be true at the same time. This is the case for the first alternation statement considered:

This phenolphthalein solution will be pink, or it will be colorless.

If any solution is pink, then it is not colorless, so the affirmation of one alternant in this case justifies denial of the other.

In view of these qualifications, an alternation statement sometimes implies that not both of the alternants are true. However, the safest thing to do, unless such an implication is absolutely clear, is to use the weak 'or' interpretation.

In evaluating an alternation argument, one proceeds by first determining whether the alternation is strong or weak. Given a strong alternation the following forms are **valid** (using '(or)' to represent the strong 'or'):

p (or) *q*	*p* (or) *q*	*p* (or) *q*	*p* (or) *q*
not *p*	*p*	not *q*	*q*
q	not *q*	*p*	not *p*

In each case the denial of the given conclusion (that is, not *q*, *q*, not *p*, and *p* respectively) would give us not only an invalid argument, but also a contradiction. Invalidity is rare with strong alternation and generally is the result of confusion when it does appear.

Given a weak alternation, the following two forms are **valid** (using simply the word 'or' for the symbol).

p or q	p or q
not p	not q
q	p

Or course the conclusions, 'not q' and 'not p' respectively cannot be validly drawn. The following forms are invalid:

p or q	p or q
p	q
not q	not p

And for the invalid forms, the conclusions, 'q' and 'p' respectively cannot be validly drawn either.

COMPREHENSION SELF-TEST

True or false? If the statement is false, change a crucial term (or terms) to make it true.

3–112. 'Not both p and not q' is a negajunction.
3–113. The affirmation of one negajunct implies the denial of the other.
3–114. The affirmation of one strong alternant implies the denial of the other.
3–115. The affirmation of one conjunct implies the denial of the other.
3–116. The denial of one weak alternant implies the affirmation of the other.
3–117. The affirmation of one weak alternant implies nothing about the other.

Symbolization Exercises. Symbolize each of the following sentences. Before writing the symbolized sentence, give a complete key.

3–118. This piece of cloth is warm and it is only 50 per cent wool.
3–119. This piece of cloth is warm, but it is only 50 per cent wool. (Note: For logical purposes, 'but' can often be treated like 'and'.)
3–120. Thomas Jefferson was a scholar; he was a gentleman; and he was an astute politician.
3–121. Either there will be rain within the week, or the crops will be ruined.
3–122. Either the two colors that you select will match, or the room will be ugly.
3–123. Either that figure is a square, or it does not have four sides.
3–124. There is not now both a rainbow and a completely overcast sky. (Or in other words—Not both of these are true: There is now a rainbow, and there is now a completely overcast sky.)
3–125. Either Abraham Lincoln thought that his Gettysburg Address was reverently received, or he thought that it was a failure.
3–126. *Alice in Wonderland* is a book for children, but it is also a book for adults.
3–127. Hamlet was not both in doubt of the guilt of his uncle and convinced that he had actually spoken to his father's ghost.

Translations. (**3–128** through **3–131**) Translate each of the four alternations in the previous group into equivalent conditionals.

Arguments to Judge. Here is a set of arguments. On a separate sheet of paper, symbolize each and put it in shape; then judge whether each is valid, explaining why you judge as you do.

3–132. This piece of cloth is warm and it is 50 per cent wool. If the dog is shivering from cold, then the cloth is not warm. Therefore the dog is not shivering from cold.

3–133. If the label on this piece of cloth reads "50 per cent wool", then it is 50 per cent wool. This morning John, who knows about such things, said that the piece of cloth is warm, but it is only 50 per cent wool. So the label certainly must read "50 per cent wool".

3–134. Thomas Jefferson did not make the mistake of which you are accusing him. If he had, then he would not have been an astute politician. But he was a scholar; he was a gentleman; and he was an astute politician.

3–135. Either there will be rain within the week, or the crops will be ruined. We can be sure that there will not be rain within the week. Hence we can be sure that the crops will be ruined.

3–136. Either the two colors that you select will match, or the room will be ugly. If I help you select the colors, then they will match. I am going to help you select the colors. Therefore, the room will not be ugly.

3–137. Either that figure is a square or it does not have four sides. I conclude that it does not have four sides, since I know that it is not a square.

3–138. There is not now both a rainbow and a completely overcast sky. The combination is impossible. The sky is now completely overcast. Therefore, you must be wrong when you say that there is now a rainbow.

3–139. Abraham Lincoln must have thought that his Gettysburg Address was a failure. The following reasons make this apparent: Either he thought that it was reverently received, or he thought that it was a failure. From his remarks made immediately afterwards, we can be sure that he did not think that it was reverently received.

3–140. If Jones likes *Alice in Wonderland,* then it is not a book for children. *Alice in Wonderland* is a book for children, but it is also a book for adults. Hence Jones probably likes it.

3–141. Hamlet must not have been in doubt of the guilt of his uncle. Consider: He certainly was not both in doubt of the guilt of his uncle and convinced that he had actually spoken to his father's ghost. Now he was convinced that he had actually spoken to his father's ghost. Hence in his mind there was no doubt of the guilt of his uncle.

∴ *Greater Complexities*

Many topics in the field of logic are more complicated and sophisticated than the ones which you have considered so far. Although many of them have little bearing on the problems of ordinary logic, some are relevant. In this section you will confront a few of these topics which are relevant. One in particular, "Material Implication", touches on some of the basic controversies in contemporary logic. You should realize that at whatever level the subject matter of logic is presented, there are qualifications which for ease of presentation and understanding must be omitted. Consequently, although the topics in the remaining part of this chapter might be regarded as qualifications to what has already been presented, they too are also subject to a number of qualifications which are beyond the scope of this book.

⁘*Step-by-step organization of arguments*

You have noted that arguments sometimes have a number of steps in reaching the conclusion. There is an orderly method for treating such arguments, a method which is particularly helpful with the more complex arguments. Recall this argument, used in an earlier exercise:

Example 3-29
If this figure is an equilateral triangle, then it has all sides equal.
I conclude that it cannot be an equilateral triangle, since not all sides are equal.
Let 'p' = 'this figure is an equilateral triangle'
Let 'q' = 'it has all sides equal'

In step-by-step form, the argument looks as follows:

Statements:	*Reasons:*
1. $p \longrightarrow q$	1. Premise
2. not q	2. Premise
3. not p	3. 1, 2, denial of consequent

When using this procedure, you make two lists which correspond to each other and which are in order. The left-hand list consists of statements which you are entitled to make, granting the premises and truths of logic. The object is to be able to write down the conclusion in this list, but you may not write it unless previous items on the list, premises, and/or truths of logic entitle you to do so. Ordinarily you first write down all the premises. When you reach the conclusion and write it down, you have achieved the goal, so nothing appears after that step.

But if the argument is invalid, then it is not possible to get as far as writing down the conclusion. Instead, on the line after the last line that it is possible to establish, you write a question mark.

On the right-hand side you indicate just what it is that entitles you to make the statement written on the left. If the statement is a premise, then you write "premise". If the statement follows from earlier statements, you write down the numbers of the earlier statements and mention the rule of logic that enables you to make the step to this latest statement on the left.

In Example 3-29 above, the first two lines consist of the two premises (the conditional and the denial of the consequent of the conditional), and the word "premise" written on each line in order to indicate that each of the statements is a premise. The third line on the left consists of the denial of the antecedent, which is the proposed conclusion ('not p'); and on the right the numbers of the statements (1, 2) which justify this conclusion and an indication of the rule that entitles one to make this step.

In this case the rule, "denial of the consequent implies the denial of the antecedent", is indicated by the phrase, "denial of consequent". In referring to a rule, you generally mention the part that refers to what one of the premises does to the other. For a conditional chain, however, the thing to do is write down "conditional chain". In spite of the specificity of the previous two suggestions, you still have considerable leeway in the specification of reasons. As you will see, you will have to devise ways of indicating your reasons. This procedure is probably more conducive to understanding than using a set list of possible reasons, although it is less rigorous.

If the argument is invalid, then on the line on which the question mark is written, the reason should indicate to the extent possible why the argument is invalid. Here is an example of the step-by-step organization of an invalid argument:

Example 3-30

If these two plants are not closely related, then they cannot be crossed. However, they are closely related. Therefore, they can be crossed.

Let 'p' = 'these two plants are not closely related'
Let 'q' = 'these two plants cannot be crossed'

Statements:	*Reasons:*
1. $p \longrightarrow q$	1. Premise
2. not p	2. Premise
3. ?	3. 1, 2, denial of antecedent

Now that you have the general idea, let us apply this method of organization to a slightly more complex argument, which you have seen before. After you read the initial presentation of the argument in this one, try to work it all the way through yourself without looking at the way it is worked here. Then compare and see if the differences, if any, are crucial:

Example 3-31

I am convinced that the lighting in the livingroom is satisfactory. There can be no doubt about this, for it follows from the following reasons: If the lighting in the livingroom is indirect, then Mrs. Smith will like it. And one thing is clear—Mrs. Smith is a fair judge. If she does not like it, then it is clearly unsatisfactory. This morning she said that the lighting in the livingroom is indirect. My conclusion is therefore obvious.

Let 'p' = 'the lighting in the livingroom is indirect'
Let 'q' = 'Mrs. Smith will like it'

Let 'r' = 'the lighting in the livingroom is unsatisfactory'

Statements:	*Reasons:*
1. $p \longrightarrow q$	1. Premise
2. not $q \longrightarrow r$	2. Premise
3. p	3. Premise
4. q	4. 1, 3, affirmation of antecedent
5. ?	5. 2, 4, denial of antecedent

Hence the argument is invalid.

This method of dealing with complex arguments presents a danger: There is no guarantee that you have exhausted all the possibilities for showing that an argument is valid. In a very complex argument there might be a way of showing that the argument is valid, but you might not see it. What this method does accomplish is the ordering of one's thoughts. It does not automatically grind out the answers. Such decision procedures do exist for some artificial systems of logic, but none exist for ordinary logic. You simply must be alert and ingenious.

COMPREHENSION SELF-TEST

True or False? If the statement is false, change a crucial term (or terms) to make it true.

3–142. In the step-by-step organization of arguments the object is to try to show that one is entitled to write down a premise as a last step.

3–143. In this method of organizing arguments, one thing that one is justified in writing down is a premise.

3–144. Ordinarily the first thing that one writes down in the step-by-step sequence is a premise.

3–145. In order to show what justifies a statement which is not a premise, one should indicate the lines from which it is derived and the rule by which it was derived.

Arguments to Organize and Judge. **3–146** through **3–165**. Take each of the following arguments from previous exercises, assign symbols (or make use of your previous assignment of symbols), organize it according to the step-by-step method, and state whether it is valid: 3–66, 3–67, 3–68, 3–69, 3–70, 3–96, 3–97, 3–98, 3–99, 3–100, 3–101, 3–102, 3–103, 3–135, 3–136, 3–137, 3–138, 3–139, 3–140, 3–141. If this practice becomes repetitive, leave out some of those in the middle.

3–166. Take the argument dealing with the relationship between the loss of the nail and the loss of the kingdom (Example 3–24) and organize it in step-by-step form.

⁘Complex sentences

As may have occurred to you, each conditional, alternation, disjunction, and conjunction, although it is composed of sentences, is itself a sentence, and might be part of a more complex sentence, such as the following:

If you did put the yeast in the dough, then if the dough has rested in a warm place for thirty minutes, it has risen.

First, the assignment of symbols:

Let 'p' = 'you did put the yeast in the dough'
Let 'q' = 'the dough has rested in a warm place for thirty minutes'
Let 'r' = 'it has risen'

In this case, the conditional, '$q \longrightarrow r$', is itself the consequent of the primary antecedent, 'p'. We can show this by enclosing the expression, '$q \longrightarrow r$', in parentheses, and writing this all down after the 'p' and the arrow, as follows:

$$p \longrightarrow (q \longrightarrow r)$$

Here is an argument which makes use of this type of symbolization:

Example 3-32
If you did put the yeast in the dough, then if the dough has rested in a warm place for thirty minutes, it has risen. Now I know you put the yeast in the dough, but it has not risen. Therefore, the dough has not rested in a warm place for thirty minutes.

Since we have already assigned symbols to all the parts of this argument, we can turn to working it out in step-by-step form:

Statements:	*Reasons:*
1. $p \longrightarrow (q \longrightarrow r)$	1. Premise
2. p	2. Premise
3. not r	3. Premise
4. $q \longrightarrow r$	4. 1, 2, affirmation of antecedent
5. not q	5. 3, 4, denial of consequent

Thus the argument is valid.

The thing that is new here is treating the simple conditional, '$q \longrightarrow r$', as the consequent in the complex conditional, '$p \longrightarrow (q \longrightarrow r)$'. The affirmation of the antecedent 'p' in the complex conditional enables us to conclude the consequent of this complex conditional, which consequent is the simple conditional, '$q \longrightarrow r$'.

Such complexities are not limited to conditional statements. The first premise in Example 3-32 can be restated to include an alternation:

If you did put the yeast in the dough; then either the dough has not rested in a warm place for thirty minutes, or it has risen.

Using the same assignment of letters, that sentence looks like this:

$$p \longrightarrow (\text{not } q \text{ or } r)$$

Worked out in step-by-step form, the corresponding argument would look like this:

Example 3-33

Statements:	*Reasons:*
1. $p \longrightarrow$ (not q or r)	1. Premise
2. p	2. Premise
3. not r	3. Premise
4. not q or r	4. 1, 2, affirmation of antecedent
5. not q	5. 3, 4, denial of alternant

The thought can also be expressed in such a way that the antecedent is a conjunction:

If you did put the yeast in the dough and the dough has rested in a warm place for thirty minutes, then it has risen.

That sentence is symbolized as follows:

$$(p \text{ and } q) \longrightarrow r$$

Using this version of the complex premise, the argument looks like this:

Example 3-34

Statements:	*Reasons:*
1. (p and q) $\longrightarrow r$	1. Premise
2. p	2. Premise
3. not r	3. Premise
4. not (p and q)	4. 1, 3, denial of consequent
5. not q	5. 2, 4, affirmation of negajunct

You can now see that with the judicious use of parentheses, sentences of greater complexity can be handled. However, one should remember that the material in the parentheses must be treated as a unit which must be established before you can deal with its parts.* For example, the following move to line three is a mistake:

Example 3-35

Statements:	*Reasons:*
1. $p \longrightarrow (q \longrightarrow r)$	1. Premise
2. q	2. Premise
3. r	3. 1, 2, affirmation of antecedent

It is a mistake because the conditional that is presumed, '$q \longrightarrow r$', in arriving at 'r' has not been established.

* A qualification of this point is presented in the section on indirect proof, but for the sake of simplicity, it will be ignored here.

Next a qualification must be made to the earlier discussion of alternation, when it was suggested that an alternation can be translated into a conditional, and vice versa. That is, it was suggested that '$p \longrightarrow q$' and 'not p or q' could be treated in the same way. This suggestion holds (assuming the weak 'or') for alternations that stand by themselves. But if the alternation is the antecedent of a conditional, then a proper interpretation of 'p or q' **can** be 'At least one of "p" and "q" is true.' Alternation with this interpretation will here be called INCLUSIVE ALTERNATION.

In the following sentence, the alternation is to be interpreted as inclusive alternation:

> If Smith is under thirty-five or he is an alien, then he is not eligible for the Presidency.

That sentence informs us that if at least one of the conditions is met, then Smith is ineligible. Thus in order to establish that the antecedent of the complete conditional is affirmed, one can establish that Smith is under thirty-five; alternatively one can establish that Smith is an alien. But one does not need to establish that there is a connection between the two alternants, which is what one would have to establish if the translation relationship between conditionals and alternations held in this kind of case.

Here is an argument put in step-by-step form, which shows how the affirmation of an inclusive alternant can be handled:

Example 3-36

If Smith is under thirty-five or he is an alien, then he is not eligible for the Presidency. Smith is an alien. Therefore, he is ineligible.

Let 'p' = 'Smith is under thirty-five'
Let 'q' = 'Smith is an alien'
Let 'r' = 'Smith is not eligible for the Presidency'

Statements:	*Reasons:*
1. $((p \text{ or } q)) \longrightarrow r$	1. Premise
2. q	2. Premise
3. $(p \text{ or } q)$	3. 2, affirmation of inclusive alternant
4. r	4. 1, 3, affirmation of antecedent

The extra parentheses were put around the alternation in order to note the type of alternation in use here, inclusive alternation.

Probably one can safely say that whenever an alternation appears as a condition, it should be interpreted in this way. This is so for the above example in which the alternation was an antecedent that gives a condition, and it is so in the following example in which the alternant is a consequent that gives a condition by virtue of the 'only if' formulation:

> Jones may attend the banquet only if he has a varsity letter or he is to receive a trophy.

The person making the above statement would not be understood to be saying that Jones may attend only if there is a connection between having a varsity letter and being about to receive a trophy. Rather the statement would be taken to mean that Jones may attend only if he meets at least one of the conditions.

A word of warning: Our language is so complex that it is dangerous to rely exclusively on rules when you want to determine the meaning of a particular occurrence of the word 'or'. You can generally expect to find weak alternation when the alternation stands alone, although emphasis on the 'or' might make it strong alternation; and an alternation as a condition is generally to be interpreted as inclusive. But the final choice of one of the three interpretations must rest upon your appraisal of the context.

∴*Indirect proof**

Frequently a proof is most conveniently constructed by assuming the proposed conclusion to be false and showing that this assumption leads to a contradiction. If the denial of the proposed conclusion leads to a contradiction, then the conclusion must be affirmed.

An understanding of the previous paragraph will enable you to deal effectively with most indirect proofs which you will meet. But in order that you can deal with complicated ones in an orderly manner, I will explain how to do so with the step-by-step method. Another purpose I hope to achieve in this section and the next one on conditional proofs is the appreciation on your part of the neatness and inescapability of even complicated deductive proofs.

In an indirect proof one first writes down the premises as usual. Then for the next step one writes down the denial of the proposed conclusion. Since the denial of the conclusion has not been established, but is simply assumed for the sake of argument, one indicates that it is an assumption by putting a star to its left. All succeeding steps up to and including the statement of a contradiction are similarly marked with the star, just to remind us that there is an assumption in the background.** We work for a contradiction, which should appear in the form, 'p and not p'. If we achieve a contradiction and it depends upon the assumption of the denial of the conclusion, then for the next step we can draw the conclusion. No star is necessary because the conclusion does not depend on the acceptance of the assumption.

Here is an example using the same argument as in Example 3-34:

* The procedure here adopted is modeled after that presented by W. V. Quine, *Methods of Logic* (New York: Holt-Dryden, 1959).

** One could star only those steps which actually depend on the assumption, but it is simpler to star all statements that are made up through the contradiction. Since this procedure does no harm and is simpler, it is used here.

Example 3-37

Statements:	*Reasons:*
1. (p and q) $\longrightarrow r$	1. Premise
2. p	2. Premise
3. not r	3. Premise
*4. q	4. Assumption
*5. r	5. 2, 4, 1, affirmation of antecedent
*6. r and not r	6. 5, 3
7. not q	7. 4, 6, indirect proof

On the assumption, 'q', we conclude 'r'. But we are given 'not r' as a premise, so we have a contradiction, 'r and not r'. Hence the assumption, 'q', must be false. Hence we can conclude 'not q'. The argument is valid.

The basic idea behind indirect proof is roughly the principle that the denial of the consequent implies the denial of the antecedent. In the starred part of the proof one tries to show that if the conclusion is false, then there is a contradiction. Since a contradiction must be denied, the falsity of the conclusion must also be denied. To deny the falsity of the conclusion is to affirm it.

The above example of an indirect proof is very simple and saved no steps in that particular argument. In fact it required more steps than the direct method. But there are times, as you will see in the exercises, that the indirect method is simpler and easier to see.

Sometimes indirect proofs become quite complicated. For example, on occasion one must make an assumption within a sequence that is already starred. To do this calls for double starring in order that we be reminded of the new assumption. This sort of thing is rather rare, though, so the simple procedure of starring which is exemplified above will handle most cases.

∵ *Proving a conditional*

The techniques which you have learned earlier enable you to judge some conclusions which are **themselves** conditionals. But unless there is a conditional chain or the conditional appears as a unit in one of the premises, you probably do not yet see how to handle such things. Consider this argument:

Example 3-38

If Congress passes that bill, then it will be ruled on by the Supreme Court, if, and only if, someone contests it. It is clear that if the Supreme Court rules on the bill, it will be declared unconstitutional. It is also clear that someone will contest it. Therefore, if Congress passes the bill, it will be declared unconstitutional.

First the assignment of symbols:

Let 'p' = 'Congress passes the bill'
Let 'q' = 'it will be ruled on by the Supreme Court'
Let 'r' = 'someone contests it'
Let 's' = 'it will be declared unconstitutional'

Next the first steps:

Statements:	*Reasons:*
1. $p \longrightarrow (q \longleftrightarrow r)$	1. Premise
2. $q \longrightarrow s$	2. Premise
3. r	3. Premise

But now what? How can we work toward the conclusion, '$p \longrightarrow s$'? One strategy that can be used is to assume the antecedent of the conclusion and see if we can derive the consequent. If we can, then we have established the conclusion, for we have shown that if the antecedent is true, then the consequent is true.

Here is the rest of the step-by-step working out of the argument, again making use of the starring procedure to remind us of the assumption that is in the background in deriving the consequent of the conclusion. In the step after the one in which the consequent is derived, the star is omitted, because this step, in which the conclusion is stated (step 8), does not itself depend upon the assumption:

*4. p	4. Assumption
*5. $q \longleftrightarrow r$	5. 4, 1, affirmation of antecedent
*6. q	6. 3, 5, affirmation of one side of a biconditional
*7. s	7. 6, 2, affirmation of antecedent
8. $p \longrightarrow s$	8. 4, 7, conditional proof

The argument is valid.

The starred steps show that if p, then s, which is the desired conclusion. So we are entitled to write down the desired conclusion at step 8.

COMPREHENSION SELF-TEST

True or False? If the statement is false, change a crucial term (or terms) to make it true.

3–167. An indirect proof starts by assuming the truth of the conclusion.

3–168. The method of indirect proof is similar in spirit to the valid form, denying the consequent.

3–169. If one conditional is the antecedent of another, then for purposes of symbolizing the complex whole, the first conditional is enclosed in parentheses.

3–170. In order to show that something has been proven in an indirect proof, one puts a star to the left of each line that has been proven.

3–171. The following constitutes a proof of a conditional: The antecedent is assumed and the consequent is shown to follow thereby.

Sentences to Symbolize. Put each of the following sentences into the symbolic form that most closely adheres to the way the sentence is actually stated. Give a key to your assignment of symbols in each case.

3–172. If Governor Smith is actually planning to throw his hat in the ring; then if the reporters asked him to declare himself, he has refused to do so.

3–173. If Governor Smith is actually planning to throw his hat in the ring; then either the reporters did not ask him to declare himself, or he has refused to do so.

3–174. If Governor Smith is actually planning to throw his hat in the ring, and the reporters asked him to declare himself; then he has refused to do so.

3–175. If Iceland has ordered the fishing vessels of Great Britain to leave the area within ten miles of Iceland's shores; then Iceland is sovereign in that ten-mile zone, only if the ships of Britain leave.

3–176. If Iceland has ordered the fishing vessels of Great Britain to leave the area within ten miles of Iceland's shores; then Iceland is sovereign in that ten-mile zone, if the ships of Britain leave.

3–177. If Jones is given the *California Test of Mental Maturity* under standard conditions; then his IQ is about 100, if, and only if, his score is about 100.

3–178. If you put this mercury thermometer in the beaker of water; then the thermometer read x, if, and only if, the temperature was x.

3–179. Either this small test piece of dough, if put in the warming pan, will at least double in size in twenty minutes, or the dough on the board will not rise sufficiently if put in the oven.

3–180. If lines AB and CD were not parallel to each other; then if a third line is drawn in the same plane, either it will cross one and only one of them, or it will cross both of them.

Arguments to Judge. Here is a set of arguments. On a separate sheet of paper, check their validity using the step-by-step method. Make sure that your assignment of symbols is clear. In each case state explicitly whether the argument is valid.

3–181. The reporters did not ask Governor Smith to declare himself. Here is why I think so: If Governor Smith is actually planning to throw his hat in the ring; then if the reporters did ask him to declare himself, he has refused to do so. Now I know from the Governor's own testimony that he is planning to throw his hat in the ring, but that he has not refused to declare himself.

3–182. If Iceland has ordered the fishing vessels of Great Britain to leave the area within ten miles of Iceland's shores; then Iceland is sovereign in that ten-mile zone only if the ships of Britain leave. Iceland has made such an order, and the ships of Britain left. Hence Iceland is sovereign in the area within ten miles of its shores.

3–183. If Jones is given the *California Test of Mental Maturity* under standard conditions; then his IQ is about 100, if, and only if, his score is about 100. Jones does not both know calculus and have an IQ of 100. But he does know calculus and his score on the test was 100. Hence Jones was not given the test under standard conditions.

3–184. If you put this mercury thermometer in the beaker of water; then the thermometer read x, if, and only if, the temperature was x. You did put this mercury thermometer in the water and it read x. Hence the temperature of the water was x.

3–185. Let me describe the test for the rising ability of the dough on the board: Either this small test piece of dough, if put in the warming pan, will at least double in size in twenty minutes, or the dough on the board will not rise sufficiently if put in the oven. The test piece did not double in size in twenty minutes, though it was put in the warming pan. The dough on the board is in the oven. Therefore, it will not rise sufficiently.

3–186. If lines AB and CD are not parallel to each other; then if a third line has been drawn in the same plane, either it will cross one and only one of them, or it will cross both of them. A third line has been drawn in the same plane, and it crosses neither AB nor CD. Hence lines AB and CD are parallel.

3–187. If X was rubbed on Y; then X is harder than Y, if, and only if, X scratched Y. Only if there are marks on Y did X scratch Y. X was rubbed on Y, and there are clear marks on Y. Therefore, X is harder than Y.

3–188. If this pronoun is the object of a preposition, then it requires the objective form. If it requires the objective form, then it should appear as 'him'. If it appears as 'he' and it should appear as 'him', then the sentence is in error. Hence the sentence is in error, if the pronoun appears as 'he', and is the object of a preposition.

3–189. If Communism were going to spread in Lower Slobbovia, then the Prime Minister would have been defeated in the recent election. He has been defeated, only if there has been an announcement of his defeat in the local newspaper. No mention of such a defeat has been made, nor will it appear. On the basis of inside information, I know for a fact that the Lower Slobbovians are discontent. On the basis of the foregoing, I conclude that the following statement is false: If the people of Lower Slobbovia are discontent, then Communism will spread in Lower Slobbovia.

3–190. The wind is not from the east. If, and only if, the contour lines are close together, is the hill steep. If the hill is steep, then there is undoubtedly turbulence on the west side, if the wind is from the west. We shall not have both turbulence on the west side and a good race close to the west shore. We must have our race on a triangular course with two buoys on the east shore, if we shall not have a good race close to the west shore. The contour lines **are** quite close together. Therefore, if the wind is from the west, then we must have our race on a triangular course with two buoys on the east shore.

❖ *Material implication*

So far I have assumed that a conditional statement suggests some kind of connection between an antecedent and consequent. If one does not make this assumption, then the logical system that one constructs can be much simpler—in that fewer basic relationships need be assumed (though it will not be simpler from the point of view of ease of understanding, as parts of the system appear to be counterintuitive).

Most contemporary symbolic logicians have chosen not to make this assumption of a connection between the antecedent and consequent, and have worked on the construction of elegant* systems of logic. Although they realize that the systems so constructed are somewhat artificial, many do so anyway because of the attraction of such systems.

This section on material implication is intended only to point out some basic features of many contemporary systems. Although various systems differ from each other in many ways, they do share the features presented here. Unless you are interested in these matters for their own sake, or are planning to go on in your study of logic, I suggest that you omit this section. It will not be of additional help to you in judging deductive arguments that are used in everyday life.

Since this topic is presumably of interest only to those who have found the material so far rather easy, the discussion that follows will be compact. P. F. Strawson in his *Introduction to Logical Theory*** has treated the topic at much greater length. Those who are interested are urged to go to Strawson's book and to some of the other items in the bibliography,*** because what follows here is sketchy and in need of qualification.

The basic feature of the approach is revealed by the definition of the conditional:

'If *p*, then *q*' means the same as 'Not both *p* and not *q*'.

In this definition the conditional is equated to a negajunction, which is a combination of negation and conjunction. As the negajunction is interpreted, it is made true by the falsity of either one of its components. There is at least some plausibility in this equation, because the conditional does imply that negajunction. If it is true that if *p*, than *q*; then it cannot be that *p* is true and *q* is false. But the trouble is that the negajunction does not imply the conditional. This is shown by the fact that the negajunction is made true by things which do not make the conditional true. So the negajunction can be true when the conditional is not. If the negajunction implied the conditional, this could not be.

To see that the negajunction is made true by things which do not make the conditional true, consider just what can make the negajunction true. The negajunction that appears in the above definition is made true by the

* 'Elegant' is not here a derogatory term. Rather it is laudatory.

** *Op. cit.*

*** At the end of Chapter 5.

falsity of 'p' or the truth of 'q'. Thus according to this interpretation the **defined conditional** is made true by the falsity of 'p' or the truth of 'q'. This is a special kind of conditional and is called the MATERIAL CONDITIONAL. The if-then relationship so defined is called MATERIAL IMPLICATION.

That material implication is special can be seen from this example of a conditional:

If I go to lunch at 2:00 P.M. today, there will be a broad selection of food.

Interpreted as material implication, this conditional is made true by the falsity of the antecedent. That is, the conditional is true if I do **not** go to lunch at 2:00 P.M. today. Under the ordinary interpretation of this conditional, however, I happen to know that the statement is false. I know that if I go to lunch at 2:00 P.M. today, there will be a small selection. And I know this to be so even if I do not go to lunch at 2:00 P.M. today. Hence the material conditional is different from the ordinary conditional.

The problem is compounded by the fact that all conditionals are interpreted as material conditionals (or in similar ways) in the views under consideration. So there is no room for the ordinary conditional.

A number of parallel situations can be pointed out: The word 'or' is interpreted in the inclusive sense; everything is supposed to be true of any class which has no members; and in fact there is supposed to be only one such class. But there is not space here to discuss each of these matters. If you would like to pursue them, you can find expositions of the positions in many contemporary books on logic. Your understanding of them will perhaps be facilitated by the above discussion of material implication.

Now that you have seen the consequences of this particular definition of the conditional, you might wonder why anyone should desire to so define it. There are several reasons:

1. As was indicated earlier, such a definition allows one to construct a much more elegant system than the one I have presented. Starting with fewer (usually two) independent logical operators, one can define all other operators in sentence reasoning. Thus there are fewer types of building blocks. Sometimes conjunction and negation are the two; sometimes inclusive alternation and negation are the two. As a matter of fact one can start with only one operator (negajunction will do it) and define all the rest.

2. Such a definition allows the development of a convenient mechanical decision procedure for judging arguments. Perhaps you have heard of truth tables. They are used in one such procedure.

3. The difficulties which I have indicated do not often give trouble in practical situations, and when they do, one who is on guard might not be caught in the traps.

4. The defined relationship, material implication, is not very far removed from our intuitive notion of implication. After all, '$p \longrightarrow q$' does imply 'Not both p and not q', and when 'Not both p and not q' is established on grounds other than the falsity of p or the truth of q, the relationship '$p \longrightarrow q$' holds.

These are important considerations, but I have still chosen to give you a logic that assumes that conditionals assert connections, primarily because this logic is intuitive and correct. The elegance of modern systems is not of much help when dealing with the problems of everyday logic.

Chapter Summary

In this chapter on sentence reasoning, you have seen in some detail the role of conditional statements in arguments. The fundamental valid types of conditional arguments are called **affirming the antecedent, denying the consequent,** and the **conditional chain**. The fundamental invalid forms are **denying the antecedent** and **affirming the consequent**. A crucial distinction is that between the antecedent and the consequent. They must not be exchanged when dealing with conditionals.

The only-if type of conditional is rather confusing in this respect, because the words 'only if' introduce the consequent—in contrast to the introduction of the antecedent by the word 'if' in the standard 'if-then' statement.

The move from a statement to its converse is not a valid move, but the move to its contrapositive is valid and often helpful in organizing arguments. In general the denial of the negation of a statement may be treated as equivalent to the straightforward affirmation of it.

Sometimes one's insight into the nature of an argument is helped by thinking in terms of necessary and sufficient conditions. In the symbolic form, '$p \longrightarrow q$', the truth of 'p' is a sufficient condition for the truth of 'q', and the truth of 'q' is a necessary condition for the truth of 'p'.

The biconditional, a statement of implication in both directions, is conveniently indicated by the phrase, 'if, and only if'. It is difficult to make a mistake in reasoning with biconditionals because valid arguments can be developed out of the affirmation or denial of the antecedent or consequent. The main danger is in confusion with negation.

Conjunction, the joining together of two statements by the conjunction 'and' (or some similar one), offers few problems. A conjunction is true, if, and only if, both conjuncts are true. The order of the conjuncts does not matter.

Negajunction, the denial of a conjunction, is a bit more confusing because of the negation. The order of the parts in the negajunction also does not matter. A negajunction is true, if, and only if, at least one of the negajuncts is false. Negajunctions and conjunctions do not express connections between their parts—or at least we so treat them.

There appear to be at least three significant types of alternation: weak alternation, strong alternation, and (⁘) inclusive alternation. Weak alternation is translatable into a conditional, strong alternation into a biconditional, and inclusive alternation into the statement that at least one of the alternants is true. The decision as to which type is in use rests heavily on the context, although inclusive alternation (while the alternants are sentences) probably does not appear except as part of a complex sentence, usually in which the alternation plays the role of a condition.

The basic units of sentence reasoning are symbolized by representing them by small letters, 'p', 'q', etc. The conditional, biconditional, conjunction, negajunction, and alternation relationships are respectively symbolized by '$\longrightarrow$', '$\longleftrightarrow$', 'and', 'not both . . . and . . .', and 'or'. A circle is drawn around the 'or' ('Ⓞr') to show that the alternation is strong, and (⁘) parentheses are put around the entire alternation if it is inclusive alternation.

The last section in this chapter, "Greater Complexities", is devoted to advanced material and considers five topics: "Step-by-Step Organization of Arguments", "Complex Sentences", "Indirect Proof", "Proving a Conditional", and "Material Implication".

⁘When arguments are long and complicated, an orderly step-by-step method has been suggested. When following this method, one lists on the left the premises and what one is entitled to conclude on the basis of the premises; on the right are given the reasons for the entitlement to write what is written on the left. Indirect proofs are handled by assuming the denial of the proposed conclusion, and by seeking to derive a contradiction from this assumption. The assumption, contradiction, and intervening lines are starred in order to keep track of what is going on. Conditional proofs (proofs of conditional statements) are sometimes effected by assuming the antecedent of the conditional and seeing if one can derive the consequent. Again starring is used to keep track of the basis on which one is proceeding. The step-by-step method does not guarantee that one will find that a valid argument is valid. Considerable ingenuity must sometimes be exercised.

⁘Complex statements can be symbolized by using parentheses to show the grouping of their parts. For example 'If p; then if q, then r' can be symbolized as $p \longrightarrow (q \longrightarrow r)$. The parentheses show that '$q \longrightarrow r$' is to be taken as a unit in the total conditional.

⁘The last topic in the chapter dealt with contemporary artificial logic systems, although no effort was made to achieve comprehensive coverage. Instead, a crucial but typical difference was briefly described. This difference is the definition of the conditional in terms of a negajunction.

Lastly you should remember that this chapter has dealt with only one kind of logic, that in which the basic units are sentences which remain essentially unchanged throughout the argument. The next chapter treats class reasoning, in which sentences change radically during the course of the argument. In some cases similar techniques can be used, but often the easiest way is to use circles to represent classes. We now turn to this method.

CHAPTER 4

Class Reasoning

You have seen what deduction is and found some techniques for handling deductive arguments in which the logical operators joined complete independent sentences or items that could be treated as such. This chapter is concerned with another sort of argument, that in which the basic units are individuals and classes, rather than sentences. Class reasoning arguments, like sentence arguments, are very common, so you should also know how to handle them.

You will find that class and sentence reasoning are related in various ways. Frequently they are combined in the same argument; some arguments can be shifted from one type to the other without serious change in meaning; and like all deductive arguments, they involve the basic relationship, which is here stated in conditional form: **If** the premises are true and the argument is valid **then** the conclusion must be true.

But each is uniquely suited to certain jobs. Class reasoning cannot handle most of the arguments considered in the previous chapter, because no classes were involved—only specific things and events. And sentence reasoning is not well suited to the following two arguments (although you can handle the first with sentence reasoning either by overlooking a difficulty, or by adding a special step). Examine these two arguments, which are valid, and see whether you can show that they are valid, using the techniques of sentence reasoning:

Example 4-1

Dough containing yeast mixed with lukewarm water rises rapidly.
Ingrid's dough contains yeast mixed with lukewarm water.

Ingrid's dough rises rapidly.

Example 4-2

All triangles inscribed in semi-circles are right triangles.
At least some of the triangles on this page are inscribed in semi-circles. [A geometry text]

At least some of the triangles on this page are right triangles.

You may have had a degree of success with the first argument, but you surely did not succeed with the second one. You might have done this with the first argument:

Example 4-3

Let 'p' = 'any dough contains yeast mixed with lukewarm water'
Let 'q' = 'that dough rises rapidly'

$p \longrightarrow q$
$\underline{p\qquad}$
q (valid; affirmation of the antecedent)

In so doing we have restated the first premise to read:

If any dough contains yeast mixed with lukewarm water, then that dough rises rapidly,

which is a fairly satisfactory restatement of the first premise. But note that what was affirmed was not the antecedent, "any dough contains yeast mixed with lukewarm water", but rather the sentence, "Ingrid's dough contains yeast mixed with lukewarm water." In fact it would not make sense to affirm the antecedent of the revised if-then sentence, because that sentence fails to refer to some dough. If you do not know what dough is referred to, how can you tell whether it contains yeast mixed with lukewarm water? Incidentally the second premise, "Ingrid's dough contains yeast mixed with lukewarm water", does refer to some particular dough, so it does make sense to affirm that.

Example 4-2, the one which concluded, "At least some of the triangles on this page are right triangles", is not at all amenable to the sentence approach. It can, however, be handled by a class reasoning approach. Although many ways of doing class reasoning may be found in the literature on logic, the one that you will read about here is probably the simplest and most intuitive. It has the additional advantage of being usable at various levels of sophistication. If a person knows just a little of it, he can make use of that.

A complicated set of techniques need not be mastered before the simplest problems can be worked.

A Simple Euler Circle System

The system you are about to study is a modification of a circle system named after Leonhard Euler, a Swiss mathematician who developed his system in order to teach deductive logic to a German princess. The basic idea is to represent a class by the area bounded by a circle actually drawn with a writing implement on a surface. All the members of the class can be treated as being **inside** that circle.

This Euler circle system is to some extent similar to another circle system —the Venn diagram system. The latter is more formal and invites difficulties that parallel the difficulties of material implication mentioned in the last chapter. Some contemporary instruction in modern mathematics makes use of a system which is called "Venn Diagrams", but which actually is a combination of the Euler and Venn approaches. I shall not examine the pure Venn approach in this chapter; if you are curious, you can find it presented in many elementary logic texts.

For purposes of simplicity in presentation of this Euler system, I shall postpone consideration of the triangle example and commence with the dough example.

Let us proceed to represent this argument with circles. Consider the first premise. "Dough containing yeast mixed with lukewarm water rises rapidly." In effect it says that the class of dough* containing yeast mixed with lukewarm water (the subject of the sentence) is included in the class of dough that rises rapidly. It is represented by assigning a circle to each class and putting the circle for the subject class inside the circle for the predicate class (See Diagram 4-1). This diagram says:

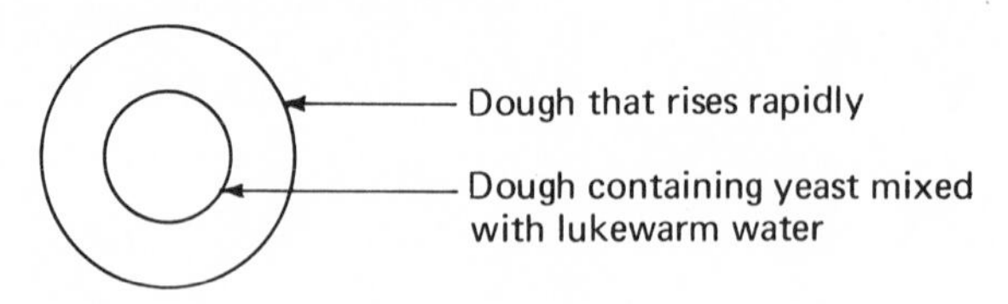

DIAGRAM 4-1

* For purposes of simplicity, I am ignoring the distinction between general terms and class terms. Strictly speaking, dough containing yeast mixed with lukewarm water is not a class, although pieces of such dough are a class. One can imagine each use of a general term to be so converted for purposes of fitting the circle model.

> All of the members of the class, *dough containing yeast mixed with lukewarm water*, are also members of the class, *dough that rises rapidly*.

Consider the second premise, "Ingrid's dough contains yeast mixed with lukewarm water." It is diagramed similarly (see Diagram 4-2). This diagram says:

> Ingrid's dough is a member of the class, *dough containing yeast mixed with lukewarm water*.

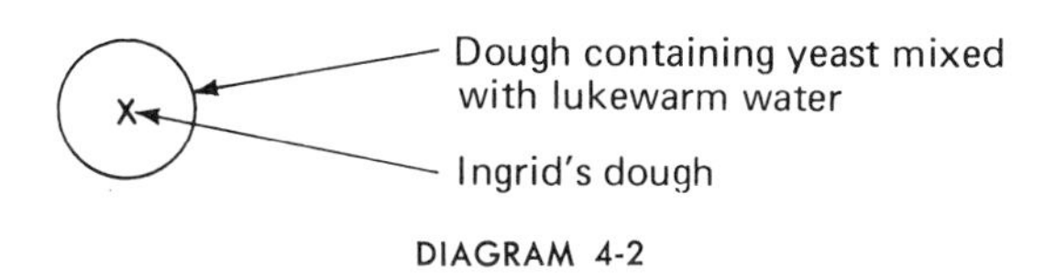

DIAGRAM 4-2

The cross, instead of a circle, was used to represent Ingrid's dough because that is not a class in this context; it is a single thing. For some situations you can ignore this distinction and use circles to bound single things as well as groups of things, but please adhere to the distinction for present purposes. It is of theoretical importance.*

Now let us combine the two premises in a single diagram. They share a circle in common so we can put them together. A good strategy is to so select your classes that the premises have circles in common. When combined the two premises look like those in Diagram 4-3. Inescapably the cross

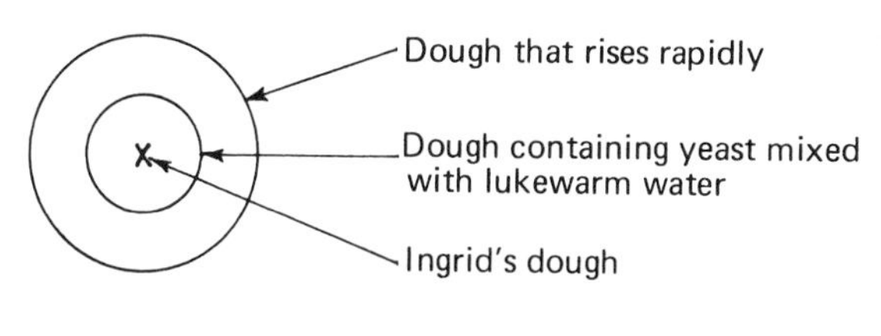

DIAGRAM 4-3

representing Indrid's dough is within the boundary of the class of dough that rises rapidly. That is, inescapably Ingrid's dough is a member of the class, *dough that rises rapidly*. Thus the conclusion is inescapably represented in the diagram and the argument is valid.

* The distinction between class membership and class inclusion, which is emphasized in set theory, is thereby preserved.

General strategy

We have now worked through one argument, applying the circle-method validity test. The general strategy to follow is this:

Try to represent the premises in one diagram. Seek common classes in different premises and take advantage of these classes to combine the premises. At all times work against the conclusion. If the conclusion is inescapably represented in the combined diagram, then the argument is valid.

In the previous argument, we were forced by one premise to put the '*x*' for Ingrid's dough inside the circle for dough containing yeast mixed with lukewarm water, and we were forced by another premise to put the latter circle inside the circle for dough that rises rapidly. Thus there was no way out. The conclusion was inescapably represented by the combined diagram.

Here is a second example of the same logical form:

Example 4-4

All of the chairs in this room are wooden.
All wooden things can burn.

All of the chairs in this room can burn.

Again the sentences must be transformed either explicitly or implicitly to fit the class relationship pattern. A predicate class must be created, and it must be connected to the subject by means of the verb, 'to be'. I shall repeat the argument, making the transformations explicit for purposes of illustration. You need not rewrite each sentence every time you check an argument, but you must think in terms of classes. Here is the transformed argument with the class relationships made explicit and the classes in italics:

Example 4-5

All *the chairs in this room* are *wooden things.*
All *wooden things* are *things that can burn.*

All *the chairs in this room* are *things that can burn.*

As you can see, the explicitly transformed sentences are somewhat stilted, but there is no doubt about their meaning. After you check the validity you can change back again.

Now that you have the transformed sentences in front of you, it would be a good idea for you to get out a piece of paper and pencil and check the argument by means of the Euler circle system. When you finish, your diagram should look like Diagram 4-4.

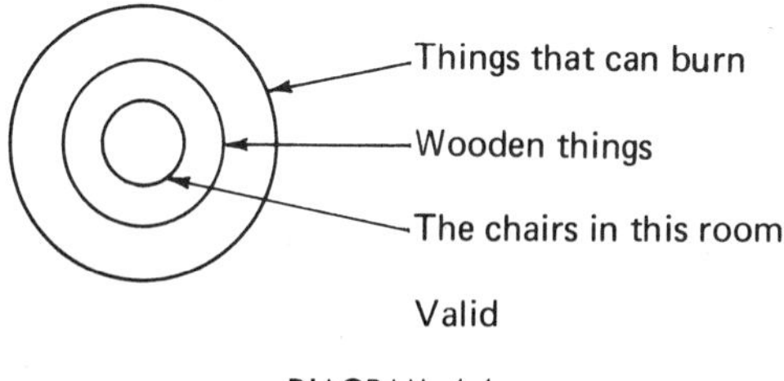

DIAGRAM 4-4

COMPREHENSION SELF-TEST

True or False? If the statement is false, change a crucial term (or terms) to make it true.

4–1. In the Euler circle system, a sentence is represented by a circle.
4–2. In a sentence of the form, "All *A*'s are *B*'s", the circle for the *B*'s would be put inside the circle for the *A*'s.
4–3. A singular thing, as opposed to a class, is represented by an '*x*'.

Diagrams. Here are a number of sentences. Using what you know so far about the modified Euler system, represent each sentence with an Euler diagram. Label each diagram. Remember that in some cases you will have to construct a predicate class.

4–4. All parallelograms are quadrilaterals.
4–5. All quadrilaterals are plane figures.
4–6. All of the books by Thomas Mann are on the top shelf.
4–7. Every one of Chekhov's short stories has fascinated me.
4–8. All acids are compounds.
4–9. All the stars in the Milky Way are far away.
4–10. Every state has two senators.
4–11. All unwanted plants are weeds.

Arguments to Diagram. The following arguments are all valid. For each argument make a labeled diagram that will show that the argument is valid.

4–12. All parallelograms are quadrilaterals. All quadrilaterals are plane figures. Therefore, all parallelograms are plane figures.
4–13. *Magic Mountain* is by Thomas Mann. All of the books by Thomas Mann are on the top shelf. Hence *Magic Mountain* is on the top shelf.
4–14. All literary works that have fascinated me have had an influence on my life. Since all of Chekhov's short stories have fascinated me, they have all had an influence on my life.
4–15. All acids are compounds and all compounds are composed of more than one element. Hence all acids are composed of more than one element.
4–16. Heavenly bodies that are far away have little or no influence on the course of

events in the world. Since all of the stars in the Milky Way are far away, they do not have much influence on the course of events in the world. (Do not be concerned with the truth of the statements; just pay attention to their meaning and the logical relationships.)

4-17. Every state has two senators. Whatever has two senators has two important votes in treaty ratification. Hence every state has two important votes in treaty ratification.

4-18. All unwanted plants are weeds. The wheat in my cornfield is unwanted. Hence the wheat in my cornfield is a weed.

Invalidity

Let us turn to an invalid argument to see how its invalidity is exposed by this Euler circle system:

Example 4-6
All of the chairs in this room can burn.
All wooden things can burn.
―――――――――――――――――
All of the chairs in this room are wooden.

Since this is such a simple argument, you can probably see already that it is invalid, because the premises allow that the chairs burn because they are made of some other material.

Remember the strategy: work against the conclusion. In this case you find that diagraming the premises does not commit one inescapably to diagraming the conclusion. An easy way to show this is to show some of the possibilities that are left open by the premises, at least one of which possibilities is inconsistent with the conclusion. Appropriately placed question marks make this situation clear (see Diagram 4-5). The circle for the chairs in this

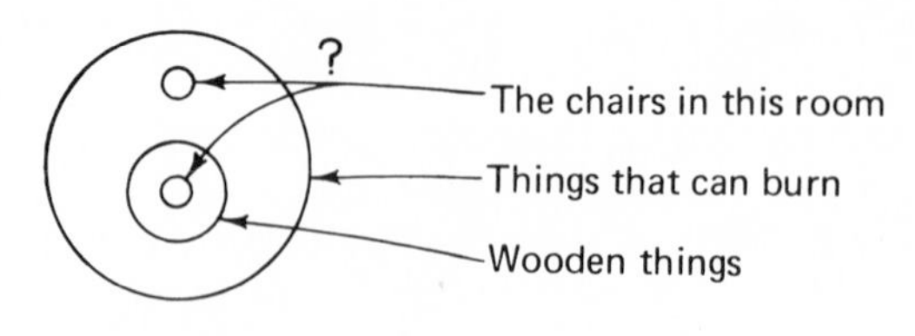

DIAGRAM 4-5

room must be in the things-that-can-burn circle, but it might or might not be in the wooden-things circle. Two of the possibilities are shown by two possible different placements of the circle for the chairs in this room.

COMPREHENSION SELF-TEST

True or False? If the statement is false, change a crucial term (or terms) to make it true.

4–19. If an argument is invalid, then it is possible to diagram the premises without diagraming the conclusion.

4–20. If an argument is valid, a diagraming of the premises inescapably results in a diagraming of the conclusion.

4–21. It is here recommended that the invalidity of an argument be shown by diagraming the argument in two ways, one of which does not represent the conclusion.

Arguments to Diagram and Judge. Here is a set of arguments, some of which are invalid. Diagram each argument, labeling each circle or '*x*', judge the validity, and show by the suggested means that the invalid arguments are invalid.

4–22. All triangles with two equal sides are isosceles triangles. Triangle *ABC* has two equal sides. Therefore, triangle *ABC* is an isosceles triangle.

4–23. All nearsighted people have defective eyes. John's eyes are defective. Hence John is nearsighted.

4–24. Birds that are unable to fly are fast runners. The penguin is a bird that is unable to fly. Therefore, the penguin is a fast runner.

4–25. Indices used to show trends in productivity should take into account changes in the cost of living. The index (percent increase in the Gross National Product) is used to show trends in productivity. Therefore, that index should take into account changes in the cost of living.

4–26. Wool clothing is warm. Clothing that is worn in winter is warm. Therefore, wool clothing is worn in winter.

4–27. The first few sentences in Mark Antony's speech to the people of Rome should be combined, because these sentences are short, and short sentences should always be combined.

4–28. The practice of lay investiture was a practice that weakened the church. Any practice weakening the church was opposed by the papacy. Hence the practice of lay investiture was opposed by the papacy.

4–29. An equilateral polygon inscribed in a circle is a regular polygon. *ABCDE* is a regular polygon. Therefore, it is an equilateral polygon inscribed in a circle.

Negatives

If we want to show that no members of a given class are members of another class, the two circles are drawn apart from each other. For example the sentence, 'No past-presidents are women', would look like Diagram 4-6. As you can see, that would also represent the equivalent sentence, 'No women have been president'.

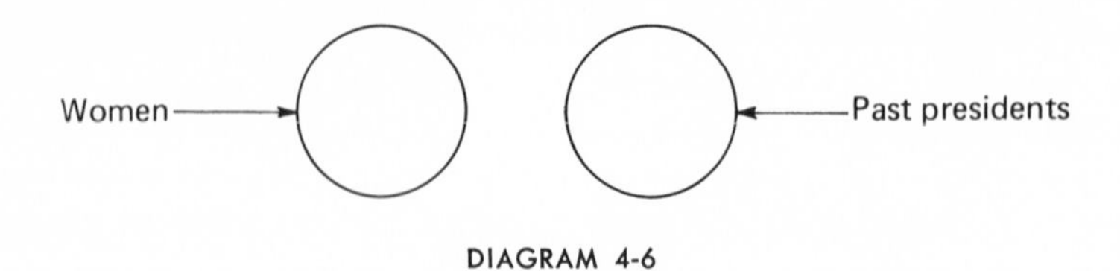

DIAGRAM 4-6

Consider this argument which uses the above sentence as a premise:

Example 4-7

No women have been president.
W. H. Harrison was a president.

W. H. Harrison was not a woman.

The diagram of this valid argument (Diagram 4-7) is such that there is no way to put W. H. Harrison into the circle for women; hence the argument is valid.

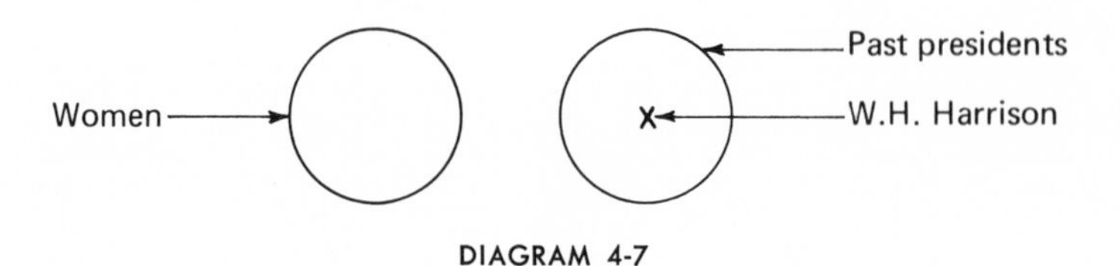

DIAGRAM 4-7

*Transformations among negatives and positives**

Sometimes in dealing with arguments, one must transform a sentence from negative form to positive form, or vice versa. Doing this is made easy by reference to Euler diagrams, but a new concept must be used, *the universe of discourse.* In effect, the UNIVERSE OF DISCOURSE is an encompassing class

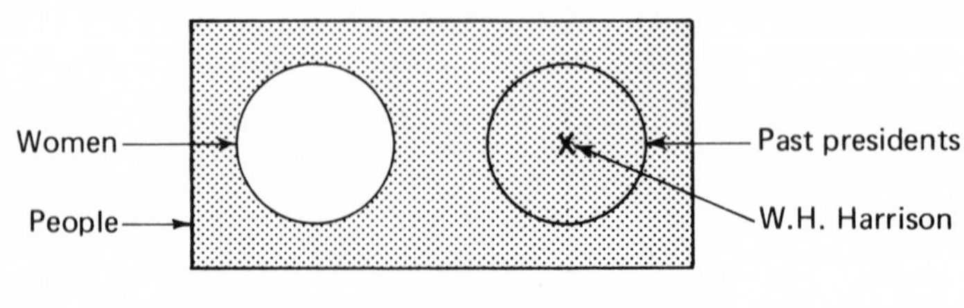

DIAGRAM 4-8

* For purposes of simplicity I shall neglect the problem of possible nonexistence of members of the subject and predicate classes. One's own grasp of the context is sufficient for proper treatment of any difficulties.

which includes members and nonmembers of all the classes involved in an argument or sentence. For example, a possible universe of discourse for the argument dealing with presidents is people. This can be shown by drawing a large rectangle around everything and labeling it 'people'. Now according to this convention, the area inside the circle labeled 'women' represents women and the area outside this circle (shaded area) represents nonwomen (who are people). Thus Diagram 4-8 shows the division of the universe of discourse, people, into two classes, women and nonwomen. Since the circle for past presidents is part of the shaded area, this diagram says that all past presidents are nonwomen (or are not women). It also says that W. H. Harrison was a nonwoman (was not a woman), since the '*x*' for W. H. Harrison is in the past-president circle, which in turn must be in the shaded area.

Now let us shade the diagram so that our attention is focused on the two mutually exclusive classes, past presidents and nonpast presidents.

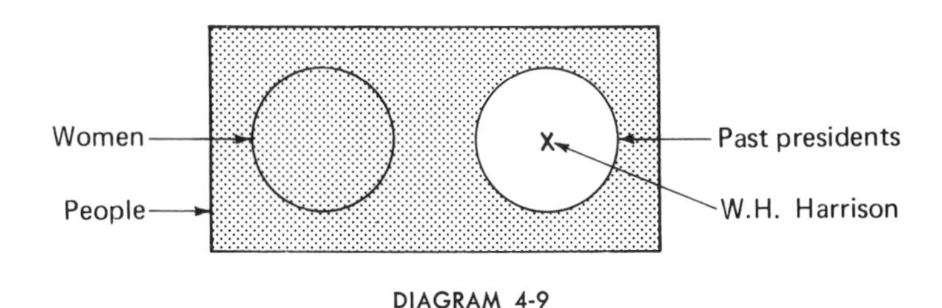

DIAGRAM 4-9

The area enclosed by the circle labeled 'past presidents' represents past presidents and the area outside this circle (shaded area) represents nonpast-presidents (who are people). Since the circle for women is part of the shaded area, Diagram 4-9 clearly says that all women are nonpast presidents, or in other words, are not past presidents.

The fact that the following sentences are all equivalent may thus be read off the original diagram (Diagram 4-7):

No past presidents are women.
No women have been president.
All past presidents are nonwomen (or are not women).
All women are nonpast presidents (or are not past presidents).

You perhaps did not need diagrams to make those transformations, but I deliberately chose a simple example to make the procedure clear. The next example is more difficult.

Perhaps you are not aware that the following two sentences are equivalent:

All wooden things can burn.
All nonburnable things are not wooden.

This can be shown by an Euler diagram (Diagram 4-10) with a universe of discourse. As an aid to your imagination I have redrawn the diagram

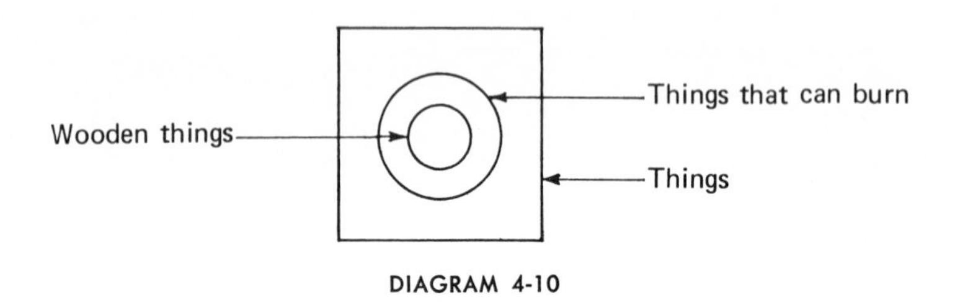

DIAGRAM 4-10

twice. The first time (Diagram 4-11) the nonwooden things are shaded. The second time (Diagram 4-12) the nonburnable things are shaded. You

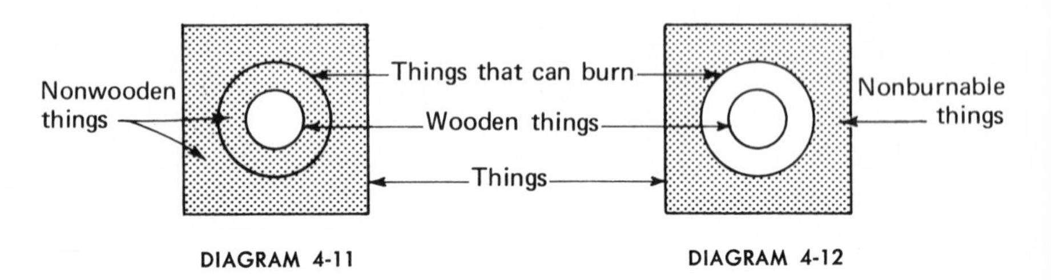

DIAGRAM 4-11

DIAGRAM 4-12

will see that the area for nonburnable things is included in the area for nonwooden things and thus that the sentence, 'All nonburnable things are not wooden', can be read from the original, Diagram 4-10.

Furthermore, a simple diagram of 'All nonburnable things are not wooden' gives us the statement, 'All wooden things are burnable'. Examine Diagram 4-13, which represents 'All nonburnable things are not wooden'. Note that the space for wooden things (all that is outside the circle for non-

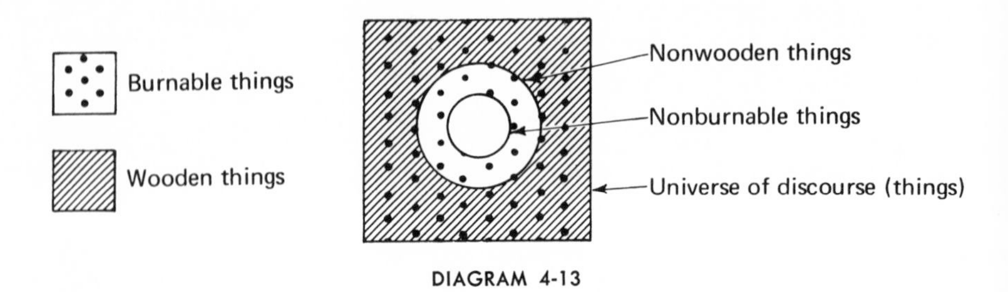

DIAGRAM 4-13

wooden things) is included in the space for burnable things (all that is outside the circle for nonburnable things). Hence the sentence, 'All wooden things are burnable', can be read from Diagram 4-13.

Since each of these sentences implies the other, they are logically equivalent. Either can be substituted for the other in an argument. Incidentally, it is interesting to note the similarity between this logical equivalence and that of contrapositives in sentence reasoning.

You should now see that if Example 4-4 had appeared in the following form we could have solved it with the same diagram as before, because we can substitute 'All wooden things can burn' for 'All nonburnable things are not wooden':

Example 4-8

All of the chairs in this room are wooden.
All nonburnable things are not wooden.

All of the chairs in this room can burn.

An alternative, of course, would be to leave the premises as they are and make a direct attack on the argument. This would put the circle for the chairs in this room outside the larger circle, because only nonwooden things are inside that larger circle. This placement requires that the circle for the chairs in this room also be outside the circle for nonburnable things, and thus be among the burnables. Thus the argument is again shown to be valid (Diagram 4-14). Sometimes it is more convenient to proceed one way, sometimes the other.

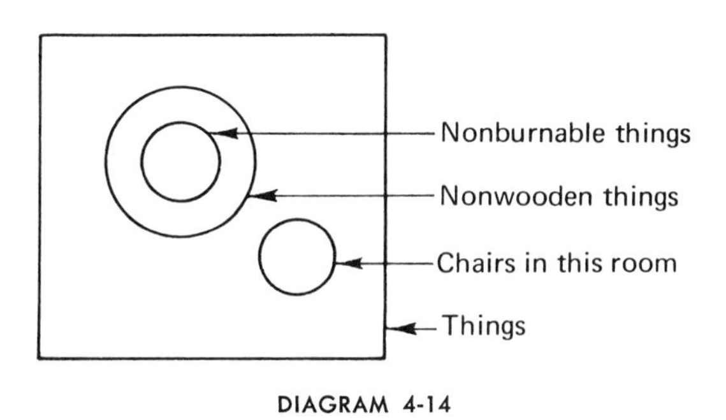

DIAGRAM 4-14

COMPREHENSION SELF-TEST

True or False? If the statement is false, change a crucial term (or terms) to make it true.

4–30. The universe of discourse is a larger class which includes all of the classes which play a role in the argument.

4–31. The universe of discourse is represented by a rectangle which appears around all circles.

4–32. 'All *A*'s are *B*'s' is logically the same as 'All non-*A*'*s* are non-*B*'s'.

Arguments to Diagram and Judge. Diagram each of the following arguments, labeling your diagram. Judge whether the argument is valid or invalid. In cases of invalidity make clear by means of alternate positions why you think the argument is invalid. In each case include a universe of discourse in your diagram.

4–33. Electric bells in complete circuits ring loudly. The front doorbell is in a complete circuit. Therefore, the front doorbell is ringing loudly.

4–34. Complementary colors are colors which when combined appear to be white. Blue and yellow are complementary colors. Therefore, blue and yellow when combined appear to be white.

4–35. Men who are not trusted by the American people are not elected president. Hence men who are elected president are trusted by the American people.

4–36. Bells in complete circuits ring loudly. The bell in my hand is not in a complete circuit. Hence it is not ringing loudly.

4–37. Men who are elected president by the American people are trusted by them. Blaine was not trusted by the American people. Hence he was not elected president.

4–38. Plants and animals which aren't closely related can't be crossed to produce hybrids. Since plants *X* and *Y* can be crossed to produce hybrids, they must be closely related.

4–39. People who know the proper rules of punctuation do well in their written compositions. Mary did not do well in her written compositions. Therefore, Mary does not know the proper rules of punctuation.

4–40. No true believers were heretics. All heretics were condemned. Therefore, no true believers were condemned.

4–41. ". . . none of woman born
Shall harm Macbeth."
". . . Macduff was from his mother's womb,
Untimely ripped."
Therefore, Macduff shall harm Macbeth.

Partial inclusion

The triangle example at the beginning of this chapter contained the key word 'some'. A seemingly obvious way to diagram sentences containing this word is to have overlapping circles, such as those of Diagram 4-15. Fundamentally this is a good idea, but precautions must be taken.

Ambiguity of 'some'

A major difficulty is that the word 'some' is used in two ways, 'at least some (and perhaps all)', and 'some, but not all'. In order to see this ambi-

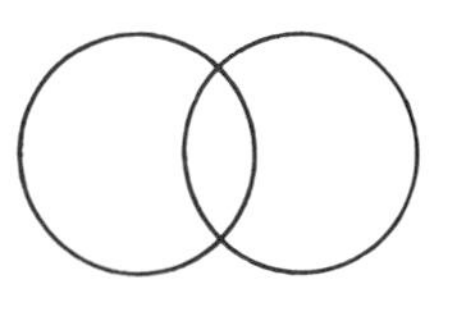
DIAGRAM 4-15

guity, consider the sentence, 'Some of the triangles on the page are inscribed in semi-circles', and say it over to yourself emphasizing different words. The latter interpretation ('some, but not all') is more common and should ordinarily be the interpretation given, if there are no clues. If possible and if there is any doubt in your mind, you should inquire about which is intended. Furthermore when **you** use the word, if any doubt might arise in the minds of your audience, you should say either 'at least some' or 'some, but not all'.

'At least some'

Suppose we want to diagram the 'some' sentence which was one of the premises in the triangle example, "At least some of the triangles on this page are inscribed in semi-circles." This relationship is shown in Diagram 4-16. The dotted line indicates a boundary about which we are somewhat

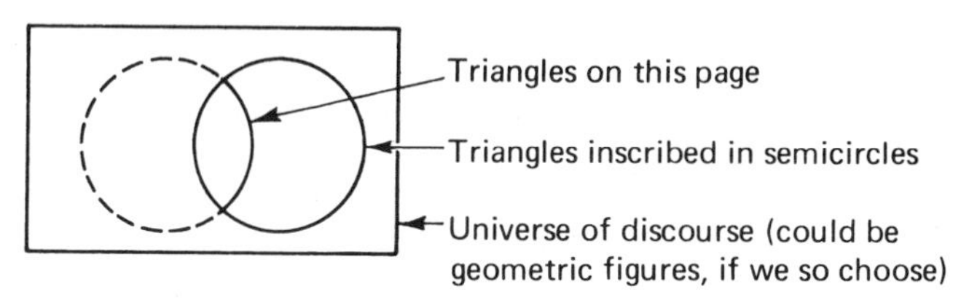

DIAGRAM 4-16

in doubt. There might be triangles on the page which are not inscribed in semi-circles; there might not be such. This indeterminacy is indicated by the dotted line. However, we do know from the premise that there are at least some which **are** inscribed in semi-circles, and the solid part of the line, which is inside the right-hand circle, so indicates.

Now we are in a position to diagram the triangle example (4-2) appearing at the beginning of the chapter. You will remember that it goes like this:

All triangles inscribed in semi-circles are right triangles.
At least some of the triangles on this page are inscribed in semi-circles.

At least some of the triangles on this page are right triangles.

The validity of the argument is shown in Diagram 4-17. There is no way to avoid putting at least a part of the circle for triangles on the page inside the circle for right triangles. Hence the argument is shown to be valid.

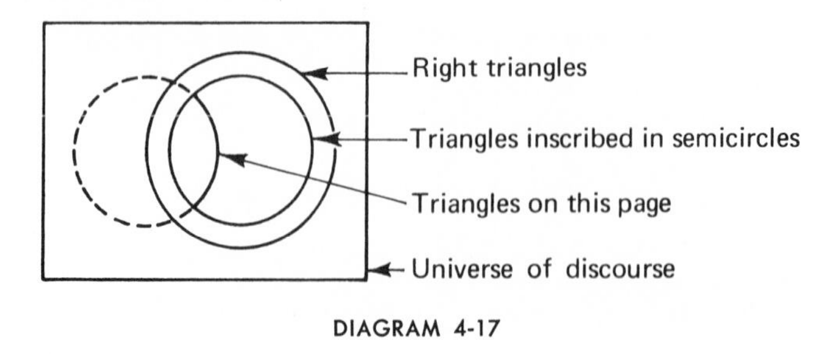

DIAGRAM 4-17

'Some, but not all'

Suppose that the previous 'some' sentence had been as follows:

Some, but not all of the triangles on this page are inscribed in semi-circles.

How should this be diagramed? Since the sentence tells us that there are triangles on this page which are not inscribed, we can diagram this by making the previous dotted line solid, as in Diagram 4-18. Part of the left-hand

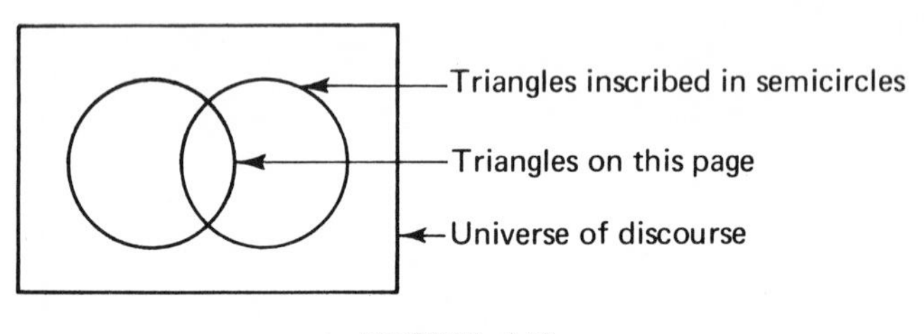

DIAGRAM 4-18

circle is definitely inside, and part is definitely outside the right-hand circle.

Consider the argument with the 'some-but-not-all' interpretation:

Example 4-9

All triangles inscribed in semi-circles are right triangles.
Some, but not all of the triangles on this page are inscribed in semi-circles.

Some, but not all of the triangles on this page are right triangles.

Is it valid? Diagram it and see.

Your diagram could look like that in Diagram 4-19. Since it was possible within the limits prescribed by the premises to put the whole circle for

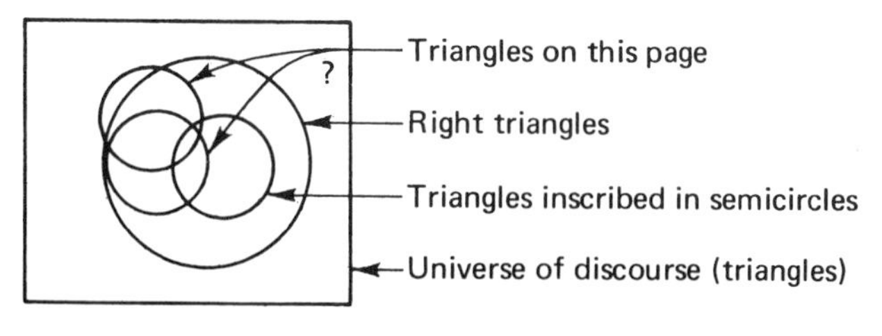

DIAGRAM 4-19

triangles on this page inside the circle for right triangles, the argument is invalid. The conclusion, since it says "but not all", calls for the appearance of part of the area of the triangles-on-the-page circle outside the right-triangle circle. Since we were not inescapably forced to show that state of affairs in the diagram, the argument is invalid.

If this is not clear, it might help to think of the argument in symbolized form. Assume the following assignment of symbols:

Let '*A*'s' = 'triangles inscribed in semi-circles'
Let '*B*'s' = 'right triangles'
Let '*C*'s' = 'the triangles on this page'

Then the argument looks like this:

All *A*'s are *B*'s.
Some, but not all *C*'s are *A*'s.

Some, but not all *C*'s are *B*'s.

From the premises we can see that it might well be that some, but not all *C*'s are *B*'s, but it could be the case that **all** the *C*'s are *B*'s. So the argument is invalid.

If, however, the conclusion were in terms of 'at least some', then the argument would again be valid. If this is not immediately clear to you, make a diagram and see that this is so.

Sometimes, when it is not clear which sense of 'some' is intended, you will find it profitable to diagram the argument several times, using the various possible interpretations. If you get the same result no matter what the interpretation, then you can be safe in making the judgment that it fits them all.

Partial exclusion

The word 'some' is used in negative sentences also. 'At least some *A*'s are not *B*'s' is diagramed as in Diagram 4-20. This diagram leaves open the possibility that at least some *A*'s are *B*'s.

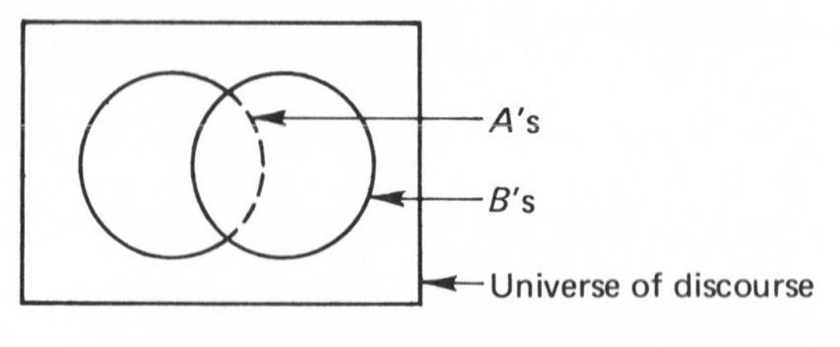

DIAGRAM 4-20

On the other hand, 'Some, but not all *A*'s are not *B*'s' is diagramed (Diagram 4-21) so that all of the circle for the *A*'s is solid. This diagram tells

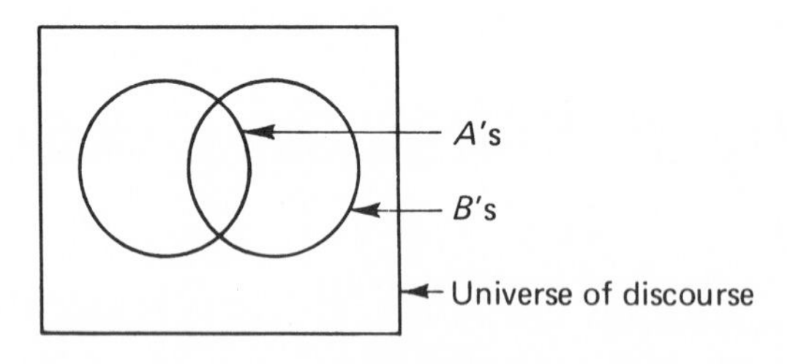

DIAGRAM 4-21

us that at least some *A*'s are *B*'s and that at least some *A*'s are not *B*'s. Since Diagram 4-21 is the same as a diagram for 'Some, but not all *A*'s **are** *B*'s', the two forms are logically equivalent.

COMPREHENSION SELF-TEST

True or False? If the statement is false, change a crucial term (or terms) to make it true.

4-42. The word 'some' is ordinarily to be interpreted as meaning 'at least some'.
4-43. A diagram for 'Some, but not all *A*'s are *B*'s' will have the circle for *A*'s dotted in part.
4-44. A diagram for 'At least some *A*'s are not *B*'s' will have the circle for *A*'s dotted in part.

Sentences to Diagram. Using a universe of discourse, diagram each of the following sentences, labeling the circles, and being careful about the placement of dotted lines.

4-45. At least some things that glitter are not gold.
4-46. Some of the poets in your text are romanticists.
4-47. Some bases are not strong.
4-48. At least some city governments are not corrupt.
4-49. At least some city governments are corrupt.

Arguments to Diagram and Judge. Diagram each of the following arguments, judging whether the argument is valid or invalid. In cases of invalidity, make clear by means of alternates why you think the argument is invalid.

4–50. Triangle *ABC* contains a right angle. Some triangles containing right angles are isosceles. Hence triangle *ABC* is isosceles.

4–51. The romanticists idealized life. Some of the poets in your text are romanticists. Therefore, some of the poets in your text idealized life.

4–52. All plants in which photosynthesis occurs need water. There are some plants, however, in which photosynthesis does not occur. Therefore, there are some plants which do not need water.

4–53. Some foods contain hydrogen and oxygen. All carbohydrates contain hydrogen and oxygen. Therefore, some foods are carbohydrates.

4–54. At least some things that glitter are not gold. The trinkets in this box glitter. Hence these trinkets are not gold.

4–55. At least some city governments are not corrupt. The government of New York, although complex, is still a city government. Hence it is not corrupt.

4–56. The liquid that I spilled on my lab table is a base. Since some bases are not strong, I can be sure that this liquid is not strong.

Multiple premises

This Euler circle system is useful for class reasoning arguments containing more than two premises. The thing to do is to look for premises with common classes and make use of the common classes to combine the premises in the same diagram. Again you work against the conclusion (but give it a chance, of course!). Here is a simple example using letters to stand for classes:

Example 4-10

All *A*'s are *B*'s.
All *B*'s are *C*'s.
All *C*'s are *D*'s.

All *A*'s are *D*'s.

The diagram looks like Diagram 4-22. The conclusion is inescapably diagramed, so the argument is valid.

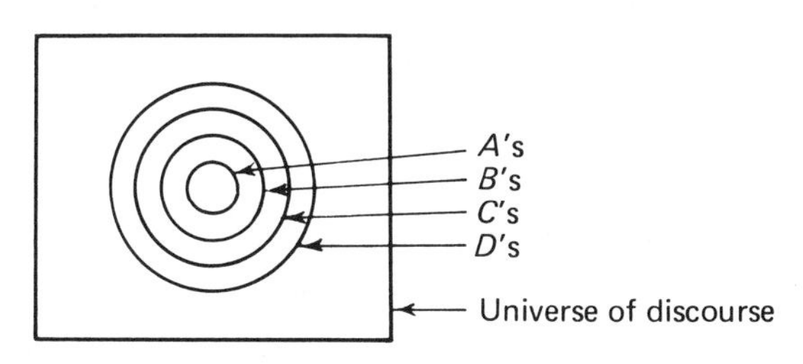

DIAGRAM 4-22

Here is a more difficult example, again using letters to stand for classes. It is more difficult because it requires a transformation on the side, which rates a separate diagram:

Example 4-11

All *D*'s are *B*'s.
All non-*D*'s are non-*C*'s.
All *B*'s are *A*'s.

All *C*'s are *A*'s.

Try to work this yourself, before reading on.

One way to start is to transform the second premise so that it will have classes in common with the other premises. Perhaps you can do this in your head, but it is safer to put it on paper (Diagram 4-23). Since the area out-

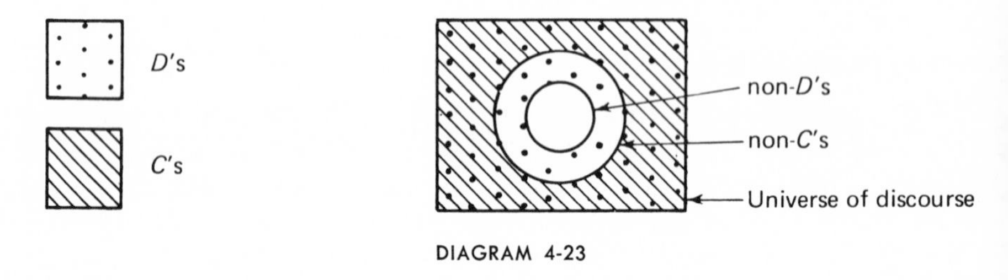

DIAGRAM 4-23

side the larger circle represents *C*'s, and the area outside the smaller circle represents *D*'s, we can say from this diagram that all *C*'s are *D*'s. If we substitute that for the second premise, then the problem becomes easy (Diagram 4-24). Since the conclusion is inescapably diagramed, the argument is valid.

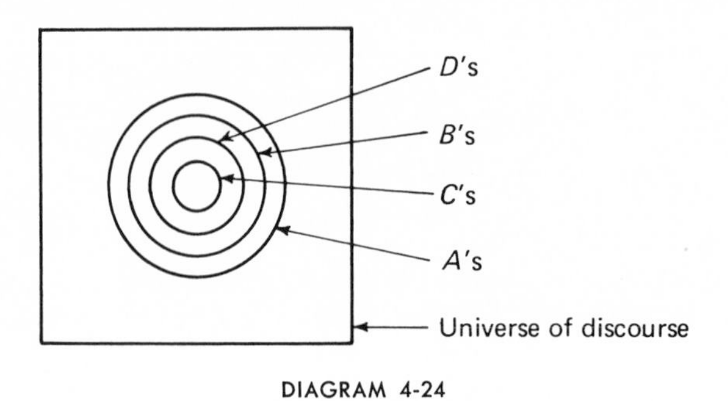

DIAGRAM 4-24

COMPREHENSION SELF-TEST

Arguments to Diagram and Judge. Diagram each of the following arguments, using a universe of discourse and labeling the circles with class terms. Judge whether the argument is valid, making clear by means of your diagram that the argument is as you judge it.

4–57. Any man who voted for Senator Smart has in effect voted against himself. John Brown voted for Senator Smart. It is obvious that anyone who votes against himself is a fool. Hence John Brown is a fool.

4–58. All genuine foods contain hydrogen and oxygen. This is also true of carbohydrates. Since all carbohydrates contain carbon, we can be sure that all genuine foods contain carbon.

4–59. Nobody who has attained historical fame has done it as a result of his own inherent greatness. All of the characters in the history book may be regarded as famous. Hence, Napoleon Bonaparte, a prominent figure in the history book, is not famous as a result of his own inherent greatness.

Note: The following arguments are a few of many similar arguments to be found in Lewis Carroll's book, *Symbolic Logic*, which was published under his real name, Charles Lutwidge Dodgson. Lewis Carroll was a mathematician and logician.

In these arguments, the conclusions are not given. You must figure out what conclusion follows necessarily and makes use of all the premises. Diagram the argument and write out the conclusion.

4–60. Babies are illogical. Nobody is despised who can manage a crocodile. Illogical persons are despised. What follows?

4–61. The only books in the library, that I do **not** recommend for reading, are unhealthy in tone. The bound books are all well written. All the romances are healthy in tone. I do not recommend you to read any of the unbound books. What follows?

4–62. No kitten, that loves fish, is unteachable. No kitten without a tail will play with a gorilla. Kittens with whiskers always love fish. No teachable kitten has green eyes. No kittens have tails unless they have whiskers.

4–63. No interesting poems are unpopular among people of real taste. No modern poetry is free from affectation. All your poems are on the subject of soap bubbles. No affected poetry is popular among people of real taste. No ancient poem is on the subject of soap bubbles. What follows?

Other interpretation problems

To express the thought behind the form, 'At least some *A*'s are not *B*'s', people frequently use a manner of speaking that strictly speaking means something else. They say, 'All that are *A*'s are not *B*'s.' For example in order to express the thought, 'At least some things that glitter are not gold', Shakespeare used the following: "All that glitters is not gold."

Strictly speaking, Shakespeare's form of words implies that everything that glitters is not gold. (If something glitters, then it is not gold.) Of course he did not mean this, so one must be careful in interpreting sentences that are of this form.

A little reflection will show you that another way of putting the same thought is in the form, 'Not all *A*'s are *B*'s.' In terms of the above example, the expression would be 'Not all that glitters is gold.' Diagram 4-25 repre-

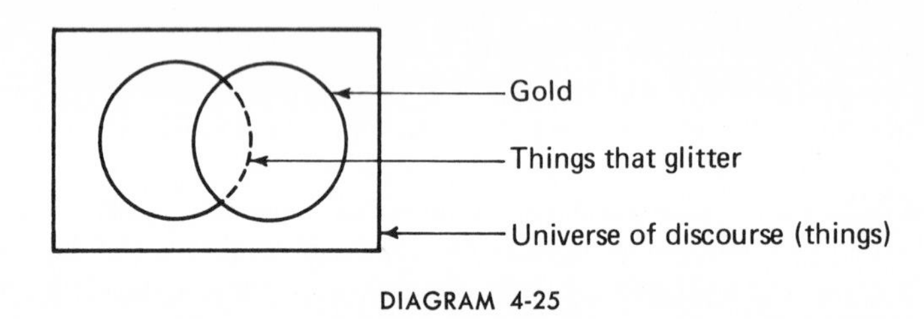

DIAGRAM 4-25

sents each of the two strict ways of expressing this thought. Examine it carefully. Each of the two sentences, 'At least some things that glitter are not gold' and 'Not all that glitters is gold' can be read from Diagram 4-25.

In traditional logic an elaborate system has been developed for determining the relationships between sentences like the above pair. Part of this system is referred to as "the square of opposition". The approach of this book is to depend upon the spatial relationships between circles, so I will not present the elaborate system, trusting that your grasp of the circle system will suffice. Some of you will find the elaborate system of interest and might consult some standard logic text for a treatment of it.* But an intelligent, cautious application of the Euler circle method should enable you to handle the practical problems for which the system can be of use.

No logical system has been organized which makes use of the distinctions in ordinary language that exist between 'few', 'much', 'several', 'many', 'most', etc. This Euler circle system is no exception. You must use common sense in applying this system to sentences containing such words.

Extent of the predicate class

So far we have ignored the ambiguity that is present in most of these sentences with respect to the predicate class. When we say that all *A*'s are *B*'s, that form of words does not tell whether there are *B*'s which are not *A*'s. It leaves open the possibility that there are *B*'s which are not *A*'s, but it also leaves open the possibility that there are no *B*'s which are not *A*'s.

* One standard text, which is as good as any other, is that by Morris Cohen and Ernest Nagel, *An Introduction to Logic and the Scientific Method* (New York: Harcourt, Brace and Company, 1934).

Hence from the form of the sentence, 'All *A*'s are *B*'s', we cannot conclude 'All *B*'s are *A*'s', nor can we conclude 'At least some *B*'s are not *A*'s'. Both possibilities are left open by the form of words, but neither is required.

Usually we can ignore this problem, but sometimes a judgment about an argument depends on our alertness to it. It is a good idea, when diagramming affirmative (as opposed to negative) statements, to remember that the extent of the predicate class is undetermined by the form of words. Sometimes it is determined by the context, and sometimes the extent does not matter. But be alert for this situation when working against the proposed conclusion.

Here is an example of an argument in which you might go wrong, if you are not alert for this situation:

Example 4-12

All right triangles can be inscribed in semi-circles.
All triangles in which the sum of two of the angles equals 90 degrees are right triangles.

At least some triangles which can be inscribed in semi-circles do not have the sum of two of their angles equal to 90 degrees.

A hasty diagram of that argument looks like Diagram 4-26. This diagram certainly suggests the conclusion, since some of the area for 'triangles that

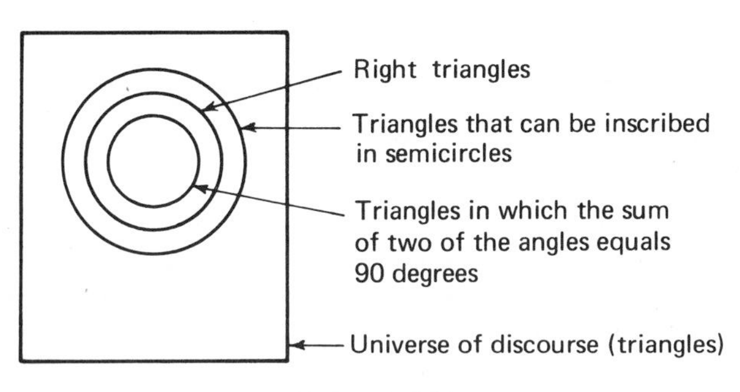

DIAGRAM 4-26

can be inscribed in semi-circles' is outside of the area for 'triangles in which the sum of two of the angles equals 90 degrees'. But to draw the proposed conclusion would be to depend on the assumption that the extent of the predicate class is greater than that of the subject class. This is an assumption which we never have a right to make on the basis of the form of the statements as they appear above, and which in this case is false for both premises.

Conclusions cannot depend on such an assumption unless it is explicitly part of the premises. When a statement of the form, 'All *A*'s are *B*'s', is made, we are left in doubt about whether at least some *B*'s are not *A*'s. That is,

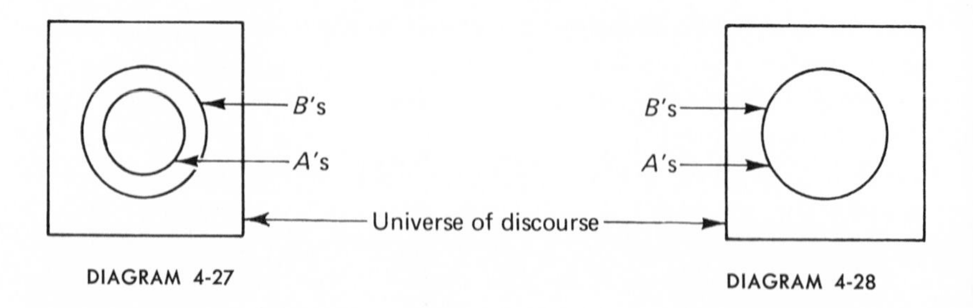

DIAGRAM 4-27

DIAGRAM 4-28

Diagrams 4-27 and 4-28 are left open as possibilities. In Diagram 4-27 the circle for the *A*'s is inside the circle for the *B*'s. In Diagram 4-28 the circles are the same size and in the same place. The two circles completely overlap, thus appearing as only one circle. This is the diagram that means that all *A*'s are *B*'s **and** all *B*'s are *A*'s. It is the possibility of this latter situation, as represented in Diagram 4-28, that makes it improper to make the above-mentioned assumption.

Taking the first premise of the example, Diagrams 4-29 and 4-30 are

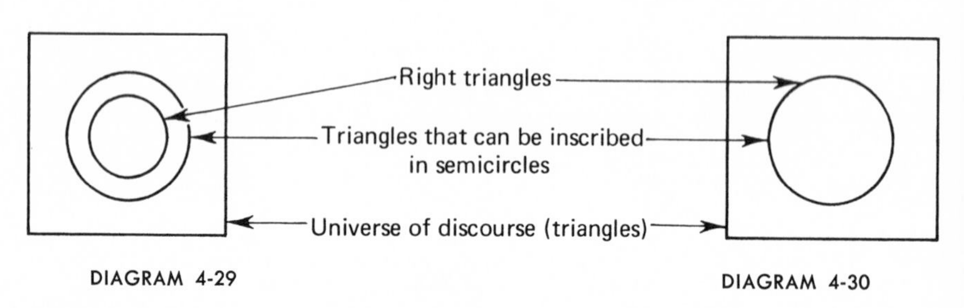

DIAGRAM 4-29

DIAGRAM 4-30

each a possibility, given only, "All right triangles can be inscribed in semicircles." The same thing can be done with the second premise. In view of these alternatives for each premise, a possible way of diagraming the premises is shown in Diagram 4-31, which does not force us to accept the conclusion. Hence the argument is invalid.

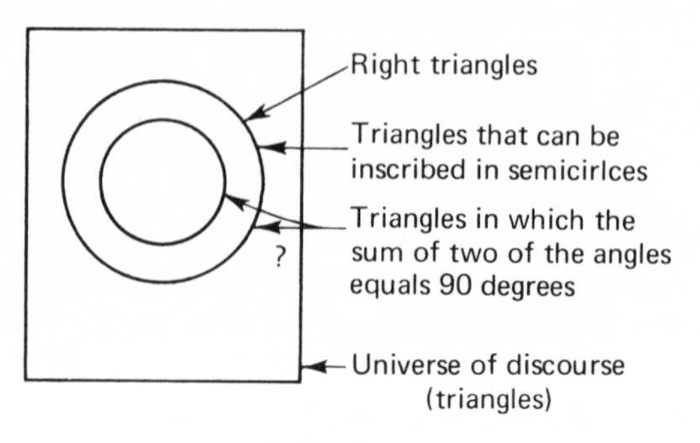

DIAGRAM 4-31

This way of working against the conclusion of an argument illustrates the fact that this system is only an aid to your judgment in dealing with arguments. It is not a strictly mechanical system, but must be used with care and ingenuity.

COMPREHENSION SELF-TEST

True or False? If the statement is false, change a crucial term (or terms) to make it true.

4–64. The Euler circle system which you have learned does not make a distinction between 'a few' and 'several'.

4–65. The use of the form, 'All *A*'s are *B*'s', implies that there are *B*'s which are not *A*'s.

4–66. Strictly speaking, 'All of the lake doesn't have fish' means that there are no fish in the lake.

Arguments to Diagram and Judge. Diagram and label each of the following arguments, using a universe of discourse. Judge the validity, making clear why you judge as you do.

4–67. Every bishop was an important church official. Many important church officials held fiefs from kings. Therefore, many bishops held fiefs from kings.

4–68. Some fiefs were held by secular lords. Many fiefs held by secular lords were hereditary. Hence some fiefs were hereditary.

4–69. Not all rhombuses are similar. *A* and *B* are two polygons that are not similar. Therefore *A* and *B* are rhombuses.

4–70. People who spell English words exactly as they sound misspell some of them. Joe misspells many English words. Therefore, Joe spells many English words exactly as they sound.

4–71. All that glitters is not gold. This case glitters. Hence it is not gold.

4–72. All of the members of the team did not break training. Only if everyone on the team broke training will we lose. Hence we will not lose. (Note: Use whatever procedures seem appropriate for this argument.)

4–73. The buildings on the campus are all of Gothic architecture. Whatever is of Gothic architecture is out of step with the times. Hence the buildings on the campus are out of step with the times, and there are things which are out of step with the times which are not on this campus.

4–74. Whatever is in the animal kingdom is not in the plant kingdom. Lobsters are in the plant kingdom. Hence there are things not in the plant kingdom which are not lobsters.

Combination of Class and Sentence Reasoning

Contemporary logic contains a system—with many variations—which combines sentence and class reasoning by elaborating sentence reasoning and introducing a more complicated symbolism. The resulting system for handling class reasoning is often called the "predicate calculus". I do not believe that one need master this system in order to handle problems in everyday reasoning, although the system is interesting in its own right and is valuable in understanding the foundations of mathematics and some of contemporary philosophy.

Part-by-part use of the two systems

You can use in combination the two systems when faced with arguments that involve both class and sentence reasoning. You might treat the diagrams as sentences which can be joined by the logical connectives you have studied. Or you might be able to work the parts separately in the different systems. For example consider this argument, again about Ingrid's dough:

Example 4-13
Only if Ingrid's dough contains yeast mixed with lukewarm water did she make the check in her book. Now we know that dough containing yeast mixed with lukewarm water rises rapidly. And we also know that she made the check in her book. Hence we know that her dough is rising rapidly.

An examination of this argument shows that, using the techniques of sentence reasoning, we can combine the first and the third sentences to produce the subconclusion, "Ingrid's dough contains yeast mixed with lukewarm water." Using the techniques of class reasoning we can combine this subconclusion with the second sentence to produce the given conclusion. I shall work it out in detail:

Example 4-14
Let 'q' = 'Ingrid's dough contains yeast mixed with lukewarm water'
Let 'p' = 'she made the check in her book'

Premises (of the sentence reasoning part of the argument):

$p \longrightarrow q$
p

Conclusion (of this part of the argument):

q (by affirmation of the antecedent)

So far we are entitled to conclude that Ingrid's dough contains yeast mixed with lukewarm water. Examination of Diagram 4-32 shows the rest of the argument, and thus the total argument, to be valid.

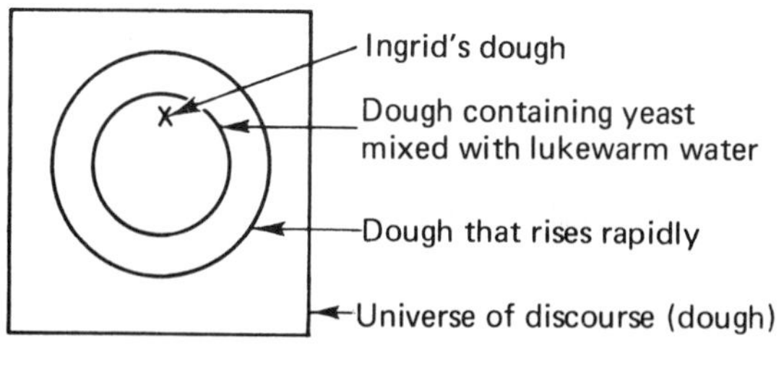

DIAGRAM 4-32

Instantiation

You will remember that one of the occasions for the introduction of the Euler circle system was in part the inability of strictly interpreted sentence reasoning to handle Example 4-1, which went as follows:

> Dough containing yeast mixed with lukewarm water rises rapidly.
> Ingrid's dough contains yeast mixed with lukewarm water.
>
> ---
>
> Therefore Ingrid's dough rises rapidly.

The problem was that a transformation of the first premise to conditional form did not produce two separate affirmable sentences:

> If any dough contains yeast mixed with lukewarm water, then that dough rises rapidly.

To say "Ingrid's dough contains yeast mixed with lukewarm water" is not to say "Any dough contains yeast mixed with lukewarm water", the latter of these looking something, but not quite, like an antecedent of the conditional, and not being meaningfully affirmable.

In contemporary logic a useful move has been developed for this kind of situation. I will describe it because it is sometimes more convenient to use this move than to use the Euler circle system, depending mainly on the form in which the premise happens to be naturally stated. This move is called instantiation. The following step from the more general to more specific statement is an example of instantiation:

Example 4-15

FROM:

> If any dough contains yeast mixed with lukewarm water, than that dough rises rapidly.

TO:

> If Ingrid's dough contains yeast mixed with lukewarm water, then Ingrid's dough will rise rapidly.

In effect the specific reference to Ingrid's dough was substituted for the variable reference to any dough. Note that we can affirm the new antecedent without uttering nonsense; thus the result of the instantiation step is suitable for use in sentence reasoning.

To INSTANTIATE a conditional statement is to give its application to a specific situation, the result being another (but specific) conditional. The move is an intuitively plausible one and removes the barrier to treating a number of deductions in sentence reasoning terms. Once we have made the move in the dough example, we can take the instantiation and use it as a premise as follows:

Example 4-16

If Ingrid's dough contains yeast mixed with lukewarm water, then Ingrid's dough will rise rapidly.
Ingrid's dough contains yeast mixed with lukewarm water.

Ingrid's dough will rise rapidly.
Valid. Affirming the antecedent.

Whether you actually choose to use instantiation or the circle method in any particular case is partly a matter of taste and partly a matter of convenience.

Ingenuity is often required in devising ways to judge arguments, but with an understanding of the ways of handling arguments presented in this and the previous chapter, you should be able to work out any long deductive reasoning problems that you will genuinely face. Generally, long arguments become simple by being broken up into parts that can be managed with the basic techniques you have seen.

COMPREHENSION SELF-TEST

Arguments to Judge. Here is a set of arguments. Using any techniques that you feel are appropriate, decide whether each argument is valid. But show all your work.

4-75. Either the present municipal airport should continue to be used for purposes of general aviation, or it should be used to provide a site for a summer festival every year, but not both. It should continue to be used for general aviation only if the other airport is to be closed down. The other airport is not to be closed down; rather it is to be expanded. Hence the municipal airport should be used to provide a site for a summer festival each year.

4-76. If Brown has a position on the Rules Committee, then all the men on this list have declined to serve. Jones is on the list, and he has declined to serve only if he was appointed to the Appropriations Committee. Since Jones was not appointed to this last-named committee, Brown has not secured a position on the Rules Committee.

4-77. Only if the piece of wood sinks in the beaker of alcohol is its specific gravity greater than one. Anything with a specific gravity greater than one will sink in water. The piece of wood sinks in alcohol. Hence it will sink in water.

4–78. Most household chemicals are safe to touch. If any chemical is not safe to touch, however, then it is so labeled. There is no label indicating danger on this bottle of citric acid. Therefore, it is safe to touch.

4–79. All of Beethoven's works are solid and deliberate. Now Frank does not like music that is solid and deliberate, and whatever he does not like he does not really listen to. He is really listening to this music only if his eyes are closed. Since his eyes are not closed, we can conclude two things: (1) Frank does not like this piece, and (2) it is by Beethoven.

4–80. All well-lighted rooms have light-colored walls. Some of the rooms in Stone Hall are small. All of the rooms in Stone Hall either have very dark-colored walls, or have no windows, or are large, or are well lighted. The rooms in Stone Hall that are not well lighted are on the east side. All of the rooms on the east side have windows. If some of the rooms in Stone Hall are small, then my room in Stone Hall is small. The walls in my room are not light colored. Therefore, the walls in my room are very dark in color.

Chapter Summary

In the system presented in this chapter, a modified Euler circle system, the classes and individuals which are the basic units in class reasoning are, for purposes of seeing relationships, represented by circles and the letter '*x*'. Often, however, sentences as they appear must be revised in order to bring out the class relationships to be put in a circle diagram. This revision most often requires that the predicate of the sentence be changed to contain a class, which is connected to the subject by the verb of inclusion (or membership), the verb, 'to be'. For example the sentence, 'This tree grows quickly', becomes 'This tree is a quickly growing thing' or 'This tree is a quick grower'.

When this sort of revision, if necessary, is accomplished, the classes are represented on paper in the form of circles. The inclusion of one class in another is represented by the inclusion of one circle in the other. The membership of one individual in a class is represented by the appearance of an '*x*' to represent the individual in the circle to represent the class.

Exclusion is represented by keeping these things separate from each other. Partial inclusion is shown by partial overlapping (with dotted lines to show where boundaries are uncertain), and partial exclusion is shown by partially separate circles (again using dotted lines to show boundaries that are uncertain).

Since a standard class inclusion statement of the form, 'All *A*'s are *B*'s', does not indicate whether there are *B*'s which are not *A*'s, one must remember that the extent of the circle for the predicate class is in doubt. That it occupies the same place as that for the subject class is not ruled out by the form, 'All *A*'s are *B*'s'.

One determines whether an argument is valid by putting the premises into one diagram, combining them where possible. In so doing one tries not to diagram the proposed conclusion, doing justice of course to the premises. If the conclusion is inescapably diagramed by the diagraming of the premises, then the argument is valid.

Combinations of class and sentence reasoning can be handled by breaking the argument into component parts and treating each part appropriately. In such combinations, as with all genuine arguments, one must use care and common sense, since the systems offered are not simply automatic. No realistic logic can be.

Instantiation, which is basically a class reasoning step, can be used to accommodate the methods of sentence reasoning to some deductions which appear in class reasoning form. In many cases the choice between the circle system and sentence reasoning (with instantiation) is a matter of taste and convenience.

CHAPTER 5

Practical Application of Deductive Logic

Perhaps you have already noticed that when you actually apply the techniques and rules of deductive reasoning presented in the previous three chapters, you run into snags. The snags are generally of two types: those resulting from the fact that much deductive-like reasoning occurs which does not strictly conform to the principles of ideal deduction; and those resulting from the fact that there are other forms of necessary inference than the ones you have studied here. This chapter treats those two types of snags.

Looseness of Reasoning

The term, 'looseness', as it appears in this chapter, is not meant to be a pejorative term. It is used simply to show recognition of the facts of life: the standards of deduction cannot be applied strictly and directly to many cases of actual reasoning that go from general statements to specific ones and appear deductive in form. This is a strong statement, the truth of which becomes evident when one tries to take these standards seriously and tries to apply them directly to respectable inference practice in most fields of study.

In what follows, I shall develop a model which makes reasonable use of deductive standards, and consider then a number of examples drawn from different fields in order to show how this model can be applied. Please realize that this problem of looseness is not one to which logicians have devoted much attention. The solution to it, even among those who recognize that it exists, has not been a subject of intense, disciplined, comprehensive treatment. Hence you should not treat what you are about to read as doctrine received and accepted by the philosophical community. Instead look at it as something placed before you in an attempt to make sense out of what is otherwise a puzzling situation.

Actually the proposed model is not at all complicated. It simply treats strict deduction as an idealized set of inference patterns to which we shift in judging the formal moves in an argument. Thus there are basically three steps in this model: (1) the shift into idealized form; (2) the judgment of the validity of the idealized form thus produced; and (3) the shift from the idealized conclusion back to the world of reality. In actual practice these three steps are not sharply distinguished. Generally one merges the three together. They are separated here so that a role for strict deduction can become explicit, and so that deviations from the strict deductive pattern can be explained.

Step 1: the shift into idealized form

In this first step the premises are put into shape, partly by revision to fit some recognizable formal pattern, and partly by eliminating implicit and explicit general qualifiers. By 'GENERAL QUALIFIERS' I mean such terms as 'probably', 'likely', 'generally', 'for the most part', 'under normal conditions', '*ceteris paribus*' ('other things being equal'),* 'by and large', and 'roughly speaking'. These are general because they are not limited to any subject matter or branch of inquiry.

Implicit qualifications are eliminated by simply ignoring them. Explicit qualifications are eliminated by dropping them off for the purposes of Step 2. Consider this statement:

Example 5-1
A wind shift from south to northwest is generally accompanied by clearing and colder weather.

* ∴It is somewhat of a simplification to group 'under normal conditions' and 'other things being equal' with the rest, but the simplification does not damage the general approach recommended here, so long as one keeps the meaning of the eliminated qualifier in mind. An alternative system suggested by Professor David Lyons would allow the retention of these two qualifiers in the general statements of the premises and for the deduction test in Step 2 would add a presumably implicit premise affirming the satisfaction of the qualifier. Then the problems discussed later under Step 3 must in part be faced when deciding whether and how strongly to endorse the implicit premise.

Deletion of the term 'generally' would effect the transformation into idealized form.

Example 5-2
Other things being equal, if the demand for a commodity decreases, the price will decrease (assuming that the supply remains the same).

In this last example deletion of 'other things being equal' effects the transformation. Note, however, that one specific condition is singled out for the requirement that it be equal (remain the same): the supply. Mention of this specific condition is not to be deleted in the transformation. The only qualifiers that are deleted are the general qualifiers. The qualifier, "the supply remains the same", is specific to the subject matter of the principle.

Example 5-3
Each one of the periods of lax financial integrity coincides with periods when a new set of frontier communities had arisen, and coincides in area with these successive frontiers, for the most part.*

Deletion of the phrase, 'for the most part', would transform this general statement into idealized form, if the phrase qualifies the entire statement. If it only qualifies coincidence in area, then we need only delete it for certain purposes. We will go into this later.

In this next example there are no explicit general qualifiers.

Example 5-4
English literature of the first fifty years of the eighteenth century was neoclassical.

However, anyone at all versed in the field of literature knows that there are always exceptions to such statements, which fact could be shown by the use of the qualifier 'generally'. But the existence of such exceptions apparently is such common knowledge that people take it for granted and do not bother to insert explicit qualifiers, leaving them implicit. Hence elimination of the qualifiers in such cases simply consists in temporarily forgetting the common knowledge that there are exceptions.

Step 1 also includes whatever else is needed to put the premises in shape for the application of techniques presented in the previous three chapters. Although no precise line can be drawn between putting the premises in shape and using deductive techniques,** there still is a distinction between

* Frederick Jackson Turner, "The Significance of the Frontier in American History," a paper read at the meeting of the American Historical Association in Chicago, July 12, 1893, and reprinted in various places, including Turner's *The Frontier in American History* (New York: Henry Holt and Company, 1921), p. 32.

** "Putting an Argument in Shape" (see Chapter 3) was one of the headings in the material dealing with deductive techniques.

the preliminary procedures requiring intelligent judgment and the application of rule-governed techniques.

Step 2: judgment of validity

This step was the subject of the previous three chapters. An explicit validity test must be applied. Consider this simple example:

Example 5-5
Premises:
A wind shift from south to northwest is accompanied by clearing and colder weather.
The wind shift that just occurred was a shift from south to northwest.
Conclusion:
The wind shift that just occurred will be accompanied by clearing and colder weather.*

The argument is valid, as can be seen by an inspection of Diagram 5-1.

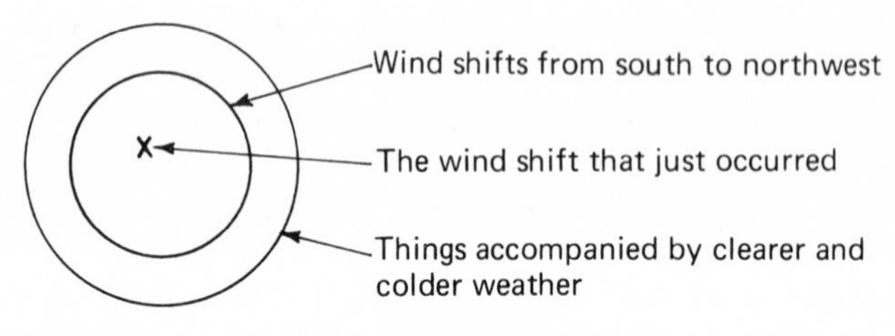

DIAGRAM 5-1

In order to adjust the first premise and conclusion to the diagram system, they were put in the form of class relationship statements:

A wind shift from south to northwest is a thing accompanied by clearing and colder weather.
The wind shift that just occurred will be a thing accompanied by clearing and colder weather.

The explicit validity test that was applied was the rule about trying to avoid diagraming the conclusion.

Step 3: the shift from the conclusion back to the world of reality

This step is the most risky and difficult one. No set procedures exist for weakening the conclusion and/or deciding whether it should be asserted.

* For purposes of simplicity I shall ignore the tense differences in the verbs here. In some cases such shifts do make a difference, so be wary.

This step requires a familiarity with the field in which the subject matter is located and experience in drawing conclusions in this field. It also depends on the context. Since there are no explicit exceptionless rules to follow, one can expect that experts in the given field will in some cases disagree on the results. This part of practical reasoning is an art which calls for the intelligent exercise of experienced judgment.

In the weather-prediction example the appropriate conclusion might well be the following:

Example 5-6
The wind shift that just occurred will probably be accompanied by clearing and colder weather.

The word 'probably' has been inserted, because the science of weather prediction calls for some sort of indication that the prediction might not be fulfilled. This word 'probably' performs the function of letting one's audience know that the asserter, although reasonably confident of his statement, does not want to guarantee it unconditionally. He explicitly disclaims full endorsement of the statement. In this case, if you were the person making the weather prediction, you would by the use of 'probably' be explicitly disclaiming full endorsement of the statement that the wind shift that just occurred will be accompanied by clearing and colder weather.* A variety of considerations can justify this disclaimer.

For example the premises might not be indentical with true factual reports, perhaps because the premises are more vague or more specific. Suppose in trying to decide whether to apply the generalization in Example 5-1, one learns that the wind was from 190 degrees (180 degrees is due south) and has shifted to being from 300 degrees (exactly northwest is 315 degrees). Has there been a shift from south to northwest? Answering this question requires familiarity with the field. Inevitably there will be borderline cases and disagreement among experts. In this case I presume that most would say that there has been such a shift and that the generalization would still apply. But in any case intelligent, informed, experienced judgment is needed.

Rejection. Furthermore under certain conditions one might justifiably decide that the conclusion, even with the word 'probably' inserted, should not be asserted. The ability to make decisions of this sort calls for expertise, familiarity, and experience. In the weather-prediction example, if the wind shift is the result of a local thunderstorm that develops in advance of a warm front, then it probably will not be accompanied by clearing and colder. Furthermore it will probably soon be followed by a wind shift back to the

* The use of the word 'probably' and terms like it is discussed in J. O. Urmson's "Parenthetical Verbs," in Antony Flew, ed., *Essays in Conceptual Analysis* (London: Macmillan & Co. Ltd., 1956), pp. 192–212; and in S. Toulmin's article, "Probability," in the same volume, pp. 157–91.

south. There are other standard exceptions as well, but mention of this one makes the point.

Uncertainty. A similar problem exists in the application of the generalization in a different type of surrounding, say Death Valley, California, or Vienna, or Tibet, or Mars. Again experience and expertise is required in deciding whether the conclusion should be asserted, even with the word 'probably' included.

Application to the Situation. In the process of applying the conclusions of practical reasoning, the problem of vagueness reappears. In order to avoid being paralyzed by a degree of imprecision in our knowledge, and/or in order to avoid unnecessary precision, we make use of ways of saying things that are to an extent vague. This leads to borderline cases and indeterminacy. Consider Example 5-6. Suppose that one wants to know whether to make plans for an airplane take-off in exactly one hour. The given conclusion does not tell one exactly when to expect the accompanying clearing. Suppose that one wants to know whether a pond will freeze overnight. The given conclusion does not specify how much colder it will be. Actually our meteorological knowledge warrants more precision than that given in the prediction of Example 5-6, but a more complicated principle must be used than the one given as the first premise in the argument, and more facts must be used as other premises.

This sort of vagueness is also a problem when dispute arises about the truth of the generalization: Someone offers as counter-evidence to the generalization the fact that it is one hour after the wind shift, but the weather actually looks more ominous and there has been a temperature drop of only one degree. Is this counter-evidence or not? Again intelligent informed judgment is required.

The Broader Logical Context. This last-described situation brings to mind another factor to which one must attend: the broader logical move in which the argument plays a role. Four such broader moves which frequently occur are prediction, retrodiction, explanation, and hypothesis-testing.

The weather case, as discussed, exemplifies prediction, and shows some of the sorts of considerations which bear upon the expressed degree of endorsement of the conclusion. Retrodiction is similar to prediction, except that retrodiction applies to the past, while prediction applies to the future. When we conclude that a certain thing probably happened and make use of reasoning processes similar to those used in prediction, we are RETRODICTING. For example suppose that we know that five days ago, when the weather was bad, the wind shifted from south to northwest. We might on this basis make the following retrodiction: The weather probably cleared up soon thereafter. And again judicious use of experience and theoretical knowledge should temper our use of 'probably'—or our complete rejection of the retrodiction.

Arguments also play a role in some kinds of explanation. If we want to explain why the weather cleared during the day, we might point out the fact that the wind shifted early this morning, and, making use of the generalization, show that the thing to be explained follows loosely from the fact and the generalization. In this case the deduction is not used to show that its conclusion is true, for we already know that it is true. What we want is an explanation of why it is true—and, given an appropriate context, this explanation is provided by the deductive argument leading to the conclusion. In this sort of situation it does not make sense to add such words as 'probably' to the conclusion, because we already know it to be true. The word 'probably' would imply that we do not **know** that the conclusion is true, but merely have good reason to believe it to be true.

Deductive arguments also play a role in the testing of hypotheses. The role is a complicated one, but let me point out here that the implications of a hypothesis often count as tests of the hypothesis. Roughly speaking if an implication turns out to be false, then by denial of the consequent, the hypothesis is thereby shown to be false (unless one of the assumptions is abandoned). And if the implications turn out to be true, then under certain conditions, the hypothesis thereby achieves a greater degree of credibility. Of course, each of these results is subject to experience and theoretical knowledge.

Granting the above brief analysis of the relation between a hypothesis and its implications, and construing the hypothesis as one of the premises in an argument and an implication as the conclusion to an argument, we then face the question of how strongly to endorse such a conclusion. In the case in which the hypothesis is something about which we are not sure, and we have not yet checked to see if the implication (the conclusion) is true, we are not in a position to endorse the conclusion, but neither are we in a position to deny it. Hence we must say something like this: "The hypothesis makes the conclusion probable", hedging against direct endorsement and denial, and instead only indicating degree of endorsement of the argument from hypothesis to implication.

These comments about prediction, retrodiction, explanation, and hypothesis are not meant to cover comprehensively all types of situations. Instead they are intended to note some significant differences in some common broad logical moves in which arguments play a role, and to suggest ways in which we attend to these differences in phrasing and endorsing conclusions to arguments.

False Premises and Invalid Arguments. You will remember from the discussion in Chapter 2 that one can have a true conclusion to a valid argument, even though the premises are false. Furthermore, it is also possible to have a true conclusion to an invalid argument utilizing true premises. And lastly one can have a true conclusion to an invalid argument containing false premises. Thus these defects in argument and/or premises do not by themselves justify rejection of the conclusion; but they do show that the conclusion is not established by the argument.

Summary

The three steps (shift to idealized form, judgment of validity, and shift from the conclusion back to the world of reality), which are treated separately for purposes of examining the problems of practical reasoning, are performed in concert in actual cases of reasoning. Furthermore, although Step 2, the application of deductive techniques, can be at times fairly difficult, it is generally the easiest step; the other two require careful, intelligent, informed judgment, which for its background and degree of specificity must depend on the context, the nature of the subject matter involved, and the knowledge of it that we possess.

Other Types of Deduction

Not all deductive arguments, even after the appropriate adjustments for looseness have been made, can be judged by the criteria given for sentence and class reasoning. There are other types of deduction. To some extent an understanding of sentence and class reasoning is helpful in dealing with other types, because one who does understand these two has a grasp of the basic idea of necessary inference and because in some cases the techniques for sentence and class reasoning loosely apply to others. For example the transitivity of the conditional chain is paralleled by the transitivity of equality and of ordinal relationships:

If $p \longrightarrow q$ and $q \longrightarrow r$, then $p \longrightarrow r$
is parallel to
If $x = y$ and $y = z$, then $x = z$
and also to
If n is greater than m and m is greater k, then n is greater than k.

In order to give warning of the types of problems that one might face, I shall describe briefly some other types of deduction. Since no successful comprehensive classification of types of deduction has to my knowledge ever been prepared, I make no claim about the comprehensiveness of this list.

Mathematics

A wide variety of deductive techniques are used in mathematical proofs: reduction of fractions, derivation of formulas, manipulating and solving equations, and many other techniques. These are deductive because, given the premises, the conclusion necessarily follows. The deductive relationship holds not only for complex mathematical proofs, but also for the very simple relationships one learns to use in his early years of schooling. This book makes no attempt to present the deductive techniques of mathematics.

*Alethic logic**

This is the logic of the relationship between possibilities. A rule in this sort of logic might be the following:

> If p is a necessary truth, and if p implies q, then q is a necessary truth.

*Deontic logic**

This is the logic of obligation statements. A possible rule is this one:

> If you are obligated to do x, and if you cannot do x without doing y, then you are obligated to do y, unless there is good reason not to do y.

*Epistemic logic**

This is the logic of relationships between knowledge, beliefs, and claims about the truth. Here is a possible rule:

> If someone knows that p is true, then p is true.

Spatial logic

This is the logic of spatial relationships. On it is based the model used for class reasoning in Chapter 4, the Euler circle model. Here is a rule:

> If a given area, A, is inside an area, B, and if the area, B, is inside an area, C, then the area, A, is inside the area, C.

Other types

Other types of deductive logic also exist, often in such unorganized form that no name has been suggested for them. For example, relationships between claims about what is good and what a person ought to do are possible rules of inference in some type of deductive logic. But in any case, systems of alethic, deontic, epistemic, and others yet unnamed are generally quite controversial. Much work needs to be done before they attain the less

* The terms, 'alethic', 'deontic', and 'epistemic' are used by G. H. von Wright, in his attempt to categorize some types of logic. See his *Logical Studies* (London: Routledge & Kegan Paul Ltd., 1957), pp. 58–74.

controversial state of sentence reasoning, class reasoning, spatial reasoning, and mathematical reasoning.

Examples of Practical Reasoning in More Detail

A look at several more examples of practical reasoning might be instructive. In developing these examples, I have consulted experts in the fields involved. This act of consultation fits in with the view expressed: that proper performance of practical reasoning requires familiarity and experience with the subject matter involved. This consultation, however, did not result in sophisticated examples that can be understood only by one versed in the field. Rather they are intentionally fairly simple so that all of them can be understood by the nonexpert. All have many more complications than will be introduced, but that is due to the nature of practical reasoning: it is not the simple, elegant thing that one hopes to find after studying pure deduction.

An aspect of the frontier thesis

Frederick Jackson Turner, an American historian who lived from 1861 to 1932, offered in 1893 the suggestion to his fellow historians that they look more closely at the frontier conditions of American life in their attempts to explain and understand events and trends in American history. One statement that he made concerned "periods of lax financial integrity" and was quoted earlier (Example 5-3) as one illustration of the use of explicit qualifiers ("for the most part"). Here is the first stage of an argument constructed on the basis of his general statement:

Example 5-7

Premises:*

P-1: Each one of these periods of lax financial integrity coincides with periods when a new set of frontier communities had arisen, and coincides in area with these successive frontiers, for the most part.

P-2: There was a great deal of lax financial integrity in the period prior to the crisis of 1837.

Conclusion:

C-1: The period prior to the crisis of 1837 coincides with the period of a new set of frontier communities.

Conclusion 1 does not take us very far, but for the time being let us concentrate only on the reasoning leading up to it. In a real situation this con-

* In order to facilitate reference to the parts of arguments, labeling systems are here adopted which are more extensive than those used in the main part of Chapter 3. Different systems are used in order to illustrate a flexibility of labeling to fit a situation.

clusion could be derived in an attempt to make a retrodiction (like a prediction, but about the past) based upon Turner's claim and serving as a test of the claim. Admittedly it would not be a very good test, because the phrase, "period of a new set of frontier communities", is vague, and because there were almost continuously new sets of frontier communities. Alternatively the conclusion could be derived in an attempt to show that Turner's claim explains the occurrence of some events around 1837. Such explanatory power is often offered as evidence in support of a hypothesis.

Step 1. The Shift into Idealized Form. In my opinion the qualification, "for the most part", only qualifies the coincidence in area and is not a qualification of the entire statement. We can then use deductive techniques leading to Conclusion 1 without removing the qualification; hence it need not be removed. But we will need to ignore the ever-present implicit qualification to generalizations in history while we use our deductive techniques. Some revision though is required in the first premise, because strictly speaking it is absurd. It sets periods of time in coincidence with areas in the second major clause:

> Each one of these **periods** of lax financial integrity . . . coincides in **area** with these successive frontiers, for the most part. [Emphasis added]

Presumably Turner meant the entire sentence to mean the following:

> Each one of these periods of lax financial integrity coincides with a period* when a new set of frontier communities had arisen, and the area of the lax financial integrity coincides with that of these successive frontiers, for the most part.

Now we have periods coinciding with periods and areas coinciding with areas. Although this revision is not needed for the derivation of Conclusion 1 it is probably best to set things straight from the beginning.

The second premise also requires some revision. It looks like this:

> There was a great deal of lax financial integrity in the period prior to the crisis of 1837.

I would revise it as follows:

> The period prior to the crisis of 1837 was a period of lax financial integrity.

This revision is made with the general premise in mind. The revision enables one to put the two premises together to produce a conclusion, because there is a common class, *periods of lax financial integrity*.

* A minor change here from plural to singular. Presumably he would have one period coincide with another, instead of a set of them.

Step 2: Judgment of Validity. The argument, reproduced below as revised, is valid, as can be seen by an inspection of the diagram.

Example 5-8

Premises:

P–1: Each one of these periods of lax financial integrity coincides with a period when a new set of frontier communities had arisen, and the area of the lax financial integrity coincides with that of these successive frontiers, for the most part.

P–2: The period prior to the crisis of 1837 was a period of lax financial integrity.

Conclusion:

C–1: The period prior to the crisis of 1837 coincides with a period of a new set of frontier communities.

Using only that part of the first premise which precedes the first comma, we have Diagram 5-2. The argument is valid.

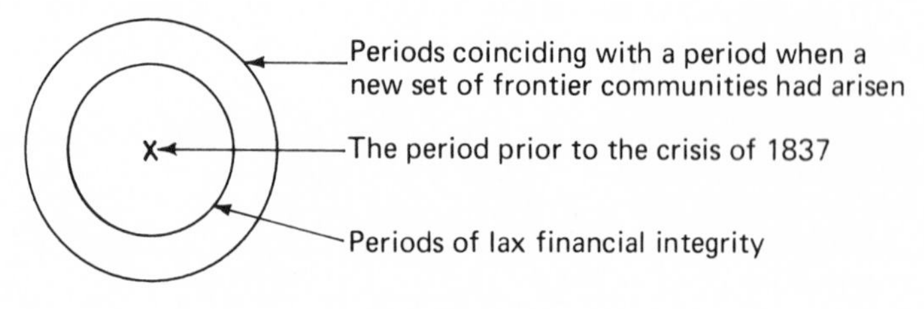

DIAGRAM 5-2

Step 3. The Shift from the Conclusion back to the World of Reality. Should the word 'probably' be inserted in the conclusion to this valid argument? That depends in part on the context. If the purpose of the argument is to generate a retrodiction, on which one might base future decisions (about what to look for, what to expect to find, etc.), then we would insert the word 'probably' (assuming Turner's general claim to be true):

> The period prior to the crisis of 1837 probably coincided with a period of a new set of frontier communities.

If, on the other hand, we know that there was a coincidence of two such periods, and are trying to explain this coincidence, then we do not insert 'probably'. If one knows that there was a coincidence, then it is misleading for him to say that there probably was a coincidence.

Remember though that this first conclusion, because of its vagueness and the frequent presence of periods of new frontier communities, is not very informative. But it is a step toward a conclusion that is more informative. Let us turn to the development of this informative conclusion.

Suppose we know that, as retrodicted (or explained), the conclusion is true in virtue of the fact that there actually was a period of new frontier communities prior to the period of the crisis of 1837, and that Cincinnati, Ohio, is one of the communities typically mentioned as a frontier community at that time. Naturally there will be some hesitation about this piece of knowledge because of the vagueness of Turner's usage of the word 'period'. But suppose that we, relying on our experience and understanding of the field of American history, judge this to be a piece of knowledge. The coincidence of the period of new communities (including Cincinnati) with the period prior to the crisis (using 'period' fairly loosely) convinces us that the conclusion to the previous argument is true. Then we can go on to make new retrodictions—or to explain other alleged facts: that the area in which lax financial integrity was to be found coincides for the most part with the new frontier area—and more particularly that probably lax financial integrity existed in Cincinnati at the time.

Look at the total argument in which everything we know is put into the premises and in which two conclusions are generated, the broad one and the particular one about Cincinnati:

Example 5-9

Premises:

P–1: Each one of these periods of lax financial integrity coincides with periods when a new set of frontier communities had arisen, and coincides in area with these successive frontiers, for the most part.

P–2: There was a great deal of lax financial integrity in the period prior to the crisis of 1837.

P–3: Cincinnati was in the area of the frontier of the period prior to the crisis of 1837.

Conclusions:

C–2: The area of these new frontier communities prior to the time of the crisis of 1837 was for the most part characterized by lax financial integrity.

C–3: Cincinnati probably was characterized by lax financial integrity.

Step 1. What needs to be done? The first two premises need the revisions indicated earlier (Example 5-8). In addition the qualifier, 'for the most part', must be dropped from the first premise. Lastly the phrase 'these successive frontiers' should be changed to 'the frontier area of the time'. This is because we are now going to use only the second part of the first premise and will be thrown off by reference to the first part. The meaning is not changed.

In order to fit a valid form of argument (and one must look ahead to Step 2 to know this), the conclusions must be reworded as well:

C–2: The area of lax financial integrity of the period prior to the crisis of 1837 coincides with the area of the frontier of the time.

C–3: Cincinnati was in an area of lax financial integrity.

The use of Conclusion 1 is now apparent. It is a presupposition to Conclusion 2; the latter would not make sense if there were no "frontier area of the time".

Next, just to be sure that all is clear, I shall rewrite the premises and conclusions in accord with changes just indicated:

Example 5-10

Premises:

P–1: Each one of these periods of lax financial integrity coincides with a period when a new set of frontier communities had arisen, and the area of the lax financial integrity coincides with that of the frontier area of the time.

P–2: The period prior to the crisis of 1837 was a period of lax financial integrity.

P–3: Cincinnati was in the area of the frontier of the period prior to the crisis of 1837.

Conclusions:

C–2: The area of lax financial integrity of the period of the crisis of 1837 coincided with the area of the frontier of the time.

C–3: Cincinnati was in an area of lax financial integrity.

Step 2. Examination of Diagram 5-3 shows the argument for the second

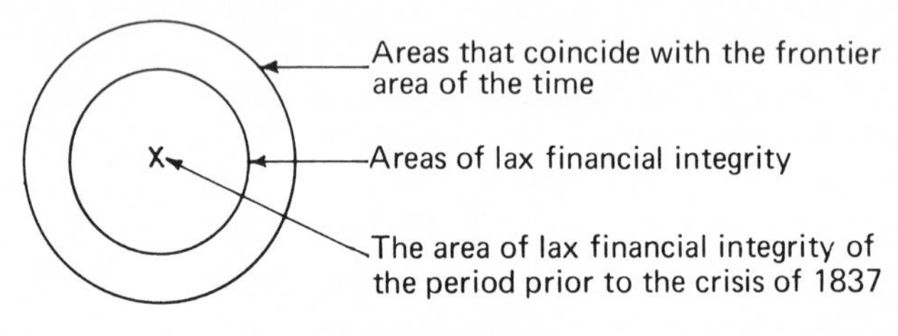

DIAGRAM 5-3

conclusion to be valid. We now can use the second conclusion as a premise to derive the third conclusion. It becomes P-4 in the following argument:

Example 5-11

Premises:

P–3: Cincinnati was in the area of the frontier of the period prior to the crisis of 1837.

P–4: The area of lax financial integrity of the period prior to the crisis of 1837 coincided with the frontier area of the time.

Conclusion:

C–3: Cincinnati was in an area of lax financial integrity.

To show the validity of this argument we first use spatial reasoning, a technique analogous to that developed in class reasoning. You will remember that spatial reasoning includes the basic technique of inclusion of areas on which the Euler circle system is based. We use a circle to represent the geographical area of lax financial integrity of the period prior to the 1837 crisis. According to the fourth premise (which is also the second conclusion), this area coincides with the frontier areas of the time, so for that area we use another circle which coincides with the first. Cincinnati, by the third premise is inside the second circle, which coincides with the first, so it is in the first. The argument so far is valid (See Diagram 5-4). Strictly speaking

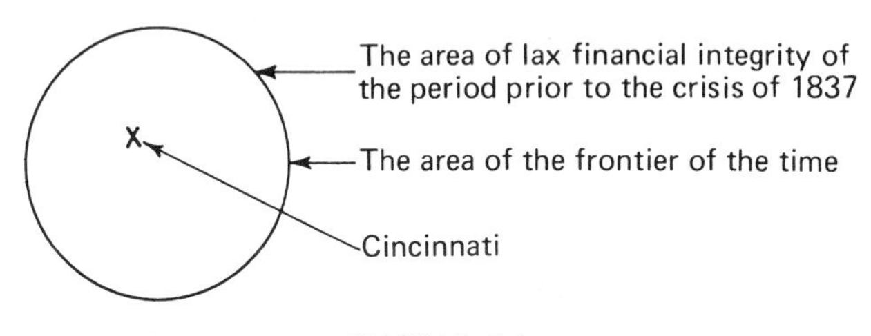

DIAGRAM 5-4

we need to go one step further, for this conclusion is that Cincinnati was in the area of lax financial integrity of the period of the crisis of 1837. The conclusion we seek is that Cincinnati was in an area of lax financial integrity. The move is a simple class reasoning move which I will not diagram.

Step 3. Next the conclusions must be revised in the light of the omitted qualifications in the premises and in the light of knowledge and experience in the field of study. This is Step 3. Certainly the qualifier, 'for the most part', should be reintroduced in the statement of the second conclusion. Turner indicated that he did not want to claim perfect coincidence in area. Other considerations are to be brought to bear, but they can be better illustrated by their application to the third conclusion.

The third conclusion reads as follows:

> Cincinnati probably was characterized by lax financial integrity.

First of all if the conclusion is a fact to be explained by Turner's claim, a fact which we accept as true, then the word 'probably' should not be there at all for reasons given earlier.

But suppose that the conclusion is one we derived from Turner's claim (and the other assumptions) in order to test his claim; then presumably the conclusion should be accepted as a conclusion to the argument. If there is as yet no determination of the truth of the implied conclusion, then the word 'probably' should be omitted, because it would indicate qualified endorsement when there should be no endorsement.* But Turner did say

* Please refer back to the discussion of 'probably' earlier in this chapter, if this point is not clear.

"for the most part". He did not strongly commit himself to such a judgment about any particular area. Some sort of qualification would be needed because a determination that Cincinnati had no lax financial integrity should not be allowed by itself to falsify Turner's statement. One might say, "Turner's statement loosely implies that Cincinnati was characterized by lax financial integrity."

After the independent determination of the truth status of the implied conclusion, then what one directly says about it depends upon the determination. One might then assert it without qualification, assert it with qualification, or reject it. But one can still say, "Turner's statement loosely implies that Cincinnati was characterized by lax financial integrity."

Next, suppose that the conclusion is derived in order to get an idea of what life in Cincinnati was like in the early part of the nineteenth century. Here the option is open to the expert to reject the conclusion completely, to accept it with the word 'probably' inserted, or to accept it with no qualifiers. He might reject it completely, if on other grounds he has good reason to believe that it is false. Suppose for example, that we generated such a conclusion about early frontier pilgrim settlements. Having sufficient knowledge about such settlements, an expert would simply reject such a conclusion—with or without 'probably'.

On the other hand, he might accept the conclusion about Cincinnati without the qualifier because the conclusion fits very well with other knowledge that the expert has about Cincinnati at the time. Or he might accept the conclusion with the qualifier included—either because he has some reason to wonder about the conclusion, or because he just does not have sufficient background information to justify an unqualified endorsement of the conclusion. The latter is the situation for most informed laymen. They, more than the experts, should make more liberal use of such words as 'probably', though it is often the other way around.

Summary. In this example one can see the three steps in the practical use of deduction, steps which are interdependent and inseparable in practice. Of particular note are the importance of the context, the provisional elimination of qualifiers during the use of strict deductive techniques, the need for intelligent, informed judgment, the use of another type of logic, and perhaps most important of all, the fact that the hardest part of the practical application of deduction is not the actual use of deductive techniques, but rather the prior and succeeding steps, the steps here numbered 1 and 3.

Supply and demand

Let us move to a different area, economics, and look at the application of one version of the law of supply and demand:

Example 5-12

Premises:

1. Other things being equal, if the demand for a commodity decreases, the price will decrease (assuming that the supply remains the same).
2. The demand for fountain pens is going to decrease.
3. The supply of fountain pens will remain the same.

Conclusion:

The price of fountain pens will probably decrease.

The problems in putting this argument in workable form reside primarily in the first premise. As stated earlier, the general qualifier, "other things being equal", is eliminated* (though later remembered), but the specific qualification dealing with the supply must remain. For convenience, however, it should be put into an 'if' clause. Then the first premise looks like this:

Example 5-13

If the demand for a commodity decreases and the supply remains the same, then the price will decrease.

But more remains to be done. The second and third premises cannot yet be used in conjunction with the first, since it talks about "a commodity" and they talk about fountain pens. This problem was raised before—in the yeast example at the beginning of Chapter 4. The solution at that time was to transform the general sentence into a class sentence. If we use the same method, the first premise, restated in class terms, looks like this:

Example 5-14

Commodities for which the demand decreases as the supply remains the same (are commodities which) will have a decrease in price.

Though awkward, this is a workable version of the first premise. After eliminating 'probably' from the conclusion we can diagram the argument

* ⁘Alternatively, the general qualification, 'other things being equal', can remain if a premise is added asserting the satisfaction of this qualification. The argument could look like this:

Premises:

1. If the demand for a commodity decreases, the price will decrease, if other things are equal, and if the supply remains the same.
2. The demand for fountain pens is going to decrease.
3. Other things are equal.
4. The supply of fountain pens will remain the same.

Conclusion:

The price of fountain pens will decrease.

In deciding whether to assert Premise 3, one faces many of the same sorts of problems that one faces in deciding whether, or to what extent, to endorse the conclusion.

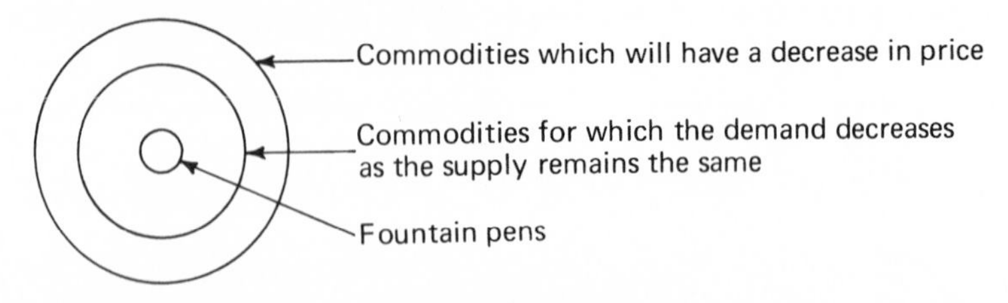

DIAGRAM 5-5

as in Diagram 5-5 (assuming that fountain pens are commodities). The following conclusion can thus be validly derived from the premises:

The price of fountain pens will decrease.

An alternative (and in this case easier) way of reformulating and judging the argument calls for the use of sentence reasoning instead of class reasoning. In order to use sentence reasoning, one must make the explicit instantiating step of putting the conditional premise in terms of fountain pens. We infer from the first premise, as found in Example 5-13, the following instantiation of it:

Example 5-15
If the demand for fountain pens decreases and the supply remains the same, then the price will decrease.

This implication of the first premise together with the two other premises (which are now the antecedent) yields the desired conclusion by means of the valid step, affirmation of the antecedent.

Next comes the most difficult part. The inevitable vagueness of the premises requires a judgment about whether the facts warrant asserting these premises. For example, did the supply remain sufficiently the same to warrant asserting the third premise? The same vagueness problem exists in the conclusion. Will the concluded decrease be sufficient to assert? Furthermore, one must judge whether other things are equal, that is whether other things stay the same. Which other things are involved? All other things? Obviously not—only the relevant ones, and it is only the experienced, informed person who is well qualified to determine which these are. Such factors as lack of price-maintaining agreements by suppliers, advertising campaigns, and national crises* are things that might occur to an ex-

* A national crisis, strictly speaking, would negate the qualifier 'under normal conditions' rather than 'other things being equal' in a period of frequent national crises. But since nobody that I know of interprets 'other things being equal' this strictly, I shall not do so; rather I shall conform to standard (and vague) usage and let the phrase be used where 'under normal conditions' would strictly speaking be more appropriate.

perienced, informed person. But even after the expert has made the relevance appraisal, he must still make a judgment about the extent to which the other (relevant) things must stay the same—certainly not absolutely immobile: minor fluctuations can be ignored. Expertise is needed to distinguish minor from significant fluctuations.

As with the argument developing out of one part of Turner's thesis, various courses are open. One is to refuse to affirm the conclusion, perhaps because one believes on other grounds that the conclusion is false or quite dubious, even though one otherwise has good reason to believe that the premises are true. Suppose, for example, that one learns that a number of leading economists have asserted that the price of fountain pens will remain the same.

A second course is to affirm the conclusion but include the word 'probably', because one is not sure enough that something will not go wrong. A third is to affirm the conclusion without the word 'probably', without any qualifications at all. If one has no reason for reservations, and is very well informed, then it is deceptive to include 'probably'.

Note that the use of the future tense in the conclusion ("the price **will** decrease") precludes the possibility of this argument's being part of an explanation. If the past tense had been used and the argument were put forward to explain a fact, then the 'probably' option would not have been open. The first option, that of refusing to affirm the conclusion, would still have been open in the sense that although one accepted the statement given in the conclusion as true, one did not believe that it was explained by the material offered—perhaps because one or more of the premises was believed false. The third option, affirming the conclusion without any qualifiers, is the standard one in the case of explanation.

Neoclassical English writing

Turning to the field of English, consider this argument:

Example 5-16

Premises:

1. English literature of the first fifty years of the eighteenth century was neoclassical.
2. Alexander Pope's *Essay on Man* is English literature written in the first fifty years of the eighteenth century.

Conclusion:

Alexander Pope's *Essay on Man* was probably neoclassical.

Since in this case no explicit changes are required to put the premises into workable form (though the implicit qualifier in the generalization must be ignored when doing the validity test), we can proceed directly to the

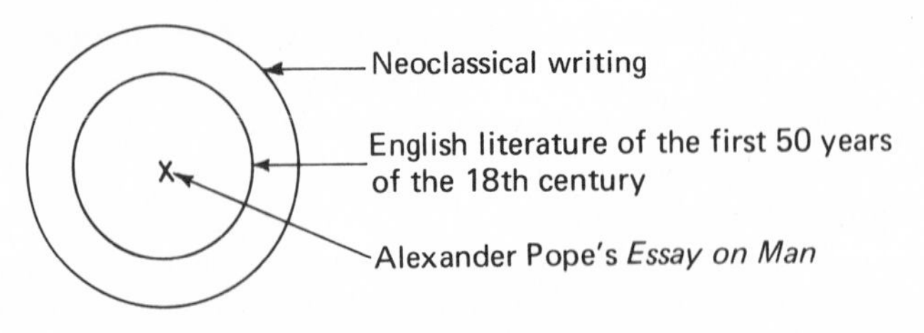

DIAGRAM 5-6

validity test. The argument is valid as can be seen in Diagram 5-6. Next we turn to the conclusion. Should the word 'probably'* be there even though there is no explicit qualifier in any of the premises?

Think of some possible contexts in which this argument might appear. Realize that even though there are no explicit qualifiers in the generalization, an exception or two will not prove it wrong. Daniel Defoe's *Robinson Crusoe*, for example, which was written in the given period, does not prove the generalization wrong. But a large number of exceptions would prove the generalization wrong. So if this argument is one of a large number which are set up to test the generalization, then we have one conceivable context in which it could be offered. In this context the word 'probably' would not be used, since it indicates endorsement, albeit weak endorsement, by the concluder.

A second context is one in which an English teacher is teaching his students the meaning of the word 'neoclassical' by means of examples. He gives his students the generalization and asks them to go through their memories to find items written by Englishmen in the first half of the eighteenth century. When a student comes up with an example, then the conclusion is drawn, and the student gets a better idea of what the word 'neoclassical' means, in virtue of his having read the item. Here the word 'probably' might be used, or even better, the phrase, 'by this principle'.

A third possible context is that in which an English teacher is trying to teach his students the categorization scheme of the history of literature. And he asks them to apply it to examples that he supplies. He supplies the example. They draw the conclusion and should include 'probably'.

So far as I can see, the argument would not be used in an explanation of why this work of Pope's was neoclassical, though it might be used to explain why someone at a low level of sophistication in the field judges the work to be neoclassical. If this argument is all the reason he has, then he should use 'probably'.

There are other sorts of contexts possible, but we will not go any further.

* Or some similar term, such as 'likely'. In this discussion 'probably' will be used to represent this family of terms.

The main idea is that with this sort of generalization in this field, one should expect exceptions, even though at a given level of sophistication the generalization is to be considered true. Qualifications and endorsements are distributed accordingly, context respected of course.

A body immersed in a fluid

A rather well-known principle of elementary physics, Archimedes' Principle has been stated as follows:

> When a body is totally or partially immersed in a fluid, it experiences an upthrust equal to the weight of fluid displaced.*

A cubic foot of wood held under water will suffice as an illustration of this principle. A cubic foot of wood will displace (occupy the same space as) a cubic foot of water. The weight of a cubic foot of water is given as 62.4 pounds. Hence we can expect, according to the principle, that the wood will experience an upthrust of 62.4 pounds. Suppose that the block of wood itself weighs 50 pounds. Then the force we would have to use to hold down the block of wood would be another 12.4 pounds.

Although this may sound quite simple and straightforward and is quite satisfactory at one level of sophistication, problems can arise, problems that can be seen without an advanced knowledge of physics. Consider this argument which formalizes the first part of reasoning used in the above explanation:

Example 5-17
Premises:
1. When a body is totally or partially immersed in a fluid, it experiences an upthrust equal to the weight of fluid displaced.
2. This cube of wood (measuring one foot on an edge) is totally immersed in this lake water.
3. When a body is totally immersed in a fluid, it displaces an amount of fluid equal to the volume of the body.
4. The weight of one cubic foot of this lake water is 62.4 pounds.

Conclusion:
The block of wood experiences an upthrust of 62.4 pounds.

Ignoring the metaphorical use of 'experience', let us concentrate our attention on the basic moves and problems in this argument. In order to avoid the further complications involved in arriving at the figure of 12.4 pounds downward force, let us limit our concern to the determination of the "upthrust".

* W. Ashhurst, *Physics* (London: John Murray, 1954), p. 35.

Step 1. Since the first premise speaks of "a body" while the second mentions a "cube of wood", the two cannot yet produce a conclusion. We could convert the first premise into a class statement that includes the class of immersed bodies in the class of bodies experiencing the state, upthrust. Alternatively we could instantiate the first premise in terms of this cube of wood and water:

> When this cube of wood is totally or partially immersed in this lake water, it experiences an upthrust equal to the weight of the lake water displaced.

Similarly the third premise can be instantiated:

> When this cube of wood is totally immersed in this lake water, it displaces an amount of water equal to the volume of the block of wood.

In this example I shall use sentence reasoning, making use of these two instantiated premises. There are no explicit general qualifiers in the premises, so Step 1 is complete.

Step 2. The reasoning is straightforward and simple. There is some simple mathematics, which I will simply note without detail. That is the computation of the volume of the cube of wood ($1' \times 1' \times 1' = 1$ cubic foot). This computation enables us to substitute 'one cubic foot' for 'the volume of the block of wood' in the instantiated third premise, since equals may be substituted for equals. The argument now looks like this:

Example 5-18

Premises:

1. When this cube of wood is totally or partially immersed in this lake water, it experiences an upthrust equal to the weight of the lake water displaced.
2. This cube of wood (measuring one foot on an edge) is totally immersed in this lake water.
3. When this cube of wood is totally immersed in this lake water, it displaces an amount of water equal to one cubic foot.
4. The weight of one cubic foot of this lake water is 62.4 pounds.

Conclusion:

This cube of wood experiences an upthrust of 62.4 pounds.

Combining Premise 1 and the affirmation of its antecedent, Premise 2, we get the following:

5. This cube of wood experiences an upthrust equal to the weight of the lake water displaced.

Combining Premise 3 and the affirmation of its antecedent, again Premise 2, we get the following:

6. This cube of wood displaces an amount of water equal to 1 cubic foot.

Making use of Premise 4 and substituting equals for equals, Statement 6 becomes:

7. This cube of wood displaces 62.4 pounds of this lake water.

Again substituting equals for equals and using Statement 7, Statement 5 is transformed into the desired conclusion.

The reasoning just described is simple enough for most people to do in their heads. The reason for going through it in detail was to show the operation of various deductive processes. As you know from working on the exercises of Chapters 3 and 4, complications in the reasoning can arise which make doing it in one's head difficult. Note that in addition to sentence reasoning, some mathematical manipulation of numbers was involved, and the equals substitution rule (a deductive rule which is used in many more areas than mathematics) was invoked. Furthermore even to make use of sentence reasoning, adjustments to the two general premises were necessary. They were instantiated.

Step 3. This step brings out the main lessons of the Archimedes example: (1) a degree of imprecision exists in specific predictions in physics and the other precise sciences; (2) unspecified factors can arise (just as in economics) which make the result so wrong that it can no longer be called an approximation; and (3) in areas of familiarity to the engineer, the state of knowledge and precision has advanced to the point that words like 'probably' are often not needed. Let us consider these lessons one at a time.

1. For most ordinary purposes the precision of the conclusion is sufficient, but a number of factors could be taken into account. First, the figure, '62.4', is an approximation. Second the weight of one cubic foot of water varies with the temperature, a factor not mentioned. Also the temperature of the water touching the cube could easily vary from one point to another, thus adding further to the imprecision. In addition, the weight of water depends slightly upon its pressure, which increases with depth. Since the pressure of the water is not constant from top to bottom of the cube of wood, it follows that the weight of the water displaced varies accordingly from top to bottom of the cube. Generally these factors are assumed to be negligible and are ignored. But note that expertise is needed to judge properly that something is negligible.

2. As we approach vastly different situations, then there is always the chance that unspecified factors can arise which throw off the entire estimate. Suppose that there is a continual up current in the lake. The upthrust then increases. This problem is usually handled by using the term 'buoyant force' (a term which covers only the force owing to the actual displacement of the fluid) instead of 'upthrust'. This terminological substitution is a move requiring expertise, for 'buoyant force' is a more theoretical term than 'upthrust'. More serious is the problem encountered when a very small body, say one that is composed of five molecules, is in the lake. Archimedes' Principle was not framed for this kind of case. Even farther removed is the case of one electron shot into the lake. The idea of buoyant force is simply inapplicable, as is the idea of volume, even though the shooting of the electron into the lake might have resulted in the displacement of some amount of water (I am assuming one can give some meaning to 'displacement' here). Thus by rigidly following Archimedes' Principle, one might generate by deduction a prediction which is absurd, even though Archimedes' Principle is true. Hence expertise is called for in deciding whether to endorse a validly deduced conclusion from true premises. Incidentally this case also shows the existence of implicit qualifiers in such principles, at least as they are understood by experts.

3. In spite of the existence of imprecision and the possibility of situational factors which nullify any prediction based on the standard methods of application of such a principle, words like 'probably' are not generally used in such conclusions. This is because within the standard-type situation the result is quite regularly predictable. In modern physics where there is a heavy use of the concept, *probability*, words like 'probably' appear more often. Often in both modern and classical physics some word like 'approximately' is introduced to give warning of the fact that various possibilities for imprecision exist.

The result then in Step 3 varies with the principle and the situation. For cases like the application of Archimedes' Principle to ordinary situations the derived conclusion can often appear without such qualifiers as 'probably' much more often than conclusions in the social sciences and some of the other physical sciences.

Chapter Summary

In this chapter on the practical application of deductive logic the major problems treated are those of putting the premises into a form for dealing with them with deductive techniques, and of deciding whether and how strongly to endorse the conclusion to a piece of practical reasoning.

In putting the premises in workable form one drops such general qualifiers as 'generally', 'other things being equal', 'under normal conditions', etc., but does not omit specific qualifiers like 'if the supply remains the same'. And, of course, one rewords, reorganizes, revises (sometimes this requires drawing out implicit parts) the premises until they fit some logical form with which one can work.

In deciding whether, in what way, and how strongly to endorse the conclusion, one must look at the purpose behind the reasoning (for example: Is it part of an explanation? Is it the basis for a prediction? etc.), and one must look at the field of knowledge for such things as limits beyond which one must be especially careful in applying the generalization, facts which contradict the conclusion or cast suspicion on it, and the sort of context in which the generalization can be fairly safely applied. One also must decide whether the facts are such as to warrant the assertion of the premises.

A related problem is that of finding the appropriate deductive techniques, since the techniques of sentence and class reasoning do not in all cases suffice. Often one can work by analogy to established deductive techniques (which include those of mathematics) and sometimes one must base one's decision simply on the basic rule of deductive argumentation: the denial of the conclusion of a valid deductive argument contradicts the assertion of the premises.

The result of this process can be many things, depending on the purpose behind the reasoning, but very often it is the assertion of, the qualified assertion of, or the deliberate nonassertion of the conclusion. Generally, the strictly logical problem is simpler than the practical application problem.

This chapter does not attempt a thorough comprehensive treatment of the practical application of logic. Instead through the use of a simple model and selected examples it attempts to suggest ways of dealing with the problems faced herein as well as others that appear in other cases. Hopefully, the suggestions will stimulate your ingenuity.

COMPREHENSION SELF-TEST

True or False? If the statement is false, change a crucial term (or terms) to make it true.

5–1. The model put forward here calls for the temporary idealization of an argument in order to make a judgment about its validity.

5–2. In putting an argument into form, one generally eliminates general qualifications from the premises but does not eliminate specific qualifications.

5–3. Rarely does one find a practical deductive argument that requires more than sentence and class reasoning techniques.

5–4. If a deductive argument is used to show how the conclusion of the argument can be explained, then the conclusion should not have the word 'probably' in it.

5–5. Since the practical application of deductive processes is relatively mechanical, anyone with a good knowledge of logic should be able to make the application.

Argument Appraisal out of Context. Take each of the following arguments, put it into form suitable for use of deductive techniques, and judge its validity.

5–6. Premises:

1. Whenever the supply of a commodity increases (assuming that demand remains constant), the price will decrease, other things being equal.

2. It is clear that the price of eggs is going to decrease.
Conclusion:
It follows, therefore, that the supply of eggs is going to increase.

5–7. Frederick Jackson Turner has stated, "The most important effect of the frontier has been in the promotion of democracy here and in Europe." By this he means in part, and says, "The frontier is productive of individualism." Since Turner apparently did not want to limit his analysis to the United States, presumably he would expect to find considerable individualism in the outback of Australia of the present day, for there we find what he would undoubtedly call a frontier.

5–8. A wind shift from south to northwest is generally accompanied by clearing and colder. Since the weather bureau has predicted rain for the next twenty-four hours, quite probably the wind will not shift from south to northwest within twenty-four hours.

5–9. Since English writing of the first fifty years of the eighteenth century was neoclassical, and since Bronte's *Wuthering Heights* is romantic rather than neoclassical, it quite probably was not written in the first fifty years of the eighteenth century.

5–10. The physics book says that a body immersed in a fluid is buoyed up by a force equal to the weight of the fluid displaced. There is a rectangular solid concrete block underwater here which measures $2' \times 2' \times 1'$. Hence there must be a buoyant force of exactly 249.6 pounds on the block.

Argument Appraisal in Context.

5–11. Take one of the above five arguments and imagine and describe a context in which it could appear. Decide whether and how strongly to endorse the conclusion and tell why you judge as you do.

5–12. Find an argument in a book in some subject matter in which you have at least a fair degree of knowledge. Reproduce the argument and write a short essay appraising it. Be sure to include your reasons.

Suggested Further Reading in Logic

The following presentations of deductive logic are arranged roughly in order of increasing difficulty:

Black, Max. *Critical Thinking*, 2nd ed. Englewood Cliffs, N. J.: Prentice-Hall, Inc., 1952. 459 pages.

An elementary, readable, and interesting treatment of deductive logic, scientific method, and semantics. Exercises are provided.

Salmon, Wesley. *Logic*. Englewood Cliffs, N. J.: Prentice-Hall, Inc., 1963. 114 pages.

An elementary book, dealing with deductive logic, scientific method, and semantics. No exercises are provided. The approach to deductive logic differs from that here in that a system of rules is provided for class reasoning. Circles are not used.

Beardsley, Monroe. *Thinking Straight*, 3rd ed. Englewood Cliffs, N. J.: Prentice-Hall, Inc., 1966. 292 pages.

The content is similar to the Black and Salmon books listed above, and is again at an elementary level. Exercises are provided. For class reasoning Venn diagrams are used.

Fisk, Milton. *A Modern Formal Logic*. Englewood Cliffs, N. J.: Prentice-Hall Inc., 1964. 116 pages.

A somewhat more advanced treatment of logic than in the above but still an introductory text. It deals only with deductive logic, and that from the same point of view as that of this book. Exercises are provided.

Copi, Irving. *Introduction to Logic*, 2nd ed. New York: The Macmillan Company, 1961. 472 pages.

An elementary presentation of contemporary symbolic logic. Exercises are provided.

Cohen, Morris, and Ernest Nagel. *An Introduction to Logic and the Scientific Method.* New York: Harcourt, Brace and Company, 1934. 467 pages.

A classic but introductory study of many topics associated with proof. Exercises are provided.

Quine, Willard Van Orman. *Methods of Logic*, rev. ed. New York: Henry Holt and Company, Inc., 1960. 272 pages.

An elegant development of contemporary symbolic logic. Exercises are provided.

❖The following chronologically ordered items are relevant to the ordinary language vs. material (and strict) implication, etc., interpretations of the logical operators:

Whitehead, Alfred North, and Bertrand Russell. *Principia Mathematica*. Cambridge (England): Cambridge University Press, 1910–13.

Lewis, C. I. "Implication and the Algebra of Logic," *Mind*, October, 1912, pp. 522–31.

Lewis, C. I., and C. H. Langford. *Symbolic Logic*. New York: Dover Publications, Inc., 1959 (first published 1932).

Strawson, P. F. *Introduction to Logical Theory*. London: Methuen & Co., Ltd., 1952.

Bennett, Jonathan. "Entailment," *The Philosophical Review*, Vol. 78, No. 2 (April, 1969), pp. 197-236.

Wright, Georg Henrik von. *Logical Studies*. London (England): Routledge & Kegan Paul, Ltd., 1957.

Smiley, T. J. "Entailment and Deducibility," *Proceedings of the Aristotelian Society*, Vol. 59 (1959), pp. 233–54.

Russell, L. J. "Formal Logic and Ordinary Language," *Analysis*, Vol. 21, No. 2 (December, 1960), pp. 25–34.

Faris, J. A. *Truth-Functional Logic*. New York: The Free Press of Glencoe, 1962 (esp. pp. 107–19).

Anderson, Alan Ross, and Nuel D. Belnap, Jr. "The Pure Calculus of Entailment," *Journal of Symbolic Logic*, Vol. 27 (1962), pp. 19–52.

Part Two

DEFINITION

Section A: functions of definitions

CHAPTER 6

An Introduction to the Functions of Definitions

A considerable amount of the time of teachers and students is spent in giving, receiving, teaching, learning, inventing, and appraising definitions, but sometimes this effort is not accompanied by a conscious understanding of what it is they are up to. Students need this understanding so that they can choose rationally among the alternatives that are open to them, and teachers need it so that, as well as choosing rationally themselves, they can help their students to do so.

This is not to suggest that all time spent on definitions is time well spent. Quite the contrary. On occasion, definitions are simply memorized without being accompanied by understanding of that which is conveyed by the definition. On other occasions, a particular phrasing of a definition is insisted on when another would do. And, of course, there are those total systems which seem to be just definitional—that is, they add nothing to our existing knowledge but a self-contained system of interrelated definitions that get us nowhere. Time is not thereby well spent.

But we cannot manage without definitions. We need them in order to indicate what we mean when we say something, to teach people the meaning of terms that are new to them, and to have organized, recorded systems of knowledge. They are needed in the development of new concepts; although it is probable that the definition follows the insight that produces a new concept, the recording of the definition fixes the concept so that it can be examined intensively.

In short, although much of our knowledge is nondefinitional, we must usually express, discover, and teach it by means of the tool we call language; and central to learning the proper use of this tool is learning to give, receive, teach, learn, invent, and appraise definitions. Part II of this book is devoted to this topic.

This part of the book has two sections. The first section is concerned with various things that we try to accomplish under the general heading, definition. Since many important jobs in the classroom can be done by definitions, since different jobs are appropriate in different situations, and since people sometimes do one, thinking they are doing another, it is well to be clear about the many functions that definitions can serve. This first section is called "Functions of Definitions", in contrast to the second section, "Forms of Definitions", which deals with the problems connected with getting definitions worded satisfactorily.

In the first section the following functions will be treated: stipulating a meaning, reporting usage, suggesting a program, interpreting basic terms, identifying names, marking limits, and describing things. This is a varied list, and one might well question whether the performance of every one of those functions is defining, particularly the last three.

The Definition of 'Definition'

The question 'what is a definition' is a difficult one to answer, but some things can be said about it. All of the above performances have been called "defining", and all fit the root meaning of the word 'DEFINE': **to end** or **limit**. Furthermore, an examination of dictionary entries suggests that these are legitimately called 'defining', since the dictionaries present lists of items that roughly cover the above list. For example, *Webster's Collegiate Dictionary* suggests the following three definitions of 'define', chronologically ordered:

1. To mark the limits or boundaries of; to make distinct or fix in outline or character.
2. To describe, expound, or interpret; to explain, hence to determine the precise signification of; to discover and set forth the meaning of, as a word.
3. To set apart in a class by identifying marks; to distinguish.*

The *Oxford Universal English Dictionary*, which presents meanings in order of first-known occurrence, provides the following list of eight entries:

1. To bring to an end.
2. (a) To determine the boundary or limits of. (b) To make definite in outline or form.
3. To limit, confine.
4. To lay down definitely; to fix upon; to decide.

* *Webster's Collegiate Dictionary*, 5th ed. (Springfield, Mass.: G. C. Merriam Co., 1947), p. 264.

5. To state precisely.
6. (a) To set forth the essential nature of. (b) To set forth what (a word, etc.) means.
7. To make (a thing) what it is, to characterize.
8. To separate by definition.*

As should be clear from these two lists, the term 'definition' does not have a single clear precise meaning, but rather has a family of meanings, related, broad in scope, and including the things with which this section is concerned. For purposes of focus and organization, and in order that certain recurrent classroom problems will receive adequate attention, the central notion of DEFINITION** with which I will be concerned in this book is **setting forth the meaning of a word** (see entries 2 and 6b respectively above). In the list of the topics of this section, the first two items, stipulating and reporting, fit directly under this notion, even though they are rather different from each other. The other items appear to deviate more or less from this notion, but still fit the dictionary definitions of 'definition'. Since these other items are related closely enough to the central notion to profit from comparison and contrast, and since they offer significant problems to the teacher, problems that are often labeled 'problems of definition', they are included in this section on the functions of definitions.

Thus the definition of 'definition' with which we will be working is a loose one—unavoidably so—because the concept *definition* is a loose concept. For purposes of focusing on facility with that crucial tool, language, **setting forth the meaning of a word** will be of central concern to us in this study of definition. But if you will think carefully about it, you will see that even that statement of central concern, which might be formally put as follows,

'To DEFINE' means 'to set forth the meaning of a word',

is less informative than you might have originally thought. For after all, what does 'meaning' mean, and what sorts of things are excluded by the phrase, 'to set forth'?

You might well wonder why I said that the last three items in the list of topics in this section appear not to fit directly under this central notion of *definition*. For example, you might wonder why the process of identifying names, such as 'Napoleon', is not setting forth the meaning of a word. And you might wonder why some descriptions are not setting forth the meaning of a word. For example why is the quality, *commonly treated by removal of the appendix*, not part of the meaning of the word 'appendicitis'?

* *Oxford Universal English Dictionary*, Vol. III (Oxford: Oxford University Press, 1937), p. 470. So many things (dates, etc.) were omitted from this selection that the ellipsis marks to so indicate would have been more confusing than helpful. Hence they were left out.

** In order to avoid confusion I have adopted (and recommend) the use of capitals to indicate a term being defined.

These are very difficult philosophical questions, but they do show that even if we were to take 'setting forth the meaning of a word' as precisely defining 'definition', there would still be questions that would be unanswered by that attempt to make our concept of definition more rigid. Such an attempt takes us just so far, but it depends on an undefined term, 'meaning', and stops there.

The upshot is that you must depend heavily on your own intuitive notion of definition at the start of your study of the use of definitions in the classroom. Presumably, the intuitive notion with which you approach this study is the loose one described. That is, it covers a number of different kinds of functions, the major ones having been listed, and is focused on setting forth the meaning of a word. But the answer to the question, "What is the meaning of 'the meaning of a word'?" is very difficult to give—and perhaps unnecessary. We can proceed in our study of definition by taking 'meaning' as an undefined term, assuming an intuitive notion that is subject to some refinement as the discussion proceeds.

Two important lessons are illustrated by this attempt to define 'definition': (1) looseness is often inevitable, and (2) the attempt to push something continuously back must stop somewhere—with either an intuitive notion or a blunt experience. In various forms, these two theses appear frequently in this book.

Let us start our study by examining an actual classroom dialogue from a social studies class. As you read this, try to imagine what you would say if you were Mr. Delta, the teacher.

An Argument Over the Meaning of a Word

Example 6-1

JIM: (Giving an analysis of the content of the previous evening's edition of the local newspaper) The theme that I want to prove is that most of the material in this newspaper is propaganda. Look at the back page—a full page advertisement. That's all propaganda. Look at the next page. Half of it is advertisements. The other half looks like straight reporting, but it's not. This story on the rehearsals of the Community Players is in effect an ingenious attempt to persuade us us to go to their show. And this article that appears to present facts about the current state of our economy is a very one-sided account intended to persuade our parents to re-elect Congressman Smith. This article on the left is intended to persuade us that within five years the sewage disposal plant will be inadequate to meet the demands of this community. The announcement of the Red Cross drive in the corner is propaganda for the Red Cross.

SALLY: (Interrupting) Wait a minute. Those last two things aren't propaganda. The article about the sewage disposal plant, according to my father, is a true and balanced account. And the Red Cross is a good cause.

JIM: I guess you don't know what 'propaganda' means. Let me quote from

Webster's New Collegiate Dictionary: "A doctrine or ideas, spread through . . . any organized or concerted group, effort, or movement . . ." There are a few other meanings here, but they are even farther away from what you think 'propaganda' means. The point is that propaganda is any doctrine or ideas that are deliberately spread. Thus these two articles contain propaganda.

SALLY: Either you have misinterpreted the dictionary or the dictionary is in error or out of date, because that's not what 'propaganda' means. That's only part of the meaning. If something is propaganda, it must appeal to emotion instead of reason and fact; and it must not be for a cause that everyone knows is good. Everyone knows that the Red Cross is a good cause, and the article on the sewage system used reason and fact in a balanced presentation. So neither one is propaganda.

JIM: You're just wrong about the meaning of 'propaganda'. Here look in the dictionary and see if you can find a definition for 'propaganda' that is anything like yours. If you won't believe the dictionary, whom will you believe?

SALLY: (After looking at the dictionary) Mr. Delta, who is right? Can a dictionary be wrong?

What should Mr. Delta say? The easy way out is to say, "This is not an important question, so proceed with the report." The choice of this course leaves the students ignorant about some important matters of conceptual strategy, so that the next time they face this kind of question, they will still be unable to handle it. But sometimes, of course, such a choice is justified by the various pressures to which teachers are subject.

Let us assume that such a choice is not made by Mr. Delta and that he decides to face the logical issues involved. What can he do? The next two chapters focus on this question.

COMPREHENSION SELF-TEST

True or False? If the statement is false, change a crucial term (or terms) to make it true.

6–1. The dictionaries offer us a single, clear, precise notion of definition.

6–2. The root meaning of 'to DEFINE' is 'to set forth the meaning'.

6–3. The central aspect of definition, as it is treated in this book, is *setting forth the meaning of a word.*

6–4. The phrase, 'the meaning of a word', is not easily definable.

Questions.

6–5. What are two practices which clearly come under the notion, *setting forth the meaning of a word?*

6–6. Is the term 'meaning' treated (for our purposes) as a defined or an undefined term?

6–7. Is *definition* a loose or a precise concept?

Complete:

6–8. When we try to keep pushing a question further and further back, eventually we must stop and be satisfied with (a) ______________________ or (b) ______________________.

Discussion Questions.

6–9. Do you think a dictionary definition can be wrong? Why?

6–10. Look up 'propaganda' in your dictionary. In what respects are the entries in accord with your concept of propaganda? In what respects different?

CHAPTER 7

Stipulating a Meaning

One way to handle a question about the meaning of a word is to stipulate a meaning. A stipulation of a meaning is a pronouncement or proposal that the given meaning is the meaning the word shall have in this particular context. Mr. Delta (in the example in Chapter 6) might either authoritatively stipulate a meaning himself or he might encourage Jim to stipulate a meaning for the word. That is, Mr. Delta might say:

> Let us all agree to the dictionary definition of 'propaganda', for purposes of this discussion.

Or with encouragement from Mr. Delta, Jim might say:

> When I use the word 'PROPAGANDA', you may understand me to mean the same thing that the dictionary means.

Each of these is a stipulation which makes use of the dictionary definition given earlier.

The Basic Move

When a definition is stipulated, no claim is made that the meaning presented is what the term **really** means. Instead, the stipulator simply announces and commits himself to intended usage, and perhaps tells the group involved that it should conform to this usage in the given situation.

Jim's stipulation announces his usage and commits him to it; Mr. Delta's in effect **tells** the others to conform as well. Mr. Delta is able to get away with this because he is in a position of authority.

Purpose

The purpose of a stipulative definition is to facilitate progress on the matter at hand. In the 'propaganda' case, this would be accomplished by giving a particular meaning to the word, thus making clear what the disagreement, if any, is about. As long as Jim and Sally understand the sentence, "Most of the material in the newspaper is propaganda", in different ways, there is no point to arguing about it. If Jim says that the statement is true, and Sally says that the statement is false, they are not necessarily disagreeing with each other, since the statements to which they are referring are **different** statements—though the same words are used to express them. Until there is agreement on what it is they are discussing, they will be talking past each other. The points that Jim makes might well be relevant to his understanding of the statement, but not relevant in the same way to the statement as she understands it.

As long as everyone conforms to the stipulated meaning of the term (sometimes very hard to do), there will ordinarily be no problem of communication. For example, if everyone were to use the word 'cat' to refer to dogs, and the word 'dog' to refer to cats, we would all understand each other. Under this new usage we would say that cats bark, and dogs are good at catching mice—which would be speaking the truth. Shakespeare captured this thought in *Romeo and Juliet* when he had Juliet say, "What's in a name? That which we call a rose, by any other name would smell as sweet. . . ." (Act II, Scene 2).

Arbitrariness of word meanings

We may stipulate meanings for words, because in an important way words are arbitrary symbols.* They are not natural properties of things. There is no justification in nature for using the symbol 'cat' to refer to cats rather than dogs. We might just as easily have developed a language in which the symbol 'cat' is used to refer to dogs, and we could now decide to do so, if we so choose. There would be inconvenience, of course, but we could do it without violating the laws or facts of nature.

The word 'cat' is not a natural property of cats. If a biologist were to study cats and make a list of their characteristics, one thing that he would not say he had discovered about cats is that they are called 'cats'. Being called 'cats' is not a natural trait of cats. This sort of fact, by the way, seems to

* As the word 'ARBITRARY' is used here, 'to be an arbitrary matter' roughly means 'to be decidable by a flip of the coin'. (This is stipulation, by the way.)

me to be the significant aspect of the frequently heard thesis of the General Semanticists:

The word is not the thing.*

Since words are not traits, we have a certain degree of freedom to stipulate meanings. How much freedom? For the time being, let us consider just the most important limitation to this freedom.

Adhering to the stipulation

The major limitation is that the stipulator may not stipulate a certain meaning for a term and then without warning slip into another usage (perhaps ordinary usage) for that term later on in the discussion. In the propaganda case, that means that Jim may not stipulate the dictionary definition for the term and then slip into the derogatory usage that Sally has suggested. To do so would be to trade on an ambiguity.

Since this sort of mistake is very common, you should be particularly on your guard against it. If, in this case, Jim were to prove his thesis, using the dictionary definition of the term 'propaganda' (and it appears that he can do this); and then were to shift the meaning of the thesis to the statement as Sally interprets it, he would appear to have established a thesis that is damaging to the newspaper. For in Sally's sense of 'propaganda', the thesis, 'Most of the material in this newspaper is propaganda', roughly means the same as, 'Most of the material in this newspaper is an attempt to persuade people to hold mistaken views, such attempt making use of irrational, emotional appeals.'

When this error of shifting meanings is made explicit in this manner, you might think that no one could make such a mistake, and that this warning is unnecessary; perhaps it is unnecessary for you, but the mistake is so common that even people who never make the mistake themselves should be on the alert for it and be ready to deal with it when it is suspected, by requesting explicit definitions throughout such a proof.

Stipulation Maneuvers

Suppose that Sally says that she is unable to agree to the dictionary definition and that she is unable to interpret what Jim says in the sense he has indicated, because that definition is just incorrect. Mr. Delta has been challenged. What is he to do then?

One thing that Mr. Delta cannot do is try to prove that he or Jim

* See for example, S. I. Hayakawa's *Language in Thought and Action* (New York: Harcourt, Brace and Company, 1949), pp. 29–31.

would be right—in the sense that either has given the correct definition of the term. Neither stipulation alleged to give a correct definition. A stipulative definition is not a statement about what is right or wrong; it is an announcement of an intention, a commitment, and a request or order. Just as it is inappropriate to say 'true' or 'false' to a request, it is inappropriate to say 'true' or 'false' to a stipulation. So too it would be a mistake for Mr. Delta to deal with this challenge directly in the way in which it is put. Rather than saying that the stipulation is correct, he might try to show that correctness and incorrectness do not apply to stipulations. He at least should avoid an apparent commitment to correctness, perhaps by inviting Sally to **suppose** that 'propaganda' means what the dictionary says.

The invitation to suppose

Since Sally in effect has been unable to obey Mr. Delta's order to accept the dictionary definition for purposes of the discussion, or has indicated an unwillingness to go along with Jim's announcement of usage, Mr. Delta, in the interest of Sally's understanding the discussion, might well retreat from his order and change it to an invitation, or make Jim's implicit invitation explicit. Either the order was fruitless, since Sally found herself unable to obey, or Jim's implicit invitation was refused. Mr. Delta might deliver the explicit invitation thus:

Example 7-1

MR. DELTA: Well, Sally, just **suppose** that 'PROPAGANDA' means any doctrines or ideas that are deliberately spread. If it were to mean that, would Jim's thesis be true? (waits for assent) You're not committed to anything you don't like, when you make that supposition. This is because the thesis now only means that the majority of the material on those two pages is deliberately intended to spread certain ideas. And you certainly will admit that the Red Cross article is intended to promote the idea that one should contribute to the Red Cross. And the article on the sewage plant is intended to convince us that it will be inadequate in five years. These are not bad things, but under this supposition, they would be propaganda.

The strategy in the above case is to get Sally to suppose the stipulated meaning, and then lead her along through the proof and application, with that meaning supposed.

If Sally boggles at even this approach, Mr. Delta might get her to suppose that some made-up term, 'propo' for example, means a doctrine or ideas that are deliberately spread. Using this term, Mr. Delta can carry through the entire proof and application as above. This certainly would avoid Sally's objection to the stipulated definition, since not even the same term is in use. Furthermore, it has the advantage of being similar to 'propaganda' and thus easier to remember than some completely unrelated symbol, such as 'glotto'.

The advantage of using an invitation to suppose the stipulated meaning of the term in question—or of some new term invented for the purpose—is that ordinarily it saves time for other things. The alternative, which is usually more time consuming, is to stop and try to convey an understanding of the nature of symbols and the extent to which their meanings are arbitrary. This is instruction that students should get somewhere along the line, but it might not be your job to give it. If it is your job (whether by curriculum decision or by your own), or if your students boggle at the invitation to suppose (indicating a need for immediate instruction), then here are some suggestions for how to go about it.

Instruction about the nature of symbols and stipulation

These suggestions for how to go about helping students to understand the degree of arbitrariness of symbols and stipulation are put forward with one advance qualification, namely, that there cannot be complete freedom to stipulate—or (what amounts to the same thing) that symbols are not completely arbitrary. If we give students a sense of freedom to stipulate, we must also give them, among other things, a sense of responsibility for communication and convenience. Unrestricted stipulation has various dangers. These will be discussed later.

Different Languages. One point that might be made in order to demonstrate the way in which symbols including words, are arbitrary, is that there are numerous languages with which we can say the same thing. For example, the word that one learns in order to refer to cats depends on the language he learns. In a sense it does not matter what word we use to refer to a cat, as long as everyone involved understands how the word is being used. We use 'cat'; the Germans use 'Kat'; the French use 'chat'; the Italians use 'gatto'; and so on. If it mattered which symbol is to be used, then some languages would be wrong in using the symbol that they use.

Changes in Meaning in Our Own Language. A second type of point that you can make is that in our own language there have been many changes in meaning adopted by accident or deliberately for reasons of convenience, style, taste, exclusiveness, popularity in a peer group, etc. Consider the following examples as possibilities for your use in instructing your students.

For the sake of convenience, various institutions and fields of study have taken standard terms and given them a technical meaning, usually related to, but always somewhat different from the standard meaning. A good example is the term 'strike', which for the game of baseball has been given a technical meaning. According to this meaning, there can be a strike even though the batter does not lift the bat from his shoulder to strike at the ball. The term 'run' has similarly been made a technical term. A man can run—all the way around the bases—without there being a run.

In basketball, the term 'basket' itself has a specialized meaning. The ideal basket in basketball is simply a hoop with net hanging down from it. It has no bottom and is of no use for holding anything.

Another good example is the term 'salt', which in ordinary usage refers to sodium chloride, the white stuff we usually find in the shaker next to the pepper shaker. The chemists have stipulated a broader meaning for that term, so that it refers not only to common table salt but to a large number of other compounds as well. Under the broader usage, in which 'SALT' means a compound formed by the union of an acid radical with a base radical, many common substances which we would not ordinarily call 'salt' become salt. Washing soda, baking soda, and limestone are a few examples.

The term 'work' has acquired a technical meaning in a specialized field of study. Physicists have redefined the term so that a man who, under orders of his employer, holds a 100-pound block of ice on his back all day, is doing no work. According to the technical definition of 'work', if there is to be any work, the force exerted must succeed in moving the object in the direction in which the force has been exerted.

Mathematics has taken the term 'RATIONAL', which originally meant 'endowed with reason or understanding', and has stipulated that 'RATIONAL NUMBER' shall mean a number expressible as an integer or the quotient of two integers. Psychology has taken the same term in its verb form, 'RATIONALIZE', and specified for it the meaning, 'to attribute one's actions to rational and creditable motives, without adequate analysis of the true motives'. These moves, which certainly are legitimate, could not have been made if the meanings of words were fixed.

The term 'demand' in economics has a special meaning, which, although related to our ordinary meaning, is different in important ways—by decision of the economists. In the ordinary sense a DEMAND is a very forceful request for something—usually backed up by something other than money. For the correct use of the economist's term, the demand must be backed by an offer to exchange money for the thing demanded and the demand need not be put forcefully at all. A request is sufficient.

In the field of history the term 'primary source' has a technical meaning which has been given to it by the historians. The uninitiated layman might expect a primary source to be the major source, as in the utterance, "The primary source of my information was Jones, although Smith was of some help." But for the historian a primary source is a particular kind of major source of information. A PRIMARY SOURCE for him is an original source of information, as opposed to a SECONDARY SOURCE, which gives information through one or more intermediaries. A Cornell University Announcement would ordinarily be considered a primary source for the course offerings at Cornell. A description of this Announcement would be a secondary source. Although historians differ on the question of how close to the original occurrence something must be in order to be a primary source, presumably most would agree to the above example of a primary source. A purist might quarrel with even that, however, for the Announcement only indicates what was intended a year in advance of the actual offerings. An interesting point here is that although a term may be made a technical term for a particular purpose, disagreement about its precise application very often remains. This situation certainly holds for the next example, 'romantic'.

The field of English has taken the term 'romantic' and made a technical term out of it. According to *Webster's New Collegiate Dictionary* (based on the second edition of *Webster's New International Dictionary*), the standard meaning of 'romantic' is vague, but things that are ROMANTIC tend to have such characteristics as being adventurous, surprising, dreamy, imaginary, picturesque. In the field of English the term has been appropriated to apply to a period of English literature, the Romantic Period, usually considered to extend from 1798 to 1832.* The works of this period in many cases could have *Webster's* sense of 'romantic' applied to them. This shows that there is a relationship between the two meanings. But certain features of the Romantic Period do not fit the meaning given by *Webster's*. Among them is an interest in external nature, or the poet himself as opposed to other men.** No such restriction may be found in *Webster's* meaning. Furthermore, and more obvious, is the fact that any literature which fits all of the characteristics given by *Webster's* definition, but which is contemporary, is not romantic in the technical sense of the term.

In addition to the deliberate specification of a technical meaning for a term in a given field, there is the gradual change of meaning resulting from its being heavily used in one restricted way. The term 'romantic' again serves as an example, for in contemporary American usage this term tends to be taken to indicate love. For example, "Jim and Joan are having a romance", or "Joan is having romantic feelings about Jim." And we would expect a newsstand magazine titled *Romance* to contain stories of requited and unrequited love. These shifts would not be possible unless the meanings of words were to some extent arbitrary.

Then there is the deliberate changing of the language by people who want to be exclusive or by leaders in style, changes often adopted by a peer group. The introduction of slang terms, many of which eventually become embedded in the language (like 'mob', 'stunning', and 'quack'***) exemplifies this way in which meanings can be arbitrary. Since contemporary slang is changing so rapidly, I need not give examples, but suggest that you select them from the slang of your students.

Enough examples have now been given of ways in which the connections

* M. H. Abrams, *A Glossary of Literary Terms* (New York: Holt, Rhinehart & Winston, Inc., 1957), p. 85.

** *Ibid.*, p. 57.

*** Reported by Simeon Potter, *Our Language* (Baltimore, Md.: Penguin Books, Inc., 1950), pp. 132, 136, 138.

between words and meanings are arbitrary—and thus can be stipulated. The examples given were chosen because they are likely to be familiar to students with even a minimal acquaintance with the fields and institutions mentioned. You can undoubtedly think of many more. After you have given several examples, it would probably be a good idea to ask your students to produce some.

Playing a Game with Words. Another way to drive home the arbitrary aspect of the relation between words and meanings is to make some sort of game out of this fact. For example, in an unsophisticated group there might be two sides, perhaps boys against girls, in a game modeled after baseball. Each side is up once in each inning. The side in the field stipulates certain meanings for a maximum of five terms and makes up a group of questions for the other side to answer. The pitcher delivers a question to the batter, who must answer it correctly within a given time limit, say five seconds. The other members of the team in the field can be preparing questions while the pitcher is delivering them. The answer to the question must be correct in accord with the **stipulated meanings** of the terms. A correct answer is a single and an incorrect answer is an out. And so on. Various elaborations of the rules can be worked out on the spot, depending on the situation.

There is a danger in the use of this technique. Students might remember facts in accord with the stipulated meanings and thus actually be remembering errors. This is another manifestation of the danger of a shift in meaning. Suppose that 'THREE' is stipulated to mean four and vice versa. Then the correct answer to the question, "When did Columbus discover America?" becomes 1392. This fact, if accidentally remembered in these terms, would be confusing. There would probably be no danger, however, if the question were, "What is the product of 32 and 93?" The answer is not something that anyone would remember anyway. Other ways to avoid the danger are to make sure that the stipulated meanings are absurd, or to frame questions about common facts in everyday life.

You have just had a chance to consider three general approaches to teaching your students that words are at least to some extent arbitrary in meaning: noting differences in languages, noting various kinds of shifts in our own language, and playing games with stipulations. All three approaches can be effective with almost any group—so long as you match the sophistication of the presentation to that of the group.

Handling suspected shifts in meaning

Now suppose that Sally has been persuaded that the stipulation move is a legitimate one and agrees to the stipulation of the dictionary definition of 'propaganda'. As indicated earlier, Mr. Delta, and hopefully the students as well, must be on guard against accidental or deliberate shifts in meaning of the term in mid-argument. In this case the danger is that Jim will shift to a derogatory sense of 'propaganda'. Suppose, for example, in a discussion of the question, "Where should one look in order to keep informed about contemporary affairs?" Jim argues that the local newspaper is not the place to look, because, as he has shown, it contains mostly propaganda; then we have a right to suspect that there has been a shift of meaning to the derogatory sense.

Making Definitions Explicit. One way to handle this situation is to ask Jim what he means by 'propaganda' (or remind him of his former stipulation), and then ask what it is about attempts to persuade that disqualifies them as ways of keeping informed about contemporary affairs. This, in effect, eliminates the word 'propaganda' from the argument and enables us to utilize the terms used in the stipulative definition. Now Jim must show why attempts to persuade are generally of little help in keeping informed. He might be able to do this, but at least the potential confusion from the word 'propaganda' has been avoided.

You will note that there is still room for confusion depending on the sense given to 'attempts to persuade'. If **any** statement of fact in a newspaper is to count for Jim as an attempt to persuade (on the ground that the newspaper is trying to persuade us of the truth of the fact), then the proof that this newspaper mostly contains attempts to persuade us of things becomes a strong proof; but there is a price to pay. The proven statement would be of no help in deciding the question of where to go to keep up on contemporary affairs. The phrase, 'attempts to persuade', would be so broad that the statement, 'The newspaper mostly contains propaganda', would be trivially true.

The explicit definitions might look like this:

> 'PROPAGANDA' shall mean any attempt to persuade.
>
> 'ANY ATTEMPT TO PERSUADE' shall mean any presentation which gives an argument, reasonable or not; or makes an emotional appeal; or asserts a fact; or does some combination of these.

Thus 'propaganda', by substitution, would mean any presentation which gives an argument, reasonable or not; or makes an emotional appeal; or asserts a fact; or does some combination of these.

If these are the definitions operating in the background, then making them explicit will guard against trading on an ambiguity. The conclusion that the newspaper contains mostly propaganda would be so clear in meaning (and innocuous), that an attempt to shift away from the stipulation to a derogatory sense for 'propaganda' would be obviously out of line.

Smoking Out Implicit Definitions by a Consideration of Cases. On occasion it is unwise to try to make the definitions explicit all the way through the proof and application of the statement to be proven. Sometimes students (or whoever it may be) are incapable of setting forth definitions that are accurate indicators of the meanings with which they are operating. And sometimes just for the sake of variety you should avoid asking 'What do you mean?', and should instead find out indirectly. And sometimes the terms involved are such basic terms that explicit definition does not help anyway.

On such occasions you can probe for meanings by advancing or asking for application of the term to possible cases. In the following dialogue Mr. Delta progressively determines the limitations of Jim's concept of propaganda, as it appears in the application of the thesis to the question of keeping informed.

Example 7-2

MR. DELTA: I take it that your assumption is that reading a particular publication is not a good way to keep informed, if the publication contains mostly propaganda.

JIM: Right.

MR. DELTA: I heard an announcement over the radio last night informing us that Mr. Jones and Mr. Smith are running for the open position of the school board. Is that propaganda? It just gave their names and addresses.

JIM: Oh no. That's information about contemporary affairs.

MR. DELTA: Then this morning I heard a presentation of the case in favor of the candidates. Was the combination of cases propaganda?

JIM: No, that is an attempt to give both sides. That's only fair.

MR. DELTA: Oh.—Now here in my hand is a circular advancing only the case for Mr. Jones. It is exactly what was read on the radio this morning. As you can see, it is a very sober, factual, unemotional presentation. Is it propaganda?

JIM: Well, not really.

MR. DELTA: How about this circular for Mr. Smith? It is quite different from the one for Mr. Jones, since there is an allegation that Jones is an "old fogey", and in large letters at the bottom we find the invitation to "join the forces of progress and win with Smith."

JIM: That definitely is propaganda. Name-calling, glittering generality, and bandwagon devices are used. They are of little use in keeping us informed about the issues. They cloud the issues.

In this dialogue Jim has revealed a shift in his meaning of 'propaganda' away from the definition which he stipulated in order to prove his thesis. Now apparently for something to be propaganda, it must be more than just any attempt to persuade; it must also be irrational in some way. When it comes to the application of a stipulated meaning to specific cases, people often shift their meaning.

For purposes of illustration the line of questioning was presented so directly that it is a bit unrealistic. Most people who are mistakenly or deliberately shifting their meanings would not fall into the obvious trap that Mr.

Delta set. More finesse would ordinarily be required in order to determine the meaning that is actually operating.

In the next chapter this technique will be considered with more thoroughness under the topic, "Determining Usage", and is called the method of example and nonexample.

Refusing the Stipulation. A third way to handle suspected shifts in meaning in the course of an argument is to refuse to accept the stipulation in the first place, and to insist that terms be used in their ordinary senses throughout the discussion. One might do this because it is sometimes extremely difficult to be flexible enough to understand and work consistently with stipulated meanings—either because the people involved are unsophisticated or emotionally involved, or because the terms are so basic that almost anyone is likely to slip up.

For example, with a whole group of Sallys, the move against Jim's original stipulation might be as follows:

Example 7-3

MR. DELTA: I'm sorry Jim, but we just don't understand 'propaganda' in that sense, even though the dictionary defines it that way. Let's stick to the contemporary meaning of 'propaganda', in order to avoid confusion. According to ordinary usage, if something is propaganda, there must at least be an irrational or emotional attempt to persuade. I'd like to hold off my comments about the other features of ordinary usage, as Sally presented them. But in any case, let's stick to ordinary usage in this one respect—the irrationality or emotionality of the presentation. If we do stick to it, then you might want to change the wording of your thesis. Would you be satisfied with this wording, "Most of the material in this newspaper is an attempt to persuade us of something"?

JIM: No, I prefer the earlier one.

MR. DELTA: Then I must insist that you include the element of irrationality or emotionality in your definition. Otherwise we just will not be able to follow you.

This move is an order to the effect that Jim and the group should stick to what Mr Delta considers to be the contemporary meaning of the term. Jim's refusal to accept the alternate statement of his thesis provides some indication that he is not going to stick to his own stipulative definition. By refusing Jim's stipulation, Mr Delta avoids the danger.

A more forceful and somewhat more dogmatic move is to say that this meaning of Jim's is just not the correct meaning of the term. This sort of move will be discussed in the next chapter, "Reporting Usage". However, let me make two points at this time:

1. This is a difficult step for a teacher to take in this instance, in view of the definitions one finds in most dictionaries. The presumption is that the dictionary is right in questions about the usage of terms. Mr. Delta would be obligated to build a case to show that the dictionary is wrong about this word.

2. Some occasions on which it **is** appropriate to be so dogmatic arise in teaching the vocabulary of a field, responding to a stipulation that is very far from usage, and dealing with a basic term.

The Uses and Abuses of Stipulative Definition

As you can now see, stipulating a meaning for a term can be of use, but it is also a process that can be abused. Several important uses and abuses have already been indicated in an off-hand manner. To be more methodical I shall present an interpreted list of uses and abuses. The list starts with major uses of stipulative definition.

Uses

Providing Clarity in a Situation Through Elimination of Ambiguity. When an ambiguity threatens the clear treatment of a subject, a stipulation is ordinarily called for. For example, the ambiguity of the word 'propaganda' calls for a stipulation in those situations in which it makes a difference which meaning of the term is intended. As indicated earlier, when the meaning is explicitly stipulated, there is more likelihood that people will understand each other, and there is a greater chance to check to make sure that no arguments depend on meaning shifts.

When the social scientist uses the word 'role', there are a number of things he could be taken to mean, since there are several different usages of this term in the social science literature. In *Explorations in Role Analysis*, Neal Gross, *et al.*, gives three types of definitions of 'role':

1. The normative culture pattern, in which a person's ROLE consists of the things **his culture expects** him to do as a result of his holding a certain position.
2. An individual's view of his situation, in which a person's ROLE consists of the things that **he thinks** he should do as a result of the group expectations for his position.
3. The behavior of actors occupying social positions, in which a person's ROLE consists of the way **he actually carries out** the requirements of his position.*

These three catagories distinguish what the group thinks one should do, what the individual thinks he should do, and what the individual actually does. Since instruments for gathering data about role, in each of the three senses, would be different, and since the interpretation of conclusions using the word 'role' would be correspondingly different, one should stipulate which, if any, of the three definitions of 'role' is in use in a particular context.

Teachers of such courses as family living, health, and psychology should

* Neal Gross, Ward S. Mason, and Alexander W. McEachern, *Explorations in Role Analysis* (New York: John Wiley & Sons, Inc., 1958), pp. 12–14.

make sure that when the word 'need' is used, it is clear which sense is intended. There are two major definitions of 'need' in common use:

1. '*X* needs *y*' means the same as '*X* wants *y*'.
2. '*X* needs *y*' means the same as '*X* ought to have *y*'.*

In order to make sure that there are no shifts in meaning and to make sure that everyone understands what is said when the word 'need' is used, a stipulative definition is necessary.

The above cases are ones in which clarity is provided by stipulating one of several meanings, no one of which is definitely preferred in a given field.

Confusion can also arise in cases where, although a definite technical meaning is preferred in a given field, a person might be in doubt about whether the technical meaning is the one in use in a given situation. Again stipulation would be called for. Please realize that in most situations the context would make quite clear which meaning is intended. An example of a situation in which it was not clear and in which a stipulation helped to clear things up is the following, in which a physics teacher and his students were trying to move a piano up onto the stage:

Example 7-4

MR. BETA: Now if we set up a ramp, there will be less work to this job.

JOHN: No, there will be more work, because we'll at least have to overcome the friction of rolling it up the ramp. If we lift it straight up onto the stage, there will be less work.

MR. BETA: I don't mean the physics concept of *work*. I mean the ordinary notion of *work*. If we push it up the ramp, it won't be hard at all.

According to the physics concept of *work*, John was right. According to the ordinary concept, Mr. Beta was right. A stipulation was needed to facilitate communication.

Providing Clarity through the Reduction of Vagueness. So much for ambiguity. Let us turn our attention to the use of stipulation to reduce vagueness. For legal purposes and research purposes, among others, it is often helpful to refine by stipulation a term that is loose in ordinary language. It is helpful to define terms in laws so that administrators and judges can carry out the law with as little independent use of judgment as possible.

In "The National Defense Education Act of 1958" the following stipulation, which may be found in a section labeled "Definitions", makes it easier to administer and judge applications of the Act:

* For a discussion of this difference see B. Paul Komisar, "'Need' and the Needs-Curriculum," B. Othanel Smith and Robert H. Ennis, eds., *Language and Concepts in Education* (Chicago: Rand McNally & Co., 1961), pp. 24–42.

> The term "SECONDARY SCHOOL" means a school which provides secondary education, as determined under State law, except that it does not include any education provided beyond grade 12. For the purposes of sections 301 through 304, the term "secondary school" may include a public junior college, as determined under State law (Section 103).

According to this stipulation, which to some extent embodies the spirit of local control in education, state law is stipulated to be the determiner of what constitutes a secondary school. However, except for the application of sections 301 through 304, this definition stipulates that no education beyond grade twelve is to be counted as secondary education. The first sentence of this definition, it is interesting to note, stipulates a meaning for 'secondary education' and then the second sentence stipulates an exception to the first. So we have a stipulative amendment to a stipulative definition! Lawmakers often find it appropriate to stipulate in such detail. Only by so doing can legislators be fairly well assured of the consequences of the laws which are before them.

Similarly, for purposes of data collection it is sometimes desirable to stipulate precise meanings for loose terms. The United States Census Bureau's definition of 'rural' exemplifies this approach:

> The URBAN population comprises all persons living in (a) places of 2,500 inhabitants or more, incorporated as cities, boroughs, and villages, (b) incorporated towns of 2,500 inhabitants or more except in New England, New York, and Wisconsin, where 'towns' are simply minor civil divisions of counties, (c) the densely settled urban fringe, including both incorporated and unincorporated areas, around cities of 50,000 or more, and (d) unincorporated places of 2,500 inhabitants or more outside any urban fringe. The remaining population is classified as RURAL.*

This is in considerable contrast to the definition in *Webster's New Collegiate Dictionary*:

> RURAL—Of or pertaining to the country, as distinguished from a city or town; designating or pertaining to country people, or country occupations, especially agriculture; rustic.**

You can see how difficult it would be for a census taker to use the dictionary definition in order to judge whether to classify someone as rural or not; it would be doubly difficult to get the census takers to be consistent with each

* Bureau of the Census of the U.S. Department of Commerce, *Census of Population: 1950*, Vol. I. (Washington, D.C.: United States Government Printing Office, 1952), p. xv. The definition has been slightly modified since then, but I cite this version because it is less complex (!), and because it can be used better to illustrate a later point about negatives in definitions.

** *Op. cit.*, p. 742.

other, using the dictionary definition. Given the need of the Census Bureau to maintain consistency among its judgments and to make judgments of classification quickly and easily, the sort of definition stipulated by the Census Bureau is a practical necessity.

Introducing New Concepts. When you present a new concept to your students, you must attach it to a term they already have or to a term that is partly or completely new to them. In any case, you use the process of stipulation to give meaning to the term.

The concept, *parallel structure,* in the field of English, is at some time a new concept for students, and might appropriately be introduced by a number of examples and nonexamples. But somewhere in the process of introduction of the concept, a definition is called for. This definition will be stipulative in spirit, as in the following one:

> By 'PARALLEL IN STRUCTURE' we shall mean the property of having all the items in a list of the same part of speech.

When the physics teacher introduces the concept *work,* as used in physics, he too must give a definition that is stipulative in spirit. The economics teacher's definition of 'demand' similarly must be stipulative in spirit when the new concept is introduced.

The examples so far presented show the need for stipulation in teaching the meanings of technical terms, that is, in introducing concepts that are new to the students. Although not appropriate at most teaching levels, there are cases of the introduction of new technical meanings which should be pointed out here because of their great importance in the advancement of knowledge. These cases are the specification of meaning for newly created concepts. The invention or discovery* of new concepts is often of signal importance in the advancement of knowledge in a field. If these concepts are valuable, then they become part of the conceptual structure of the field and eventually are taught to students as part of the organized body of knowledge. But at the time of their original introduction they are not taught to any but the most advanced students, because great sophistication is ordinarily required to understand why they are proposed, and because the time of the less-advanced student is often better spent learning concepts that have stood the test of time and are less likely to be discarded a few years hence.

Familiar examples of concepts which have stood the test of time are *imaginary number* in mathematics, *neutron* in physics, *valence* in chemistry, *nucleus* in biology, *noun* in languages, *counter-cyclical fiscal policy* in economics, *contour-*

* I say "invention **or** discovery" because I do not see the need to take sides on the question, "Are concepts invented or discovered?" This is a very interesting philosophical question which has not been settled. Since our discussion can take place without assuming an answer to the question, it is best to allow it to do so.

plowing in agriculture, *role* in sociology, *romantic* in literature, *Enlightenment* in history, and *protein* in home economics.

At the time each of these concepts was introduced, the logically correct way to deal with them was to stipulate a meaning for them. This is not to make the historical claim that in each case the person or persons who proposed the concept were aware that they were stipulating a meaning for the terms they used; for they might not have been. The claim is simply that they had the right only to stipulate a meaning, and that so doing was quite useful in the advancement of knowledge in the field.

Avoiding Shifts in Meaning in the Course of a Discussion. In the earlier discussion of the nature of the local newspaper, Mr. Delta found it easier to keep Jim from shifting his meaning of 'propaganda' by securing a stipulative definition from him, a definition to which Jim could later be held. A safeguard against meaning shifts is the explicit defining of terms. Since often people cannot reach an agreement on what is the standard usage of a term, a retreat to stipulative definition is often satisfactory, for such a definition provides a basis for consistent communication. Such was the case in the propaganda discussion.

Avoiding Fruitless Arguments over the Meaning of a Term. Countless wasted hours have been spent arguing over the meaning of a term. Sometimes it matters what meaning we shall attach to a term, as you will soon see if this is not already clear. But it often does not matter, and the stipulation of a meaning enables the discussion to proceed.

Shorthand. Often it is convenient to stipulate that a short term shall mean the same as a long one, thus enabling us to say what we want to say more quickly and sometimes to grasp complex ideas more readily. For practical reasons the term 'DDT' has been stipulated to mean **d**ichloro-**d**iphenyl-**t**richloro-ethane. We are thus enabled to refer to that compound with less trouble.

Consider the word 'Enlightenment', which is the name for an eighteenth century movement that was characterized by a lively questioning of authority, much theorizing in the sphere of politics, and emphasis on empirical method in science. The statement, "There is much of the Enlightenment with us today", carries with it a host of ideas; it even vaguely suggests some causal relationships in a situation in which it appeared. It would be more difficult to comprehend the thought expressed by that statement if we had no shorthand term for that period in history.

Dangers and abuses of stipulation

A number of dangers and abuses are attached to the process of stipulation, as you might well have suspected. Every powerful tool has its problems.

The Invitation to Ambiguity in Reasoning. When we stipulate a different meaning for a standard term, the danger always exists that we will forget about the stipulation. This was illustrated by the possibility that Jim would shift to some derogatory sense of 'propaganda'.

Consider the case of 'rural', for which you will remember, the Census Bureau has stipulated a more precise technical meaning. There is a danger attached to this stipulation.

The size of our rural population in 1960 was 54,041,888. A politician who did not attend to the technical (and stipulated) sense of 'rural' in that statement might be inclined to weight agricultural interests more heavily than is appropriate when he makes his campaign speeches and makes his decisions as a public official. He might conclude that there are more than 50 million rural people (justifying this on the basis of the Census figures) and then apply this conclusion using the dictionary definition. This would be a mistake, because many who are classified as rural by the Census definition are not agriculturally oriented. An indication of this situation is the number of people classified as rural nonfarm in 1960, 40,596,990, as compared with 13,444,898 classified as rural farm. Now some of the rural nonfarm were agriculturally oriented (for example, farm implement dealers, milk wholesalers), but many were simply suburban and were less likely to respond like agricultural people than our public official might have expected. Using the dictionary definition of 'rural', 'rural nonfarm' even borders on being a self-contradictory term.

Ways to avoid the temptation to ambiguity would be to invent a partially or wholly new term, and to stipulate the meaning for that term. For example, instead of using the term 'rural' for the technical term, the Census Bureau might have used 'ruralcen' or 'lar'. Then there would be much less likelihood of confusion from ambiguity.

On the other hand, then a new kind of confusion would arise—particularly from the wholly new term: The unfamiliarity of the new language would puzzle people and would make it difficult for them to remember the new term. Probably the best compromise in most cases is to change the term slightly, as was done for 'ruralcen', so that there is a memory association without the invitation to ambiguity. Regrettably, this course is not more often followed by language manipulators.

Misleading One's Audience. When one's audience has not had sufficient chance to learn about the stipulations with which one is operating, it is deceptive to use terms in the stipulated sense. As Richard Robinson* pointed out, the title of W. H. Auden's *The Oxford Book of Light Verse* is deceptive in that one expects to find a collection of verse that is not serious in nature. In his introduction Auden stipulates a special meaning for the term, 'light

* Richard Robinson, *Definitions* (Oxford: Oxford University Press, 1954), p. 76.

verse', which would enable us to include very serious things under the classification, *light verse*. His definition runs as follows:

> When the things in which the poet is interested, the things which he sees about him, are much the same as his audience, and that audience is a fairly general one, he will not be conscious of himself as an unusual person, and his language will be straightforward and close to ordinary speech. When, on the other hand, his interests and perceptions are not readily acceptable to society, or his audience is a highly specialized one, perhaps of fellow poets, he will be acutely aware of himself as a poet, and his methods of expression may depart very widely from the normal social language.
>
> In the first case his poetry will be 'LIGHT' in the sense in which it is used in the anthology.*

According to Auden's usage, if a poet's interests coincide with those of his audience, if the audience is a general one, if he is not conscious of himself as an unusual person, and if his language is straightforward and close to ordinary speech, his poetry will be light verse, even though it be about the most serious of subjects. In the anthology, for example, we find A. E. Housman's angry poem, "The Laws of God", and his poem, "The Stars", which, if not angry, is at least very serious. Therefore, we might be misled.

Here is another example. When a student proposes a title for a paper that he wants to write, or a topic that he wants to investigate, we have a right to expect him not to be keeping any odd stipulations in the back of his mind, stipulations that would in effect make a considerable difference in the topic being investigated. This stricture also holds for teachers. They must not propose topics, keeping in the background certain stipulative definitions that make a difference in the nature of the suggestion.

It would be inappropriate to propose as a topic, "The Justification of *Laissez-Faire* Child-Rearing Practices", and by 'JUSTIFICATION' mean the extent of practice, unless this stipulation is clearly signaled in some way or other. For otherwise, one would expect this investigation to be about whether *laissez-faire* is justified rather than about the extent to which it is practiced.

Similarly, a number of euphemistic stipulations are misleading. Here are two examples:

1. Stipulating that 'HEAT ENGINEER' shall be the word for the occupation of people who install furnaces in homes.
2. Stipulating that 'CUSTODIAN' shall mean janitor.

Of course, certain advantages are to be achieved by stipulating euphemisms, but these advantages depend on the deception of euphemisms. Ironically,

* W. H. Auden, *The Oxford Book of Light Verse* (Oxford: Oxford University Press, 1938), pp. viii-ix, by permission of the Clarendon Press, Oxford.

as soon as their misleading nature is exhausted (which tends to happen over a period of time), they lose their utility as euphemisms.

The Loss of Concepts. If the Census Bureau's stipulated meaning for 'rural' is generally accepted, there is danger that we will be without the loose concept *rural*, which the Census Bureau, for its purposes, has replaced. That this is a useful concept can be seen in an attempt to propose a person as candidate for senator from Iowa. The fact that he had a rural background was a point offered in favor of his candidacy. Using the ordinary sense of 'rural' this statement tells us more about his value orientation, his understanding of problems faced by farmers, etc., than it would using the Census Bureau sense of 'rural'. It is, therefore, useful to have this word 'rural' to use in situations of this sort. It communicates information to us that is not communicated by the Census Bureau term.

This is not to say that we would be completely unable to communicate this sort of information if the ordinary sense of 'rural' were eliminated. But things would at least be less convenient without it. It is a useful tool.

Deliberate Restriction. The danger becomes greater if people deliberately try to restrict us to the stipulated meaning. A common disease among people who have some training in a field is believing that this field has identified the "real" meanings of the terms it uses. In effect this belief often results in the loss of useful concepts. Interestingly enough, we rarely find this disease among people who know a field well enough to be doing basic research in it. They are usually well aware of the stipulative nature of the meanings in a field. Perhaps this is because they are continuously trying out modifications of concepts. In order to do this they must have developed a flexibility not required by the person who has simply absorbed the results of others' investigations.

Here are some examples of this disease:

1. A student who has some training in geometry is asked at a class meeting to draw a line under two words that he has just written on the board. He smugly remarks, "You mean line segment, I suppose."

For those uninitiated to the definitions of geometry a word of explanation is in order. According to the current formalization of geometry, the distinction between a line which extends to infinity in both directions and one that is finite in length is marked by the terms, 'line' and 'line segment', respectively. In accordance with this stipulated usage it would be proper to say, "Please draw a line segment under those two words", but of course almost nobody does.

2. A person with some training in the field of English literature hears a contemporary novel described as romantic. He points out that the describer does not know what 'romantic' really means, since it is used to apply to a certain period of English

literature. Neglecting the fact that the objector is talking about 'Romantic' with a capital '*R*' (which fact would not be directly observable in speech), he is apparently trying to force the perfectly good stipulated meaning of the field of English upon ordinary speech.

3. The person with some training in home economics is told by a friend that she is going to the store to buy some baking powder to make some dough for some bread. This purchaser is informed that she does not know what 'dough' really means, for by definition dough is not made with baking powder, but only from yeast. Again we have a case of a person's forgetting the stipulative nature of the definitions of technical terms in a field and treating the technical meaning as the real meaning.

In the first example, the broad concept *line*, as we now have it, is what is threatened. This concept includes the modern geometrician's concepts, *line* and *line segment*. For most purposes the distinction is not necessary. To insist upon it is to make things unnecessarily complicated.

In the second and third situations the ordinary concepts, of which we might be temporarily deprived, are *romantic* and *dough*. Each is useful—and dispensable only with inconvenience.

Loss of Basic Concepts. The danger of the loss of concepts is still greater when the concept is a really basic one. Examples of really basic concepts are *sameness*, *difference*, *good*, and *justice*. A person who makes the following stipulation,

'*X* is GOOD' is to mean the same as 'I like *X*',

and then insists upon our accepting it, is threatening us with the loss of a basic concept. Replacing the word 'good' after this linguistic imperialist has appropriated it would be very difficult, because we do not have a range of words to substitute for it.

Perhaps some of you are wondering what is wrong with the above attempt to define the word 'good'. Among other things such a definition leaves us without a term in which to express disagreements about what is good. (This point assumes that other value terms would be similarly defined in terms of personal likes and dislikes.) Imagine two students arguing about mercy killing:

Example 7-5

FRANK: Mercy killing is very definitely not a good thing. It is wrong to take a life.

JOAN: No, Frank, you're mistaken. Mercy killing is a good thing. It is very cruel to leave someone in permanent misery. The taking of such a life is not wrong.

Regardless of the merits of the arguments pro and con, the relevant point to be made here is that there definitely is a disagreement between Frank and Joan on this question. When Joan says, "Mercy killing is a good thing", she is contradicting Frank's statement, "Mercy killing is very definitely not a good thing." But according to the proposed definition, there is no contradiction between the two statements. Using that definition the statements may be translated as follows:

> FRANK: I very definitely do not like mercy killing.
> JOAN: I like mercy killing.

There is no contradiction between Joan's saying that she likes something and Frank's saying that he does not like it. To put it another way, to say "Joan likes something, but Frank does not" is not a self-contradiction. But to say "This thing is good and it is not good" is a self-contradiction.

Thus the definition does not capture the meaning of the word 'good' as it is ordinarily used and threatens us with the loss of an important concept. If other value terms, such as 'valuable', 'desirable', 'worthwhile', etc., were similarly defined in terms of personal (or societal, for that matter) likes and dislikes, then we would really be without our evaluative concepts, a serious loss.*

Perhaps some of you are now wondering what 'good' really does mean, if it is not so connected to personal preferences. I shall postpone attempting to answer this question until Chapters 9 and 21. But the question does not have to be answered in order to make my point, which depends on showing that the previous definition of 'good' is not satisfactory. The point is that stipulation of a meaning for a basic term is dangerous because it might force us to be without a basic concept.

Inflexibility of People. As indicated in the discussion of 'propaganda', a practical disadvantage of stipulating a meaning is that often people have great difficulty in thinking in terms other than those to which they are accustomed. Sally had great difficulty in using and understanding the term 'propaganda' in the way Jim wanted her to. People generally have this difficulty to a greater extent with basic terms and with terms which have an emotional tinge to them in ordinary usage (such as 'freedom', 'democracy', 'elegant', and 'army brass'). Because of our difficulty in changing our habits, it is usually better to use words in their ordinary sense, other things being equal. Since other things often are not equal, we often need to stipulate a meaning and must face the inflexibility problem.

Pretentiousness and/or Mere Verbiage. Stipulation can easily be used in order to be pretentious rather than to make communication more effective. We are all familiar with many examples of unnecessary technical terms, not all of which are **deliberately** pretentious. Some authors and speakers are completely unaware of their excesses. Here are some examples of probable pretentiousness and/or mere verbiage introduced by stipulation:

* For an enlightening discussion of attempts to define value terms in this way, see G. E. Moore's *Principia Ethica* (Cambridge, England: Cambridge University Press, 1903), especially pp. 1–21.

1. The use of 'cathected' to mean the same as 'wanted', as in the sentence, 'The new automobile is a cathected object among teenagers'.
2. The use of the term, '*non sequitur*'. To say that an argument is a NON SEQUITUR is nothing more than to say that the conclusion does not follow.
3. The use of 'traumatic' to mean shocking, as in 'I just had a traumatic experience'.

Chapter Summary

As you can now see, in some situations much is to be gained from stipulating a meaning for a term, that is, proposing (with varying degrees of authoritativeness) a meaning for a term—and much to be lost in other situations. Stipulation enables us to provide clarity through the elimination of ambiguity and reduction of vagueness, provides us with a vehicle for the introduction of new concepts, helps us to avoid shifts in meaning in the course of a discussion, helps to avoid fruitless arguments over the meaning of a term, and enables us to make use of shorthand reference to complex things. On the other hand, it can serve as an invitation to ambiguity in reasoning, it can mislead an audience when the audience does not have a chance to see the stipulation in advance, and it can effectively deprive us of concepts, obstruct communication with an inflexible audience, and result in pretentiousness and/or mere verbiage.

There is no hard-and-fast rule to tell us when to stipulate, nor to tell us whether, when stipulating, to use existing terms, modifications of existing terms, or completely unique terms. Vague general rules (which have many exceptions) are the following:

1. Do not stipulate unless you have good reason.
2. Generally pick a modification of an existing term, rather than an unmodified, existing term, or a completely unique one.

In applying these rules, keep in mind the above uses and abuses of stipulation, and pay close attention to such situational features as level of sophistication and flexibility of students, basicness and emotional tinge of terms, time available, cruciality of adherence to the technical meanings of the term, and need for ease of application of the term. Although there is no precise universal formula for making decisions about stipulation, an understanding of the bearing of these factors on the cases discussed in this chapter should be of considerable help in your handling such problems with your students.

COMPREHENSION SELF-TEST

True or False? If the statement is false, change a crucial term (or terms) to make it true.

7–1. A person giving a stipulative definition implies that he has captured the correct meaning for the term.

7–2. A stipulative definition can be in the form of each of the following:

a. A request.
b. A command.
c. A commitment.

7–3. Since words are arbitrary symbols, we have complete freedom to stipulate any meaning we want for any word.

7–4. It is never appropriate to say "true" to a stipulation.

7–5. When a student finds himself unable to obey the teacher's command to accept a stipulation, the teacher should retreat gracefully and try another device.

Questions.

7–6. Give two other techniques which might work if the command to accept a stipulation fails.

7–7. State one advantage of inventing a new term, instead of stipulating a new meaning for an existing term.

7–8. State a disadvantage of inventing a completely unique symbol and stipulating a meaning for it.

7–9. Give three general reasons that you can advance in support of the contention that words are arbitrary symbols.

7–10. In guarding against ambiguity in the use of stipulative definitions, under what condition(s) would you:

a. Make the stipulations explicit?
b. Leave them implicit but investigate them?
c. Reject the stipulation?

7–11. List five uses of stipulative definitions.

7–12. List four dangers in the use of stipulative definitions.

Discussion Questions.

7–13. Go to the chapter summary. The first paragraph contains a list of uses and abuses of stipulation. For each item, write one or two paragraphs in which you exemplify that use or abuse, using terms from some area that you have taught or will teach. Treat the clarity provided by elimination of ambiguity and reduction of vagueness as two items.

7–14. Give an example from your field in which it was best (when stipulating) to use an existing term as is rather than alter some term. Justify.

7–15. Give an example from your field in which it was best (when stipulating) to modify an existing term rather than use an existing term as is. Justify.

7–16. Can you find an example in your field in which what had previously been a nonsense syllable became a technical term? If so, give it. If not, try to explain why you have not been able to find such a thing.

7–17. Read the chapter on stipulative definitions in Richard Robinson's *Definition* (Oxford: Oxford University Press, 1954), pp. 59–92. Select a thesis of his with which you agree or disagree, and defend your agreement or disagreement in a two-page paper.

7–18. Read the section entitled "On Nominal Definition" in Carl Hempel's *Fundamentals of Concept Formation in Empirical Science* (Chicago: University of Chicago Press, 1952), pp. 2–6. Select a thesis of his with which you agree or disagree and defend your agreement or disagreement in a two-page paper.

7–19. Read Robinson's and Hempel's views on stipulative definitions (see above two items for source) and write a two-page paper comparing and contrasting their views.

CHAPTER 8

Reporting Usage

In the previous chapter on stipulating a meaning you saw how stipulation might be used to resolve the difficulty arising from different meanings of 'propaganda'. You also saw that a number of kinds of situations occur in which stipulation can be useful—but not without attendant dangers. One of the suggestions made was that as an alternative to stipulation, Mr. Delta might have somewhat dogmatically said about some definition of 'propaganda',

This is what the term means.

You will note that this sort of thing is radically different from stipulation. It is not a request, not a proposal, not a commitment (though it does involve a commitment), and not even an order. It is an assertion. It is the sort of thing to which someone can respond 'true' or 'false'. Therefore, we must have a new set of criteria for evaluating such definitions.

But what does it mean to say, "This is what the term means"? Well, it could mean a number of things, but one common interpretation, the one to be pursued in this chapter, is,

This is the established usage of the term.

This chapter deals with claims about the way terms are actually used, that is with reported definitions. For our purposes 'REPORTED DEFINITION' shall mean a definition which is alleged to report the way a term is actually used. This stipulative definition of 'reported definition' is consistent with established usage among those who study definitions. Note that this definition of 'reported definition' does not limit reported definitions to reports of **established** usage. It permits as a reported definition a definition which is simply a report of an actual usage which is **not** established. However, for practical reasons we are most often concerned with **established** usage.

Another thing to note is that the definition does not specify whose usage is being reported. Usually it is some standard (but vague) reference group, and usually the context makes clear which group, if any, is the reference group.

Now it would certainly be a legitimate move for Mr. Delta to give a reported definition of the term 'propaganda', a reported definition that purported to give an established usage for the term. Communication is possible because there is a large body of established usages for terms. People are familiar with them, can expect to be interpreted in accord with them, and can expect to be addressed in terms that are in accord with them. When Humpty Dumpty in Lewis Carroll's *Through the Looking Glass* attempts to violate some of the standard meanings of terms (for example, he defined 'glory' as 'nice knock-down argument'), he causes nothing but confusion, but if he had violated them all, he would not even have been able to express his right to violate them. To express his right to violate conventions he had to make use of them, as in the passage:

> "When **I** use a word," Humpty Dumpty said, in rather a scornful tone, "it means just what I choose it to mean—neither more nor less."

In that passage the words with which he expressed his disdain for linguistic convention were used conventionally. Otherwise he would have failed to communicate. Without adherence to convention, communication breaks down.

Turning to a Dictionary

Ordinarily in situations in which people disagree about the meaning of a word, the appropriate thing to do is to turn to the dictionary and look it up. If it is a common term, we look it up in a general dictionary; if it is a technical term, we can often find it in a general dictionary, but for a fuller and more precise account we should turn to a dictionary of technical terms for the field in which it is a technical term.

A source of conventions

This appeal to the dictionary is reasonable, because the dictionary supposedly gives us the conventions in accords with which we talk and write.

Since language is a matter of convention, why not go to the place where scholars have recorded what they find the conventions to be? Thus it is reasonable for every teacher to have a dictionary or two on his desk—a general dictionary, and one for technical terms, if he teaches a subject at anything but an elementary level.

Problems with dictionaries

But as every teacher knows, it is not that simple. Here are four major problems:

1. Dictionary definitions are circular for some people.
2. Formal dictionary definitions often lose some of the nuances of a word.
3. The dictionaries often disagree with each other.
4. Dictionaries are sometimes out-of-date.

Let us examine these problems.

Circularity. We all know well the experience of looking up a word in the dictionary, being unclear about the meanings of the term or terms used to clarify the original term, looking up these terms and finding that they are defined by use of the original term. Sometimes if we try hard enough and follow all the leads, we can get out of the circle, but sometimes it is very difficult to do so.

When a student of mine once tried to look up 'depreciatory', which appeared in the sentence, "That word is a depreciatory word", he ran into trouble. Under 'depreciatory' he found 'tending to depreciate or disparage'. The reappearance of the first nine letters ('d-e-p-r-e-c-i-a-t') of the word he was pursuing discouraged him a bit, but this was not really circularity because he only had to look up the nearby entry, 'depreciate', in order to make progress. He did so and found the following entry:*

> DEPRECIATE . . . to lessen in price or estimated value; also to undervalue; disparage, belittle. —Syn. See 'decry'.— Ant. Appreciate.

Feeling that price and value had nothing to do with what he was looking for, not understanding 'belittle', and again finding a reference to 'disparage', he decided to look up that word. This is the entry he found:

> DISPARAGE . . . To lower in rank or estimation by actions or words; hence to speak slightingly of; to depreciate. —Syn, See 'decry'.

He did not understand the first two of the three definitions and found that

* This and the other entries in this part on circularity are from *Webster's New Collegiate Dictionary* (Springfield, Mass.: G. & C. Merriam Co., 1958).

the third referred him back to 'depreciate'. So far, the process was for him circular.

There are two ways out: (1) to figure out either of the first two definitions of 'disparage', and (2) to look up 'decry', which had been mentioned by both entries. It turned out that the second course was easiest for him, because under that word, the following statement appeared:

> 'DECRY', 'DEPRECIATE', 'DISPARAGE', 'DEROGATE FROM', 'DETRACT FROM', 'BELITTLE', 'MINIMIZE' mean to express one's low opinion of something.

This student understood what it is to express one's low opinion of something and then was able to suggest that a depreciatory word would be one used to express one's low opinion of something. Although he did not have the full meaning of 'depreciatory', he had made considerable progress in his bout with the dictionary. The initial circularity was overcome by his perseverance and by the dictionary's elaborations.

Another young student had a more difficult problem—to figure out the meaning of 'abstract'. He found the following entry, which failed to enlighten him:

> ABSTRACT . . . 1. a. Considered apart from any application to a particular object; as, **abstract** truth. b. Ideal; abstruse. c. **Math**. Used without reference to a thing or things, as the **abstract** number 10. 2. Of words, names, etc., not concrete: a. Expressing a quality apart from any object (**honesty, whiteness**). b. General, as opposed to a particular (**reptile**). 3. Dealing with a subject in its theoretical considerations only. 4. **Art**. Presenting or characterized by nonrepresentational designs depicting no recognizable thing, only geometric figures, or abstruse diagrams, or mechanical or amorphous creations.—Ant. Concrete.

Being mystified by the above interpretation, the student tried looking up the antonym, 'concrete'. The entry under 'concrete' he found equally mystifying, even after eliminating the first and fourth definitions, which are irrelevant:

> CONCRETE . . . 1. United in growth; compounded or coalesced; solid. 2. a. Naming a thing, or a class of things, as opposed to naming a quality or attribute; thus, "man" is a **concrete** term but "human" is abstract. b. Having a specific application; particular; as a **concrete** term or number;—opp. to abstract or general. 3. Of the nature of, or characterized by, immediate experience; belonging to actual things or events; real; not abstract or ideal; also dealing with that which is concrete; not abstract or general; as **concrete** ideas. 4. Pertaining to or made of concrete.—Syn. See 'special'.—Ant. Abstract.

The word 'abstract' appears five times in the definition of 'concrete'. Not only this, but there is a set of words which seem to be defined in terms of each other, but the definitions for the most part do not seem to reach out intelligibly beyond these terms: 'abstract', 'concrete', 'ideal', 'general', 'particular', 'specific', 'immediate experience', and 'real'. Except for two things under the *2a* part of the definition of 'concrete', we seem to be in a tight circle, and each of these two things embodies a problem:

1. In the definition of 'concrete', the implied characterization of abstract terms as naming a quality or attribute is inaccurate, though seemingly intelligible. We would not call the words, 'solid', 'heavy', and 'red', abstract terms, but they are qualitative words just as much as 'human' is; they are used to attribute qualities to things.
2. The use of the examples, 'man' and 'human', as concrete and abstract terms could be very helpful. The problem is that when presented out of context, the word 'man' can easily be interpreted as an abstract term, as in 'Man is a rational animal'. Given more space the dictionary might well have used the word 'man' in a sentence in which it is clearly a concrete term, such as, 'That man is Mr. Hyde'.

Thus circularity is a potential problem in the use of dictionaries. A teacher can do two things to minimize this problem:

1. Encourage students to keep trying and to pursue the various leads presented by the various definitions. Usually a way out of the circularity can be found. That is, there is usually a way from the unfamiliar word to familiar ones.
2. Make larger dictionaries available to students, because the larger dictionaries tend to have more complete examples and comments about the terms. In a very important way the shortest dictionary is the most obscure. Some good large dictionaries are *Funk & Wagnall's New "Standard" Dictionary of the English Language*, *Webster's Third New International Dictionary*, and the *Oxford English Dictionary*, the latter being so large that it is unlikely to be available in most school libraries. *A Dictionary of Contemporary American Usage* by Bergen and Cornelia Evans is also quite useful in this respect because of its extended discussions. However, it has many fewer entries than the other dictionaries.*

Since circularity is primarily a problem of the form of a definition, any further discussion of it belongs in Section B of Part II, "Forms of Definitions". For the time being, be content with the observation that the danger of circularity is reduced to the extent that the dictionary departs from the traditional, precise, brief, definitional forms and makes use of examples, contrasts, use in a sentence, and the like.

Loss of the Nuances of Meaning. It is really very difficult to capture the full meaning of a word, particularly the rich terms of everyday speech, in a short definition. We have all seen cases of the use of terms in sentences in which they just did not fit, but which use seemed to be sanctioned by the dictionary definition of the term. For example, the following statement appeared in a student's paper:

* Publication information on these dictionaries appears shortly.

The trees were senescent.

The use of the word 'senescent' here is inappropriate. The word should not be applied to trees, but this fact is not evident in the following dictionary definition:

SENESCENT . . . growing old, aging.

This problem is also to some extent handled by reference to those dictionaries which tend to give more of the flavor of words than dictionaries with short entries. The problem is handled even better by repeated exposure to and practice with correct usage in different situations. Forms of definition which give lengthier definitions are helpful too, and will be examined later (Part II, Section B).

Disagreement among Dictionaries and the Degree to Which They Are Out-Of-Date. One of the first lessons to be learned about dictionaries is that they often disagree among themselves. For example one may find the following two definitions of 'cultural relativism' in two social science dictionaries:

CULTURAL RELATIVISM—the point of view in which each cultural group is evaluated in terms of its own value system.*

RELATIVISM, CULTURAL. The principle that experience is interpreted by each person in terms of his own background, frame of reference, and social norms, and that these factors will influence perception and evaluations, so that there is no single scale of values applicable to all societies.**

The second definition, in contrast to the first, does not attribute to cultural relativism the view that each cultural group is to be evaluated in terms of its **own** value system. It merely says that there is no **one** value system by which all can be evaluated, allowing for the possible view that there are, say, two value systems, in accord with one or the other of which all cultures are to be evaluated. Furthermore an empirical explanation of the differences in what people actually do value and see is not made part of the first definition, whereas it is part of the second definition.

Our now controversial term 'propaganda' receives varied treatment at the hands of the general dictionaries, although there are, of course, a number of points of agreement. Here is a list of the dictionaries I consulted in my study of the treatment of the word 'propaganda':

1. *The American College Dictionary*. New York: Random House, 1960.

* John T. Zadrony, *Dictionary of Social Science* (Washington, D.C.: Public Affairs Press, 1959), p. 78.

** Charles Winick, *Dictionary of Anthropology* (New York: Philosophical Library, 1956), p. 454.

2. Evans, Bergen and Cornelia Evans. *A Dictionary of Contemporary American Usage.* New York: Random House, 1957.
3. *Funk & Wagnall's New "Standard" Dictionary of the English Language.* New York: Funk & Wagnall's Company, 1961.
4. *The Oxford English Dictionary.* Oxford: Oxford University Press, 1933.
5. *Thorndike-Barnhart Comprehensive Desk Dictionary.* Garden City, N. Y.: Doubleday & Company, Inc., 1962.
6. *Webster's New Collegiate Dictionary* (based on *Webster's New International Dictionary,* Second Edition). Springfield, Mass.: G. & C. Merriam Co., 1958.
7. *Webster's Seventh New Collegiate Dictionary* (based on *Webster's Third New International Dictionary*). Springfield, Mass.: G. & C. Merriam Company, 1963.
8. *Webster's Third New International Dictionary.* Springfield, Mass.: G. & C. Merriam Company, 1961.

These dictionaries essentially agree on the capitalized use of 'propaganda' as it appears in the title, "The Congregation of Propaganda", a body of Roman Catholic Cardinals instituted in 1622 by Pope Gregory XV and having charge of missions, and the title, "College of Propaganda", a college to educate priests for missions. But on five other types of entries, they disagree. No one of these other five is found in all the dictionaries consulted. Sometimes the disagreement may be attributed to attempts to save space, though it is, of course, difficult to be sure of the explanation, but some of the disagreements are clearly matters of inconsistency. When the *Oxford English Dictionary* omits four of these five types of entries, you can be sure that this is not the result of an effort to save space.

Here is a list of the types of entries appearing under 'propaganda':

a. the reference to the **special Roman Catholic sense.**
b. **institutional,** as in "'PROPAGANDA' means an institution devoted to the spreading of doctrines, etc."
c. **activity or effort,** as in "'PROPAGANDA' means the effort to or activity of spreading doctrines, etc."
d. **doctrines or material,** as in "'PROPAGANDA' means that doctrine, etc., so propagated or the material used to effect the propagation."
e. **a hint at derogation,** as in "'PROPAGANDA' means the dissemination of ideas, information, or rumor..." and "'PROPAGANDA' means the doctrines, ideas, arguments, facts, or allegations spread by deliberate efforts. . . ." Such entries indicate that the term might be used in a derogatory manner by the use of the words, 'rumor' and 'allegations', in the definitions.
f. **definite derogation,** usually attached to *d* or *c* above.

Using these types of entries, I have constructed a table which somewhat oversimplifies the situation, but which in the main represents the degree of agreement among these dictionaries (see Table 8-1). In this table dictionaries are arranged from left to right in order of increasing adherence to

TABLE 8–1 The Extent of Agreement Among Leading Dictionaries on the Meaning of 'Propaganda'

	Oxford Eng. Dict. 1933	*Funk & Wagnall's* 1961	*American College Dict.* 1960	*Thorndike-Barnhart* 1962	*Webster's New Collegiate* 1958	*Webster's Third New Internat.* 1961	*Webster's 7th New Collegiate* 1963	*Dict. of Contemp. American Usage* 1957
a. Special Roman Catholic sense	X	X	X	X	X	X	X	X
b. Institutional	X	X	X		X	X*		
c. Activity or effort	X	X		X	X	X	X	X**
d. Doctrines or material		X	X	X	X	X	X	X**
e. Hint at derogation						X	X	
f. Definite derogation								X

The presence of an 'X' in a column indicates a dictionary entry.

* Labeled 'archaic'.

** But not without derogatory overtones.

contemporary American usage (assuming that willingness to attach the label 'propaganda' to doctrines or materials, and readiness to treat it as a derogatory term, are symptoms of a more contemporary treatment). Using these criteria, one may group the dictionaries into four groups. This grouping is fairly obvious when the dictionaries are arranged in this order.

Dictionary 1, the *Oxford English Dictionary*, differs from all the rest by not being willing to apply 'propaganda' to doctrines or materials, thereby limiting its definition of the common noun 'propaganda' to institutions. Dictionaries 6–7 on the other hand, relegate the definition that involves the institution to an inferior status ("archaic", according to *Webster's Third New International Dictionary*; omitted altogether in *Webster's Seventh New Collegiate Dictionary*, the abridged dictionary based on *Webster's Third*). These two dictionaries also include *doctrines* and give a slight hint that the word can be used in a derogatory fashion. The large middle group, 2–5, which includes an earlier edition of the *Webster's* series, includes *doctrines or materials*, but gives no indication of any derogatory aspects of the term. The only dictionary of the set which definitely treats 'propaganda' as a derogatory term is 8, which in its title indicates its concern with contemporary usage.

From this study of the treatment of the word 'propaganda' by these eight dictionaries, two theses emerge: (a) that the dictionaries do not always agree among themselves, and (b) that dictionaries, even those with recent publication dates, can be out-of-date. Now just suppose Mr. Delta has sent his students to consult these dictionaries in order to determine the meaning of 'propaganda'. How can he handle the conflicting reports he is bound to get if their investigations are at all careful?

Established Usage

One of the lessons of the previous chapter is that when there are various definitions, it is appropriate to stipulate one in order to avoid the possibility of ambiguity. But another lesson was that sometimes stipulation is a mistake—perhaps because of inflexible people, presence of basic concepts, greater utility of one concept, wide adoption of one definition, and so forth. Let us suppose that this class situation is a case in which two of these reasons hold—that the class is a bit too inflexible with this word for there to be freedom of stipulation, and that one particular definition is widely accepted. In this case, the issue, somewhat oversimplified, is whether propaganda is a derogatory term, so Mr. Delta should not just arbitrarily stipulate an answer, if the assumptions of inflexibility and wide acceptance do hold.

These assumptions in this case are not at all far-fetched. Most students with whom I have dealt are not flexible enough to work with Jim's stipulative definition. And furthermore, as seems fairly clear, the derogatory sense of the term is almost universal.* But in any case, whether you find these assumptions far-fetched or not, you certainly can imagine cases in which they are not far-fetched.

The problem is what to do when disagreements exist about the established usage(s) of a term, if the avenue of stipulation is not open to us. This problem has two parts: (1) the determination of usage, and (2) judging whether a particular usage is established.

Determining usage

The problem of determining the usage of a particular group or person is rather different if we are not able to address questions to the group or person. Under that condition the problem is ordinarily more difficult, because we must hunt around for chance occurrences of the term without the assurance that the aspects of its meanings have had a chance to show themselves. The makers of dictionaries are to some extent in this position, especially when they try to determine historical meanings of terms.

But this job is not one that the classroom teacher has to perform, so let us narrow the problem down to determining the usage of people or groups who are accessible. The reasoning can thereby be less complicated.

In the stiuation which we are considering, the problem arises from the inflexibility of the class and from the (assumed) predominance (at least in their environment) of one particular usage. If Mr. Delta (or a student) is able to discover one common usage among the members of his class, then he will have made an important step toward securing a clear discussion. For he can then report a definition as the one actually operating in the class, and everyone will have an agreed-upon criterion for judging whether a particular piece is propaganda.

If he finds that the people in the class really are not in agreement, then he will have to be alert to the possibility that they will be talking past each other. Stipulations, translations, interpretations, and the like will be in order.

But in any case it will be helpful for Mr. Delta to determine the usage of the members of the class, especially Jim and Sally. Hence in this case it is the usage of accessible people that is in question. To the extent that communication with and understanding of **inaccessible** people is involved, we must depend on a dictionary.

There are two major techniques for determining a person's usage:

1. *Requesting a Definition.* One obvious step is to say,

> Would you please give me a definition of 'propaganda' as you use the term?

* This claim is corroborated by numerous checks that I have made with people in all walks of life, and it is the claim made by Bergen and Cornelia Evans in *A Dictionary of Contemporary American Usage*, *op. cit.*, p. 397.

Sometimes this works; sometimes it does not work. Most people have difficulty in framing definitions at all; and all of us have considerable trouble in originating a definition that accurately conforms to our own usage. But even so, requesting a definition is often a good first step.

Suppose that Jim and Sally give the following definitions of 'propaganda', feeling that these definitions at least accurately report their usage of the term. Sally as well feels that her definition is a report of the established usage of the term.

Example 8-1

JIM: To me 'PROPAGANDA' means any attempt to persuade people.

SALLY: But 'PROPAGANDA' really means an attempt to persuade people of mistaken doctrines through the use of devices that appeal to the emotions rather than fact.

Drawing out those definitions is a good first step in the attempt to determine the way(s) in which Jim and Sally use the term, because there is now a basis on which to work. Frequently people are too inarticulate to do even as much as Jim and Sally have done. In such cases the teacher or other investigator must hypothesize reported definitions instead.

Usually, however, there must be a refinement of the first attempt to report usage, whether the attempt is made by the user or an investigator. For usually the first attempt does not capture a person's usage of a term. In order to do this refining, we must consider clear cases in which it would be appropriate to use the term, and clear cases in which it would not be appropriate, and we must see if the proposed reported definition gives the correct guidance in those cases. This may be called the method of example and nonexample.

2. *Calling Forth Examples and Nonexamples.* An example of a table is the one at which I am working. A nonexample of a table is the chair on which I am sitting. The use of examples is very common. The use of nonexamples, particularly crucial ones, is far less common, though very useful. It is useful because it gives an indication of what is on the other side of the boundary line and thus a rough indication of the location of the boundary line.

It is often helpful to present a related example and nonexample in a pair that reveals an important point. The following pair is instructive:

a. An orange crate which one uses for a writing surface when living in a tent is a TABLE.

b. An orange crate on which one sits when living in a tent is a chair—not a TABLE.

This pair shows the importance of **function** to the concept, *table*.

A complementary move to the method of example and nonexample is that of following up with the question, 'Why?'. When a person gives an example or a nonexample, if he is then asked why it is an example or nonexample, he often indicates a general criterion which is part of the definition of the term as he uses it. The way in which he indicates his definition and the method of determining a general criterion from the answer to a 'why' question are rather complicated topics—to which much of Part III of this book is devoted. Please be content for the time being with the unclarified use of the question, 'Why?', to dig out the general principles that are operating.

In checking to see if Sally's definition of 'propaganda' is in accord with her own usage, Mr. Delta might pursue the following line of questioning. Read this dialogue very carefully to make sure that you see the logical relevance of each move made by Mr. Delta:

Example 8–2

MR. DELTA: Sally, would you give us some examples of propaganda?

SALLY: That article about the current state of our economy, and the advertisement for that washing machine are two examples.

MR. DELTA: Do you feel that Congressman Smith should not be re-elected?

SALLY: Yes.

MR. DELTA: Then your definition seems to fit that example. How about the washing machine. Do you think the Maticwash is a poor washer?

SALLY: Oh, no. My mother has one and likes it.

MR. DELTA: But in your definition you mentioned "mistaken doctrines". So how can you say that the washer advertisement is propaganda if you think that the Maticwash is a good washer?

SALLY: Uh——well, I suppose I didn't mean to say "mistaken doctrines". It might be a good doctrine. I guess I should not say anything about the doctrine at all. Here's a better definition: 'PROPAGANDA' means an attempt to persuade people through the use of devices that appeal to the emotions rather than fact.

MR. DELTA: Hmm. That's a bit closer to Jim's notion. Now, Sally, you've already suggested two nonexamples of propaganda, the announcement of the Red Cross drive and the article on the sewage system.

SALLY: That's right.

MR. DELTA: Is the article on the sewage system propaganda, according to your new definition?

SALLY: No.

MR. DELTA: Why not?

SALLY: Because it's not done in an emotional or distorted way. There is simply a balanced and sober presentation of the facts. Although the author does reach a conclusion, which he recommends to us, he is not trying to use any tricky devices. It seems clear to me that if the facts pointed the other way, he would have drawn the opposite conclusion. He's not just trying to ram a conclusion down our throats regardless of the facts.

MR. DELTA: That's very interesting. Your reasons mention more than the manner in which the presentation is made. You talk also of the intent of the person making the presentation. But that's a refinement that we might well ignore, for the time being. Your reasons by and large do fit in with your definition. But your Red Cross nonexample puzzles me. Is the Red Cross announcement propaganda?

SALLY: I said it wasn't.

MR. DELTA: Well, think about it some more.

SALLY: The Red Cross is a fine organization.

MR. DELTA: So?

SALLY: Oh——I see. By my last definition that announcement **is** propaganda—— I guess I'll stick with my definition this time. Because I think so highly of the Red Cross, maybe I didn't want to admit that it could engage in propaganda. But I suppose it can—and does—with good reason, I think.

MR. DELTA: Then you think that sometimes the use of propaganda can be justified?

SALLY: Yes. Sometimes we are justified in engaging in strictly emotional appeals.

MR. DELTA: Some people would disagree with that, but I don't think it affects your definition. Propaganda might not by definition be always bad, though some people might well make the value judgment that it is always bad.

In the above dialogue Mr. Delta used the method of example and nonexample in association with the use of the question, 'Why?'. First he sought examples, one of which did not fit Sally's definition. Sally realized that her definition needed to be changed to fit the example, the Maticwash advertisement, which to her was a clear case of propaganda.

Then Mr. Delta reminded her of some nonexamples that she had previously offered. He used the 'Why?' question to get a more explicit check on her proposed definition and found that her answer in the main was consistent with her definition, although she made use of the notion of intent in her answer. This he decided to ignore, feeling that it would make matters even more complicated. This was probably a wise decision on his part, although in contemporary ordinary usage the notion of intent is probably involved.

The Red Cross case, obviously inconsistent with the new definition, was then directly challenged. The alleged nonexample of the Red Cross announcement failed, because according to Sally's latest definition, the Red Cross announcement is propaganda. This time Sally stuck to the definition and with some reluctance withdrew the nonexample. Two interesting points are illustrated by this maneuver:

1. Sometimes people make mistakes about what they claim to be clear examples and nonexamples. This makes the task of determining their usage that much more difficult.
2. The boundaries for terms in everyday use are not absolutely precise. Some doubt might still exist in Sally's mind about whether to call the Red Cross announcement propaganda. It is either a borderline case or close to being one. Under the topic, "Range Definitions", in the next section you will learn more about looseness of terms and a form of definition that is particularly accommodating to looseness.

At the end of the dialogue Mr. Delta brings out the point that calling something propaganda (using Sally's latest definition) does not automatically imply that it is bad. This is a sophisticated point which rests on the distinction between a definition and a value judgment.* Strictly speaking, if this point is right, propaganda is derogatory only on the assumption that mere appeals to emotion are in some way wrong. In this chapter I make that assumption.

You can probably now see that attempts to ascertain a person's usage can lead to a number of difficult questions. Whether these should be pursued depends on the sophistication of the students and the goals for that class. For the time being let us confine our interest to the rough determination of usage, something which has been accomplished for Sally.

Jim's definition of 'propaganda' is radically different from Sally's and from the ordinary contemporary notion. Mr. Delta is aware of this in the following line of questioning, in which he checks to see if Jim's definition accurately represents Jim's usage:

Example 8-3

MR. DELTA: Jim, would you give me an example of propaganda that is not from last night's newspaper?

JIM: OK. Last week the city councilmen got out a pamphlet in which they tried to prove that overnight parking on the city streets was harmful. That was propaganda.

MR. DELTA: Now why was that propaganda? Don't you think that was a fair presentation?

JIM: Definitely not. They certainly did not give both sides. They forgot to mention all the people who don't have garages.

MR. DELTA: Is that why it's propaganda?

JIM: Yes. It's an attempt to persuade, isn't it?

Note that Jim is wavering here. Mr. Delta ran together two questions at once ("Now why was that propaganda?" and "Don't you think that was a fair presentation?"), which could be run together under the contemporary sense of propaganda, but which under Jim's explicit stipulation cannot be run together. Jim does not complain about putting the two questions together, but, on the other hand, he does not clearly accept putting them together. And he ends up by restating his criterion, "attempt to persuade". So the result of this exchange is not clear. Perhaps Jim's stipulation conforms to his usage; perhaps not. Let us follow the dialogue further. Mr. Delta tries what he thinks is a nonexample, but which would be an example in Jim's usage, if it conforms to his stipulation.

* More will be said about this distinction in Chapter 17, "Types of Explanation", Chapter 18 "Testability/Applicability", and Part IV, "Justification".

Example 8-4

MR. DELTA: Last Saturday at the football game, you persuaded the referee that your opponent had stepped out of bounds by showing the referee your opponent's footprint and by getting testimony from the people on the sidelines. Were you propagandizing?

JIM: No, of course not.

MR. DELTA: Why do you say that?

JIM: He did step out. I saw it and all the evidence pointed to it.

MR. DELTA: But you were attempting to persuade the referee, weren't you?

JIM: Of course I was. Did you expect me to let it go by?

MR. DELTA: But the point is that here is a case which fits your definition, but which you do not want to call propaganda. How do you explain that?

JIM: I don't know. Let me think———I guess I'll have to change my definition, because that certainly was not propaganda.

Mr. Delta has shown that Jim's usage is inconsistent with his stipulation by picking something in which Jim was deeply involved. This is often a good move. People are less able to keep up a front when the example gets close to home.

Incidentally Mr. Delta has just proposed what we shall call a counter-example. A COUNTER-EXAMPLE is a case which counts against what is proposed. In this situation the counter-example was something that under the proposal should have been an example (of propaganda), but which actually was a nonexample in Jim's usage.

If Jim had stuck to his definition and held that his efforts to persuade the referee were propaganda, then either the definition did conform to his usage, or he was sufficiently on guard to avoid contradicting himself. He might have been able to do this because the game's being somewhat in the background enabled him to sit back and look at it objectively—and stick to his guns about 'propaganda'.

A final potential counter-example is Mr. Delta's comment at the end of Jim's report:

Example 8-5

MR. DELTA: (very seriously) Jim, your whole report is propaganda about the local newspaper.

Mr. Delta has come up with a potential counter-example that is connected with Jim's current involvement. If Jim now agrees to Mr. Delta's comment, then he will have weathered the storm of potential counter-examples and will have given us good evidence for the conclusion that his usage is accurately reported by the definition he offered. But it is really unlikely that any contemporary Jim would actually agree to this statement; a disagreement would show that his usage does not conform to his definition. The probable result of Mr. Delta's use of the method of example and nonexample would be considerable agreement among Jim, Sally, and Mr. Delta on the meaning of 'propaganda'.

If he can achieve this agreement, then he has made a more significant advance than would be made by a simple stipulation. For he would have a basis for agreement on which he can depend. Stipulation as a basis for agreement, as you saw in the last chapter, is not nearly so dependable, because it often interferes with old habits—instead of conforming to them.

You will find that it sometimes helps, when thinking about examples, nonexamples, and counter-examples, to think in terms of Euler circles. When Jim reports his definition, "'PROPAGANDA' means any attempt to persuade people", the implication is that the circle representing propaganda and the circle representing any attempt to persuade people occupy one and the same area—that is, that they are coextensive (Diagram 8-1).*

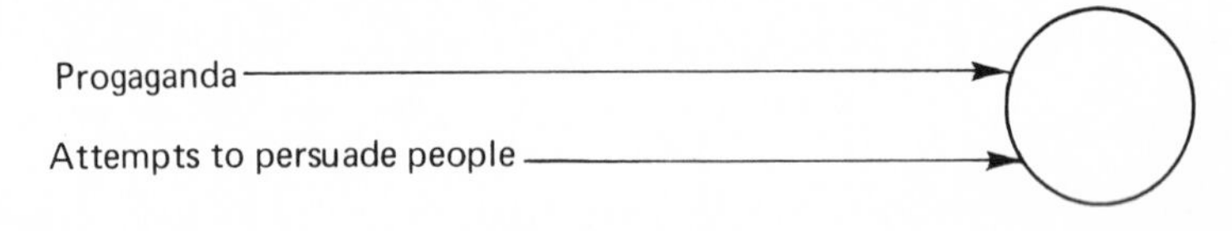

DIAGRAM 8-1

Sally's original reported definition, "'PROPAGANDA' really means an attempt to persuade people of mistaken doctrines through the use of devices that appeal to the emotions rather than fact", does not make the propaganda circle coextensive with the circle representing attempts to persuade people. Rather it includes the propaganda circle inside the latter circle and makes the propaganda circle coextensive with a different circle (Diagram 8-2).

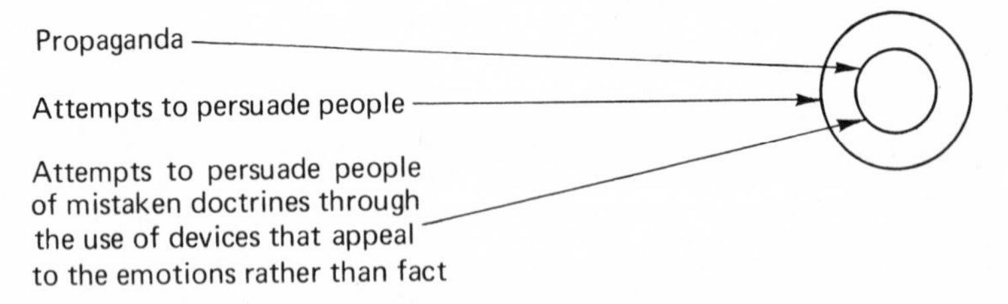

DIAGRAM 8-2

Mr. Delta never says what he considers to be the established usage of 'propaganda', but it does appear that he regards the relationship between propaganda (as ordinarily used) and attempts to persuade people as one of

* Later on you will see other kinds of relationships which definitions can allege, but the one under consideration in this chapter is coextensiveness.

class inclusion (Diagram 8-3). Mr. Delta's proposed football-game counter-example to Jim's definition consisted of a nonexample of propaganda (according to Mr. Delta's beliefs about local usage) which, according to Jim's definition would be an example of propaganda. This counter-example is depicted by an '*x*' in Diagram 8-3.

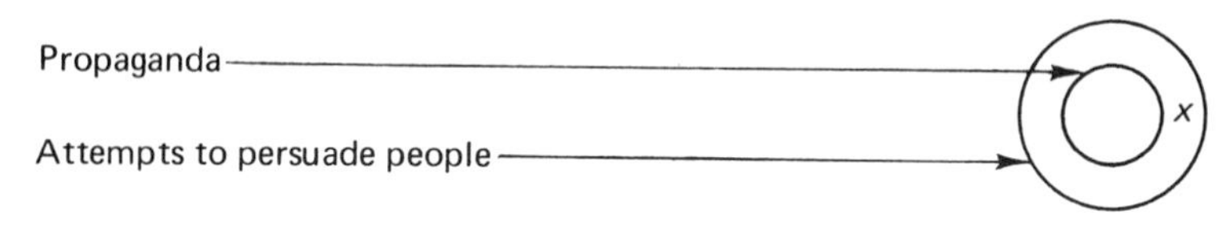

DIAGRAM 8-3

Other types of counterexamples and relationships between the two parts of a definition can be represented by Euler circles. Instead of exemplifying each I shall show the possibilities, using symbols. Assuming that the proposed reported definition is of the form, *A*'s are *B*'s (where '*A*' is the term being defined), the relationship alleged by this definition is as shown in Diagram 8-4. Diagrams 8-5, 8-6, and 8-7 represent the possible actual (not just alleged), relationships between *A* and *B* assuming at least some

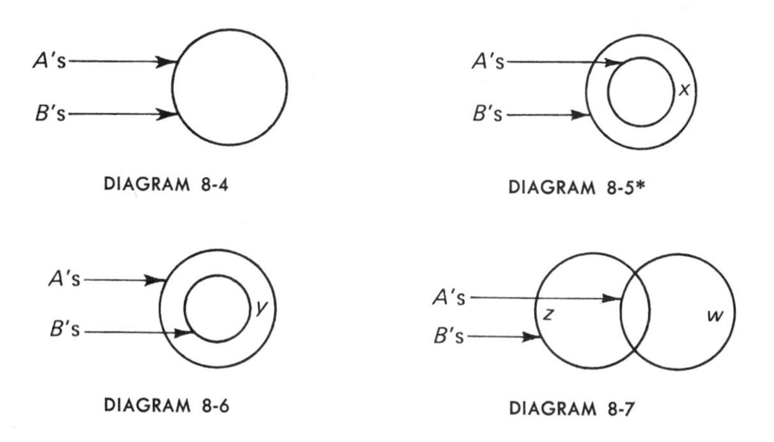

DIAGRAM 8-4

DIAGRAM 8-5*

DIAGRAM 8-6

DIAGRAM 8-7

overlap; *x*, *y*, *z*, and *w* represent types of possible counter-examples to the proposed definition, *A*'s are *B*'s. Can you think of some proposed reported definitions which, although they allege coextensiveness, actually present concepts which are related as in these three diagrams? Can you think of counter-examples which play the roles of '*x*', '*y*', '*z*', and '*w*'? If so, then you have a good picture of the logical relationships involved in the method

* Diagram 8-5 is the symbolized form of Diagram 8-3.

of example and nonexample. There are also exercises at the end of the chapter to test your skill.

You might be wondering if one can put forth any general rules for the method of example and nonexample. Not much more can be said than has already been said—or implied, but perhaps it will be helpful to make a list:

1. The job is easier if the subject gives a definition with which to start.
2. Examples and nonexamples should ordinarily be requested. The term 'nonexample' will be unfamiliar to most people, so the question might be put in the form, 'Can you give me an example of something that comes close, but is not an *X*?' If the nonexample does not even come close, then it is likely to be uninformative.
3. Suggest crucial cases yourself.
4. The question, 'Why?', is useful after the examples and nonexamples have been offered, because it tends to draw out principles which might very well be the definition sought.
5. Do not expect to achieve a perfect statement that is immune to all counter-examples and borderline cases. For many purposes such a statement is unnecessary, and in many cases unattainable.
6. When dealing with a person who is trying hard to maintain a definition that you believe he does not really adhere to, think of cases with which he is closely involved personally and see if he sticks to his pretended usage in those cases.
7. There is no formula for the automatic generation of crucial cases. That is an art which can be cultivated, but which depends on one's flexibility, creativity, and familiarity with situations. Practice helps.

Establishing the usage

Let us assume that Mr. Delta has found that he, Jim, and Sally use 'propaganda' in essentially the same way. He is not yet entitled to say, "This is what the term means . . . ", which you remember is interpreted in this chapter to mean the same as, 'This is the established usage of the term. . . . ' He may not do this because he would only have shown that he has identified **a** usage. No evidence has yet been offered to show that it is **the established** usage, or in other words, to show that he has identified **the** meaning. He has not yet even shown that he has identified **an** established usage, or **a** meaning (without qualifications). He has, of course, identified **their** meaning or **a** meaning of the term for these three people. (The qualification, 'for these three people', makes it all right to say '**a** meaning'.)

If a child were to use the term 'horse' to refer to any four-legged animal, we would not say that 'any four-legged animal' was a meaning of the term 'horse'. We would say that the child is wrong, or that 'any four-legged animal' is what **he** means by 'horse' or that it is **a** meaning for him; but not that 'any four-legged animal' is **a** meaning of 'horse' (without qualification), nor that it is **the** meaning of 'horse'.

To be elevated to the status of **a** meaning or **the** meaning, a usage must in some way be shown to be legitimate. (The phrase 'a meaning' implies that more than one legitimate usage might exist; 'the meaning' implies that there is only one.) Although the line marking legitimacy is hard to draw and there are many borderline cases, some ascertainable group or culture must have as its usage this possible meaning of the word. If some tribe used 'horse' to refer to any four-legged animal, then that would be a meaning of 'horse'.

Admittedly this criterion is vague, but a teacher can insist that if a usage is to be elevated to the status of **the** meaning or **a** meaning, then the usage must be the usage of **some** group. Note that this criterion is a necessary condition, not a sufficient condition, for elevation. On the other hand, if the group is a large one, and exhausts a particular culture, then we have a sufficient condition for elevating a usage to the status of **a** meaning or **the** meaning. The minimum size of the group and the extent of usage in a culture that turn the necessary condition into a sufficient condition are not matters that can be specified.

Unless there is some group that uses 'propaganda' in the way defined in a dictionary, then that way is not currently even **a** meaning of the word. Now Mr. Delta is in no position to determine that no group uses the word in a way given in some dictionary. But he is in a fair position to determine the usage for his own environment. If he finds that the entire class is in agreement on one usage and that is their only usage (assuming that the members of the class represent their parents and others in his environment), then he has a good case for claiming identification of an established usage in that environment. If he makes this case, then the thing to do is say: "This is a meaning of the term. Since it is the meaning in this area, it is the way that we will use the term."* In so doing he will have avoided the potential confusion arising from diverse stipulations. He should, of course, be aware that when he says, "the meaning in this area", he is saying nothing more than, "This is the established usage of the term in this area."

In summary a quick consultation with the dictionary will usually suffice. When it does not, then the teacher must make an effort to determine **the** established usage of the term. If he can make this determination, then he can state the meaning. If he can only determine **an** established usage, or if he can find only confusion, then he should stipulate in order to make progress in the matter at hand.

* Note that if he says this, he is giving a reported definition and then stipulating that reported definition (using the report to justify the stipulation). The reported definition is, "This is a meaning of the term. . . ." The stipulated definition is, ". . . it is the way we will use the term."

Advantages and Disadvantages of Reported Definitions

A major **advantage** of the use of reported definitions is that they are conducive to consistency of usage. They help to preserve the *status quo* in language. If all words meant different things to different people, language would be a useless instrument. We would not be able to understand one another. The more words shift in meaning the more difficult it is to understand and be understood. Similarly, adherence to reported definitions, and thus to accepted patterns of language, keeps down the number of meanings one must remember for each term, a danger of overfree use of stipulation. And it is inefficient to have students spend time learning new meanings for old terms if the important things to be learned can be stated using the meanings with which students are familiar.

The major **disadvantage** of reported definitions is that rigid adherence to the *status quo* in language can impede the development of new empirical knowledge, since new ideas frequently require new concepts, which require new words or redefinition of old words. Furthermore, adherence to the *status quo* in language can reduce our ability to express new thoughts effectively through the literary arts.

The concept *work* exemplifies the need for adjustment of language in the advance of empirical knowledge. The word 'work' was redefined by the physicists to fit the new concept, as was pointed out earlier. Similarly the development of the concept *romantic* in a much different field called for a new definition for the term 'romantic'.

Through the use of metaphor the literary artist is continually reshaping language in order that his works may be fresh, beautiful, and expressive. But in his use of metaphor he is in conflict with reported definitions. When Winston Churchill introduced the metaphor 'iron curtain', he was very effectively saying what he wanted to say, but strict adherence to the spirit of reported definitions would not have permitted this.

Another disadvantage of the reported-definition approach is the danger that in using it we will either force concepts into overprecise molds, or else we will abandon the quest for reported definitions as a hopeless task. Most terms are somewhat indefinite in application. The attempt to report a usage for a term might founder on the fact that there are borderline cases and there are cases which we who use the term do not know how to handle. The dialogues in which the method of example and nonexample was used were beginning to arrive at the point at which the looseness of the term 'propaganda' was revealing itself. Mr. Delta stopped the investigation at this point, but if he had continued it, the looseness would have been revealed. This in turn might have resulted in stipulating a definition of 'propaganda' that is overprecise for most purposes (like the Census Bureau's definition of 'rural'), or it might have resulted in the feeling that it is not worthwhile to try to get a definition anyway.

Here I will only mention these problems. In the section on forms of definition they will be considered more thoroughly. This postponement is appropriate because the solution to the problems often involves the selection of the proper form of definition.

Chapter Summary

Since communication requires agreement on the meanings of terms, it is usually wise to adhere to those definitions which are reports of widespread or universal usage. Such definitions are called reported definitions. They make empirical claims about usage of standard groups, although these groups are not clearly identified. These claims can be right or wrong, unlike the proposals of stipulative definitions, which are simply useful or convenient.

Dictionaries, both general and technical, are the best source of information for reported definitions. Major problems in the use of the dictionary as an authority are that dictionary entries are for some people effectively circular; short dictionary entries miss some of the nuances of words; and dictionaries are sometimes in disagreement with each other or are out-of-date.

The first two problems may be dealt with by perseverance and extended dictionary entries, including examples, nonexamples, and use in context. The other problems, disagreement and out-of-dateness among dictionaries, require a retreat to stipulation, or an independent determination of the facts, or some combination of the two.

This independent determination of the facts is an investigation of established usage. Two good ways of determining usage, best used in combination with each other, are: (1) creating and amending definitions, and (2) using the method of example and nonexample (including use of the question, 'Why?'). The judgment about whether a usage is established is a difficult one to make, partly because of the limited access that most people have to usage and partly because the reference group that legitimizes a usage is vague. But it is simpler to investigate established usage when there is a given limited reference group—such as a given class, or the students in Ithaca High School, or the people in Ithaca—but even this is a difficult task. Often the best a teacher can do is to locate **an** established usage and stipulate it. Progress is thereby facilitated without long-range interference with communication.

COMPREHENSION SELF-TEST

True or False? If the statement is false, change a crucial term (or terms) to make it true.

8–1. Since reported definitions make empirical claims, the words, 'true' and 'false' may be applied to them.

8–2. 'REPORTED DEFINITION' is defined as 'a definition which gives the established usage of a term'.

8–3. People have a right to use any word in any way they choose in all situations.

8–4. In seeking a reported definition of a term, a dictionary is ordinarily the best place to look first.

8–5. The longer the entries in a dictionary, the more likely they are to be effectively circular.

8–6. If a teacher finds that two students give different definitions of a key term, his only recourse is to stipulate a meaning for that term.

8–7. The use of the question, 'Why?', while using the method of example and non-example to determine usage, is usually a mistake, because the result is usually confusion rather than clarification.

8–8. A definition is not satisfactory if there are borderline cases which it does not decide.

Questions.

8–9. Give four problems in the use of dictionaries as a source of reported definitions.

8–10. What is a nonexample?

8–11. What is a counter-example?

Matching: Match each item on the left to one (but only one) of those on the right.

8–12.	
a. A usage	the meaning
b. An established usage	a meaning for someone
c. The established usage	a meaning
	meaningless

Discussion Questions.

8–13. Assume that each of the following has been offered as a reported definition of the underlined term. Supply a counter-example to each. In each case tell whether it is:

1. An example which according to the definition would be a nonexample, or
2. A nonexample which according to the definition would be an example.
   a. A CIRCLE is a plane curved figure.
   b. The PROBABILITY of a coin's turning up heads is the number of times it has turned up heads in the past divided by the number of times it has been tossed.
   c. A GLACIER is a large body of ice.
   d. 'SCIENTIFIC METHOD' is defined by the following traits. If any are missing, the method is not scientific. If all are there, then it is.

1. Stating the problem.
2. Formulating a solution or hypothesis.
3. Running controlled experiments.
4. Drawing a tentative conclusion.
5. Testing the conclusion in practice.

e. A POEM is a literary work with meaning beyond the actual literal meaning of the words.
f. 'NOUN' means the name of a person, place, or thing.
g. A SOVEREIGN state is one with complete control over all its affairs.
h. '*X* CAUSES *Y*' means the same as 'Whenever there is an *X*, there is a *Y*'.

8–14. Invent and write out a dialogue between you and a student in which you, using the method of example and nonexample in conjunction with the judicious use of the question, 'Why?', force him to refine a report that he has offered of his own usage. Select a term that is likely to cause trouble in your field.

Be prepared to act out this dialogue in front of the class, and in order to do so, select people from the class to play the other part(s). You should play the role of the person using the method of example and nonexample.

8–15. Read Richard Robinson's chapter on lexical definition in his book, *Definition* (Oxford: Oxford University Press, 1954), pp. 35–52. Choose a thesis of his with which you agree or disagree and in a two-page paper defend your view.

CHAPTER 9

Shades of Definition

In Chapter 6 you became aware of the fact that the term 'definition' is a rather broad and vague one, with a number of associated meanings. The meaning that was stipulated for purposes of the discussion of stipulating a meaning (Chapter 7) and reporting usage (Chapter 8) was setting forth the meaning of a word. In teaching and discussion, as in all forms of communication, setting forth the meaning of a word is a crucial step.

But in ordinary usage the term 'definition' covers many more activities than setting forth the meaning of a word. For two reasons you should become familiar with the more important of these activities:

1. The danger of confusion between one activity and another always exists. That is, a person might set out to give one kind of definition. Even if he succeeds, he might be taken, either by himself or others, to have accomplished a different definitional feat.
2. When these other types of definitional activity are undertaken, we must be able to evaluate the products on their own terms, just as we had to be able to evaluate stipulative definitions on their own terms—rather than as reported definitions.

In this chapter a number of other definitional activities will be considered. In a way you will already be familiar with them, since you have presumably heard people claim to be defining when they were doing these things, and have probably done these things yourself and labeled them 'definition'. But unless you have thought a great deal about the topic, you probably have not explicitly made the necessary distinctions. On some occasions you might very well have sensed the fact that something was going wrong, but were not able to put your dissatisfaction into words, and were not able to ask the right questions or make the right points that would reveal the error and show the way to proper handling of the problem. From this chapter, together with the previous two chapters, you should not only develop insight into definitional problems; you should develop an insight into the principles behind them; and you should develop a facility at asking the kind of question and making the kind of point that will tend to set matters straight.

Here is a list of the activities to be considered in this chapter. Think about them, and see for yourself how each activity can properly be fit under the broad sense of 'definition' presented in the two dictionary definitions quoted in Chapter 6, which may be roughly summarized as follows: A definition is an attempt to mark off, to bound, to limit something.

Suggesting a program
Interpreting basic terms
Marking limits
Identifying
Describing

Each of these activities is often called 'definition' in the classroom. Let us consider them in turn.

Suggesting a Program

In the following classroom dialogue more is going on than setting forth the meaning of a word. And a great deal is at stake.

Example 9-1

FRANK: I think that the new zoning ordinance is a terrible thing because it cuts into our freedom. We have little enough of that left now.

JANE: It doesn't cut into our freedom. In fact it results in greater freedom. It's very democratic.

FRANK: Greater freedom! That's wrong. Look at what's happening. We have a trailer in our side yard rented out, and we make good money on it. Now we have to take it off our land and sell it. And there's a wrecked car in our back yard that I can get parts from. We have to take it away. We can't keep chickens any more, either. I thought this was supposed to be a free country.

JANE: It *is* a free country. Those restrictions increase the freedom of your neighbors and increase your own freedom too. Your neighbors will be more free to enjoy the beauty of their surroundings when your ugly trailer, wrecked car, and noisy chickens are gone. You'll have the same freedom too. And you and your neighbors will be free to improve your property with the knowledge that you'll get your money back if you sell it.

FRANK: That's not freedom. I'm being restrained.

JANE: 'Freedom' doesn't mean lack of restraint. That's a meaningless idea. There are always restraints. You were restraining your neighbors from enjoying their homes and improving their property. True FREEDOM is the power to do. Now both you and your neighbors have the power to enjoy and improve your homes.

FRANK: According to Herbert Spencer, 'FREEDOM' means lack of restraint on an existing power and desire. That's the foundation on which our country was built. 'Freedom' doesn't mean what you say.

JANE: Yes, it does. That's what the philosopher, John Dewey, says. By what you say, there always is someone who is denied freedom, because there is always someone who is restrained. Mr. Delta, doesn't 'freedom' mean power to do?

What is Mr. Delta to say? Is he to stipulate a meaning for 'freedom'? He cannot legitimately do this, because this is a case in which each side wants to secure the word for its own purposes. 'Freedom' is a word toward which we are positively inclined. Capturing the word as a label for one's program is an aid in getting one's program adopted. This is a case in which not just any sound will do. This particular one is sought after as a banner for a program. Hence a stipulation would beg the question.

Will a reported definition settle the question? Not really. Even if Mr. Delta were to show that the ordinary usage of 'freedom' conformed to the meaning suggested by Frank, 'lack of restraint', Jane might very well say that she is redefining 'freedom' and giving it a more satisfactory meaning, on the ground that the old meaning is out of date. In effect she would then be seeking to apply this term, 'freedom', to her program, which she feels is a better program than the one represented by the term as ordinarily used. And she would be trying to discredit the program represented by this term as allegedly ordinarily used.

She is offering a PROGRAMMATIC DEFINITION.* It is called this because, although it has the form of a definition, it is more than this. It assumes a program and somehow embodies the endorsement of this program in the definition. Often a term towards which we have a positive attitude (such as 'freedom') is defined so that the program can have the term applied to it. Sometimes a term toward which we have a negative attitude is defined so that it applies to programs which are opposed to the program being promoted by the definer. Furthermore, the procedure is used with terms that are embedded explicitly or implicitly in statements of what shall be or ought to be done (by law, by custom, by order of the school board, and so forth). Attempts to define 'history', 'science', 'grammar', 'home economics',

* This term, 'programmatic definition', was suggested by Professor Israel Scheffler in his book, *The Language of Education* (Springfield, Illinois: Charles C Thomas, 1960), pp. 19–22. The idea of a programmatic definition is similar (but with some important differences) to Stevenson's idea of a persuasive definition. See C. L. Stevenson, *Ethics and Language* (New Haven: Yale University Press, Inc., 1944), pp. 206–26.

'mathematics', etc. (once the law, a directive, or a custom has specified their inclusion in a school curriculum) exemplify programmatic definitions, if the purpose is to serve as a guide to what is to be included in the curriculum.

A proposal

In effect a PROGRAMMATIC DEFINITION is a proposal (that is, a request, or command, or entreaty, etc.) for adoption of a program or a point of view. It is similar to a stipulative definition in that it is a proposal; but it is quite dissimilar in its complete lack of arbitrariness. What is wanted is to attach a particular word to a program or point of view in order to make it more (or less) palatable or in order simply to adjust the emotive aspects of our language to the programs or points of view that have already been adopted. And such a definition is not simply a report, for that would be a statement about what people actually do support rather than the **proposing** of some program or point of view. When Jane says that true freedom is the power to do, she is not alleging to report what people actually do support. She is proposing something herself.

The value question

How then is Mr. Delta to answer her question about what freedom really means? Unless he is blatantly trying to indoctrinate people with one view or the other, he should probably make clear the fact that each is proposing a different program. Thus the discussion should focus on which notion of freedom would be a better guide for life, and more specifically, on whether living with zoning would be better than living without it.

The question has at least two aspects: determination of the effects of zoning and, (taking these effects into account) making the value judgment about zoning. Neither part of the question raised by a programmatic definition is easy to answer, but the important thing for the present is to recognize that these elements are involved, the question of fact and the value question.

This is not to say that in every case of disagreement over a programmatic definition, there is a disagreement about both aspects. Usually when people disagree about programmatic definitions, an underlying disagreement about values exists. Often disagreement about the effects of the program can also be found; and even if there is agreement on the likely effects of a given program, there is disagreement about the importance of some effects in contrast to other effects. Thus Jane was emphasizing the importance of getting rid of the trailer, the wrecked car, and noisy chickens, and maintaining property values; while Frank was emphasizing the importance of avoiding restraints by outside forces.

Now if each did not realize that the other was right in claiming that the alleged effects would result, then there might be a basis for settling the dispute on the basis of an investigation of the facts. In the above dialogue, Jane realized that Frank was correct in alleging that increased restraint (of one sort) would result; whether Frank realized that Jane was right too is not clear. If he had not realized this, then the dispute might have been settled by making him come to realize the truth of Jane's factual claims.

But if each realizes that the other was right in his claims about the results, and disagreement still exists, then there is a value disagreement to be faced. Somewhat oversimplified, the value issue is this: Is life with restraints (of one sort) and maintained property values, but without the trailer, the wrecked car, and the noisy chickens, better than the opposite? This is a very difficult question to answer, but very important. Mr. Delta should guide them to a realization that this is the basic value issue that must be faced, assuming they agree on the facts. If one wants to call this an issue about what meaning shall be set forth for the term 'freedom', then one should be clear that this is a different kind of setting forth the meaning of a term than is involved in stipulative and reported definitions.

For the present let us hold in abeyance the problem of settling value questions. This problem will be treated in Part IV, but do not expect to find a pat answer there, for none is forthcoming. Suggestions will be made, however.

Interpreting Basic Terms: 'A Good X', 'The Same X', and 'Different X's'

Requests for the definition of good, same, and different, frequently appear in the course of settling difficult questions. The adjectives, 'good', 'same', and 'different', are among the most basic ones that we have, so we might suspect that they will raise special problems. Other terms are often defined in terms of one or more of these three, a fact which frequently makes these crucial. Since the problems for 'good' are different from the problems for 'same' and 'different', they are grouped accordingly.

Defining a good x

The phrase, 'the definition of a good *X*', or a similar phrase commonly appears in classroom discourse, as in the following examples:

Would you give me a definition of a good piece of cloth?
Please define good government.
Here is the definition of a good proof.
Good weather is defined as that weather in which the wind is less than 20 miles

per hour, the sky is less than 1/4 cloudy, and the temperature is between 70 and 80 degrees Fahrenheit.
A good flame on the Bunsen burner is defined as one in which the tip of the cone is about one inch above the mouth of the tube and in which the flame is blue and about five inches long.
Would you please define a good poem for me?
That depends on your definition of a good dictionary.
How do you define a good tractor?

When someone asks for the definition of a good piece of cloth, presumably he knows what the words, 'piece of cloth', mean; and presumably he knows that the word 'good' is the most general adjective of commendation.* What he is asking for is what to look for in choosing a piece of cloth, assuming the characteristic uses of cloth. He is not asking someone to set forth the mean ing of a word; he is asking someone to mark off the limits of, to tell him how to identify, commendable pieces of cloth. Thus this definitional activity fits the general notion of definition, but not the restricted one of setting forth the meaning of a word.

Not an Arbitrary Matter. As with programmatic definitions, the decision about how to define a good *X* is not an arbitrary one, which is to say that it is not properly decided by such means as a flip of a coin. A careful exercise of judgment is required, because criteria for commendability are at stake. Selection of these criteria requires either a value judgment or a judgment about the characteristic purposes or functions of an *X*, and sometimes also requires a judgment about what is the most effective way of achieving the purpose or function.**

The definition of a good government at least calls for a value judgment about the ways in which men ought to live together. The definition of a good Bunsen burner flame depends on the characteristic purpose of this flame: to heat things in a laboratory. And this definition further depends on just what kinds of flame are most effective in providing heat. These examples should indicate the kinds of considerations to bring to bear on judging the definition of a good *X* in your field. Certainly the above three judgments are not arbitrary.

Thus the process of giving a definition of a good *X* is in many respects like that of giving a programmatic definition. When the definition of a good *X* involves a value judgment, then it is also a programmatic definition. The

* *Oxford Universal English Dictionary*, Vol. III (Oxford: Oxford University Press, 1937), p. 287.

** This statement is somewhat simplified for purposes of presentation here. Underlying it are some difficult questions. For an introduction to the topic, see R. M. Hare, *The Language of Morals* (Oxford: Oxford University Press, 1952), and P. Foot, "Goodness and Choice", *Supplementary Volume XXXV, The Aristotelian Society* (London: The Aristotelian Society, 1961), pp. 45–60.

difference lies in the fact that the definition of a good *X* does not necessarily assume or require a value judgment in the background. To see this just think of a person who is offering the previous definition of a good Bunsen flame, even though he does not care about heating things in a laboratory. In effect he is saying, "If you want to heat things effectively with a Bunsen burner (and most people who use them do want this goal), then setting your flame in the way indicated will best achieve your purposes." This does not commit him to any value judgment.

You need not remember the distinction between a programmatic definition and a definition of a good *X*, nor is the term, 'programmatic definition', particularly important to remember. The important thing to remember is that these kinds of definitions are not arbitrary matters, something which Mr. Delta fails to realize in the following dialogue.

A Case of a Nonarbitrary Matter Being Treated As An Arbitrary One.

Example 9-2

MR. DELTA: A basic question behind your discussion of zoning is this one: "Is the zoning law a good law for Thiston?" The answer to that question, of course, depends on your definition of good law. If this is your definition of good law, then the zoning law is not a good thing:

A GOOD LAW is a law which does not change the *status quo*.

On the other hand, if this is your definition of good law, then the zoning law is a good thing:

A GOOD LAW is a law which is approved by the majority of the people covered by the law.

So take your pick. What do **you** mean by 'good law'?

FRANK: By GOOD LAW I mean a law which does not change the *status quo*.

JANE: By GOOD LAW I mean a law which is approved by the majority of the people covered by the law.

MR. DELTA: Well, that's all there is to it. It's simply a matter of defining 'good law'. For Frank, the law is bad, and for Jane, the law is good. If we are flexible in permitting various meanings for a given term, there is no serious problem. Its simply a matter of definition.

Obviously, something has gone wrong here. The problem cannot be solved so simply.

In one sense of 'definition', the problem **is** one of the definition of good law. When we define good law in this sense of 'definition', we are trying to specify the characteristics of a good law. We are in this case making a value claim about the presence or absence of these characteristics. Jane is claiming, for example, that if, and only if, a law is approved by a majority of the people whom it covers, it is a good law. In this sense of 'definition' a definition of good law does not simply give us words which may be substituted in a statement without changing the meaning of the statement (which is roughly the case for most definitions); instead a definition of good law in this sense of 'definition' claims to tell us what kinds of laws **are** good.

In this sense of 'definition' Mr. Delta did not make much logical progress when he said, "The answer to that question of course depends on your definition of good law." In effect this is to say, "The way to tell whether a law is a good law is to see what are the characteristics of a good law." This move does put us at a more general level, but the question that is the difficult one still lies before us: What does make a law a good one? In his terms, "What is the definition of good law?" is the difficult question.

Everything is all right up to this point, although not much progress has been made. But then Mr. Delta shifts to a different definition of 'definition', 'setting forth the meaning of a word' and then treats the question as a matter of arbitrary stipulation. If everyone were supremely flexible, intelligent, informed of the way in which others are using terms, and possessed of no prior commitment to any term, then it would not matter what each means by the term 'good law', and his superficial way of handling the matter would be acceptable up to a point—although he would not have made any progress. For the question that would then face us is this one:

> Are "good laws" the kind we ought to have?

And this question is the same as the question which we previously put in these terms:

> What is the definition of a good law?

Mr. Delta's approach skirts this question, whichever way it is phrased. The answer to that question requires a value judgment, not just capricious ruling.

Defining the same X and different X's

As with the word 'good', the words 'same' and 'different' are fully clear in meaning to any normal English-speaking person. When such a person asks the question, "What do **you** mean by same (or different) *X*?" he is not going to be enlightened by synonyms, such as 'alike' and 'identical' (or 'unlike'), for these could not be any more clear than 'same' and 'different'. Instead he must be asking something to this effect: 'What are your criteria for judging whether these things are the same (or different)?' Or he might be asking for the **proper** criteria for judging whether these things are the same, in which case the question could be rephrased, "What is the definition of the same (or different) *X*?" Consider the following dialogue in which such a question arose.

Example 9-3

DONALD: Democracy is not really a different form of government from dictatorship. Each is a tyranny: democracy, a tyranny by the majority; dictatorship, a tyranny by one. Historically both forms of government have engaged in violation of the civil rights and liberties of people.

ALLAN: Oh, no. There is a vast difference between the two. In our democracy, for example, we have freedom of speech, press, and religion.

DONALD: Is it freedom of speech if a man's job is jeopardized by declaring himself in opposition to our foreign policy? Is it freedom of the press if the press is controlled by its advertisers? Is it freedom of religion if polygamy is prohibited to people whose religion endorses it? Your democracy is essentially the same type of government as a dictatorship.

ALLAN: What do you mean by the same type of government?

Here Allan is asking for Donald's criteria for judging whether two types of government are essentially the same.

Here is another dialogue from a different field in which a similar question arose:

Example 9-4

WAYNE: (giving a report) Here are the readings that I obtained:

30.12″
30.09″
30.07″
30.04″
29.93″

As you can see, they are all different.

THOMAS: (interrupting) Nonsense. They are essentially the same. Look at them. They're all within twelve hundredths of thirty inches. That makes them the same. You're being overprecise.

WAYNE: I'm not being overprecise. These are different readings.

THOMAS: What do you mean by different readings? (pause) Mr. Beta, would you define different readings for us?

Again we have a request for criteria for judging whether *X*'s are the same or different.

Context. In dealing with such questions the most important thing to consider is the context in which they arise—in particular the sorts of decisions that depend on the selection of the criteria. The sorts of decisions involved reveal the background purpose(s) of the discussion. Without an indication of the sorts of decisions and the background purpose, such questions are essentially undecidable—or else only trivially decidable.

They are trivially decidable in that everything is different from everything else in some respect—though it be only time or place of occurrence. If we look hard enough, we can always find differences. The question is whether, admitting these differences, two things are essentially the same or essentially different. And that question is undecidable without some assumption of a background purpose and of the sorts of decisions on which the selection of criteria rests.

For example, the measurements hovering around thirty inches might be judged essentially the same or essentially different, depending on the context. If they are mercury barometer readings to be used to predict the weather, then they are essentially (and, of course, absolutely) different. If, on the other hand, they are measurements of the height of a five-foot cross-bar above the laboratory table, the purpose being to support weights and pulleys for block and tackle demonstrations, and if the teacher has suggested that they set the bar level at a height of thirty inches, then the measurements are essentially the same—and Wayne has been overprecise.

Comparisons. Given the establishment of the context in which the question about sameness and difference is a genuine question, the teacher should see that comparisons are presented which are made relevant by the specification of context. Often it helps to compare the consequences in later decision-making of the alternative answers to the present question.

If the various measurements are judged the same (perhaps assuming a criterion that specifies that discrepancies up to 1/8″ are to be ignored), then a consequence in the case of weather prediction is a prediction that current weather conditions will stay with us for a while, which would be an unfortunate prediction on which to base our plans for the next few days. The consequence of a much stricter criterion, in which variations of 1/100″ are to be recorded, is probably a prediction of the approach of bad weather. These consequences are quite different, and since we are interested in accurate prediction, we should be ill-advised to follow Thomas' rough criterion.

If our purpose, on the other hand, was the setting up of the bar for laboratory demonstration purposes, then a comparison of the consequences of the two levels of strictness shows that no damage is done by the loose criterion and that time is wasted by invoking the strict one.

Application to a More Difficult Case. The sort of things just discussed are frequently forgotten in the heat of classroom exchange. Let us try to apply them to the democracy-dictatorship comparison, in which, because of the basic value conflict involved, one can easily go astray.

First, significant features in the context must be brought out. What are the background purposes? What sorts of decisions might turn on the judgment about the similarity or difference between democracy and dictatorship? Here are some decisions in everyday life which turn on the judgment: whether to vote for measures that will preserve democracy, whether to serve in the military forces (or, if forced to serve, whether to put forth full effort), whether to emigrate, and so forth; in summary, whether to support one type of government or the other.

The background purposes that are relevant here are the basic value commitments of people, which for us tend to include the following: equality of opportunity, freedom to criticize and compliment, and prevention of pain to others and ourselves. Other background purposes are conceivable.

A scientist might be only concerned with the conditions which will enable him to do his work (assume that it is not politically controversial); a chess player might be only concerned with conditions that will enable him to play chess.

The comparisons of the effects of the alternative decisions rests heavily on the background purposes which are assumed. The person with the first set of purposes is likely to see a difference between democracy and dictatorship, because these purposes are more likely to be achieved if democracy rather than dictatorship is supported. On the other hand, the apolitical scientist and chessplayer might from their point of view understandably judge that there is no difference in the consequences of support of one rather than the other (although particular instances might differ) and thus that the forms of government are essentially the same. Whether democracy and dictatorship actually are the same depends then on which purposes are the right ones, and this is, therefore, at least in part a value question.

Thus we have this general strategy for examining differences of opinion about whether two things are the same or different: Investigate the background purposes and kinds of decisions which turn on the question at hand; compare the two candidates, paying particular attention to the consequences in the decisions to be made. Sometimes (as in the democracy-dictatorship case) the determination of the background purposes is a value issue, and thus like the disputes about programmatic definitions and many of those about the definition of a good *X*, depends on settling the value question.

A teacher should: (1) be aware of and make use of this strategy, (2) avoid thinking that settling such questions is an arbitrary matter, and (3) respect the value issues that often underlie these questions of definition.

Marking Limits

The following locutions make use of this shade of definition:

> Please define your problem.
> The boundaries of the school district are defined on the east by Route 89. . . .
> The Constitution defines the authority of the executive branch.

This sense of 'define' conforms to the broad definition of 'DEFINITION', reported earlier: "to mark off, to bound, to limit something". There is little to be said here about defining in this sense. Naturally it is important to have the proper limits and boundaries, but these matters, to the extent that they are logical questions, will best be treated in a later section of this book. To claim limits often requires justification, the general topic of Part IV.

Identifying

Occasionally we find teachers putting requests for identifications in language making use of the term 'definition', as in the following part of a quiz:

> Define the following (5 points apiece):
> French Revolution
> XYZ Affair
> The Civil War

Each of these items is a proper noun, naming one and only one thing. What is requested is some way of marking off this one thing from all other things, thus making the process at least like defining.

Whether it is properly called defining is disputable. We do not here need to decide the question with finality, but it would probably be better to phrase such things as requests for **identifications** rather than definitions. A possible confusion may arise in using the term 'definition', although various clues in the context usually serve to avoid the confusion. The confusion can arise when the term in question has an independent meaning, like the terms, 'depression' and 'romantic'.

In the following question there is the possibility of this confusion in the first item:

> Define:
> Depression
> AAA
> Francis Perkins

Although the context suggests otherwise, a student might legitimately give a reported definition of the term, 'depression', which would not make any reference to specific conditions in the 1930's. To make sure that he identifies **the** Depression, it is probably best to say "Identify".

Describing

The term 'definition' is sometimes applied to attempts to give an identifying description of something or some quality, but which could not be a case of setting forth the meaning of a word, because the meaning of the word was known before the description was known. For example the following identifying fact about the color red (in the ordinary sense of 'red') might be called a definition in this sense of 'definition':

> Red is that color which produces light with wave lengths ranging from 6,500 A to 7,000 A.

As a result of laboratory investigation, the range of hues which we call red was found to produce predominantly the indicated range of wavelengths when exposed to white light, and only this range of hues was found to produce predominantly this range of wavelengths. Therefore, a criterion was discovered which could be used to identify the color red.

To call a statement of this criterial relationship a definition is again to fit into the broad, but not the narrow, sense of 'definition'. Of course, someone could stipulate the above as a definition (in the narrow sense) of a technical term 'red', but that would be a different meaning from the ordinary one. For if we found something that was green, but which somehow produced light that was predominantly in the given range, we would be permitted to call it red (in this technical sense) without contradicting ourselves.

As with other shades of definition, definition that might also be called description is not an arbitrary matter. Such definitions are empirical statements and are subject to proof and disproof, topics discussed in Part IV.

Chapter Summary

You have had a chance to consider five different activities which are labeled defining: suggesting a program, interpreting basic terms, marking limits, identifying, and describing. Each of these activities serves a different function from that of setting forth the meaning of a term, yet each is more or less appropriately labeled defining, and of course the arbitrary element is not present in these activities (with a few minor exceptions). In judging definitions of this kind, you saw the frequent importance of context, empirical facts, and basic value judgments.

The main lesson to be learned from this chapter is that these activities involve serious questions and cannot be dispatched with the attitude often expressed in the following words: "It's simply a question of definition."

Although techniques for revealing underlying value questions were presented, the actual settling of value issues was not discussed. This problem is dealt with in Chapter 21, starting from where the freedom dialogue leaves off in this chapter. You might find the discussion in Chapter 21 relevant now.

COMPREHENSION SELF-TEST

True or False? If the statement is false, change a crucial term (or terms) to make it true.

9–1. In ordinary usage the term 'definition' is limited to setting forth the meaning of a word.

9–2. Stipulation is never the appropriate way of settling a dispute about a programmatic definition.

9–3. The central issue in a dispute about a programmatic definition is ordinarily a value question.

9–4. There is always a dispute about what the facts are when there is a disagreement about a programmatic definition.

9–5. Settling a programmatic definition is never an arbitrary matter.

9–6. Settling a dispute about the definition of a good *X* is usually an arbitrary matter.

9–7. Settling a dispute about the definition of the same *X* is usually an arbitrary matter.

9–8. In at least a trivial sense, everything is different from everything else.

9–9. A descriptive-type definition alleges to state a fact.

Questions.

9–10. Give the five functions (and types) of definition discussed in this chapter.

9–11. What are the two phases of investigation in settling a dispute about the definition of the same *X*?

9–12. What is the recommended way to phrase requests for identification of things named by proper nouns?

9–13. Why is this locution preferable to "Please define:"?

Discussion Questions.

9–14. Choose one of the following terms and give two conflicting programmatic definitions of it. Describe a situation in which these conflicting definitions might be advanced, and state the value proposition underlying each of the definitions.

a. Grammar
b. Literature
c. Art
d. Proof
e. Science
f. Definition
g. Education
h. Responsibility
i. Justice
j. Equality of opportunity
k. Experiment

9–15. Do the same for a second term. Whether the term you chose for 9–14 is from your field or not, the second term should be from your field and need not be from the above list.

9–16. Write out a dialogue from a class you have taught or might teach. Develop a dispute about the programmatic definition of some term (perhaps the one you used in 9–14 or 9–15) and show what you as teacher would do about it. Be prepared to act out this dialogue for the class in cooperation with other members, whom you may choose.

9–17. Give and defend in writing a definition of one of the following:

a. A good piece of cloth.
b. Good government.
c. A good proof.
d. Good weather.
e. A good titration.
f. A good Geiger counter.

g. A good poem. h. A good paragraph.
i. A good dictionary. j. A good tractor.

9–18. Prepare a dialogue from a class you have taught or might teach. Develop a disagreement about the definition of the same *X* (or different *X*'s). Show what you as teacher would do about it. Be prepared to act out this dialogue for the class in cooperation with other members, whom you may choose.

9–19. Read C. L. Stevenson's *Ethics and Language* on the topic, persuasive definition, and read Israel Scheffler's *The Language of Education* on the topic, programmatic definition. In a four-page paper compare and contrast the two approaches to the problem.

9–20. Read pp. 1–27 in G. E. Moore's *Principia Ethica* (Cambridge: Cambridge University Press, 1903), in which he discusses the definition of 'good'. Select a thesis of his with which you agree or disagree and defend your view in a two-page paper.

9–21. Read Chapter II of Rupert Crawshay-Williams' *Methods and Criteria of Reasoning* (London: Routledge and Kegan Paul, 1957), in which there is an introduction to the contextual features involved in making judgments about sameness and difference. Select a thesis of his with which you agree or disagree and defend your view in a two-page paper.

Section B:
definition
forms

CHAPTER 10

Equivalence Forms: Synonym and Classification Definition

So far we have been concerned with the content of definitions, paying particular attention to the function that the definition is intended to serve, different functions calling for different types of definitions. Now we will consider various forms that classroom definitions can take. There are two major kinds of definitional forms—those that attempt to provide equivalence of some sort, and those that attempt to provide concrete interpretation. In this chapter you will be presented with first two of the four major equivalence-providing forms, which are synonym definition, classification definition, equivalent-expression definition, and range definition. Chapter 11 will deal with the other two. In Chapter 12 three major concrete-interpretation forms will be examined: examples and nonexamples, operational definition, and conditional definition. One main point to be made is that there is no one ideal form of definition. All have disadvantages for some circumstances. The form to be used in a particular situation depends upon the context and the nature of the concept involved.

Equivalence is generally regarded as a desirable relationship between the two parts of a definition; namely the term being defined, the DEFINIENDUM (pronounced deh-fin-ee-en′dum), and the material offered as interpretation of the term, the DEFINIENS (pronounced deh-fin-ee-enz′). For example in the following stipulative definition of 'propaganda', 'propaganda' is the definiendum and 'an attempt to persuade' is the definiens:

> 'PROPAGANDA' shall mean an attempt to persuade.

Presumably the person doing the stipulating intends the definiendum and definiens to be taken as equivalent.

Equivalence between the parts of a definition is an ideal for definitions, because when it exists, we know that the full meaning of the term in question has been presented—not just part of the meaning. Assuming the ideal of equivalence, the stipulative definition of 'propaganda' given in the previous paragraph implies that any attempt to persuade and only attempts to persuade are to be regarded as propaganda. It implies that there is no qualification such as 'which is put forward in an emotional or distorted way' incorporated in the meaning of 'propaganda' as stipulated. When equivalence is achieved, we know where we stand.

Another advantage of equivalence, which is related to the first, is that with equivalence between definiens and definiendum, one is ordinarily substitutable for the other. Substitution enables us to simplify and/or reorganize arguments and statements in order to make them more manageable and/or understandable. For example, in Chapter 7 Jim's notion of *propaganda* was clarified by showing the import of one possible meaning of 'attempt to persuade', and by **substituting** this meaning in his definition of 'propaganda'. His definition of 'propaganda' went as follows:

> 'PROPAGANDA' shall mean any attempt to persuade.

One possible definition of 'any attempt to persuade' is the following:

> 'ANY ATTEMPT TO PERSUADE' shall mean any presentation which gives an argument, reasonable or not; or makes an emotional appeal; or asserts a fact; or does some combination of these.

If the last actually is Jim's definition of 'any attempt to persuade', then the pair of definitions can be combined by substituting the definiens of the second definition for the definiens of the first (which is the definiendum of the second). The result of the substitution makes more clear one of the alternative interpretations of Jim's notion of *propaganda:*

> 'PROPAGANDA' shall mean any presentation which gives an argument, reasonable or not; or makes an emotional appeal; or asserts a fact; or does some combination of these.

The following is a case in which sheer reduction in size and complexity of a statement is made possible by the equivalence of the definiendum and definiens. The simple statement is the formula, "Work in = work out", which is short and easy to grasp (once one understands what work is). The equivalence definition of 'work' is,

> 'WORK' means the product of the force exerted and the distance moved in the direction in which the force is exerted.

When one tries to test the formula experimentally, the thing that he is testing is the following complicated statement (in which the phrases for which 'work' may be substituted are italicized):

> *The product of the force exerted and the distance moved in the direction in which the force is exerted* in equals *the product of the force exerted and the distance moved in the direction in which the force is exerted* out.

Since the definiendum 'work' is equivalent to its definiens, we may substitute 'work' in the above statement, making it much easier to grasp. Numerous examples of this sort of advantage of equivalence can be found in the exact sciences and mathematics.

On the assumption that you are now convinced that equivalence is a desirable trait of definitions, let us proceed to examine the forms of definition that to a greater and lesser degree attain this ideal.

Synonym Definition

The synonym, the one-word definiens, is the obvious first candidate for equivalence, since a synonym is supposed to mean the same thing as the definiendum. That is what it is to be a synonym. The trouble is that synonyms rarely do mean exactly the same thing. An example given earlier illustrates this point. A synonym of 'senescent' is 'aging', but 'senescent' cannot be used to modify 'trees', whereas 'aging' can be so used. It would be an inefficient language that has a number of pairs of words that are identical in meaning, so we should not be surprised about the lack of strict equivalence between synonyms.

Another occasional disadvantage of synonyms (and antonyms) is that they remain at the same level of abstraction as the definiendum. A synonym of 'concrete' is 'specific' and an antonym is 'abstract'; but all of these terms are themselves rather abstract. If a person does not understand one of them, he probably does not understand the other, as illustrated in the chapter on reported definitions. What such terms often need is some sort of concrete interpretation.

On the other hand, synonyms can be helpful because they are brief (the briefest of definitions), and they usually come close enough to the meaning to be helpful. Furthermore the fact that they remain at the same level of abstraction is not a problem if the person for whom they are intended already knows how to operate with the definiens at that level, but just does not happen to know the meaning of the definiendum. Like the other forms of definition, synonyms are not universally good, nor are they universally bad. Because of their weaknesses, they are used less frequently than the next form, classification definition, which is commonly used and is the form generally recommended by logic books.

Classification Definition

Here are some definitions which exemplify common faults in definitions which appear in the classroom. Assume that they are reported definitions. (For purposes of clarity in this book the term being defined appears in capital letters. This is in addition to any other appropriate punctuation.)

> A METER is how long something is.
> A TARIFF is when you pay extra for something you buy.
> IRONY is where an author insults somebody by saying something that just sounds nice.
> AD is a MEDIAN.

Frequently teachers encounter definitions like these. Let us analyze them to see why something should be done about them.

The definition of 'meter' fails to tell us what kind of thing a meter is, although it does indicate that 'meter' has something to do with length. And it is a grammatical mismatch: A meter is neither "how" nor "how long". A meter is a unit of length.

Neither does the definition distinguish a meter from other units of length. Even if a person knows that a meter is a unit of length, he cannot tell from this definition how to use the term 'meter'.

Similarly, the definition of 'tariff' fails to indicate that a tariff is a sum of money, and it fails to distinguish tariffs from other sums of money. The definition of 'irony' fails to say explicitly that irony is a mode of expression, though we must realize that in this case the error is not so serious from a practical point of view. That irony is a mode of expression is in a way implicit in the definition. The fact remains, however, that the words used present an absurdity. Irony is not "where"; it is not a place.

Assuming that the fourth example is an answer to a request for a definition of 'median', the definition does implicitly, though not explicitly, suggest that a median is a line segment, but it fails to distinguish this kind of line segment from others—for example, altitudes. The weakness of a definition by example is that it is inevitably incomplete.

What can be done

Definitions such as these provide incomplete analyses of the meanings of the terms in question. Now an analysis of the meaning of a term has the advantage of exposing its constituents, but an incomplete analysis exposes only part of the constituents. When analyses are complete and accurate, they ordinarily assume a definitional form which is called classification definition. A CLASSIFICATION DEFINITION is one which gives a general category which holds for all the things to which the term is applicable; it also gives features that distinguish these things from others in that category. The word 'classification' is used to name this form of definition, because of the many similarities between such definitions and systems of classification. Perhaps you have met this type of definition under the name, 'definitions by division', or the name, 'definition *per genus et differentiam*'.

In order to bring a student to provide complete and accurate coverage in an analysis, two fairly standard approaches can be used, separately or in combination: raising probing questions that challenge the completeness and correctness of the proposed definition, thus driving him toward a complete and correct analysis; and teaching him a set of rules that can serve as guides to construction and evaluation of classification definitions.

Raising Probing Questions. Examples of standard challenges to 'where' and 'when' definitions are:

Is a tariff a **time**?
Is irony a **place**?

These challenges are appropriate because the words, 'when' and 'where' indicate time and place. The student is forced by the obvious absurdity to **classify** tariffs and irony.

Once the student has them classified, further questions can be raised to force him to narrow or broaden his definition. Suppose that the new definitions are:

A TARIFF is a sum of money paid extra for something you buy.
IRONY is a mode of expression in which the author insults somebody by saying something that just sounds nice.

The first of these definitions includes more than should be included, while the second is too restricted. This can be brought to light by bringing up counterexamples:

Is the gasoline tax a tariff?
Was Mark Twain being ironic when, in *Huckleberry Finn*, he said that a person who helps a slave escape is a bad person?

In the first case, the overbroad scope of the definition is shown by the example of the gasoline tax, which by the given definition should be called a tariff but which actually should not be so called (remember we are assuming these to be reported definitions). In the second case, the overly restricted scope of the definition was shown by an example which by the given definition should **not** be called irony, but which actually should be so called.

These kinds of questions either expose a student's ignorance, or drive him to a definition that does justice to the term in question. If the answers to these questions are respectively "yes" and "no", then, assuming that the questions are understood, ignorance of the meaning of the terms in question and the need for instruction has been shown. If the answers are respectively "no" and "yes", then understanding of the meaning of the terms in question has been shown, but the definitions are obviously defective and in need of repair.

A similar approach can be used to handle the other two definitions, as exemplified by the following dialogues:

Example 10-1

MR. BETA: You say that a meter is how long something is. That doesn't make sense.

JANE: Well, a meter is a unit of length.

MR. BETA: Any unit of length?

JANE: It is a unit of length approximately equal to 39.37 inches.

MR. BETA: That's better.

Example 10-2

MRS. ALPHA: Is *AD* a distance? A line segment? Must it be straight?

ARNOLD: It's a straight line segment. That line segment is a median.

MR. ALPHA: But how do you distinguish a median from some other line segment? Is *AD* a median here?

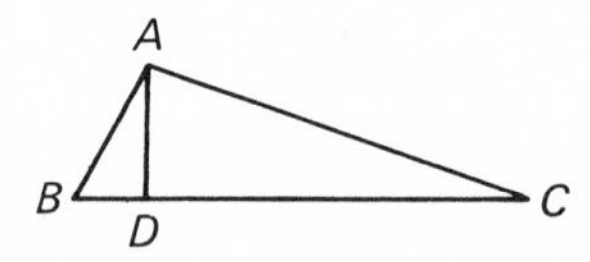

ARNOLD: I think so.

MRS. ALPHA: Let's talk some more about it. . . .

In the 'meter' example the student was driven to do justice to the term 'meter', whereas in the 'median' example his ignorance was revealed. What a teacher does with the ignorant student depends upon the specific situation, but presumably he will set out to teach the concept of a median.

The general logical strategy that has been examplified runs as follows: In raising questions about definition, aim first at the general category and, when this is clear, see that the proper discriminating features are presented.

A useful procedure for accomplishing each of these tasks is to produce counter-examples. These are generally of two types: items which the definition includes but which should be excluded, and items which the definition excludes but which should be included.

As you can see, it might be more efficient to have taught students a simple set of rules that can serve as guides to construction and evaluation of their classification definitions. This is not to suggest that the challenge-question approach should never be used, but if students know and understand a set of rules, the challenge-question approach will be needed less often. We will now consider the rule approach.

Giving Two Basic Rules for Classification Definition. The following set of rules is intended to bring out the classification and equivalence aspects of this form of definition.

In a classification definition,

1. **the definiens should give**
   a. **a general class, and**
   b. **features that are supposed to distinguish what is referred to by the term from other members of the general class;***
2. **the definiens and definiendum should be equivalent; that is,**
   a. **the definiens should not be broader, and**
   b. **the definiens should not be narrower.**

The reason for beaking the rules up into so many parts is that doing so enables students to indicate efficiently the errors in a set of definitions, which is good drill in judging definitions. The student is enabled to identify each of four types of errors by using a shorthand label:

'1a' for 'A general class is needed.'
'1b' for 'Distinguishing features are needed.'
'2a' for 'The definiens is too broad.'
'2b' for 'The definiens is too narrow.'

Each of the definitions at the beginning of this chapter violates Rule la, since none provides a general class—though, as noted before, this is more serious for the definitions of 'meter' and 'tariff'. The definitions of 'meter'

* The decision about whether a particular characteristic is to contribute to marking off the general class or the distinguishing features is often arbitrary. For example, the words 'of length' in the definition of meter might be regarded as part of that which names the general class, or it might be regarded as part of that which names the distinguishing features. If the former, then the general class is *unit of length;* if the latter, then the general class is *unit*, and the distinguishing features are the rest of the definiens grouped together.

and 'median' also violate Rule lb, since they do not attempt to provide distinguishing features. Since the latter two definitions violate both parts of Rule 1, it is hard to apply Rule 2, the equivalence rule, to them.

The original definitions of 'tariff' and 'irony' might be said to make an attempt to provide distinguishing features, although this is not at all clear, since it is difficult to conceive of distinguishing features when there is no explicit mention of a general group within which certain ones are to be distinguished from the others. Let us say in this kind of case that the definitions definitely violate Rule la, and that it is not clear whether they violate Rule lb. Thus they too are not really in form for us to apply the equivalence test.

The first revisions of these definitions are in such form and look like this, you will remember:

> A TARIFF is a sum of money paid extra for something you buy.
>
> IRONY is a mode of expression in which the author insults somebody by saying something that just sounds nice.

Applying the equivalence rule to the revised definition of 'tariff', we find that Rule 2a is violated since the definiens is too broad. There are sums of money that augment the prices of some purchases, but that are not tariffs—for example, the gasoline tax and some salesman's commissions. The distinguishing features fail to eliminate these things.

The definition of 'irony', on the other hand, violates Rule 2b for at least two reasons. The definition excludes that kind of irony in which the surface meaning is derogatory, though the real meaning is just the opposite, and it limits ironic statements to statements about people. When patched up to conform to the rules, the definitions of these four terms might look like this:

> A METER is a unit of length approximately equal to 39.37 inches.
>
> A TARIFF is a sum of money which is levied as a tax against imports or exports.
>
> IRONY is a mode of expression in which the implied attitudes are the opposite of those literally expressed.
>
> A MEDIAN is a straight line segment extending from an angle of a triangle to the middle of the opposite side.

Note that in each case there is a general class, a distinguishing feature, and at least a fairly good equivalence between the definiendum and definiens.

Thus there are two basic logical strategies in getting students to define terms in the classification form, raising probing questions and giving them two basic rules to learn to apply. When the rules have been learned, the probing questions can, of course, refer to them, as in the following four examples:

Is there a general class in the defining part of your definition of 'meter'?
A definition should have equivalent parts. Is **anything** that one pays extra a tariff?
The definiens should not be narrower. Was Mark Twain being ironic when he expressed disapproval of those who helped slaves to escape?
What are the distinguishing features that set a median off from other line segments?

The first two rules and their application at the simple level so far considered are fairly obvious. But difficult problems do arise in arriving at adequate definitions that fit this form. We now turn to these problems.

Problems in framing classification definitions

Some common problems faced in arriving at a good classification definition are these:

1. Can the definition contain a negation or must it always be in positive terms?
2. Is it permissible to repeat the term being defined (or any part thereof) in the definiens? In other words, just what is circularity?
3. How should a definition be punctuated?
4. Can exceptions and borderline cases be avoided?
5. Should material be permitted in the definition if it goes beyond the bare minimum necessary to mark off the concept? In other words, should the ideal of parsimony be observed?

These problems are not unique to classification definitions, but since they are focused most clearly with respect to classification definitions, it is well to consider them here. The last three problems have aspects that, if pushed, take us into some difficult problems in philosophy.

Negation. Frequently we find as one of the rules for definitions the claim that definitions should be stated in positive terms—that there should not be any negative terms in a definition. Generally this is good advice, because the use of negation often results in our producing a definiens that is broader than the definiendum. When a term is defined as 'everything which is **not** X', we are likely to find some things included which should not be.

For example suppose the following definition of 'median' to be proposed:

> 'MEDIAN' means a straight line segment drawn from one angle of a triangle to an opposite side, which line segment is **not** an altitude or a leg of the triangle.

The word 'not' appears in the last clause and serves to exclude altitudes and legs of triangles, but also serves to allow the inclusion of all other straight line segments drawn from one angle of a triangle to an opposite side. The way to avoid this is to say what a median **is**, not what it is not. We simply need to replace the negative clause with one that indicates the point to which a median is drawn.

But some terms are most conveniently defined with the use of negatives or the equivalent; and some terms can only be defined in this way. So we cannot insist that all definitions should be in positive language. An example of a term most conveniently defined with the use of negation or its equivalent is the term 'rural' in the sense in which the Census Bureau uses it. You will remember that the Census Bureau's definition lists a number of sufficient conditions for a person's being classified as urban. Then it goes on to say that all other people (that is, all people who are **not** urban) are rural.

Now some might hold that this example is not a good counter-example to a universal rule forbidding negation in a definition, since no specifically negative term (like 'non', 'not', and 'no') actually appears in the definition of 'rural'. But this would reveal too narrow an interpretation of such a rule, because the reason behind the rule would apply to definitions using locutions like the one actually in the definition:

1. The remaining population is classified as rural.

Other ways of stating the same idea are the following:

2. All other people are rural.
3. All of the nonurban population is rural.
4. Everyone who is not urban is rural.

The reason behind the prohibition of negation is that the use of negation tends to allow too much included in the definiens. The locutions, 'remaining' and 'all other', as they appear in the above four examples, run the same risk as the locutions, 'non' and 'not', in the above examples, since sentences 1-4 are equivalent in meaning. When we speak of the "remaining population" and "all other people", we run the risk of opening the door too wide, because they, just like the specifically negative forms, allow all of a certain group who (or which) are not specifically excluded.

Thus, this definition of 'rural' is a successful counter-example to a universal rule prohibiting negation, and it is also useful in showing that the rule, even when cut down to a general rule, should be interpreted broadly enough to suggest an avoidance, if possible, of forms that have the same meaning as those specifically containing negations.

There is one difference between definitions that specifically contain negation and those that contain phrases which are equivalent, a difference which does make it somewhat more dangerous to include specific negation than its equivalent. Specific negation tends to slip by a little more easily than such forms as 'all other', because sometimes we forget that the negation allows **all others,** but we cannot forget that the phrase 'all other' allows all others.

Then there are terms, the definition of which **must** use some form of negation or its equivalents. An example is the term 'bachelor'. One distinctive feature of a bachelor is something that he has **not** done, so the definition must heed this fact; the following one does so:

'BACHELOR' means a man who has not yet married.

It should now be quite clear that a rule forbidding negation will be subject to so many exceptions that some word of warning should be included. In the following rule, which is Rule 3, the word 'generally' serves this function:

3. Generally negation and its equivalents should be avoided in definitions.

Add this rule to your list of rules for classification definition.

Circularity. CIRCULAR DEFINITIONS are definitions that do not get anywhere because they lead back into themselves. (Note the use of a negative in this definition of 'circular definition'!) Here are some examples:

Set 1
ORGANIC MATTER is matter that is really organic.
An EX POST FACTO LAW is a law passed *ex post facto.*
BLANK VERSE is poetry that is blank.
PARALLEL LINES are lines that are parallel.
A CUT ON THE BIAS is a cut that is made along a bias.

These definitions conform to Rules 1 and 2, but in most circumstances they would be deemed circular. They would not provide clarification because the key term is repeated. Though the circularity is rather obvious in these definitions, it is frequently less obvious. Consider this sequence:

A COMMUNITY is a contiguous area the boundaries of which mark off a group of people characterized by very little noncommunal conflict.
What is noncommunal conflict?
NONCOMMUNAL CONFLICT is conflict which is sufficiently severe to result in the disruption of a community.

Since 'noncommunal conflict' and 'community' are defined in terms of each other, there is less enlightenment than needed; the definition of 'community' is circular.

On some occasions, however, it is perfectly all right to repeat a word. We may do this when there are two or more words in the term to be defined and the repeated word is not the one in need of clarification. For example, the following definitions of the above terms are ordinarily satisfactory:

Set 2

ORGANIC MATTER is matter that is a part of, or comes directly from, anything that has life.

An EX POST FACTO LAW is a law passed after an act has been done and which makes the doing of that act at that time a crime.

BLANK VERSE is verse that does not rhyme.

PARALLEL LINES are plane straight lines that do not meet however far extended.

A CUT ON THE BIAS is a cut made along a diagonal line that proceeds across a fabric.

In these definitions the words 'matter', 'law', 'verse', 'lines' and 'cut' are repeated, but the definitions are not circular.

The question of circularity depends heavily upon the context. In the first set of definitions, which would ordinarily be deemed circular, the words that are crucial and in need of clarification in most school contexts have been repeated; thus the definitions in the first set are circular for most contexts. The definitions in the second set repeat words that for most school contexts are already clear and thus those definitions are not circular for most contexts.

You might be wondering how there can be any context in which any of the first set of definitions would not be circular. One kind of context would be one in which the person giving the definition assumes that the meanings of the individual terms are clear, and is trying to indicate that a special technical sense is not in use.

For example the definition of 'cut on the bias' in Set 1 might be used to indicate to people who are familiar with the term 'bias' that the term 'cut on the bias' is to be taken the way one might well guess it to be meant. That is, a cut on the bias is a cut that goes along the bias and is not, say, a short cut that crosses it.

Similarly the definition of 'organic matter' given in Set 1 might not be circular in a special context. A nontechnical sense of the term 'ORGANIC MATTER' is *matter that is a part of, or comes directly from, anything that has life.* But as the field of chemistry developed and it was discovered that almost all organic compounds, as defined above, contained carbon, and as it became possible to synthesize identical compounds, the meaning of 'ORGANIC MATTER' was changed to *compounds containing carbon* (an oversimplification, but it will do for present purposes). With this new meaning many things are organic that are not organic in the primitive sense of the term.

Suppose that an agriculture teacher and a chemistry student are talking about the care of lawns and the teacher advises the student (who is quite ignorant about growing things) to gather organic matter in one corner of his yard. If the student should wonder if that might include some old nylon rope that he is about to discard, the teacher's appropriate retort might very well be the definition given in Set 1: "ORGANIC MATTER is matter that is really organic."

The word, 'really', usually gives us warning that something special is going on. In this case the special thing is the invitation to return to a more primitive meaning of a term, both meanings of which are thoroughly familiar to both parties.

Obviously, we must be cautious in leveling the charge of circularity. Judgments of circularity cannot be made mechanically. Attention must be paid to the context. To remind us of that moral, the word 'ordinarily' is inserted in this fourth rule for classification definition:

4. The definiens should ordinarily not use any crucial part of the definiendum.

Punctuation of Definitions. Sometimes definitions are confusing unless they clearly show that one is **talking about**, rather than **using**, a word. For example the following is ambiguous:

> When I use propaganda, I shall be condemning something.

If that sentence is regarded as a partial definition (in which case the speaker would be **talking about** the word), then we may probably understand the speaker to be stipulating that 'propaganda' is for him a derogatory term. If, on the other hand, it is not a definition (in which case he would be **using** the word), then we may understand him to be telling us about his policy in the use of propaganda. If he otherwise defines 'PROPAGANDA' as 'an attempt to persuade that is somehow irrational', then he is informing us that he plans to use irrational methods of persuasion only when he is condeming something —not when he is supporting something.

In order to avoid the ambiguity, some convention is necessary to show when we are talking about, rather than using, a word. One convention, the one in use in this book, is the use of single quotes around the word and inside the punctuation of the sentence in which the word appears. In accord with this convention, the above sentence, if it is to be a partial definition, looks as follows:

> When I use 'propaganda', I shall be condemning something.

Note that the quotes are closed before the comma, because the speaker is not talking about the comma—only the word. The use of single quotes (') for talking about a word enables us to reserve double quotes (") for enclosing material that is being quoted.

Sometimes in definitions we are not talking about a word, so the quote convention is not always to be used. Consider the following previously given sentence, which is intended to be a reported definition of the word 'median':

> A MEDIAN is a straight line segment extending from an angle of a triangle to the middle of the opposite side.

Because the verb 'is' appears in that sentence rather than the verb 'means', the definer is not talking about the word 'median'. If he were, he would be saying the word 'median' is a straight line segment, which it is not. The word 'median' is used to **refer** to certain straight line segments, but it is not itself a straight line segment. (The written word 'median' is, of course, composed of a number of straight and curved line segments, but that is obviously different from **being** a straight line segment.)

Because not all definitions talk about the word being defined, and some, such as the above definition of 'median', **use** the word, another convention is used in this book to indicate which word is being defined—that of capitalizing the word in question. This convention was introduced earlier and was used in the above definition of 'median'.

It would be a good idea for you to adopt both of the conventions so far discussed: quotes to indicate that a word is being talked about rather than used; and capitalizing to show which word is being defined. In your teaching you might decide to neglect the quote convention for unsophisticated students, if the distinction between using and talking about a word is difficult for them. And for sophisticated students capitalization is in many cases unnecessary, so you might decide to neglect it for such students. When both conventions are in use, there can be some redundancy, as in the following example:

> 'MEDIAN' means a straight line segment extending from an angle of a triangle to the middle of the opposite side.

In this example, 'median' is in quotes because it is being talked about and it is capitalized because it is being defined.

Since the appropriate punctuation convention is dependent upon the level of sophistication of students, the rule to be suggested is deliberately vague:

5. Definitions should be punctuated so that they are clear in context. (For purposes of the exercises in this book interpret this rule to be a request to use both conventions.)

⁘ *Two Further Conventions.* You will notice that two other conventions are in use in this book, conventions which are based upon reasons which are somewhat controversial. I will try to clarify the conventions so that you will understand what they will signify, but will not make any serious attempt to justify them. To do so would be to go beyond the deliberately limited scope of this book.

These conventions are connected with the logical status of concepts and meanings and give a way of showing whether we are talking about such things.

The first convention is to italicize words which refer to concepts, as in the following example:

The concept, *blank verse,* is fairly easy for students to master.

This is not the same as saying that the term, 'blank verse' is easy to master, but is rather more like saying that the meaning (or the proper use) of the term, 'blank verse', is easy to master. This convention is not used in the following definition because the concept, *blank verse,* is not being talked about; rather blank verse is the subject of the sentence ('blank verse' is capitalized not italicized):

BLANK VERSE is verse that does not rhyme.

Since italics are also used for book titles and foreign words, some attention to context is necessary to determine whether the italics are used to indicate a reference to a concept.

The difficult problem beneath this convention is whether we can successfully distinguish between a word ('blank verse'), a concept (*blank verse*), and the thing or stuff (blank verse). Little can profitably be said here, but you might find Peter Geach's *Reference and Generality** of interest, if you would like to look into the topic.

The second convention which is based upon controversial doctrines is that which is evidenced in the following two alternative definitions of 'blank verse':

1. 'BLANK VERSE' means verse that does not rhyme.
2. 'BLANK VERSE' means the same as 'verse that does not rhyme'.

The second definition talks about two sets of words and equates them; the definiens and the definiendum are the same sort of thing—words. In the first definition the definiens and definiendum are different sorts of things: the definiendum is words, but the definiens is the meaning of the words. Formally the differences are two: the first definition uses the locution 'means', while the second uses 'means the same as'; and the first definition does not put single quotes around the definiens, while the second one does use single quotes around the definiens.

* Peter Geach, *Reference and Generality* (Ithaca, N.Y.: Cornell University Press, 1962).

You might find the distinctions behind the preceding two conventions quite unclear, but do not worry about it. For present purposes all you need to know is that these conventions enable us to make these distinctions if we so choose. Ignore both the conventions and the distinctions if you like. They are explained here only so that you will not be surprised by their use.

Exceptions and Borderline Cases. You cannot ignore problems resulting from exceptions and borderline cases, however, because most definitions when given at one level of sophistication have exceptions at a higher level of sophistication, and all definitions have borderline cases when applied to concrete objects.

You will face the exceptions problem when you have students who at a lower level of sophistication have previously studied what you are teaching them, and who then come up with definitions that are not rigorous enough for the level at which you want them to operate. You will see and point out exceptions to these definitions, and, I hope, will not belittle the efforts of your predecessors—unless they were operating at an unreasonably low level of sophistication or were confused. In such situations a teacher can easily play the role of the big-time Charlie who is unable to see how his predecessors could be so ignorant, but it is better if instead he tries to show his students that there are various levels of understanding of a field and that they are moving to a higher level where there are qualifications to the simplified material learned earlier; it is still better if he admits that there are still more qualifications and refinements which they are missing at the level at which he is operating. The ironical thing about the teacher who scorns the efforts of his predecessors operating at a lower level of sophistication is that since there is almost always another level of sophistication higher yet than the one at which he is operating, the scorn, if justified, applies to him as well.

This is not to say that all teachers operate at a high enough level of sophistication, for that is certainly not true. I am simply pointing out that subject matter for purposes of teaching is almost inevitably simplified to some extent no matter what the level at which it is taught. As students mature in a given field, they can grasp more and more of its complexities. Thus we can expect exceptions not only in the definitions that students bring to us, but also in the definitions that we give them, when viewed from a higher level of sophistication.

An obvious example of a definition with exceptions is the definition of 'meter' given previously:

> A METER is a unit of length approximately equal to 39.37 inches.

According to that definition a unit of length which was exactly 39.371 inches would be a meter, since 39.371 inches is approximately 39.37 inches. So the definition which is quite appropriate for introducing the concept of a *meter* fails when carefully checked.

Similarly the definition of 'tariff' given earlier would have exceptions since it limits tariffs to sums of money, whereas a certain percentage of an import might be a tariff. *Webster's New Collegiate Dictionary* uses 'duty' as the general class term, but if a student does not know what a 'duty' is, then the definition using 'sum of money' is more likely to communicate at least a substantial part of the meaning of 'tariff' to him.

'Irony' also was defined in a simplified manner. A glance at M. H. Abrams' *A Glossary of Literary Terms** reveals that only one kind of irony is marked off by that definition. For example understatement is a form of irony, but the implied attitude is not the **opposite** of that literally expressed; instead it is **greater** than that literally expressed. Thus understatement constitutes an exception. But again the given definition is appropriate at a certain level of sophistication.

The definition of 'median', you will remember, limits medians to triangles. Thus the median of a trapezoid constitutes an exception to that definition, which again is appropriate at a given level of sophistication.

We can go on and on in this way. You will find it helpful to take several definitions from a book you use or will use in instruction and try to find counter-examples to them. This should not be difficult. It is much more difficult to construct classification definitions to which you and your colleagues cannot find any counter-examples. It will be profitable to try to do that also.

In doing these things you will find that it is not possible to construct an exceptionless classification definition when you try to put the definiens at a more concrete level than the definiendum, but that it is often possible, though difficult, to construct an exceptionless classification definition when remaining at the same level of abstraction as the definiendum. Admittedly this advice is vague and on the brink of being circular or empty, since I am offering no formula for judging whether two items are at the same level of abstraction. For the time being I appeal to your intuitive notion, and plan to supplement it with examples and nonexamples as we proceed.

Here are three examples of classification definitions, which I think are exceptionless. The definiens and definiendum in each case are at the same level of abstraction:

A BACHELOR is a man who is not yet married.
A TRIANGLE is a closed plane figure with three straight sides.
A TARIFF is a duty imposed on exports or imports.

Even exceptionless classification definitions have borderline cases when applied. The above definitions of 'bachelor', 'triangle', and 'tariff' exemplify this fact. Suppose that we have an American male, age twenty-three, who

* M. H. Abrams, *A Glossary of Literary Terms* (New York: Holt, Rinehart & Winston, Inc., 1961), pp. 45–47.

has not yet married. He is clearly a bachelor. On the other hand, an American male, age eight, is clearly not a bachelor. Somewhere in between those ages are the borderline cases, perhaps mostly among seventeen- and eighteen-year-olds. There are borderline cases of bachelors, because there are borderline cases in determining whether a male is a man or not. As long as we stay at the same level of abstraction, there are no borderline cases of bachelors, but as soon as we apply the terms of the definiens to concrete cases, borderline cases can arise, because we are moving from a given level of abstraction in the definiens to a lower level in the application.

Similarly the definition of 'triangle' has borderline cases in application because there are borderline cases of closed figures, straight lines, and planes. And the definition of 'tariff' has borderline cases because there are borderline cases of duties, imports, and exports. It would be valuable for your comprehension of the point for you now to stop reading and imagine borderline cases that can arise in the application of each of the terms in the definiens of 'triangle' and of 'tariff'. The above suggested borderline cases of men should serve as an example to get you started.

No special rule for definitions arises out of our consideration of the problems of exceptions and borderline cases. Rather you should have developed, as a result of the problems raised, a tolerance for a degree of looseness in definitions and a greater respect for the role of the context in determining just what is to be a satisfactory definition in a given situation.

Parsimony. The fifth problem is concerned with the point at which we should stop in defining a term. Should one stop with the bare minimum for logically delimiting a term (and thus be parsimonious)? Should one allow a few redundancies? Or should one go further by providing a number of examples, nonexamples, and statements of fact about the things named by the term?

For several reasons teachers, students, and textbook authors often provide more than enough information when they claim to be defining. So doing often facilitates initial comprehension by a learner, though it frequently results in fuzzy thinking if the definition is not later made more concise. Sometimes students, teachers, and authors offer all the associations that they have for a term in order to demonstrate the vast knowledge that they have acquired. And on some occasions many connections with a concept are given because the person is not able to give only essential features of the concept. This might be because although the concept is clear and precise, the person is not clear about it, or it might be because the concept itself is a loose one.

Of course, we may expect extra material to cause some difficulties. Other things being equal, it wastes time and space. The inclusion of extra material results in a failure to isolate the essential features and thus may make the presented concept appear to be complicated when it might be simple. Furthermore, the extra material might justifiably be taken as a necessary condition and thus might result in a judgment which is quite the opposite of that which would result if an elegant definition were provided.

The following definition of 'square' provides an example of the first two difficulties (waste and complication):

> A SQUARE is a four-sided polygon with all sides equal, with four right angles, and with opposite sides parallel.

That the opposite sides are parallel is implied by the fact that the four angles are right angles. Hence the information about the parallel sides is extra, though true. An elegant definition would omit it, though at a certain stage in teaching we might include it in order to help a student grasp connections.

The alert reader will have noted that after we omit this information, the definition still contains more material than is needed to distinguish squares from all other things. We need only say that one of the angles is a right angle. That the other three are right angles follows, then, from the specification of the equality of the four sides. However, it is matter of debate whether the mention of the other three angles is extra material. Some would say that the essence of the concept *square* includes four right angles and, therefore, all should be mentioned in the definition. Others would say that since the concept *square* can be distinguished by mentioning only one angle, the definition should mention only one angle, if elegance is to be achieved. I lean toward the former view. What do you think?

In any case, here is the sixth rule for classification definition:

6. Extra material should not be included in the defining part, if elegance is to be achieved.

⁘ *Conceptually mistaken extra material*

However one decides this debatable matter, one should see that there is a potential objection to the presence of extra material in a definition that does **not** hold for any of the extra material in the definition of 'square'. This objection is that a person facing something that **fits** the parsimonious part of the definition, but **does not fit** the extra material, does not have proper guidance from the definition in making a decision about whether the term applies.

Consider this definition, which contains what is called 'synthetically related extra material':

> A CONCAVE LENS is a lens with both surfaces curved inward, and which diverges parallel light rays.

The extra material is that which follows the comma. Once we have determined that a lens has both surfaces curved inward, we have thereby established that it is a concave lens. The fact that parallel light rays are diverged by passing through such a lens is extra. But this is not the relatively innocuous sort of extra material found in the definition of 'square', since we would not be involved in a contradiction if we claimed to have found a lens which has both surfaces curved inward, but which does not diverge parallel rays.

If, and only if, it is logically possible for the extra material not to hold when the parsimonious definiens does hold, then the extra material is SYNTHETICALLY RELATED. This sort of extra material is a serious problem. Even though it may help a student to develop associations, it leaves him with a fuzzy or mistaken notion. It either puts him in the position of not knowing what to say in some cases, or of being required to say the wrong thing. If a student armed with the above definition of 'concave lens' were faced with a lens with both surfaces curved inward, but which **converged** parallel rays,* he would be required to say that it is not a concave lens. This consequence is unfortunate, for a student should call that lens a concave lens.

Thus, although a definition containing synthetically related extra material does give a student associations and connections, it should be avoided because it seriously misrepresents the concept. If you desire to make these associations for your students, do not do it in the form of a definition.

On the other hand, the objection under discussion cannot hold against the extra material in the given definitions of 'square', because it is logically impossible for something to fit the parsimonious definition without also fitting the other material. If something is a polygon with four equal sides and one right angle, then it is logically inevitable that it has three other right angles, and that its opposite sides be parallel. So this objection cannot apply to this definition. The extra material in the definition of 'square' is what is called 'ANALYTICALLY RELATED'. Extra material in definitions does not lead to mistaken judgments if the extra material is analytically necessary.

Here are some other examples of definitions with analytic extra material —probably acceptable in a classroom. Only if we are seeking to present an elegant system would they be defective. The extra material is in brackets:

> A METER is a unit of length approximately equal to 39.37 inches. [It is greater than one yard.]
>
> 'LITERATURE' is defined as 'everything in print'. [Newton's book, *Principia Mathematica*, is thus literature.]
>
> The GROSS NATIONAL PRODUCT is the sum total of all goods and services produced in a given year. [A haircut and an automobile produced this year are part of this year's Gross National Product.]

* Such a situation arises, by the way, when the lens is in a medium of greater density than the lens.

For contrast here are some other examples of classification definitions with synthetically related extra material in brackets:

> PARALLEL LINES are plane straight lines that do not intersect however far extended [often occurring in engineering projects].
> IRONY is a mode of expression in which the implied attitudes are the opposite of those literally expressed [and which is likely to get one in trouble with dull-witted authorities].
> A TARIFF is a sum of money which is levied as a tax against imports or exports [usually used in order to protect industries from competition].

More will be said about the presence or absence of extra material in a definition in the next chapter, in discussion of the definition of loose terms, and more will be said about the analytic-synthetic distinction in the chapter on types of explanation. No special rule is needed to prohibit synthetically related material. It is already forbidden by Rule 2b, since it has the effect of narrowing the definition.

An appraisal of classification definition

Advantages. The reasons for the common preference for classification definitions are quite plausible: Such definitions are brief and complete; and the form is teachable, provides for at least the appearance of precision, and allows for substitution of one part for the other in standard substitution situations.

Brevity is, of course, desirable, since brief statements are ordinarily more understandable and less wasteful of time and space. Completeness is also desirable. We want the full meaning of a concept to be exposed by a definition. Otherwise students might think they understand the full meaning when they do not; and teachers often cannot tell whether students who give incomplete interpretation have mastered the full meaning.

Teachability of the form is an added convenience provided by the simplicity of the concept of classification definition and by the existence of a simple set of rules.

Precision is desirable so that one can tell in specific situations whether a concept applies. There is no vagueness of application of the following definition, if we are able to identify four-sided polygons and parallel lines:

> A PARALLELOGRAM is a four-sided polygon with opposite sides parallel.

If, and only if, something meets the criteria specified in the definiens, then it is a parallelogram. That is precision.

Substitutability is desirable for purposes of clarification, understanding, and/or compactness of statement.

Difficulties. Though classification definitions have a number of advantages, they are frequently not satisfactory for classroom work. First, they are appropriate only for nouns. Verbs, adjectives, conjunctions, etc., may not be defined this way, although alterations sometimes may be instituted so that a noun is being defined. Such an alteration was performed in the earlier definition of 'parallel lines', if one treats it as in reality a definition of the adjective, 'parallel':

> PARALLEL LINES are plane straight lines that do not meet however far extended.

The alteration in this case involved adding the noun 'lines', the meaning of which is not in question, and then defining the term, 'parallel lines', instead of simply the term, 'parallel'. This making of alterations leaves up to the person receiving the definition the job of inferring the meaning of the term that is in question ('parallel') from the meaning of the defined term ('parallel lines'). Thus in making such alterations, the resulting definition looses some of the attractive straightforwardness of classification definition. Often, however, we can ignore this slight loss.

Such alterations do not work for some important particles. Try to give a classification of if . . . then, or, notwithstanding, etc. This is not a problem for most areas of study, but it is a problem for the fields of logic, grammar, and mathematics.

Furthermore, classification definition of relational terms, such as 'harder than' and 'inversely proportional', in spite of the usually required alterations, tends to have awkward results. You will see if you try to define either of these two relational terms. The next form of definition to be considered, equivalent-expression definition, is particularly adapted to relational terms.

A second weakness of classification definitions is that they are usually more difficult for the beginner to understand than some other forms of definition, if used to introduce a concept. A person completely unacquainted with the meaning of the word 'parallel' is not best instructed by being given the above definition of 'parallel lines'. He is better instructed by examples and nonexamples of parallel lines—perhaps in conjunction with the above definition or with a challenge to formulate a definition.

A third weakness, which is part of the cause of the second weakness, is the elusiveness or lack of concrete content when such definitions are used to define abstract terms. We shall see that to insert such content, retaining the equivalence, warps the concept.

A fourth weakness of the classification definition is one mentioned earlier, that the appearance of precision and accuracy is often deceiving. A classification definition that is applied to the world of men, things, and events becomes vague at some point. At least borderline cases develop. Exceptions often do too. This difficulty is avoided by using one of the concrete-interpretation forms of definition, which make no pretense of providing complete precise boundaries, and thus cannot mislead by appearances.

A fifth and related difficulty is the inappropriateness of a precise mold for an imprecise concept. For such concepts the range definition, which is presented in the next chapter, is better suited.

As you can see, some other form can be used if one desires to avoid given specific weaknesses inherent in the classification form. But, all in all, the classification form is a **very** useful general-purpose form, and is probably the first one to be taught to students.

Chapter Summary

In this chapter you examined two equivalence forms of definition—synonym definition and classification definition, and some standard problems of definition. Equivalence forms are those which enable us to construct a definition of two more-or-less equivalent parts. The term being defined is called 'the definiendum', and the part doing the defining is called 'the definiens'. Equivalence forms are aimed at making the definiens and definiendum equivalent.

Equivalence is regarded as a goal in definition because it provides a complete marking out of a concept and usually enables us to make clarifying substitutions with or for the definiendum. Synonym definition, the simplest form, has the advantage of being brief and the disadvantages of the usual absence of an exact synonym, and the frequent failure of synonyms to clarify because they do not analyze a concept.

Classification definition does analyze a concept and is still brief and complete. The form is teachable, provides, for at least the appearance of precision, and allows for substitution. On the other hand, this form is not usable for particles, and is more or less inconvenient for parts of speech that are not nouns. For the introduction of a completely new concept other forms should probably precede the classification form, since the classification form does not provide concrete interpretation of terms. And lastly this form's appearance of precision is deceiving when application to cases is involved.

The following are guidelines for classification definition:

1. The definiens should give
   a. a general class, and
   b. features that are supposed to distinguish what is referred to by the term from other members of the general class.

2. The definiens and definiendum should be equivalent; that is,
   a. the definiens should not be broader, and
   b. the definiens should not be narrower.

3. Generally negation and its equivalents should be avoided in definitions.

4. The definiens should ordinarily not use any crucial part of the definiendum.
5. Definitions should be punctuated so that they are clear in context.
6. Extra material should not be included in the defining part, if elegance is to be achieved.

The first two of the above rules give the essence of classification definition. ⁂Synthetically related extra material is prohibited by Rule 2b.

COMPREHENSION SELF-TEST

True or False? If the statement is false, change a crucial term (or terms) to make it true.

10–1. There is no one ideal form of definition.
10–2. Synonym definition is the ideal form of definition.
10–3. A definition should never contain a negative term, since negatives can always be converted into positives.
10–4. The truth of a charge that a definition is circular is always context-dependent.
10–5. To indicate that a word or words are being talked about, quotes are used herein.
10–6. For your work in this course the closing of quotes that are used to indicate reference to a term should ordinarily appear after other punctuation such as commas and periods.
10–7. A well-formed definition inevitably has conceivable borderline cases when applied to concrete objects.
10–8. Most well-formulated classroom definitions have exceptions.
⁂**10–9.** Analytically related extra material is likely to lead to mistaken judgments.

Questions.

10–10. What does the term 'definiendum' mean?
10–11. What does the term 'definiens' mean?
10–12. State two advantages of the use of equivalence forms of definition.
10–13. Punctuate the following sentence:
Propaganda is a derogatory term although propagation a term with the same root means the spreading abroad of anything and is thus not a derogatory term.
10–14. Here is a list of reported definitions for you to judge by the rules for classification definition. For each definition indicate the rule violated or indicate that the definition is satisfactory. Assume that the definer offered these definitions as reports of established usage. If you think that more than one rule is violated, pick the earlier one in the list given in the chapter summary, since the earlier ones are more essential. If you feel you need to qualify your answer, then do so.

a. CONDENSATION is where water forms.
b. CONDENSATION is a process.
c. CONDENSATION is the process of the formation of water.
d. CONDENSATION is the process of condensing.
e. CONDENSATION is the process of becoming more compact, as the process in which steam becomes water.
f. Do you see those water drops on the side of that cold glass? That's CONDENSATION.
g. A METAPHOR is when you do not say what you mean.
h. A METAPHOR is a figure of speech.
i. A METAPHOR is a figure of speech in which a word or phrase has a meaning analogous to, but not the same as, its literal meaning.
j. A METAPHOR is a word used in a way which is not literally correct.
k. A POLYGON is a figure with equal sides.
l. A QUADRATIC EQUATION is an equation in which the unknown is squared.
m. SOVEREIGNTY is when a country is able to do what it wants.
n. PERSONALITY is the combination of traits, habits, values, and tendencies that make an individual uniquely himself.
o. PERSONALITY is the combination of traits which vary from one person to the next.
p. A LABOR UNION is a union of laborers.

10–15. For each of the definitions in 10–14 which you marked defective frame a question of challenge.

10–16. For each of the following classification definitions identify the extra material, if any. Even if the definition is not in your field, do your best with the existing cues. If you are putting your responses on a separate sheet of paper, you might write the first and last words of the extra material connected by three dots. Using this convention the answer to the first is ", which . . . activities".

a. The ADRENAL GLAND is the gland which produces adrenalin, which serves to speed up body activities.
b. An ATOM is the smallest part of a chemical element which still retains the chemical properties of the element.
c. A CIRCLE is a plane figure which may be inscribed in a square and which has all of its points equidistant from a given point.
d. An EQUATION is a statement of equality between two quantities, often used to solve algebraic problems.
e. A PARALLELOGRAM is a plane figure with four straight sides and with opposite sides parallel.
f. IRONY is a mode of expression in which the implied attitudes are the opposite of those literally expressed, and which most frequently appears as disapproval which is literally expressed as praise.
g. A GERUND is a verbal noun which can be used as the subject of a sentence.
h. A SIMILE is a mode of expression in which two essentially different things are explicitly held to be similar.
i. NATIONALISM is the devotion to the unity, independence, and interests of a country that is commonly found among the people of new countries.

j. SELF-DETERMINATION is the currently popular method of control by the people of an area over the key decisions that relate to that area.
k. THE PRINCIPLE OF CUMULATION is that principle which holds that a change in a given direction in one set of conditions results in a change in another set of conditions, which latter change results in further change in the given direction in the first set of conditions.
l. RATIONALIZATION is the process which so many of us use of finding good reasons to use in place of the real ones.
m. PROJECTION is thinking to see our weaknesses in others.

Discussion Questions.

⁘ **10–17.** For each of the definitions in 10–16 that contains extra material, tell whether the extra material is analytically or synthetically related, and indicate whether Rule 2b is violated by the definition.

10–18. Frame a classification definition in your teaching area which is exceptionless and airtight.

10–19. Frame a definition in your teaching area which is perfectly suitable for teaching at a given level, but which has exceptions. State one counter-example.

10–20. Frame a classification definition of a term in your teaching area which is best defined with the use of a negative.

⁘ **10–21.** Frame a classification definition in your teaching area that contains analytically related extra material. Label the extra material.

⁘ **10–22.** Frame a classification definition in your teaching area which contains synthetically related extra material. Label the extra material.

10–23. Frame a classification definition in your teaching area which is intended to give the meaning of a word which is not a noun, and makes appropriate adaptations. Identify the key word in addition to underlining the definiendum.

10–24. Select a thesis from this chapter with which you agree or disagree and state your reasons in a two-page paper.

CHAPTER 11

Equivalence Forms: Equivalent-Expression Definition and Range Definition

At the end of the previous chapter you were told that some of the problems with classification definition could be handled in part by switching to alternate forms of definition. This chapter is devoted to two forms which approximate the ideal of equivalence, but not in the precise-appearing way of the classification definition. These two forms are the equivalent-expression definition and the range definition.

*Equivalent-Expression Definition**

One of the problems with classification definition is its inability to handle particles, such as, 'if . . . , then', 'or', and 'notwithstanding'; a second was

* This form of definition is usually called 'contextual definition' in the field of philosophy. I have chosen the term 'equivalent-expression definition' because 'contextual definition' tends to suggest to people the idea that such definition is accomplished simply by using a word in context. In order to avoid confusion I am stipulating that 'equivalent-expression definition' shall mean contextual definition.

its awkwardness in handling terms denoting relationships, such as 'inversely proportional', 'series' (in electricity), 'anonymous', and 'role'. Try to frame a satisfactory classification definition for these terms. You should see that you simply cannot do it for the particles.

Defining particles

When a definition of a particle is needed, the best form to use is ordinarily the equivalent-expression form. With this form, one puts the term in question in a larger expression and provides another expression which is alleged to be equivalent in meaning to that larger expression. For example, one can give the following equivalent-expression definition of 'if . . . , then' (in which '*x*' and '*y*' stand for sentences):

> 'IF *x*, THEN *y*' means the same as '*x* implies *y*'.*

'If *x*, then *y*' is the larger expression which incorporates the term to be defined. This larger expression is equated in meaning to the expression, '*x* implies *y*'. The result is an equivalent-expression definition. Probably this definition does not enlighten you about the meaning of 'if . . . , then', since you already have a good grasp of this basic term. But definitions like this can be used in discussions of some aspects of the meaning of the word 'if'.

Similarly the terms 'or' and 'notwithstanding' might be defined as follows, when a definition of either is needed:

> 'Either *x* OR *y*' means the same as 'At least one of *x* and *y* is true, but not both are true' (the strong 'or').
>
> 'The heat NOTWITHSTANDING' means the same as 'in spite of the heat'.

In each case the key term is incorporated in a larger expression, which is equated to another expression. The last term, can also be defined by synonym definition, but classification definition certainly will not do.

Defining relational terms

Perhaps you **are** able to frame classification definitions of the relational terms, 'varies inversely', 'series' (in electricity), 'anonymous', and 'role'. Yours might look like these:

> INVERSE VARIATION is that relationship between two variables such that as one increases, the other decreases, and *vice versa*.
>
> (Alternately and more elegantly) INVERSE VARIATION is that relationship between two variables such that their product is constant.

* To be technically correct I should say 'That *x* implies that *y*', but do not do so, because the word 'that' might at first be interpreted by some as an adjective rather than as a conjunction, and thus might cause confusion.

SERIES is the state of being so connected that the same electricity passes through all parts that are in this state.

ANONYMITY is the state of being an unknown author.

'ROLE' means the normative culture pattern consisting of the things a person's culture expects him to do as a result of his holding a certain position.

Once one has surmounted the noun-conversion problem set by 'varies inversely' and 'anonymous', there is another problem that these definitions set for us. They have a formalistic, artificial flavor, which is not really a grievous fault, but which is bothersome.

The phrases, 'relationship', 'state of being', and 'normative culture pattern', are extremely abstract and difficult for some people to work with. Perhaps this is just a matter of taste, but the following definitions, making use of the equivalent-expression form, seem to have more vitality and less artificiality than the previous ones:

'*x* VARIES INVERSELY as *y*' means the same as 'As *y* gets larger, *x* gets smaller, and *vice versa*'.

(Alternately and more elegantly) '*x* VARIES INVERSELY as *y*' means the same as 'The product, *xy*, is constant'.

To say that elements are in SERIES is to say that they are on the same electrical path.

'The author of this poem is ANONYMOUS' means the same as 'The author of this poem did not reveal his name'.

'*X*'s ROLE is *y*' means the same as 'In *X*'s culture, a person holding a position like *X*'s is expected to do *y*'.

(With concrete content) 'Mr. Macmillan's ROLE is to preside over meetings of the council, to carry out the decisions of the council, and to make day-to-day decisions subject to review of the council' means the same as 'By virtue of his position Mr. Macmillan is expected by our culture to do those things just mentioned'.

Convenience

Perhaps your taste still leans toward the classification definition. Even if this is so, you should still develop a facility at the spontaneous framing of equivalent-expression definitions, since you will find them extremely convenient at times. Even if you prefer the classification form, you will sometimes have a great deal of trouble finding a general category on the spur of the moment; the equivalent-expression definition relieves you of the burden.

Herein lies a danger, for one can easily use the equivalent-expression form when the classification form would be most informative. The equivalent-expression form leaves it to the hearer of the definition to **infer** the meaning of the term in question, since it is not the term that has been equated, but rather an expression containing the term.

A spurious advantage of equivalent-expression definition

Another criticism that is leveled at classification definitions such as those of 'inversely proportional', 'series', 'anonymous', and 'role' is that the use of such general terms as 'relationship', 'state of being', and 'normative culture pattern' is not only artificial, but assumes or implies a mistaken doctrine: that these latter terms stand for vague metaphysical entities, whose status is dubious. The equivalent-expression definition, since it avoids the use of such categories, is felt to avoid this alleged difficulty. According to the complaint, which some of you perhaps feel, the use of these terms commits us to the existence of the entities, *relationship*, *state of being*, and *normative cultural pattern*. The hard-headed empiricist frequently wants to disassociate himself from the alleged implication of these entities, since he does not know how to locate them; he does not even know what would count as evidence for or against their existence.

Although some people do hold that there are entities to correspond to these terms, there is no reason to say that everyone who uses them is committed to the existence of such entities. We can regard the use of such terms as a manner of speaking which enables us to talk about things in general. After all does the following definition of 'hamburger' imply the existence of an entity, *sandwich*?

> 'HAMBURGER' means a sandwich composed of a cooked, ground-beef patty between two halves of a bun.

This definition does not refer to any particular sandwich, so the criticism, if it holds against the definitions using 'relationship', 'state of being', and 'normative cultural pattern', would hold just as well here, which is absurd. This criticism, if taken seriously, would eliminate our use of general categories.

The suggestion of a context

In any case the equivalent-expression form is on many occasions more convenient and less artificial. Furthermore it has the added advantage of indicating a context in which the term can legitimately be used. Thus, it provides protection against neglect of the nuances of a term. You will remember the case of the synonym definition of 'senescent', which failed to state anything about the kind of thing for which this word can be used in description. An equivalent-expression definition could be used to indicate that the expression can be used to describe people, as in the following case:

> To say that a person is SENESCENT is to say that he is growing old.

Note that this definition does not explicitly rule out applying the word 'senescent' to trees, but it does assure us of one kind of thing to which it can be applied; in that respect it is somewhat of an improvement over the earlier definition.

As you perhaps realize, this form has a correlative disadvantage which takes the form of a dilemma: the use of this form leaves one in doubt about the scope of the term being defined, or else it leaves one with too narrow a notion of its scope. Take the definition of 'anonymous'. Either one does not know to what sorts of things this term can be applied in addition to authors of poems, or else one is misled into thinking that the term can be applied only to authors of poems. This danger is inherent in the use of the equivalent-expression form and in the use of the classification form when terms are modified by adding another term (as in the case of the addition of 'lines' to enable us to make a classification definition of 'parallel'). So we must be on guard when making these definitional moves. One helpful device is the use of a series of equivalent-expression definitions, indicating various contexts in which the term can be used.

Helping a student in search of a category

When a student is having trouble finding a general category for a term to be defined (perhaps because it is a particle or a relationship term), you can help him by pushing him toward an equivalent-expression definition. One way to do this is to put the term in a longer expression and ask him what that means. For example, a student struggling for a definition of 'anonymous' might be helped by your suggesting:

> Perhaps you might tell us what it means to say that the author of a poem is anonymous.

This move might be accompanied by your urging your students to adopt the equivalent-expression form as a means of handling difficult definitional problems.

Range Definition

Sometimes it just seems to be impossible to come up with a satisfactory, precise, equivalence definition. That is, sometimes the exceptions to any equivalence definition we are able to formulate are so embarrassing that we are tempted to abandon our efforts and declare the term indefinable. Witness the following dialogue:

Example 11-1

MR. BETA: Your reading assignment for today contained a definition of 'scientific method'. I wonder if you have any questions about it.

TONY: Yes, I do. The definition says that. . . .

MR. BETA: (interrupting) Wait a minute. Will you all open your books to page 20, and look at this definition. Esther, please read it aloud.

ESTHER: (reading) 'SCIENTIFIC METHOD' is the process of following these steps:

1. Stating the problem.
2. Formulating a solution or hypothesis.
3. Running controlled experiments.
4. Drawing a tentative conclusion.
5. Testing the conclusion in practice.

MR. BETA: All right, Tony, what is your question?

TONY: I was reading in an astronomy book about a conclusion that was announced by Gerard Kuiper. He said that Pluto is a former satellite of Neptune. I read about how he came to this conclusion and didn't see any mention of controlled experiments. In fact how could there be any controlled experiments, since he was not in a position to manipulate the planets?

ESTHER: Well, maybe he did some controlled experiments in his laboratory with balls tied to strings or something like that.

TONY: Maybe he did, but that sort of thing is not mentioned in the description of what he did. Anyway let's suppose that he didn't do anything like that. Suppose that he never went near a laboratory. You certainly wouldn't then say that this great astronomer did not use the scientific method in his work. It just wouldn't make sense to say that a competent scientist doing research was not using the scientific method.

ESTHER: There's something to what you say. How about it, Mr. Beta?

MR. BETA: Let's think about it. Tony do you have any other criticisms?

TONY: Yes, I do. There is another step which I do not think must always be present, step number five, "Testing the conclusion in practice". Some scientific conclusions are just not the sort of thing that can be tested in practice. The conclusions drawn by geologists, historians, anthropologists, and archeologists about what happened in the past are usually like this. Take the archeologist's conclusion that Hissarlik is located at the site of ancient Troy. How can that conclusion be tested in practice? I see how it can be tested, but the idea, **in practice,** just does not fit. So the words 'in practice' should be eliminated from the definition of 'scientific method'. Only generalizations can be tested in practice.

MR. BETA: Does anyone see any reasons not to remove those two words? (No response) How about step number three, "Running Controlled Experiments"? Should we remove that also?

ESTHER: I guess we'll have to, now that I think about it.

ERIC: But if we do, what's left? Stating a problem, formulating a solution, drawing a tentative conclusion, and testing the conclusion. That's so vague that it is not much guidance. All it says, in effect, is, "Be clear about your goal, and check to see if you have achieved it." Even more briefly it says, "Be careful." These eliminations result in a formula that is just common sense and is not distinctive of science at all. I think we shouldn't try to define 'scientific method'. It's an undefinable term.

In the above dialogue, somewhat streamlined in order to make it short and clear, Mr. Beta's students have made a number of good points. They have put him on the horns of a dilemma. Either accept a definition with obvious exceptions; or amend it by making it so broad that it is not discriminating; or abandon the effort. Is there a way out?

Retaining looseness

The way out is to adopt a form of definition that allows loose concepts to exhibit their looseness. *Scientific method* is a loose concept. Any attempt to force it into the precise-appearing mold of classification definition will give problems. Either the definiens will be too narrow (as in the book definition) or too broad (as in the amended definition).

A survey of the literature on scientific method reveals many precise-appearing definitions of the term. They all fail because the term is not a precise one, yet the spirit of testing reported definitions with examples and nonexamples pushes us toward trying to make it a precise term. It is this sort of thing which prompts James B. Conant to say in *On Understanding Science*: "I am inclined to think that, on the whole, the popularization of the philosophical analysis of science and its methods has led not to greater understanding but to a great deal of misunderstanding about science."*

The abandonment of efforts to define 'scientific method' would be a mistake, for the term 'scientific method' is a meaningful term. We must use a form that will convey that meaning.

'Scientific method' is not the only term like this. Examples of others are 'rural', 'Romanticism', 'elegance', and 'sovereignty'. Such terms will be referred to as 'range terms', because their boundaries are like those of a mountain range, imprecise but, loosely speaking, there.

Now we are all familiar with the admonition to avoid vagueness, to give clear and precise definitions. Ordinarily this is good advice. But when we are faced with a range term, what else are we to do but give a vague definition—provided that we desire to do justice to the concept. We can build precision into a term, but then we have a different concept. Remember the illuminating case of the term 'rural' as ordinarily used, and its fate in the hands of the United States Census Bureau.

Terms like those under discussion are most briefly defined using a form called 'range definition'. The range definition is a form named by Max Black** when he faced the task of defining 'scientific method'. A range definition consists of a set of criteria, **most of which** can be expected to hold for any given application of the term.

* James B. Conant, *On Understanding Science* (New York: Mentor, 1951), p. 27.

** Max Black, "The Definition of Scientific Method", in his *Problems of Analysis* (Ithaca: Cornell University Press, 1954), pp. 3–23.

The major advantage of such a definition is that it retains the imprecision of many of our concepts and thus fits them better. The weakness is the other side of the coin. Such definitions are not self-applying. Human judgment, based on a thorough knowledge of the field and the situation, is necessary.

Black's definition of 'scientific method' might well serve as an example. He lists experimentation, observation, generalization, the hypothetico-deductive use of assumptions, measurement, the use of instruments, and mathematical construction as characteristics which:

> . . . are neither necessary nor sufficient, but . . . may be present in higher or lower degree and they contribute to what we recognize as science. Their diminution removes from an activity the feature we apprehended as scientific; their joint presence in high degree creates conditions recognized as pre-eminently scientific.*

Thus the resolution of Mr. Beta's dilemma lies in the use of a range definition of 'scientific method'. Although his psychological strategy will vary with the context, the idea he should try to get across runs as follows:

Example 11-2

MR. BETA: These points you make are good points. 'Scientific method' is a loose term, but the form of definition used in your book made it appear to be a precise one. Using this form, we are inevitably pushed toward an overly vague definition. If instead we use a loose form, we can do justice to the term. Here is a possible definition of 'scientific method':

SCIENTIFIC METHOD is characterized by experimentation, observation, generalization, deductive reasoning from assumptions and hypotheses to data, measurement, the use of instruments, and theories that are mathematical in form.

This definition lists a number of items, each of which is more specific than the amended book definition; but since no one of them is to be regarded as a necessary condition, the counter-examples proposed by Tony will not defeat the definition.

Here is a range definition of 'romanticism', which does more justice to the term than the simplified definition presented in Chapter 7:

> ROMANTICISM is an artistic approach characterized by: (1) a sturdy and plainly expressed belief in the brotherhood of man; (2) a deep sympathy with humble lives, human and animal alike; (3) a sense of the independent spirit of man and his natural right to freedom; (4) existence around the early part of the nineteenth century; (5) expression of individual emotional experience; (6) de-emphasis of form; and (7) concern with national consciousness.

* Reprinted from Max Black: *Problems of Analysis*. Copyright © 1954 by Cornell University. Used by permission of Cornell University Press.

Note that a general class has been provided (artistic approach) and thus that this definition gives one necessary condition of romanticism. The situation is standard. An appropriate general class can be put forward, and should be if clarification is thereby provided. In the 'scientific method' definition, the addition of a general class (perhaps *approach*) would not have provided clarification, and so was omitted.

The looseness inherent in most terms

But did you not learn that all definitions of terms that apply to the world of things, men, and events often have exceptions and always have borderline cases in application? And if this is so, should not the classification form be abandoned completely? The answer to this question is a rather pragmatic one. When there are enough exceptions at the level at which we are operating, then the thing to do is to retreat to the range definition. If not, stick with the classification form or some other precise-appearing form.

Chapter Summary

In this chapter you were faced with two other equivalence-type forms of definition, equivalent-expression definition and range definition. Each is somewhat of a departure from the precision that is usually associated with equivalence; the first because of the inference that is required in going from the meaning of the expression in which the term is embedded to the meaning of the term; the second because the equivalence is between two loose items, the definiens and the definiendum.

Equivalent-expression definition is useful for defining parts of speech other than nouns, especially particles, and for defining terms that denote relationships. It is also a convenient crutch when one is unable to come up with the category necessary for a classification definition. The equivalent-expression definition puts the term to be defined in a larger expression and then gives a meaning for the larger expression.

Range definition gives a list of criteria most of which are expected to hold for any given instance of a term. A common form is, "x is a y which is characterized by z, v, and w". Range definition is useful for defining terms that are loose at the level at which we are operating.

COMPREHENSION SELF-TEST

True or False? If the statement is false, change a crucial term (or terms) to make it true.

11–1. Particles are definable.

11–2. Terms used to express relationships are definable.

11–3. Loose terms are indefinable.

11–4. The use of the term, 'state of being' necessarily assumes the existence of a corresponding entity.

11–5. An equivalent-expression definition suggests a context in which the term can be used.

11–6. The characteristics listed in a range definition are not all expected to hold in all cases.

11–7. Loose concepts are generally improved by making them exact.

Questions.

11–8. Define 'equivalent-expression definition'.

11–9. Using variables for which terms can be substituted, give a general form for equivalent-expression definition.

11–10. Define 'range definition'.

11–11. Using variables for which terms can be substituted, give a general form for range definition.

11–12. State an advantage that equivalent-expression definition has over classification definition.

11–13. State an advantage that range definition has over classification definition.

11–14. State a disadvantage of equivalent-expression definition.

11–15. State a disadvantage of range definition.

Exercises.

11–16. For ten of the following relationship terms, frame a classification definition and an equivalent-expression definition.

a. varies directly
b. necessarily follows
c. congruent
d. symmetrical
e. transitive (as applied to relationships)
f. transitive (as applied to verbs)
g. compatible
h. meaning
i. connote
j. denote
k. abstract (as opposed to concrete)
l. concrete
m. self-evident (as in the Declaration of Independence)
n. cause (as used in an analysis of the Civil War)
o. integrate
p. status
q. instrumental value
r. intrinsic value
s. resistance
t. eclipse (as in 'eclipse of the moon')
u. tide
v. malleable

11–17. Pick two particularly awkward classification definitions of the terms in 11–16, assume that one of your students has given them, and for each, frame a question designed to drive the student to the use of the equivalent-expression form.

11–18. Give a true reported range definition of three of the following terms:

a. sovereignty
b. elegance (as used in mathematics)

c. elegance (as used with respect to people, clothing, and buildings)
d. sophistication
e. experiment
f. plot (of a novel, for example)
g. poetry
h. democracy
i. chemistry
j. home economics

11–19. From your field pick a term that is not on the above lists, and has not been discussed in the text, and is best defined by equivalent-expression definition. Give such a definition of the term. Justify in writing your use of the form for that term.

11–20. Do the same (as in 11–19) for a term best defined by range definition.

CHAPTER 12

Concrete Interpretation Forms

Although equivalence forms of definition tend to provide a definiens that is roughly at the same level of abstraction as the definiendum, the range definition in particular tends to depart from this tendency by listing criteria that are usually more concrete than the term being defined. This chapter treats definition forms that are distinguishable by their emphasis on giving concrete interpretation. Definitions that give concrete interpretation sacrifice the combination of brevity and completeness which is characteristic of classification definition.

If one attempts to approach completeness and gives a definiens that is more concrete than the definiendum, then brevity must be sacrificed. If, on the other hand, one aims at brevity when giving a definiens that is more concrete than the definiendum, then completeness must be sacrificed. The first case would be illustrated by a long list of examples; brevity would be sacrificed. The second case would be illustrated by a single example; completeness would be far from realized.

The Need for Concrete Interpretation

But there are times when we must be willing to foresake this combination of completeness and brevity, so that we can descend to a more concrete level. It is helpful to do this for psychological and logical reasons. Consider this chain of interrelated definitions given in a geometry course:

A SURFACE is the boundary of a solid.
A LINE is the intersection of two surfaces.
A POINT is the intersection of two lines.
A RAY is that part of a straight line which extends from a point in one direction only.
A LINE SEGMENT is that part of a straight line contained between two of its points.
A broken line that encloses a portion of a plane is a CLOSED LINE.

The presentation to the beginner of such a list of classification definitions of the technical terms in a subject is usually forbidding and unintelligible. The beginner in geometry finds the above array unenlightening, if it is presented without concrete interpretation. For this reason geometry texts accompany such a definition series with drawings and comparisons, interspersing various descriptive material in order to relate these concepts to concrete material. The concept, *solid*, an early one in the above series of definitions, is introduced in one geometry text by mentioning that books, pencils, and bricks are solids and by providing a three-dimensional line drawing of a rectangular solid.

A single classification definition can be forbidding too. Imagine introducing the concept *irony* to an average seventh grader by using this previously given definition of 'irony' and nothing else:

IRONY is a mode of expression in which the implied attitudes are opposed to those literally expressed.

It is likely that this definition, though in good classification form, would not provide clarification.

In part, these are psychological facts. It is very difficult to take a list of interrelated classification definitions and master interrelationships between the terms. And, of course, even a single definition cannot provide clarification, if it is in terms that the student does not know.

The logical problem

This is also a logical problem, because abstract descriptive terms must have some concrete interpretation. It is not claimed that most definitions, in order to provide meaning, must give a concrete interpretation, but rather that a concrete interpretation, if not given **by** the definition, must **be available**. Furthermore, if the definition is to communicate the meaning, there is a practical necessity: that the person(s) addressed can supply this interpretation, if it is not already supplied.

Concrete interpretation is not always available. Consider this dialogue from a civics class:

Example 12-1

MR. DELTA: And in New York State there has been a concerted effort to organize school districts so that they have the same boundaries as communities. Fred?

FRED: What's so hard about that? The boundaries of communities are well known. They're marked on maps. Voters are grouped in accord with these boundaries, and the tax rolls are organized that way. It looks to me as if any other way would be more difficult.

MR. DELTA: Those aren't community boundaries you see on the map. Those are political boundaries.

FRED: Do you mean that the sign saying, "You are entering the City of Ithaca", is wrong and that the boundary of Ithaca is somewhere else?

MR. DELTA: That sign marks the political boundary of Ithaca, but it does not mark the boundary of the community.

FRED: I don't understand.

It is about time for Mr. Delta to offer a definition of 'community'. Suppose he proceeds in the following fashion, which I shall refer to as 'Style A':

Example 12-2

MR. DELTA: 'COMMUNITY' is defined as an integrated unity of specifics.

FRED: I still don't understand.

MR. DELTA: Well does that road sign mark the boundary of an integrated unity of specifics?

FRED: I don't know how to tell.

Fred's response is an appropriate one. The basis for integration needs to be clarified, and what is to count as a specific must be made clear. In other words, we need to be able to tell whether something is or is not a specific and whether a group of these specifics is integrated. Unless this clarification is available, the term is not one that can be used to communicate information. The communication of information with a noun requires that we be able to identify examples **and** things that are **not** examples. The above definition does not give a basis for judging that any randomly selected group of objects is **not** a community. Without concrete interpretation, it does not exclude anything. A person who is told to stay in his community (using the above definition, uninterpreted) will not know whether he is obeying the direction.

Unless concrete interpretation is available, then, the term is without sufficient meaning. One caution: Without investigation, it is best to say only that this term (so defined) might very well be one for which no concrete interpretation is available; Mr. Delta could conceivably have something in mind, although he has not told his class yet. Style A is not automatically deficient, but it is suspect.

Consider another approach, which provides more concrete interpretation. Let us call it 'Style B':

Example 12-3

MR. DELTA: A COMMUNITY is a group of people and their institutions such that: (1) the people live adjacent to each other, and (2) the group of people is characterized by very little noncommunal conflict.

FRED: I can understand what you said about living adjacent to each other, but what is noncommunal conflict?

MR. DELTA: 'NONCOMMUNAL CONFLICT' is defined as conflict that is sufficiently severe to result in the disruption of a community.

This definition chain is circular, because in order to determine whether we have a community and whether we have noncommunal conflict, we first have to determine the other. Thus Style B, although it provides some concrete interpretation in the first condition (adjacency), is deficient because the the second condition (little noncommunal conflict) does not provide a way of making connections to the concrete world.

For his last definition Mr. Delta, might instead have pursued this line, which I shall call 'Style C':

Example 12-4

MR. DELTA: NONCOMMUNAL CONFLICT is conflict that is serious.

FRED: I see, I think. But how do I tell whether a given conflict is serious?

MR. DELTA: Serious conflict is conflict in which people are badly hurt.

FRED: But don't people disagree about what it is to be badly hurt?

MR. DELTA: Very good! To say that a conflict is serious is to make a value judgment about the situation. And people do disagree about this particular value judgment.

Let us pause to reconsider these three styles of answer. In each style the answer was not sufficient to guide an objective examination of the situation in New York State to justify or test Mr. Delta's claim that there has been a concerted effort to organize school districts so that they have the same boundaries as communities. In each case this difficulty exists because there is no objective way to identify communities. So if we want to conduct a scientific study, all three styles are defective.

Style A (Example 12-2) gives no guidance whatsoever. If concrete interpretation is available for the concept, *community*, it has not been presented. No way is given to tell whether something is a community, and no information is conveyed by the claim that a certain thing is a community. These two difficulties go together. Generally when there is no way to tell about a given claim, then there is no information conveyed when the claim is made, and *vice versa.**

Style B (Example 12-3), a less extreme approach, is more common. The clause referring to adjacency is probably satisfactory in this situation, because it can call to mind examples and nonexamples of adjacency. But the clause referring to noncommunal conflict needs concrete interpretation; this is not provided by the circular definition of 'noncommunal conflict', although one might be led to miss the difficulty by the imposing pair of definitions. Thus Style B is still useless until concrete interpretation is available for 'noncommunal conflict'.

Style C (Example 12-4), on the other hand, is not useless for all purposes, but it is useless for any objective study and prediction that requires identification of communities. In effect Style C incorporates the speaker's value judgment about the kinds of conflicts that he perceives. This is often interesting and important, but since such judgments vary from person to person, it cannot be the basis for such study and prediction.

The 'etc.' definition

Now look at Style D, which would provide concrete interpretation for many purposes:

Example 12-5

MR. DELTA: A community is characterized by its occupying one small geographical area and being made up of people, the majority of whom do their shopping, have their frequently seen friends, etc., in the area.

FRED: I think I get the idea.

Style D, although vague, enables us to make some rough decisions about whether an area is a community by examining the shopping habits and friendships of people. And concomitantly, the initial statement by Mr. Delta to the effect that there has been a concerted effort to organize school districts so that they have the same boundaries as communities becomes a meaningful statement. It communicates information.

The use of the term 'etc.' in the above example might bother some people. It enables us to get by without giving a full list of criteria. It is thus conducive to definitions that are even more vague than standard range definitions, which at least attempt to give a complete list of criteria, most of which hold in a given case. This 'etc.' interpretation of 'community' does not even claim to have given a full list. In effect a person who uses 'etc.' in clarifying the meaning of a term is saying: "These are some of the criteria. You get the idea,

* This generalization, by the way, is subject to qualifications that will be presented under the topic, testability, in Part III.

don't you?" Some degree of this open-endedness is inevitable in giving concrete interpretation; but the word 'etc.' is used only when one wants to indicate that the interpretation being given is particularly open-ended, and that there are other criteria which he could give on the spot, but chooses not to, because the given list seems good enough for the situation. This use of 'etc.' enabled Mr. Delta in Style D to give concrete interpretation for 'community' without committing himself and his audience to a more complete list, yet probably with enough clarification for the situation.

The 'etc.' definition may be regarded as a cross between the range definition and the more concrete forms. It makes use of the idea expressed by 'characterized by', and thus is like the range definition; but its use of 'etc.' makes possible the use of rather specific items. *Shopping habits* and *friendship patterns* are rather specific concepts. They are more concrete in this context than the concept, *community*. The use of 'etc.' avoids the commitment to have made complete coverage of the concept and thus enables such items to be fairly specific.

The meaning of 'concrete interpretation'

This is not to say that such interpretive items are as concrete as they can be. The most concrete kind of interpretation consists of examples and nonexamples, but since such concepts as *shopping habits* and *friendship patterns* in this context indicate what would be examples and nonexamples, they satisfy the need for concrete interpretation.

Perhaps you are wondering just what exactly is concrete interpretation. So far I have left your interpretation of the term, 'concrete interpretation', up to your prior understanding, because it is a basic, abstract term with which you are presumably fairly well acquainted. But I will say a bit about it before examining two standard approaches to concrete interpretation, examples and conditional definitions. In what follows note the **use** of concrete interpretation and a range definition to interpret this fairly abstract term, 'concrete interpretation'.

Concrete interpretation varies from one field to another. Colors, pushes, and distances, for example, are concrete interpretation in the physical sciences; and colors, roots, breathing, etc., in the biological sciences. In English we find such things as words, poems, authors, and emotions serving as concrete interpretation. The social sciences make use of decisions, battles, hunger, joy, bullets, and proclamations. In the vocational subjects, children, wheat, pistons, cloth, food, and money are the sorts of things that serve as concrete interpretation.

In mathematics in its early stages, marbles, table tops, chickens (to be counted), etc., serve as concrete interpretation. After one advances in the field, points, surfaces, numbers, and relationships can play this role. A point is abstract for the beginner in mathematics, but more concrete for the advanced person. What is true of mathematics is also true to some extent of other fields: That which is concrete interpretation depends on the level of sophistication of the treatment of the subject and thus is relative to the situation. This fact seems most pronounced in mathematics.

Roughly speaking CONCRETE INTERPRETATION is characterized by familiarity, incompleteness, specificity, physicalness, and relativity to the situation. Its availability for terms used in descriptive discourse is absolutely essential. Its actual presentation is sometimes time consuming, sometimes confusing because of its occasional complexity, and never a complete interpretation of an abstract term. You will note these traits in the coming discussion of two primary forms of concrete interpretation, examples and conditional definitions. And you noted these traits in the definition of 'community' presented earlier in Example 12-5 as Style D, the definition which was like a range definition but which made use of the word, 'etc.'. Furthermore, you can see some of them in the range definitions that were discussed in the previous chapter. This fact should suggest to you that the line between concrete interpretation forms and equivalence forms is not a sharp one. The difference is one of emphasis.

*Examples (and Nonexamples)**

The most common form of concrete interpretation of terms is the example. Less frequently used, but quite important, is the nonexample, the instructive case to which the term does not apply.

In an English class Miss Gamma might use the following quotations from Shakespeare to give an example and a nonexample of irony:

Example 12-6

MISS GAMMA: An example of irony is the use of the word 'noble' in this line of Antony's speech to the populace: "The noble Brutus has told you that Caesar was ambitious."

A nonexample would be Hamlet's use of the term, 'slings and arrows', in his phrase, "the slings and arrows of outrageous fortune".

These do not stand well alone, however, because it is not clear what aspects of the example and nonexample are important, so examples and nonexamples are often used in conjunction with an equivalence-type definition. The reasons for the fit of the example and the only partial fit of the nonexample are thereby out in the open. It is particularly helpful to **show the explicit con-**

* This sort of definition is sometimes called 'ostensive definition'. I do not see any need to introduce this new term, so am not doing so.

nection between the example and the equivalence definition, and to show the aspects of the nonexample that **do** fit and that do **not** fit the concept. In the following cases of showing the connection between the classification definition and the example and nonexample, assume that the previously given classification definition of 'irony' is before the class (IRONY is a mode of expression in which the implied attitude is opposed to that which is literally expressed.):

Example 12-7

MISS GAMMA: Marc Antony says 'the noble Brutus', but he actually means 'the ignoble Brutus'. Thus his literally expressed attitude of admiration is opposed to his implied attitude of disgust. In Hamlet's reference to "the slings and arrows" he also does not mean the terms literally. That is, he is not referring to any physical slings and arrows. But this is not an example of irony because there is no implied opposed attitude. The attitude is expressed openly in a straightforward manner.

The problem is more difficult when using a range definition in conjunction with examples and nonexamples, because usually no one single item is given by a range definition as a necessary condition, so it might seem hard to show why a nonexample is a nonexample. The problem is handled by referring to the definition as a whole.

Assume that the range definition of 'Romanticism' given in Chapter 11 is before the class. The problem might be handled as follows:

Example 12-8

MISS GAMMA: Wordsworth, Byron, Shelley, and Keats are clearly Romantics, for they fit all the characteristics in the definition. On the other hand, Pope, Addison, and Kipling are clearly not Romantics, since they are not characterized by too many of those items listed in the definition. They do not show particular concern for brotherhood, they demonstrate little sympathy for humble lives, and they emphasize form and constraint instead of freedom.

An example and nonexample would help to make even more concrete the interpretation of 'community' given in Example 12-5 as Style D ('etc.' definition). The dialogue might have proceeded as follows:

Example 12-9

MR. DELTA: For example the boundaries of the Ithaca City School District roughly bound a community, but the boundaries of Ulysses Township do not bound a community. Half of the people in Ulysses Township shop and have their frequently seen friends in the geographical area with Trumansburg as its center; for the other half, these things are located in the geographical area centering around the City of Ithaca.

FRED: Does that mean that Ulysses contains parts of two communities?

MR. DELTA: Yes, it does.

This dialogue illustrates the fact that there can be different degrees of concrete interpretation (the 'etc.' definition provided some; the examples are even more concrete), and it again illustrates the combination of the example approach with a different type of definition. If the example and nonexample alone had been used, one would wonder just what about the example and nonexample is significant.

Examples and nonexamples you will remember are also useful in finding out whether a student has mastered a term and in getting him to apply his knowledge and thus retain it. You can show or describe something, and ask him if the term applies, and then ask "Why?" The thing shown or described can be an example or a nonexample, although it is often a good idea to give both; and it can, if you desire, call for considerable discrimination. And you can request an example **and** a nonexample **from** the student. Again the question, "Why?", is appropriate.

You can undoubtedly see the great utility of examples and nonexamples in giving and checking for the meaning of terms. Perhaps you have wondered whether to call these things definitions. Some people do and some do not. As long as we remember that they are not the kind of definitions that give equivalences and two-way substitutability, I can see nothing wrong with calling them definitions. This approach is consistent with the broad notion of definition presented in Chapter 6. If you choose not to call these things definitions, and would rather characterize them as useful concrete interpretations, that will be all right too. For purposes of this book I stipulate them to be definitions.

The next form of definition, the conditional definition, comes closer to the strict notion of definition because of its rigor. Even though it too does not provide completeness (nor thus two-way substitutability), there is little reluctance to call it definition. But perhaps that is because some have thought that it does provide completeness.

∵Conditional Definition

The conditional definition gives concrete interpretation in a more rigorous form than examples and nonexamples, but again it does not provide completeness. These traits can be seen from an analysis of its standard form.*

The initial condition

A conditional definition commences with an if-clause which specifies

* A more extensive treatment of this topic appears in my paper, "Operational Definitions," *American Educational Research Journal*, Vol. I, no. 3 (1964), pp. 183–201. There you can find a bibliography and many of the reasons for what is presented here.

a condition under which the rest of the definition is to hold. This initial condition might simply be something that could be observed, or it might be something that is deliberately brought about by an investigator. In the latter case the devices used by the investigator should ordinarily be mentioned in the specification of the initial condition, which is called an operation. When a conditional definition's initial condition is an operation, the definition is an OPERATIONAL DEFINITION.

Here are some examples of if-clauses that can serve to specify initial conditions:

1. If a mercury thermometer is put in a substance, . . .
2. If the *California Test of Mental Maturity* is administered to a student under standard conditions, . . .
3. If Iceland orders the fishing vessels of Great Britain to leave the area within ten miles of Iceland's shores, . . .

The first two conditions indicate operations performable by an investigator, and thus can be parts of operational definitions. The third condition does not specify an operation performable by an investigator; hence it is not part of an operational definition—it is part of a nonoperational conditional definition.

That conditional definitions provide only partial interpretation can be seen in part from an examination of the meaning of the word 'if' in the if-clause. The use of this word to introduce the initial condition indicates that fulfillment of this condition is **sufficient** for the relationship given in the rest of the definition to hold. But it does not say that fulfillment of this condition is **necessary** for the relationship to hold. It leaves open the possibility that there might be other sufficient conditions for the relationship. This is one of the reasons for saying that conditional definitions provide only partial interpretation. Another reason depends on the analysis of the relationship that is given by the rest of the definition, the next topic.

The relationship between an observation and the term being defined

Given the initial condition, the conditional definition provides a relationship which in standard form holds between two parts, a part specifying an observation or type of observation, and a part containing the term to be defined. This relationship is such that the observation is a necessary condition, a sufficient condition, or a condition that is both necessary and sufficient. The following operational definition of 'temperature' makes use of the third type of relationship, necessity **and** sufficiency (shown by the use of the phrase, 'if and only if'):

Example 12–10

If a mercury thermometer is put in a substance, the thermometer will read x, if and only if, the TEMPERATURE of the substance is x.

In other words, given the fact that a mercury thermometer is put in a substance, a reading of x is necessary and sufficient for the temperature's being x. This definition ties the concept *temperature* down to a type of operation and consequent observation.

Thus a CONDITIONAL DEFINITION has four major parts, listed below and exemplified by the parts of the definition of 'temperature':

1. Initial condition in an if-clause: "If a mercury thermometer is put in a substance, . . ."
2. Phrase or clause indicating an observation or type of observation: ". . . the thermometer will read x, . . ."
3. Specification of the relationship: ". . . if and only if, . . ."
4. Phrase or clause containing the term being defined: ". . . the TEMPERATURE of the substance is x."

The phrase, 'if and only if', is significant for what it says and for what it does not say. It says: "necessary and sufficient"; it does not say: "means the same as", which would be the standard relationship in equivalent-expression definitions. Thus, no claim is made that the meaning has been completely covered, nor is the more limited claim made—that the meaning has been completely covered given the initial condition. (Whatever that limited claim might mean, it has not been made by this form using 'if and only if'.)

Other examples, showing variations

Here is another example of a conditional definition that uses the relationship, necessity and sufficiency:

Example 12–11

If the *California Test of Mental Maturity* is administered to a student under standard conditions; the student's score will be x, if and only if, his IQ is approximately x.

You should stop now and identify the four parts of this definition of 'IQ'.

In this next example the part indicating the observation is presented as a necessary condition, but not claimed to be a sufficient condition. The term being defined is 'sovereign':

Example 12–12

If Iceland orders the fishing vessels of Great Britain to leave the area within ten miles of Iceland's shores; Iceland is probably SOVEREIGN, only if Britain's vessels leave.

In this example the observation statement was put after the statement containing the term 'sovereign' in order to avoid the slight awkwardness of the following definition:

Example 12-13

If Iceland orders the fishing vessels of Great Britain to leave the area within ten miles of Iceland's shores; only if Britain's vessels leave is Iceland probably SOVEREIGN.

They are logically equivalent, however, and each is satisfactory.

The following example is of the same logical form as the previous example, but differs in its generality. It gives a more general formula for an application of the term 'sovereign', though still not very general—still a rather incomplete interpretation of the term.

Example 12-14

If a country orders the vessels of another country to leave the area within ten miles of the former's shores; then the former is probably SOVEREIGN, only if the vessels leave.

The reason for giving the observation in the preceding series of definitions of 'sovereign' as a necessary rather than sufficient condition and rather than a combination of the two is that under the condition specified, we would not want to take the departure as sufficient proof of the sovereignty of the ordering country. The lack of departure would ordinarily be sufficient disproof of sovereignty (making departure a necessary condition), but departure might well be the result of some other circumstance—bad weather, no fish, full load of fish, and so forth.

Qualifiers

Note that there is a qualification (the word 'probably') explicitly inserted in the definitions of 'sovereign',* so that we are not unalterably bound to deny the application of the word every time the initial condition is met and the necessary condition is not met. We should not be so bound because some extenuating circumstance might develop which would justify deviation from strict adherence to the necessity of departure. For example, some of the vessels might break down; or they might recognize the ordering country's sovereignty and apply for and be granted permission to remain. In each case an uncompromising commitment to the unqualified definition would require a judgment that the ordering country is not sovereign.

Similarly the definition of 'IQ' contained one, perhaps two loosening

* The general problem of the meaning and bearing of such qualifications on deductive reasoning was considered in Chapter 5.

qualifiers. The word 'approximately' releases us from the commitment to saying that the IQ is exactly equal to the score. We all know how scores vary from administration to administration. And the phrase 'under standard conditions' might also be a loosening qualifier depending on whether there is a set list of standard conditions. If not, then it is a loosening qualifier which allows us a way out in case the unforseen (unspecified) develops. If there is a set list, then probably some other loosening qualifier is needed to allow for unspecified extenuating circumstances.

The definition of the word 'temperature', you will notice, did not explicitly contain any loosening qualifiers. When it is quite unlikely that anything will go wrong, qualifiers are not explicitly inserted. This is the case for the term 'temperature' in the contexts in which I am accustomed to using the term. Every conditional definition, however, should be regarded as containing at least implicitly some loosening qualifiers. This is because something unforseen can always go wrong. In this case, for example, the substance might be hot enough to melt the thermometer, or it might be cold enough to freeze the mercury in the thermometer, or to carry the mercury off the scale. The bore might be uneven in one place making the thermometer inaccurate there. Or the context might be one requiring more precision than one can achieve with a mercury thermometer (in which case the word 'approximately' should be introduced).

Thus conditional definitions are not as rigorous as they might have first appeared. The introduction of the qualifiers made necessary by the open-endedness* of our empirical concepts reduces the rigor. It would be nice if things were otherwise, but we must accept a degree of vagueness and imprecision at some level when we are dealing with the empirical world.

The utility of conditional definitions

In the classroom, conditional definitions are useful in tying down abstract concepts as rigorously as possible. Furthermore, given a conditional definition, one can often reason deductively, as can be seen in some of the exercises in Chapters 3 and 4, exercises with which you are presumably already familiar.

Operational definitions are particularly useful in that they reveal the connection between the meaning of key abstract concepts and the operations (and instruments) we use in deciding whether and how to apply the concepts. The operational definition is a convenient device for showing students how dependent some of our concepts are upon our instruments and manipulations.

I have already used the terms 'temperature' and 'IQ' to exemplify this fact. 'Meaning', 'grammatical', 'social class', 'hardness', 'pressure altitude', and 'compression' (in a cylinder of an internal combustion engine) are other

* The open-endedness of empirical concepts is discussed in Frederich Waismann's "Verifiability" in Antony Flew, ed., *Essays in Logic and Language* (Oxford: Basil Blackwell, 1952), pp. 117–44.

examples of terms which are dependent upon operations for the interpretation to be accorded them.

The meaning of 'meaning', for example, depends on what sort of investigation is performed and on what counts as evidence in the investigation. The dispute about whether 'infer' means the same as 'imply' reveals different approaches to the term 'meaning', differences which can be most dramatically revealed by different programmatic operational definitions. Similarly, contemporary conflict about what is grammatical can be clearly presented through such definitions, because the methods of the investigator are so crucial.

Social scientists are always quick to point out that the meaning to be attributed to an occurrence of the term 'social class' depends heavily on the methods in use by the investigator who is making use of the term. This holds for the use of the term by any layman as well. His meaning is revealed by the way he would go about making judgments about social class position. To the extent that he is unclear about how he would do it, he is unclear about the meaning of 'social class'.

The meaning of the technical term 'hardness' is dependent upon an operation, the operation of rubbing one substance against another. 'Pressure altitude' is tied to the operation of setting an altimeter to 29.92″. Among automobile mechanics the term 'compression' is associated with the use of the compression gauge.

These examples show how in a wide variety of fields concepts frequently are dependent upon our instruments and manipulations. Naturally not all concepts are dependent in this way, but students should understand this dependence when it appears. It is an important feature of the logic of their subject matter.

The use of conditional definitions in the classroom has disadvantages also. Such definitions are often long, and they are difficult for a beginner to construct. Once he can construct them, however, he will have another tool in his kit for understanding and working with his subject at a higher level of sophistication. He will also have another means of expressing himself with greater clarity in his subject.

Some common misconceptions

In order to emphasize some key features of conditional definitions I shall present some definitions that for one reason or another are not successful. As you examine them, try to see why they fail as either operational definitions or as nonoperational conditional definitions.

Example 12-15

If Iceland orders the fishing vessels of Great Britain to leave the area within ten miles of Iceland's shores; Iceland is probably SOVEREIGN, only if Britain's vessels leave.

This definition of 'sovereignty', which appeared before as Example 12-12, fails as an operational definition because the first clause does not specify an operation performable by an investigator. The definition is formally satisfactory as a nonoperational conditional definition, however. Next, consider this proposed operational definition of 'mastery of the denial-of-the-consequent principle':

Example 12-16

If a student has studied logic; then if he has MASTERED THE DENIAL-OF-THE-CONSEQUENT PRINCIPLE, he understands that principle.

First of all this proposed definition cannot be an operational definition because the first clause does not specify an operation performable by an investigator. It is the student, not the investigator who does the studying. But the definition is not satisfactory as any kind of conditional definition, for the clause which is supposed to provide the observation statement does not do so. The clause, "he understands that principle", is not an observation-type statement. Hence, the desired concrete interpretation is not provided.

Another difficulty with Example 12-16 is that the rest of the definition does not depend on the fulfillment of the initial condition. Presumably mastery implies understanding whether a student has studied logic or not.

The next example is an attempt to improve upon the previous definition:

Example 12-17

If a student is asked to examine an argument embodying the denial-of-the-consequent principle; then if he has MASTERED THE PRINCIPLE, he will be able to answer significant questions about the argument.

Although the first clause does attempt to specify an operation performable by an investigator, it is not clear what the operation is. Suppose that you were working as an investigator and were asked to perform that operation. Just what would you do? The problem is that the particular argument is not specified. Hence the first clause is not satisfactory whether the definition is supposed to be operational or simply a nonoperational conditional definition. The specification of the initial condition is too vague.

Similarly, the observation condition is too vague. The observation statement must be more explicit than "he will be able to answer significant questions about the argument". The questions should be specified and a way of telling whether the person has answered these questions must be provided. Of course, there inevitably is some vagueness in any conditional definition, but the vagueness in Example 12-17 is excessive.

The following definition is a formally satisfactory operational definition of 'mastery of the denial-of-the-antecedent principle':

Example 12–18

If a student is given the *Cornell Conditional-Reasoning Test, Form X*, under standard conditions; then if he has MASTERED THE DENIAL-OF-THE-CONSEQUENT PRINCIPLE, he will give the keyed answer for at least four of these six items: 8, 16, 22, 29, 35, and 39.

Chapter Summary

In this chapter you have seen the need for the availability of concrete interpretation for terms of descriptive discourse, and you have examined several ways of supplying this interpretation.

The 'etc.' definition is a modified range definition, although it is ordinarily more concrete. Because it deliberately leaves more gaps in specifying the meaning of a term, those parts that **are** specified can be more concrete. But still the specification does not get as concrete as examples.

The example and nonexample approach is the ultimate in concrete interpretation. Its weaknesses are its cumbersomeness and its usual inability to stand alone. The latter problem is resolved by making use of other forms of definition in conjunction with the question, 'Why?'.

⁘Conditional definitions provided more rigorous concrete interpretation, although they are still incomplete. One form of the conditional definition, the operational definition, is particularly valuable for its ability to expose the connection between abstract concepts and the way we go about deciding how and when to apply them. The conditional definition consists of four parts:

1. An if-clause containing the initial condition.
2. An observation phrase or clause.
3. A relationship between parts two and four (necessity, sufficiency, or both).
4. A phrase or clause containing the term to be defined.

COMPREHENSION SELF-TEST

True or False? If the statement is false, change a crucial term (or terms) to make it true.

12–1. Every definition must include concrete interpretation.

12–2. The meaning of a term used in descriptive discourse is lacking to the extent that methods for judging how it applies do not exist.

12–3. The 'etc.' definition is more like a classification definition than any other form you have studied.

12–4. Example-nonexample definitions need complementation by equivalence forms, if full meaning is to be conveyed.

∴**12–5.** The conditional definition ordinarily commences with a statement of a relationship between an observation and an operation.

∴**12–6.** Operational definitions are useful for terms which describe operations.

Questions.

∴**12–7.** List the four parts of a conditional definition in standard order.

∴**12–8.** Using the operational definition of 'IQ' given in this chapter (Example 12–11), exemplify each of the four parts of a conditional definition in standard order.

12–9. What is a weakness of an 'etc.' definition?

Discussion Questions.

∴**12–10.** Making use of the hints given in this chapter, prepare operational definitions of two of the following terms (if they are stipulated definitions, make them at least reasonable):

a. Meaning
b. Grammatical
c. Social class
d. Pressure altitude
e. Compression

12–11. Select a term from your field which is amenable to conditional definition. Give three definitions of this term: an 'etc.' definition, an example definition, and (∴) a conditional definition. If your field is mathematics, select a term in applied mathematics.

∴**12–12.** Read one or more selections on operationism in Chapter 2, "The Present State of Operationism," in Philipp G. Frank, ed., *The Validation of Scientific Theories* (New York: Collier Books, 1961) (first edition in 1954), pp. 45–92. Prepare a two-page critique of one or more selections.

∴**12–13.** Read the article, "Operational Definitions," *American Educational Research Journal*, Vol. I, no. 3(1964), pp. 183–201. Select a thesis with which you agree or disagree and justify your stand in a four-page paper.

CHAPTER 13

Definition: An Overview

Although definitions are important in classrooms in many different ways, and although one example cannot illustrate all of these, you will find the following dialogue of help in looking broadly at the classroom use of definitions. As you read the dialogue, think about what you would do if you were Mr. Beta, the ninth-grade science teacher.

Example 13-1

MR. BETA: To start out today we have a report and demonstration by Phil P., who is going to show us how baking soda works in the rising of dough.

PHIL: (in front of class) I have here some equipment which I will use to show you the action of baking soda in the rising of dough. Baking soda is only one ingredient in baking powder, so my demonstration is oversimplified, but it's interesting anyway. (seeing Nancy's hand) You have a question already, Nancy?

NANCY: Yes. Well, not a question. But anyway you're not talking about dough if you use baking soda to make it rise. In home ec. we learned that yeast is used in dough, not baking soda, baking powder, or any other artificial agent.

PHIL: But Mr. Beta suggested that I show you the action of baking soda in the rising of **dough**. See, I have it right here in my notes. Besides I don't care what you learned in home ec. My Mom uses baking powder when she makes dough. Just yesterday she made some dough for my sister's birthday cake. And I know she used baking powder. She certainly did not use yeast.

NANCY: Then it wasn't dough. It was batter.

PHIL: My Mom said it was dough. She never called it batter.

NANCY: Then your Mom is wrong. Mrs. Epsilon taught us what dough is. And she has a degree in home economics. Does your Mom have a degree in home economics?

PHIL: No, but Mr. Beta has a degree in chemistry. He ought to know. And he said "dough". (seeing Fred's hand) Fred?

FRED: In my folks' store we sell some ready-made biscuits. On the label it says, "The dough used to make these biscuits contained no artificial preservative." On the label also is a list of ingredients. One of them is baking soda. I suppose that Nancy thinks the bakers don't know what they're doing either.

EVELYN: (interrupting) You boys, you think you're so smart. This time you're wrong. "DOUGH is a moist mixture of flour and other ingredients, including yeast." That's a direct quote from my home ec. book.

The discussion from which this dialogue was reconstructed continued, but no additional reasons were provided—only restatements, insults, and misunderstandings. What would you have done if you had been Mr. Beta?

Is another definition needed? If so, what function? (Stipulation? Report? Program embodiment?) What form? (Synonym? Classification? Equivalent expression? Range? Example and nonexample? (⁘) Conditional?) What should be Mr. Beta's stance toward the definition quoted from the home ec. text? Assume that Mr. Beta was previously ignorant of the accepted usage of the term 'dough' in home economics and decide on appropriate action.

The very framing of this range of questions makes more explicit a fact that has been implicit in the discussions of function and form of definition: the fact that every definition in a context has both a form and function. It has a form—that is, a logical arrangement of its parts—and the person putting it forward assumes a certain stance—that is, he used the words (and actions, if any) in the definition to perform a function in the context. Actually the qualifications of the person offering the definition are a third variable. If Mr. Beta offers it, he can perform certain functions in virtue of his position of authority, which the students cannot perform, but some of them can perform a function which he cannot perform: to report the meaning of this term, 'dough', as used in home economics. He is operating as an expert in chemistry. Since he was unaware of usage in home economics, he was in no position to report that usage.

Function

First consider the three major functions that definitions perform: stipulating, reporting, and embodying a program. In this context a programmatic definition would not be relevant, for no program is at stake. No particular way of making bread or cake would be advanced or hindered by acceptance of either of the competing notions of dough. So we can rule out a programmatic definition.

Would a reported definition be of use here? To some extent it might be of use, but the major goal in this context is to get on with demonstrating how baking soda works, no matter what we call the stuff in which it works. It is presumably not one of Mr. Beta's goals to teach a (or the) meaning of 'dough'. Hence there is no immediate contextual requirement for an accurate report of usage. So a meaning should be stipulated for the term. Here are some ways it could be done:

Example 13-2

MR. BETA: Since Evelyn remembers the definition of her home ec. book, let us accept that definition and change Phil's topic to "The Action of Baking Soda in the Rising of Batter". Go ahead with your demonstration, Phil.

Mr. Beta has stipulated the use of the term 'dough' in accord with Evelyn's reported definition. Alternatively he could have stipulated Phil's notion of dough:

Example 13-3

MR. BETA: For our purposes it doesn't matter what we call the stuff in which baking soda functions. The important thing is to understand what happens. Since Phil is making the presentation, let us respect his choice of meaning for 'dough'. After all, the dictionary defines 'DOUGH' in the following way: (reads) "Paste, esp. for bread, thick enough to knead or roll." Let's get on with the demonstration.

Mr. Beta suggested deference to the speaker's choice of definition, especially since he did not find it at variance with what he took to be ordinary usage. Another plausible move would have been to ask Phil to handle the problem (if Phil is sophisticated enough):

Example 13-4

MR. BETA: How would you like to handle this, Phil?

PHIL: Actually I don't think that it matters very much. What I want to show is the action of baking soda. Just to make the girls happy I won't use their word 'dough'. Instead I'll invent a word which is pronounced the same, 'dowe'. By 'DOWE' I shall mean a pasty mixture generally containing mostly flour, a leavening agent, some moisture, and often one or more of the following: eggs, vanilla, sugar, shortening, and milk. Now I shall try to show how the leavening agent, baking soda, produces its effect in dowe.

Mr. Beta's confidence in Phil was fairly well justified. Phil handled it as a situation requiring stipulation, let the girls have the word 'dough' to define as they pleased, and invented a new word to which he attached the meaning he had previously attached to 'dough'. He was being a bit high-handed in picking a word that is pronounced the same way, and thus inviting ambiguity, but in this case his move was probably innocuous, because it held only for this situation, a situation in which it did not really matter very much what definition was attached to 'dough'.

In all three of these possible ways of handling the difficulty, you should note that even though stipulation was the main move, respect was paid to reports of usage. In the first example, Example 13-2, Mr. Beta stipulated Evelyn's reported definition; a reason might be that he thought that doing so would produce less confusion among those working in the field where 'dough' is a technical term, home economics; another (though not a logically relevant reason) might be that he wanted to maintain good relations with his colleague Mrs. Epsilon; a third might be that he felt that the people in home economics have worked out a consistent and useful set of distinctions, which are marked by their technical definitions of their terms, and thus that the rest of us should adopt such terminology when feasible in order to avoid ambiguity.

In the second example, Example 13-3, Mr. Beta stipulated the adoption of what he took to be Phil's usage and cited the report in the dictionary to show that he would not be doing a grave injustice to the word. Hence two reports backed up that stipulation: the report of the usage of the person making the presentation (to whom some deference is owed) and the report in the dictionary.

In the third example, Example 13-4, Phil paid his respects to the usage reported by Nancy and Evelyn, and then went on to stipulate for his new word the definition that he would previously have reported for 'dough'. Again two reports are in the background of the decision to make the stipulation.

Although the major move to be made in this situation was the stipulative move, in a home economics class the major move might have been a report of the standard usage of home economists. Suppose that the class is composed of people who want to learn home economics: they want to learn the facts, principles, and terminology of home economics. Then a true report of the usage in home economics would have sufficed. In a situation where this desire for learning the field does not exist, then a pure report would not have sufficed. It would need to have been accompanied by an implicit or explicit invitation (or order) to use the word in accord with the report.

Form

The forms of definition appearing in the original dialogue and the examples were classification, range, and a cross between the two. Evelyn's report was in classification form; Phil's stipulation was essentially in range form; and the dictionary entry (a report) was a combination of the two. These forms are all fairly appropriate, given the context, in which the question was whether the presence of yeast is a necessary condition for something's being dough. Evelyn's classification definition form made the presence of yeast a necessary condition, and the other two definitions did not do so.

Evelyn's use of the classification form has its drawbacks, since this form implies precision, and 'dough' is not a precise term. The result is a definition that does not convey what is probably the home economist's intent, for it places no limits on what the other ingredients are, not even suggesting what sort of ingredients they are. Furthermore it gives no indication of the proportions involved. (Would a mixture containing 1 per cent flour, 1 per cent yeast, 10 per cent ethylene glycol (antifreeze), and 88 per cent sodium chloride (table salt) be dough?) But to have given an indication of other ingredients and the proportions involved in classification form would have resulted in overprecision, because there is no definite list of other ingredients and there is no definite proportion, nor is there a definite range of proportions of flour to other ingredients. On the other hand, the classification form is simple. In this context complexity was not needed. There was, thus, no need for a conditional definition. And there was no need for an equivalent-expression definition, because dough is a simple noun for which it is fairly easy to find an appropriate class. A synonym definition would probably not have been an accurate report and would have made it at least very difficult to specify the presence of yeast as a necessary condition.

Phil's use of the range form (Example 13-4) was quite appropriate to his purposes. He wanted to define 'dowe' just the way he would have defined 'dough', had he not given away that word. Since *dough* is a range concept for Phil (and probably for the girls as well), he needed a range definition in order to avoid boundaries that are too sharp, boundaries that would warp the concept. The added complexity of the range definition was then justified by his purpose: to stipulate an accurate report of his own usage. If he had not wanted to get the better of Evelyn and Nancy, a much simpler (and less accurate) definition would have sufficed.

In Examples 13-2 and 13-3 Mr. Beta, not seeking to put anyone down, but simply seeking to further the learning of science, picked what is probably the two wiser courses. In each case he used the classification form and tried to pass over the question as quickly as possible, in one case endorsing Evelyn's classification definition, and in the other citing with endorsement the simple form used by the dictionary, which is almost classification form. (The phrase, "esp. for bread", is what moves it away from pure classification definition in the direction of a range form. But there was no point in omitting that phrase, since he might well then have been asked whether he left anything out. Not having done so, he could just say 'No'.)

If one of Mr. Beta's goals was to teach his students some sophistication about definitions, then this episode could have been an appropriate place to begin, depending on how much time Phil's demonstration was going to take. But assuming that the goal was to impart some understanding of baking soda and other carbonate compounds and perhaps also to develop Phil's confidence in himself, a quick stipulation on Mr. Beta's part, probably in classification form, is most appropriate in this context.

Thus the appropriate move with respect to form and function depends not only on the concept under consideration, but also on such contextual features as purpose, level of sophistication of students, and the qualifications of the person offering the definition.

COMPREHENSION SELF-TEST

For each space in the following grid find a definition from a text or situation in your field. Write down the definition, and explain why the definition is of the function that you claim it to be. If you cannot find a definition to correspond to a space, explain why you had such difficulty, making reference to the nature of your field.

	A. Stipulated	B. Reported	C. Programmatic
13–1. Synonym			
13–2. Classification			
13–3. Equivalent expression			
13–4. Range			
⁘ **13–5.** Operational			
⁘ **13–6.** Nonoperational conditional			
13–7. Example and/or nonexample			

Suggested Further Reading on the Topic, Definition

Introductory

Black, Max. *Critical Thinking*, 2nd ed. Englewood Cliffs, N. J.: Prentice-Hall, Inc. 1952, chap. xi, "Definition".

An introductory treatment which considers the classification form of definition, occasions for definition, and the problem of communicating word meanings.

———. *Problems of Analysis*. Ithaca, New York: Cornell University Press, 1954, chap. i, "The Definition of Scientific Method".

Black introduces and justifies the range form of definition.

Bridgman, Percy W. *The Logic of Modern Physics*. New York: The Macmillan Co., 1927.

This is the first naïve statement of Bridgman's views about operational definitions, views which have been quite influential in the social sciences.

Cohen, Morris R. and Ernest Nagel. *An Introduction to Logic and Scientific Method*. New York: Harcourt, Brace and Company, 1934, chap. XII, "Classification and Definition".

An introductory treatment of classification definition.

Hospers, John. *An Introduction to Philosophical Analysis*. Englewood Cliffs, N. J.: Prentice-Hall, Inc. 1953, Part I, "Words and the World".

A general introductory treatment of problems of definition.

Robinson, Richard. *Definition*. Oxford: Oxford University Press, 1954.

Robinson deals with the dispute between those who profess to define things and those who profess to define words, and he describes various purposes and methods of definition. This is written for the general reader.

Scheffler, Israel. *The Language of Education*. Springfield, Illinois: Charles C Thomas, Publisher, 1960, chap. I, "Definitions in Education".

Scheffler treats the three basic functions of definition discussed in *Logic in Teaching*, stipulative, reported (which he calls "descriptive"), and programmatic, and considers possibility of overlap in function.

Stevenson, Charles L. *Ethics and Language*. New Haven: Yale University Press, 1944, chap. IX.

Stevenson's discussion of persuasive definition has been influential and popular.

More advanced

Benjamin, A. Cornelius. *Operationism*. Springfield, Illinois: Charles C Thomas, Publisher, 1955.

Benjamin surveys the literature on operational definitions up through about 1955, paying particular attention to the development of the views of Percy Bridgman.

Caton, Charles E., ed. *Philosophy and Ordinary Language.* Urbana, Illinois: University of Illinois Press, 1963.

A collection of selected articles by J. L. Austin, Gilbert Ryle, P. F. Strawson, J. O. Urmson, Leonard Linsky, and others, dealing with problems related to definition and meaning.

Cronbach, Lee and Paul E. Meehl. "Construct Validity in Psychological Tests," *Psychological Bulletin,* Vol. LII, no. 4 (1955), pp. 281–302.

Cronbach and Meehl, who are practicing psychologists, present an imaginative view of concept development and justification of tests for the application and use of the concept.

Ennis, Robert H. "Operational Definitions," *American Educational Research Journal,* Vol. I, no. 3 (1964), pp. 183–201.

Here I develop and defend the view about operational definitions which is presented in *Logic in Teaching.*

Hempel, Carl G. *Fundamentals of Concept Formation in Empirical Science.* Chicago: University of Chicago Press, 1952.

The title is self-explanatory. A careful treatment of the problem.

Moore, G. E. *Principia Ethica.* Cambridge: At The University Press, 1954 (first edition, 1903), pp. 1–21.

In this well-known selection Moore suggests that it is fallacious to define 'good' using nonevaluative terms. To do so is to commit what he calls "the naturalistic fallacy".

Quine, Willard Van Orman. *From a Logical Point of View.* Cambridge, Massachusetts: Harvard University Press, 1961.

In this book and the next Quine proposes and defends significantly different positions from those assumed in *Logic in Teaching,* questioning such notions as synonymity and translatability.

———. *Word and Object.* Cambridge, Massachusetts: The M.I.T. Press, 1960.

Waismann, F. "Verifiability." In Antony Flew, ed., *Logic and Language.* Oxford: Basil Blackwell, 1952.

Waismann contends that all empirical concepts are in a way "open-textured" and thus are not susceptible to precise definition using lower order terms.

Part Three

EXPLANATION

CHAPTER 14

Basic Kinds of Explanation

Part II of this book, "Definition", dealt with one kind of explanation. Construed broadly, as it was in Part II, the word 'DEFINITION' means the explanation of the meaning of terms. We may call this INTERPRETIVE EXPLANATION, because the explanation interprets or clarifies.

Part III is concerned primarily with a second kind of explanation, REASON-GIVING EXPLANATION, so called because this process of explanation involves the giving of reasons. As you will see, the existence of a variety of types of reasons results in a variety of types of reason-giving explanations. But more about this later. First let us examine a third kind of explanation and then see how to distinguish among the three.

Descriptive Explanation

This third category of explanation should be noted partly in order to avoid confusing it with that of reason-giving explanation, but also in order to make a few general suggestions. It may be called descriptive explanation. A DESCRIPTIVE EXPLANATION does not interpret the meaning of a term; it does not give reasons; instead it describes a process or a structure. Here are some examples of explanations, which when presented, would be descriptive explanations:

Explaining how a bill becomes a law (which involves stating the steps in the process).
Explaining how sulphuric acid is made (which involves stating the steps in the process of making sulphuric acid).
Explaining the structure of the United Nations (which involves giving the parts of the organization and their relationships).
Explaining how to diagram a sentence (which involves listing the steps and stating the criteria to use to make the appropriate decisions).
Explaining how to do short division (which involves listing the steps and specifying the criteria for making the decisions).
Explaining the structure of a Shakespearian sonnet (which involves stating the number of lines and giving the rhyme scheme).
Explaining how to make meatloaf (which involves specifying the steps, listing criteria for decisions, and describing things to guard against).
Explaining the nature of a sentence used in class reasoning (which involves showing the parts and their relationship).
Explaining how to bisect an angle (which again simply calls for listing—and perhaps demonstrating—the steps to take).
Explaining the functioning of the carburetor (calling for a description of what the carburetor does under the variety of conditions under which it operates).*

A distinguishing feature about all of the above explanations is that they do not require the giving of reasons. They simply require stating facts, listing steps, supplying purposes, giving relationships, specifying criteria, etc.

Of course, the three kinds of explanation can be combined in one explanation sequence. When **explaining how** a bill becomes a law, one might well give **reasons why** certain steps, rather than others, take place, and one might well **explain the meaning** of some of the terms involved. But each of the three kinds, considered separately, raises different problems, so they are treated as distinct in this book.

Many of the problems of descriptive explanation are unique to the particular thing being explained, so we cannot discuss them here. But there are a few general (though vague) pieces of advice that can be given, which are to some extent organized common sense:

1. The thing to be explained should be broken up into parts by the explainer, parts which can be made clear in and of themselves.

* This explanation, although the word 'functioning' is used here, is not what is ordinarily called a functional explanation (for example, explaining the function of the heart). Functional explanations appear to make reference, either implicitly or explicitly, to purpose. They are not discussed in this book, because at the time of writing, I can find no full satisfactory account of such explanations. Professor John Canfield has in conversation given me an account that sounds very good in its outline form, but I prefer not to include it until the details are available. He has sketched out this account in his *Purpose in Nature* (Englewood Cliffs, N.J.: Prentice-Hall, Inc., 1966), pp. 6–7.

2. The type of relationship between the parts should be settled upon by the explainer.
3. The parts should be presented in a carefully chosen order, which depends greatly upon their relationship to each other. In the explanation of processes, this would ordinarily be chronological. In the explanation of some structures a choice must be made between presenting the parts in order of increasing generality and decreasing generality. In explaining the structure of the United Nations, for example, one must decide between starting at the top and starting at the bottom. Combinations of these strategies can be used too, but without an explicit statement of the fitting together of the relationships there is a danger of confusion.
4. Models can be used to provide clarity by use of analogous things which presumably are already clear. Diagrams composed of boxes and lines are frequently of help. The structure of the United Nations can be represented by such a model, boxes being used to represent the various units of the United Nations and lines connecting the boxes to show lines of authority. The process of making sulphuric acid can be represented by boxes, one for each step in the process, and lines to show the flow from one step to the next. In the chapter in this book dealing with class reasoning, class relationships were descriptively explained by means of circles, which are models for classes. The letters, '*abab—cdcd—efef—gg*', give a model for the rhyme pattern of the Shakespearian sonnet.
5. Every model has its dangers, since it is analogous, not identical, to the thing being explained. The explainer should be aware of the places where the analogy does not hold and should point out those that are not obvious. For the Euler circle system, for example, the relative size of the circles does not indicate anything about the number of things that are, or could be, members of the class. Similarly the size of the boxes in a structural diagram of the United Nations does not ordinarily show the size of the parts of the United Nations.

Cues

You should now be fairly clear about the differences among the three major kinds of explanations. But this alone is not enough. You must also become adept at requesting explanations unambiguously, and at ascertaining the meaning of others' requests for explanations. Although you might be clear about what you want, your students will not be clear unless your requests are. Of course you might not always be clear about what you want, in which case what follows should have the doubly helpful effect of forcing you to be clear about what you want and helping you to make this intent clear to your students.

Here is an unclear request:

Explain the Civil War.

It could be interpreted as a request for a descriptive explanation or for a reason-giving explanation. That is, it could be a request for an account of the major events of the Civil War, or it could be a request for the reasons for the Civil War. A teacher who asks a question like that is inviting the student to tell all he knows about the Civil War, but at the same time he is hinting that there is some particular unspecified aspect which he wants explained, thus leaving the student in a quandary.

Here is another unclear request:

> Explain the thunderstorm.

This could be interpreted as a request for a description of the parts of a thunderstorm and their relationships, or it could be a request for the causes that bring a thunderstorm into being, or perhaps it is a request for something else.

A possibility in each of these examples is that what is requested in each case is both kinds of explanation. If that is what a teacher wants, then he is less likely to puzzle his students if he asks specifically for each.

How does one ask for the different types of explanations? There is no exact pattern, but there are general guides. If a person keeps in mind just what it is that he seeks, the way of phrasing the request tends to come out correctly, but the following suggestions and comments about explanation cues can be of help.

Interpretive explanation

A clear way to indicate that an interpretive explanation is sought is to make explicit reference to meaning, as in "Please explain the meaning of 'sovereignty'". In this case the word 'meaning' provides the cue to the type of explanation desired.

Another way to show that such an explanation is wanted is to put the thing to be explained in quotes. This works only if the audience understands the use of quotes to show that you are referring to a word rather than using it. Accompanying this use of quotes, it is convenient to use a colon preceding the thing to be explained:

> Explain: 'sovereignty'.

Naturally one can so phrase this kind of request without using the word 'explain' at all. One can simply ask for a definition, or one can ask for the meaning of the word:

> Please define 'sovereignty'.
> What is the meaning of the word 'sovereignty'?

Descriptive explanation

The most common locution for expressing a request for a descriptive explanation is 'Explain how . . .'. This is particularly appropriate for explanations of processes but can be used for structure explanations as well. For example, "Explain how sulphuric acid is made", "Explain how to do contour plowing", and "Explain how the United Nations is organized" make use of this locution.

Its use, however, is not an infallible cue for a descriptive explanation. It can also be used to request a reason-giving explanation when certain other words are used as well. For example, the request, "Explain how it is possible that electricity can leap across this three-inch gap", seeks a reason, as does the request, "Explain how you know that the derivative of the sine of an angle is the cosine of the angle." Explanations of possibility and of alleged knowledge provide reasons and can be sought by the use of the phrase, 'Explain how . . .' with certain additions.

Another clear way to request process or structure explanations is to mention the terms, 'process' or 'structure' in the request, without making use of the word 'explain', as in the following examples:

Describe the process of making sulphuric acid.
Describe the structure of the United Nations.

Reason-giving explanation

The most common cue to a reason-giving explanation is the word, 'why'. Not only is it the most common cue, but is is also a very dependable one. Here are some examples of the use of this universal caller-forth of reasons:

Explain why angle *AEF* is equal to angle *EFD*.
Explain why the fuse blew.
Explain why 'compelled' is spelled with two 'l's.
Explain why Germany was indifferent to our entrance into World War I.
Explain why Ingrid's dough rose rapidly.
Explain why these burlap bags should be treated with methyl bromide.

The word 'why' can function without the use of the word 'explain' in requesting reason-giving explanations, as in the following examples. You can see that the requests are essentially the same as the corresponding ones above:

Why is angle *AEF* equal to angle *EFD*?
Why did the fuse blow?
etc.

Reason-giving explanations can be requested in other ways, as you can see from the following examples:

How do you know that angle *AEF* is equal to angle *EFD*?
What accounts for the blowing of the fuse?

What is the reason for spelling 'compelled' with two 'l's?
How is it that Germany was indifferent to our entry into World War I?
What caused Ingrid's dough to rise rapidly?

Thus there are these other cues to signify reason-giving explanation: 'How do you know . . .?', 'account for', 'reason for', 'How is it that . . .?', and 'cause'. These cues of course are not identical in meaning; they tend to call for different types of reason-giving explanations, but at least they all call for reasons of some sort, which is our interest at the moment. In future chapters you will see the importance of the differences among these cues.

You should now have a feeling for the differences among the three major kinds of explanation and in context should be able to state and recognize unambiguous requests for each. Presumably you are also sensitive enough to vague or ambiguous requests to seek clarification when they appear. Such clarification can be achieved by simply stating one interpretation of the request and asking if that is what is intended.

COMPREHENSION SELF-TEST

True or False? If the statement is false, change a crucial term (or terms) to make it true.

14-1. The three different kinds of explanation, interpretive, reason-giving, and descriptive, should not be mixed in a given teaching sequence.

14-2. The main point of a descriptive explanation is to give the meaning of a term or other linguistic expression.

14-3. Models used in descriptive explanations can never catch all aspects of the thing being explained.

14-4. 'Explain why' is more dependable as a cue to reason-giving explanation than is 'Explain how' as a cue to descriptive explanation.

14-5. It is usually not possible to phrase a request for an explanation without the use of 'explain' or 'explanation'.

14-6. The following is clearly a request for a descriptive explanation: "Explain how to treat burlap bags to eliminate the presence of golden nematode."

14-7. The following is clearly a request for an interpretive explanation: "Explain the Marbury *v.* Madison decision of the United States Supreme Court."

Practice: Formulate explanation requests which will call for the specific type of explanation of the thing listed.

14-8. A reason-giving explanation of the structure of the United Nations.

14-9. An interpretive explanation of 'inverse variation'.

14-10. A descriptive explanation of the organization of the material in a dictionary.

14-11. A reason-giving explanation of the organization of the material in a dictionary.

14–12. A request that clearly combines the requests in 14–10 and 14–11.
14–13. An interpretive explanation of the term 'weed'.
14–14. A reason-giving explanation of the power-stroke movement of the piston in a Diesel engine.
14–15. A descriptive explanation of the proper threading of a needle.
14–16. An interpretive explanation of the concept, *cubism.*

Basic Features of a Reason-Giving Explanation

We now turn to the main topic of Part III, reason-giving explanation. In the remainder of this chapter you will see the two basic aspects of appraising such an explanation. The other chapters in Part III are devoted to an elaboration of these two aspects. From now on in this book, **please understand the word 'explanation' to indicate reason-giving explanation,** unless otherwise specified.

Completing explanations

An explanation has two parts, the EXPLICANDUM (the thing to be explained) and the EXPLICANS (the material actually offered in explanation). In the following short explanation episode, the equality of angles *AEF* and *EFD* is the explicandum, while the fact that they are alternate interior angles of parallel line segments is the explicans:

Example 14-1
MRS. ALPHA: Why is angle *AEF* equal to angle *EFD*?
JANE: Because they are alternate interior angles of parallel line segments.

By way of interpretive explanation for those who have forgotten their geometry, ALTERNATE INTERIOR ANGLES are those angles, occurring in pairs, which are formed on opposite sides of a line (in this case line segment *GH*) intersecting a pair of parallel lines, which angles share a common side (in this

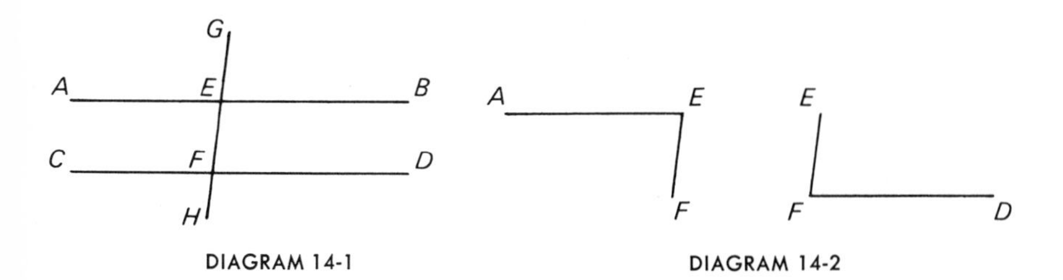

DIAGRAM 14-1

DIAGRAM 14-2

case line segment *EF*), and which have for their other sides parts of different parallel lines (in this case *AE* and *FD*). Angles *AEF* and *EFD* are drawn separately in Diagram 14-2 as if they were lifted out of Diagram 14-1.

One thing that is not explicitly included in the above explanation episode is a statement of the connection between being alternate interior angles of parallel lines and being equal. This gap may be focused on by the teacher, Mrs. Alpha, by some such request as the following:

MRS. ALPHA: And what does that have to do with it?

or

MRS. ALPHA: Tell me how that explains their equality?

or simply

MRS. ALPHA: So?

These alternate requests possess varying degrees of intimidating force, which can of course be much altered by the tone of voice and the atmosphere, but they all do call for the making of an explicit connection between the explicans and the explicandum.

The most likely connector in this case is the theorem, "Alternate interior angles of parallel line segments are equal." Henceforth we shall call such connectors GAP-FILLERS.

If Jane had explicitly stated the principle in addition to the answer she gave, then the explanation would have been complete and there would have been no gap to fill. To have a COMPLETE EXPLANATION as the term 'complete' is here used, is to have sufficient material to make what is essentially a deductively valid argument yielding the explicandum as the conclusion.

Here is a reordering of the material in the complete explanation in order to show the deductively valid argument:

Example 14-2

Premises:

They (angles *AEF* and *EFD*) are alternate interior angles of parallel line segments (Jane's explicans).

Alternate interior angles of parallel line segments are equal (gap-filler).

Conclusion:

Angles *AEF* and *EFD* are equal (explicandum).

An Euler diagram shows this to be a valid argument (Diagram 14-3).

An incomplete explanation, then, is one in which the explanatory material does not by itself logically imply the explicandum. Explanations can be completed by adding material which together with the explicans does imply the explicandum.

Please be clear that 'complete' is here a technical term. To say that an explanation is incomplete is not to say that it is defective. It is merely to say that the connection between the explicans and the explicandum has not yet been made explicit. And to say that an explanation is complete is not to praise it. Some complete explanations are very bad explanations.

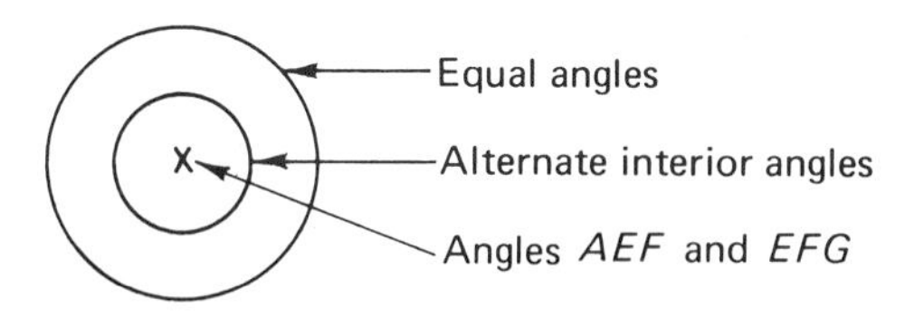

DIAGRAM 14-3

The point of completing explanations is to get the whole structure out in front of us for evaluation. A person who offers an explanation which is incomplete is generally obliged to defend not only the explicans, but also his answer to the question, "And what does that have to do with it?" The gap-filler is the answer to that question. If the gap-filler (or the explicans) is false or otherwise defective, then he has not offered a good explanation. Consider the following episode:

Example 14-3
MRS. ALPHA: Why is angle *AEF* equal to angle *EFD*?
JACK: Because they have a common side.
MRS. ALPHA: And what does that have to do with it?
JACK: Angles with a common side are equal.

We now have a complete explanation. The explicans plus the gap-filler imply the explicandum. The Euler diagram is shown in Diagram 14-4. In this case the gap-filler is false. It is not true that all angles having a common side are equal. The defect in the explanation lies not in the explicans—for that is true. The defect lies in the gap-filler, that is, in the relationship that Jack alleges to hold between having common sides and being equal. We want to bring the gap-filler out in the open so that it can be considered and judged.

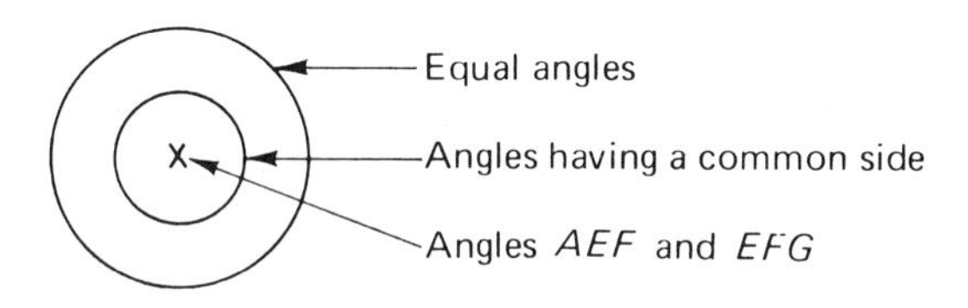

DIAGRAM 14-4

Applying evaluation criteria

The second basic aspect of appraising reason-giving explanations is the application of the appropriate criteria for evaluating them. Not all of the following criteria apply to every explanation, but the first four generally hold: (1) truth, (2) proper level of sophistication, (3) noncircularity, (4) proper function and type, and (5) testability/applicability.

The first three criteria are the easiest to grasp. The fourth criterion (proper function and type) is also fairly easy to grasp, but the distinctions among functions and types of explanations must be made with care, for the distinctions are sometimes hard to draw. In addition different criteria apply to different types. The fifth criterion is fairly subtle and difficult to apply, but crucial in some situations.

Discussion of these criteria is lengthy and is reserved for Chapters 16, 17, and 18. In the following chapter the process of inferring gap-fillers is examined.

COMPREHENSION SELF-TEST

True or False? If the statement is false, change a crucial term (or terms) to make it true.

14–17. The EXPLICANS is the material explicitly offered as explanatory.

14–18. The EXPLICANDUM is the thing to be explained.

14–19. A COMPLETE EXPLANATION, in the sense in which 'complete' is used here, is one in which the explicandum follows from the explicans, perhaps together with an explicit gap-filler.

Exercises. For each of the following explanation episodes, add a gap-filler that will make the explanation complete. In each case show by means of symbols or circles why the argument from explanatory material to explicandum is a valid argument. Label your diagrams and give a key for your symbols. The first one is done as an example.

14–20. MRS. EPSILON: Why did Ingrid's dough rise rapidly?
JOAN: Because Ingrid's dough contained yeast mixed with lukewarm water.

Proposed gap-filler: Dough containing yeast mixed with lukewarm water rises rapidly.

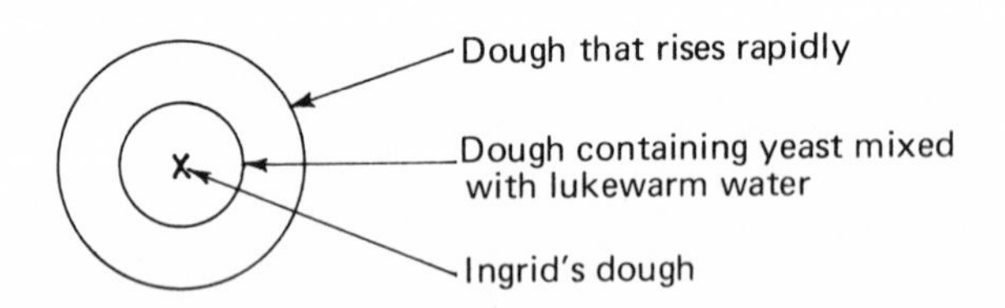

14–21. MR. ZETA: Why is the wheat in my northeast field a weed?
DICK: Because there it is unwanted.

14–22. MR. DELTA: Why won't the Senate stand by the President in his efforts to get the tax legislation passed?
JOHN: Because he is going to veto the pork barrel bill that just arrived on his desk.

14–23. MISS GAMMA: Why is 'going' a gerund in that sentence?
JONATHAN: Because it functions like a noun there.

14–24. MR. BETA: Why did the fuse blow?
SID: Because its rated capacity was exceeded.

14–25. MRS. ALPHA: How do you know that this figure is an equilateral triangle?
BETTY: It has three equal sides.

14–26. MISS GAMMA: Why is 'compelled' spelled with two 'l's?
SALLY: 'Compel' is accented on the last syllable.

14–27. MR. DELTA: Explain why Germany was indifferent to our entrance into World War I.
MOLLY: We were already supplying the Allies with all the materials that Germany thought we could. We were not mobilized and Germany thought we could not mobilize effectively before she expected the war to be over.

Chapter Summary

In this chapter you were introduced to the distinction between three basic kinds of explanation, and were presented with some basic facts about two of them, descriptive explanation and reason-giving explanation. The third, interpretive explanation, was the focus of Part II of this book, "Definition".

A descriptive explanation describes a process or a structure. Some rough and ready rules were presented, which included general recommendations to:

1. Break the thing to be explained into parts;
2. Be clear about the relationship between the parts;
3. Choose the order of presentation of parts carefully;
4. Use models when the analogy can be helpful; and
5. Pay heed to the misleading analogies that are ever-present in models.

The above fairly vague pieces of advice must be applied with full attention to the subject matter being explained.

A reason-giving explanation explains by giving a reason. There are two parts: the explicandum, which is the thing to be explained; and the explicans, which is the explicit explanatory material. An explanation is not complete unless the explicandum follows from the explanatory material. 'Complete' here is a technical term. Incompleteness of an explanation does not make the explanation defective, nor does completeness make it satisfactory. But in order to judge an explanation, one should see that it is completed. When not present, completion is accomplished by the addition of one or more gap-fillers, the topic of the next chapter.

Criteria for judging reason-giving explanations are: (1) truth, (2) proper level of sophistication, (3) noncircularity, (4) proper function and type, and (5) testability/applicability. They are discussed in later chapters.

Cues for identifying basic kinds of explanations are often not reliable apart from considerations of context. The word 'meaning' generally indicates an interpretive explanation, and the word 'why' always calls for a reason-giving explanation. On the other hand, the word 'how', although it is most generally associated with descriptive explanations, can be used for the other kinds as well. The words 'structure' and 'process' are more reliable cues for descriptive explanations. When requesting an explanation, you should be clear just which kind you seek, and you should try to see whether, in that context, the phrasing of the request could be misinterpreted. In interpreting a request for an explanation, one must pay close attention to context and cues.

CHAPTER 15

Gap-Filling

In doing the comprehension self-test at the end of the last chapter you probably noticed that there is more than one possible way to complete an explanation. Another way of putting this fact is that there are a number of logical possibilities for the assumption(s) of an incomplete argument.* In this chapter we will focus on filling the gaps in an explanation, and, to the extent possible, will defer treatment of the actual evaluation for correctness until later chapters. Since gap-filling and evaluation are interdependent, we cannot even here neglect evaluation, as you will see. The purpose of this chapter is to help you become more adept at gap-filling.

Using the gerund example, here are four possible completed explanations (the gap-fillers are in brackets, a convention I shall henceforth observe):

Example 15-1

MISS GAMMA: Why is 'going' a gerund in that sentence?

JONATHAN: Because it functions like a noun there. [If 'going' functions like a noun, then it is a gerund.]

Example 15-2

MISS GAMMA: Why is 'going' a gerund in that sentence?

JONATHAN: Because it functions like a noun there. ['Going' is a verbal. All verbals that function like nouns are GERUNDS.]

* This point is discussed in greater detail elsewhere. See my "Assumption-Finding" in B. O. Smith and Robert H. Ennis, eds., *Language and Concepts in Education* (Chicago: Rand McNally & Co., 1961), pp. 161–78.

Example 15-3

MISS GAMMA: Why is 'going' a gerund in that sentence?

JONATHAN: Because it functions like a noun there. ['Going' is a verbal ending in 'ing'. All verbals which end in 'ing' and which function like nouns are GERUNDS.]

Example 15-4

MISS GAMMA: Why is 'going' a gerund in that sentence?

JONATHAN: Because it functions like a noun there. [Any word that functions like a noun is a GERUND.]

The explicandum and the explicans are the same from one case to the next. In each case the explicans and the gap-filler together imply the explicandum. But the gap-fillers are quite different.

If Miss Gamma attributes the first gap-filler to the explanation, then the explanatory material is true and it does explain the thing to be explained, although we would like our students to have a more general conception of gerunds than that demonstrated by the gap-filler, "If 'going' functions like a noun, then it is a gerund." (This is not to say that the first gap-filler implies a narrow conception of gerunds; it simply fails to demonstrate a broad conception.)

If Miss Gamma attributes the second gap-filler to the explanation, then she is pinning a false gap-filler on the explanation. She is attributing a false view to the explainer. On the other hand, the gap-filler is much more general than the first and is close to the truth. The view is false because infinitives are verbals and function like nouns. But they are not gerunds.

The gap-filler in the third explanation is true and is more general than the first. Knowledge in this form is much preferable because it has wider applicability. To attribute this gap-filler to Jonathan's explanation is to credit him with a satisfactory understanding of why 'going' is a gerund in that sentence.

The fourth gap-filler is just false. It is the most general of the gap-fillers but unfortunately too general, since, in addition to gerunds and infinitives, it covers all words that function like nouns, including ordinary nouns and pronouns, which are not gerunds.

Now in order to evaluate an explanation which is complete as it stands, a teacher (or a student) must evaluate the gap-filler. If there are several choices for the gap-filler (assuming that it has not been explicitly stated), then how is he going to know which one to attach to the explicans? That is the dilemma one faces when gap-filling reason-giving explanations. Two of the above gap-fillers are false and two are true. Some are more general than others. Which is Miss Gamma to attribute to Jonathan?

There is one fairly easy way out. That is to make an explicit request for the explainer to complete his own explanation. Various locutions for making this request were presented in the previous chapter. But we do not always use them—for several different reasons.

Reasons for Not Always Directly Securing Completion by the Explainer

First of all the explainer is often not immediately at hand. He might be the author of a book or article that is being read (although if he is alive, one can sometimes reach him and probe his explanation). Or he might be a student who has written a paper which the teacher is reading at home.

A case in which the gap-filler was obvious in the context in which it was actually presented, as I remember that context, is the explanation of why the wheat in the northeast field is a weed, the gap-filler being, "Unwanted plants are WEEDS." The completed explanation looks as follows:

Example 15-5
MR. ZETA: Why is the wheat in my northeast field a weed?
DICK: Because there it is unwanted. [Unwanted plants are WEEDS.]

The gap-filler, "Unwanted plants are WEEDS", was obvious **in that context** because it was a simple completion and because the definition was one that was often explicitly stated by the teacher.

Secondly when the explainer **is** right at hand, it frequently seems to be a waste of time to seek and secure the completion of the explanation, since the gap-filler often seems so obvious. Now sometimes the gap-filler is obvious to everyone concerned, although this occurs less often than one might expect from the prevalence of incomplete explanations.

A third reason, one which is most relevant to the next section, is that it frequently saves time to infer what the gap-filler is, rather than explicitly to request it and wait for an answer, since such inferences can be made by an experienced person in a split second. Drawing the line between a gap-fillers' being obvious and its being inferable is difficult, however. Those gap-fillers that must be consciously inferred by some of us often seem obvious to one who is experienced at gap-filling. You might, therefore, look at the next section as an attempt to help you increase the likelihood that an inferable gap-filler will be obvious to you.

A fourth reason for not always demanding the completion of the explanation is that sometimes we are interested only in the primary feature that is thought to account for the thing to be explained. In the gerund explanation in the context in which it occurred the primary feature was that of functioning like a noun. Sometimes we are only interested in getting out this primary feature, thinking that this is good enough, given the situation. If a student has grasped the fact that this is the primary feature, then for the time being we are satisfied. After all, first things first, we think; we have to deal with other students and must teach so many other things.

From the point of view of the person who is receiving a reason-giving explanation for the first time, it is also, on occasion, desirable to receive only the primary feature. A complete and correct explanation might be too much to grasp at the moment. For example, an essentially complete and correct explanation of the spelling of 'compelled' might go like this:

Example 15-6

SARAH: Why is 'compelled' spelled with two 'l's?

MISS GAMMA: 'Compel' is accented on the last syllable. [Monosyllables, and words of more than one syllable accented on the last syllable, when ending in a single consonant (except *h* and *x*) preceded by a single vowel, double the consonant before a suffix beginning with a vowel; 'ed' is a suffix beginning with a vowel; l is a single final consonant preceded by a single vowel.]

Now if Sarah is young and completely unacquainted with this way of telling whether to double a final consonant, this complete explanation might be too much for her to grasp, unless considerable time is devoted to exemplifying it. But she might well profit from the reference to the primary feature, the location of the accent. (If you do not think that this **is** the primary feature, then substitute your own. The point still holds.)

This fourth reason for not always demanding the completion of explanations is often legitimate. It is forced on us by practical considerations. People cannot learn everything at once, or in one year, or in one lifetime. And teachers cannot present everything at once. Choices must be made. Sacrifices must be made. Sacrifices in completeness of content must be accepted in order that the limitations of learners be respected.

A fifth reason for not securing completion by the explainer—at least directly—is that he might not be able to state directly what he knows to be the proper relationship, although under questioning he might reveal this knowledge. Complicated principles, such as the one given by Miss Gamma in Example 15-6 to explain the spelling of 'compelled', are not easily set forth (unless memorized). Careful probing can sometimes elicit them where direct request would fail.

A last reason for not explicitly requesting completion is that teaching is often more effective if various kinds of indirect probes are utilized. Later on the use of such probes will be discussed and exemplified.

Thus, different considerations can justify not making a direct request for the gap-filler. Granting that no direct request is to be made, one either might make an indirect request, or might try to infer the gap-filler without further inquiry. This latter move is the subject of the next section.

Inferring the Gap-Filler

You will remember there were alternative gap-fillers for the explanation of why 'going' is a gerund in a particular sentence. Which of these gap-fillers should be attributed to Jonathan's explanation? Here they are, as a reminder:

1. If 'going' functions like a noun, then it is a gerund.
2. 'Going' is a verbal. All verbals that function like nouns are GERUNDS.
3. 'Going' is a verbal ending in 'ing'. All verbals which end in 'ing' and which function like nouns are GERUNDS.
4. If any word functions like a noun, then it is a GERUND.

Rules of thumb

Unfortunately there is no automatic way to tell what gap-filler to attach to an explanation. The following rules of thumb can be of some help, though admittedly they are somewhat vague:

1. Pay close attention to the context.
2. Other things being equal, select the simpler of two gap-fillers.
3. Be fairly generous to the explainer, but not overgenerous.

Since virtually no context has been supplied to you for the gerund explanation, you will have trouble applying the second and third suggestions. Perhaps you can see how the results might vary from one context to the next.

The reason that simplicity is a criterion of gap-fillers is that we have a right to expect a person to refer to all the important features in giving an explanation, unless there is good reason not to do so. If a person does refer to all the significant features, and if they do provide sufficient reason, then the simplest completion should do the job.

Two related problems arise. First of all, competing gap-fillers might seem equally simple, like the first and the fourth gap-fillers in the above series. How to choose between them? That depends on the context. If Jonathan is known to be a person who knows about pronouns, then he probably is not using the fourth gap-filler, and it should not be pinned on him. Or suppose (as was the case in this teaching episode) that Miss Gamma has set things up in the beginning by placing before the class a list of fifteen sentences, each of which had either a gerund or a participle in it, the class being asked to determine which. Then pinning the fourth gap-filler on Jonathan would be unfair, since he is not under the circumstances committed to pronouns' being gerunds. These two cases illustrate supplementing the principle of simplicity with the use of context and the principle of generosity.

A second problem lies in the phrase which appeared two paragraphs above and which is in quotes in the following sentence: A person is expected to refer to all the significant features, "unless there is good reason not to do so." How do we tell if there is good reason not to refer to all the significant features? That depends very heavily on the context.

Again assume the context of the fifteen sentences and compare the first, second, and third gap-fillers. To demand without warning that a reference be made that excludes infinitives would not be fair. They have already been excluded by the context. Similarly, to insist on a gap-filler that implies that infinitives are gerunds would not be fair, even though such a gap-filler has not explicitly been excluded by Jonathan's answer. Hence, if Miss Gamma has limited the concern to participles and gerunds, then it would be unfair to Jonathan to pin the second gap-filler on his explanation.

Thus, the combined application of the rules of context, simplicity, and generosity can provisionally eliminate some gap-fillers—in this case, the second and fourth. This is not to say that the second and fourth are **not** gap-fillers in such contexts; they could be what Jonathan had in mind. Rather what has been shown is that one would in such contexts have no right to attribute those gap-fillers to the explanation without some additional strong reason.

We still have the first and third gap-fillers as candidates for the completion of the explanation. Can the three rules help to choose between them? Given the context as it has so far been specified, it does seem a bit overgenerous to credit Jonathan with the third gap-filler, although it would also seem undergenerous to deny it to him. Pinning the first gap-filler on his explanation might seem somewhat undergenerous, since it is a fairly narrow statement. It is not completely specific, however, for it does make an assertion about the occurrence of 'going' in **any** sentence in which it functions as a noun—not just this sentence.

Given the context as so far specified, probably the best thing to do is to agree that Jonathan is at least committed to the first gap-filler and is obligated to defend that, even though his actual gap-filler, upon questioning might turn out to be considerably broader. Judgment about attributing the third gap-filler should probably be suspended.

If, however, the following two rules had been written on the blackboard, then we probably should attribute the third gap-filler to Jonathan:

1. All verbals which end in 'ing' and which function like nouns are GERUNDS.
2. All verbals which end in 'ing' and which function like adjectives are PARTICIPLES.

Given those two rules out in the open, the only significant feature that needs to be referred to is the function which the word fulfills. Attributing this third gap-filler under these circumstances, of course, does not bring as much credit to the explainer as otherwise, for after all, the rule is right in front of him.

Two warnings about the application of the principle of generosity should be mentioned. Time pressures and the desire not to discourage students might result in overgenerosity. We might ourselves supply an implicit reference to significant features that the explainer would not have thought relevant. In so doing we might convert a poor explanation into a good one. Hence one should be wary—not overgenerous.

On the other hand, we should not expect a learner to be generous at all when a new idea is being presented to him. If a person is to be expected to get the full explanation, then all of the relevant features must be mentioned. When an instructor provides a 'why' explanation for a learner, the learner has a right within contextual limits to take the simplest completion to be the one intended. A teacher who gives a 'why' explanation will do well to refer to all the features that he wants the student to know are involved. It might also be helpful for the teacher to give the complete explanation, supplying the gap-fillers as well. Then there is no danger that the student will insert the wrong gap-filler. Thus, an English teacher might give the complete rule for spelling words like 'compelled' when explaining why 'compelled' is spelled with two 'l's, if he is to make sure that students know why.

On the other hand, the English teacher might ask the students to fill in the gap, as a learning experience. It is not appropriate here to recommend the psychologically more effective way of teaching the spelling rule—or some other rule, principle, or generalization. This is an empirical matter that varies with different kinds of students, teachers, situations, and subject matter. The point here is simply to clarify the logical relationships involved, so that the alternatives are clearly understood.

Summary

The rules of context, simplicity, and generosity are hints which must be applied with discretion in trying to infer without further inquiry just what is the gap-filler in an incomplete reason-giving explanation. Such rules cannot be applied mechanically. After all what we are looking for is a statement that connects the explicans and the explicandum, and which the explainer should be willing to defend if he wants to stand by his explanation. This is not something that can be mechanically determined. But probably an understanding of the logical relationships and practice in applying the rules to concrete situations will make you better able to do on-the-spot inferring of gap-fillers.

The Focus of an Explanation

So far we have been discussing explanations in contexts in which the **subject matter to be learned** was in the form of statements that cover more than one case. The spelling rule covers many cases, as do the statements about what a gerund is, the definition of 'weed', and the alternate interior angles theorem. But in history as it is commonly taught, the subject matter often consists of singular statements. Generalizations are avoided. That is, history texts and textbooks focus on the learning of specific, rather than general, statements. The merits and demerits of such an approach to history are beyond the scope of this chapter, but the bearing, if any, on the present discussion should be considered, because reason-giving explanations are common in history. Singular subject matter is, of course, not restricted to history and the other social sciences; it is very common in literature and is found in historical aspects of science.

In such cases the generalizations that complete good explanations often border on being common sense. The student ordinarily knows these before he comes into the course. Note for example a general gap-filler for the explanation of Germany's indifference to our entry into World War I: "A country at war will be concerned about an additional enemy only if the country thinks that an increase in enemy material or of the enemy's fighting force will result before the war is over." When a teacher asks a student to explain Germany's indifference, he is not focusing on the above truism. He is focusing on the particular situations that led Germany to be indifferent. So the criterion of understanding is not whether the student refers to the significant features of the truism, but rather whether he refers to the significant features of the situation in 1917.

The important point here is that even if the explanation is in a field in which the focus is on the singular statements, one should still be aware of the gap-filler.

Suppose the student had said:

Example 15-7
Because the United States had a high productive capacity.

Please pause here and figure out what is the likely gap-filler.

Here is one possibility:

Example 15-8
Countries at war tend to be indifferent to the entry into the war of an enemy with a high productive capacity.

In this last case, the student either did not have the common-sense knowledge, or he made a mistake in fitting the situation into his knowledge. No matter what the problem, it is helpful to be aware of the likely gap-filler.

Necessity

So far the question of the kind of following has been left unanswered. Must the fact to be explained follow **necessarily** from the explanatory materials? The answer to this question appears to vary within subject-matter areas. This you probably expected, in view of the discussion in Chapter 5 of the application of deductive logic to everyday reasoning.

In much of mathematics and those explanations in other areas which depend essentially on definitions, necessity is appropriate. But in most situations necessity is inappropriate, since most generalizations and rules have exceptions. In such cases, a looser notion of following is desirable.

For the fuse explanation at the end of the last chapter, you probably filled the gap with something like this:

Fuses blow when the rated capacity is exceeded.

But we well know that fuses do not **always** blow when the rated capacity is exceeded, yet they almost always do; and the generalization about the blowing of fuses is to be interpreted in this sense. The fact that the fuse blew follows from the complete explanation, but it does not follow from the generalization with absolute necessity, since the generalization, though true, must be understood to have exceptions.* The safest thing to say is that the fact to be explained follows with a reasonable degree of strictness from the explanatory material (gap-filler plus explicans).

Those people who are pushing back the frontiers of knowledge are searching for and discovering the qualifications and exceptions to be added to rules and generalizations; but, except in limited areas such as traditional grammar, they discover also that more qualifications and revisions are yet to be made. For this reason, as well as for the reason that subject matter in the classroom must be simplified (thus rules and generalizations are presented with exceptions deliberately neglected), the teacher must operate in most cases with the looser kind of following.

Even in these cases, however, it is helpful to know what **would necessarily follow** if the rule or generalization were without qualification. This knowledge is helpful because it provides guidance in deciding what **does follow**. In the example below, knowing that C_1 **necessarily follows** in the first example helps us judge that C_2 **follows** in the second.

Example 15-9

Case 1: A_1 The rated capacity of this fuse was exceeded.
B_1 Fuses **always** blow when their rated capacities are exceeded.
C_1 Therefore, this fuse blew.

Case 2: A_2 The rated capacity of this fuse was exceeded.
B_2 Fuses blow when their rated capacities are exceeded.
C_2 Therefore, this fuse blew.

In other words, the rules of deductive logic are useful in the process of filling in explanations. They provide us with a model from which we depart

* You are referred back to the discussion in Chapter 5 of this sort of generalization.

more or less when making judgments about what follows from explanatory material.

To what extent **can** you permit departure from the necessity model? This depends in part on the particular subject matter under consideration and in part on the sophistication of the student. In most of mathematics no departure at all should be permitted. This is also the case for much of grammar and holds for those explanations which appeal to definitions. (For example, why is the unwanted wheat a weed? Because 'weed' means a plant that is not wanted.) Most explanations in the physical sciences and the social sciences are likely to be less strict, although the former tend to be more strict than the latter. Those aspects of English literature which are historical would be comparable to those of history, which either is, or is comparable to, a social science in this respect. Explanations of aesthetic, ethical, and 'ought' statements are common in English and social studies, but also appear in physical science and mathematics classes. These explanations in general are the least strict of all because there are so many exceptions to the rules and generalizations involved. But there is still a logical structure to them. The student who explains why he thinks that Sandburg's *Fog* is a good poem by giving the reason, "Because it is short", can ordinarily be called upon to defend the simplest gap-filler, "Short poems are good poems", or at least to supply another gap-filler.

In summary, a strict logical necessity is usually not a characteristic of the reasoning involved in a satisfactory explanation, but it provides a good guide for that reasoning.

Chapter Summary

The gap-filler to an explanation is what the explainer intends (or would intend) to use in completing the explanation. In this chapter you saw that gap-filling is not an automatic process, but rather one that calls for an intelligent decision. Although frequently the easiest way to get the gap filled is to ask of the explainer such questions as "What does that have to do with it?", one often wants to (or has to) figure out for himself just what completion is actually the gap-filler.

Some rules of thumb for gap-filling are:

1. Pay close attention to the context.
2. Other things being equal, select the simpler of two gap-fillers.
3. Be fairly generous to the explainer, but not overgenerous.

Usually gap-fillers are general statements, rather than specific ones, but sometimes the explicans is general and the explicandum is specific, in which case the gap-filler contains at least one specific statement. In the teaching context the focus of the explanation is often the generalization(s). But in some subject-matter areas, especially history, the focus is on the specific statement, since the generalizations are usually truisms and the things to be learned are the specific statements and their interconnections.

In most cases of explanation, as with most practical uses of deduction (discussed in Chapter 5), the explicandum is not expected to follow necessarily without qualification from true, qualificationless explanatory material. Instead the relationship is such that the explicandum, if it had no qualifications, would follow necessarily from the explanatory material, if it had no qualifications. The judgment as to whether the explanatory material then does explain the explicandum is a practical one which, like those discussed in Chapter 5, calls for a knowledge of the context and subject matter.

In spite of these difficulties, one can become proficient in gap-filling, and, though there are risks, be right most of the time.

COMPREHENSION SELF-TEST

True or False? If the statement is false, change a crucial term (or terms) to make it true.

15–1. Each combination of explicans and explicandum has its own unique gap-filler, determinable on the basis of the words used and their meanings.

15–2. Other things being equal, the simpler of two gap-fillers is ordinarily the one to attribute to an explanation.

15–3. In the evaluation of an explanation, the gap-filler does not usually need to be evaluated, because it is usually not explicitly present.

15–4. In historical explanations in contexts in which crucial parts of understanding are singular statements, the general gap-fillers are often truisms.

15–5. A teacher does not have the right to expect as much generosity from his students (when he is by means of an explanation introducing new subject matter) as they have a right to expect from him when some of the significant features are obvious.

15–6. In reason-giving explanation, a fact in mathematics (such as the equality of alternate interior angles of parallel lines) can generally be expected to follow from the explanatory material with a greater degree of strictness than a fact in history (such as the Supreme Court's reversal on child labor laws).

Exercises.

15–7. State the three "rules of thumb" to use in inferring the gap-fillers in reason-giving explanations.

15.8. to 15.30. For each of the following explanations supply a gap-filler. Follow the rules of thumb, inventing contextual details where necessary. Not all of these explanations are good ones, a fact which will be made clear by the gap-fillers you provide.

15–8. T: Why was Blaine never elected president?
P: The American people never did trust him.

15–9. T: Why did that electric bell ring?
P: You completed the circuit containing the bell and a live battery.

15–10. T: Why is triangle *ABC* an isosceles triangle?
P: It contains a right angle.

15–11. T: Why should the return address be on the front of the evelope?
P: The example in the text puts it there.

15–12. T: Why is wool worn in winter?
P: Because wool is warm.

15–13. T: Why should the index, *per cent increase in the Gross National Product*, take into account changes in the cost of living?
P: Because it is used to show trends in productivity.

15–14. T: Why is the penguin a fast runner?
P: Because it is unable to fly.

15–15. T: Why is the Atlantic Ocean salty?
P: It contains salt.

15–16. T: Why do blue and yellow when combined appear to be white?
P: Because blue and yellow are complementary colors.

15–17. T: Why is the sewing room well lighted?
P: Because it has light-colored walls.

15–18. T: Why is the direct-lighting method unsatisfactory?
P: Because it does not remove glare by having a reflector made of translucent material.

15–19. T: How do you know that plants *X* and *Y* are closely related?
P: Because they can be crossed to produce hybrids.

15–20. T: Why will Macbeth never be vanquished?
P: Because Birnam wood will never come to Dunsinane hill.

15–21. T: Why was Macduff able to harm Macbeth?
P: Because no one born of woman was able to harm Macbeth.

15–22. T: Why did many bishops hold fiefs from kings.
P: Because every bishop was an important church official.

15–23. T: Why were no true believers condemned?
P: Because true believers were not heretics.

15–24. T: Why is it that a circle cannot be inscribed in *A*?
P: Because *A* is not a regular polygon.

15–25. T: Why are *A* and *B* rhombuses?
P: Because they have equal sides and equal angles.

15–26. T: Explain why you can screw a nut on a bolt tighter with a wrench than you can with your fingers.
P: There is more mechanical advantage with a wrench.

15–27. T: Why is "childrens'" incorrect?
P: The apostrophe is after the '*s*'.

15–28. T: Why is "stewdents'" incorrect? (In "The stewdents' book was red.")
P: The apostrophe is after the '*s*'.

15–29. T: Would you like "The Gift of the Magi" better if the last paragraph were removed? Why?

P: Yes. Stories are better if you must figure out the moral.

15–30. T: Why did the American people not trust Blaine?

P: Because there were too many incidents in his career that called for apologies and explanations.

CHAPTER 16

Introductory Evaluation and Probing of Reason-Giving Explanations

Although it is risky to judge an explanation without a thorough knowledge of the context in which it is offered, these following attempts at explanation are presented as examples of explanations that are at least usually defective. See if you can tell what would ordinarily be wrong with each.

Example 16-1
MRS. ALPHA: Why are angles *y* and *z* equal?
FRANK: Because they are supplementary.*

Example 16-2
MR. THETA: (in a physics class) Why is the fuse wire broken?
JOHN: Because its capacity was exceeded.

Example 16-3
MR. OMICRON: Why does opium produce sleep?
LARRY: Because it has dormitive power.

* SUPPLEMENTARY ANGLES, by the way, are any two angles which together add up to 180°.

In the discussion that follows, the defects of these explanations will be treated, together with some standard ways of probing explanations.

The Interdependence of Completion and Evaluation

In order that logical relationships could be made clear, the discussion of gap-filling neglected, for the most part, the interdependence of gap-filling and evaluation. Our discussion of evaluation must pay more attention to this interdependence.

The completion of an explanation which is incomplete as presented, requires that we know which of the possible gap-fillers make the explanation a poor one (so that we do not pin an implausible one on an explanation when a plausible one may reasonably be attributed to it). Thus the decision about how an explanation should be completed depends on an evaluation of possible completions. And the evaluation of an explanation ordinarily requires that it be completed.

This interdependence does not make the evaluation of explanations an impossible process. But it does make it a more difficult one than it would be if there were simply a series of steps, no one of which depended on a later step. What is often required is a series of successive possible completions and consequent evaluations. If the first gap-filler makes the explanation a poor one, one should cast about for a gap-filler which may be reasonably attributed to the explanation, and which makes it a satisfactory explanation. Only after a reasonably thorough search has been made should the explanation be declared unsatisfactory.

With this interdependence in the back of our minds, let us proceed to the four basic criteria for the evaluation of explanations: truth, proper level of sophistication, noncircularity, and proper function and type. Accompanying this examination of these criteria will be discussions of the probing of explanations to see if the criteria are met. Discussion of a fifth criterion is left until Chapter 18.

Truth

An explanation with a part that is false is ordinarily not an adequate explanation. Example 16-1 above has the following false statement as its simplest gap-filler:

> Supplementary angles are equal.

If that **is** the gap-filler, then the explanation is defective because this part of the explanatory material is false. In most situations that gap-filler would be attributable to the explanation, so in **most** situations the explanation would be defective. False explanatory material ordinarily disqualifies an explanation.

Qualifications

You may be wondering how the explanation given in Example 16-1 could **ever** be satisfactory. It would be satisfactory in a situation in which we are considering a group of angles that are related in various ways to a given right angle (for example, adjacent, opposite, and so forth), and in which it is well established that one of the two angles mentioned in the explanation request is the right angle. It would then be sufficient to mention that the two angles are supplementary, since supplementary angles **are** equal, if one of them is a right angle. The gap-filler (including contextually supplied material) would be:

> Supplementary angles are equal, if one of them is a right angle.

This gap-filler is true, making the explanation satisfactory in this special context. Hence one qualification is that an explanation can be satisfactory, even though the simplest filler of the gap is false.

A second qualification: Truth of all the explanatory material is not always used as a necessary condition for something's being an explanation. One kind of case is that in which the ability of a hypothesis to explain the data is used as a criterion for judging the truth of the hypothesis. In such a case, we obviously cannot be assured in advance that the hypothesis which is supposed to explain the data is also true. If we were so assured, then there would be no point to seeing if, as a test of the hypothesis, it could explain the data.

For example, in trying to decide about the hypothesis, 'Shakespeare intended Iago to be a **non**melodramatic villain', one might say that it would explain why Emilia displayed trust in Iago throughout most of *Othello.* This explanatory power of the hypothesis is urged as evidence in favor of the hypothesis. We cannot first assume the hypothesis to be true in judging that it would successfully explain Emilia's display of trust, since the explanatory power is urged as evidence in favor of the hypothesis.

Another kind of case in which truth is not used as a criterion is that in which we believe that the explanatory material is false. A person who is sure that the above hypothesis about the interpretation of Iago is false might nevertheless admit that it **would** explain Emilia's display of trust.

Thus truth of the explanatory material is not always necessary for something to qualify as **an** explanation. There can be explanations which do not have true explanatory material, and the other aspects of these explanations can be judged. But note that we do not commit ourselves fully to such explanations—unless we are convinced of the truth of the explanatory material. We tend to use the subjunctive in order to show our reservations. We do not say, "That **does** explain . . .", when there is a question about the truth of the explanatory material. We say, "That **would** explain . . .", or sometimes grant, "That is **an** explanation."

Thus with the aforementioned reservations an explanation should satisfy the criterion of truth. This criterion can be applied directly to the explicans and to gap-fillers that can be established without further investigation. As you realize, however, further investigation is frequently necessary. The explanation must be probed in order to ascertain the gap-filler, so that the criterion of truth can be applied. Let us now interrupt our treatment of the criteria for evaluation of explanations to take a look at the basic operations involved in probing explanations.

Probing

In addition to the direct request for completion of an explanation, two standard methods of probing an explanation exist, with many variations, of course. One is to propose a possible gap-filler yourself, checking to see if that is the one, and the other is to suggest implications of a possible gap-filler, checking to see if the explainer wants to accept these implications.

Proposing a Gap-filler. In order to check to see if the gap-filler that you have pinned on the explanation is the correct one, and often in order to provoke thought on the part of the explainer, you might propose a prospective gap-filler and ask about it:

> You're assuming that supplementary angles are equal?
> Are supplementary angles equal?

Although this is a good approach, there are two difficulties. First, it gives direction to the explainer's thought; sometimes it is better to explore without pushing him in a given direction. Second, people usually interpret such probes as challenges that imply a disagreement. Students who are not accustomed to examining and defending their views tend to retreat when such a probe is delivered. In order to avoid these consequences in conducting classroom discourse one should mix in a number of such probes in which the prospective gap-filler **is** satisfactory. Then your probe will not serve as a cue that indicates a defective explanation.

Such probes **can**, of course, be used as direct challenges of explanations, challenges which sometimes force a person to realize without being told directly that his explanation is unsatisfactory. This is what happened in the following dialogue:

Example 16-4

MRS. ALPHA: Why are these two angles equal?

FRANK: Because they are supplementary.

MRS. ALPHA: Are supplementary angles equal?

FRANK: Uh—Wait a minute. No, they're not. I guess that's not the reason. It's because they are supplementary and one of them, the one on the left, is a right angle.

MRS. ALPHA: That's better.

The above probe, "Are supplementary angles equal?" served to show Mrs. Alpha that she had located the gap-filler, and it also made Frank realize that his explanation was defective, because the gap-filler he had in mind was false.

Suggesting an Implication of a Gap-filler. If you want to challenge a gap-filler that you have pinned on an explanation, or if you want to check to see if you have the correct gap-filler, your probes might suggest an implication of the gap-filler, as in the following examples. (The gap-filler is: "Supplementary angles are equal.")

Would angles *a* and *b* then be equal? *a* / *b*

Is an exterior angle of a triangle always equal to its adjacent interior angle?

Since the correct answer to each of those probes is 'no', and since the answer 'yes' is implied by the proposed gap-filler, 'Supplementary angles are equal', they constitute challenges to the explanation (if the suspected gap-filler actually is the gap-filler).

Such probes can also help to tell you whether you have identified the correct gap-filler. If the student says 'no' to these questions, if he knows what 'supplementary' means, if he can do simple deductive reasoning, and if he sits silently or wonders why you ask, then you can presume that he does not hold as the gap-filler, 'Supplementary angles are equal', since an answer of 'yes' is called for by that gap-filler under those conditions. If you have any doubt that the antecedents (the 'if' clauses) in the preceding sentence hold, you might check to see if they do hold:

You said 'no', didn't you?

What do you mean by 'supplementary'?

Is this a valid argument form (or: Does this conclusion follow necessarily?):

If two angles are supplementary, then they have trait *x*.

These two angles are supplementary.

Therefore, these two angles have trait *x*.

Does anything bother you about saying that angles *a* and *b* are not equal, although you say that the reason that angles *y* and *z* are equal is that they are supplementary?

If, on the other hand, the student affirms the implications of the gap-filler (in this case, that angles *a* and *b* are equal, and that an exterior angle of a triangle is always equal to its adjacent interior angle), then one has evidence (in this case fairly strong evidence) that 'Supplementary angles are equal' is the gap-filler to his explanation. But one also has reason to suspect in this case that something is peculiar, for it is difficult to see how in the ordinary case a student can look at that diagram and say that the two angles are equal. He does not know the meaning of 'equal', one might think. In general, though, affirmation of the suggested implications is evidence that the gap-filler has been identified (especially if it is probable that the implications would be affirmed only if the suggested gap-filler is believed).

As you can perhaps already see, the suggestion of such implications is also a way of determining what the explainer means by the gap-filler, assuming that you have correctly guessed it. Suppose that a student, in answer to the probes about angles *a* and *b* and the exterior angle of a triangle, had said:

> No, they aren't equal. Why do you ask? They aren't even supplementary angles.

Then you would know that he does not know what 'supplementary' means. Similarly, as suggested before, an answer of 'yes' makes one suspect that he does not know the meaning of 'equal'.

This implication-suggestion method of probing does not require that the suggested implications always be false. First of all **negative** responses to probes that supply true implications are of help, since they indicate that the gap-filler is not held. And **positive** answers can be of help as well, if the implication is one that a person is not likely to believe if he does not believe the suspected gap-filler. Such implications are not always easy to locate, but you might be helped in looking for them if you think of yourself as searching for surprising consequences of the gap-filler. For example, a surprising consequence of the gap-filler, 'All unwanted plants are weeds', might well be that the strawberries in the cabbage patch are weeds. A positive answer to the question, 'Are the strawberries in the cabbage patch weeds?', could well indicate that the gap-filler, 'Unwanted plants are weeds', is held by the respondent, and presumably was in the background of the explanation.

In brief, one indirect way to probe to see if the suspected gap-filler is the one to pin on the explanation is as follows: Identify crucial implications of the suspected gap-filler and see if the explainer assents to them. If he does not, then, granting certain qualifications, you have probably misidentified the gap-filler; if he does assent to them, then you might well have identified it. Naturally you cannot be sure that you have identified it, because other possible gap-fillers might also carry the same implications.

One advantage of this implication-suggestion method of probing is that you are not as likely to put words into students' mouths as you are if you directly suggest a possible gap-filler. Furthermore, when students have accepted the gap-filler and do not accept its implications, they are forced to think.

COMPREHENSION SELF-TEST

True or False? If the statement is false, then change a crucial term (or terms) to make it true.

16–1. A fully satisfactory explanation must have true explanatory material.

16–2. If a student denies the truth of implications of a possible gap-filler, then, with qualifications, one has evidence that it is not the gap-filler for his explanation.

16–3. If a student assents to an implication of a possible gap-filler for his explanation, then one has conclusive proof that this is the gap-filler for his explanation.

Exercises.

16–4 to **16–8.** Do each of the following for five of the explanations given in the "Exercises" at the end of the previous chapter (Chapter 15).

a. Supply a possible gap-filler that is false.
b. Frame a probe of the explanation such that the probe suggests a false implication of the gap-filler supplied for *a*, above.
c. Supply a gap-filler that is true.
d. Frame a probe of the explanation which provides an implication of the possible gap-filler supplied for *c*, the response to which probe could provide evidence about whether the possible gap-filler supplied for *c* is the gap-filler to the explanation. Tell why you think it could provide evidence.

16–9 to **16–18.** Do the same for ten more of those explanations.

Proper Level of Sophistication

The explanation of the broken fuse wire (Example 16-2) is quite appropriate in some contexts—when children are just learning about fuses, for example. But in other contexts, it is hardly satisfactory It does not go very deeply into the matter. The explanation request could have been a request for an account of the pertinent characteristics of the metal used in the fuse wire. Or it might even have been a request for something more sophisticated than that—so that a reference to the kinetic theory of heat would have been appropriate. Thus, some explanations are unsatisfactory because they are not at the appropriate level of sophistication.

If the context does not make obvious the appropriate level for the explanation, the questioner is obligated to make this clear. In the sophisticated context of a physics class, the reference to the exceeding of the capacity is ordinarily too shallow. The person requesting the explanation should not have to warn about this in advance. But in a ninth-grade general science class the person requesting the explanation would probably need to specify more depth, if he wants it. To request a deeper explanation he could say, "Referring to the characteristics of fuse metal, explain why the fuse blew."

Situations might arise even in the physics class in which the explanation is perfectly all right. Suppose that a board designed to illustrate a complicated combination of series and parallel circuits has a fuse as a safety device. Suppose further that by mistake its capacity is exceeded. When the fuse wire breaks and an explanation is sought, the answer, 'Because its **capacity***
was exceeded', can be quite appropriate. It rules out damage by a blow, for example.

What are the major factors bearing on the level of sophistication of a piece of subject matter? One is the degree of abstractness. This is exemplified by the difference between an explanation that uses the kinetic theory of heat and one that refers to the specific characteristics of fuse metal, the former being more abstract.

A second factor is the degree of refinement of the subject matter. A generalization about the characteristics of fuse metal is more refined than the one about exceeding the capacities of fuses. Degree of refinement is also exemplified in the comparison between the following version of the spelling rule and the version presented as a gap-filler in Chapter 15 (Example 15-6):

> Words accented on the last syllable double a single final consonant which is preceded by a single vowel before adding a suffix beginning with a vowel.

This last version, which could also serve as a gap-filler in the spelling explanation, neglects the exceptions, words ending in *h* and *x*. But for a given level of sophistication, the last version is a satisfactory rule. It serves most of the time.

As was pointed out in the discussion of exceptions and borderline cases in definitions, the varying degrees of refinement of subject matter are at least in part responsible for the feeling that most college students have about their elementary and high school education—that they were misinformed about many things. Frequently subject matter, which is in need of qualification at a higher level of sophistication than that at which the student is capable of operating, is presented (and/or received) as the final truth on the matter. The later discovery that there are many qualifications and refinements which were not presented earlier is disappointing to one who has not been disabused of the view that he is receiving the final truth.

* If you are bothered by an apparent circularity here, then substitute 'rated capacity' for 'capacity'. More about circularity later.

Unfortunately this insight into the nature of subject matter is often not pressed home in college either, so that frequently a student who thinks he was misled in elementary and high school believes in college that he is finally learning the unqualified truth. He, of course, is in for more shocks, unless he closes his mind to further qualification.

You are reminded that the material in this book is like other subject matter when presented at a given level of sophistication: there are many unstated (and probably many more undiscovered) qualifications and refinements to the subject matter of logic in teaching.

In summary, an explanation that misgauges the level of sophistication appropriate for the audience is in that respect unsatisfactory, although sometimes it is the explanation request that is at fault. Almost all principles (including those in this book) require qualification when treated at more sophisticated levels. Unfortunately, teachers at all levels too often fail to make this fact clear to their students.

Noncircularity

If an explanation is circular, it is defective. A CIRCULAR EXPLANATION is one which, given the context, gets nowhere because it simply restates what is already given. Example 16-3 is a standard example of a circular explanation. It is reproduced here with a gap-filler which makes obvious the circularity:

MR. OMICRON: Why does opium produce sleep?
LARRY: Because it has dormitive power. [DORMITIVE POWER is sleep-producing ability.]

The explanation is tantamount to saying that opium has the power to produce sleep, because it has the power to produce sleep. We are not helped by the introduction of the term 'dormitive power', since it covers no more than is already implied in the request for explanation.

The importance of context

The following would be a borderline case:

Example 16-5
MR. OMICRON: Why do birds migrate south in the winter?
BOB: Because they have a south-flying migratory instinct.

Except for the reference to instinct, this is blatantly circular. But the instinct reference suggests that the south-flying tendency is an inherited rather than an acquired trait. If in the context there is no doubt about the instinct question, but it is the direction (south) for which explanation is sought, or if instinct is assumed and the reason for it sought, then the explanation is circular. Our judgment about the circularity of this explanation thus depends on what the context reveals to be in need of explanation. Naturally a teacher should make clear the feature on which to concentrate. He can obviate the reference to instinct in the explicans by explicit mention of it in the explanation request (for example, 'Why do birds have an instinct to migrate south in the winter?').

Here is another case that depends on the context:

Example 16-6

MRS. ALPHA: Why is triangle *ABC* a right triangle?

ALAN: Because it is a triangle containing a right angle. [Triangles containing a right angle are RIGHT TRIANGLES.]

When students are first learning about right triangles, this explanation could be satisfactory because it shows that Alan understands the definition: A right triangle is a triangle containing a right angle. But suppose that a circle is drawn on the board and that a diameter of the circle serves as one side of the triangle and that the triangle is inscribed in the circle. (See Diagram 16-1.) When students have progressed to the point that they deal with that kind of situation, to say that *ABC* is a right triangle is the same as saying that it is a triangle containing a right angle. In this case, then, the explanation is circular because it does not take us any further than the request for the explanation took us.

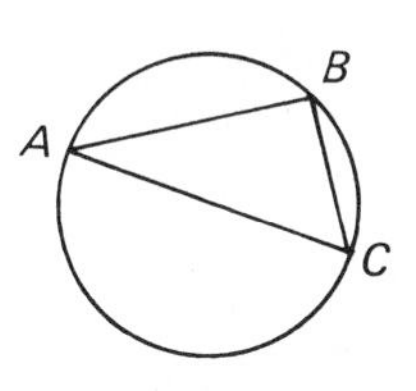

DIAGRAM 16-1

Consider this case from an English class:

Example 16-7

MISS GAMMA: Explain why you think that Mark Antony is being ironical when he says that Brutus is an honorable man.

TONY: Because his implied attitudes are opposed to those literally expressed. [If a man's implied attitudes are opposed to those he literally expresses, then he is being IRONICAL.]

By now you should be able to imagine a situation in which this answer would be acceptable, and a situation in which this answer would be circular. Try to do so.

Here is a case from a home economics class:

Example 16-8

MRS. EPSILON: Explain why this nylon blouse is smooth.

JANE: Because it's made of nylon. [Things made of nylon are smooth.]

Try to imagine circumstances in which this explanation would be acceptable and circumstances in which it would be circular.

The earlier example of the explanation of the breaking of the fuse wire might have been thought circular by some, since one might well argue that to say that its capacity was exceeded is to offer no further information than has been given in the explanation request. The wire could not break unless its capacity was exceeded. To say that the wire broke is to imply that the capacity was exceeded. Thus the reply that explains the breaking by saying that the capacity was exceeded does not seem to take us any further than the original request for explanation.

Analogously, we might say that to explain by saying that there was too much current flowing through it does not get us anywhere. This sort of problem is common to all explanations that make use of such expressions as 'too much', 'not enough', 'capacity', etc. Such explanations seem true simply by virtue of the meaning of the above-mentioned terms.

The wisdom in such a challenge is that the terms mentioned do not by themselves take us beyond the original request for explanation. But in context and in association with other terms in an explicans, they often serve to point out a significant feature of the situation which accounts for the thing to be explained. An explanation of the breaking of the fuse wire which speaks of "too much current" in the wire points to a significant feature, the amount of current. Similarly in context the explanation which referred to the exceeding of the capacity implied that the amount of electricity flowing through the wire was the significant factor, instead of, for example, the wire's frailty when dropped, or someone's having broken it with his hands.

Such explanations are still open to challenge, because they neither give nor suggest as much explicit information as is sometimes desired (though they sometimes give all that can be expected). For example one might want to know how much electricity it takes to cause the fuse wire to part, rather than simply that it was the amount of electricity rather than something else that was responsible. Thus an explicans that indicated that the reason was that the current was greater than fifteen amps would be preferable, because it is more explicit than the answer given. It gives a way of predicting such occurrences. Similarly an explicans that said that the **rated** capacity was exceeded would have been better than the one given. This is so because the probable gap-filler, 'Fuse wire breaks when the rated capacity is exceeded', gives a way of predicting when a fuse wire will break. The rated capacity is information that is available. It is printed on the fuse.

These refinements in the explanation are matters of the proper degree of sophistication. Once we have established that an explanation gets us beyond the explanation request, then the explanation is not circular. It might still be unsatisfactory because it is not sophisticated enough (in the broad sense of 'sophisticated' used in the previous section), but it is not circular.

In summary, the justifiability of the circularity charge depends heavily on the context in which the explanation is offered. But even if an explanation is cleared of the charge of circularity, it might still be defective because its level of sophistication is too low.

Probing: level and circularity

When level of sophistication and/or circularity are in question, standard probes are those that call for more about the situation. Here are some examples:

Can you tell me a little more about that?
Could you be more explicit please?
Do you mean just any kind of capacity?
How does one determine the capacity?
Can you see the connection between this and the molecular theory of heat?

The first two are general probes which are surprisingly effective in many different kinds of situations. They are strongly recommended as ways of searching out more details and depth. The other probes are specific to the particular explanation under consideration, but exemplify the sort of thing that can be done.

COMPREHENSION SELF-TEST

True or False? If the statement is false, change a crucial term (or terms) to make it true.

16–19. To say that an explanation is circular is to say that at least one term appears in both the explicans and the explicandum.

16–20. It is quite appropriate to omit some of the qualifications to statements when operating at a low level of sophistication.

16–21. Unless the context rules out an explicans of a low level of sophistication, a teacher who seeks an explanation at a higher level should so specify.

Problems.

16–22. Describe a situation in which the irony explanation (Example 16-7) is not circular, and describe a situation in which it is clearly circular.

16–23. Do the same for the nylon explanation (Example 16-8).

16–24. Go to a textbook from which you might teach or have taught and find an explanation which is not circular in the context in which it appears. Write it down and explain why it is not circular. Then imagine and describe a situation in which the same explanation would be judged circular.

16–25. From the same textbook take and write down an explanation which is at the correct level of sophistication. Then imagine and describe a situation in which the explanation is at too low a level of sophistication. Then supply an explanation with the same explicandum, but which is at the appropriate level of sophistication for this imagined situation.

Proper Function and Type

A fourth and dual criterion of explanation is that the explanation be of the proper function and type. In the following two examples this criterion is violated. Try to see why.

Example 16-9

MR. DELTA: In our study of various cultures, we have seen that different groups have valued different things. The Spartans valued bravery and feats of physical strength and skill; the Zunis valued cooperativeness and submerging oneself into the group; the Kwakiutls valued the man who could prove himself superior by demonstrating his great wealth; and we in the United States value the twin ideals of freedom and responsibility.

JANE: Mr. Delta, do you value freedom and responsibility?

MR. DELTA: Yes, Jane, I do.

JANE: Why?

MR. DELTA: Because a man tends to take on the values of his milieu. That's reasonable, isn't it?

Example 16-10

MRS. ALPHA: Jim, will you please explain why you are late?

JIM: Because I wanted to see what the halls are like when they are empty.

MRS. ALPHA: That's no explanation.

JIM: But that is why I was late. I wanted to see the empty halls.

In the next example it is not clear whether the criterion is violated or not. The explanation must be probed.

Example 16-11

MISS GAMMA: Can you tell me why Dylan Thomas came to the United States to read his poetry?

ARTHUR: He was driven by a basic unconscious desire to receive public adulation.

Two functions of reason-giving explanations: accounting for and justifying

Examples 16-9 and 16-10 are cases in which, in the context in which they appeared, the explicandum was accounted for rather than justified.* The

* Strictly speaking the explicandum that was accounted for is different from the explicandum for which justification was sought. In Example 16-9 the fact that he **does** value freedom and responsibility was accounted for. What was sought was justification of the claim that freedom and responsibility **ought to be** valued. In slipping from one function to the other, one also changes the explicandum, if it is stated precisely and unambiguously.

distinction between these two functions of explanations is an important one to know because it frequently happens that people change the subject by offering one when the other is appropriate.

In Example 16-9 Jane wanted to know the justification of the values, freedom and responsibility, as Mr. Delta saw it. (Granted: that Jane wanted this is not absolutely clear from the dialogue here given; but it was quite clear in the context in which the request occurred.) Instead Mr. Delta accounted for the fact that he had acquired these values, making no attempt to justify them.

Mrs. Alpha in Example 16-10 sought a justification of Jim's tardiness. He instead accounted for his tardiness by giving his reason for his action. In that context he could not have reasonably thought that such a reason was a justification.

In the situation from which Example 16-11 is taken, Miss Gamma used the 'why' question as an opener, an attempt to provoke a discussion. Hence there was little context to depend on in interpreting her question. But it does seem at least clear that she wanted someone to account for Dylan Thomas' visit to the United States and that Arthur did attempt to account for this visit. Hence the last example does not violate the criterion of proper function. The function that is sought is provided. Later we shall consider whether the explanation is of the proper type.

Here are some more examples with a discussion of each from the point of view of this distinction between accounting for and justifying:

Example 16-12

MRS. ALPHA: Why is angle *A* equal to angle *B*?

AL: Because they are alternate interior angles of parallel lines. [Alternate interior angles of parallel lines are equal.]

Often in the field of mathematics reason-giving explanations have the function of justifying—or proving—something. In the above example, Mrs. Alpha is seeking a justification (or a proof) of the claim that angle *A* equals angle *B*. This justification is supplied by the explicans together with the gap-filler.

Example 16-13

MR. BETA: Why is the resistance 8 ohms?

MIKE: Because the voltage is 16 volts and the current is 2 amperes. [RESISTANCE is voltage divided by current.]

Since the context is not supplied, you cannot tell from the explanation request whether a justification is requested or not. But Mike has taken the request in that way and supplied a justification of the claim that the resistance is 8 ohms. Had Mr. Beta said, "Explain why you think that the resistance is 8 ohms?" then the request would have clearly been a request for a justification.

The request that actually was used by Mr. Beta could be also used to secure an explanation of the other sort. Suppose, for example, that in the laboratory each person is instructed to wire a set of resistors in some arrangement which will result in an overall resistance of 12 ohms. Suppose further than an ohmmeter shows the overall resistance of Mike's set of resistors to be 8 ohms. Mr. Beta wants Mike to understand what he has done to produce the 8-ohm resistance. Under these circumstances the request, "Why is the resistance 8 ohms?" is a request for Mike to account for the fact that the resistance is 8 ohms. There is no call at all to prove or justify the claim that the resistance is 8 ohms. That is assumed.

Thus, the function which is called for by an explanation request is not simply dependent on the language of the request but also upon the context in which the request appears. Given the laboratory context specified in the previous paragraph, Mr. Beta does not need to be more precise in order to have requested Mike to account for the 8-ohm resistance. In a less definitive context, however, he could have made one of the following more precise requests:

How did it come to be that your resistance is 8 ohms?
Account for the fact that you have an 8-ohm overall resistance?
What is causing your overall resistance to be 8 ohms?

When the context does not make clear what is wanted, then the more precise request is in order.

Example 16-14
KEN: Why ought I treat the burlap bags with methyl bromide?
MR. ZETA: Because that is the cheapest way to stamp out golden nematode. [You ought to do what is the cheapest way to stamp out golden nematode.]

In this example the request is clearly for a justification, and Mr. Zeta has tried to supply one. The request is unambiguous, even out of context, primarily because of the use of the word 'ought'.

Example 16-15
MR. DELTA: Why was Blaine never elected president?
HELEN: The American people never did trust him. [A man who is not trusted by the American people will not be elected president.]

Mr. Delta in this last example wants someone to account for the fact which he obviously assumes needs no proof, that Blaine was never elected president. Helen has given an answer which aims at this function. There is no ambiguity in the request and the reply is intended to fulfill the account-for function.

Example 16-16

MR. BETA: Why did the electric bell ring when you pushed the button?

RON: Because pushing the button closed the circuit. [This electric bell rings when the circuit is closed.]

Again we have an unambiguous request for someone to account for something —in this case the ringing of the bell when the button was pushed. The request was so understood and the response aimed at the function desired.

Example 16-17

MRS. EPSILON: Why is the sewing room well lighted?

SARAH: Because it has light-colored walls. [Rooms with light-colored walls are well lighted.]

This is an interesting example because the whole sequence can be interpreted in two ways: in one way the request and reply fit the justification function. In another way they fit the function of accounting for something. Mrs. Epsilon might well have been asking for a justification of the claim that the sewing room is well lighted, a request that could have been put more explicitly as follows:

> Explain why you think that the sewing room is well lighted.

Given that sort of request, Sarah's response can be construed as a justification of the claim that the sewing room is well lighted. On the other hand, Mrs. Epsilon might well have been asking Sarah to account for the fact that the sewing room is well lighted, on the assumption that this fact is well established. The following might represent her thought:

> Now that we know that the sewing room is well lighted, having applied the standards for well-lighted rooms, I wonder if anyone can account for the fact that it is well lighted.

Given that as the situation, again Sarah's response can be satisfactory, because it can be interpreted as a causal explanation of the good lighting in the sewing room: The light-colored walls cause the room to be well lighted.

This last example emphasizes the fact that the same words can be interpreted in different ways. Not only can the words of the request be ambiguous, but so can the words of the reply, even when the gap-filler is added. Sarah is safe, no matter what Mrs. Epsilon meant.

To sum up, there are two basic functions of reason-giving explanations, and ordinarily when one is sought, the other is not appropriate. The functions are giving a justification and accounting for something. Roughly speaking, the sign that an accounting-for explanation is desired is the indication that the thing to be explained is to be accepted as a fact; and a sign that a justification explanation is desired is the indication that the explicandum needs to be shown to be true.

Proper type of explanation

Another way to classify explanations is according to type, such as causal explanation, reason-for-acting explanation, and value explanation. (A reason-for-acting explanation gives a person's reason for doing something.) Generally speaking, knowing the type of explanation does not automatically determine the function. For example, causal explanations can be used to account for something, but they can also be used to justify or prove something.

In this section you will be introduced to some of the types of reason-giving explanation, and some important distinctions will be suggested. The next chapter will go into the idiosyncrasies of the various types of explanation, mentioning some of the unresolved problems, problems that will be ignored in this brief discussion.

In Example 16-11, Arthur offered an account-for explanation of Dylan Thomas' coming to the United States to read poetry. His explanation appealed to "a basic unconscious desire to receive public adulation". Since an account-for explanation was requested, Arthur's explanation did not violate the criterion of proper function.

However, whether Arthur provided an explanation of the proper type is not clear. This is in doubt because Miss Gamma did not make clear which type she desired. Perhaps it did not matter to her what type was offered. Perhaps she was only trying to provoke a discussion which would stimulate interest or would serve as a vehicle for some important points that were in the back of her mind.

In any case, her request was not clear. Arthur offered a causal explanation of Thomas' visit in an attempt to account for it. Another type that could have been offered would be one that gave Thomas' consciously held reason for making the trip, which reason might not have had anything to do with public adulation. Such an explanation would be what we shall call a 'reason-for-acting explanation'. Had Arthur said, "Because he wanted to make money", then he would have been giving a reason-for-acting explanation.

These two explanations of Thomas' visit are not incompatible. They might both be true. But they are of different types. If one type is requested and the other supplied, then the explanation has failed, even though it might be true. Since in this case Miss Gamma did not specify the type she seeks, Arthur's reply does not fail the criterion of type, although it might fail to meet the criterion of truth.

Turning to Example 16-9 in which Jane (let us assume) sought a justification of the values of freedom and responsibility, we can see not only a failure to meet the function criterion, but also a failure to meet the type criterion. The request was for a value explanation, which perhaps might have been handled by reference to some higher value; but the response was a scientific explanation of some sort, perhaps a causal explanation, perhaps some other type of empirical explanation.

In Example 16-20 Mrs. Alpha was seeking some kind of justification of Jim's tardiness:

> MRS. ALPHA: Jim, will you please explain why you are late?
> JIM: Because I wanted to see what the halls are like when they are empty.

Actually Jim in a way does explain why he was late. He gives his reason for making the decision that he made. However, as is clear from the context, Mrs. Alpha wants more than an accounting for Jim's lateness. She wants him to provide a justification of the proposition, "Jim's lateness was excusable", or, "Jim was not obliged to be on time." This he made no attempt to provide. Hence Jim's answer fails the function criterion. Since a satisfactory explanation might have included a reason for acting (for example, he wanted to help a student who had fallen on the stairs), his explanation cannot be judged to have violated the type criterion. More about types of explanations in the next chapter. As you might suspect, the topic can be quite complex.

Nondeductive justification explanation

Since there are various ways of justifying statements, not all of which are deductive in form, there must be justification explanations which do not fit the deductive model. However, as the topic "justification" is one which we have not yet explored (except for deductive justifications) and will not explore until Part IV, the evaluation of such explanations must be neglected at this point.

Summary

This brief discussion of functions and types of explanations should serve to make clear the distinction between the two functions of explanations: accounting for something and justifying; and it should serve to introduce the topic of the next chapter, types of explanation. In the background of all this discussion is the function-type criterion for judging explanations: An explanation should be of the function and type appropriate to the situation, which means most usually that it should be of the function and type that is requested.

COMPREHENSION SELF-TEST

True or False? If the statement is false, change a crucial term (or terms) to make it true.

16–26. Generally, reason-giving explanations have but one function: to justify something.

16–27. The presentation of a cause in an explanation can only serve to account for something.

Problems.

16–28. Pick one of the explanations from the completion exercises in the last chapter and describe a context in which that explanation would be used to justify something.

16–29. Using the same explanation describe a context in which it would be used to account for something.

16–30. Pick and copy a reason-giving explanation from a text from which you have taught or might teach. (Do not choose a nondeductive justification explanation.)

a. Complete it.

b. Apply the criteria of truth, level of sophistication, noncircularity, and proper function and type. State how each explanation fares when these criteria are applied. Be sure to specify the function of the explanation, and the type, if you can.

Chapter Summary

This chapter introduced the four most commonly needed criteria for the evaluation of reason-giving explanations: truth, proper level of sophistication, noncircularity, and proper function and type. The statement of these criteria in general terms is simple and obvious, though their application in particular cases is sometimes difficult and quite context-dependent. The importance of context can be seen from the fact that every example considered in this chapter could, given suitable context, be interpreted in a different way from that presented. Hopefully this dependence will not be confusing in the establishment of the basic theses of this chapter.

Each of the criteria has qualifications, the most important of which were presented, but inevitably there are others. Explicitly, the criteria are as follows:

1. The explicans and the gap-filler, if any, should ordinarily be true.
2. They should be at the proper level of sophistication.
3. The explanation should not be circular.
4. The function and type of the offered explanation should be that which is requested.

A reason-giving explanation might have the function of accounting for something, or it might have the function of justifying something. Types of reason-giving explanation mentioned in this chapter are causal, reason-for-acting, and value explanations. These and other types will be elaborated on in the next chapter. Evaluation of nondeductive justification explanations actually comes under Part IV, "Justification".

Since explanations as presented have gaps in them which can be filled in various ways without violating the canons of logic, they must sometimes be probed in order to determine the complete explanation. Probes can serve as challenges as well. Two methods of probing which were discussed are explicitly proposing a possible gap-filler, and suggesting an implication of a possible gap-filler, which implication might be true or might be false, depending on the circumstances.

CHAPTER 17

∴Types of Explanation

In the previous chapter the point was made that one of the criteria of a satisfactory explanation is that it should be of the type called for in the situation. In this chapter, the major types of explanation will be described and discussed, not only from the point of view of the application of that criterion, but also from the point of view of the particular problems raised by each of the types. The types of explanation to be discussed are analytic, empirical, causal, reason-for-acting, value, and obligation.

This system of categorizing types of explanation depends on the type of general statement on which the explanation is primarily based. So we will start out by making explicit distinctions among some major types of statements.

Analytic and Synthetic Statements

The first distinction to consider is that between analytic and synthetic statements. Next are the distinctions among types of synthetic statements. Both topics are covered in this section. The analytic-synthetic distinction was briefly described in Chapter 10, and more fully here, though certainly not exhaustively. There is a vast literature on the topic.

Analytic statements

ANALYTIC STATEMENTS are those which are in a given context correctly taken as true simply as a result of the meanings of the words appearing in the statement. They are not statements that can be tested, because no conceivable test could exist for them. Here are examples of sentences that at least in most contexts are used to make analytic statements:*

1. A square has four sides.
2. A BACHELOR is a man who is not yet married.
3. Alternate interior angles of parallel lines are equal.

The first example is part of a definition. It lists one of the defining qualities of a square. The second example is a complete classification definition. The third example follows necessarily from the definitions and postulates of Euclidian geometry, the postulates themselves being regarded in the context of Euclidian geometry as analytic statements.

To deny an analytic statement in the context in which it is offered is to contradict oneself. For instance, if you were to state 'Not all squares have four sides' (using the terms in their ordinary sense), then you would be involved in a self-contradiction. The falsity of the previous contradictory statement can be determined merely by reference to the meanings of the words which form the statement, just as the truth of the statement 'All squares have four sides' follows from the meanings of the terms which constitute that statement. The latter is a logically true statement, whereas contradictory statements such as 'Not all squares have four sides' and 'Certain bachelors are married' are logically false.

So, if you were to deny that a square has four sides, you might be contradicting yourself, but more probably you are showing that you are not using the word 'square' in the way most people do. When someone actually does challenge the truth of a statement that you are regarding as analytic, that is usually a good indication that he is attaching meanings to the word(s) different from those that you are. (Of course, if the statement is one which follows necessarily from other analytic statements, then he might simply not have seen that it follows.)

The criterion for an analytic statement is not that the statement be obviously true, but that there be no conceivable counter-examples. Most people regard the following as an obvious truth:

If you throw a heavy stone up in the air, it will come back down.

But, one can **conceive** of a counter-example to that statement. Conceivably, a stone might be thrown up into the air and remain suspended—up there.

* In this discussion I am using a distinction between sentences and statements, 'sentence' referring to the symbols being used and 'statement' referring to what is said with the symbols. Note that the analytic-synthetic distinction is made between statements, not sentences, since sentences vary so much in meaning from one context to another. My practice roughly follows that of P. F. Strawson, in *Introduction to Logical Theory* (London: Methuen and Co., 1952).

We all know that this will not happen, yet we can conceive of it by forming a series of images in which the stone is thrown up and just stays there. Although such a happening is not empirically possible, it is logically possible, and the logical possibility of a counter-example disqualifies a statement from being analytic. Counter-examples to the three analytic statements listed above are not logically possible, if the statements are taken in the sense that most people take them.

Some people might initially have the inclination to mistakenly judge a statement such as 'London is the capital city of England' to be analytic (perhaps because it is so indisputably factually true)—but beware; remember that the criterion for determining whether the statement is analytic is **not** whether the statement is factually accurate, but whether it is logically true. If you were to deny the previous statement, you could be charged with ignorance or misinformation, but not with self-contradiction; for it is quite conceivable that the seat of government might be transferred to some other city. It is the **logical** possibility of a counter-example to that statement which disqualifies it from being analytic. We call it a synthetic statement.

Synthetic statements

SYNTHETIC STATEMENTS (the other part of the analytic-synthetic distinction) are any and all statements that are not analytic. Here are some examples of sentences which in most contexts would be used to make synthetic statements:

1. If you throw an object into the air, it will come back down.
2. Plugging in the iron caused the fuse to blow.
3. Marshall's reason for his actions in the Marbury *v.* Madison case was that he wanted to establish the Supreme Court's right to interpret the Constitution.
4. *You Can't Take It With You* is a good play.
5. You ought to set forth a complete interpretation of the symbols on your map.

Ordinarily none of the above sentences would be used to make an analytic statement, because as ordinarily used they all can be denied without self-contradiction. Their truth, if they are true, does not follow simply from the meanings of the words used.

You might wonder about questions and commands (for example, "Where is Macedon?" "Divide both sides by 'a — b'."). Since these are not statements, the question about whether they are analytic or synthetic cannot arise.

Applying the distinction between analytic and synthetic statements

Since this is a distinction between statements that are made in a given context, we sometimes stumble when trying to apply it to sentences that appear out of context. Sometimes the same set of words which makes up a sentence can be used to make an analytic statement in one context and a synthetic statement in another context without violating established usage in the particular context.

The following is an example:

Pure water freezes at 32 degrees Fahrenheit.

In some contexts the temperature at which pure water freezes (at sea level) is taken as the defining characteristic of the 32-degree point on the Fahrenheit scale. In such situations the statement made with that sentence is analytic.

However, in other situations that sentence is used to express a fact about water. Suppose that a child has learned the use of the thermometer by associating its readings with the way the air feels to him—and this is the way we do generally learn the use of the thermometer. He has a vague understanding of the 32-degree point on the Fahrenheit scale. For him it is a discovery that water freezes at 32 degrees Fahrenheit. For him, as for most laymen, the sentence, "Pure water freezes at 32 degrees Fahrenheit," would be presumed to be used to make a synthetic statement. And when laymen make a statement with that sentence, they are making a synthetic statement. An unsophisticated layman can easily conceive of what he thinks to be a good Fahrenheit thermometer immersed in a beaker containing a mixture of water and ice, such that the reading on the thermometer is, say, 40 degrees.

Hence in applying the analytic-synthetic distinction one must pay close attention to the context and the intent of the person who commits himself to the statement. If, according to the way he is using the words, a denial of the statement would be a contradiction, then he is making an analytic statement. If the denial would not be a contradiction, then he is making a synthetic statement.

One must be on guard against a person who makes an analytic statement and justifies it as such, and then reinterprets it as a synthetic statement later on. This is one way of interpreting what Jim did in the discussion about propaganda in earlier chapters of this book. For him the following statement at the beginning of the discussion was analytic:

1. PROPAGANDA is any attempt to persuade.

Then later on the statement made with that sentence became synthetic and false, when Jim was operating under a new definition of propaganda:

2. PROPAGANDA is any illegitimate attempt to persuade.

The statement made with the original sentence became false and synthetic under the new definition, since there are attempts to persuade that are legitimate.

Thus Jim's conclusion, "The newspaper is full of propaganda," was proven by treating 1 as analytic; then his conclusion was applied in condemning the newspaper, assuming 1 to be synthetic and 2 to be analytic. Such a shift was improper.

The categorization of explanations

The analytic-synthetic distinction is the first basic distinction in our categorization of explanations. The main reason for using this distinction in our category system is that analytic explanations (or more strictly the analytic parts of explanations) are not subject to the criterion of testability/applicability, which is discussed in the next chapter. Briefly the idea is that a statement that is not expected to play the role of a synthetic statement is not forced to meet a criterion that synthetic statements should meet.

In the category system that follows, explanations are grouped according to the type of general statement that is basic to the explanation. A more precise system would not group explanations according to type, but would look at each of the statements involved in an explanation and judge it on its own merits, considering the role it is expected to play in the explanation. Such a system would be more precise primarily because there can be complicated explanations containing basic generalizations of more than one type. But for our purposes it is simpler to think in terms of types of explanations, assuming that we will generally work with the simpler kinds of explanations.

Once the analytic-synthetic distinction is made, the other distinctions are among types of synthetic statements. Here are five types of synthetic statements, which incidentally correspond to the five examples given earlier of five sentences which would be generally used to make synthetic statements:

1. Empirical (but not causal)
2. Causal
3. Reason-for-acting
4. Value
5. Obligation

Thus we will be considering six types of explanation: analytic explanations, and explanations corresponding to each of the five listed types of synthetic statements. In the following discussion the distinctions among these types of statements will provide the basis for the distinctions among types of explanation.

COMPREHENSION SELF-TEST

True or False? If the statement is false, change a crucial term (or terms) to make it true.

17–1. It is self-contradictory to deny an analytic statement.

17–2. It is not self-contradictory to deny a synthetic statement.

17–3. If a sentence is used to make a true synthetic statement in one context, then it can only be used to make synthetic statements in other contexts.

17–4. All statements are either analytic or synthetic.

Classification. For each of the following sentences, judge whether it would be ordinarily used in contexts familiar to you to make an analytic statement or a synthetic statement. Be able to describe the context which justifies your judgment.

17–5. The main United Nations building is located in New York City.

17–6. A straight line is the shortest distance between two points.

17–7. The first word in a sentence should start with a capital letter.

17–8. In German all nouns are capitalized.

17–9. An irregular verb is a verb which is not conjugated in the regular way.

17–10. The sense of smell is of extremely slight service to man.

17–11. The crossing of forms, which have been exposed to slightly different conditions of life or which have varied, favors the size, vigor, and fertility of the offspring.

17–12. Vaccination is inoculation to induce immunity to smallpox.

17–13. A concerto is a musical composition (usually in symphonic form with three movements) in which one instrument (or two or three) stands out in bold relief against the orchestra.

17–14. Beethoven's Fifth Piano Concerto is a mechanical, uninteresting piece of music.

17–15. If a batter swings at a pitched ball and misses it completely, then he has made a strike.

17–16. In order to hit the ball squarely, it is best to swing level.

17–17. A pentagon has five sides.

17–18. The pentagon shape is used rarely in buildings.

17–19. The building in Washington, which is called "The Pentagon", has five sides.

17–20. The pressure is the force on each unit of area.

17–21. The pressure of the water in a lake varies directly as depth.

17–22. If the pressure is kept constant, the total force varies directly with the area considered.

17–23. A sonnet is a lyric poem consisting of fourteen lines written in an elaborate rhyme scheme.

17–24. Most people use the word 'propaganda' as a derogatory term.

17–25. If there is enough cultural lag, a revolution will result.

17–26. A social class structure is based upon the status positions of people.

17–27. Slavery was the principal cause of the Civil War.

17–28. A sibling relationship will be found among brothers and sisters in the same family.

Discussion Question.

17–29. Find a sentence in your field that could be used to make an analytic statement and could also be used to make a synthetic statement. Then:

a. Give the sentence.
b. Describe a context in which it is used to make an analytic statement.
c. Describe a context in which it is used to make a synthetic statement.

Analytic Explanations

If the basic general statement in an explanation is analytic, then we shall consider the explanation to be analytic. Here are three examples of analytic explanations. You have seen them before:

Example 17-1
MR. OMICRON: Why does opium produce sleep?
LARRY: Because it has dormitive power. [DORMITIVE POWER is sleep-producing ability].

Example 17-2
MRS. ALPHA: Why is triangle *ABC* a right triangle?
ALAN: Because it is a triangle containing a right angle. [Triangles containing a right angle are RIGHT TRIANGLES.]

Example 17-3
MISS GAMMA: Why is 'going' a gerund in that sentence?
JONATHAN: Because it functions like a noun there. ['Going' is a verb ending in 'ing'. All verbals which end in 'ing' and which function like nouns are GERUNDS.]

In each of these explanations the basic general statement is presumably analytic. Immediately one of the dangers in analytic explanations becomes apparent. They can easily be circular. Example 17-1 is quite clearly circular, as was indicated earlier. The request was for an explanation that would account for the sleep-producing power of opium. The thing supplied did not get us anywhere. It stated a fact that was already known to the person requesting the explanation, though he may not be familiar with the terms used to express the alleged explanatory fact. It depended simply on a definition—an analytic statement. What was wanted was something that depends upon an empirical, perhaps causal law. Hence the first explanation, though analytic, is defective because it is circular.

As you will remember, the second example, the one dealing with a right triangle, might be circular in some contexts and not so in others. The gap filler to which it appeals is an analytic statement, a definition of 'right triangle'. In some contexts a definition appealing to this sort of analytic statement is perfectly satisfactory; in others a more sophisticated analytic statement is called for. Recall the situation as presented in Example 16-6.

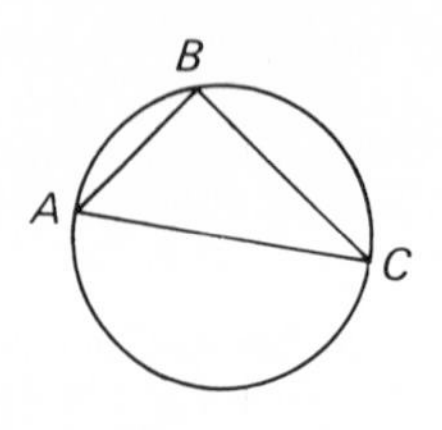

The diagram on p. 306 is on the board. Mrs. Alpha has asked why triangle *ABC* is a right triangle. The class already knows what a right triangle is. They have already proved that a triangle inscribed in a circle, if one of its sides is a diameter of the circle, is a right triangle. Then the following answer, which also makes use of an analytic statement as a gap-filler, might well be acceptable, while the one given in Example 17-2 is unacceptable:

Example 17-4

ALAN: Because *AC* is the diameter of a circle and the triangle is inscribed in that circle. [If a triangle is inscribed in a circle and if one side is a diameter of that circle, then the triangle is a right triangle.]

The explanation in the third example, the one dealing with a gerund, would ordinarily be quite satisfactory. Miss Gamma's request would ordinarily be taken to call for an answer that would make use of an analytic statement about what gerunds are—generally a definition of 'gerund'. And Jonathan supplied an answer that used an analytic statement as a gap-filler.

Thus the three cases are of different sorts. The first would generally be circular; the second would be in some circumstances, but not in others; and the third would generally not be circular. Two conclusions can be drawn from these examples:

1. Analytic explanations are potentially circular explanations.
2. Whether they are circular depends upon the context of the request and the request itself.

Analytic explanations must also meet the other three criteria presented so far: truth, proper level of sophistication, and proper function and type. Nothing further needs to be said here about the application of the latter two criteria, but a word about truth is in order. If a statement is analytic, then it satisfies the criterion of truth, for to deny an analytic statement would be to contradict oneself. Other parts of the explanation might be judged to fail this criterion, but not the analytic statement itself.

The important point is that in a way it is inappropriate to call analytic statements true; for this might be interpreted to mean the same as it means when we call synthetic statements true. If, when we say that an analytic statement is true, we mean something like the following, then the word 'truth' may be applied to analytic statements:

> If a statement expresses the way the words are being used in a given context—or follows solely from such expressions, then it is true in the way analytic statements can be true.

Consider the following example, referring back to the 'propaganda' discussion in Chapters 6, 7, and 8:

Example 17-5

MR. DELTA: Jim, why do you call the Red Cross announcement propaganda?

JIM: Because it is an attempt to persuade. [PROPAGANDA is any attempt to persuade.]

In a way it is not appropriate to call that gap-filler true, since although analytic, it is so because of Jim's stipulation in the context. As he is using the language, it would be contradictory to deny that gap-filler. On the other hand, one might well have qualms about calling it true. Let us say that it is a linguistic truth, as Jim is using the language. Hence we will say that the criterion of truth shall be satisfied by analytic statements.

Analytic explanations are quite common in teaching situations. They are the typical sort of explanations that demonstrate understanding of the concepts of a field and show how a person is using a term. They have dangers, but we cannot do without them.

Empirical Explanations

Empirical explanations are those which depend on an empirical general statement. Now just what is an empirical statement? The sort of thing that scientists discover is put in the form of empirical statements. Historians make claims about what has happened. When they do, they are making empirical statements. Newspapers try to tell us what happened at a given place at a given time, and in so doing make empirical statements. Roughly speaking, empirical statements are characterized by being about the world, by being checkable by observation, and by being grounds for making predictions. When someone asks you to give him the facts, and not to make any value judgments about them, he is asking you to make empirical statements.

Here are some examples of empirical statements:

Columbus discovered America in 1492.

The United States is the world's greatest consumer of oil.

If dough does not rise after yeast has been introduced, then the yeast is probably dead.

Modern writers generally do not obey the rule that prohibits ending a sentence with a preposition.

A body immersed in a fluid is buoyed up by a force equal to the weight of the fluid displaced.

The first two of the above examples are singular empirical statements. They cover only one specific fact. The other three are general in scope. They cover a number of cases.

Example 17-6

Here is an example of an empirical explanation:

MR. BETA: Why did the liquid in the jar not freeze when the temperature was minus 10 degrees Centigrade?
FRANK: Because it is alcohol. [Alcohol does not freeze when the temperature is minus 10 degrees Centigrade.]

Note that the general statement is an empirical statement, but also note that it is not a causal statement. It simply gives a characteristic of alcohol, which, at least at lower levels of sophistication, is not analytically related to the concept, *alcohol.*

Empirical explanations are expected to satisfy all four of the criteria mentioned in the previous chapter. And there is no special way of interpreting the criterion of truth. The empirical statements in an explanation must be true in a straightforward sense, if the explanation is to be satisfactory. Empirical explanations must also satisfy the criterion of testability, which will be discussed in the next chapter.

Causal Explanation

Causal explanations are like empirical explanations in many respects, but because of certain peculiar problems in dealing with causal statements, they will be treated separately. If explicit reference to causation appears, then the explanation shall be deemed a causal explanation. For example, the following are causal explanations:

Example 17-7
MR. BETA: Why did the fuse blow?
SID: Plugging in that 5-ohm resistor caused it to blow.

Example 17-8
MR. BETA: Why did the fuse blow?
ARDYSS: You plugged in that 5-ohm resistor. [Plugging a 5-ohm resistor into a 110-volt, 15-amp circuit causes the fuse to blow.]

Presumably the following is also a causal explanation:

Example 17-9
MR. BETA: Why did the fuse blow?
FRED: You plugged in that 5-ohm resistor. [Whenever a 5-ohm resistor is plugged into a 110-volt, 15-amp circuit the fuse blows.]

Under the circumstances, on the assumption that Fred was trying to account for the blowing of the fuse, he probably thought that he was giving a cause, even though the words in Example 17-9 do not include the word 'cause' or any similar term (like 'results in', 'produces', and so forth). The words in this explanation do not necessarily commit Fred to a causal explanation, but since people using words this way usually do mean to indicate a causal relationship, we will usually be right in treating such explanations as causal.

Causal language

The language which we use to express causal relationships is rich, partially because for reasons of style we want to have different ways of saying the same thing, partially because there are a number of different sorts of things we want to say about causal relationships, and partially because, causal relationships being difficult to establish, people sometimes want to be vague in their claims.

Synonyms and Vagueness. Such locutions as 'produces', 'results in,' 'follows from', and 'brings about' are causal terms. They are generally used for purposes of variation in style, but people sometimes use them because they have a prejudice against the word 'cause' and at the same time want to make causal claims. When the latter situation obtains, they do not really avoid making a causal claim; they simply satisfy their prejudice.

Here are some examples of statements using the above locutions:

> Increasing taxes without a thorough public relations campaign **produces** an angry electorate.
>
> Neglect of the basic needs of young children **results in** maladjustment.
>
> Vigorous growth **follows from** the introduction of fertilizer.
>
> Heavy emphasis on an art form or method soon **brings about** a reaction in the opposite direction.

Henceforth we shall neglect locutions of this sort in order to simplify the discussion. But remember that the same sort of problems hold for statements using locutions like the above, as for statements explicitly using the word 'cause'.

Other locutions are vague enough to enable one to avoid being committed to the existence of a causal relationship. Examples are 'If . . . , then', 'Whenever', 'is followed by', 'is correlated with'. These expressions can be used when causal relationships hold, but do not by themselves commit the speaker to a belief in the causal relationship. Consider the following empirical statement:

> Whenever the red light of this traffic light goes off, the green light goes on.

The extinction of the red light does not cause the green light to go on. Instead they have a common cause—to be found in the mechanism operating the light. This example shows that the 'Whenever' locution (and the others as well, for similar statements could be made with them) does not require that one of the indicated events or things be a cause of the other indicated event or thing. But the following example shows that this locution (and the others as well) can be used when a causal relation is believed to exist:

> Whenever taxes are increased without a thorough public relations campaign, the electorate gets angry.

When we know that there is a relationship, but do not know that it is a causal relationship, these locutions are quite useful. For the sake of style they are also useful. Even when we do know of the existence of a causal relationship, the relationship can be indicated in these ways, as it was in Example 17-6. But these expressions are also ways of avoiding public commitment to causal assertions that we really would make, if it were not for a prejudice against doing so.

When causal generalizations are asserted, there is always an implicit qualifying phrase, 'under normal conditions'. This is a vague phrase, but it serves to protect the generalization against odd challenges. No causal generalization can hold in the face of odd challenges unless it has some sort of implicit (or explicit) protective phrase. Let me clarify using an example:

> Inserting a piece of paper in an oven set at 300 degrees Fahrenheit causes the paper to char.

One very quickly thinks of conditions under which this generalization does not hold. Suppose that there is no electricity (or gas) connection to the oven. Suppose that the paper is wet. Suppose that the paper is made of asbestos. Suppose that the paper is only in for two seconds. Suppose that the paper is enclosed in an insulated container like a vacuum bottle. Suppose that the paper has a cold blast of air blown upon it. Suppose the oven door is not closed. And so forth.

We might want to sharpen up the generalization a little bit:

> Inserting a piece of ordinary dry paper in an operating oven set at 300 degrees Fahrenheit causes the paper to char.

But we cannot allow in advance for all the possible things that can go wrong.

No matter how many qualifications are added to the generalization, an ingenious person can think of conditions under which it would not hold. Yet there is a ring of truth to the generalization as it was first stated. And there certainly is a strong element of truth in the revision. But since complete insulation against all contingencies is impossible, there must be an implicit or explicit vague qualifier such as 'under normal conditions'. Another good idea is to insulate in advance against known possibilities that might occur. That was done in the revision. But since there are always other conceivable possible conditions under which the generalization does not hold, a vague qualifier must be invoked as well.

This vague qualifier may be invoked in different ways. It can be made explicitly. Secondly, it might be left implicit on the assumption that the person addressed knows that there are inevitably unstated qualifications to any empirical generalization, a fact which unfortunately most people do not explicitly know. A third way of invoking it is, when an odd challenge is made, to say, "You know very well what I mean." A fourth way is to introduce the term 'generally', or 'tends to', or some similar term, in the causal statement. But this last results in a weaker statement (which, of course, is sometimes wanted) than the 'under normal conditions' qualification, for it allows that even under normal conditions the causal generalization sometimes does not hold.

Because there are always conceivable conditions under which causal generalizations do not hold, some people claim that we should not make such generalizations (though they themselves, of course, do make them in their everyday lives). A more discreet course is to make use of causal generalizations but to realize that they are true only if one has such implicit or explicit escape clauses as are mentioned in the previous paragraph.

The Cause—As Opposed to a Partial Cause. The locution, 'a partial cause' ('contributory cause', etc.) is invoked to mark the fact that the thing identified as a cause was (is) not by itself sufficient to bring about the effect, and that all of the partial causes together were (are) sufficient to bring about the effect. To call something '**the** cause' is to imply that under the given conditions, it was sufficient by itself.

When giving a causal explanation we must choose between giving a cause as **the** cause and giving a cause as **a partial** cause. In the social sciences, including history, we often choose the latter course, because the relationships between events are so complex and unclear to us, because the other factors are not regularly present, and because to assert that something or someone is **the** cause, when dealing with human affairs, is often to ascribe responsibility to the alleged cause. Social scientists often want to avoid ascribing responsibility.

Aside from the responsibility aspect, the decision should be made on the basis of the extent to which the other factors are known to be regularly present. We give economic complaints as a partial cause of the Revolutionary War, because the other factors are both not all known and not all known to be regularly present. On the other hand, we give the application of the match to the combustible paper as the cause of the fire even though we are well aware that without the presence of an oxidizing agent (generally oxygen) there would be no fire. We neglect the oxidizing agent because it under normal conditions is the only other factor and is regularly present. (The three factors are: kindling temperature, oxidizing agent, and a combustible material.) If it were not known to be regularly present, then we would say that the application of the match was **a partial** cause of the fire.

The Fundamental Cause (also called 'the basic cause', 'the underlying cause', 'the decisive cause', and 'the real cause'). This type of cause may be contrasted with the immediate cause (also called 'the proximate cause' and 'the occasion'). The difference between the fundamental and immediate cause is a relative one. The event of which each is alleged to be the cause allegedly would have occurred anyway if the immediate cause had not been present, whereas its occurrence (at least at that time) allegedly was much **more** unlikely if the fundamental cause had not been present. Thus the difference between the immediate cause and the fundamental cause is like the difference between the likelihood of the event's not occurring given the absence of each.

For example, when firing on Fort Sumter is given as the immediate cause, and slavery as the fundamental cause of the Civil War, the implication is that the war would have come anyway, even if Sumter had **not** been fired upon (there would have been another immediate cause); but that there might well have been no war at all, if the institution of slavery had not been present. Incidentally, I do not here imply that slavery actually **was** the fundamental cause of the Civil War; all that is suggested is **what it means to say** that slavery was the fundamental cause of the Civil War.

*Empirically Necessary and Sufficient Conditions**; *General and Singular Causal Statements.* To say that a condition was empirically necessary for another condition is to say that without the first, the second could not have occurred. For example, the presence of an oxidizing agent was an empirically necessary condition for the fire. To say that a condition was empirically sufficient for another is to say that under the conditions in existence, given the occurrence of the first, the second was bound to have occurred. For example, given the presence of the oxygen and the dry paper, and given the application of the match (sufficient condition), the fire was bound to have occurred.

Empirically necessary and sufficient conditions are to be distinguished from logically necessary and sufficient conditions. The latter are analytically related to that for which they are necessary and/or sufficient (for example, being a bachelor is a logically sufficient condition for being unmarried). The former are empirically related. It is conceivable, and thus logically possible, that a fire could occur without the presence of an oxidizing agent; but such an occurrence is an empirical impossibility. Our concern here is with empirically necessary and sufficient conditions.

In discussions of causation it sometimes helps to use the language of necessary and sufficient conditions, because this language is more clear. This is not to imply that the meaning of 'cause' can be exhausted by a definition using this language; but the allegation that x caused y does roughly

* You are reminded of the discussion in Chapter 3 of deductive reasoning with necessary and sufficient conditions.

imply a statement in the language of necessary and sufficient conditions, and this statement is easier to test than the causal statement.

To say that x caused y* is to **imply** that under the existing circumstances the occurrence of x was a sufficient condition for y. It is also loosely to **imply** (unless y was overdetermined) that the occurrence of x was a necessary condition under those circumstances for the occurrence of y **at the instant it occurred**. If x was an immediate cause, then its occurrence was not a necessary condition for all time—just for that instant and perhaps a short period before and after. If x was a fundamental cause of y, then for a long period of time—perhaps forever—y would not have occurred if x had not occurred. In other words, a fundamental cause is necessary for a longer period of time than an immediate cause. You can now see more clearly why these are relative notions. The more fundamental, the more necessary; the more immediate, the less necessary.

Let us use this language to talk about the causes of the Civil War.** The firing on Fort Sumter is held by many to have been at that instant a sufficient and necessary condition for the occurrence of the war, but (they hold) since the war would have occurred even if Sumter had not been fired on, it would not long have been a necessary condition. Something else would have come along which would have been a sufficient condition for the occurrence of the war. These people hold that the firing on Fort Sumter was the immediate cause.

Further back in the causal chain (they hold) we find the institution of slavery, which was a sufficient and necessary condition for the occurrence of the war. Under the conditions in the United States at that time the existence of that institution was sufficient to bring about the war; furthermore, if that institution had not existed (and since it was the fundamental cause), it is very doubtful (they would hold) that there would have been a war between the North and the South. They hold slavery to be the fundamental cause of the war.

A weaker claim is made by others, who claim that slavery was only a partial cause of the war; that is, by itself it was not sufficient. A conjunction of it and several other partial causes was sufficient and necessary, however. Furthermore, each of them was necessary at the time, but perhaps less indispensible than if it had been **the** cause.

Please be clear that the above discussion of the causes of the Civil War

* The locution is not the general one '*A* **causes** *B*'; it is the specific one, 'x **caused** y'. Discussion of this distinction will appear shortly.

** See Howard K. Beale's "What Historians Have Said About the Causes of the Civil War," Chapter III in *Theory and Practice in Historical Study: A Report of the Committee on Historiography* (New York: Social Science Research Council, 1946) (Bulletin 54), pp. 53–102. This article is an enlightening discussion of various views about the causes of the Civil War. It discusses the substantive issues instead of the logical ones which are discussed here.

is only intended to show in terms of necessary and sufficient conditions the logical content of certain causal claims.

For practice, you should now take some singular causal statement from your field (unless your field is mathematics) and state what it implies in terms of necessary and sufficient conditions. A singular causal statement is of the form '*x* caused *y*', where single things or events are to be substituted for '*x*' and '*y*'.

General causal claims are of the form, '*A* causes *B*', where '*A*' and '*B*' can be replaced by terms for classes or types of things or events. The following is a general causal claim:

> Inserting a piece of ordinary dry paper in an operating oven set at 300 degrees Fahrenheit causes the paper to burn.

The inserting of a piece of ordinary dry paper in an operating oven set at 300 degrees Fahrenheit is one type of event. It is a fairly carefully limited type, but it is still a type; it is not one particular occurrence. The burning of the piece of paper is again a type of event. The causal generalization relates events of the first type to events of the second type.

What does this sort of statement imply in terms of necessary and sufficient conditions? It generally implies that an event of the first type is a sufficient condition for the occurrence of an event of the second type. But it does not imply that an event of the first type is a necessary condition for an event of the second type. In terms of the above example, the statement implies that the inserting of some particular piece of dry paper in the 300-degree oven is a sufficient condition for the burning of the particular piece of paper. But it does not imply that inserting that piece of paper in that oven is a necessary condition for its burning. It might burn without being put in the oven. It might be held over a lighted candle and catch fire as a result of that.

Unfortunately the locution form, '*A* causes *B*', has an ambiguity in its ordinary use. Sometimes people use the phrase when they do not mean to imply that a case of *A* under normal conditions is by itself a sufficient condition for the occurrence of a case of *B*. Instead they only would claim that a case of *A* **can be** a sufficient condition, given the right circumstances, of the occurrence of a case of *B*. For example, when the posters say, "Drunken driving causes accidents", presumably the writers do not mean to imply that every time someone is drunk and drives, there is an accident. Instead they only mean to imply that, given the right conditions, drunken driving is a sufficient condition for an accident, that drunken driving **can** cause accidents.

Hence one must be on guard in the use of this locution. In order to avoid a possible misunderstanding, unless the context does the job for you, it does not hurt to insert such terms as 'usually', 'always (under normal conditions)', or 'sometimes', as the case may be. And it does not hurt to ask another speaker what he has in mind, if the context does not make it clear.

With the reservation about this ambiguity in mind, we can say that the general causal statement of the form '*A* causes *B*' gives a type of event that would be a sufficient condition but not necessarily a necessary condition. The singular causal statement of the form, '*x* caused *y*', gives something that under the existing circumstances was sufficient and necessary (if *y* was not overdetermined) at that point in time.

Hopefully you have now mastered the language of necessary and sufficient conditions as a way of putting some of the implications of causal allegations. If so, then you will find it easier to discuss and evaluate the gap-fillers in causal explanations.

The Generality of a Singular Causal Claim. Consider the simple singular causal claim, 'Plugging in that 5-ohm resistor caused the fuse to blow'. To what does the language of this singular causal claim commit the speaker? Suppose he offers it in an answer to a request for an explanation of why the fuse blew. Usually a singular statement offered in explanation needs some general statement to complete the explanation. Is that the case here?

No, it is not. You will remember that the need for a gap-filler was shown by the question, 'What does that have to do with it?' But such a question is inappropriate when a single causal claim has been offered in explanation, if the event alleged to be caused is the one for which explanation is sought. Consider this dialogue, which illustrates the point:

Example 17-10
MR. DELTA: Why did the fuse blow?
FRANK: Plugging in the 5-ohm resistor caused it to blow.
MR. DELTA: What does that have to do with it?
FRANK: I just told you. It caused the fuse to blow.

There was no gap to be filled in that explanation. It was complete as it stood.

Of course, if Mr. Delta had meant to be asking why plugging in the 5-ohm resistor caused the fuse to blow, then there is a reply to that question, but such a reply would not be a gap-filler. It would be an explanation of the fact that is offered in explanation. It would not attempt to make the connection between the offered explanatory material and the fact to be explained, which is the role of a gap-filler.

Although no gap-filler is needed, some claims are implied by a singular causal statement. First of all, such a statement presupposes that both the alleged cause and the effect actually occurred. In this case that means that the facts that a lighted match was applied to the piece of paper and that the paper caught fire are presupposed. Of course, the second of these presuppositions was also presupposed by the request for an explanation.

A degree of generality is also implied by the singular causal assertion. Some sort of general relationship between events like applying a match to paper and events like the paper's catching fire is implied. What is this general relationship? It is this: If, under the same circumstances, an event which is just like the explaining event were to occur, then an event which is just like the explained event would occur. Applying this formula to the fuse example, the generalization implied by the allegation of the causal relationship between the specific events is this: If, under circumstances like the ones obtaining at the time of the blowing of the fuse, there were to be a plugging of a 5-ohm resistor into a similar circuit, then the fuse would blow.

To see why this generalization is implied, imagine it to be false. If it is false, then if the general statement is interpreted narrowly enough; the statement of specific causal connection must be false also.* Thus the narrow interpretation of the generalization is implied. Notice that this is not to say clearly just what is implied, since the question of the amount of similarity necessary is left open.

Why this concern about the presupposition and implication of a specific causal claim? One reason is that in evaluating an explanation of this type one should know what a person who offers the explanation is committed to. If either the presupposition or the generalization is false, then the explanation is unsatisfactory.

Another reason is that in discussions of the nature and value of history, a rather basic disagreement has arisen about the function of generalizations in history.** One school holds that historians are committed to generalization when they explain; another school holds that historical explanations do not necessarily commit historians to generalizations, and, furthermore, some would assert, historians that do commit themselves to generalizations are poor historians because of the perils of generalizing about human events.

The previous analysis does not touch on the perils of generalizing; and surely the dangers and temptations are great. But it does deal with the commitment question.

If a historian claims that event *x* caused event *y*, then he is committed to saying that under the same circumstances, if an event just like *x* were to occur, then an event just like *y* would occur. Now this in a way is a compromise position between the above-mentioned two schools. It is in line with the generalization school because the implied statement is a generalization; but it is in line with the other school because the scope of the generalization is vague and can be very narrow. It does not specify **how** similar the circumstances and the events must be. Thus the generalization might be so narrow

* On the assumption of the uniformity of nature. If this assumption is rejected, then the argument does not work.

** See especially the works of Hempel, Dray, Gardiner, and Scriven listed in the references at the end of Part III.

that it has only one actual instance—although many **logically possible** instances. It is this narrowness that is sought by the other school.

Let us put the idea of the previous paragraph in terms of an example. If one claims in answer to the question, 'Why was there a war between the states in the early 1860's?', that the existence of slavery caused the war, the following is implied: Under circumstances similar to those of the early 1860's, if there also is a condition of slavery to the degree then present, a war occurs. Since the degree of similarity of circumstances and the extent to which the degree of slavery is identical are both unspecified, the generalization may be taken very narrowly, thus satisfying both positions.

How broadly it should be taken depends on the context and the field. In history we generally construe the generalizations quite narrowly, because true broad generalizations about the lives of people are so difficult to make. In the physical sciences on the other hand, because true and broad generalizations are common, we tend to construe the implied generalizations more broadly.

Gap-filling and probing a causal explanation

At the beginning of the section on causal explanation you saw examples of three different sorts of causal explanation, those which explicitly use a singular causal statement, those which make use of an explicitly causal generalization (but no singular causal statement), and those which do not use an explicitly causal statement, but which are probably causal because they attempt to account for an occurrence by citing another occurrence and/or by citing a constant relationship between occurrences of the type cited and the type explained. These three sorts of causal explanation are exemplified by Examples 17-7, 17-8 and 17-9. We shall now look at the processes of gap-filling and probing such explanations.

Singular Causal Explanation. There is no gap to fill in singular causal explanations (for example, "Plugging in that 5-ohm resistor caused it to blow.") as has already been shown by Example 17-10, in which the question, "What does that have to do with it?", was an inappropriate question. A person offering a singular causal explanation has a degree of generality to defend, but until he specifies how much, one cannot offer a clear challenge.

One can, however, probe such an explanation by asking questions that reveal the degree of general commitment:

1. Does plugging a 5-ohm resistor into a 110-volt, 15-amp circuit always cause the fuse to blow?

2. If I plug a 5-ohm resistor in this circuit, will the fuse blow?

3. I plugged a 5-ohm resistor into the 110-volt, 15-amp circuit on the desk and the fuse did not blow. Why not?

The first probe explicitly suggested a generalization, asking if it is true; the second asked for a prediction in a circumstance somewhat similar; and the third gave a counter-example to the broad generalization suggested in the first probe. Each of these probes will get at the degree of generalization and enable one to evaluate the explanation. If the explainer is not willing to assert any degree of generality, then the body of knowledge with which he is working does not in this sort of case give us any basis for making predictions about future occurrences. Whether this is actually a deficiency is a controversial issue, but what is not controversial is that if any field of study wants to claim any insight into what is going to happen, its relevant, singular causal explanations must be to some extent generalizable.

The four basic criteria (truth, proper level of sophistication, noncircularity, proper function and type) and also the criterion of testability* all apply to singular causal explanations.

General Causal Explanations. This sort of explanation is illustrated by Example 17-8, which made use of the generalization, "Plugging a 5-ohm resistor into a 110-volt, 15-amp circuit causes the fuse to blow." This generalization served in the context as the gap-filler showing the connection between the offered explanation ("You plugged in that 5-ohm resistor.") and the fact to be explained (the fuse blew). The gap-filler made explicit reference to causation. The problems and suggestions mentioned in earlier chapters apply to the explanation under discussion: Gap-filling, probing, and evaluating are interdependent processes. Taking account of the context, the person filling the gap should be reasonably generous. Probing can take a number of different forms: directly asking for a gap-filler, suggesting one, supplying counter-examples to suspected gapfillers, and checking to see how borderline cases are handled. The four basic criteria (truth, proper level of sophistication, noncircularity, proper function and type) and also the criterion of testability are applicable in the evaluation of the final product.

Since the generalization is explicitly causal, its truth, of course, definitely depends on whether there actually is a causal relationship. The generalization which is found in Example 17-9 and which is not explicitly causal is different:

> Whenever a 5-ohm resistor is plugged into a 110-volt, 15-amp circuit, the fuse blows.

The explained fact and the offered explanatory fact were the same as those of Example 17-8. Since the gap-filler in Example 17-9 does not make explicit reference to causation, there is a problem with evaluating it which does not apply to the explicitly causal explanations. The problem is that we must

* To be discussed in Chapter 18.

guard against the claim that no causal allegation was intended. In applying the criterion of truth, we can expect that the occurrence of a case of *A* be truly sufficient **evidence** for the claim that a case of *B* will occur. (This, of course, also holds for the explicitly causal generalization). But if we expect that the occurrence of a case of *A* be truly a sufficient cause of a case of *B*, then we should add the proviso in the evaluation, 'on the assumption that a causal relationship is alleged'. As was indicated earlier, the general statement that is not explicitly causal might not actually be expressing a causal relationship. We cannot insist that a person defend a claim that a causal relationship exists when he has not explicitly so alleged.

Again the same general procedures of gap-filling, probing, and evaluating, as developed in previous chapters, can be applied.

Asking for a causal explanation

Sometimes the question, 'Why did *x* occur?', is clear enough to indicate that a causal explanation is desired. A safer procedure is to say, 'Please give me a causal explanation of the occurrence of *x*' or 'What caused *x* to occur?', thus making use of the word, 'cause'. If we ask a question such as 'Why did President Washington cross the Delaware?', the request might understandably be answered with a reason-for-acting explanation or an empirical noncausal explanation, so it is best not to use this type of question, unless the context clarifies the kind of explanation desired. The problem is similar with the request, 'Explain why President Washington crossed the Delaware', which can be answered with different kinds of reason-giving explanations.

But, as should be clear from the previous discussion of various kinds of causes, it sometimes is not enough to make clear that a causal explanation is desired. Sometimes we must indicate that we want a fundamental explanation; and sometimes we should say that a partial cause will do. If we want to be sure that a student knows the scope of the causal generalization to which he is going to appeal, we should call for an explicit statement of the generalization in the explanation. The point is that if we want to check a particular aspect of understanding, we should ask for it specifically.

Fields in which causal explanation is used

The natural sciences abound with causal explanations. A basic doctrine of these sciences in their elementary and intermediate forms is that all phenomena have causal explanations. The causal explanation is the basic logical building block for subject matter in the natural sciences. As they become more sophisticated, the physical sciences in particular veer away from the use of causal formulations, preferring precise mathematical relationships. These can often generate causal statements (for example, from the law of gravity, $F = \gamma\, mm/r^2$, we can say that doubling the distance between two objects causes the force of attraction to be one-fourth of what it was), but we have to understand what we are about (because we cannot say from the law of gravity that reducing the force of attraction to one-fourth **causes** the distance to double). The most sophisticated statements in modern physics, since they deal with probabilities, are not subject to causal interpretation.

Some of the contemporary social sciences (sociology, psychology, economics, anthropology, etc.,) make heavy use of the concept *cause* in their explanations and investigations because they, like the natural sciences, are interested in control (in the social science case—of behavior and institutions), and thus are forced to be interested in causation. They are also interested in prediction, an activity made possible by, among other things, a knowledge of causal relationships. To the extent that these social sciences are built into literature (as depth psychology is built into modern literature), literature is interested in causal relationships also.

History is much less interested in control of behavior and institutions than the above social sciences, but it is very much interested in understanding of the past, and to some extent, many people would say, in prediction of the future course of events. Knowledge of causal factors contributes to understanding and, to the extent that the causal relationships are general, prediction. This goes for history of literature as well.

The vocational subjects are quite interested in causation, because at the practical level, which is the level at which causal interest is greatest, we want to control many things. Mathematics, on the other hand, is not interested in causation at all, although mathematical techniques such as correlation, algebra, trigonometry, calculus, etc., can be used to help establish or refute causal claims.

COMPREHENSION SELF-TEST

True or False? If the statement is false, change a crucial term (or terms) to make it true.

17–30. If an explanation is analytic, all parts are analytic.

17–31. If an explanation is empirical, the generalization is empirical.

17–32. If an explanation is causal, there is a generalization—either explicitly stated or as a gap-filler—and this generalization is causal.

17–33. If a statement gives the cause of an event, then it has not given a proximate cause.

17–34. All causal generalizations, if they are to be accepted, must be understood to have an implicit qualification such as 'under normal conditions'.

17–35. A statement of the form, '*m* caused *n*', is a singular causal statement.

17–36. A general statement of the form, '*R* causes *S*', implies that the occurrence of a case of *R* is a necessary condition for the occurrence of a case of *S*.

17–37. A statement of the form, 'If p, then q', is a causal statement.

17–38. If a cause is alleged to have been the fundamental cause of an event, then the implication is that the event would not have occurred (for a considerable time at least) without the occurrence of the alleged fundamental cause.

17–39. If a cause is alleged to have been the proximate cause, then the implication is that the caused event would not have occurred (for a considerable time at least) without the occurrence of the alleged proximate cause.

Discussion Questions.

17–40. From the explanations that are given at the ends of Chapters 14 and 15 pick one that could be interpreted as a causal explanation and which has not been examined in this chapter.

a. Fill the gap, using causal language. Be generous, but not overgenerous.
b. Indicate whether you think it gives a fundamental cause or an immediate cause. Tell why you think so.
c. Indicate whether you think it gives **the** cause or a partial cause. Tell why you think so.
d. In terms of necessary and sufficient conditions, state what is implied by the alleged causal relationship.
e. Give another answer to the request for that explanation. This other answer should be complete in itself because it is of the form, 'because x caused y'.
f. State the implications of this new answer in terms of necessary and sufficient conditions.
g. Decide what type of causal explanation (for example, fundamental, partial, etc.) you think would be appropriate as an explanation of the event in question, and frame an explanation request that explicitly calls for that kind of causal explanation.

17–41. Do all of the above for an explanation that you find in a text book.

Reason-for-Acting Explanation

Explanations of why a person did a particular thing are sometimes causal explanations. For example if an explanation of Irishman Dan Breen's participation in the attack on the British Barracks in Drangan in 1920 appeals to the early anti-British indoctrination that he experienced, then that explanation would most probably be a causal explanation, because it would appeal in part to some causal generalization such as the following: "If a person like Dan Breen is indoctrinated against a ruling country at an early age, generally such indoctrination causes him to participate in later hostile acts against the ruling country." The indoctrination causes the hostile acts.

But a reason-for-acting explanation can be given to account for this act also. Consider this explanation:

Example 17-11
Dan Breen's reason for his participation in the 1920 attack was that he wanted the British to leave his country.

His wanting the British to leave is given as **his** reason for his action. **His** purpose is given; hence we have a reason-for-acting explanation. A REASON-FOR-ACTING EXPLANATION is one that appeals to a person's purpose.

Each of the two explanations would account for his actions (though in different ways), and both might be true. The truth of one does not rule out the truth of the other. Causal explanations and reason-for-acting explanations can be provided for the same actions, and both can be true, but they are different sorts of explanations, as can be seen in the above examples. A reason-for-acting explanation gives a person's purpose in doing something, while a causal explanation tells what caused him to do it, which might well not be his purpose, but something else (such as his early indoctrination). Whether reason-for-acting explanations are also causal is a controversial question. But we do not need to settle it here in order to make the distinction. For if reason-for-acting explanations should turn out to be causal explanations, they would be a special kind of causal explanation, a kind to be given when an explanation in terms of a person's purposes is sought. Reason-for-acting explanations can be used to account for an action and to justify a belief that an action occurred or will occur.

Gap-filling, probing, and evaluating

Consider the following dialogue:

Example 17-12
MR. DELTA: Why did Dan Breen engage in the attack on the Drangan barracks in 1920?
TIM: Because he wanted the British to leave Ireland.

How do we fill the gap in Tim's reason-for-acting explanation? The answer is not simple. Although various different general statements could be used in filling the gap, all of them are rather complicated. Let us pause to examine some of the factors.

First of all, it does not particularly matter in gap-filling and evaluating this explanation whether Breen's action did actually contribute to the departure of the British. The explanation depends instead on Breen's **beliefs** about the likelihood of his actions contributing to the departure of the British. It would be odd to say that Breen took part in the attack because he wanted the British to leave Ireland, but that Breen did not believe that his taking part in the attack would contribute to the departure of the British.

Secondly, given that Breen wanted the British to leave Ireland, the question arises about his selection among the possible means. If at the time several ways were open to him to contribute to the departure of the British, his wanting to contribute to the departure does not by itself explain why Breen chose the means he chose: participation in this particular attack.

There are a number of different ways he could have selected the means he did. Here are some of them:

1. He could have decided that several different actions would have made the same degree of contribution, but that the one he chose would have the least undesirable consequences for his other goals (for example, the preservation of his life).

2. He could have decided that several courses of action would have the same degree of undesirable consequences for his other goals, but that one would make a larger contribution than the others to the achievement of his stated goal.

3. In a combination of 1 and 2 he could have decided that the degree of contribution of one means (which was perhaps less than that of an alternate means) together with its lesser degree of undesirable consequences for other goals warranted its selection.

4. Then he might have taken into account also the **degree of likelihood** of his action making any contribution at all, and the **degree of likelihood** of undesirable consequences.

These and other ways are methods that lead to the decision that the means selected is **the best means, all things considered**.

A third factor is the person's ability to do the act—and his belief in his ability. A person does not do something he cannot do—and generally does not do something that he thinks he cannot do.

A fourth factor is the person's rationality at the time of action. If a person is not rational at the time of the action, he might not pursue what he thinks is the best means to achieve a goal of his.

Putting these factors together, we can construct the following general statement which is part of the completion of many reason-for-acting explanations. This general statement, incidentally, is not offered as an empirical truth; it is intended to be an analytic statement which expresses in part the meaning of the word 'rational'. (Because of its complexity, the parts are numbered.)

1. If *X* wants something, *Y*;
2. if *X* believes the doing of *Z* to be the best means of (or at the time the best contribution to) achieving *Y*, all things considered (including his other desires);
3. if *X* can do *Z*;
4. if *X* believes that he can do *Z*;
5. and if *X* is acting rationally at the time;
6. then *X* will do *Z*.

Refinements can yet be made in this statement, but for present purposes it will suffice. One thing should be clear, however. It is not the only possible general gap-filler in a reason-for-acting explanation. The construction of others is left as a challenge to your ingenuity.

Making use of the above general statement the explanation can be completed as follows:

MR. DELTA: Why did Dan Breen participate in the attack on the Drangan barracks in 1920?

TIM: Because he wanted the British to leave Ireland. [He believed the participation at that time to be the best contribution he could make to the departure of the British from Ireland, all things considered.
He was able to participate.
He believed that he was able to participate.
He was acting rationally at the time.
(Add to this the previously given generalization, which I will not repeat here.)]

This example should suffice to show that the process of gap-filling this kind of explanation is complicated and difficult. Remember that the given general statement is not the only possible one that can be used. It is just one that is commonly assumed in a reason-for-acting explanation. Hence a person can not be sure that this is the general statement to use in identifying the specific factual conditions.

When gap-filling and evaluating a reason-for-acting explanation, the best general procedure is to investigate the agent's other desires and his beliefs about the best means; to estimate the explainer's beliefs about those desires and beliefs of the agent; to frame a general explanatory statement that when applied to the case makes use of the estimated beliefs of the explainer; and to check to see if the general statement and the estimated beliefs of the explainer are true. As usual, be generous, but not overgenerous.

One can usually safely simplify by ignoring the last three 'if'-clauses: the ability clause, the belief-in-ability clause, and the rationality clause. The truth of the ability clause is implied by the request for explanation. The truth of some belief about ability, which, although not necessarily the belief indicated in the given general statement, is implied by the request for explanation, if the person was acting rationally. The rationality clause generally holds, but when it does not hold, this sort of explanation just does not work.

As with other types of explanation the process of gap-filling a reason-for-acting explanation is an exploratory one, often accompanied by appropriate probes. The advice previously given about the general processes of gap-filling and probing holds here, but of course the process is generally more difficult because of the complexity of the task.

In the evaluation of the resulting explanation the same general criteria hold. The explanatory material must be true, noncircular, at the proper level of sophistication, and of the proper function and type. The empirical material (though not the analytic generalization) must also satisfy the criterion of testability.*

The rationality assumption is difficult to evaluate. More often it is simply accepted. People are usually rational to the extent required.

Requesting a reason-for-acting explanation

As should be clear from the Dan Breen example, the use of the word "why?" does not by itself make clear that a reason-for-acting explanation is sought. The request, "Why did Dan Breen participate in the 1920 attack?" could understandably be answered by giving a cause, such as an early indoctrination, or a series of, say, thyroid pills he had taken during the previous month. Neither of these things would be his reason for acting. Hence the request did not unequivocally call for a reason for acting.

Here are some ways of making a request that is more clear:

1. What was Dan Breen's reason for participating in the 1920 attack?
2. What purpose was Dan Breen trying to achieve through his participation?
3. What was Dan Breen's motive in his participation in the attack in 1920?

For present purposes we will neglect the shades of difference among these three requests, simply capitalizing on the fact that all three call for what Breen had in mind, which is the main thing we seek in a reason-for-acting explanation. Admittedly the three requests do not necessarily call for an explanation, but for our purposes this fact can generally be neglected. A clear, but somewhat awkward, request which certainly does call for an explanation is the following:

4. Why, in terms of his reason(s), did Dan Breen participate in the 1920 attack?

The explicit use of the word "why" makes it clear that an explanation is requested, and the explicit use of the phrase "his reason(s)" makes it at least fairly clear that a reason-for-acting explanation is sought. The phrase "**the** reason(s)" (as contrasted with the phrase "his reason(s)") does not succeed in specifying a reason-for-acting explanation. "The reason" might very well not be the person's purpose; "his reason" will be his purpose or goal.

Historical explanation

Under the heading, "Causal Explanation", the nature and degree of generality of historical explanation was discussed. You will remember that with the use of singular causal statements a very limited generalization can lie behind the causal explanation, thus providing a compromise position

* To be discussed in Chapter 18.

between those who claim that historians are committed to laws when they explain and those who deny this.

Many historical explanations are reason-for-acting explanations, so we can expect the problem to arise here also. To what is a historian committed who offers a reason-for-acting explanation? The first thing to note is that he is committed to no more and no less than you and I when we offer such explanations of the behavior of our associates. All that historians are trying to do is to extend the scope of our understanding of human action backwards in time.

Secondly, note that there is no empirical law behind these explanations. The only general part of the explicans is an analytic general statement, such as the one used to gap-fill the Dan Breen explanation. Such general statements are rather like truisms, since they only express linguistic facts that we all know anyway.* Hence the historians (and the rest of us) are committed, when giving reason-for-acting explanations, only to some such truistic generalization as the one in the Breen explanation. From the point of view of the historian and the ordinary man giving an explanation (though not from the point of view of the philosopher), such explanations do not commit us to any significant general statements. Thus again there is truth in what each side says in the controversy about the degree of generality behind historical explanations. There is a truistic general statement of some sort, but, of the parts of the explicans that are significant to the historian, there need not be any generalization. The important parts (from the point of view of the historian) of a reason-for-acting historical explanation can be, and usually are, quite unique.

Summary

In giving an explanation of some action, reason-for-acting explanation offers a man's purpose or end. Gap-filling and evaluating such an explanation is quite difficult because of the complexity of the totality and because an assumption of a degree of rationality is made but is hard to establish as a truth. Criteria for evaluating such explanations are the four basic ones: truth, noncircularity, proper level of sophistication, and proper function and type; furthermore the criterion of testability (to be discussed in Chapter 18) must be applied to the empirical material. In requesting a reason-for-acting explanation, one can make one's request more clear by referring to the agent's reason, his purpose, or his motive.

The only generalities that are required to be in the explicans are truistic. Hence the historian in giving such explanations is not necessarily committed to any generalizations that he considers significant.

* Michael Scriven suggests the appellation, 'truism', for such nonsignificant (to the historian) backings for explanations. See "Truisms as the Grounds for Historical Explanation," in Patrick Gardiner, ed., *Theories of History* (New York: The Free Press of Glencoe, Inc., 1959), pp. 443–71.

COMPREHENSION SELF-TEST

True or False? If the statement is false, change a crucial term (or terms) to make it true.

17–42. Reason-for-acting explanations of human actions refer to a person's purpose in doing the thing to be explained.

17–43. Gap-filling a reason-for-acting explanation is a fairly simple operation, compared to gap-filling other types of explanation.

17–44. The following is not clearly a request for a reason-for-acting explanation: Explain why President Wilson tried to get the United States into the League of Nations.

17–45. When a historian gives a reason-for-acting explanation, he is unavoidably thereby committed to an empirical generalization of some sort.

Questions.

17–46. Complete the following explanation in as plausible a way as possible without being overgenerous to its source, a high school text in American history: Although Washington had retired from public life, he accepted the Presidency of the United States, because he wanted the new nation to survive.

17–47. Evaluate the complete explanation of 17–46 using the four basic criteria.

17–48. Locate a reason-for-acting explanation in some text. Complete and evaluate it.

Challenge Question.

17–49. See if you can frame a general analytic statement that is different from the one offered in the completion of the Dan Breen explanation, but that could be used in completing some reason-for-acting explanation. Construct a complete explanation using your general analytic statement.

Value and Obligation Explanation

VALUE and OBLIGATION EXPLANATIONS are so classified because they respectively attempt to explain statements of value and obligation. Here is an example of each:

Example 17-13

MISS GAMMA: Why is *You Can't Take It With You* a good play?

MARY: Because it moves rapidly, without ever dragging, has numerous humorous situations, and is believable. [A play that moves rapidly without ever dragging, that has numerous humorous situations, and is believable is a good play.]

Example 17-14

EMILE: Why do you say that my map ought to have a complete interpretation of its symbols?

MR. DELTA: If you don't present a complete interpretation, then people will not be able to understand the map. [People ought to be able to understand maps.]

The fact that the statement, "a play that moves rapidly without ever dragging, . . . is a good play", is a value statement, makes Example 17-13 a value-type explanation. The word 'good' indicates a value statement, as would the word 'bad' and other evaluative terms.

Example 17-14 is an obligation explanation, because the statement, "People ought to be able to understand maps", is an obligation statement. The word 'ought' indicates an obligation statement. Other words sometimes used to make obligation statements are 'should' and 'must'. Since all of these words can also be used for predictions and descriptions (for example, "Smith must be on his way now"), there are no foolproof verbal cues to the identification of obligation statements. The key feature is the expression of an obligation endorsed by the person making the statement.

Gap-filling

You will remember that in filling the gap in an explanation, one generally looks for a proposition that is true and that makes the argument from explicans to explicandum a valid deductive argument. In making this search, one is expected to be generous to the explainer, but not overgenerous. When gap-filling value and obligation explanations, you will find that the problem of looseness in deduction, discussed in Chapter 5, becomes prominent. As a result truth, deducibility, and generosity are intertwined, calling for particularly intelligent judgment on the part of the person trying to fill the gap.

Truth. The problem of looseness, you will remember, results from the fact that many general statements, though acceptable as they stand, either have exceptions, are to some extent vague, or both.* The gap-filler supplied in the example dealing with the play ("A play that moves rapidly . . . ."), though acceptable to Mary as it stood, would also have been recognized by Mary to have exceptions. Suppose that some play, in addition to meeting the criteria specified in the general statement, were also flimsy and superficial. Then presumably Mary would not want it to count as a good play, and she might then want to amend her general value statement by adding the word 'generally'.

The situation is somewhat similar with respect to the general obligation statement used to gap-fill the map explanation, although vagueness is more pronounced with this one. Certainly the gap-filler does not mean that every

* See H. L. A. Hart, "The Ascription of Responsibility and Rights" and Friedrich Waismann "Verifiability"; both are in Antony Flew, ed., *Logic and Language* (First Series) (Oxford: Basil Blackwell, 1952), pp. 145–66, 117–44.

conceivable person should be able to understand every conceivable map. Hence the coverage of the general terms, 'person' and 'map', is not clear. That is, it is not clear just what is to be the range of exceptions, of which there must be some.

The problem is not simply that of failing to state the general value and obligation claims properly; instead it is that, no matter how stated, the general claims will be recognized by a reasonable person to have exceptions, or to be vague, or both—though acceptable (in general) as they stand. As Aristotle observed, in a passage quoted earlier, "We must be content, then . . . to indicate the truth roughly and in outline, and in speaking about things which are only for the most part true, and with premises of the same kind, to reach conclusions that are no better."*

Aristotle is not recommending the abandonment of standards. He is only asking us to accept the exceptions and vagueness that are generally to be found in value and obligation statements. In brief, the criterion of truth here becomes the criterion of "for the most part" truth.

Deducibility. The criterion of deducibility, when applied in judging whether an explanation is complete, must then be applied to an idealized form of the explanation under consideration. You will remember this approach in Chapter 5. From a vague and/or exception-laden general statement (such as those in the above examples) one cannot deduce the sorts of things that one can deduce from a clear universal statement. So one idealizes the explicans, making the general statement into a clear exceptionless universal in order to see whether the deduction is valid. If so, the explanation is complete. If not, it is incomplete. After making the judgment about completeness, one then returns the general statement to its more vague and/or exception-laden status, and proceeds to handle the explanation in the usual manner: evaluating, perhaps probing, perhaps revising the gap-filler, and so forth. Each time a new gap-filler is proposed, then for purposes of testing completeness, the gap-filler (if it is also a general statement) must also be idealized into an exceptionless and clear universal for purposes of establishing completeness, and then returned to its proper status.**

Evaluation of value and obligation explanations

These two types of explanation should satisfy the four basic criteria: truth, noncircularity, appropriate level of sophistication, and proper function

* *Nichomachean Ethics* (Ross translation), Book I, chap. iii.

** You should be made aware of the fact that the view here presented is not a universally accepted account of value and obligation statements, nor is the account of their application to particular cases universally accepted. For ages men have sought universal value and obligation statements (see Immanuel Kant's *Foundations of the Metaphysics of Ethics*) and recently Stephen Toulmin has proposed what he views as a nondeductive account of the justification of value statements. See *The Place of Reason in Ethics* (Cambridge: Cambridge University Press, 1950). Nelson Pike provides an interesting evaluation of Toulmin's view in "Rules of Inference in Moral Reasoning," *Mind*, Vol. LXX, no. 279, pp. 391–99.

and type; they should also satisfy the criterion of applicability;* but there are qualifications to keep in mind when actually carrying out an evaluation. First of all as was pointed out earlier, we are dealing with things which are "for the most part true". Secondly this "for-the-most-part" truth, as you know, calls for temporary idealization of the general statement in applying the deducibility criterion of completeness. Thirdly, since some justifications are not deductive in nature (a point noted in the previous chapter), their completion, if any is needed, requires fitting the gap-fillers to the type of proof involved. Fourthly, should the justification be other than deductive in nature, then an additional criterion in evaluating the explanation is the satisfactoriness of the argument.

Asking for value and obligation explanations

In Example 16-6 in the previous chapter Mr. Delta did not give Jane the function and type of explanation she sought. She wanted him to give a value-type justification explanation of two of his values, freedom and responsibility. He replied with a causal-type explanation accounting for his values:

JANE: Mr. Delta, do you value freedom and responsibility?
MR. DELTA: Yes, Jane, I do.
JANE: Why?
MR. DELTA: Because a man tends to take on the values of his milieu. That's reasonable isn't it?

Given the actual situation in which the above dialogue occurred, it was quite clear to me what type of explanation Jane was seeking. But Mr. Delta missed the point of her question. At least in part the reason was that her question, neglecting context, is ambiguous. Given the above section of the dialogue only, a possible interpretation is that she sought a causal-type explanation in which he would account for his values. In effect her potentially ambiguous question was, "Why do you value freedom and responsibility?"

In order to avoid the possibility of misinterpretations when context is insufficient, or the listener is not alert, the request can be made more explicit. In this sort of case, the locution, "Why do you think . . .?", will not suffice, because a causal answer is plausible—we are accustomed to causal explanations of beliefs about values. Here are examples of fairly clear requests:

1. How do you justify your values, freedom and responsibility?
2. Why are those two values justified?
3. Please justify the values, freedom and responsibility.

Note that although the first two requests use standard explanation cues, 'How?' and 'Why?', the third does not. The words, 'justify' and 'value',

* To be discussed in Chapter 18.

are here key cues in an explicit request for value-type justification explanations.

A more direct approach is to put the question explicitly in value terms, using such words as 'good', 'bad', and 'valuable':

4. Why are freedom and responsibility good?
5. Why is the absence of freedom and responsibility bad?
6. Why are freedom and responsibility valuable?

We should distinguish between the words 'valued' and 'valuable'. The sixth request would not have been a request for a value-type justification explanation if the word 'valued' had been used instead of 'valuable'; it would have then been a request for a standard empirical, or perhaps causal explanation. It would have then been the sort of request to which Mr. Delta's original answer was appropriate. In using the word 'valued', the speaker is explicitly not committing himself to the endorsement of the value, although of course he might endorse it anyway. To say that something is valued is to state an empirical fact about it—not to place a value upon it.*

Even though one uses 'valuable' instead of 'valued', the language of the sixth request does not make absolutely clear that a value-type justification explanation is sought. One might, for example, tell why a particular painting is valuable without committing himself to valuing it—or thinking it good, for one might simply think that the painting is capable of commanding a high price on the market. Hence, even though the use of the word 'valuable' in a request such as the sixth will ordinarily be interpreted as a request for a value-type justification, the safest way to make the request is to use the word 'good' (or 'bad'), as in the fourth (or fifth) request. Of course, no way is infallible. Some people (for example, the Mr. Delta in the original example) will persist in misinterpretation—and will treat all value questions as empirical questions. This topic will be discussed at greater length in Part IV of this book.

Somewhat similar remarks can be made about requests for obligation explanations. Consider these three examples:

7. Why ought my map have a complete interpretation of its symbols?
8. Why am I obliged to have a complete interpretation of the symbols on my map?
9. Why is Frank obliged to appear before the judiciary board of student government?

The seventh, in virtue of the use of the word 'ought', is quite straightforwardly a request for an obligation-type justification explanation. The ninth request could easily not be a request for a justification explanation, but

* See G. E. Moore's *Principia Ethica* (Cambridge: Cambridge University Press, 1903), pp. 66–67, for a discussion of a comparable distinction: desired *vs.* desirable.

instead a request to account for the empirical legal fact that Frank is obliged (ordered, required) to appear. In the sense in which the explicandum is not an obligation statement (in other words in the sense in which it is an empirical-fact statement), the propounder of the explicandum could without contradiction say that Frank is obliged to appear, but he ought not appear. The locution used in the ninth request allows this empirical-fact interpretation of the explicandum.

From this one can see that the words, 'is obliged to', do not necessarily signal an obligation statement. Hence they can not be depended on to make the eighth request unambiguous. In a context the request might be unambiguous, but out of context, not so. The most dependable way of specifying an obligation-type justification explanation is the use of the word 'ought'. There are other things that can be said on the topic, but given the above discussion, one should be able to figure out the degree to which other locutions are suitable.

Probing value and obligation explanations

Since the value and obligation general statements in these explanations tend to be more vague and exception-laden than those in other explanations, one can expect probing to be a less precise task. That is, even though the prober finds that there is an apparent counter-example to one of these general statements, that general statement might still be the gap-filler—with the full knowledge and acceptance of the explainer of the alleged exception. Suppose for example a prober had said to Mr. Delta in the map example, "Do you mean that your one-year-old daughter ought to be able to understand this map?" Mr. Delta's reasonable response could be that the prober knows very well that Mr. Delta does not mean that: yet Mr. Delta, even after making that response could understandably stand by the wording of the general statement: "People ought to be able to understand maps."

With the above qualification, probing these types of explanations is like probing other types. One must be on guard against switching the interpretation of some ambiguous sentences back and forth between their value or obligation interpretation and their empirical-fact interpretation. Something that is a counter-example on one interpretation is not a counter-example on the other interpretation. The fact (if it is a fact) that most people do not like Shakespeare's plays would not serve as a counter to the claim that Shakespeare's plays are good plays, though it would serve as a counter to the claim that Shakespeare's plays are highly valued by our society.

Summary

Value and obligation explanations are those which use value and obligation general statements respectively in the attempt to explain. Some problems in dealing with them arise from the fact that general value and obligation statements are as a rule somewhat vague and exception-laden; the fact that not all justifications are deductive; and the fact that often the language used to express value and obligation statements is ambiguous, being interpretable in empirical-fact language as well.

In gap-filling a value or obligation explanation that fits the deductive model, one looks for statements, which when the explicans is idealized, deductively imply the explicandum. Since not all do fit the deductive model, even this loose procedure does not always suffice.

Probing and evaluating, although generally the same as with other types of explanations (except that applicability, rather than testability, is used as the appropriate aspect of the fifth criterion), must be conducted with an awareness of the above special facts about these types of explanation. In particular, in probing one must be aware that apparent counter-examples sometimes do not make a dent in the armor of a general statement; and in evaluating, one must be aware that for nondeductive justification explanations another criterion must be applied—the criterion of a satisfactory argument. This criterion replaces the deducibility requirement for completeness.

In requesting value and obligation explanations, one must be particularly careful to make clear that the explicandum is not an empirical fact. Sometimes the context suffices, but often it is as well to use language that leaves as little doubt as possible.

COMPREHENSION SELF-TEST

True or False? If the statement is false, change a crucial term (or terms) to make it true.

17–50. VALUE EXPLANATIONS are those which attempt to explain why something is valued.

17–51. According to the point of view expressed in this book, general value statements, if accepted as true, should be precise and applicable without exception.

17–52. The phrase, 'is obliged to', is ambiguous, since by itself it might not imply that its user endorses the obligation.

17–53. In gap-filling an obligation explanation, one looks for a general obligation statement that one thinks the explainer would be obliged to hold to be universally true.

17–54. In gap-filling a value explanation one tries to complete a set of statements from which the explicandum can be straightforwardly and strictly deduced.

Exercises. 17–55 to 17–60. For each of the following explanations supply a fairly simple gap-filler (or gap-fillers), assuming the deductive model. Try to be generous, but not overgenerous. Assume some context with which you are, or could be, familiar.

17–55. P: Why is "Trees" a bad poem?
T: Because the imagery is inconsistent and mawkish.

17–56. P: Why should I make the same measurements on this row of beans that does not get any fertilizer?
T: If you don't, then you won't know whether to attribute the size of the other beans to the fertilizer or to something else.

17–57. T: Why is it better to cut on a bias than to cut parallel to the threads?
P: Because it's better if the threads don't unravel.

17–58. P: Why ought we read more than one newspaper?
T: If you read only one newspaper, you will be less likely to understand both sides of contemporary issues.

17–59. P: Why should we show all of our work?
T: So that I can tell whether you know what you are doing.

17–60. T: Why ought students be permitted to wear whatever clothes they choose? Whenever they choose?
P: It's a free country, isn't it?

Problems.

17–61. Evaluate one of the above explanations.

17–62. Locate a value or obligation explanation in a text with which you are familiar. Complete and evaluate it.

Discussion Question.

17–63. Prepare a short paper in which you consider the question, "Can value and obligation explanations be used only to serve the justification function?" In your paper give your reasons and cite specific examples.

Loose Ends

In attempting to set before you some of the major considerations in working with different sorts of explanations, I have left several things unsaid, which should be noted. First, and perhaps most important, one need not spend time memorizing the distinguishing features of the various presented types of explanation. This system of categorization was developed primarily to give some order to the presentation, but it is not comprehensive, nor are the types mutually exclusive. The important thing to be learned is to pay particular attention to what is meant in a given context, and to apply the criteria of evaluation in a reasonable manner, gap-filling and probing with care and ingenuity.

A second loose end is the evaluation of nondeductive justification explanations. Since they are basically the topic of Part IV, "Justification", I must leave this problem undiscussed for the time being.

A third item is the question of whether all of the types can be used to perform both the account-for and the justification function. At the moment I think (but am not sure) that all except the value and obligation explanations can, and that those two can only perform the justification function.

A related question is whether there can be nondeductive, reason-for-acting explanations. I do not think so, but again am not sure.

These last two items are indicative of a general feature of the material in this chapter: the topics have not been fully investigated to the point that there is a generally agreed-upon solution to the problem of the nature of explanation. In particular the extent of conformity to the deductive model is a controversial issue.* I think that I have found a satisfactory middle ground between contending factions, but my solution has not at the time of writing been subjected to the careful and lengthy scrutiny of others who specialize in this problem. I think that my approach is basically right, but should not be surprised to find other's scrutiny to uncover some further qualifications.

Chapter Summary

In this chapter you saw an elaboration of the distinction between analytic and synthetic statements, a distinction that was introduced in Chapter 10. This distinction represents analytic statements as those which are so, simply in virtue of the meanings given to the words in the statements in the context in which they appear; hence they would be contradictory to deny. Synthetic statements, on the other hand, would not be contradictory to deny. On the basis of this distinction, together with distinctions among types of synthetic statements, several types of explanations were delineated and discussed. These types are analytic, standard empirical, causal, reason-for-acting, value, and obligation explanations. Generally the type of explanation depended on the nature of the general statement behind it. This is a rule-of-thumb criterion, since there is sometimes more than one generalization behind an explanation, and sometimes no generalization behind a justification explanation. A more precise system for categorizing types of explanations would be unnecessarily complicated for purposes of this book.

One reason for introducing this categorization was to focus attention on one way that explanations can go wrong: giving an explanation using one type of generalization when another is sought. A second reason for the categorization is to provide an organization for the detailed discussion of particular problems of explanation. Some of these problems are as follows:

1. How to make an unambiguous request for an explanation.

* See some suggested reading at the end of Chapter 19.

TABLE 17-1 Types of Explanation: A Simplified Summary*

Type of explanation	*Criterion for identification*	*Possible cues*	*Possible function*	*Generality of the significant part of explanatory material*	*Criteria for evaluation*
Analytic	Analytic general statement in explanatory material	1. "Why is that called . . . ?" 2. Mathematical context	Justify, account for	Can be quite general	Noncircularity, level of sophistication, proper function and type, and in a special way, truth
Standard empirical	Empirical general statement in explanatory material	"Why?" (applied to an empirical statement)	Justify, account for	Often general	The four basic criteria (truth, noncircularity, level of sophistication, proper function and type) and testability**
Causal	Causal statement in explanatory material	"Why did . . . occur?"	Justify, account for	If causal statement is singular, significant part can be very limited. If causal statement is general, significant part can be general.	The four basic criteria, and testability**
Reason-for-acting	Focus in explanatory material on person's reason for doing something	"Why did he do that?"	Justify, account for	Significant parts often all specific.	The four basic criteria and testability (though testability does not apply to the analytic generalization)
Value	General value statement in explanatory material	"Why is that good?"	Justify***	Often general	The four basic criteria, and applicability**
Obligation	General obligation statement in explanatory material	"Why ought he do that?"	Justify***	Often general	The four basic criteria, and applicability**

* Neglecting nondeductive justifications in particular.

** Testability and applicability are discussed in the next chapter.

*** Perhaps also: Account for.

2. How to find out what sort of explanation is desired by someone else.
3. The extent to which an explainer is committed to a significant general statement.
4. How to gap-fill explanations of various sorts.
5. The extent to which a completed explanation must be a pure deduction.
6. The meaningfulness of the word 'cause'.
7. Particular problems of probing and evaluation that are unique to particular types of explanations.
8. Completing nondeductive justification explanations.
9. Evaluation of the analytic, noncausal empirical, causal, value, and obligation statements that are found in an explicans.

The eighth and ninth problems are only touched upon in this chapter. They are the concerns of Part IV of this book. Table 17-1 summarizes, with some qualifications omitted, the treatment of the other seven problems.

CHAPTER 18

⁘Testability/ Applicability

A fifth criterion to apply to the nonanalytic material in the explanatory material is testability/applicability, testability applying to empirical statements, applicability to value and obligation statements. These ideas are similar, so they are looked on as one criterion, but will be treated separately for purposes of exposition.

Testability

Standard empirical and causal explanations, which are common in the physical and social sciences (including history), the vocational subjects, and literature, are intended to explain a fact or generalization about the world of things, men, and events. In order to succeed at this task of explaining, they must themselves contain (explicitly or implicitly) an empirical generalization which covers the thing being explained.* This generalization may be broad or narrow, but it at least must conceivably cover more than the one case being explained—even if this coverage extends only to conceivable cases identical to the one being explained.

To summarize what is to come, the generalization must do more than cover other cases; it must **exclude** some conceivable cases. If it does not do

* Except for nondeductive justification explanations.

both, then it is UNTESTABLE. It is, therefore, useless in making predictions, and even useless in telling us that the thing to be explained was to be expected. Thus an explanation containing an untestable but allegedly empirical generalization does not really explain at all. Put in the form of a slogan, "That which explains everything conceivable, explains nothing" (and of course that which cannot conceivably explain anything also explains nothing).

Similarly, any nongeneral, allegedly empirical material must also be testable if it is to be useful in guiding our decisions. Someone must know what it would be like for the material to be false.

The concept, *testability*, is a difficult one to grasp, as is the material in the preceding two summarizing paragraphs. The major part of this chapter is devoted to qualifying and clarifying this concept.

Practical testability

Another sort of testability does not apply here, and it should be marked off: practical testability. The following generalization is not practically testable (at least not directly so):

> If there were no air resistance, all unsupported bodies in the earth's atmosphere would fall to earth with the same acceleration.

This is not yet practically testable because we are not yet able to eliminate air resistance **completely**. But we can conceive of what it would be like to run such a test. We know what would count as evidence for **and** against the generalization. Imagining that air resistance were completely removed, the arrival of a piece of tissue paper and a marble at the same place at the same time, after having been dropped from the same place at the same time would be evidence for the generalization. Their arrival at different times would be evidence against it.

The practical impossibility of such a test, given the current state of technology, presents practical difficulties for experimenters. But the generalization is testable in a way because we are able to imagine, to conceive of, what would count as evidence for **and** against the generalization. In order to distinguish the two sorts of testability, one might say that the generalization is **conceptually testable,** but **practically untestable**. Henceforth we shall be concerned with conceptual testability.

Conceptual testability

The above generalization is conceptually testable. Here is one that appears to be untestable:

> A body that is simultaneously going in two opposite directions will alternately appear and disappear.

That seems to be untestable because we do not think we can imagine what it would be like for there to be a body that is simultaneously going in opposite directions. Thus we do not know how to identify a body on which we can perform a test. **A test appears inconceivable**.

Note, if we could identify such a body, then the rest of the statement is capable of being tested. Even though we do not believe that bodies can alternately appear and disappear, we can imagine what it would be like for a body to do so, and we know what it is like for a body not to do so—that is, to continually remain in sight. The difficulty with an untestable statement should now be apparent—at least in this extreme example. The given statement about a body going in opposite directions cannot perform the functions of empirical statements. It gives us no information about the world of things, men, and events, and is useless as a basis for predictions. We have no information from this statement and can make no predictions from it because we do not know how to make use of it. We do not know how to identify a body that is simultaneously going in two opposite directions, so we can generate no predictions, and get no information from the statement.

Of course, if some meaning is assigned to the notion of a body going in two opposite directions simultaneously, say the body is elongating like a worm and both ends move outward from the middle, then the statement becomes testable and capable of generating predictions. If true, it would also give us information. But until we have some such construal of the words, then the statement appears untestable—and therefore useless for communicating information.

Here is an explanation example, taken from a history class:

Example 18-1

MR. DELTA: Why did the United States go to war with Spain?

JANE: Because it was the manifest destiny of the United States to do so. [A country acts in accord with its manifest destiny.]

Is the generalization serving as a gap-filler testable? In order to conceive of a test of this generalization we must at least be clear about the meaning of "manifest destiny". The testability of the generalization depends on the meaning of that term. Suppose that 'to act in accord with one's manifest destiny' means 'to do what one is going to do'. Under that interpretation the generalization becomes untestable; it says:

A country does what it is going to do,

which is much like saying:

A person does what he does.

Now these generalizations are untestable, because **one cannot conceive of evidence against them**. One cannot conceive of something that a person does and does not do. One cannot conceive of something that a country is really going (not merely intending) to do, but which it does not do. Furthermore, one cannot use these generalizations in making predictions, because once one knows what a country or a person is going to do, which one needs to know in order to apply the generalizations, then one already knows all that the generalizations pretend to tell us. And if one does not know what a country or person is going to do, then the basic element for the application of the generalization is missing.

An interpretation could be given to "manifest destiny" which would make the generalization testable. For example, if 'to act in accord with one's manifest destiny' is taken to mean 'to do what will strengthen one's power', the generalization is testable. We can conceive of evidence that would count for the generalization **and** of evidence that would count against it. A country which continually did things that increased its power would constitute evidence for the generalization; and a country that continually did things that reduced its power would constitute evidence against it. Now you might contend that you cannot believe that a country could fail to do things that would increase its power. But the important thing is that you could describe such a country, even though you may think that its occurrence and survival are empirically unlikely. It is the possibility of making such a description that makes the generalization testable and capable of generating predictions.

Compare the two sorts of problems with untestable statements: meaninglessness and analyticity. The generalization about a body moving simultaneously in both directions was without sufficient meaning to apply it. The manifest destiny generalization, as first interpreted, was simply analytic; one can apply its parts, but it does not get us anywhere.

In each case, you will remember, no predictions could be generated that make use of the statement in question. Actually the criterion should be somewhat broadened. Instead of saying that the generalization must permit one to generate predictions, we should say that the generalization must permit one to generate, or **to have generated**, predictions. A generalization, such as, "Fourteenth-century mathematicians did not know calculus", could have generated predictions about what one would find in talking to fourteenth-century mathematicians; hence that generalization is testable. The ability to have generated predictions is a sufficient condition for testability.

Here is another example, from a literature class. With this example we will go more deeply into strategy for dealing with testability:

Example 18-2

MISS GAMMA: In Shaw's *Man and Superman* why did Jack Tanner finally succumb to Ann Whitefield's charms?

BRONWYN: I'm not sure, but I think that the Life Force was expressing itself through her.

MISS GAMMA: That does seem to be what Shaw says. How does that explain it? (Miss Gamma, you will note, is here asking Bronwyn to complete her own explanation.)

BRONWYN: The Life Force operates through women in effecting the propagation of the race. It gives women special alluring powers with which they capture men and secure their cooperation in the fulfillment of this purpose. Men are but insignificant pawns in this game.

MISS GAMMA: Frank?

FRANK: What does Life Force have to do with it? What Bronwyn is saying is that women have the desire to propagate the race and that they have the power to catch the man they select to cooperate with them in this venture. That's the part of the explanation that makes sense, even though it's false. But that Life Force business. Ugh!

MISS GAMMA: Is that right, Bronwyn?

BRONWYN: No. The doctrine of the Life Force makes good sense. The Life Force is the actuating power of life. It is in continual search of improvement and self-realization. Thus the propagation of the race becomes necessary. The Life Force, being concerned with propagation, has selected women as the bearers of this mission.

FRANK: Life Force! You don't know what that is.

BRONWYN: I do so. I just told you.

FRANK: Nonsense!

MISS GAMMA: Frank, can you do better than that?

What can Frank (or Miss Gamma) do in order to seek understanding of Shaw's doctrine of the Life Force, as interpreted by Bronwyn? Is the doctrine testable? Does it convey information? Can it generate predictions?

Strategy. What is the strategy for dealing with the explanation that makes use of the Life-Force doctrine (or the manifest-destiny doctrine)? First we make an effort to put the explanation into complete form. Then we check to see if the propositions are testable. This can be done by either of two approaches: (1) **asking for** examples of conceivable evidence for **and** against the propositions, or (2) **suggesting** possible examples of conceivable evidence for and against the propositions and asking if these examples, if true, would count for and against the propositions. The first approach will be called the "conceivable-evidence approach"; the second, the "counter-example approach". In effect, each asks for a concrete interpretation of the propositions involved.

If, during this process of interpretation of a proposition, the proposition as interpreted turns out to have predictability, then we judge the explanation testable in the sense interpreted. It has passed this test. If the proposition does not have predictability, then we judge the explanation untestable. Whichever way it turns out, a decision about the value of the explanation must still be made. If the proposition is testable, then the other four criteria are to be applied: truth, proper level of sophistication, noncircularity, and proper function and type. If the proposition is not testable, the explanation might still be of value, because it might, for example, be an analytic explanation, or a reason-for-acting explanation (in which case there is an analytic general statement). Naturally if the explanation is untestable because of a meaningless statement, then the explanation is defective. One caution: In judging the value of an explanation, be sure not to allow the sentences in question to shift in meaning in such a way that one interpretation is used when the explanation is applied, and a different interpretation when it is evaluated.

All the way through one must be ready to complete the explanation with a different and better gap-filler, if one can find it—unless of course the explainer has supplied the gap-filler himself.

This sounds like a very complicated process—one that is impossible for a teacher to perform when faced with the pressures of a classroom situation. But it is not impossible; it is, in fact, rather easy when one understands the nature of the problem, has had practice, and is dealing with the kinds of explanations that do appear in classrooms.

Let us proceed to apply the conceivable evidence approach, taking account of what Miss Gamma and Frank have done.

The Conceivable Evidence Approach. Miss Gamma asked Bronwyn to complete her explanation by saying, "How does that explain it?" She used this probe because she did not feel able to make a good guess about the gap-filler for the explanation. The simplest completion seemed unfair to Bronwyn. It would make the explanation look like this:

Example 18-3

Why did Jack Tanner finally succumb to Ann Whitefield's charms?

Because the Life Force was expressing itself through her. [Any man will succumb to a woman through whom the Life Force is expressing itself.]

This seems unfair because it commits Bronwyn to the prediction (assuming that her explicit answer is testable) that all men would succumb to Ann's charms. Now as a matter of fact, in *Man and Superman* many men did succumb to Ann's charms, but Hector Malone did not, so Bronwyn probably would not hold that gap-filler.

Unfortunately Bronwyn's explicit answer to the probe requesting completion of the explanation did not complete the explanation; instead she gave an exposition of the doctrine, from which we might infer a completion. The completion that Frank inferred makes no use of the concept *Life Force*, but it is testable, and Frank regarded it as false.

Let us pause to see why it is testable. Consider its two explicit propositions one at a time. The first proposition is that women have the desire to propagate the race. If a survey were conducted in which all the women in the world were asked if they have this desire, an overwhelmingly affirmative answer would count as evidence for the proposition, and an overwhelmingly negative answer would seem to count as evidence against it. (The term, 'would seem', was used because the proposition might have been about an **unconscious** desire, in which case the overwhelmingly negative answer would not count as evidence against the proposition. In that case, however, we might suspect the proposition of being untestable; the person advancing the doctrine would then owe us a conceivable state of affairs that would count as evidence against the proposition.)

The second proposition is that women have the power to catch the man they select to cooperate with them. Suppose that a woman wants to catch a particular man; suppose further that she tries to do so. If she succeeds, we have under most circumstances evidence in favor of the proposition; if she fails, we have under most circumstances evidence against the proposition. Note that the evidence conceived does not have to be conclusive; it just must have **some** bearing.

Thus the material that Frank put forth is testable. That is why Frank said that it makes sense. Note that the propositions, if they were testable **and** true, would be useful in our attempts to understand and live in the world about us. Frank, of course, went on to say that they are false, and thus rejected on different grounds than nontestability the part of the explanation that he rescued.

Bronwyn, however, did not accept this rescue, perhaps because she recognized the implausibility of the material suggested by Frank and wanted to insulate the doctrine against attack, or because she wanted to be sure to include a reference to Life Force. So let us make another effort to complete her original explanation, making use of the concept, *Life Force,* and of her attempted interpretation. As you know, there are many ways of filling in such an explanation, so it is not fair (without probing) to brand her explanation as untestable on the basis of our first efforts at gap-filling. In the end though, she owes us a testable interpretation of the doctrine that completes her explanation. If she cannot produce it, then we have a right to be suspicious of the explanation.

But we owe her something more than Frank's comment, "Nonsense." We owe her some reasonable inquiries into the doctrine. As a second attempt at completion, one that makes use of the material in her exposition, let us gap-fill the explanation to read as follows:

Example 18-4

MISS GAMMA: Why did Jack Tanner finally succumb to Ann Whitefield's charms?

BRONWYN: Because the Life Force was expressing itself through her. [If the Life Force is expressing itself through a female, and if that female selects a given man to cooperate with her in the propagation of the race, then that man is likely to succumb to her charms. Ann Whitefield picked Jack Tanner to cooperate with her in the propagation of the race.]

That seems like a fairly reasonable completion. The two parts about which questions of testability arise are the two clauses containing 'Life Force': (1) ". . . the Life Force was expressing itself through her." and (2) ". . . the Life Force is expressing itself through a female . . . ." If the first of these two is untestable, then the explanation is definitely untestable, since Bronwyn explicitly provided that material. So let us concentrate on this first clause. The second clause raises other complications, because by itself it is not a statement at all. It only expresses a condition upon the fullfillment of which the rest of the complicated conditional sentence supposedly depends.

Frank could have asked Bronwyn what sort of thing she would count as evidence against her claim that the Life Force was expressing itself through Ann Whitefield. He does not need to ask what sort of thing would count as evidence **for** the claim, since an example is contained in the request for explanation. Jack's succumbing to Ann Whitefield's charms counts with Bronwyn as evidence that the Life Force was expressing itself through Ann. If Bronwyn holds that nothing conceivably could count as evidence against the proposition (perhaps, for example, because by definition the Life Force expresses itself through every woman), then that statement becomes untestable. If Bronwyn intended it to be an empirical statement instead of the analytic statement* it has now become, she has made an error.

Suppose that instead her answer was that a failure to succumb would have counted as evidence against the proposition. If so, then we would know that it is not an analytic proposition, but then we might inquire what role the concept, *Life Force*, plays in this explanation. One might wonder if there is a difference between saying that the Life Force was expressing itself through her and saying that a man succumbed to her charms. If there is no difference, then the concept, *Life Force*, does no work in the explanation; in addition the explanation would be circular, since it roughly would be giving the thing to be explained as the explanation of itself.

If there is a difference, then perhaps it is because some reference is made to Ann's power. Another way of putting the statement then might be that Ann had the power to capture any man she chose. If we translate it that way, however, we have again dispensed with the concept, *Life Force.*

Let us examine what has happened. We have picked the explicit and specific part of Bronwyn's explanation to see if it is testable. We have discovered that its testability depends on the interpretation given to it. Under

* You are referred back to the treatment of analytic and empirical statements in the previous chapter in order to refresh your memory. Untestable, allegedly empirical statements are either analytic or meaningless.

one interpretation, it is not testable and thus of no use in prediction and postdiction, since we cannot tell whether it is true.

Under two other interpretations, it is testable, but the concept, *Life Force*, has ceased to play a role. But once the testability has been established, we can proceed to evaluate the explanation on other grounds (circularity and truth especially are weaknesses in these two cases).

Here is the way the dialogues might have gone:

Example 18-5 (showing untestability)

MISS GAMMA: What could count as evidence against your claim that the Life Force was expressing itself through Ann Whitefield?

BRONWYN: Nothing could.

MISS GAMMA: Then you have not excluded any conceivable states of affairs by your statement. You give us no information.

Example 18-6 (eliminating the concept, *Life Force*, and leading to circularity)

FRANK: What could count as evidence against your claim . . . ?

BRONWYN: If Jack didn't succumb, that would have been counter-evidence.

FRANK: Then 'the Life Force was expressing itself through her' means the same as 'Jack succumbed to her charms'?

BRONWYN: Yes.

FRANK: Then your explanation is circular.

Example 18-7 (eliminating the concept, *Life Force*, and challenging the truth of the result)

FRANK: What could count as evidence against your claim . . . ?

BRONWYN: If Jack didn't succumb, that would have been counter-evidence.

FRANK: Then 'the Life Force was expressing itself through her' means the same as 'Jack succumbed to her charms'?

BRONWYN: No. It means that she had the power to capture any man she chose.

FRANK: Then your view could be expressed without any use of the concept, *Life Force*. Why introduce extra terminology? And besides the statement is dubious. I don't think she could have captured Hector Malone.

Though the dialogue might well develop in many possible directions, the basic strategy to follow (assuming that Bronwyn is requested to supply conceivable evidence and counter-evidence) is to proceed slowly, to make clear what she is saying, and to be on the lookout for these alternatives:

1. Untestability.
2. Dispensability of the doctrine.
3. Falsity.
4. Ambiguity that occurs when doctrine is proven in its untestable form, and applied in its testable (and perhaps false) form.

A similar approach can be made with the first 'if'-clause in Example 18-4 ("... the Life Force is expressing itself through a female, ..."). One can ask Bronwyn how one would identify a case of the Life Force expressing itself through a female, which is the same as to ask what would count as evidence for and against the judgment that the Life Force was expressing itself through a given female. One must be able to identify such a case in order to test the generalization (the first complete sentence of the gap-filler in Example 18-4), since the test of the generalization can occur only under the condition that the 'if'-clause is true.

Suppose the 'if'-clause held analytically (perhaps by definition?). In that case then we could dispense with the concept, *Life Force*, since it would perform no function in the explanation—and the explanation would then be reduced to the original one that Frank suggested.

To elaborate—if the clause analytically held in all conceivable cases, then, since it is the antecedent in a complex conditional statement, we could (by affirmation of the antecedent) conclude the consequent in all cases. The working part of the law would then be the consequent, "If a female selects a given man to cooperate with her in the propagation of the race, then that man is likely to succumb to her charms." This is the working part because in order to make a prediction about a man's succumbing, we only need establish that some female has selected him to cooperate with her in the propagation of the race. The concept, Life Force, plays no role, so the proposed law has been reduced to its working part, which is roughly what Frank suggested in the first place, and presumably, is false.

Next suppose, in order, two nonanalytic interpretations of that first 'if'-clause, interpretations that parallel the nonanalytic interpretations of Bronwyn's explicit answer:

1. '... the Life Force is expressing itself through a female ...' means the same as 'a man is going to succumb to the charms of a female'.
2. '... the Life Force is expressing itself through a female ...' means the same as 'a female has the power to capture any man she chooses'.

Under these interpretations the total generalizations become the following:

1. If a man is going to succumb to the charms of a female, and if that female selects that man to cooperate with her in the propagation of the race, then that man is likely to succumb to her charms.
2. If a female has the power to capture any man she chooses, and if that female selects a given man to cooperate with her in the propagation of the race, then that man is likely to succumb to her charms.

The first generalization is obviously untestable and useless. Once the truth of the first 'if'-clause is established with respect to a given man and a given woman, then there is no point in predicting the consequent, "that man is likely to succumb to her charms". One cannot conceive of any situation in which the first clause is satisfied and in which the final consequent is not satisfied.

The second generalization seems untestable as well. Presumably once we have established that a given female has the power to capture any man she chooses, we know simply in virtue of the meaning of the words that if she selects a given man, he will succumb to her charms. But the second generalization could well not be useless, because it analytically spells out a consequence of the possession of such power. It seems to advance the explanation.

The first generalization does not get anywhere because the first and last clause use virtually the same language. Hence an explanation that uses the first generalization is useless. The second generalization, though also presumably analytic, could conceivably carry along the explanation because of its tracing out the meaning of 'power' in this sort of situation. Hence it is not necessarily useless. Making use of the second generalization, we have an analytic explanation with an explicit premise, "Ann had the power to capture any man she chose", which is perhaps false. But if true then we have an explanation that is satisfactory at a certain level of sophistication.

As you no doubt now realize, a large number of possibilities exist, no one of which can be pinned for certain on an uncompleted, uninterpreted explanation. But if one is careful and attentive to all parts of the explanation at once, and uses some memory aid—such as the blackboard—to keep track of the alternative gap-fillers and interpretations, then the nature of the explanation can be tracked down, and can be quite enlightening to students.

Some of you might now be thinking that since Frank's original comments were quite appropriate, there is no point in going on as we have been doing. The reason, of course, is that Frank had no defense ready for his comments. His intuition was correct, but if we only go that far, then rational discussion stops when intuitions clash. What must be done is to go beneath intuitions and look carefully at the possible interpretations of the statements involved, keeping in mind the fact that there are alternate ways of filling the gap, and keeping in mind the logical tools which you are acquiring or have acquired: the notion of testability, the rules of deduction, patterns of explanation, the practical application of deduction, the distinctions among analytic, synthetic, and meaningless statements, the distinctions among types of synthetic statements, and at a more concrete level, the discreet use of counter-examples.

But perhaps we have still not gone far enough in dealing with Bronwyn. There might be a clash of intuitions over the utility of untestable statements, or, which is more likely, the charge that a statement is untestable might just pass over the heads of many people. This problem might well arise in Example 18-5 above, in which Miss Gamma pointed out that Bronwyn's statement did not exclude any conceivable states of affairs, whereupon Miss Gamma concluded that the statement gave no information. Many people just will not see the connection between not excluding any conceivable state of affairs and not providing any information. So the last-named tool in the previous paragraph must often be brought into play: the discreet use of counter-examples.

The Counter-example Approach. This strategy, as compared to the conceivable evidence approach, is much more difficult to employ successfully: (1) because its employer cannot make use of such sophisticated concepts as *logical possibility, conceivable evidence, exclusion of conceivable states of affairs, testability,* and so forth; (2) because an audience that is unaware of these concepts, is in addition likely to be less sophisticated in general; and (3) because a proof using only the unsophisticated notion of a counter-example is much more lengthy and difficult to construct, just as a proof in any other field is difficult to construct without the use of considerable conceptual apparatus in the background. Be that as it may, let us examine how the dialogues might have proceeded along the lines of the counter-example strategy:

Example 18-8a

MISS GAMMA: Now, Bronwyn, is this the complete explanation, as you would like it to be? (points to completed explanation, Example 18-4)

BRONWYN: Yes.

MISS GAMMA: Let's look at what you explicitly said, which was, ". . . the Life Force was expressing itself through her." Suppose that Ann Whitefield chose to be a career woman—say a lawyer. And suppose that she became a lawyer, a good one. Would that have shown that the Life Force was not expressing itself through her?

BRONWYN: No. The Life Force would have been expressing itself through her.

MISS GAMMA: Well, suppose that she failed to become a lawyer. Would that have shown that the Life Force was not expressing itself through her?

BRONWYN: Oh no. That would only have shown that the Life Force was not expressing itself in that way.

MISS GAMMA: Suppose that Ann never married, worked in a factory all day, and spent her nights making her own clothes. Would that be evidence against your statement that the Life Force was expressing itself through her?

BRONWYN: Not at all. The Life Force can be expressed in many ways, an infinite number of ways. No matter what she does, the Life Force will inevitably be expressing itself through her, because she is a woman.

MISS GAMMA: Do you mean to say that whatever any woman does, the Life Force will be expressing itself through her?

BRONWYN: Yes, I do.

Miss Gamma now has evidence that seems sufficient to warrant the conclusion that Bronwyn's explicit statement offered in explanation is untestable.

But there is no point in simply telling Bronwyn this fact, because the information will not mean anything to her. So she must try to show that the claim as Bronwyn has interpreted it is of no use in explaining or predicting.

One is tempted here to try to show immediately that Bronwyn cannot generate predictions and cannot explain, but that move will not work yet, because the complete explanation (which includes the gap-fillers) does generate predictions under the interpretation just given by Bronwyn. The troubles are that the predictions are false and are generated without making use of the Life Force doctrine. Thus again we have two major problems for which one should be alert: uselessness and falsity. This time the problems appear together. Often in doctrines suspected of untestability they do not appear together; instead they appear alternatively: on one interpretation of the doctrine it is useless, and on the other interpretation it is false.

In this case we find that on the same interpretation uselessness and falsity both appear. How can Miss Gamma show this, still avoiding the use of sophisticated terminology? Since falsity is easier to understand than uselessness of a concept, she should probably go to work on that first in order to make Bronwyn see that a problem exists here.

Example 18-8b

MISS GAMMA: You have just held that no matter what any woman does, the Life Force is expressing itself through her. Then it seems your gap-filler is clearly false. Look at the complex sentence (pointing to the board), "If the Life Force is expressing itself through a female, and if that female selects a given man to cooperate with her in the propagation of the race, then that man is likely to succumb to her charms." According to you, the first 'if'-clause is always satisfied; hence you must hold that if any female selects any man and so forth, then he is likely to succumb. That is simply false. Hector Malone was not likely to succumb to Ann Whitefield's charms, even if she had selected him. You should know from your own experience that not just anyone you select to try to charm is likely to succumb to your charms.

Bronwyn next makes a move that is very frequently made: to insulate the statement against counter-examples, and thus to begin to transform a statement that looks straightforwardly empirical (the gap-filler without the first 'if'-clause) into an untestable statement:

Example 18-8c

BRONWYN: But because the Life Force is expressing itself through us, we females never select a man who is not likely to succumb.

MISS GAMMA: Now the first sentence of your gap-filler is beginning to look useless. The generalization you are assuming takes on the appearance of circularity. Suppose you wanted to predict whether a man would succumb to your charms. As I first interpreted the generalization, it warrants a prediction to the effect that it is likely that the man will succumb if you will only try to charm him. But now it seems that you have to know whether he is likely to succumb before you will select him as recipient of your charms. In other words, using this generalization, you must know whether he is likely to succumb before you can predict that he is likely to succumb. Not much use, that.

Note that Miss Gamma has not completely dispatched this latest move of Bronwyn's; she has only shown the statement's uselessness when Bronwyn herself tries to make a prediction. But she has also indicated the way to reveal its probable uselessness under other conditions. I said "probable" because the statement, given proper interpretation, can still be saved from the charge of uselessness. But then, under all the reasonable interpretations that I can think of, it would be false.

Next Miss Gamma proceeds to show that the Life Force doctrine is useless as Bronwyn has interpreted it:

Example 18-8d

BRONWYN: But someone else might be able to predict that a particular man would be likely to succumb to my charms.

MISS GAMMA: Well, there are difficulties there too, but I'd like to pass over them for now, because the key question is the Life Force doctrine, which seems to play no role in whatever it is that you are doing. You said that whatever any woman does the Life Force will be expressing itself through her. Hence the first 'if'-clause of your generalization is always fulfilled. Since that is so, there is no point in your saying that the Life Force was expressing itself through Bronwyn. According to the way you mean 'Life Force', the first 'if'-clause does not need anything to show that it holds. Furthermore, since that first 'if'-clause always holds, regardless of the facts, and since it is an antecedent of a conditional, it can be dispensed with. The working part of your proposed law is, "If a female selects a given man to cooperate with her in the propagation of the race, then that man is likely to succumb to her charms." That, together with the other gap-fillers implies the explicandum. And all this makes no use of the doctrine of Life Force. So why introduce it?

BRONWYN: Because Shaw did.

MISS GAMMA: But now you can see that it only serves to waste time and energy.

BRONWYN: Well, I can see that at least as I've interpreted it, it does not help to explain why Tanner succumbed. Perhaps Shaw meant it in a different way. I'll have to think some more about it.

And so it goes. Doctrines can always be reinterpreted to avoid given embarrassments. Again the main things to watch out for are the following:

1. Untestability.
2. Dispensability of the doctrine.
3. Falsity.
4. Ambiguity that occurs when a doctrine is proven in its untestable form, and applied in its testable (and perhaps false) form.

More can be said by each side in the above dialogue, but the main ideas of each of the strategies should be fairly clear: One checks the proof and application of the claim, making sure that the claim does not change meaning in the process. A doctrine which gives no basis for predicting one thing over its opposite, or for the accounting for one thing instead of its opposite, although impossible to prove false, cannot play the role of an empirical statement. The conceivable-evidence strategy is more efficient at pointing out this defect when it exists, but requires more conceptual sophistication on the part of its audience than the counter-example strategy, which simply makes judicious use of counter-examples and a demand for consistency.

Applicability

The criterion, applicability, which is somewhat like testability, is applied to obligation and value explanations. Roughly it goes like this: If there are not conceivable examples and nonexamples of that sort of thing which is judged obligatory or which is judged good (or bad), then the explanation making use of general 'ought' and value statements is defective. Consider this example, which again makes use of the concept, *manifest destiny:*

Example 18-9

MR. BETA: Why do you think it was a good thing for the United States to go to war with Spain?

LARRY: Because that was to act in accord with our manifest destiny. [Acting in accord with our manifest destiny is a good thing.]

You can readily see that the applicability of this gap-filling generalization depends on the meaning of 'manifest destiny' as did the allegedly empirical explanation that we examined earlier. If 'to act in accord with our manifest destiny' means the same as 'to do what we are unavoidably going to do', then there are no conceivable nonexamples of acting in accord with our manifest destiny. That is, we cannot conceive of something which we are unavoidably going to do but which we do not do, at least in the rather standard senses of these terms. If there is something which we do not do, then we were not unavoidably going to do it. Thus under that interpretation, the explanation fails to meet the applicability criterion.

If, on the other hand, 'to act in accord with our manifest destiny' means 'to do what we can to increase our power', then we can easily think of both an example of so doing and a nonexample. Thus under the second interpretation, the explanation satisfies this criterion.

How do we probe explanations about which we are in doubt? One thing to do is to ask for operational or conditional definitions of the key terms. Another thing to do is simply to ask for an example and a nonexample of the thing judged obligatory or good. Thirdly, we can suggest possible examples and nonexamples and check to see if they actually are such. These probes are presented in order of decreasing sophistication.

Here is an interesting example of probing and its results, taken from Mark Twain's *The Adventures of Huckleberry Finn*. In it Huck goes after Tom Sawyer for making a recommendation that fails to pass the applicability criterion. Then the recommendation is made to pass the test by the invention of a meaning for the key term 'ransom'. One lesson to be learned from this passage is that, although certain value or obligation statements apparently fail to satisfy the applicability criterion, a meaning can be given, enabling discussion to proceed.

Example 18-10

"Must we always kill the people?"

"Oh, certainly. It's best. Some authorities think different, but mostly it's considered best to kill them. Except some that you bring to the cave here and keep them till they're ransomed."

"Ransomed? What's that?"

"I don't know. But that's what they do. I've seen it in books; and so of course that's what we've got to do."

"*But how can we do it if we don't know what it is?*"

"Why blame it all, we've got to do it. Don't I tell you it's in the books? Do you want to go to doing different from what's in the books, and get things all muddled up?"

"Oh, that's all very fine to say, Tom Sawyer, but how in the nation are these fellows going to be ransomed if we don't know how to do it to them? That's the thing I want to get at. Now what do you reckon it is?"

"Well I don't know. But perhaps if we keep them till they're ransomed, it means that we keep them till they're dead."

"Now, *that's something like*. That'll answer. Why couldn't you said that before? We'll keep them till they're ransomed to death—and a bothersome lot they'll be, too, eating up everything and always trying to get loose."

"How you talk, Ben Rogers. How can they get loose when there's a guard over them, ready to shoot them down if they move a peg?"

"A guard. Well, that is good. So somebody's got to set up all night and never get any sleep, just so as to watch them. I think that's foolishness. Why can't a body take a club and ransom them as soon as they get here?"

"Because it ain't in the books so—that's why. Now Ben Rogers, do you want to do things regular, or don't you?—that's the idea. Don't you reckon that the people that made the books knows what's the correct thing to do? Do you reckon you can learn 'em anything? Not by a good deal. No, sir, we'll just go on and ransom them in the regular way."

"All right. I don't mind; but I say it's a fool way, anyhow. Say—do we kill the women, too?"

"Well, Ben Rogers, if I was as ignorant as you I wouldn't let on. Kill the women? No—nobody ever says anything in the books like that. You fetch them to the cave, and you're always as polite as pie to them; and by-and-by they fall in love with you and never want to go home any more."

"Well, if that's the way, I'm agreed, but I don't take no stock in it. Mighty soon we'll have the cave so cluttered up with women, and fellows waiting to be ransomed, that there won't be no place for the robbers. But go ahead, I ain't got nothing to say."

Chapter Summary

A general synthetic statement in an explicans must be either testable or applicable, the former if the statement is supposed to be empirical, and the latter if it is supposed to be a value or obligation statement. If a supposedly empirical statement is untestable, or if a supposedly value or obligation statement is inapplicable, then it is either meaningless or analytic. Analytic statements are useful in many ways, but they cannot be used to play the role of empirical statements. Meaningless statements are generally useless.

The testability discussion dealt with conceptual testability, rather than practical testability. A general statement is CONCEPTUALLY TESTABLE if, and only if, evidence both for and against the statement is **conceivable**. Evidence might be conceivable, even though impossible to gather from a practical point of view. Practical impossibility of the gathering of evidence makes a statement untestable practically. The impossibility of conceiving evidence is what makes a statement conceptually untestable.

A general value or obligation statement is INAPPLICABLE when one cannot specify conceivable examples and nonexamples of the sort of thing judged good, bad, or obligatory. The **actual** nonexistence of either examples or nonexamples is irrelevant to the question of applicability. Only the **conceivable** existence is relevant.

Parallel considerations apply to specific (as opposed to general) synthetic statements. For an empirical singular statement to be testable, one must be able to conceive of a state of affairs that would show it true, and a state of affairs that would show it false. These states of affairs need not be practically possible—only conceivable. For a singular value statement to be applicable one must be able to identify the thing judged good or bad, and to distinguish it from other things. For a singular obligation statement to be applicable, one must be able to conceive of a situation in which the alleged obligation had been satisfied and a situation in which the alleged obligation had not been satisfied.

When dealing with a sophisticated audience which understands such concepts as *testability*, *logical possibility*, *conceivable evidence*, etc., the discussion about whether a statement is testable or applicable can proceed more quickly and efficiently than it can when these concepts are not understood. In the latter situation one must make discreet use of possible examples and counter-examples in order to search out the meaning and weaknesses of statements that are made. Primary difficulties to be avoided, whatever the strategy, are the following:

1. Untestability or inapplicability.
2. Dispensability of the doctrine or concept.
3. Falsity.
4. Ambiguity in transition from proof to application.

This, the criterion of testability/applicability, is then a fifth criterion to use in evaluating explanations. Like the other four criteria, its applicability is not limited to explanations, but it is limited to material performing the function of synthetic statements. Analytic statements performing an analytic function—including definitions—are not subject to this criterion, whether in explanations or not.

COMPREHENSION SELF-TEST

True or False? If the statement is false, change a crucial term (or terms) to make it true.

18–1. If an alleged empirical general statement is practically untestable, then it is either meaningless or analytic.

18–2. The criterion of testability applies particularly to analytic explanations.

Problems.

18–3. For the following explanation frame a probe that would help to see if the explanation satisfies the criterion of testability:

FRANK: Our society is headed for collapse.

JOAN: Why do you think that?

FRANK: Because there is too much cultural lag at present. You know what cultural lag is, don't you? When the nonmaterial part of a culture (for example, laws, customs, knowledge, morality, and so forth) lags behind the material part (for example, tools, machines, and the like), cultural lag may be said to exist.

18–5. Frame an answer that Frank could give that suggests that his explanation satisfies the testability criterion. Explain why the proposed answer suggests that the criterion is satisfied.

18–6. Frame an answer that Frank could give that suggests that his explanation does not satisfy the criterion. Explain why the proposed answer suggests that the criterion is not satisfied.

Discussion Question.

18–7. Examine one of the following doctrines, reading primary source material, and try to decide whether the doctrine is testable or applicable. Write a paper in which you defend your view.

a. The doctrine of manifest destiny, as set forth in the United States at the end of the nineteenth century by President William McKinley among others.
b. George Bernard Shaw's doctrine of the Life Force.
c. William Fielding Ogburn's cultural lag doctrine, as expressed in his book, *Social Change.*
d. The phlogiston theory, which was offered in explanation of burning, among other things. A good start in your examination of this theory is the pamphlet edited by James B. Conant, "The Overthrow of the Phlogiston Theory," Case 2 of *Harvard Case Histories in Experimental Science* (James B. Conant, General Editor), (Cambridge, Mass.: Harvard University Press, 1950).
e. Social Darwinism, as developed by William Graham Sumner in *What Social Classes Owe to Each Other.*

CHAPTER 19

Explanation: An Overview by Way of Application

In this chapter I will not try to summarize the content of the chapters on explanation, since a summary appears at the end of each chapter. Instead, as in the final chapter on definition, I shall present a classroom dialogue, modified to eliminate some irrelevancies and to make the flow of thought more clear. As you read this dialogue, put yourself in the place of Miss Gamma, an eleventh grade English teacher, focusing your attention on her logical, as opposed to psychological, moves. What would you have done differently, if anything? (Entries are numbered for later reference.)

A Dialogue

1. Miss Gamma: Well, now, you all should have finished reading *1984*, and I have heard from some of you that you think that this is a valuable book with a lesson for us. Several people also told me that they were disappointed in the way it ended. I hope that today we can discuss the value and impact of the book as a whole. The first and preliminary question I'd like to put to you is this one: Is this book literature? (Pauses) Hilary?

2. Hilary: I don't really think that it is.

3. Miss Gamma: Why not?

4. Hilary: Because there are inconsistencies in it. For example, Winston Smith in the beginning of the book is supposed not to be sure of what year it is, yet further on we learn that his daily job gives him frequent contact with dates on recent newspapers.

5. Miss Gamma: And what do you think, Neil?

6. Neil: I think that it's literature, because it is fictional, it has an organization, it expresses the author's feelings, its main purpose is not practical, and it exploits the medium here, the written novel.

7. Miss Gamma: Oh, I see that you remember Wellek and Warren's concept of literature. I suppose that this should remind us that opinions can differ on whether a particular work is literature. Virginia?

8. Virginia: But there **was** a practical purpose in Orwell's book. He was trying to persuade people that socialism is bad for England. He used the term "Ingsoc" to refer to the doctrines of Oceania and treated that term as synonymous with 'English socialism'. The whole thing is one big repetitive complaint about the political situation in England.

9. Sam: That's right. Some of us interested in radio and television were talking before class and I know that we no longer think that it's a good idea for the British government to control radio and television the way it does.

10. Miss Gamma: Hold on now. We have several things going here. For the time being let's stick to the question of whether this book is literature. Hilary said that it isn't, and Neil said that it is. Virginia said that one of Neil's points is wrong. Sam, you said that the book **had** a particular effect upon you, but let me remind you that the important question here is whether the book is primarily **aimed** at doing such things. So let's return to your point later. Now Hilary, you gave as your reason for thinking that this is not literature the existence of inconsistencies. What does that have to do with it?

11. Hilary: That means that it is not literature.

12. Miss Gamma: Well, we know that you think that, but **why** does the existence of inconsistencies mean that it is not literature?

13. Hilary: It just does.

14. Miss Gamma: Does anyone share Hilary's opinion and feel able to tell me what the presence of inconsistencies has to do with it? (Silence)

15. Peter: Well, I agree with her, but I can't say any more than she did.

16. Miss Gamma: You remember last month we read *The Adventures of Huckleberry Finn* and thought that we found some serious defects in Mark Twain's work. Is that literature?

17. Peter and Hilary: No.

18. Miss Gamma: Oh, then you are assuming that a necessary condition for something's being literature is that it be of high quality?

19. Hilary: Yes, that's it.

20. Miss Gamma: I assume that I did not make my question clear then. I meant to be asking a question of classification, according to some scheme like Wellek and Warren's, not a question of evaluation. As you are using the term 'literature', the phrase 'bad literature' is then inconsistent, and the phrase 'good literature' is redundant. I meant to ask whether one could classify *1984* as literature, leaving aside for the moment the question of whether it is good or bad. Neil, I suppose that you were using Wellek and Warren's range definition of 'literature'?

21. NEIL: That is correct.

22. MISS GAMMA: Would you refresh the memories of the rest of us?

23. NEIL: O. K. They said something like this (glancing at his notes): LITERATURE is an art form characterized by organization, personal expression, realization and exploitation of the medium, lack of practical purpose, and fictionality. That's not the same order I used, but I covered the points.

24. MISS GAMMA: Any questions about that, class?

25. TONY: I agree with Virginia about the purpose. Orwell had a very practical purpose: persuading the English to reject socialism.

26. NEIL: Even if you're right, why does that show that *1984* is not literature? You're assuming that Wellek and Warren's definition gives us a list of **necessary** conditions.

27. TONY: This one is considered to be a necessary condition. Let me quote from the bottom of page 13: "It seems, however, best to consider as literature only works in which the aesthetic function is dominant." The word 'only' shows that they **are** giving a necessary condition. That's why I think that this book is not literature.

28. MISS GAMMA: A good point. Hans?

29. HANS: I don't really see what difference it makes. Who cares whether we call it literature or something else? Why bother with this question?

30. MISS GAMMA: I can see why you don't particularly care about it, but it does make a difference. Remember that this is a course in literature. Some of the English teachers have been wondering whether we should be reading this book in this course at all. My reason in bringing up this question is to get help in making up my mind about whether to include this book in the reading list in future years.

31. HANS: Oh, I see. Well then I think we should talk about whether Virginia is right about Orwell's principal purpose. Anyway I think that's an interesting question, whether or not we are trying to decide whether *1984* is literature.

32. MISS GAMMA: Agreed, Virginia?

33. VIRGINIA: That political persuasion was his primary purpose explains why he depicted so many things offensive to Englishmen, many of which are also offensive to us. The use of dollars as the currency in London would offend any Englishman. And the practices of rewriting history, of thought control, of deprivation of privacy, of summary arrests and torture of political prisoners, of promoting slogans like "War Is Peace", "Ignorance Is Strength", and "Freedom Is Slavery" are all very offensive. They can be explained by a primary purpose of political persuasion, but not by a primarily aesthetic purpose.

34. MISS GAMMA: That's a strong argument, as I understand it. You hold that Orwell believed that the use of these offensive items would be an effective way to persuade English people that socialism is bad, but that he could not have believed that these things would achieve an aesthetic purpose, since there is so much ugliness and dullness among them.

35. VIRGINIA: That's right.

36. Miss Gamma: Anyone disagree? (Pause) Sam?

37. Sam: I think that my earlier point was relevant, since it supports Virginia's assumption that Orwell believed that the use of these offensive items would be an effective way to persuade English people that socialism is bad. I was saying that Orwell made an effective persuasive instrument. Since experienced people like Orwell tend to believe what is true, my evidence supported Virginia's assumption about Orwell's beliefs.

38. Miss Gamma: Oh, I see. Then let's consider whether Orwell was correct in his belief that the use of these offensive items would be an effective way to persuade English people that socialism is bad. Why did the book persuade you, Sam, to change your mind about control of the radio and television by the British Government?

39. Sam: The things that the government of Oceania was able to do with the telescreens caused me to change my mind.

40. Virginia: That's true of most people. If somebody shows you in detail the extremes of anything, your mind will probably change about it.

41. Neil: It didn't change my mind.

42. Virginia: Well, you're not most people.

43. Miss Gamma: Virginia, do you mean people's minds are generally changed by the depiction in detail of the extreme possibilities of a system?

44. Virginia: That's it. Neil doesn't fit a number of generalizations that I know about.

45. Miss Gamma: I see, but let's get back to this generalization that you stated. How does it explain what happened to Sam?

46. Virginia: That telescreen business is the—what did you say—the depiction in detail of the extreme possibilities of the system.

47. Miss Gamma: I just wanted to be sure. Neil?

48. Neil: I think that Virginia has too little trust in people. People aren't generally swayed just by extreme pictures. They know better.

49. Miss Gamma: Do you think that the members of this class weren't generally swayed by Orwell's book?

50. Neil: Moved, but not swayed.

51. Virginia: What do you mean?

52. Neil: I believe that we are an intelligent group, and that although many of us found the book moving, it did not alter our political opinions.

53. Virginia: It altered Sam's and mine.

54. Neil: So?

55. Virginia: Doesn't that mean anything to you?

56. Neil: It means that you think that the book altered Sam's and your opinions.

The discussion continued with the attempt by Virginia to justify her generalization, but I shall interrupt it here because justification is the topic of Part IV. Before examining the appropriateness of the moves made by Miss Gamma, I shall make a few general observations about the dialogue:

(a) As you can see, the three basic logical aspects of teaching that are treated in this book (definition, explanation, justification) are closely intertwined in this dialogue. This is frequently the case.

(b) The dialogue contains a large number of explanations of a number of different types, more explanations than are to be found in a random selection of classroom dialogues, since so many classroom dialogues (at least at the period of writing) are dominated by fact questions and answers.* The frequency of explanations found in this dialogue is not exceptional in discussions that **involve** students in making judgments and defending their views. The quality of the discussion here, however, is still atypically high, partly because I have refined this dialogue, leaving out much irrelevance; adding, subtracting, and changing points in order to lay bare a rational set of logical moves and to maintain anonymity. An actual transcription of a class session is always much less comprehensible, partly because some crucial words are missed; partly because the speakers leave much of their communication to their intonations, leaving the reader mystified about what is actually occurring; and partly because irrelevancies are more frequent in oral discussions.

(c) On the whole Miss Gamma did a good job as discussion leader. She kept the discussion from skipping all around, yet did permit development of related ideas.

(d) Note in this discussion how the use of the word "Why?" and other explanation requests provoke thought.

(e) There are more explanations and explanation-relevant moves in the dialogue than you may think. Before going on, look through it to see how many sentences are related to some explanation, and try to be clear in each case what the explicandum is.

(f) Although this particular dialogue took place in a literature class, there is much to see in it that is generalizable to other subject-matter areas.

(g) Since many justification problems arise in the preceding dialogue, it will be used as a springboard into the next part of the book. As you think about the dialogue, consider how one could justify some of the statements made therein.

Analysis

In the following analysis, I shall summarize the exchange concerning each explanation, and comment on this exchange. In contrast to the discussion in the previous chapters about explanation, I shall take the problems as they come, dealing with each in the way that seems best suited to it. I shall make incidental comments about some psychological features of Miss Gamma's

* See B. O. Smith and Milton Meux, *A Study of the Logic of Teaching* (Urbana, Illinois: Bureau of Educational Research, College of Education, University of Illinois, no date), p. 54.

teaching, but will concentrate on the logical features. Inevitably, not all aspects of explanations are mentioned—or even relevant.

Miss Gamma set the direction of the discussion with her question at the end of Entry 1, "Is this book literature?" She immediately followed Hilary's negative answer to the question with a "Why not?", thus bringing forth the first explanation of the dialogue. Hilary's explicans, "Because there are inconsistencies in it", was followed by comments, answers, and suggestions by Neil, Virginia, and Sam, which appeared to work the discussion gradually away from the central topic, so Miss Gamma discreetly brought them back to Hilary's suggestion (Entry 10). There she asked Hilary to gap-fill her own explanation by saying, "What does that have to do with it?"

Hilary's answer (Entry 11), "That means that it is not literature", was correctly though discreetly declared circular by Miss Gamma. In asking for the gap-filler Miss Gamma had explicitly asked for an explanation of why the alleged inconsistencies were supposed to explain why the book was supposed not to be literature. In other words, the request for a gap-filler was a second-order request for an explanation: "Why did the explanation explain?" was in effect what she asked. The answer to this did not advance the discussion, since it simply repeated the claim made by the first explanation, and hence was properly judged circular.

Upon requestioning Hilary declared herself unable to fill the gap in her first explanation and was joined by Peter. Miss Gamma set about probing, suggesting an item (*The Adventures of Huckleberry Finn*), the classification of which might well reveal the gap-filler that Hilary and (perhaps) Peter were using. It was a crucial case, since most people would call Twain's work literature, and yet given the suspected gap-filler, "All literature is of high quality" (and assuming some decisions that had previously been made about the quality of this work), it would not be literature. This was a good move on Miss Gamma's part. She did not put words into Hilary's mouth without first having good reason to think that they belonged there.

Of course, Miss Gamma could have taken the time to get Hilary or Peter to state the criterion, perhaps by getting them to consider a range of examples, trying to see what similarly classified things had in common. But given the judgment about Twain's work, she had good reason to know what criterion they were using, and apparently felt that she did not want to spend much time dealing with that criterion. Instead she tried to make clear that she did not want a value explanation, which they had in effect given her, but did want an explanation dependent on a nonevaluative classification system (⁘ an analytic explanation).

She was deceiving herself to some extent here, since the term 'literature' in this context was a value term in the way that programmatically defined terms are value terms. In her later response to Hans' wondering what difference it makes whether *1984* is literature, she made clear that a programmatic definition was involved, so she really had asked something of a value question in the first place. Wellek and Warren did a similar thing, when they said in their *Theory of Literature*, "Classification [of something] as art should be distinguished from evaluation"*, so Miss Gamma had a precedent. Wellek and Warren (and Miss Gamma) are, of course, doing an important thing: attempting to preserve the logical possibility of bad literature. Hilary's approach makes bad literature a logical impossibility, as Miss Gamma noted.

On the whole, Miss Gamma's handling of Hilary's explanation was good.

Neil's explanation in justification of his positive answer to Miss Gamma's question quite obviously made use of Wellek and Warren's definition of 'literature', which served as the simple gap-filler to his explanation. The criteria of simplicity and generosity, given the context (the class had previously studied Wellek and Warren's view), justified the attribution of that gap-filler to his explanation. Miss Gamma, presumably for some psychological reinforcement purpose, asked him (Entry 22) to state the gap-filler, though she did not put the request as a request for a gap-filler, probably because it was so obvious to her and Neil that the Wellek and Warren definition was the gap-filler. If she had said, "What does that have to do with it?", as she did to Hilary, she would have in this case been talking down to him and perhaps insulted him. Different logical moves often have different psychological effects.

The gap-filling aspects of her handling of Neil's explanation are quite good, though not particularly difficult.

In his explanation, Neil said that Orwell's main purpose was not practical. Virginia challenged this and explained why she did so by mentioning what she took to be Orwell's purpose (persuading people that socialism is bad for England) and justifying her claim that this was Orwell's purpose. The kind of justification she was presenting was not deductive, but rather a type of justification to be discussed in Part IV.

Neil's response was to interpret the Wellek and Warren definition as a range definition, so that the failure to satisfy one of the conditions did not disqualify something as literature. The deductive structure of his explanation then became much looser, but still satisfactory, a topic discussed in Chapter 5. But Tony did not let Neil get by with the range definition move—at least insofar as purpose goes, pointing out that Wellek and Warren, regardless of how they treated the other features, took having a dominant aesthetic purpose to be a necessary condition for something's being literature. Miss Gamma's proper role here, since the students were making good logical moves, was that of background superintendence, a role she adopted. Tony

* René Wellek and Austin Warren, *Theory of Literature*, 2nd ed. (New York: Harcourt, Brace & World, Inc., 1956), p. 15.

(Entry 27) gave a justification explanation of why *1984* is not literature. His explanation is completed by Virginia's claim (already given) that Orwell's purpose was not aesthetic. He not only offered his explanation but defended his claim that having an aesthetic purpose is a necessary condition by citing a quote from Wellek and Warren. Thus Tony, making use of Virginia's claim about Orwell's purpose, offered a complete explanation and defended his explicans, presumably leaving to Virginia the defense of the claim that Orwell's purpose was not aesthetic. Tony's moves were appropriate and received Miss Gamma's approval. The discussion later returns to the claim about Orwell's purpose, but before it does, Miss Gamma is called upon to explain why they should bother with the question of whether *1984* is literature (Entry 29).

In reply to this challenge by Hans, Miss Gamma says, "My reason in bringing up this question is to get help in making up my mind about whether to include this book in the reading list in future years." Filled out to some extent her explanation could look something like this (I have added some gap-fillers and freely revised her explicit statements, but do not think I have done injustice to her thought):

Example 19-1

Explanatory material:

1. If the question, "Is *1984* literature?", is relevant to a decision about whether to include *1984* in the reading list for future years, then the question is important for this class to consider.
2. The question, "Is *1984* literature?", is relevant to a decision about whether to include *1984* in the reading list for future years.
3. We should bother with questions that are important for this class to consider.

Explicandum:

We should bother with the question, "Is *1984* literature?".

I interpreted Miss Gamma to be attempting to justify the consideration of the question in her class, and filled out the explanation as a value explanation. Even though she used the word "reason", I did not take her to be attempting to account for her action—but rather to justify a value statement.

The explanation is complete as it stands in Example 19-1. One might well want to challenge the truth of the first and second premises, a fact which the completion helps us to realize. I shall not here argue the pros and cons about these two premises, but will leave that to you.

In Entry 33 Virginia gives a justification explanation of why she thinks that political persuasion was Orwell's primary purpose. This justification makes use of the fact (in Virginia's eyes) that her view explains a feature about the book, a feature that the alternative (the purpose was primarily aesthetic) is unable to explain, because the alternative is inconsistent with that feature. There is here an explanation within an explanation. The ability of Virginia's view to explain the feature explains (in part) why Virginia holds the view, one explanation being an account-for explanation and the other being a justification explanation. You will see in Part IV more about this type of justification, which depends in part for its strength on the explanatory power of the thing being justified.

⁘The issue about primary purpose is, in terms used in Chapter 17 in this book, an issue about Orwell's reason for acting. The question is: What was Orwell's primary reason for writing the book? Virginia holds that the political persuasion reason explains (presumably by a reason-for-acting explanation) why he depicts so many offensive things, whereas the alternative (aesthetic purpose) does not explain this and is in fact inconsistent with it.

⁘I shall sketch out a possible completion of Virginia's explanation. You will note that the analytic generalization used here talks about an "effective means" rather than a "best means", as was done in Chapter 17. You will remember that in Chapter 17 you were informed that a number of slightly varying analytic generalizations could be used. The one here is different from the one used there, because it does not seem plausible to say that Orwell thought that his device was the best means.

⁘Example 19-2

Explanatory Material:

1. Orwell's primary purpose was to persuade English people that socialism is bad.
2. Orwell believed that the depiction of many offensive things would make an effective contribution to this purpose without overly interfering with his other purposes, all things considered.
3. Orwell truly believed that he was able to depict many offensive things.
4. Orwell was rational.
5. If a man has x as his primary purpose; if he believes that doing y would make an effective contribution to x without overly interfering with his other purposes, all things considered; if he truly believes he is able to do y; and if he is rational; then he will probably do y.

Explicandum:

Orwell depicted many offensive things.

The only part of the above explanatory material that Virginia explicitly offered was the first premise. The rest, although complicated, is fairly routine, and much of it is truistic. It was included only for purposes of exemplification. The only crucial things are the explicans (first premise) and the explicandum. There is little doubt that her explicans, if true, would explain the explicandum. She has provided an account-for, reason-for-acting explanation.

⁘Virginia also claimed that the alternative theory not only did not explain the depiction of many offensive things, but was inconsistent with this characteristic of the book, that is, that the alternative theory would explain (and predict) just the opposite: the absence of the depiction of many offensive things. I shall not fill out that explanation (or argument for a prediction), but instead will leave it to you to do.

Miss Gamma appropriately endorsed Virginia's moves.

Sam next (Entry 37) offers a justification explanation of why his earlier point was, he thinks, relevant. I will leave the filling out of that explanation to you, accepting it, as Miss Gamma did, and move on to the causal explanations which come next. The question providing the focus of the discussion was stated by Miss Gamma in Entry 38: "Then let's consider whether Orwell was correct in his belief that the use of these offensive items would be an effective way to persuade English people that socialism is bad." This focusing move was appropriate, because it made it more likely that the discussion would not stray.

Miss Gamma in the same entry asked Sam for a causal explanation of his change of mind: "Why did the book persuade you . . . ?" Sam's answer (⁘ a singular causal explanation) attributes his change of mind to the things that the government was able to do with telescreens. Since he is in a good position to know what caused him to change his mind (⁘ and since his answer does not necessarily commit him to more than that under identical circumstances the same thing would happen again), I shall, like Miss Gamma, register no complaints about his explanation; but I would like to note that it advances the discussion only to the extent of providing one instance of the generalization under question.

Next, Virginia attempts to generalize (Entry 40) about most people. Neil's attempted counter-example (himself) is rejected by Virginia on the ground that it is only one case. This is a question of inductive justification, however, so I will bypass it, referring you to Chapter 5 and to Part IV.

Virginia's generalization is offered as a causal explanation of what happened to Sam (and Virginia). Miss Gamma (Entry 45) asks Virginia to add to its completion by saying, "How does it explain what happened to Sam?". Virginia's response is to assert that the "telescreen business" is an instance of "the depiction in detail of the extreme possibilities of the system". There is a difficulty in this attempted completion, which Miss Gamma ignores up to the end of the presented part of the dialogue. If you have not noticed it already, turn back to Entry 46 and reconsider that entry now.

The difficulty to which I refer is the failure of Virginia to instantiate her generalization. The "telescreen business" is the depiction in detail of **one** extreme possibility of the system—not of the extreme possibili**ties**. A proper instantiation of that generalization would mention most (or all) the extreme possibilities of a given system. Actually Virginia needs a different generalization—or an extraordinary interpretation of the one she provides. The generalization as given does not account for Sam's change in view.

Perhaps Miss Gamma let this go by with the intent of catching it later, or perhaps she decided to overlook the flaw, feeling that time did not permit dealing with it, or perhaps she just did not notice it. In any case her ignoring this flaw is a possible weakness in the logic of her handling this situation, depending on why she let it go by.

Regarding the evaluation of an explanation like Virginia's (when it is revised to make it complete), the criteria to apply do not require that the generalization be true for the explanation to be satisfactory for this situation, since in this case the generalization is the hypothesis under question. Virginia is trying to show the worth of the hypothesis by showing its explanatory power. In judging the explanation, we cannot first insist that the hypothesis be true. Strictly speaking (assuming that the explanation were complete and that the rest were true) we should say that the hypothesis **would** explain Sam's change of mind.

The dialogue ends on a dispute about the strength of the justification provided by Virginia.

Chapter Summary

On the whole Miss Gamma did an excellent job in dealing with the explanation problems in the dialogue. She kept the discussion on the track, called for the completion of explanations where appropriate, and in the case where the student was unable to complete her explanation, Miss Gamma suggested a crucial implication of the suspected gap-filler, thus avoiding putting ideas into Hilary's head, but eventually supplying Hilary with the words to express the idea that she probably had.

Miss Gamma's own justification explanation of the importance of the question under discussion is a somewhat dubious explanation, because the truth of her premises is questionable, but she was the teacher and might have had other reasons which she did not feel appropriate to reveal to the students.

For some reason, Miss Gamma ignored Virginia's failure to complete the explanation of Sam's change of mind, but we do not know the reason.

Hopefully in reading the dialogue and the analysis you were able to see the logical structure utilized in evaluating the explanations, which structure has these features:

1. The explicans plus the gap-filler(s) imply (often with qualifications) the explicandum.

2. The explicans is either singular or general. If the explicans is singular, then there is usually a generalization in the gap-filler(s). If general, and if the explicandum is singular, then a singular statement must appear in the gap-filler(s).

3. If the explicans is itself something that the explainer is trying to prove (in virtue of its explanatory power), though the explicandum is implied, the explicans is not; the explicans might be **justified** by its explanatory power. Such justification is to be discussed more elaborately in Part IV.

4. When the explicans is itself something that the explainer is trying to prove (in virtue of its explanatory power), the criterion of truth is not applied to the explicans.

❖**5.** Analytic general statements, found in analytic explanations and reason-for-acting explanations, are not subject to the criterion of testability.

6. In general the criteria of truth, proper level of sophistication, noncircularity, proper function and type, and (❖) testability/applicability should be applied to the explicans and the gap-fillers.

7. Of course, like every other communication, an explanation should be understandable by the person for whom it is intended.

Given an understanding of these structural features and given practice, you should become competent to make quick, accurate decisions concerning requesting, gap-filling, probing, evaluating, and reacting to explanations.

Suggested Further Reading about Explanation

A good deal has been written about the deductive model of explanation, some of which you might find interesting. The following items support the use of this model in fairly pure form, Carl Hempel being the most frequently mentioned advocate:

Brown, Robert. *Explanation in Social Science.* Chicago: Aldine Publishing Company, 1963.

Gardiner, Patrick. *The Nature of Historical Explanation.* Oxford: Oxford University Press, 1952.

Hempel, Carl and Paul Oppenheim. "The Logic of Explanation," in Herbert Feigl and May Brodbeck, eds., *Readings in The Philosophy of Science.* New York: Appleton-Century-Crofts, Inc., 1953, pp. 319–52.

Hempel, Carl. "The Function of General Laws in History," in Patrick Gardiner, ed., *Theories of History.* New York: The Free Press of Glencoe, Inc., 1959, pp. 344–56. Also in Herbert Feigl and Wilfrid Sellars, eds., *Readings in Philosophical Analysis.* New York: Appleton-Century-Crofts, 1949, pp. 459–71. Also in Hempel's *Aspects of Scientific Explanation.* See below.

———. *Aspects of Scientific Explanation.* New York: The Free Press of Glencoe, Inc., 1965.

Hospers, John. "What Is Explanation?" in Antony Flew, ed., *Essays in Conceptual Analysis.* London: Macmillan & Co., Ltd., 1956, pp. 94–119.

A number of people (myself included) have expressed reservations about the pure deductive model, and some reject it completely. Most of the disagreement has been about its applicability to history, with William Dray taking the lead among philosophers. Michael Scriven and Israel Scheffler have also criticized the applicability of the pure deductive model, as described by Hempel, to the physical and other social sciences.

Dray, William. *Laws and Explanation in History.* Oxford: Oxford University Press, 1957.

———. "The Historical Explanation of Actions Reconsidered," in Sidney Hook, ed., *Philosophy and History.* New York: New York University Press, 1963, pp. 105–35.

Scheffler, Israel. "Explanation, Prediction, and Abstraction," *British Journal for the Philosophy of Science,* Vol. VII (1956–57), pp. 293–309.

Scriven, Michael. "Truisms as the Grounds for Historical Explanations," in Patrick Gardiner, ed., *Theories of History.* New York: The Free Press of Glencoe, Inc., 1959, pp. 443–75.

———. "Explanations, Predictions, and Laws," in Herbert Feigl and Grover Maxwell, eds., *Minnesota Studies in the Philosophy of Science.* Minneapolis: University of Minnesota Press, 1962, pp. 170–230.

The distinction between accounting for and justifying has been used by Scheffler in his article mentioned above ("Explanation, Prediction, . . .," footnote 13), and has been described by Hempel in the title article of his book, *Aspects of Scientific Explanation* (pp. 334–35), which is also mentioned above. I make use of it in the following article:

Ennis, Robert H. "Enumerative Induction and Best Explanation," *The Journal of Philosophy,* Vol. LXV, no. 18 (1968), pp. 523–29.

⁘You might be interested in other attempts to categorize explanations. Here are two:

Brown, Robert. *Explanation in Social Science.* Chicago: Aldine Publishing Company, 1963.

Smith, B. Othanel and Milton O. Meux, eds. *A Study of the Logic of Teaching.* Illinois: Bureau of Educational Research, College of Education, University of Illinois. Project No. 258 (7257). United States Office of Education.

⁘The problem of testability is a long-standing one. At the level at which the problem is treated in this book there are a number of helpful statements, including the following:

Brown, Robert. *Explanation in Social Science.* Chicago: Aldine Publishing Company, 1963, chap. *VI,* pp. 58–74.

Hospers, John. *An Introduction to Philosophical Analysis.* New York: Prentice-Hall, Inc., 1953, chap. ii, pp. 86–158 and chap. iii, pp. 159–220.

⁘At a more sophisticated level testability requires some qualifications which are not fully developed in this book. The problem is widely discussed and is closely related to the analytic-synthetic distinction. Here are some items dealing with testability and the analytic-synthetic distinction:

Donnellan, Keith. "Necessity and Criteria," *The Journal of Philosophy*, Vol. LIX, no. 22 (1962), pp. 647–58.

Grice, H. P. and P. F. Strawson. "In Defense of a Dogma," *The Philosophical Review*, Vol. LXV, no. 2 (1956), pp. 141–58.

Hempel, Carl. "Problems and Changes in the Empiricist Criterion of Meaning," in Leonard Linsky, ed., *Semantics and the Philosophy of Language*. Illinois: The University of Illinois Press at Urbana, 1952, pp. 163–85.

Putnam, Hilary. "The Analytic and the Synthetic," in Herbert Feigl and Grover Maxwell, eds., *Minnesota Studies in the Philosophy of Science*. Minneapolis: University of Minnesota Press, 1962, pp. 358–97.

Quine, Willard Van Orman. *From a Logical Point of View*, 2nd ed. Cambridge, Mass.: Harvard University Press, 1961, chap. *II*, pp. 20–46.

White, Morton. "The Analytic and the Synthetic: An Untenable Dualism," in Leonard Linsky, ed., *Semantics and the Philosophy of Language*. Illinois: The University of Illinois Press at Urbana, 1952, pp. 272–86.

Part Four

JUSTIFICATION

CHAPTER 20

Early Stages of Justification Decisions

Our concern in this, the last part of the book, is with how to tell when a statement is justified and how to make use of this knowledge in a classroom. Since there are different kinds of statements, and they are offered in different kinds of circumstances, there are also a variety of tests for the justification of a statement. In discussing these tests, we will be concerned only with the truth aspect of statements. (White lies are sometimes justified, but that is not our sort of concern.)

Justification and Truth

To say that a statement is justified (assuming it is intended to be true) is not the same as to say that a statement is true. Consider the statement that the earth is flat. Even though it was not (and is not) true, a resident of the North American continent 4000 years ago would have been justified in making that statement, because the evidence that he had available strongly supported that statement in that context. You and I are not justified in making that statement, because the evidence that we have available refutes the statement. Lack of truth and lack of justification coincide when **we** make the statement, but they did not when it was made in North America 4,000 years ago. Truth was lacking then; justification, however, was present. Thus justification and truth are different.

Probably you have heard it alleged that truth changes.* This is a misleading way of putting the insight that what is justified can change as times change. The statement that the earth is flat was justified in the earlier context, but is not justified in our context. The truth, however, has not changed. It was (and is) true that the earth is not flat.

The connection between justification and truth can be made as follows (assuming a concern only with the truth aspect of a statement): If a person says about a statement (which he is at the time prepared to make) that it is fully justified, then he (though not necessarily someone else) is committed to saying at least that it is quite probably true. Furthermore, if a person says that a statement is true, then he (though not necessarily someone else) is committed to admitting that he is fully justified in making it. This is fairly complex, but it does show the connection between truth and the kind of justification that is to be our concern in this chapter.**

Basically there are four steps to follow in evaluating a statement to see whether it is justified: First, one must be clear just what the statement is; second, one must determine the evidence and/or reasons that are offered in its favor; third, the basic evidence and/or reasons must themselves be evaluated; and fourth, one must appraise the strength of the argument that goes from the basic evidence and/or reasons to conclusion (the statement under consideration). In this chapter we shall look at the first three of these steps, leaving the fourth for the ensuing chapters.

What the Statement Is

The need to be clear about just what the statement is, although obvious, is easily forgotten when we are involved in a discussion. Sometimes the statement is put incoherently, sometimes with self-contradictions, sometimes with vague or ambiguous terms, and sometimes it is not put at all. We often have to figure it out—and must then be sure to do so because what are apparently slight differences often loom very large when the evaluation is being done. You will remember Jim's statement that the newspaper is full of propaganda, and will also remember that the justification of this statement depended very much on just what the statement actually was, which in turn depended on Jim's definition of 'propaganda'. There the problem was ambiguity.

* See for example Karl Mannheim, *Ideology and Utopia* (New York: Harcourt, Brace and Company, 1936), in which this view takes the name, "sociology of knowledge".

** For an interesting collection of discussions of the concept *truth* itself, see George Pitcher, ed., *Truth* (Englewood Cliffs, N. J.: Prentice-Hall, Inc., 1964).

Vagueness and ambiguity

The following dialogues, although they differ greatly in sophistication, both illustrate the problem of vagueness on the part of the student. Note how Mr. Delta handles them:

Example 20-1

RON: I think that there's going to be another small war very soon.

MR. DELTA: Why is that?

RON: Well, my Dad says that important things happen in threes. There are now two small wars, so there's bound to be a third.

MR. DELTA: (writing on board) "Important things happen in threes." Why does he say that?

RON: Because they just do happen in threes.

MR. DELTA: How important does something have to be to happen in threes?

RON: You know, important. Important to you or to me.

MR. DELTA: Well, it was very important to me to have been offered the position to teach in this school. Yet it was the only offer that I received.

RON: I mean **really** important—matters of life and death. Like Mr. Brown and Mr. Smith dying right together like. And then Mrs. Jones the next day.

PHYLLIS: But Mr. King died the day after that. That makes four.

RON: Well, he must have been in another group of three.

PHYLLIS: But people are dying all the time. How do you know how to group them? How close together do the events have to be? How much alike?

RON: You have to tell by looking at the individual case.

MR. DELTA: That doesn't help me very much. How soon must this next war be? How big must it be to count as a war? Wars of varying intensity are happening all the time. So unless you make your principle more clear, it only tells us something that we already know: that there will be another war of some intensity in the near future.

Thus do Mr. Delta and Phyllis find Ron's principle too vague to judge as justified or unjustified. The inquiry cannot commence without a meaningful statement. Mr. Delta did succeed in getting the notion of important things narrowed down to matters of life and death. Phyllis followed up by asking key questions of application that Ron was unable to answer, thus showing that his principle was too vague to be evaluated, and also showing that the principle is useless in making predictions—an inevitable result of excessive vagueness.

In this next dialogue Betty makes a statement which has an important insight lurking therein.

Example 20-2

MR. DELTA: Approximately 5 per cent of the Gross National Product of the United States is devoted to education, as contrasted to a figure of approximately 8 per cent for Russia.

BETTY: (interrupting) But you can't compare.

MR. DELTA: Why not?

BETTY: The two countries are just not comparable. The economy of the United States is a mature economy, whereas Russia's is not.

MR. DELTA: Since I did compare the two, you certainly don't mean that I am unable to do so. I don't even think that you mean that one should make no comparisons, since you just did—with respect to the maturity of the two countries. Perhaps you mean that in making comparisons between countries one should be careful, and should remember that single comparisons can be very misleading—especially without a thorough understanding of the countries involved.

BETTY: Yes, I guess so.

MR. DELTA: Then let's write it down. (writing) "One should be careful in making comparisons between countries." Is that all right, Betty?

BETTY: Yes.

MR. DELTA: I fully agree with you on that. Can you suggest some reasons why we should be careful in our interpretation of the comparison of percentages that I gave?

Note that in each of these dialogues Mr. Delta used the question "Why?" to get a justification explanation of the original statement. The reply in each case gave him a picture of what was going on in the mind of the maker of the original statement. He also in each case made effective use of counter-examples to narrow down the statements, thus eliminating apparent implications that obviously were false. Lastly he took the time to write down the statement on the board, thus guaranteeing that they were at least discussing the same set of words. When, as in the 'propaganda' example, the definition of a key term is crucial, it is extremely helpful to write down in addition the definition or definitions, as the case may be. More generally, the three probing strategies suggested in earlier chapters are appropriate aids in ascertaining the meaning of the statement. These strategies, with examples, are as follows:

Directly Asking for Clarification. Such questions as, "Would you elaborate on that?", "Would you tell me a little more about that?", and "Could you put that in other words?" are often helpful. If the person is quite unsophisticated, as was Ron, then what he says in response might give others a clearer picture of what he has in mind, even though he is unable himself to state it clearly. A sophisticated person like Betty might, as a result of such a minor prod, realize some of the deficiencies in her own statement and revise it so that it comes closer to saying what she actually means.

Suggesting Possible Implications. The proposal of counter-examples is one way of doing this. Another is the suggesting of surprising implications, which are not counter-examples, but which are probably not accepted by the offerer of the statement unless he also accepts a particular interpretation of the statement offered. Mr. Delta's inquiry about Jim's attempt to persuade the referee was such a case. If Jim actually meant that 'propaganda' means any attempt to persuade, then he was engaging in propagandistic activity when he tried to persuade the referee to change the decision.

Asking "Why?". The reasons a person gives for what he says often clarify what he says (as well as provoking him to think more about it). You will remember that a request of a person to complete his own explanation is in effect a request of him to tell **why** his explanation explains. The answer makes more clear what he has in mind. Similarly here, when the statements are not explanations, but just assertions, the answer to the question "Why?" often clarifies, if clarification is to be had. Ron's reply to the question, "Because they just do happen in threes", gave warning that perhaps clarification of his statement was just unobtainable, which later turned out to be the case. Betty's reply, "The economy of the United States is a mature economy . . .", suggested that she saw dangers in making comparisons, so Mr. Delta accordingly better knew what sort of claim he was dealing with.

As was indicated in earlier chapters, there are possible threats implicit in the use of these strategies, threats which must be adjusted by the teacher to the situation with judicious use of tone of voice and selection of words. Sometimes threatening questions are helpful, sometimes not. I leave that to your knowledge of practical psychology and of your students.

The problem of determining which of several possible interpretations of an ambiguous statement is the one to accept, is a problem which was discussed at some length in the section on definitions. The above three strategies, you will remember, are quite appropriate.

Types of statements

Although no precise and satisfactory system of classification of statements has yet been produced, some rough distinctions among the following will be quite helpful: value statements, empirical statements, conceptual statements, and miscellaneous performatives. The main reason for distinguishing is that different criteria are used to evaluate the different types.

Value Statements. VALUE STATEMENTS characteristically use value terms such as 'good', 'bad', 'should', 'right', and 'ought'. Since each of these terms has nonevaluative uses, the appearance of one of them does not necessarily signify a value statement, although such appearance usually does so. Here are some examples of sentences which in context are usually used to make value statements:

Stealing is bad.
One ought to fulfill the terms of a contract.
One should be careful in making comparisons between countries.
It is good to tell the truth.

Mr. Delta's establishing that Betty's statement in Example 20-2 was a value statement ("One should be careful in making comparisons between countries") was a first step in evaluating the statement, since different criteria can be expected to apply to that statement than to other possible interpretations of Betty's original words.

Significant differences exist among the terms, 'good', 'should', 'right', 'ought', and the like, but I am grouping them together as value terms (terms which most frequently are used to express values), because of the similarities in later treatment, as compared with empirical terms.

Empirical Statements. An EMPIRICAL STATEMENT is one about the universe of things, men, and events. Ultimately it is testable by appeal to observations, although empirical statements can be very general and theoretical.* Here are some examples of empirical statements:

The tree stump is five inches thick at the top.

Columbus discovered America in 1492.

Approximately two-thirds of this newspaper is advertising.

As you go higher, the air pressure reduces.

The price of electricity is generally lower when it is produced by hydroelectric stations than when it is produced by steam plants.

Contemporary writers are revolting against tradition.

The force of gravitational attraction between two bodies varies directly as the product of their masses and inversely as the square of the distance between them.

Of the above statements only the first and second are what I shall call observation statements. Consider the first, for example. It is an observation statement because it can be established by a simple observation—setting a ruler on top of the stump (with one end even with an edge of the stump, etc.) and seeing how far on the ruler it is to the other side of the stump. It is a specific statement about one thing. In addition observation statements are generally checkable by an impartial observer. If two people disagree about such statements (understanding them to mean the same), then we are justified in saying that something is wrong with one of the people or with the conditions of observation. Observation statements are simple descriptions of the world about us. They are essentially reports of what one can directly see, hear, feel, etc.

The other statements in the group of empirical statements above are more general in scope than an observation statement, but they depend upon observations.** The last one, which is Newton's Law of Gravity, is the most

* This is the philosopher's use of 'empirical'. Many scientists use the word 'empirical' for low-level, nontheoretical statements and approaches to research.

** I have not classified the statement about the content of the newspaper as an observation statement, since multiple measurement **and** calculation are required to arrive at the statement. The distinction between observation and other statements can get tricky and will be discussed more fully later on.

theoretical of all, since it uses a number of theoretical terms, but it is still based upon observations. These more general empirical statements are also checkable by an impartial person. Supposedly people who know the field, when given the evidence, should be able to come to agreement about the justification of the statements. In fact many heated disagreements occur among scientists about some general empirical statements, even when the scientists are faced with the same evidence. But such statements are generally neither fully proven nor disproven at the time of controversy. They are frontier-of-knowledge statements. The notion of agreement by impartial people is still an **ideal** upon which all are agreed.

This ideal incidentally does not hold for value statements. We do not hold that value statements are things upon which all men, given the evidence, will agree. There are challenges to what I have just said, but I am not sure how else to put the matter, and do think that what I have said does characterize (as in a range definition) value statements and empirical statements well enough for one to proceed with a treatment of justification of statements.

Conceptual Statements. This next category of statements is difficult to characterize and murky in its boundaries. Roughly speaking, CONCEPTUAL STATEMENTS express systems of language or parts of systems of language. Strictly speaking they are not reported definitions, which are **empirical** statements about the way terms are used. Stipulated definitions are conceptual statements, a sort which are not at all to be regarded as true or false. Other conceptual statements have elements of stipulation but also elements of truth-falsity in them as well, because they are more or less established on the basis of their ability to be useful (as presuppositions) in formulating other kinds of statements.

The Newtonian statement, "There are fixed points in space", and the relativity statement, "Space is curved", express parts of different conceptual schemes, different ways of viewing the world. According to contemporary physicists, the Newtonian way is inadequate to the facts which have been discovered (presumably without some complex assumptions which they are unwilling to accept). So there is an element of empirical truth-falsity in conceptual statements. But there are also some very pragmatic elements of workability, simplicity, and convenience.

Wellek and Warren's proposed definition of 'literature', as provided by Neil in the dialogue in Chapter 19, is a conceptual statement. Tolstoy's definition of 'art' indicates a broader, but different, conceptual scheme: "Art is a human activity, consisting in this, that one man consciously, by means of certain external signs, hands on to others feelings he has lived through, and that other people are infected by these feelings, and also experience them."*

In sum, conceptual statements are characterized by being about meaning,

* Leo Tolstoy, *What is Art?* (trans. by Aylmer Maude), (London: Walter Scott, Ltd., 1899), p. 50.

by being expressions of parts (or wholes) of conceptual schemes, by being only partly (if at all) empirical, by having a degree of truth-falsity, by having a degree of stipulation, and by having strong pragmatic requirements (for acceptability) as well. In this book I shall say very little about the evaluation of conceptual statements other than what was said above and in Part II, "Definition". The problems are complicated, difficult, and unsolved (at least in detail). In the bibliography at the end of Part IV, you will find some suggested reading, if you want to pursue the matter.* Benjamin Lee Whorf's *Language, Thought, and Reality* makes an interesting starting point.**

Miscellaneous Performatives. A number of types of statements are not aimed at being true, but rather are, in effect, performances. Here are some examples:

I nominate Brown for the presidency.
I now pronounce you man and wife.
I bid three clubs.
I sentence you to three months in jail.

These statements, when made in the appropriate circumstances by an appropriate person, are complete actions, just as scoring a touchdown in a football game is an action. They accomplish something. Of course, making value statements and empirical statements are actions too, but they are conventionally aimed at expressing truths,*** whereas these miscellaneous performatives are not aimed at expressing truths. They are aimed at and accomplish other things. In the first case, for example, what is accomplished is the nomination of Brown, given the proper circumstances.****

* ⁘Those of you who have been following the ⁘ material should be reminded of analytic statements by the above discussion of conceptual statements, since analytic statements are conceptual statements. But the category, conceptual statement, covers more, because there are empirical elements of some conceptual statements. When a particular person is using a particular sentence to do a particular job on a particular occasion, then the distinction between analytic and empirical statements can be clearly drawn. But when a conceptual proposition is part of a usable theory but is not employed at the time, then I am not ready to insist that it must be either analytic or empirical. It combines elements of both. Even Carl Hempel has challenged the sharpness of this distinction for some situations. "A Logical Appraisal of Operationism," in Philipp G. Frank, ed., *The Validation of Scientific Theories* (New York: Collier Books, 1961), p. 66.

** Benjamin Lee Whorf, *Language, Thought, and Reality* (Cambridge, Mass.: The Technology Press, 1956).

*** That value statements can express truths is, I believe, correct, according to the way we ordinarily use 'truth'. Since some will disagree, let me stipulate that 'truth' is applicable to value statements, understanding that 'truth', so interpreted, applies where they would have applied 'correct evaluation'.

**** J. L. Austin discusses performatives in his *How To Do Things With Words* (Cambridge, Mass.: Harvard University Press, 1962). The term 'performative' as applied to language is generally attributed to Austin, although he in this book indicates a preference for the term 'illocutionary act'.

Questions of justification can be raised about performances like these. (Was I justified in nominating Brown? Was I justified in marrying them?) But these questions are not focused on truth; the concepts, *true* and *false*, do not apply to such statements. Only in a joke would someone say "That's true" in response to "I nominate Brown for the presidency", when the speaker is actually nominating Brown for the presidency. Hence we shall be concerned with the justification of such performatives only as a special case of the justification of value statements about the actions they accomplish (for example, the value statement, "You did the right thing in nominating Brown for the presidency.").

Summary

In determining what the statement is, one should focus on what it says and on what sort of statement it is. One should make its interpretation as specific as possible without forcing the statement into a mold of greater specificity than the statement-maker wants it to have. Open-ended requests for clarification, requests for examples, suggestions of counter-examples and other possible implications, and asking for justification explanations are all helpful in making clear what the statement is. The type of statement is important to determine because different appraisal procedures are appropriate for different types of statements. Types discussed here are value statements, empirical statements, conceptual statements, and miscellaneous performatives. Later on various kinds of empirical statements will be further distinguished.

The basic idea here is that a necessary condition for deciding whether a statement is justified is the determination of just what the statement is.

COMPREHENSION SELF-TEST

True or False? If the statement is false, change a crucial term (or terms) to make it true.

20–1. True statements are always justified, given the sort of justification with which we are here concerned.

20–2. False statements are always unjustified, given the sort of justification with which we are here concerned.

20–3. Empirical statements are about things, men, events, etc.

20–4. Performative statements are neither true nor false.

Application.

20–5. From a book in your field or from a classroom dialogue with which you are familiar, choose an example of each of the following four kinds of statements: value statements, empirical statements, conceptual statements, and miscellaneous performatives. In each case explain why it is classified in the way you have chosen.

The Reasons

Along with getting clear about just what the statement is, one must try to be clear about what the reasons are. In general, a statement with no reasons to back it up is to be regarded with suspicion. If we make the statement ourselves, then we should be clear what our reasons are. If someone else makes the statement, then generally we should find out his reasons. Exceptions are: (1) matters too technical for us to understand, in which case we should do the best we can in evaluating the credentials of the statement-maker as an authority (to be discussed shortly); and (2) immediate perceptions or reports of feelings. For example, if a person tells us that he has a headache, we do not ask for his evidence.

People often act as if they were unaware of the importance of finding reasons, perhaps because of their emotional state. A crucial step in the evaluation of a statement is seeking out reasons for it. Questions such as "What is the evidence?", "What are your reasons?", and "Why do you say that?" are simple, effective ways of bringing forth the support for a statement.

In the remainder of this chapter we shall be concerned with some of the standard types of answers to these questions: observation statements, statements by alleged authorities, and assumptions. Arguments are often complex—with many stages—but they do start somewhere. It is to the starting points that we now turn.

Observation Statements

Although observation is considered by many to be the basis for much of our knowledge, mistakes in observation reports are notorious. Presumably, most of you are familiar with various demonstrations of this fact. If not, arrange for the occurrence of a striking event in your class, and ask each student to write down exactly what he saw and heard in the order in which it occurred.

Observations and conclusions from observations

One problem that always develops is distinguishing observations from conclusions based upon observations. For example, suppose that the events being observed consisted of measuring the thickness of two tree stumps, one of which is five inches across, and the other of which is eight inches across. One of your students might say that the eight-inch stump had lived longer than the five-inch stump. This conclusion might be true and it might be false, but the point is that it is not an observation. Conclusions are generally less dependable than the observations on which they are based. Since the conclusion depends on the observation, it can go wrong not only in the observation stage but also in the inferring stage.

There are exceptions to the rule that conclusions are less dependable than the observations on which they are based. One kind of exception is that in which the inference is so unavoidable that the conclusion is as dependable as the observation. Consider counting the number of apples in two very small baskets, one containing three apples and the other containing four apples. The conclusion that there are seven apples in the two baskets is just as dependable as the separate counts. A second kind of exception is one in which, although the observation itself is fairly undependable (because it might well be off by a bit), the conclusion would be strongly supported by any of the observations in the neighborhood of the one made. To illustrate this sort of exception consider the case of a blood count to determine whether a person (with appropriate symptoms) is ill with appendicitis. The count itself is not exactly accurate, but is close enough to provide a basis for a reasonably dependable inference. Putting it more strongly, the count will almost certainly be inaccurate, but the conclusion will probably be correct.

I mention these cases so that you will be ready for the student who thinks of such cases. The advice about conclusions generally being less dependable than observations still holds. It is one of the first lessons which teachers must teach if they want their students to have a respect for and understanding of the nature of proof or justification in most subjects. In legal proceedings, conclusions inferred by witnesses—as opposed to observations—are generally ruled out of order because of the notoriously greater undependability of witnesses' conclusions that their observations. (Exceptions are made for conclusions drawn by authorities.)

Drawing the Line. In applying this advice about the relative general dependability of conclusions and observations you will undoubtedly run into the problem of drawing the line between the two. For example, some contentious person might claim that the statement about the thickness of the tree trunk is in reality a conclusion. What was observed was that a certain line on the ruler coincided with the edge of the tree trunk when the end of the ruler was even with the other edge of the trunk. That the tree trunk is five inches thick at the top is a conclusion based upon the appearance of the number '5' next to the line on the ruler and an assumption: either that the trunk is circular or that the measurement was made on the thickness dimension. An even more contentious person might say that the line did not coincide with the edge of the trunk at all since the line is straight and the edge of the trunk is curved. Assuming that the ruler is transparent (except for the lines), he might say that what was observed was an apparent touching of the two lines at one point. But he might be even more difficult, noting that the edge of the trunk is very rough and that the ruler line, as seen under a magnifying glass, is also quite uneven. From here it is easy to go all the way and say that there is really no such thing as an observation after all, and that everything should be put in terms of appearances and conclusions.

If one wants to talk this way, he can, but there is still the distinction to be made between the starting point and the conclusion of an argument. There is an important difference in the immediacy of our knowledge of the thickness of a tree trunk and of the age of a tree trunk. This difference must somehow be recognized, as must the primacy of our knowledge of the thickness of the tree trunk. A good way to recognize it is with the use of the term, 'observation'.

In drawing the line between observations and conclusions, I recommend a pragmatic approach similar to that used in Chapter 8 in dealing with judging whether two things are the same or different. You will remember that there it was important to be clear about the purpose of the discourse and to see what are the consequences, given that purpose, of calling two things the same (or different). Here the purpose is the securing of reliable knowledge. Given that purpose, the question, "What is an observation statement?", resolves into the question: "In this field of inquiry, what sort of statement closely dependent on the senses can be relied on because of the likelihood of getting quick agreement among experienced people?" The important pragmatic question is: "Is something likely to go wrong if we take this sort of statement as a starting point?"

Consider the case of trying to measure electrical resistance. On the basis of an ohmmeter reading we might, in an experiment in which the resistance determination does not have to be precise, declare the following to be an observation statement: "The resistance is 2.3 ohms." On the other hand, if the measurement must be very precise, we might have to take account of instrument error and calculate an adjustment of the initial reading, in which case a statement about the pointer reading would be the observation statement and the report of the calculated result would be a conclusion of a sort.

Or consider a (supposed) case of a statement written in the diary of Napoleon's aide: "The general left for Paris today." In an attempt to find out on what exact day Napoleon left for Paris, a historian would treat that as an observation statement. But if a historian had good reason to believe that Napoleon did not leave for Paris at all, and that Napoleon had deliberately deceived his aide, then the statement would be considered a conclusion, one that showed the effectiveness of Napoleon's deceit.

The determination of just what is an observation statement varies from field to field. In the hard sciences, statements about pointer readings, colors, comparative sizes, etc., are observation statements. In the social sciences and history, statements about test scores, actions of people (with a minimum of interpretation), the departure of an army, the reported net worth of a bank at the end of a day, and so forth are observation statements. (Note with respect to the net-worth example that the net worth is not observed. The **reported** net worth is observed.)

The attempt by historians to emphasize primary sources is an attempt to keep close to observation statements. Some primary sources contain observation statements (for example, the diary of Napoleon's aide containing the statement, "The general left for Paris today", when the historian is trying to find out when Napoleon left for Paris); and some primary sources are things about which the historian himself can make important observation statements (for example, the draft of the Bill of Rights as presented to the original states, about which the historian can say: "The draft of the Bill of Rights contains twelve proposed amendments, not ten."). The pursuit by historians of reliable knowledge is facilitated by separating off this group of observation-related materials, primary sources, and by placing heavy emphasis on their use. In context historians do successfully distinguish observations from conclusions.

Let us apply the observation-conclusion distinction to parts of the dialogue in Chapter 19, which dealt with the question, "Is *1984* literature?". Virginia's statement in Entry 8, "He was trying to persuade people that socialism is bad for England", is a conclusion and not an observation statement. That she treated it as a conclusion is shown by the fact that in Entry 33 she offered a number of pieces of evidence which the proposed statement was supposed to explain. In some situations people might have made the mistake of treating her statement as an observation statement, but she did not make that mistake.

Consider next some of her evidence, which she treated as starting points in her argument. She held that the deprivation of privacy is offensive to people. Although probably no one will challenge that statement, it is not an observation statement. It is a generalization which might be inferred from observation statements such as: "Brown said that he finds deprivation of privacy offensive."

The statement, "Orwell used the phrase, 'Freedom is Slavery'", is in this context an observation statement, and is one quite suitable starting point for Virginia's argument to her conclusion about Orwell's purpose. I said "in this context" because in advanced literary criticism (where there might be a question about whether Orwell actually wrote the book, or whether that particular phrase was his or the editor's) that statement could be a conclusion. In such a case a more observational-type statement is: "The phrase, 'Freedom Is Slavery', appears in this copy of this book with Orwell's name on the cover." You can immediately see the impracticality of using such narrow observation statements in the dialogue in Miss Gamma's class, but presumably can also see their necessity in some instances of literary criticism.

Fact and Opinion. One rather unhelpful distinction which is often promulgated is that between "fact and opinion". This distinction is sometimes used to separate value statements from empirical statements, even though many empirical statements are not facts, and some value statements do not deserve the ordinary implications of the word 'opinion'. The distinction is also used to separate observation statements from statements of inferences, each of which are sometimes facts and sometimes opinions. The use of the fact-opinion distinction does not advance our evaluation of a position—other than reminding people that some things are better established than others—because the fact-opinion distinction only separates what we know from what we believe. In order to use this distinction, the important evaluative work must already be done. We must already have ascertained that something is known before we can label it a fact.

Reliability of observation statements: criteria

Historians, lawyers, philosophers, and scientists have over the years built up a set of principles for determining the reliability* of observation statements. I have attempted to combine their insights into one loosely framed set of rules, which, when applied with discretion, can be of help in a classroom and might well be made available to your students, if your field is one in which observations are used. The importance of **discretion** in the use of the rules should be emphasized. They are rules of thumb to which there **are** exceptions:**

1. Observation statements tend to be more reliable if the observer:
   a. Was unemotional, alert, and disinterested.
   b. Was skilled at observing the sort of thing observed.
   c. Had sensory equipment that was in good condition.
   d. Has a reputation for veracity.
   e. Used precise techniques.
   f. Had no preconception about the way the observation would turn out.

2. Observation statements tend to be more reliable if the observation conditions:
   a. Were such that the observer had good access.
   b. Provided a satisfactory medium of observation.

3. Observation statements tend to be more reliable to the extent that the statement:
   a. Is close to being a statement of direct observation.
   b. Is corroborated.
   c. Is corroboratable.
   d. Comes from a disinterested source with a reputation for veracity.

4. Observation statements, if based on a record, tend to be more reliable if the record:
   a. Was made at the time of observation.
   b. Was made by the person making the statement.
   c. Is believed by the person making the statement to be correct—either because he so believed at the time the record was made, or because he believes it was the record-maker's habit to make correct records.

Notice the use of the phrase, "tend to be", at the beginning of each section. It is there because no one criterion is a sufficient condition of reliability of

* I use the term 'reliability' in the ordinary sense. The testing specialist who uses the term in a special sense should not interpret it here in his sense.

**From my "A Concept of Critical Thinking," *Harvard Educational Review,* 32:1 (Winter, 1962), p. 90. Copyright © 1962 President and Fellows of Harvard College.

an observation statement, and most are not necessary conditions. The rules are general guides which suggest things to consider about the observer, the observation conditions, the nature of the statement, and the record, if there is a record.

The Observer. For example, Rule la dealing with the observer suggests that the observer should not have been emotionally distraught at the time of observation. But fulfillment of that condition does not guarantee a reliable observation, nor is fulfillment absolutely required. We all know of times when we were emotionally distraught, but were still perfectly reliable observers. This rule also suggests that it is best if the observer is disinterested. By this is meant not that he is uninterested, but that he does not stand to profit in any special way by making one observation statement rather than another. Of course, he can profit by having his reputation improved by his turning out to be correct, but that is a different matter. If he stands to profit in a way other than having his reputation improved by being right, then his observation statement is suspect.

Rule lb, which deals with skill in observation, applies primarily to those kinds of observation in which a special skill is required, such as noting the height of a mercury column, or making a blood count. Of course every type of observation requires some skill or background of experience (in order to observe that "Freedom Is Slavery" appears in one copy of Orwell's book, one must be able to recognize the letters), but the rule is primarily aimed at special skills.

Rule 1f, dealing with preconceptions, must be used warily. Trained observers frequently know just what to expect because of their vast experience in a field. Having this preconception should not disqualify their observations. On the other hand, they might become inattentive and miss something. Missing something because something else was expected is more common among untrained observers than among trained ones.

Observation Conditions. The two rules for observation conditions are somewhat truistic as stated. Their main function is to remind us of two kinds of problems that frequently beset an observer: poor access to the thing to be observed, and poor medium of observation (for example, dim light, fog, etc.). These criteria were both satisfied in Virginia's noting the appearance of 'Freedom Is Slavery' in her copy of *1984*.

The Nature of the Statement. I have already mentioned the problem addressed in Rule 3a, dealing with directness of the observation. Of the following two statements, the second, because it is more direct, is more likely to be reliable (in the situation of Miss Gamma's class), although much more inconvenient to use:

1. Orwell used the phrase, "Freedom Is Slavery".
2. The phrase, "Freedom Is Slavery", appears in this copy of this book with Orwell's name on the cover.

Rule 3b suggests that an observation statement on which there is agreement is more likely to be reliable than one on which there is not. On the other hand, rule 3c prefers a statement on which it is possible to get agreement, to one on which it is not possible. For example, one can obtain agreement on the statement, "The phrase 'Freedom Is Slavery' appears in this book." But one cannot obtain observational agreement on the statement, "Virginia was depressed after reading *1984*", since the latter observation is one for which Virginia alone has a privileged position.

Rule 3d, dealing with interest and reputation, does not simply repeat corresponding parts of Rule 1, because observation statements are often not made by the original observer. Rule 1 deals only with the observer.

Records. Not all observation statements are based on records. However, because of man's notoriously fallible memory, a record should be made, if the statement is not made on the spot. This record, again because of our bad memories, is better made at the time of observation than afterwards. So that we can know when records are made, a common practice is to write down the time of observation.

Since room exists for misinterpretation of the records, the safest course is to have the record-maker report on the observation. He knows his own special habits of record-keeping and knows first-hand some of the odd situations which arose in gathering the information, situations which are often masked by the format in which the records are kept.

The last rule (4c) about records is an interesting one that is drawn from legal practice.* It presumes that the person making the observation statement has some skill at evaluating the sort of observation statement being made, and gives some credence to his evaluation of the statement. You can imagine the use of this rule in court cases, but there are many other applications as well. An historian's statement that Napoleon left for Paris on the day indicated in the aide's diary would to some extent obtain credence from the belief by the historian in the truth of the statement, such belief perhaps being based in part on his belief that it was the aide's habit to make correct records.

Summary

Although the distinction between an observation statement and a conclusion depends on context, the distinction can be useful. At first approximation an observation statement is one made rather directly on the basis of perceptions, whereas a conclusion is the result of an argument or an inference. In general, observation statements are more reliable than the conclusions based upon them. The attempt to draw the line precisely requires a look

* See John H. Wigmore, *A Students Textbook of the Law of Evidence* (Brooklyn: The Foundation Press, Inc., 1935), sections 115–18.

at the consequences in context of a particular decision. The pragmatic question is the following: "Is the extra caution worth the trouble, given that our goal is maximizing the likelihood that the starting points in an argument will be safe?"

You saw a number of loose guides to deciding about the degree of reliability of observation statements. These guides, which assumed that the observer is not necessarily the observation statement-maker, dealt with qualifications of the observer, the observation conditions, the nature of the observation statement, and the records made of the observation. In general observation statements are one good place to start in a careful justification of an empirical statement.

I have not here devoted much space to examples of the actual use by a teacher of these criteria, having assumed that applications to particular cases will be clear to you upon consideration of the following things:

1. The observation-conclusion distinction
2. The criteria of reliability of observation statements
3. The importance of securing reasons (or evidence) for what people say (the importance of asking "Why?")
4. My previous advice about the use of methods of probing definitions and explanations, including the judicious use of counter-examples
5. The nature of the customary starting points in your own subject.

Furthermore, I have not given psychological advice about the use of, and insistence on, observation statements. Observing and making records can be quite involving and exciting, but when procedures are followed mechanically they can also be dull and routine. Inspiration, excitement, adventure, and involvement are important factors in dealing with observation statements in a teaching situation. The suggestions made here concern only the logical aspects of the problem.

COMPREHENSION SELF-TEST

True or False? If the statement is false, change a crucial term (or terms) to make it true.

20–6. An observation statement is more likely to be reliable if the observer is uninterested, as opposed to interested.

20–7. The distinction between facts and values corresponds very closely to the distinction between observations and conclusions.

20–8. Conclusions are generally less reliable than the observation statements on which they are based.

20–9. The distinction between observations and conclusions is dependent upon context.

Applications. From some book in your field or some classroom episode with which you are familiar pick an observation statement.

20–10. Rate the statement on each of the criteria for observation statements. If a particular criterion is not applicable, explain why.

20–11. Describe a situation in which the sentence used to make the observation statement which you rated above is used to make a statement of a conclusion.

Statements by Alleged Authorities

A second sort of answer to the question, "What are your reasons?", is a reference to a statement by an authority. Although some logic texts and propaganda analysis guides would have us believe otherwise, statements by authorities are often quite acceptable as a basis for dealing with a question. Think of all that we take on authority, and try to imagine what it would be like if we took nothing on authority, but instead insisted that we be shown. Life would be chaotic and extremely primitive. We could not exist in a civilized state. Most (although perhaps too much) of our knowledge acquired in school is taken on authority. The question is not whether we should take anything on authority, but rather what safeguards we should accept—what guidelines we should use in deciding whether to take a particular judgment as authoritative.

Ambiguity of 'authority'

When I am talking here about an AUTHORITY, I mean someone who, in virtue of his knowledge and training, is likely to know about the matter in question. I do **not** mean someone who, in virtue of his position, has a right to give orders or to be in charge. I am talking about a cognitive authority rather than a power-type authority. Thus for present purposes a statement by an authority is a statement made by a person who, in virtue of his knowledge and training, is likely to know about the content of the statement. The basic problem here then is to determine whether a person who speaks as an authority on a question actually **is** an authority on that question.

Criteria for authorities

In deciding whether a statement should be accepted because it was offered by an alleged authority, the following criteria apply. No one criterion is necessary, nor is any one sufficient, but the joint satisfaction of all the criteria makes a very strong case for accepting the statement on the ground that it was offered by an authority.

A person is an authority with respect to a particular statement to the extent that:

1. He has a good reputation.
2. The statement is in his field.
3. He was disinterested.
4. His reputation could be affected by his statement, and he was aware of this fact when he made his statement.
5. He studied the matter covered by the statement.
6. He followed the accepted procedures in coming to decide that he was entitled to make his statement (although there are legitimate exceptions to this requirement).
7. He was in full possession of his faculties.
8. He is not in disagreement with others who meet the above criteria for authorities.

Application. Let us try to apply these criteria to Sam's citation of George Orwell as an authority on the effect of Orwell's writing on the reading public (Entry 37 in Chapter 19). First of all Sam did not presumably know anything about Orwell's reputation as a purveyor of sociological (or psychological) truth, though he probably knew that Orwell was an established novelist of some repute. It is Orwell's reputation as a purveyor of sociological (or psychological) truth that counts in this instance, since the proposition in question at the time was of that sort: "Orwell's book is an effective persuasive instrument."

The second criterion was probably satisfied in Sam's mind. Orwell, since he is known as a writer of persuasive instruments, has this sort of thing as a field. Sam, in saying that Orwell was an experienced person, presumably had something like this in mind.

Sam did not apply the criterion of disinterestedness, but because this is a tricky criterion, let us see how it might go. Naturally Orwell was interested in the truth of the proposition in question, but this does not mean that he was not disinterested. He was just not **un**interested. What sort of situation then would justify a judgment that Orwell was not disinterested? The following is an example: Suppose that Orwell was trying to sell his book to a foundation for a large amount of money. Suppose further that the foundation's policy was strongly antisocialistic. Then it would have been to Orwell's financial interest to have the proposition in question be believed by the officials in the foundation. In such a case he would not have been disinterested.

The fourth criterion (impact on his reputation) strictly speaking does not apply in this case because Orwell did not actually make the statement, to our knowledge. Instead, Sam was saying that it is one that Orwell, since he is an authority, would have endorsed. But the application of the criterion would be clear in a situation in which Orwell actually made the statement.

The fifth criterion (study of the matter) does apply, and Sam presumably applied it. Orwell certainly must have thought long and hard about the effect his book would have upon the reading public.

The sixth criterion (adherence to accepted procedures) is difficult to apply. Since the statement is one of practical sociology (or psychology), there are no established field-specific canons of inquiry. There are, of course, the general canons for judging the justification of statements, which canons are the topic of this part of the book. We do not know whether Orwell applied them (or more precisely—whether Orwell would have applied them before uttering such a statement).

The seventh criterion (full possession of faculties) also does not directly apply, but there is no reason to think that Orwell was not in full possession of his faculties at the time he wrote the book and was considering such propositions as this one.

Sam did in a way apply the eighth criterion, that dealing with agreement among reputed authorities. Sam assumed the role of an authority himself on the question. This he to some extent had a right to do since the area of inquiry here is practical sociology (or psychology) and we are all to some extent experts in this area. There was not full agreement, as can be seen by Neil's objections.

You can see in this application of these criteria how important the context is, not only in making the individual judgments, but in deciding whether the criterion is applicable at all. In this case, since Sam was not using an explicit statement by Orwell to buttress his own argument, but rather was alleging that Orwell was an authority and, therefore, would be likely to believe what Sam held to be true, some of the criteria do not straightforwardly apply.

Trust. In accepting the word of an authority, we are placing our trust in someone else. Generally we are not in a position to check authorities' statements to the extent that we can check observation statements.

Establishment. The use of these criteria depends upon tradition, established practice, and approval by people generally regarded as authorities. This dependence upon what is established is often a good idea, because the people upon whom we are depending make it their business to be right about the things in question. But significant dangers exist. Established practice sometimes is frozen by inflexible people; sometimes it gets very esoteric and irresponsible just because it is stimulating to the alleged authorities; sometimes the established people neglect their ultimate responsibility to observations; and sometimes they become selfish.

The case of Galileo's disagreement with established practice comes to mind. People recognized as authorities refused to look into the telescope, because this method was contrary to accepted procedures. What Galileo was suggesting about the nature of the solar system was contrary to accepted beliefs held by existing accepted authorities. Hence Galileo would have been disqualified as an authority by the blind use of the above rules.

On the other hand, consider the case of contemporary medical practice. Physicians are regarded as authorities on matters of physical health. When a physician says that one has appendicitis, while a local soothsayer says that one is inhabited by evil spirits, and if the two come up with different recommendations, we justifiably take the word of the physician. He is an accepted authority and represents the established practice.

The rules for judging authorities work against the minority, the one who raises radical questions about established practice. The rules must, therefore, be used with discretion.

Nature of the statement

My last comments deal with the nature of the claims made by alleged authorities. The given rules most appropriately fit empirical statements, because these are the ones that often call for expertise and on which agreement among experts is an attainable ideal.

Value statements, on the other hand, are ones upon which there is often a deep and radical disagreement even among people who have given much thought to the issues and who make them their field. Even in a very homogeneous society, although we might find considerable intrasocietal agreement, this agreement does not make justified the value judgments by those who are treated as authorities in the society. If the alleged authorities teach that it is appropriate to capture and eat humans who are not members of the society, they are wrong. Such a judgment is not justified. Hence citing alleged authorities for value statements is a very tricky business, one on which I hope to shed a little light in the next chapter. We cannot take the word of an alleged authority on a value statement with the same confidence as the word of an alleged authority on an empirical statement, other things being equal.

Conceptual statements are things on which we can justifiably cite authorities, even though they are more likely to disagree with each other on these than on empirical statements. Our citation of authorities on a conceptual statement gives less support to the statement than to an empirical statement, other things being equal. Neil's (and Miss Gamma's) citation of Wellek and Warren (in Chapter 19) as authorities on the meaning of 'literature' was a legitimate move. But be clear that the legitimate claim that they can make on the basis of what Wellek and Warren say is not that the given definition is what the term 'literature' really means. You should be wary of such claims now after your study of definitions in Part II. The most that Neil and Miss Gamma are entitled to claim is that this conceptual system advanced by Wellek and Warren is a workable one, worthy of use, and probably fruitful—that students will gain insights for their study of written works of art if they think in the terms proposed by Wellek and Warren.

A conceptual scheme in science is similarly supportable by authorities—to an extent, but not so strongly as to say that a given scheme is clearly true. Instead we say, for example, that the Newtonian conceptual scheme of fixed points in three-dimensional space is workable for the phenomena encountered by most of us most of the time, but that it is not workable for certain clearly established cases. The emphasis is more on workability than truth, though there is an element of truth as well.*

Summary

Authorities are people who because of their training and experience in a given area are likely to know about the truth of statements made in that area. To accept the word of an authority is often necessary, because of one's own ignorance or lack of time, but there are attendant dangers. One is thereby placing trust in the established ways, and although this trust is usually justified, it is not always. One must maintain a healthy scepticism toward authorities, though not a continuously antagonistic rejection of all authorities. Other things being equal, empirical statements can receive strong support, conceptual statements can receive moderate support, and value statements can receive at most weak support from alleged authorities.

Assumptions

An ASSUMPTION (a third kind of starting point in a line of reasoning) is a starting point for which no defense is offered. Some assumptions are explicitly recognized and stated by the assumer (EXPLICIT ASSUMPTIONS). Others are not so recognized and stated, but are in some way needed or used by an argument (IMPLICIT ASSUMPTIONS).

Although the word 'assumption' is sometimes used pejoratively, I shall not do so. In Entry 26 of the dialogue in Chapter 19, Neil used the term 'assuming' pejoratively: "You're assuming that Wellek and Warren's definition gives us a list of necessary conditions." Neil is here trying to convey both the impression that Tony's position depended on this alleged assumption and that the alleged assumption is suspect. This pejorative tone frequently accompanies the use of the word 'assumption', but please do not infer its existence in this chapter.

Note an ambiguity in the word, 'assumption'. Sometimes the word is not used to refer to a starting point in an argument, but rather to a conclusion which is held with some reservations. For example in Entry 20, Miss Gamma said, "I assume that I did not make my question clear then." She was here

* The topics of the justification and nature of conceptual statements are difficult and controversial. See the bibliography for further references.

drawing a conclusion on the basis of Hilary's reaction to the question as first stated. I shall not be using the term 'assumption' to refer to conclusions. With these two restrictions on the topic of this section, let us proceed to look at explicit and implicit assumptions.

Explicit assumptions

Sometimes the reason that no defense is offered for an explicit assumption is that the assumer thinks that the assumption is obvious and needs no defense. For example, in Entry 33 in the dialogue in Chapter 19 Virginia assumed that the practices of rewriting history, thought control, deprivation of privacy, etc., are all very offensive. She did not offer a defense of this assumption presumably because she thought it was obvious. She did not call this an assumption, by the way, but it is an explicit assumption.

Sometimes the reason that no defense is offered is that there is, given the circumstances, too limited an amount of time or space to provide it. I presume that the supposed "offense to any Englishman" that would result from the use of dollars as the currency in London (explicitly assumed by Virginia in Entry 33) was not defended because it, although perhaps not immediately obvious to that audience, would have taken more time to defend than she felt she could (or wanted) to spend on it.

Sometimes explicit assumptions are not defended because the assumer does not know how to go about defending them, although he is confident of their truth. Sam's statement in Entry 37, "Experienced people tend to believe what is true", exemplifies such an explicit assumption. The defense of such a statement is very difficult to provide, yet the statement seemed true to Sam.

Another reason for not defending explicit assumptions is that often we do not want to endorse them. This sometimes happens when we, in order to avoid quarreling about one part of a person's argument, assume (or grant) that part "for the sake of argument", because we think that there are more suspicious parts of his argument elsewhere, or else because we want to get the whole argument out in front of us before evaluating it. Other times the assumption in a deductive argument is a hypothesis which is up for test. It is tested by seeing whether its implications are born out in experience (more about this in a later chapter). In determining what these implications are, one assumes the hypothesis without endorsing it. Stipulated definitions are explicit assumptions that often are not endorsed. They are simply accepted as a way of operating. When in Chapter 13 Mr. Beta suggested making use of Phil's definition of 'dough' just so that the demonstration could continue, he was not endorsing that definition but simply requesting its acceptance for pragmatic reasons. You might say that he was endorsing its use in that situation, but still he had no reason to defend the definition as the best definition of 'dough'. The definition needed no justification, though its use in that situation might have needed justification. Lastly note that in an indirect proof we assume that which we are trying to disprove. We then try to show that an implication of the assumption is false. By denial of the consequent the assumption must then be false. Such an assumption we do not want to endorse.

Thus, a number of different kinds of circumstances can justify explicitly making use of an assumption in an argument without trying to justify it at the time. Hence my earlier advice about getting the reasons out in the open must be tempered by the realization that sometimes one should not be expected to get out into the open the reasons for explicit assumptions. There are times when the reasons for explicit assumptions should be sought—relentlessly pursued—but not always.

The difficulty with evaluating explicit assumptions is that by definition the reasons for them are not offered. There is no argument advanced on their behalf. When defense is needed for an explicit assumption, then generally the first thing to do is to ask the assumption-maker for the defense with the standard question, "Why?". When the assumption-maker is not available, we must do the best we can with it, suggesting possible defenses and appraising them. I am not here suggesting that every time we find an undefended assumption, we should go to work on it, applying all the evaluative apparatus at our disposal. There are too many of them for such an approach. But sometimes it matters a great deal whether a particular assumption is justified. Then we should seek an argument on its behalf and evaluate the argument according to procedures and criteria being suggested in this part of this book.

*Implicit assumptions**

Implicit assumptions are more difficult to cope with, because they not only provide the same problems of evaluation as the explicit assumptions, but they also must be detected. The problems of detecting the implicit assumptions (gap-fillers) in explanations are typical of the problems of one kind of assumption-detection, which I shall now describe.

Implicit Psychological Assumptions. Some implicit assumptions, which I shall call IMPLICIT PSYCHOLOGICAL ASSUMPTIONS, are already **in the mind** of the assumption-holder; so, given access, verbal ability, and honesty on his part, one quizzes him in the various ways suggested earlier: ask for completion of the argument (or explanation), suggest counter-examples or implausible implications of proposed assumptions, and/or suggest one's own completion of the argument. In effect, one is doing an empirical inves-

* This discussion of implicit assumptions is a bit more complex (and advanced) than the discussion in Chapter 15, "Gap-Filling". Some distinctions are made here which were ignored there.

tigation of the thoughts of the assumption-holder. The product of this investigation may in the initial stages be looked on as an **hypothesis** which explains why the assumption-holder said what he said or did what he did. In Chapter 19 when Miss Gamma decided that Neil was **assuming** Wellek and Warren's definition of 'literature', she was suggesting what he had in mind. Thus she had an **hypothesis** like this: "Neil is assuming that 'literature' means . . . ." In Chapter 22 I shall discuss strategy and criteria for hypothesis evaluation, so will not suggest criteria here.

Implicit Logical Assumptions. Another kind of implicit assumption exists, however—that which the argument (or procedure) somehow **needs** in order to be reasonable. When we claim to have identified an assumption of this type, then we are not making a claim about what the assumer had in mind (or would bring to mind if challenged); we are not making an empirical claim at all. For example, when F. C. Copleston (in part of the following debate with Bertrand Russell) held that the scientist assumes an ordered and intelligible universe, Copleston was not alleging an empirical fact about what goes on in every scientist's mind. He was saying that the arguments (or procedures) used by scientists would be unreasonable, or less reasonable, without being based on this alleged assumption.*

Example 20-3

COPLESTON: . . . I cannot see how science could be conducted on any other assumption than that of order and intelligibility in nature. The physicist presupposes, at least tacitly, that there is some sense in investigating nature and looking for the causes of events, just as the detective presupposes that there is some sense in looking for the cause of a murder. . . .

RUSSELL: There seems to me a certain unwarrantable extension here. A physicist looks for causes; that does not necessarily imply that there are causes everywhere. A man may look for gold without assuming that there is gold everywhere; if he finds gold, well and good, if he doesn't, he has had bad luck. The same is true when the physicists look for causes. . . . I do think the notion of the world having an explanation is a mistake. I don't see why one should expect it to have, and I think what you say about the scientist's assumption is an overstatement.

COPLESTON: It seems to me that the scientist does make some such assumption. When he experiments to find out some particular truth, behind that experiment lies the assumption that the universe is not simply discontinuous. There is the possibility of finding out a truth by experiment. The experiment may be a bad one; it may lead to no result, or not to the result that he wants, but at any rate there is the possibility through experiment of finding out the truth that he assumes. And that seems to me to assume an ordered and intelligible universe.

RUSSELL: I think you're generalizing more than is necessary. Undoubtedly

* Bertrand Russell and F. C. Copleston, S. J., "A Discussion on the Existence of God" (first broadcast on the Third Programme of the British Broadcasting Corporation, January 28, 1948).

the scientist assumes that this sort of thing is likely to be found and will often be found. He does not assume that it will be found, and that is a very important matter in modern physics.

COPLESTON: I think he does assume, or is bound to assume it tacitly, in practice. It may be that, to quote Professor Haldane, "When I light the gas under the kettle, some of the water molecules will fly off as vapor, and there is no way of finding out which will do so", but it doesn't follow necessarily that the idea of chance must be introduced except in relation to our knowledge.

As you can see, this second kind of implicit assumption does not depend on the psychological facts about the person supposedly making the assumption. Whereas implicit psychological assumptions are those which are already in the mind of the assumption-holder, or would be called to mind if he were challenged, IMPLICIT LOGICAL ASSUMPTIONS are those which are needed by an argument, position, procedure, etc. These two categories can (and often do) overlap, although they are conceptually distinct. It frequently happens that a person has in mind that which is needed by his argument.

In Entry 18 Miss Gamma said to Hilary, "You are assuming that a necessary condition for something's being literature is that it be of high quality?". This could well have been both a psychological and logical assumption: callable to mind **and** needed. In Entry 26 Neil said to Tony (pejoratively, you will remember), "You're assuming that Wellek and Warren's definition gives us a list of necessary conditions." Neil was here contending that Tony's position needed the assumption, although it turned out, as Tony showed, that the position did not really need the proposed assumption. Neil might also have been contending that Tony had it in mind (or would bring it to mind on being challenged). If so, then it was also alleged to be an implicit psychological assumption.

Copleston was not alleging that he detected a psychological assumption. It did not matter to him very much what scientists actually **do** think about the matter. He was concerned with what they were committed to think. This is shown by his use of the phrase, "is bound to", as well as by the whole tenor of his approach. He, of course, is pleased to know of any scientist who does think that this is an ordered and intelligible universe, but he wanted something much stronger—that every scientist **is committed to** the alleged assumption.

The problem of how to detect the logical kind of implicit assumption is a relatively unexplored one. Actually it would probably be better not to even phrase it as a problem of detection, for the word 'detection' implies that we are looking for something which is already there, whereas assumption-finding of this sort is more of a suggestive and creative activity. Criteria which I can tentatively suggest are the following three: gap-filling ability, credibility, and simplicity, in that order of priority. First, the proposed assumption must fill a gap in an argument for, or a defense of, a position or procedure (although there might be other ways to fill the gap, or there might be other arguments or defenses which would have different gaps). Second, the proposed assumption must be among the more credible of the possible gap-fillers. Furthermore, where there are a number of equally credible gap-fillers, the proposed assumption should probably be chosen from among the simpler ones.

Note that this set of criteria might produce several candidates for this kind of implicit assumption, since there might be several credible, fairly simple gap-fillers. In such a case we cannot claim to have established that a particular one is **the** assumption, but that it is one of several candidates. It is fairly difficult to be sure that one has succeeded in establishing that a given thing is an implicit logical assumption. For example, Neil in alleging (in Entry 26) that he had uncovered an implicit logical assumption of Tony's, had not eliminated one plausible (credible, simple) alternative gap-filler in Tony's argument: Wellek and Warren hold aesthetic purpose (and not all of the criteria) to be a necessary condition.

F. C. Copleston has no right to be sure on the basis of what he said that he has **established** that the scientist is committed to the belief that this is an ordered universe. An alternative, equally credible, and perhaps equally simple proposition is that the scientist is committed to the hope (not belief) that the **part** of the universe he is investigating is ordered. Russell's answer to Copleston was instructive. He proposed a counter-example to what, I suspect, he (Russell) thought to be Copleston's logical assumption: Whenever a person is looking for something, he assumes that it is everywhere. Russell's counter-example was the gold prospector, who searches for gold in the hope that it is there (where he is looking, not everywhere). But was Russell correct about this alleged logical assumption? Did Copleston need that very general statement? I think not. Can you see why?

One important lesson to be learned from these examples is that it is best to be tentative about the results of a logical assumption hunt. If possible, present your results tentatively to the alleged assumption-holder—or someone sympathetic with his position—as Miss Gamma did with Hilary. Neil was a bit overconfident, as were Copleston and Russell.

Summary

In order to focus on starting points in a line of reasoning, I have neglected the concluding sense and the pejorative use of 'assumption'.

Explicit assumptions are starting points which are stated, but which for a variety of reasons are left undefended in a particular context. They present the same problems of evaluation as statements which are offered without reasons to back them up.

Implicit assumptions which are alleged to have been in the mind of the assumer are empirical. That is, a claim that x is such an assumption is an empirical claim—a psychological claim; hence the name, 'IMPLICIT PSYCHOLOGICAL ASSUMPTION'. In addition to the evaluational problems of explicit assumptions, implicit psychological assumptions must be uncovered and established as assumptions. The claim that *x* is an implicit psychological assumption must be evaluated just like any other hypothesis, a topic to be covered in Chapter 22.

IMPLICIT LOGICAL ASSUMPTIONS are those which an argument or a procedure needs in order to be reasonable—or to be least unreasonable. Criteria for them are their ability to fill some gap, their credibility, and their simplicity. This kind of assumption has the same evaluational problems as explicit assumptions in addition to the problems associated with establishing that the alleged assumption is an assumption, a difficult thing to establish.

Since all kinds of statements can be assumptions, the evaluation of assumptions can involve all the problems to which this entire part of the book is addressed. They are provisional starting points behind which we often must go to find more basic starting points. But we cannot always go behind the assumptions; for then we would never go forward.

COMPREHENSION SELF-TEST

True or False? If the statement is false, change a crucial term (or terms) to make it true.

20–12. An authority, in the sense in which we are here concerned with authorities, is a person who in virtue of his experience and training is likely to know about the matter in question.

20–13. An authority is more likely to be right, other things being equal, if he is disinterested in the outcome.

20–14. It is a mistake to depend upon authorities.

20–15. To rely on authorities is to rely on established practice, among other things.

20–16. Authorities do not need to make assumptions.

20–17. An explicit assumption for which no reasons are offered should be rejected.

20–18. For some alleged implicit assumptions the question of whether they actually are assumptions is empirical. All other implicit assumptions are held by the assumption-finder to be needed by the argument, procedure, position, etc., for which it is alleged to be an assumption.

Application.

20–19. Find a statement in your field that is made by an authority. Describe the context. To what extent does this authority conform to the criteria for authorities given in this chapter?

20–20. Find a statement in your field that is not made by an authority. Describe the context. To what extent does this nonauthority conform to the criteria for authorities given in this chapter?

20–21. Find an example of an explicit assumption in a textbook in your field. Had you been writing the textbook, would you have left that statement as an assumption or would you have given an argument in its defense? Why?

20–22. Find an allegation of an implicit assumption from some work in your field. Describe the context. Tell what kind of implicit assumption it is. Do you agree with the assumption-finder that the alleged assumption is actually an assumption? Tell why you agree or disagree as well as you can.

20–23. Suggest why the assumption that I suspected Russell attributed to Copleston is not needed by Copleston. That alleged assumption is: "Whenever a person is looking for something, he assumes that it is everywhere."

Chapter Summary

In this chapter the beginning stages in judging the degree of justification of a statement were focused upon, an interest in the truth aspect of justification was assumed, and the distinction (though close relationship) between justification and truth, noted.

The reason for placing such emphasis on the beginning stages of an appraisal is that mistakes are so common in the beginnings. It is worth remembering the old adage: "Well begun is half done." For instance, unless we are clear about what is under consideration, there is no hope for the rest of the appraisal. We must know what the statement is and what kind of statement it is. I have described value statements, empirical statements, conceptual statements, and miscellaneous performatives. If we do not know whether we have a value statement or an empirical statement on our hands, then there is not much hope for the rest.

Although the simple question, "Why?", is usually easily asked, a failure to ask it, assuming we do not know the answer, is often disastrous. Without knowing the reasons that a person has for his statement, it is difficult to appraise the statement; it is difficult sometimes to know what it means; and it is difficult to help the maker of the statement, if he is mistaken, to see why he is mistaken. Of course there are times when the reasons are just unobtainable, and times when truth-supporting reasons do not exist.

Given an understanding of the statement, and given the reasons that are advanced in favor of the statement, we then look at the reasons and the argument leading from the reasons to the statement that is under consideration. In any particular argument the reasons are generally of three kinds: observation statements, statements by alleged authorities, and assumptions.

The criteria given in the body of this chapter for judging observation statements and statements by authorities must be used with discretion. They cannot be used to crank judgments out mechanically. No criteria exist for deciding when to override the criteria for judging observation statements and statements by alleged authorities. This is an art requiring intelligence and experience.

The category, explicit assumptions, includes a variety of kinds of statements. The point in focusing on explicit assumptions is that it should be made clear that undefended beginning points occur in just about any argument. It is good to know what these are so that they can be scrutinized.

Implicit assumptions are starting points which were not part of the explicit defense of the statement. The desirability of bringing them forth again is a result of the value of getting as much as is practical out in the open. The determination of implicit psychological assumptions is a process like the establishment of hypotheses, to be discussed in a later chapter. The determination of implicit logical assumptions is quite difficult to do with certainty, since so often one can come up with alternatives to a simple credible gap-filler.

The basic approach in this chapter has been to help you become clear about logical problems and criteria; I have implicitly relied heavily on advice in previous chapters about probing, the seeking of clarification, application of principles, judicious use of counter-examples, and the like for the application of the material in this chapter. Every teacher is faced with problems of justification. Being equipped with a set of criteria and an understanding of some basic problems should better enable you to handle the starting points of justifications of statements in your area.

CHAPTER 21

Value Statements

A zoning ordinance was under consideration in Mr. Delta's class in a dialogue in Chapter 9. Jane and Frank disagreed about the worth of the new ordinance, which prohibited trailers, junk cars, and chickens. Jane thought the ordinance was a good thing while Frank thought it was bad. The discussion became a dispute over a programmatic definition of 'freedom', each party having assumed that freedom is a good thing; but the basic question was whether the zoning ordinance was a good thing.

Questions of value arise in all areas. Here are some examples:

Should one be encouraged to read Shakespeare instead of Mickey Spillane?
Is it right to teach people not to say "ain't"?
Should a national, government-supported radio network be established in the United States with an avowed purpose of elevating the taste of people?
Should the physicists have refused to cooperate in the development of atomic weapons?
Are farmers wrong to destroy milk in a strike?
Is it wrong to require manufacturers to label the fibre content of clothing?
Is fluoridation of community water supplies a good thing?
Should the United States have stayed out of World War I?
Is it right to promote democracy in nondemocratic lands?
What is the value of geometry?

Cues used in the above set of sentences which indicate (though not infallibly) the presence of a value question are the words, 'should', 'right', 'wrong', 'good', and 'value'. Compare the above set with the next set, which are about the same topics, but which do not use such terms:

Do people generally respond to encouragement to read Shakespeare instead of Mickey Spillane?

If parents and peers say "ain't", will a teacher's efforts to teach a student to do otherwise generally be successful?

Does a national, governmentally supported radio network with an avowed purpose of raising people's taste exist in Great Britain?

Did many physicists cooperate in the development of atomic weapons?

Have farmers ever destroyed milk in a strike?

Are manufacturers required to label the fibre content of clothing?

What are the effects on teeth of the fluoridation of water supplies?

Who would have won World War I, if the United States had stayed out?

Under what conditions is it possible to develop democracy in a nondemocratic land?

Does the teaching of geometry result in the improvement of ability to think?

This second set of questions is a very different sort from the first set. Admittedly, some serious problems must be settled before one can set about trying to find answers to the second set, most notably problems of definition of key terms and elimination of vagueness. But these problems are radically different from the additional problem of the first set—the value problem. The answers to the value questions do not follow simply from the answers to such questions as those in the second set. There is more to it. Just what this is—is difficult to say. But in any case teachers must face questions with this additional element. No matter what the subject area, the question of its justification (or the justification of some part) arises and will be raised by students one way or another, as exemplified by the questions about Shakespeare, "ain't", and geometry. The value of its application can be questioned as well (atomic weapons). Some public policy questions are of strong interest to people in given fields, and their subject-matter content has considerable bearing on many of these questions(government-supported radio network, milk destruction, clothes-labeling, fluoridation, World War I, and democracy). In sum, teachers cannot avoid being faced with value questions, although they might refuse to offer explicit answers to them.

Unfortunately, the problems are difficult, controversial, and in many cases unclear. As Aristotle said in his major work on ethics:

> Our discussion will be adequate if it has as much clearness as the subject matter admits of, for precision is not to be sought for alike in all discussions, any more than in all the products of the crafts. Now fine and just actions, which political science investigates, admit of much variety and fluctuation of opinion, so that they may be thought to exist only by convention, and not by nature. And goods also

give rise to a similar fluctuation because they bring harm to many people; for before now men have been undone by reason of their wealth, and others by reason of their courage. we must be content, then, in speaking of such subjects and with such premises to indicate the truth roughly and in outline, and in speaking about things which are only for the most part true and with premises of the same kind to reach conclusions that are no better. In the same spirit, therefore, should each type of statement be **received**; for it is the mark of an educated man to look for precision in each class of things just so far as the nature of the subject admits; it is evidently equally foolish to accept probable reasoning from a mathematician and to demand from a rhetorician scientific proofs.*

Hopefully, you will take what is said here in the spirit in which it is offered: It is the most that I feel entitled to say, it is subject to controversy, and it is offered as true "only for the most part".

Value Questions and Statements Delimited

The two sets of questions above provide a definition of 'value question' by example and nonexample. Since the term 'value' is such a basic one, a more formal definition would not be of much help. One thing that can be explicitly specified, however, is the restriction of the term in this context to questions of value of human actions as opposed to questions of aesthetic value. Furthermore, so far as specific value statements are concerned, I am limiting us to statements which commit the statement-maker to an action if he were ever to be in like circumstances. For example, in the range of specific value statements under consideration here, a person who says that it is wrong for a particular farmer to destroy milk in a particular strike is himself committed not to destroy milk if he were in like circumstances. This restriction enables us to bypass some very difficult problems, but not the most important one: the problem of what we should do.

In presenting this second restriction, I made use of a distinction between specific and general value statements. Here specific statements are about a particular human action; general statements are statements of principles of action. Sometimes it is not clear whether a particular sentence is specific or general but this can usually be clarified with some probing questions. For example, the question, "Should one be encouraged to read Shakespeare instead of Mickey Spillane?", could be either specific or general, depending on whether it is about one particular person or an indefinite group of people. The question, "Do you have anyone in mind in particular?", can often clarify the situation.

I am here merging value statements (those using 'good', 'bad', 'right',

* *Nicomachean Ethics,* (Ross translation), Book I, chap. iii.

etc.) and obligation statements (those using 'should', 'ought', etc.) under the heading 'value statements'. However, one should bear in mind that only where an evaluation of value of an action (or type of action) is asserted do we have what I am here calling a value statement. The statement, "If you want to get to town, you should turn left at the next junction", is not a value statement. Take this as a stipulation, which simplifies the task without violating the main points.

Strategies

The zoning discussion, you will remember, consisted of a disagreement between Jane and Frank about the rightness of the new zoning ordinance, which among other things, prohibited the trailer, the wrecked car, and the chickens in Frank's yard. What could Mr. Delta have done in that situation?

Obtain the reasons

My first suggestion is to get the reasons for each position out in the open. To write them down in separate lists on the board is a good idea, simply because it helps everyone to see more clearly what is going on. In particular, writing down the reasons gives us a more complete position to appraise than simply a statement of the value conclusion drawn by each. It is less easy to be taken in by a written statement than an oral one. Writing down the reasons provides a way to check methodically the reasons that a person has. Finally, writing down the reasons facilitates attempts to work out a compromise position that might satisfy the important reasons held by each side.

Check the facts

A second suggestion is to check the alleged facts that are presented. One of the alleged facts in the zoning discussion is that the new ordinance requires the removal of the trailer, the car, and the chickens. But perhaps it does **not** require this. Perhaps it requires only the removal of the car and the nonexpansion of the chicken and trailer facilities. If so, then Frank's position might be different. Perhaps one of Frank's alleged facts is that they make money on the chickens. Perhaps he can be shown that they actually **lose** money on the chickens, because it is such a small operation. One of Jane's alleged facts is that the chickens wake people up in the morning, but perhaps this is not so. Value decisions are difficult enough without basing them on mistakes.

Of course the facts are not always simple to check. Of the above three alleged facts, the first is probably easiest to check—unless the zoning ordinance is vague on the point, which is an unlikely possibility in view of our vast experience with zoning ordinances. But it could be very difficult to determine whether Frank's family is making or losing money on the chickens, because this determination depends on which factors you take into account. Of course you take into account the cost of the feed, the baby chicks, the marketing expenses, and the like, but do you take into account the taxes on that part of the real estate occupied by the chickens? Do you take into account the interest lost from other investments because of the capital tied up in the chickens (including again the land occupied by the chickens)? Do you take into account the cost of Frank's labor, which he could otherwise sell, but has so far chosen not to? Do you take into account the (possible) decrease of the value of the land resulting from the presence of chickens in a residential area? In this context, in which after all we are so far only seeking agreement (instead of justification), presumably these questions must be answered by Frank, but a key move is to make him aware of the possibilities —to show him the factors that could be involved.

Apply a general principle

Another fairly obvious move is to apply an accepted general principle to the case, that is, a principle that is accepted by all the parties in the case. Perhaps the following principle might be one: People should be free to do what they like so long as their exercise of this freedom does not interfere with someone else's exercise of his freedom. Probably both parties would agree to a statement of this principle, but because of different interpretations of the word 'freedom', this agreement would not settle the case. Sometimes, however, simply reminding people of a principle to which they are attached brings them around.

Perhaps a higher principle will do the trick. Try this one: Each human being is of infinite worth. That might work, but probably not in this case, for each side presumably will claim that its worth is being transgressed upon by the actions of the other side. The principle is vague, and at least at an elementary level of understanding will lead to inconsistencies, for there will be times (such as this one) where interests that are of infinite worth conflict.

Higher principles generally are vague. Consider for example, "All men are created equal" and "Honor your father and mother". As we are well aware, vigorous dispute exists about just what these principles, which many people accept, imply in actual practice. This is not to say that such principles are empty, for there are clear cases, which we all recognize, of treating men unequally and of dishonoring one's father or mother. Such clear cases are forbidden by the principles.

You will remember the discussion of application of principles in Chapter 5, where I suggested a three-step process: idealization, judging validity, and application in reality. Given Frank's notion of freedom, the application of his principle of preservation of freedom goes as follows:

Example 21-1

Basic Argument:

1. Whatever interferes with freedom is wrong (other things being equal).
2. The zoning ordinance interferes with freedom.
3. Therefore, the zoning ordinance is wrong.

Idealization:

1. Whatever interferes with freedom is wrong.
2. The zoning ordinance interferes with freedom.
3. Therefore, the zoning ordinance is wrong.

Application in reality:

Taking other things into account Frank presumably still would endorse the conclusion: the zoning ordinance is wrong. But in doing so, he would assume that other things were essentially equal, or in other words, that other considerations do not outweigh this one.

The difference between Frank's and Jane's application of this principle (assuming for the time being that both were thinking of negative freedom) is that, while Frank is ready to assume that "other things are equal", Jane is not ready to do so. Jane would emphasize attractive neighborhoods and quiet more than Frank. Thus in the third step, they would part company. This can happen with reasonable people especially where value judgments are concerned, because although they might both endorse a principle, one might give much more weight to it than another.

Thus the application of a principle, even if there is agreement on the principle, does not guarantee agreement on the application. Value principles are such that even when they are endorsed unequivocally (people rarely bother to say "other things being equal"), the endorsers are willing to allow exceptions. We act as if our principles were "for the most part true", as Aristotle said. We treat the principles we cite as rules of thumb. Citing a principle will probably not achieve agreement here.

Examine the consequences in detail

Another important approach is to look in detail at the results of adhering to each of the proposals. For example, one might go to a community with such a zoning ordinance and compare it with another community without such an ordinance, talking to people to get their reactions. This can often be done vicariously through pictures, tape recordings, videotapes, articles, books, and various other media which depict things vividly. One of the main functions of the study of history in the schools is to depict vividly the quality of life which men have lived under different systems, at least awakening us to the existence of a variety of possibilities, some of which are quite undesirable, but not apparently so until they are vividly depicted.

The inevitable danger of this approach is that it is difficult to distinguish the consequences of the position under consideration from the consequences of other factors, which are not being considered. Suppose we visit a community with zoning. What are we to look at? Obviously the appearance of the area, but should we also consider the happiness of the people there? A crucial question is whether the constraints of zoning result in happier people. Suppose though that we find happy people. Is this to be attributed to zoning or to the type of work that the people do in the community? Their nationality? Their religion? Because of this sort of difficult problem historians are reluctant to try to generalize from their narratives of past events. The situation which concerns us is always in some respects different from the one from which we seek to learn.

In spite of the dangers attendant upon attempts to depict vividly the consequences of accepting a given value statement, I recommend this approach highly. In the zoning case we can at least be fairly sure about the prospective appearance of the neighborhood. We can get a sense of the type of life people lead, not only from visits and pictures, but from novels and sociological studies. The advantage of this approach is that it tries to show as clearly as possible the quality of human life that would exist, given adherence to the principle, and this is very important.

Take other general goals into account

Although Frank indicated opposition to the zoning ordinance because of its interference with his pursuit of one of his general goals, freedom (defined as 'lack of restraint'), a possibility exists that the ordinance will promote his pursuit of one or more other general goals and that this will outweigh his loss of freedom in his present home. Perhaps for example it can be shown that with a minimum of trouble, now that the zoning ordinance is passed, his family could sell its house at a great profit and buy another one out in the country away from the middle-class sort of neighbors they have now and not feel the financial need to raise chickens, rent trailers, and use wrecked cars for parts. Thus general goals of wealth and compatible neighbors would be promoted with a minimum of reduction of trouble-free existence.

On the other hand, the same sort of considerations might go for Jane. The resistance and acrimony resulting from the passage of the zoning ordinance, together with the large number of nonconforming uses* might result in less than full satisfaction of the goal of having what her family considers a beautiful neighborhood, but might also result in unpleasant relationships with neighbors. Hence the goal of pleasant neighborly relationships might be better pursued by abandoning attempts to get the ordinance passed or by moving somewhere more receptive to such an ordinance. As with Frank's case moving might be convenient, or might be quite inconvenient.

* A NONCONFORMING USE is one which exists at the time of passage of the ordinance and is permitted to remain, although not permitted to be expanded, or replaced in the event of destruction.

Summary

This discussion actually reduces to these three basic suggestions: **Explore the possibilities, apply accepted principles, and look at the details.** Hopefully you have noticed that this discussion was not focused on the **justification** of value statements, but rather on attempting to reach **agreement** among apparently competing interests. Often problems can be settled simply by a careful exploration of the possibilities, application of accepted principles, and examination of the details. Generally, settling a problem by reaching agreement is good enough. But not always. I do not want to maintain that agreement on a value statement is a sufficient condition for its justification (nor that its assertion by some particular person makes the statement justified). It is to this sort of problem that we now turn.

Relativism

Although a variety of differing doctrines pass under the name 'relativism', two relativistic ethical doctrines (with variants) appear repeatedly in classrooms and are significant enough to deserve discussion. These two doctrines are called 'cultural relativism' and 'personal relativism'. Roughly speaking, these doctrines hold that what is right (or good) depends exclusively upon what a group or individual approves.

Cultural relativism

Elementary Relativism. In Zadrony's *Dictionary of Social Science* we find the following definition:

> CULTURAL RELATIVISM—the point of view in which each cultural group is evaluated in terms of its own value system.*

Although the phrase 'in terms of' is ambiguous, I shall for the time being interpret it so that cultural relativism implies that a practice or act of a person or group is supposed to be judged **by** the standards of the culture of that person or group, no other standards being considered applicable. I shall call this view ELEMENTARY CULTURAL RELATIVISM. One clear statement is provided by William Graham Sumner: "In the folkways, whatever is, is right."** For example, the fact that many people in the West believe that eating the meat of cattle is all right makes it all right, according to this view, for them to eat the meat of cattle. Whereas the fact that many Hindus in India believe

* John T. Zadrony, *Dictionary of Social Science* (Washington, D.C.: Public Affairs Press, 1959), p. 78.

** William Graham Sumner, *Folkways* (Boston: Ginn and Company, 1940) (original edition, 1906), p. 28.

that eating the meat of cattle is wrong makes it wrong for them to eat the meat of cattle. Furthermore, it follows from this that it would be wrong for the people of the West to try to induce Indians to eat the meat of cattle, just as it would be wrong for the Indians to try to prevent Westerners from eating the meat of cattle.

In terms of the zoning ordinance, a cultural relativist might contend that the middle-class culture has no right to impress its values (neatness, orderliness) on the lower class, and that since keeping trailers, wrecked cars, and chickens is approved by the lower-class culture, it is right for members of that culture to do so. There is an initial plausibility to elementary relativism. However, under careful examination, its basic implausibility emerges.

For one thing, according to elementary relativism, all moral reformers are wrong, because they are proposing things which are disapproved by the culture which the reformers are trying to change. Thus according to the view, a person who tried to get rid of slavery at a time when slavery was accepted by a culture was at that time wrong. It is a suspicious view which condemns reforms without looking at their individual merits and demerits.

Secondly, the view is self-contradictory in the case where it requires us to impress its value (noninterference) on a culture which is committed to interfering with the way of life of another people, for here relativism both requires and prohibits interference with the interfering culture. For example, a culture which tries to spread its religion, or its respect for human dignity, and so forth, would be trying to interfere with another culture, but the elementary relativist would then try to interfere with the interferer, even though elementary relativism implies that **all** kinds of interference with another culture are wrong. This difficulty could perhaps be avoided by specifying an exception in the case of interference with a culture that is trying to interfere with another culture (although one then wonders why elementary relativism deserves such a special privilege). Such an exception would avoid the self-contradiction, but would then require all cultures not to interfere with a culture which practiced slavery, say, of people of one particular skin color, and managed to so debilitate the wills of the enslaved that the enslaved did not object.

Thirdly, elementary relativism implies that a particular act became wrong in a particular culture only when the people in that culture came to think that it was wrong. But assuming that Brutus' murder of Caesar was wrong, it was wrong when it was done, not just when the Romans came to think it was wrong.

Each of these three points could be explored more fully, and the arguments can get very complex.* But for our purposes, I shall leave the rebuttal of elementary relativism at that. In his *Value and Obligation* Richard Brandt

* Most of these points (along with some more elaborate arguments) are suggested by W. D. Ross in his *Foundations of Ethics* (Oxford: Oxford University Press, 1939), pp. 22–26, 59–63.

describes three kinds of cultural relativism (though he uses different terminology), one of which, elementary relativism, he does not elaborate and discuss, because he contends it "is extremely implausible".* I examined it, because despite its implausibility, it is rather popular.

Empirical Relativism. The basic principle of EMPIRICAL RELATIVISM, the second type of cultural relativism, is specified by Brandt as follows: "The ethical judgments supported by different . . . groups are often different and conflicting in a very fundamental way."** This is an empirical statement, but not so obvious as some might think. For example, in some primitive societies in the South Pacific, sons kill their fathers as a matter of duty. This practice is not clearly in conflict with ours of protecting our fathers. As Brandt points out, one must make sure that the conflicting appraisals be of the same things, "that is, of events or actions or situations which are the same in the sense of having the same meaning for both parties".*** The South Pacific son might well think that the father will continue to live in an afterlife with a body in exactly the same state as that in which it is when he dies. The son is then doing his father the favor of enabling him to go into afterlife with a body in good condition. Thus the act of killing one's father has a very different meaning for the South Pacific son that it does for us. We, therefore, cannot say that his ethical judgment is in conflict with ours because he is judging an act that is radically different from the act that we judge.

Although this type of relativism makes an empirical claim, it is relevant to value statements because, should the empirical claim turn out to be false, then the elementary relativist and his opponent would have hope of coming to an agreement, since people then would be disagreeing only about the facts, which can in principle be settled. I am inclined to believe that empirical relativism is true. The zoning situation is a case in point. Opposed groups of people who come from somewhat different cultures, but who see quite clearly what would be the effects of a zoning law, often disagree rather strongly about the desirability of these effects. However, the fact of empirical relativism (if it is a fact) does not establish either elementary relativism or sophisticated relativism.

Sophisticated Relativism. "When the judgments of different . . . groups disagree, there is not . . . any way of establishing some one of them as correct; on the contrary, . . . coflicting principles are equally valid or correct.**** This

* Richard Brandt, *Value and Obligation* (New York: Harcourt, Brace & World, Inc., 1961), p. 434.

** *Ibid.*, p. 433.

*** *Ibid.*, p. 434.

**** *Ibid.*, p. 433. I have deleted certain key terms from Brandt's characterization of sophisticated relativism in order to make it a stronger view. As Brandt actually describes it, the view is rather innocuous.

is the principle of SOPHISTICATED RELATIVISM. It takes a sophisticated value position, and is difficult to prove wrong or right without already assuming that it is wrong or right. A moral skeptic, who does not see any way of establishing any moral view as correct, belongs in this camp, as does that person who does not think that any particular principle can ever be shown to be more valid than a conflicting self-consistent one (the equal-validity position). The moral skeptic does not see any way of justifying value statements. The equal-validity man, on the other hand, although he might allow ways of justifying value statements, thinks that conflicting statements can be equally justified, even if all the empirical facts are known.

In responding to sophisticated relativism, I shall not try to appeal to an authority, because (among other things) any authority I select, regardless of who he is, would be suspect to a large segment of my readers. So I would like to pursue the more precarious course. To begin with, I do not think that any person whom I have heard express this position actually believes it, as evidenced by his own strongly held views about various contemporary issues that affect him. And there are such issues for all those I have heard express the position. Self-respect, employment, war, military service, education, taxation, honesty, medical treatment, delinquency, imperialism, equality, capital punishment, genocide, birth control, and euthanasia are likely areas for locating issues on which people expressing sophisticated relativism do have a stand which they are willing to defend by giving reasons. That a person is willing to take a stand and give reasons implies that he thinks he has at least a degree of justification for the position and that the position is better than the alternatives.

In any practical situation with students, then, the location of a particular issue on which a sophisticated relativist is willing to take a stand and give reasons should convince him that he does not really accept sophisticated relativism. In the event that we should uncover a person who sincerely was unwilling to take a stand (and give reasons) on any issue, then I do not think that there is anything to do but wait until he becomes a human being.

Sophisticated relativists, although they generally are willing to take stands and give reasons, attaching to relativism in their uninvolved moments, often do seek stronger reasons for what they do. Is there something that a teacher can say to them, other than pointing out that they in all probability do not really doubt that there is strong support for some of their deeply felt positions? Well, perhaps what they are really seeking is some basis that they can use in arguing with people who disagree with them and who do not accept the offered reasons, or do not see these reasons as particularly relevant. The only suggestion that I have to offer—after reasons seem to mean nothing because they are offered with respect to different systems of principles—is that they make use of the technique of vivid depiction of the consequences. When justification by appeal to principles fails, then appeal to vivid depiction of consequences is a final court of appeal. The details must speak for themselves. They often speak loudly.

Personal relativism

Similar in logical form to elementary cultural relativism, personal relativism locates its ultimate justification in the approval of the person making the value statement. Instead of "Whatever is approved by the culture, is right", the doctrine is "Whatever is approved by me, is right". There is an initial plausibility to this view as well, for it would be very odd for a person to say (without qualification), "I approve of something that is wrong" (not merely judged wrong by others, but really wrong in the opinion of the speaker). Try saying to yourself about some particular action: "I approve of that action, even though it is really wrong."

One trouble with the view is that it seems to suggest that the speaker's approval or disapproval makes something right or wrong, rather than vice versa; for example, it is **my** disapproval of Brutus' act that makes it wrong rather than the nature of the act itself. A related problem is that personal relativism appears to imply that Brutus' act was not wrong when he did it, and did not become wrong until the speaker (the 'me'), perhaps centuries later, came to disapprove of the act. A third problem arises when we consider a situation in which one person claims that a particular act or thing is good, while another claims that it is bad. (Take our zoning case, for example.) The nature of this third problem depends upon the way in which we construe personal relativism, as a definition of 'right' or as a doctrine setting forth a nondefinitional sufficient condition for something's being right.

In the definition case, all ethical disagreement disappears, because the apparent contenders are simply talking about different things: the reaction of one and the reaction of the other. When Jane says that zoning is good, she would simply be saying that she approves of it; when Frank says that it is bad, he would simply be saying that he disapproves. Given this definitional interpretation of personal relativism, each party would have to admit the truth of the other's contention (assuming that Jane does approve and that Frank does disapprove). That is, Jane would have to admit that Frank disapproves of zoning, and Frank would have to admit that Jane approves of it. Thus each would have to admit all that the other had supposedly claimed. The disagreement that we all know exists has been whisked away by definitional personal relativism. When Frank says that zoning is bad and Jane says that zoning is good, it should be clear that they really are disagreeing and that neither does in fact think that what the other is saying is true.

Given the nondefinitional, sufficient condition interpretation of personal relativism, then, either contradictory judgments are both judged correct, or the man advancing the position is rather arrogant. If Jane's approval is a sufficient condition for zoning's being good, and Frank's disapproval is a sufficient condition for its being bad, then personal relativism generates and endorses conflicting views: Zoning is both good and bad. If, on the other hand, it is only the approval and disapproval of the person advancing personal relativism that matters, then his view does not generate such a conflict, but it is arrogant.

Thus personal relativism has its difficulties.*

Absolutism vs. relativism

One common form of argument offered in favor of relativism is exemplified by the following statement:

> We cannot assume that there are absolutes in morals. In fact it is obvious that there are no absolutes. Look at all the differences among cultures which are reported to us by anthropologists. For example, Margaret Mead tells of sexual freedom on Samoa. Point to an absolute and I will show you that you do not really regard it as an absolute. You say that one should honor his father? I ask you then to think of the father who introduces his son into a life of crime. Should that son honor his father? Obviously not. Absolutism is false. Relativism is the only other way.

We should note first of all that this argument assumes that there are only two alternatives: that either it is to be absolutism or relativism. But there are several ways in which the term 'absolutism' can be taken in this argument, so we must look at the argument as a whole using each of these senses of 'absolutism' all the way through the argument. I shall interpret 'relativism' to mean sophisticated (cultural) relativism, in order to keep things fairly simple:

1. If absolutism is the belief that all cultures **are** agreed on a basic set of values, then, although absolutism might be false, the alternation, either absolutism or relativism, is false as well, for a person who denies this sort of absolutism might consistently believe that there still is one **proper** way to do things. Hence the argument's assumption is false, when 'absolutism' is interpreted as the denial of empirical relativism.

2. If absolutism is the belief that there is a set of principles that we know and which can be applied **clearly** and **without** exception, then again absolutism is probably false. Value principles generally **do** have exceptions and borderline cases. But is it the only alternative to relativism? No. A person could believe that there is a set of rough principles—not exceptionless—which are basically correct. Thus again the assumption is false, given this interpretation of 'absolutism'.

* Several of the above-mentioned difficulties are discussed by W. D. Ross, *op. cit.*, pp. 22–24, 59–61.

3. Lastly make the unlikely supposition that absolutism is the belief that the principles by which we operate are at least roughly true ("for the most part true"), and that although there are many borderline cases, there are at least some things that are clearly wrong and some that are clearly right.* In this case, the assumed strong alternation might in fact be true, but absolutism in this sense has not been shown false.

My rebuttal to the pro-relativist argument is basically a denial of the assumed alternation, absolutism or relativism (unless 'absolutism' is interpreted in a very special way (the third way), in which case, absolutism has not been shown to be false). Thus relativism is not shown true (whichever way we interpret the argument). Although this presentation is simplified and the points and counterpoints can get much more complex, the basic strategy indicated does take care of this somewhat popular dichotomization.

The zoning case

The zoning discussion continued in a way that raised questions of relativism. Would you have handled things as Mr. Delta did?

Example 21-2

MR. DELTA: You seem to have reached an impasse. Frank resents the supposed intrusions on his freedom provided by the zoning ordinance, while Jane resents the supposed intrusions on her freedom provided by Frank's trailer, car, and chickens. Perhaps the word 'freedom' has lost its usefulness here. Let us instead look more closely at the facts of the case to try to decide whether the zoning ordinance is a good thing. Fred?

FRED: The whole idea is simply one set of people trying to interfere with the lives of another set of people. If a group of people has a set of ways of living, then nobody ever has the right to tell them to do differently. How can the town council say what's good for someone else?

MR. DELTA: I see. Well, you may have a point. Jane?

JANE: Not at all. If one set of people don't want to pay any taxes to support schools, the police, and fire departments, and things like that, they still must be made to pay. But anyway, I brought some pictures of Yarlboro, which has had zoning like this for ten years. And I brought some pictures of some houses in our town. (She then proceeds to show her slides.)

FRANK: (after the slides are seen) Well, that's a snooty place, Yarlboro. If you want to live there, go ahead. Have you ever walked down the streets there? The people make you feel like two cents. Here people respect you.

MR. DELTA: That's interesting, but you'd adjust to the change here. Now really, Frank, don't you think that a beautiful environment is essential to the good life? That's all that the zoners are trying to achieve—some pleasant surroundings—and an increase in property value.

* Even though this is an unlikely interpretation of 'absolutism', people often suggest what amounts to this. Hence we must consider it.

FRED: How can you say that such an environment is essential to the good life? Who are you to say, I mean really? You say one thing, Frank another. There's no way to prove anything. If they make us do it, then we have to do it, but there's no point in discussing it.

MR. DELTA: You certainly do have a lot of strange ideas. You didn't get those ideas from your father, my boy. Zoning is the accepted thing in this country nowadays.

FRED: Mr. Delta, you and Jane are assuming that there are absolutes in morals and ways of living together, but there aren't. For one thing look at all the different ways that people all over the world have of handling marriage, birth, death, and male-female relationships. Where is the absolute and how can you know that you have an absolute when you have one? Even we, who supposedly regard human life as of ultimate worth, excuse all sorts of murders: on the battlefield, in the execution cell, and in self-defense, to name some things. Is murder then absolutely wrong? If it isn't, then how can you say that Frank is wrong for wanting to raise his chickens?

MR. DELTA: Just a minute, there, Fred. There are higher principles on which these things are based. I think that we've had enough out of you for now.

Without judging whether zoning is appropriate for this town, we can see pretty clearly that Mr. Delta in each of his responses to Fred did not deal with the relativistic issues Fred raised. Fred raised difficult questions. Mr. Delta (perhaps wisely) avoided the first one (though Jane came through with two good moves: a counter-example, and some details through her pictures). His response to Fred's second move was unfortunate, because Mr. Delta not only failed to meet the issue, but he introduced an irrelevance and hinted himself at holding an elementary relativistic point of view. His third response (to the charge of absolutism) was weak and unhelpful. What would you have done?

Justification

Granted then that the strategies for securing agreement, even when effective, do not always produce justified value judgments. What guarantees of justification can we find? The limitation that I have set in facing this question is that we shall make no appeal to authorities or accepted doctrines, for at least the reason that no matter which authority or accepted doctrine is selected, there will be a sizeable group of readers who reject it. Working within this limitation, however, we find that the desired guarantees are not obtainable.

Even when operating on the basis of worthy principles, one can find no guarantee that the particular application will be justified, because there might very well be extenuating circumstances (as discussed in Chapter 5). Ultimately the judgment must depend on the consequences, and each person must make his own judgment, bearing the responsibility thereof. I do not mean to imply that a person must start fresh with each decision. On the contrary, he has a backlog of experience and the wisdom of his culture to suggest the right path. But the making of a value judgment is a personal thing, though not an arbitrary one nor a matter of whimsy. This decision is more likely to be justified if it is based upon worthy principles and a careful examination of the consequences. If there are no worthy principles on which to draw, then at least a careful consideration of consequences is required.

Similarities exist between the position just advocated and personal relativism, but some crucial differences also exist. The personal relativist holds that his approval is a sufficient condition for the judgment that the act under consideration is right, whereas in the view I just presented, it is only a necessary condition—of a sort. I say "of a sort" because (and this is the second difference) implicit in the position is the assumption that the resulting judgment might be wrong. The proposed position calls for tentativeness, nonarrogance, and acceptance of responsibility.

Chapter Summary

The justification of value judgments is a difficult and controversial topic. I have tried to give it "as much clearness as the subject matter admits of" without leaning on authorities and received doctrines, which would be rejected by at least some sizeable segment of my readers.

I emphasized strategies for securing agreement on values, because often that is good enough. Recommended strategies included the following: get the reasons; check the facts; apply a general principle; examine the consequences in detail; and take other general goals into account.

But empirical agreement is not always sufficient, for tradition and group approval are sometimes in error. To treat the justification of a value statement as relative to opinion, whether it be the opinion of the majority or of one, is to take a relativistic position, cultural or personal respectively. Three related doctrines which go by the label 'cultural relativism' were examined. Although elementary relativism (the doctrine that whatever is in the folkways, is right) is implausible, it is often espoused and often confused with the other two types of cultural relativism: one holding that there are significant empirical differences in value judgments among cultural groups (empirical relativism), and the other holding that there is no way to show that some value statements are more valid than others (sophisticated relativism). Empirical relativism is not simply obvious, but is, I believe, true. Sophisticated relativism is difficult to argue against, but the strongest weapon is the fact that all relativists (that I have known) do not really believe it. The next strongest weapon and the closest that we can come to ultimate justification (given the limits I have set, and assuming that attempts to find a covering principle have failed) is the vivid depiction of the kind of human life that we can expect to accompany an action under consideration.

Personal relativism, which is similar to elementary cultural relativism, faces a variety of difficulties which make it equally implausible.

The idea of absolutism is sometimes raised in an effort to frighten us into a relativistic position. Although absolutism is a vague notion, I do not think that the move succeeds. An alternative to the dichotomy (absolutism vs. relativism) is the position that, given a careful examination of the alternatives, given a vivid depiction of the details, and having a tolerance for some borderline cases and disagreements, there is an establishable value position on many issues. This is neither relativistic nor absolutistic, as these terms are ordinarily used.

Given the limitations within which we have been working, a value judgment is more likely to be justified to the extent that it is in accord with worthy principles and is based upon a careful consideration of the consequences. Each person must make his own judgments, drawing upon his own experience and that of his culture, but must bear the responsibility for what he decides.

The handling of value questions by a teacher is extremely difficult because the issues are often complex and controversial. One solution is to avoid dealing with these issues. Sometimes this is appropriate, but sometimes this leaves a vacuum which is filled by emotion and bigotry. One must choose.

COMPREHENSION SELF-TEST

Classification. Classify each of the following sentences in accord with whether it is more likely to be used to make a value statement or an empirical statement. If there is doubt, explain why you think so.

21–1. The Gross National Product of the United States has increased by about 4 per cent per year for the last several years.

21–2. Both candidates have taken an appropriate stand on the issue.

21–3. The order of an individual policeman should be obeyed just as much as an order of the Supreme Court.

21–4. The critics have almost universally judged it to be a good play.

21–5. In contemporary society 'FREEDOM' must mean the power to do something, and cannot simply mean the lack of restraint.

Application.

21–6. Prepare a short talk for some group of students in which you answer one of the value questions listed at the beginning of this chapter.

21–7. If you were Mr. Delta, how would you have handled Fred's first set of relativist comments in the dialogue in this chapter (the one in which Fred said: "The whole idea is simply one set of people trying to interfere with the lives of another set of people.")?

21–8. If you were Mr. Delta, how would you have handled Fred's second set of relativist comments in the dialogue in this chapter (the one in which Fred said, "Who are you to say . . .?")?

21–9. If you were Mr. Delta, how would you have handled Fred's third set of relativist comments in the dialogue in this chapter (the one in which Fred charged that Mr. Delta and Jane were absolutists)?

21–10. Find a sentence in a text in your field which, out of context, could be used to make either a value or an empirical statement. Tell which it is being used to make in the context in which you found it, and explain why you think so. Imagine and describe a context in which it would be used to make the other kind of statement. Again explain why you think so.

CHAPTER 22

Material Inferences

The processes of inferring to empirical conclusions are varied. When these inferences are intended to follow other than simple deductive paths (whether strict or loose), they are what I shall call MATERIAL INFERENCES.* Sometimes the product of a material inference is general in nature, such as "People's minds are generally changed by the depiction in detail of the extreme possibilities of a system". Otherwise the product is specific, such as "The ancient city of Troy once stood where Hissarlik now stands".

Not all materially inferred conclusions which students face are true, whether they be presented in school, created by the student himself, or presented by influences external to the school and the student. This chapter assumes that teachers should help students develop a facility in evaluating materially inferred conclusions, and that teachers should have such a facility themselves.

Material inferences may be divided into two main categories: those which simply generalize the evidence which is offered, and those which move to a conclusion which receives its support basically from its power to explain the evidence which is offered in its support. Some empirical conclusions can receive support both ways, but for convenience I shall discuss them separately.

Although no mechanical test of material inference validity (in the ordinary sense, as opposed to the deductive sense of 'validity') is available, there

* Sometimes they are called "inductive inferences", but because this term suggests to many that the product must be a general statement, I have chosen the less-deceptive, although less-familiar term, 'material inferences'.

are criteria, which must be applied intelligently by a person with knowledge and experience in the field of the inference. In this chapter I shall not focus on (nor ignore) a teacher's use of the criteria, since you should be fairly adept now at application of principles (the criteria are principles), at probing, at assumption-finding, at exploring positions with examples, nonexamples, and counter-examples, at clarifying, and, of course, at asking "Why?". Instead I shall focus on the criteria themselves.

Generalizing

The first kind of material inference to be examined is called GENERALIZING, a move in which we simply generalize the common features in multiple cases without introducing technical terms that are not present in the raw descriptions of the original cases. Roughly the common form of the argument goes as follows: Some amount of **observed** *A*'s are *B*'s; therefore, some amount of *A*'s are *B*'s.

*Types of generalizations**

There are three basic ways in which the generalization, '*A*'s are *B*'s', can appear: as a **universal** generalization (all *A*'s are *B*'s); as a **prevalence** generalization (generally *A*'s are *B*'s); and as a **probabilistic** generalization with a number attached [the probability that an *A* is a *B* is m/n (m/n being a fractional number)].

Universal generalizations cover every single case. Words such as 'all', 'every', 'always', and 'never' signal this kind of generalization. Class logic, presented in Chapter 4, is ideally suited to applying these generalizations, of which the following are examples:

Every action has an equal and opposite reaction.
Writers who imitate the style of another always reveal the unnaturalness of the process with inept phrases.
No one who has always been rich can know what it is like to be poor and hungry.
Every man has his price.
Acids always turn litmus red.

* Please note the distinction between generalizations and general statements, which I am introducing for the purposes of this chapter. The category, *generalizations*, implies something about the type of argument used to reach a general statement. The category, *general statement*, implies nothing about the type of argument used. General explanatory hypotheses are general statements, but often not generalizations in this sense. For example, the statement, 'In any given system, energy is conserved', does not simply generalize raw descriptions, but it **is** a general statement.

Societies always develop class systems, even when started out with the goal of being classless.

Dodo birds are extinct.

The boiling point of methyl alcohol is about 87°C at standard pressure.

Note that the last two examples do not explicitly contain universal cues, but they are still universal empirical generalizations. Can you see why?

The prevalence generalization is the most common one in the everyday world, because in that world, there are very few universal empirical truths and most of us do not make much use of probability (with a number attached). Prevalence generalizations can be expressed without any qualifier (*A*'s are *B*'s), or with such explicit qualifiers as 'generally', 'usually', 'tendency', 'under normal conditions', and so forth. Class logic is suited to prevalence generalizations, but only if the generalization is idealized for the purposes of the deductive test, as described in Chapter 5. The statement which caused disagreement at the end of the dialogue in Chapter 19, "People's minds are generally changed by the depiction in detail of the extreme possibilities of a system", is a prevalence generalization. Here are some other examples:

Rain is generally accompanied by cooling.

Lower-class rural residents are generally opposed to zoning.

The primary motivation of nation states is usually self-interest.

Under normal conditions in a free market when the demand for a commodity increases and the supply remains the same, the price increases.

Potatoes tend to grow better when planted by the dark of the moon.

Metals expand when heated and contract when cooled.

Contemporary writers are more radical than writers of thirty years ago.

(Note that there are no explicit qualifiers in the last generalization, yet it would ordinarily be taken to be a prevalence generalization.)

Probabilistic generalizations are identifiable primarily by the use of the word 'probability' with a number attached, although the phrases 'the odds are' or 'the chances are', also often indicate probability generalizations, if a number is attached. Here is a probabilistic generalization: "The probability that a tossed coin will turn up heads is $\frac{1}{2}$." Actually the concept of *half-life* in physics is a probability concept. To say that radon has a HALF-LIFE of three days is to say that the probability of the disintegration of any particular atom of radon within three days is $\frac{1}{2}$. Class reasoning techniques cannot be used with probabilistic generalizations.

A few words of caution: The word 'probably' and the phrase 'it is probable that' never indicate a probabilistic generalization, although they could be used to qualify one: for example, "It is probable that the probability of getting a two on the next roll is $\frac{1}{6}$." Furthermore, the word 'probability' is sometimes used (without a number attached) to indicate the same type of qualification as given by 'probably' and 'it is probable that': "The probability is that this tree is dead." The last example could easily be rendered as follows: "Probably this tree is dead." When no number (such as $\frac{1}{2}$, $\frac{1}{6}$, etc.) is included in the statement containing the word, 'probability', the chances are that it is not a probability generalization.* But not always. Consider: "The probability of rolling four sixes in a row is very low." In this case no number is mentioned explicitly, but an indication is given of the sort of number that it is (very low).

The application of probabilistic generalizations to the next case, and the precise meaning of such generalizations are topics which I shall not discuss. There is a vast literature on each, and the question of precise meaning is still quite controversial. However, this much should be intuitively clear: that given only the long-run goal of winning, if the probability of getting heads is really $\frac{1}{2}$, then it would not be irrational to bet (though perhaps only a small amount) on heads, if the payoff is more than twice the bet; and it would be irrational to bet on heads, if the payoff is less than twice the bet.

Justification of generalizations

There is a complicated literature on the establishment of probability generalizations, making use of statistical concepts which are beyond the scope of this book. Any standard introductory statistics book should give you an idea of how to go about this, should you so desire. In many fields, the techniques for establishing probability generalizations are crucial. If this is so in your field, then you probably are already familiar with probability statistics. In any case I shall deal here only with the basic criteria which apply to all generalizations.

Basic Criteria. The following list of criteria are applicable to all three kinds of generalizations, although the application is more strict for universal generalizations. The criteria are, like earlier lists of criteria, just guidelines which must be applied intelligently. After listing them, I shall discuss them.

An empirical generalization is justified:

1. To the extent that there is a bulk of reliable instances of it. The greater the variability of the population, the greater the bulk needed.
2. To the extent that it fits into the larger structure of knowledge.
3. To the extent that there is a variety of instances consonant with variety in the population.

* What kind of a generalization is this one that I have just stated?

a. One standard way to seek variety within a limited population is through the use of procedures of unbiased sampling.
   (1) A pure random sample is unbiased.
   (2) A systematic sample is unbiased if a careful investigation suggests that there is not a relevant cycle or trend followed by the sampling procedure.
   (3) Stratification of a population on relevant variables (if known) and unbiased sampling within the strata is likely to be more efficient than a pure random sample or a pure systematic sample.
   (4) An unbiased sampling of clusters of the population and unbiased sampling (or complete enumeration) within the clusters is likely to be a workable way of sampling when access to separate individual units is difficult.

b. Given an unlimited population, or one which is not amenable to sampling:
   (1) A portion can be selected for sampling to determine the nature of that portion;
   (2) but in any case an extension is required beyond known portions of the population in which one has an interest, such extension (the "inductive leap") to be based upon background knowledge and context.

1. Bulk of Reliable Instances. A generalization should be based on a sufficient number of cases, although the number needed varies considerably with the subject matter, particularly with the variability of the items or material talked about. A commonly recognized error, generalizing from one or two cases, is particularly serious when done about items or material with a great deal of variability from case to case. We must be wary about generalizations such as the above one about lower-class rural residents, because it is about people—and people vary considerably. A large number of cases would be needed to establish the generalization (assuming that the problems of definition had been settled). On the other hand, the generalization about the boiling point of methyl alcohol does not need a large number of cases, assuming liquids are known to have fixed boiling points. We do not need a large and varied set of samples of methyl alcohol. One pure sample is enough for us to be fairly sure, given that the equipment is in good shape and that the investigator is competent. Several competent replications which are in agreement then make the conclusion fully justified. Of course, more precision can be obtained with more refined techniques, but the point is that some things have more variability than other things, requiring a much greater bulk of evidence.

Not only must there be a sufficient number of instances, but they must be reliable, a topic considered in Chapter 20, "Starting Points". Since generalizations are usually based upon observation statements and sometimes statements by authorities, those two topics are particularly relevant.

The idea of a bulk of confirming instances requires alteration for application to a probabilistic generalization. Suppose for example that the generalization under consideration is: "The probability of getting heads with this coin is $\frac{1}{2}$." Would one toss which comes out heads be a confirming instance? Obviously not. No **one** instance gives support at all. What it takes to support that probability generalization is a long series of tosses, about half of which are heads. So for probability generalizations, I shall interpret the requirement of a bulk of confirming instances to mean a large number of total occurrences such that the ratio of favorable occurrences to total occurrences is approximately equal to the probability provided in the generalization. Statistical procedures are available for making intelligent estimates of the probable range of the actual probability, given a number of total occurrences, but we will not deal with them here. Any standard statistics text will describe these procedures for you. I shall simply assume that you find it reasonable to question an estimate of a probability based upon two cases—one heads and one tails; and that you find it reasonable to say that 498 heads out of 1,000 tosses supports the above probability conclusion.

2. Fitting into a Larger Structure of Knowledge. If a generalization fits in with other things that we know or believe with good reason, then that helps. If it does not fit in, then we have reason to suspect the generalization. The generalization about potatoes and the dark of the moon (the period of a new moon) does not fit in with the rest of our knowledge, in that our knowledge about the movements of the moon, the planets, and the sun does not provide any sort of explanation of the alleged fact that potatoes grow better if planted by the dark of the moon. Of course, this alleged fact is not inconsistent with our knowledge of the movements in the solar system (if it were, that would count much more seriously against it), but the lack of explanation in terms of some broader theory makes the alleged fact suspect.

The concept, *fitting in*, as used here, is somewhat vague. If an alleged fact is explained by our larger body of knowledge, then it fits in. If this larger body of knowledge somehow makes it unsurprising, then it fits in. But if it contradicts, or is not explained by and is surprising in the light of our larger body of knowledge, then it does not fit in. The difficulty is in specifying what makes something surprising or unsurprising. This is the vague part of the concept and must be left so. 'Surprising' is too basic a term to provide criteria for its use, but it is still usable and communicative.

3. Variety of Instances; Sampling. Variety in the cases upon which the generalization is based is important, so that the likelihood of the selection's being representative is increased. If not much variety exists in the subject group of the generalization, then not much is needed in the observed group. But if considerable variety exists in the subject group, as occurs with people, then considerable variety must be found in the observed group. When dealing with limited populations, unbiased sampling is a systematic way of achieving representativeness through variety.

An UNBIASED SAMPLE is here defined as one produced by procedures which are fair. However, no guarantee exists that an unbiased sample will actually produce a **representative** sample. For example, tossing a fair coin five times might produce all heads (although this is very unlikely), so that the sample of coin tossings is not representative of all coin tossings with a fair coin, but still was produced in an unbiased way. In sum, an unbiased sample is one selected properly, although it is not necessarily representative. The only way that we can know that it actually is representative is to first establish the generalization being inferred from the sample. If we could do that, however, there would be no point in drawing the sample.

(a) A RANDOM SAMPLE is one in which every remaining possible member of the group or population has an equal chance of being selected at each draw. In drawing a number or set of numbers out of a hat, in shuffling cards and drawing several, in selecting items in accord with a table of random numbers,* and so forth, we aim at the ideal of equal chance for every member of a population. The assumption of equal chance (or sufficiently equal chance) is one of the starting points in an argument dependent on sampling. It is this basic assumption that people are concerned about when expressing concern about randomness of a sample.

Suppose that a seed corn company wants to check to see what percentage of a certain batch of seed corn will germinate. Assuming that the size of the batch is manageable, the company would find it helpful to take a random sample of the seed corn and test it. The conclusion about the germination propensity of the whole batch of seed corn would be based on the assumption that each piece of corn had a sufficiently equal chance of being chosen. Suppose that 95 per cent of the sample germinates under test. Then the generalization that might be concluded is that there is a probability of .95 that any particular piece of the remaining corn will germinate. In this sort of case a random sample is appropriate and, given a physically manipulable batch of seed corn, easy to draw. But it is not always this easy.

Just to give an idea of the difficulties in securing random samples in some fields, consider what we would have to do to get a random sample to test the generalization that Sam and Virginia proposed in the dialogue in Chapter 19: "People's minds are generally changed by the depiction in detail of the extreme possibilities of a system." The first problem is to determine the group from which to draw the sample. The generalization does not specify a particular culture or epoch or age, so it presumably covers all cultures, all epochs, and all ages. To get a random sample, if this is the coverage, is impossible. We cannot get a sample of dead people and people who

* Tables of random numbers are standard items in the hands of statisticians. They are built by elaborate procedures which justify the assertion that each number had an equal chance of being selected for its position in the sequence. Items in a table of random numbers might look this: "49762410 . . ." To use them in selecting names from a telephone book, one might take the fourth name, then the ninth name after that, then the seventh name after that, and so forth.

are yet unborn. Even if it were limited to people who are alive now (which probably was not the intention), the job would be impossible, because many people are inaccessible—either physically or through our means of communication—and we are unable to procure a complete list of all the living people, which list we would need in order to draw our sample. Furthermore some of the people selected would be dead by the time we got around to investigating them, and young babies would be uninvestigable because we have no way of knowing whether their minds are changed about systems. Do they even have views about systems?

One practical move is to restrict the population we study to a more accessible group—perhaps current United States residents who are beyond the age of eighteen. Then, if we were to be successful in securing a random sample of this group, we would either limit our conclusion to this group, or we would perhaps extend our conclusion beyond this group because we have good reason to believe that the group to which we are extending the conclusion is **similar enough** to the one from which the sample was drawn. This 'similar enough' judgment is a practical judgment requiring experience and knowledge in a field, just like the judgments in Step 3 in the practical application of deduction (Chapter 5).

Although limiting our population studied to United States residents above the age of eighteen will make things a bit easier, the random sample would still be extremely difficult to draw. Try to imagine how you would secure an **investigable** sample from this group such that at **each** drawing of a name each unselected member of the total group had a sufficiently equal chance of being chosen. The task is difficult.

(b) A systematic sample would be slightly easier. To get one of these, you might secure a list of all United States residents over eighteen and pick every thousandth name for study—or perhaps every hundred-thousandth name for study. The point is that you would systematically (instead of randomly) select the members of your sample. Once the first name had been selected, the selection of the others is predetermined. Although the selection process is slightly different, the problem of securing access to the individuals selected is still gigantic, so much so that the job is rarely attempted.

(c) Stratified sampling is a device used to make the required size of

	1	2	3	4	5	6	7
Northeast							
Midwest							
Farwest							
Southeast							
Southwest							

the sample smaller while still getting reliable results. The entire population would be stratified on relevant variables—perhaps social class and geographical area of residence, and unbiased samples would be drawn within each stratification cell. Suppose that we broke the United States up into five geographical areas (Northeast, Midwest, Farwest, Southeast, and Southwest) and seven social class groups, estimated on the basis of occupation, using Warner's scale.* There are thirty-five cells. Once everyone is assigned to one of these cells, we draw an unbiased sample (perhaps random or systematic) from each cell and then have a stratified sample based on (estimated) social class and geographical area. The number to be drawn from each cell is proportional to its weight in the total population. The advantage of this approach is that it makes sure that each cell gets a proper representation. Under a pure random sample system, the only way to make sure that each cell gets proper representation is to take a very large sample.

As you no doubt realize, stratification can be very difficult to execute. Grouping according to the above five geographical areas is not too difficult (although our currently mobile population gives some problems), but grouping according to these social class estimates would be quite difficult. It is difficult to assign a social-class relevant occupation** to many people: for example, housewives, students, unemployed, and military personnel. Some people have two occupations. Warner's scale gives numbers to owners of businesses and farms in accord with the size of the business or farm. This size is very difficult to determine before the person is selected. There are many other difficulties with this, one of the simplest methods of estimating social class status.

We also need to have some assurance that the variables we selected for stratification are relevant. If not, it does not matter particularly whether each cell is proportionally represented. On the basis of general knowledge about Americans, I think that these two selected variables are relevant. But perhaps more are as well. More difficulties!

In sum, a stratified sampling procedure can lessen the number of people investigated (an important concern in this case), if the variables selected are relevant, but often the actual job of assigning the population to the strata is quite difficult.

(d) A cluster sample is an easier procedure, but with attendant risks. In making a cluster sample, one divides the entire area up into groups or clusters, takes an unbiased sample of the clusters, and takes an unbiased sample or performs complete enumeration within the selected clusters. In our case we might take counties for our clusters. After taking an unbiased

* See W. Lloyd Warner, *Social Class in America* (New York: Harper & Brothers, 1960), pp. 141–42.

** I should point out that using occupations simplifies things greatly. To make a social class estimate by most other means is far more difficult.

sample of all counties in the United States (random, systematic, or stratified), we could then take unbiased samples within each selected cluster. Following such a plan we would not have to list the names of all residents in the United States who are over eighteen, but only all those in the selected counties. This would still be a large order.

Difficulties with a cluster sampling procedure are the difficulty of securing clusters of roughly equal size, and the danger of securing an unrepresentative sample of clusters, since a small number of clusters is generally chosen in order to maintain sampling ease. The political statistician's dream is the location of one cluster which is representative of the country as a whole. To sample or enumerate within one cluster only is obviously cheaper, but, equally obviously, dangerous.

In summary, the sampling approach to securing a representative set of instances on which to base a generalization is methodical, clear, and fairly dependable, if used properly. It can be used for some generalizations, but for others it is impossible or impractical. It is useful in obtaining a generalization about the population **from which the sample was drawn**. But so many of our generalizations go beyond the data, so to speak, and cover instances which are not members of the population from which we have a sample. Look back at the example generalizations provided at the beginning of this section on generalizations. Almost none are about a population from which a legitimate unbiased sample can practically be drawn. This holds even for the one about potatoes, because it is about all potatoes. We can draw a random (or other sort of) sample from only a given batch of potatoes. If we do generalize to all potatoes on the basis of what we find out with a sample drawn from the batch, then another step is involved, classically known as the "inductive leap".

The Inductive Leap. If the conclusion is an ENUMERATIVE GENERALIZATION, that is, if it is only about the individuals which were actually examined, then no inductive leap is performed. The generalization, "All of the bottles on this shelf contain acids", asserted after an examination of every one of the bottles, is thus an enumerative generalization. Furthermore if it is only about a population from which we have drawn a large unbiased sample, then again no inductive leap is performed, although some care must be exercised depending on the size of the sample and the variability of the sample. But when we go beyond the population sampled or the group examined, the problem is one of good judgment based on a background of **experience and knowledge**. Although this step, the inductive leap, has attracted the attention of many philosophers, no satisfactory routinization has been developed to tell us when we can make the leap and when we cannot.

We operate continuously with generalizations reached by inductive leaps, and we would be in very difficult circumstances if we did not. Think of five of the reliable generalizations which you have used today and ask yourself how you came to know them. Generally we make a few observations, and if the thing is a regular sort (such as the pressure required on auto brakes) we generalize—not absolutely—but firmly. If it is a complex irregular sort of thing—such as human behavior—we generalize tentatively and operate on the basis of a quite tentative generalization, so that when we apply it we are suspicious of the result.

Virginia's generalization about the changing of people's minds by extreme depictions is this latter sort of generalization because it is in the area of practical psychology. Once the vaguenesses of the generalization have been resolved (that is, what sort of system, what is an extreme possibility, and so forth?), a person with experience at changing people's minds measures it up against his experience. If his experience is not sufficiently pertinent to the generalization, he might run a few studies in which he carefully determines the opinions of a variety of people about some issues pretaining to systems, exposes them to depiction in detail of extreme possibilities of one or a few systems, and sees what happens to them. He must keep very close tabs on them and not allow any of the measuring of their attitudes to be done mechanically.

Ultimately, the decision that the generalization is justified (or is not justified) must be made by each person for himself, whether he be expert or layman. He can decide to take another's word about the inductive leap, or he can decide whether he has a right to make it himself, taking into account the criteria given and his own experience and knowledge. But he must decide, bearing the responsibility for the consequences that come from the decision.*

Miss Gamma's students are not really in a position to evaluate the generalization that Virginia proposed. They are relatively inexperienced and in no position to conduct the sort of inquiry I described. Miss Gamma might lead them to see the difficulties, or she might take charge of some sort of investigation, limiting the population to a manageable group, perhaps the students in the school. But she is an English teacher and quite probably will feel that she has no time to do research in practical psychology. A more plausible approach would be to approach an authority on the subject—perhaps an educational psychologist—and ask his opinion as an authority, perhaps securing references to start a pursuit of the topic in a neighboring library. If I were Miss Gamma, I would have assigned the task to Virginia after attempting to show the difficulties involved in making the judgment in that class.

When the generalization is within the scope of the teacher's competence,

* Up until this paragraph, nothing that I have said about material inference is controversial, but the comments in this paragraph about each person's having to decide for himself and bearing the responsibility for what he decides, are controversial. This is the best that I can do with the problem of making the inductive leap. See the bibliography at the end of Part IV for references on this difficult topic.

and sufficient experience either has been had by the students or such experience is made desirable by the curriculum goals set for that class, then the appraisal might reasonably become a discussion topic, with argument going back and forth about whether the generalization conforms to the accumulated—or developing—experience of the students. Samples might be taken and experiments run. The logical point is that without considerable experience, the members of that class are not in a position to evaluate the generalization, although they might well be in a position to evaluate authorities who evaluate the generalization. If it is worth taking the time to give them the experience, then they might evaluate the generalization directly. And a compromise can be struck between the two extremes. They might obtain or already have sufficient experience to judge whether the statement by an authority is plausible, or to try to improvise the application of a not-quite-directly-applicable principle which comes from an acceptable authority.

Summary

EMPIRICAL GENERALIZATIONS are general statements which are about the world of things, men, and events, and which summarize the data on which they are based. Sometimes they are universal, sometimes prevalence, and sometimes probabilistic generalizations. The degree of justification of such generalizations depends on the bulk and variety of reliable instances of the generalizations and on the degree to which they fit in with existing knowledge. The standards for universal generalizations are stricter than the standards for prevalence generalizations, because universal generalizations make stronger claims. The determination of the degree of accuracy of probabilistic generalizations about limited populations is beyond the scope of this book, but is discussed in standard statistics texts.

One good (but often difficult) way to achieve sufficient variety of instances is through the use of random, systematic, stratified, or cluster sampling procedures—with the proper safeguards. Random samples are those such that for each draw, every unselected item has an equal chance of being drawn. Systematic samples are those drawn at regular intervals from some previously assigned ordering. Stratified samples are those drawn in an unbiased and properly weighted way from each of a set of strata. Cluster samples are those in which groups are picked in an unbiased way from a larger number of groups, followed by sampling or total examination within the selected groups. A variety of complicated combinations of the above four basic types of sampling are possible, the idea being somehow or other to give every member of a population a fair chance to be selected with the least trouble to the sampler. The goal: a representative selection efficiently investigable.

Sampling procedures apply only to finite populations, and very often are applied to a much smaller population than that about which we want to generalize. For estimating values of infinite populations, or populations larger than those sampled, or for making generalizations about things not amenable to sampling procedures, an inductive leap must be made. It should be based upon background knowledge and experience. Where this is not possessed, it should be secured; alternatively or in combination, one might seek out reliable authorities for a judgment about the degree of justification of a generalization.

COMPREHENSION SELF-TEST

True or False? If the statement is false, change a crucial term (or terms) to make it true.

22–1. A universal generalization must hold of every case, if it is to be true.

22–2. A true prevalence generalization must hold of every case.

22–3. A random sample taken from a given population must be taken so that every remaining member has an equal chance of being chosen on each draw.

22–4. A stratified sample taken from a given population must be taken so that the population is divided in groups, a sample of the groups is selected, and the members of the selected groups are either enumerated or sampled.

22–5. A justified inductive leap must be based upon knowledge and experience.

Application.

22–6. From a textbook find an empirical generalization; classify it as universal, prevalence, or probabilistic; and write an essay describing a hypothetical set of evidence which you would regard as justifying the conclusion.

Inferring to Explanations

The second basic type of material inference is the move to an empirical conclusion that is alleged to be the best explanation of something. When a detective judges that, say, Smith has stolen the rubies, he does so primarily on the ground that this hypothesis best explains the facts that he has uncovered (for example, the presence of Smith's fingerprints on the safe, the presence of the rubies in Smith's closet, the fact that Smith stayed home from work on the day that the rubies were stolen, and so forth). Here are some empirical conclusions which (as I shall later illustrate) can get their support basically from their ability to explain the facts:

Hissarlik is at the site of Troy.

The pressure in a liquid varies directly as its depth, assuming the pressure at the surface to be zero.

Emilia did not suspect Iago to be a villain until the end of *Othello.*

*Criteria**

Here is a list of criteria for judging explanatory conclusions:

An explanatory conclusion is justified to the extent that:

1. It explains a bulk and variety of reliable data.
2. It is itself explained by a satisfactory system of knowledge.
3. It is not inconsistent with any evidence.
4. Its competitors **are** inconsistent with the evidence.
5. It is simpler than its competitors.

When an explanatory conclusion is proposed but not yet established, then it is called an HYPOTHESIS. When it is established (shown to be justified), it is called a fact, a law, a truth, or some such endorsing name. I shall call explanatory conclusions 'hypotheses' in the following illustrations, because, for purposes of illustration, they are not established.

Hypotheses can be either specific (as in the case of the detective's hypothesis about the ruby thief and the statement about the site of Troy) or general (as in the case of the statement about the relationship between pressure and depth). In order to illustrate the criteria, I shall apply them one at a time to a specific hypothesis (the one about Hissarlik) and a general hypothesis (the one about pressure).**

1. *Explaining a Bulk and Variety of Reliable Data.* Hissarlik is only an hour's walk from the sea. Thus the hypothesis, "Hissarlik is at the site of Troy", explains the reported ability of the Greeks to go back and forth from Troy several times a day. And it explains why there are ruins at Hissarlik. These explanations make use of gap-fillers which I am willing to accept as true:

Example 22-1

Hissarlik is at the site of Troy.
Hissarlik is one hour's walk from the sea.
People are able to walk back and forth several times a day between places that are one hour's walk apart.

Therefore, the Greeks were able to go back and forth from Troy several times daily.

Example 22-2

Hissarlik is at the site of Troy.
A large city when abandoned tends to leave ruins.

Therefore, there are ruins at Hissarlik.

*Adapted from my "A Concept of Critical Thinking," *Harvard Educational Review,* 32:1 (Winter, 1962), 91-94. Copyright © 1962 President and Fellows of Harvard College.

**Sometimes a third category, theory, is introduced, but I shall treat theories as general explanatory conclusions which are particularly sweeping and usually quite abstract.

In each case the facts to be explained by the proposed hypothesis are the conclusions to practical deductive arguments as described in Chapter 5. Hence we can say that the hypothesis explains* these two facts, granting certain assumptions. The ability to explain only those two pieces of evidence is not enough to establish the hypothesis. More explained evidence of different types must be provided.

The pressure hypothesis explains why water spurts farther from a hole near the bottom of a tank than from a hole in the middle of a tank. It also explains the proportional relationships between the following sets of readings of pressure gauges attached to the supply tank in a water system:

Distance from top of tank (ft)	*Pressure reading* (lb/sq in)
0	0
5	2.1
10	4.2

These data can be derived from the hypothesis together with acceptable assumptions:

P–1. The pressure varies directly as the depth.
The greater the pressure at a hole, the farther the liquid will spurt.
The bottom hole is at a greater depth than the middle hole.

Therefore, the water spurts farther from the hole near the bottom.

P–2. The pressure varies directly as the depth.
The depth at 10 ft is twice that at 5 ft.

Therefore, the pressure at 10 ft (4.2 lb/sq in) is twice that at 5 ft (2.1 lb/sq in).

Again the explanation of these data alone does not establish the hypothesis. More explained data of various types are needed.

2. *Being Explained by a Satisfactory System of Knowledge.* If the Hissarlik hypothesis could itself be tentatively explained by established facts and generalizations, it would then be more acceptable. For example, suppose one could show that the traits of the Trojans and the facts about the geography, climate, and nearby civilization at the time make it probable that the Trojan city would have developed at Hissarlik at the time that Troy was supposed to have existed. If it were possible to show that, the Hissarlik hypothesis would thereby receive support.

* Strictly speaking, when dealing with a hypothesis whose truth is in question, we say that the hypothesis **would** explain.

Similarly the pressure hypothesis is supported by showing that it can be explained, and thus derived, as follows:

Pressure in a liquid is the equivalent of the weight of a regular column of liquid extending to the top of the container.
The weight of a column of liquid varies directly with its depth.

Therefore, the pressure in a liquid varies directly with the depth.

3. *Not Being Inconsistent with Any Evidence.* The Hissarlik hypothesis would be weakened if no springs could be found in the area of Hissarlik, since *The Iliad* mentions two springs in the area, one hot and one cold. The reasoning might go as follows:

Hissarlik is at the site of Troy.
There were probably at least two springs at Troy, one hot and one cold.
Springs tend to remain in existence over the years.

Therefore, there are probably at least two springs at Hissarik, one hot and one cold.

Note that in using the absence of springs as evidence against the hypothesis, we are assuming that springs tend to remain and that the report of *The Iliad* is reliable. Either of these could be wrong. The less dependable these auxiliary assumptions are, the less dependable is our counter-evidence.

The pressure hypothesis would be weakened by the discovery that water spurted out the same amounts at the middle and the bottom, since the hypothesis implies otherwise. That is, it would be weakened if we did not previously have so much by way of other evidence built up in favor of the hypothesis—so much that in this case, one would have a right to suspect such data.

The signifiance of a fact which appears inconsistent with the conclusion is a particular problem in making a judgment about justification. If the explanatory conclusion is a universal one, as the pressure hypothesis appears to be, then an inconsistency such as the one mentioned in the previous paragraph refutes it, if the evidence is very clearly established and if the assumptions are not changed. One fact which is inconsistent with a universal hypothesis, by denial of the consequent, requires the rejection or modification of the hypothesis. If, however, the hypothesis is a prevalence hypothesis, such as "Cold fronts in the summer generally bring thundershowers",* then one example of a cold front in the summer which did not have any accompanying thundershowers would not require rejection or modification of the hypothesis. The adjustment of hypotheses to possible counter-examples

* Note that this particular explanatory hypothesis is also a generalization and would be subject to generalization criteria as well as explanatory criteria.

—either by rejecting or modifying the hypotheses, changing the assumptions, or making more emphatic the general qualifying terms (for example, changing 'almost always' to 'generally')—is a process of practical judgment requiring experience, knowledge, and intelligence. No rules exist, nor can they be framed, to make this process mechanical.

4. *Its Competitors' Being Inconsistent with the Data.* A competitor of the Hissarlik hypothesis is the hypothesis that Bunarbashi is at the site of Troy. This competing hypothesis is not consistent with the data that Bunarbashi is a three-hour walk from the sea and that the Greeks were able to go back and forth several times daily, if we assume that the Greeks walked.

A competitor of the earlier-stated pressure hypothesis might be one to the effect that the pressure increases directly as one gets closer to the surface of the earth. This hypothesis is inconsistent with pressure gauge readings on two independent tanks, one over the other, when the top tank has the pressure gauge at its bottom, and the bottom tank has its gauge at the top. The alternative hypothesis implies that the gauge in the upper tank would give the smaller reading. The data are just the opposite.

A controlled experiment is designed to rule out most competing hypotheses by producing data inconsistent with them. When we test the hypothesis that a new fertilizer will increase the growth of corn, we put the fertilizer in a corn patch, develop a companion corn patch (the control area) identical in every respect possible except for fertilizer, and watch the results. If there is a difference, the fertilizer hypothesis can explain it. But it would not be explained by heavy rainfall, warm weather, sunlight, and the like, since both patches supposedly received the same amount. These alternative hypotheses would justify a prediction of no difference and would thus be inconsistent with the data.

One cannot develop a perfectly controlled experiment, since the perfect isolation and variation of a single variable is not possible. The important thing might be a **combination** of weather and fertilizer, or the important thing might have slipped by unnoticed. But we can still see in the controlled experiment an attempt to approximate the logical goal of eliminating hypotheses by turning up data that is inconsistent with them. The controlled experiment is an efficient way of eliminating hypotheses by this method.

5. *Being Simpler than its Competitors.* It is very difficult to give any interpretation of the term 'simplicity' that will clarify your existing understanding of it. A number of philosophers have tried, but the matter is yet rather controversial.* But, leaving 'simple' undefined, most are agreed that, other things being equal, a simple hypothesis is to be preferred to a complex

* See, for example, Nelson Goodman, *Fact, Fiction, and Forecast* (Cambridge, Mass.: Harvard University Press, 1955) and Israel Scheffler, *The Anatomy of Inquiry* (London: Routledge & Kegan Paul Ltd., 1964).

one. The standard example is the preference of the Copernican view of the universe, which places the sun at the center of the solar system, to the Ptolemaic view, which places the earth as the center of everything. According to the Ptolemaic view, the earth is fixed and all heavenly bodies go around the earth in circular paths, some with a variety of aberrations which are called epicycles. According to the Copernican hypothesis, the earth and the other planets go around the sun in circular paths, again complicated by epicycles. The Copernican system has fewer epicycles in describing the movement of the planets. Because of these fewer epicycles, it was a less complicated view and thus was to be preferred.

Note that simplicity is not the same as intuitive plausibility or naive acceptability. The Ptolemaic system, which treats the earth as a body at rest, is far more plausible and acceptable, given the limited experience of most people at the time of Copernicus, than a theory which asserts that the earth is in fact a spinning body revolving around another body and not hanging from anything.

To apply the idea of simplicity to our Hissarlik example, suppose that the Bunarbashi hypothesis were amended to take care of the distance that Bunarbashi is from the sea. Suppose that the amendment takes the form of some auxiliary assumptions: All the Greeks had chariots which were transported to Troy in ships that are mentioned in a section of *The Iliad* that was lost. The chariots were pulled by horses which were captured in the neighborhood of Troy, although the capture was described in a section of *The Iliad* that was lost. Furthermore, the word now translated as 'walk' meant either walk or ride at the time of the writing of *The Iliad*—or alternately editors of early texts of *The Iliad* have changed the language (for example, 'ride' to 'walk') in order to accommodate the fact that the extra ships and the horse capture were not mentioned. Many other inventions would be necessary to accommodate this new set of suppositions to the existing text and established facts, but a plausible and very different account could be constructed, which would be considerably more complex. According to the criterion of simplicity, the simpler account should be preferred, other things being equal.

Given only the data already given for the pressure hypothesis under the topic, "Explaining a Bulk and Variety of Reliable Data", an equally plausible hypothesis (except for its nonsimplicity) is the following:

Assuming that $P = D$, when $D = 0$; then

$$P = D - 3.9, \qquad \text{when } 0 < D < 10;$$

and

$$P = D - 5.8, \qquad \text{when } D \geqq 10;$$

where 'P' means pressure in lb/sq in and 'D' means depth in feet.*

* Ignoring the problem of equating different units (lb/sq in and feet), which could be handled by making things even more complex.

This is a complicated hypothesis which yields the same data. Given those data and not any other data, the 'varies directly' hypothesis is still to be preferred because of its simplicity.

Causation

One particular kind of explanatory conclusion which gives trouble is the causal conclusion. Presumably you have heard leveled the charge that a concluder is committing the "post hoc fallacy", which is a way of saying that the concluder has judged that something **caused** something else when he merely showed that it **came after** and did not have any reason to conclude that there was a causal relationship. "Post hoc" is a convenient term to use to label this mistake, but the danger in its use is that the concluder (and perhaps the labeler) will take the label as a reason for saying that a mistake has been made, whereas the label is only a label. Often we have a right to conclude that one thing caused another, given that the second came after the first in certain circumstances. The important thing to try to be clear about is the nature of the circumstances that justify an inference to a causal relationship.

Some people go even further than the typical post-hoc labeler and state that there is no such thing as a causal relationship—or that we can never show that one exists. Such people in making such statements are simply oblivious to much of their own reasoning in the practical world about them. Here is a sample dialogue, which everyone will recognize as one in which a causal relationship might well have been established.

Example 22-3
MRS. BROWN: What caused the car to skid?
MR. BROWN: You ran over a patch of ice when rounding the corner.

We have all been in circumstances such as that of the Browns' in which causal relationships have been established beyond a shadow of a doubt. The question becomes one about the kinds of circumstances that justify an allegation of a causal relationship.

The Meaning of 'Cause'. Causation is a practical notion which is closely connected with our ability and interest in controlling things. Douglas Gasking likened general causal statements to recipes,* a helpful analogy. Roughly speaking to say that *A*'s CAUSE *B*'s (generally or always) is to say that bringing about an *A* is a recipe for bringing about a *B*. There are two basic terms in that definition, 'bringing about' and 'recipe', each of which has in a way the notion of causality already built in. But so it must be. This family of causal notions cannot be reduced to noncausal notions, just as value statements cannot be reduced to descriptive statements. There is really no point

* "Causation and Recipes", *Mind,* Vol. LXIV, no. 256 (Oct., 1955), pp. 479–87.

in trying to go any further with a term which all of you intuitively understand anyway.

*Singular and General Causal Statements.** It is helpful however to distinguish between singular causal statements ('This *x* caused this *y*') and general causal statements ('*A*'s cause *B*'s'). In terms of the skidding example, 'Your running over that patch of ice when rounding the corner caused the car to skid' is a singular statement; and 'Running over a patch of ice when rounding a corner generally causes a car to skid' is a general causal statement. The singular statement, although it does imply at least some general statement (minimum: 'Under conditions **identical** to these, your running over a patch of ice **identical** to this one will cause the car to skid'), does not imply as general a coverage as the general statement. Hence the general statement is easier to disprove. A counter-example to the specific statement, if the person who offers it wants to restrict the implied generalization to the minimum coverage, is very difficult to develop—or even give a chance to develop—because providing identical conditions is so difficult.

Correspondingly, unless we derive the singular causal statement from a general causal one, the singular statement is difficult to justify. We in effect must eliminate all other possible competing causes of the event in question. To show that there could have been no other cause and thus that the one suggested is the one—is a very difficult task. Suppose, for example, that you were Mr. Brown, had made the previous single causal explanation, and were challenged by Mrs. Brown to prove that her running over that patch of ice when rounding the corner caused the car to skid. How would you do it without appealing to (or establishing) a causal generalization? You probably would consider all the possible factors and one way or another eliminate all but the running over a patch of ice when rounding the corner. Now how do you eliminate other factors? Basically two ways: (1) by showing that a given possible factor was not present and thus not a possible candidate in this case; and (2) by showing that those factors that were actually present could not be the cause, because you can produce justified negative causal generalizations (for example, 'The presence of radar does **not** cause a car to skid'), because by trying some possible factors you develop some negative causal generalizations, or because common sense tells us that there could be no connection. This last appeal—the one to common sense—is the most difficult to elaborate, but surely it **is** common sense not to consider the position of Jupiter—or the birth of a baby at a nearby hospital—as a possible causal factor. Perhaps you would like to call the elimination of such factors as these by another name than 'common sense'. Do so if you choose. But the point is that there are infinitely many factors that we justifiably do not

* Those who have been following the ⁘ material will recall that this distinction was made in Chapter 17.

consider as possible causal factors—and we would be foolish to do otherwise. This again is a point where background knowledge and experience in the field becomes essential. Because of our background knowledge and experience, we do not even consider such things as the position of Jupiter and the birth of a baby at the nearby hospital.

General causal statements are handled rather like other general explanatory hypotheses. It is much easier to develop tests of general causal hypotheses than of specific ones because conditions do not have to be identical for general ones, but rather can vary a great deal. For the generalization under consideration we could construct a number of situations with ice on the road at a turn and see whether a skid develops, as the hypothesis predicts. If so, then the hypothesis can explain the data and it obtains support. If not, then the data count against the hypothesis.

But the counter-data can also be used to limit the hypothesis. Suppose that the turn was only three degrees and no skid developed. We would not conclude that the hypothesis is refuted. We would instead let that fact limit the hypothesis to turns sharper than three degrees.

As in the case of singular causal statements, one crucial problem with trying to establish general causal statements is that of avoiding the post hoc fallacy. The notorious Hawthorne studies illustrate this problem: A number of changes in working conditions were provided for a group of workers at Western Electric's Hawthorne plant and each change was followed by an improvement in productivity. The temptation was to conclude that each of the changes caused an increase in productivity. However it was discovered that when the last change was made, which in fact was a change back to the original conditions, productivity increased again. Hence it was not the nature of the particular changes which was the cause of the increases, even though an increase **came after** each change. Perhaps it was the demonstrated interest of management in the conditions of the workers, as shown by the changes and the special treatment that any experimental group inevitably receives.*

To put the problem generally, there is a danger that an experimenter will, in obtaining the conditions in which he is interested, accidentally obtain conditions which are the true cause of the effects that he attributes to the deliberately obtained conditions. In order to help handle this problem, one can institute ingenious controls (such as the one in the Hawthorne study). But ultimately again one must still depend in part on his background experience and knowledge for the judgment: "Yes, this factor is what brings about the effect. Its manipulation is what produces (or would produce) the effects in which I am interested."

* The Hawthorne studies are described in "The Western Electric Researches", in *Fatigue of Workers: Its Relation to Industrial Production* by the Committee on Work in Industry of the National Research Council (New York: Reinhold Publishing Corp., 1941).

As you can see, the judgment about whether a causal statement is justified, like other empirical judgments, requires much dependence on background knowledge and experience: for specific causal statements, such background is used in judging that infinitely many other things are not causal factors, and in knowing about some negative causal generalizations which rule out other factors; for general causal statements, such background is used in judging that a particular piece of counter-data should be used to limit, rather than refute, the generalization, in judging that insufficient counter-examples have been discovered to refute a prevalence hypothesis, in ruling out as false a number of possible competing hypotheses, and in judging that a cause, not simply a correlate, has been identified. For both singular and general statements, background knowledge and experience are required in making judgments about plausibility and about simplicity.

Fields Using Causal Statements. Historians are notoriously suspicious of causal statements in history for reasons which should be clear as a result of the previous discussion: The difficulty of proving or disproving singular causal statements leaves them open to suspicion anywhere in which we do not have an intimate knowledge of the situation. The difficulty of finding true causal generalizations about people makes them suspect as well. A common course followed by historians is to immerse themselves in a period or series of events so that they can have the intimate knowledge required for singular causal statements; to be very cautious by using such qualifying phrases as 'tended to produce' and 'probably contributed to'. (If you have not been following the ⁘ material, and are interested in various causal locutions, you might read the section on causation in Chapter 17, which discusses the distinctions between a **partial** cause and **the** cause, between a **fundamental** and a **proximate** cause, and between **necessary** and **sufficient** conditions as related to causation. This discussion should clarify even further the verbal devices used by historians to handle their difficult problems.) But in any case historians are interested in causation, because full understanding of past human actions requires the use of causal notions.

The physical and biological sciences make frequent use of causal language and show no guilt in doing so. This is because in these fields one frequently finds very well-established causal statements. The subject matter being what it is, one can manipulate and control the objects studied sufficiently to obtain reliable causal statements.

Social scientists (psychologists, sociologists, economists, etc.) are intensely interested in causal relationships because of the ultimate practical desire of many of them to predict and control human behavior. But because it is so often difficult to manipulate and control their subjects (people), they frequently have insufficient evidence for causal statements. Generally they admit this when it is so. Frequently, however, they go beyond this justified caution and **say** that they have only correlations, but really **believe** that they have causal relationships and so imply between the lines. And often they go way out and deny the possibility of establishing causal relationships (it is from these fields that we so often get the claim that causal language is meaningless), when there are very obvious causal relationships staring at them. Such supercaution is unfortunate, but understandable, given the difficulty of controlling human beings.

The applied sciences, such as engineering, agriculture, home economics, and education, have a particular need for causal language because of their very practical interests. Sometimes they use terminology like 'brings about' and 'produces', but causal matters are of supreme interest. To the extent that they draw on the physical (as opposed to social) sciences for their basic generalizations and theory, they are more given to the use of straightforward causal language. In education because of our dependence almost exclusively on the social sciences, we understandably hedge with all sorts of qualifiers; the causal knowledge that we do have is so loose that such hedging is required.

Mathematics and logic have no use for causal language. They are not empirical subject-matter areas.

Summary

Empirical conclusions which are not taken on authority, which are not inferred generalizations, and which are not deduced from established starting points must be evaluated as explanatory hypotheses. This is not to imply that one cannot also often apply the criteria for authoritative statements, inferred generalizations, and deduced conclusions. Generally a combination of the sets of criteria should be used. But this support by explanatory power is an important way of justifying a conclusion, which can be either singular or general in scope.

An explanatory hypothesis is justified to the extent that: (1) it explains a bulk and variety of reliable data; (2) it is itself explained by a satisfactory system of knowledge; (3) it is not inconsistent with any evidence; (4) its competitors are inconsistent with the evidence; and (5) it is simpler than its competitors. Many explanatory hypotheses are causal in nature, requiring care that more than a correlation has been established. Singular causal statements are more difficult to test than general ones, but each has its place and utility, causality being basically a practical concern.

The decision as to whether an explanatory hypothesis actually is justified is a difficult one to make, requiring background knowledge and experience in the field as well as thoughtful application of the criteria. It requires a practical judgment for which there is no mechanical substitute. Each person must decide for himself whether and to what degree to commit himself to an explanatory conclusion, bearing the consequences that result from his decision.

COMPREHENSION SELF-TEST

True or False? If the statement is false, change a significant term (or terms) to make it true.

22–7. Empirical explanatory conclusions are general statements.

22–8. To explain a fact is to show that it can be derived from acceptable statements and assumptions.

22–9. The simplest hypothesis is the one that appears most plausible.

22–10. A controlled experiment is designed to eliminate one or some hypotheses which are competitive.

22–11. There is no mechanical formula for judging when an explanatory hypothesis is justified—or not justified.

22–12. 'This *x* caused that *y*' is the form of a singular causal statement.

22–13. 'This *x* caused that *y*' implies 'Under identical circumstances an identical *x* will cause a *y*'.

22–14. The elimination of causal language is a worthy goal for any field.

Application.

22–15. Find a **singular** explanatory conclusion which you find in a textbook and write an essay in which you describe in detail the evidence which substantiates or refutes it. For each piece of evidence make clear which of the presented criteria you are using to make it relevant. Make explicit the assumptions used in the explanations. Give a proper footnote citation for the conclusion you are considering.

22–16. Do the same for a **general** explanatory conclusion.

Chapter Summary

The basic idea of this chapter is that although there are guiding criteria which aid in the making of judgments about material inferences, these criteria do not enable one to grind out an answer mechanically. Background experience and knowledge combined with intelligence are necessary as well. The need for this background experience and knowledge disqualifies many students from being in a position to make a proper judgment about many empirical conclusions with which they are faced. One logical alternative is to make judgments about the authorities who make empirical statements. Another is to try to develop in students sufficient experience and knowledge to qualify them to make some judgments. A third is to encourage them to make judgments about justification before they have sufficient experience, and have them thereby (since the judgments will often clash with those of others or with raw experience) develop a respect for the experience required for justified judgments. The alternative to choose depends on the nature of the statement, the maturity of the students, the knowledge and experience of the teacher, and the curricular goals for the class in question.

No conclusion is more justified than its starting points, so a consideration of them is required along with the various criteria set forth in this chapter.

CHAPTER 23

Justification: Two Cases

Instead of presenting a classroom dialogue for your consideration at this time, I shall present two cases of attempted justifications which might possibly occur in one of your classes—or those of the teacher next door—and then try to show how the previous discussions of justification bear upon these cases. The main reason for not examining another classroom dialogue to exhibit a problem of justification is that by now you should be accomplished at such logical skills as probing, suggesting possible counterexamples, asking "Why?", handling definitions, evaluating explanations, and locating assumptions. The point of the cases in this chapter is to make more firm your understanding of the criteria and their application. Because the cases are complex, a dialogue would take more space than it would be worth at this point in the book.

In the following two cases many of you will not have the background experience and knowledge to make a fully justified judgment about the conclusions reached. But the important things to see are the broad applicability of the criteria, the need for experience and background knowledge, and the existence of unique features in each case.

One reason for presenting fairly sophisticated examples is to challenge the teachers who read this book. I do not imply that the criteria and advice are applicable only at the upper levels of education. They are applicable at all levels, though they must be somewhat simplified for lower levels.

Iago's Character

In Shakespeare's *Othello** a variety of interpretations have been given to the character of the villain, Iago. In his book, *Shakespearean Tragedy*, A. C. Bradley presents an argument supporting the view that Iago is not a melodramatic villain; that is, Iago is not "a person whom everyone in the theatre knows for a scoundrel at the first glance".** In order to support this interpretation Bradley mentions a number of points in the play in which confidence is expressed in Iago: Othello, when Cassio was found fighting with Montano, noted that "honest Iago looked dead with grieving". When Desdemona was in trouble she sent for Iago to help her. The word 'honest' is applied to Iago some fifteen times in the play. All of these facts are explained by Bradley's thesis about Iago's characterization, but seem inconsistent with the thesis that Iago is a melodramatic villain. I shall not detail these explanations and apparent inconsistencies, leaving that to you, but shall proceed to examine more carefully what Bradley apparently thinks is a stronger argument.

This stronger argument consists of two parts: a deductive inference, and a material inference, the material inference being used to establish one of the premises in the deductive argument. First the deductive argument:

Example 23-1

Premises:

1. If Iago were a melodramatic villain, then his wife, Emilia, would at least suspect him to be a villain throughout the play.
2. Emilia did not suspect him to be a villain until the end of the play.

Conclusion:

3. Iago was not a melodramatic villain.

Granting the premises, the conclusion follows necessarily—on the assumption that we are willing to take the second premise as a denial of the consequent of the first premise. The first premise in the deductive argument is left undefended by Bradley, presumably because he thinks it obvious that if a man is known by everyone in the theatre as a scoundrel at first glance, then

* A brief summary of the plot: Othello, in charge of the defense of Cyprus, is married to Desdemona. He has appointed Cassio as his lieutenant, and not Iago. Iago plots against Othello, and, using among other devices a stolen handkerchief, leads Othello to believe that Desdemona is having a romance with Cassio. Othello orders the murder of Cassio and kills his wife, Desdemona, with his own hands. Emilia, who is Iago's wife, realizes Iago's treachery and exposes him to Othello, for which Iago kills her. Othello, after wounding Iago, kills himself, and is replaced as commander by Cassio, who actually was not murdered.

** A. C. Bradley, *Shakespearean Tragedy* (London: Macmillan and Co., Ltd., 1937), p. 213. I am indebted to Prof. Bruce Warner for stimulating my interest in Bradley's thesis.

his wife should certainly suspect him. Since I am only trying to illustrate the formal structure of arguments, I shall not take a position on this premise. I merely point it out as an assumption and thus a starting point in Bradley's argument.

The second premise is the part of the argument for which Bradley provides further defense. He does this in a material-inference argument leading toward this second premise as an **explanatory hypothesis**. That Emilia did not suspect Iago to be a villain is urged on the basis of its explanatory power. In the following relevant passage, the sentences are numbered for later reference:*

Example 23-2

(1) There is no sign either that Emilia's marriage was downright unhappy, or that she suspected the true nature of her husband. (2) No doubt she knew rather more of him than others. (3) Thus we gather that he was given to chiding and sometimes spoke shortly and sharply to her (III. iii. 300 f.); and it is quite likely that she gave him a good deal of her tongue in exchange (II. i. 101 f.). (4) He was also unreasonably jealous; for his own statement that he was jealous of Othello is confirmed by Emilia herself, and must therefore be believed (IV. ii. 145). (5) But it seems clear that these defects of his had not seriously impaired Emilia's confidence in her husband or her affection for him. (6) She knew in addition that he was not quite so honest as he seemed, for he had often begged her to steal Desdemona's handkerchief. (7) But Emilia's nature was not very delicate or scrupulous about trifles. (8) She thought her husband odd and 'wayward', and looked on his fancy for the handkerchief as an instance of this (III. iii. 292); but she never dreamed he was a villain, and there is no reason to doubt the sincerity of her belief that he was heartily sorry for Cassio's disgrace. (9) Her failure, on seeing Othello's agitation about the handkerchief, to form any suspicion of an intrigue, shows how little she doubted her husband. (10) Even when, later, the idea strikes her that some scoundrel has poisoned Othello's mind, the tone of all her speeches, and her mention of the rogue who (she believes) had stirred up Iago's jealousy of her, prove beyond doubt that the thought of Iago's being the scoundrel has not crossed her mind (IV. ii. 115–147). (11) And if any hesitation on the subject could remain, surely it must be dispelled by the thrice-repeated cry of astonishment and horror, 'My husband!', which follows Othello's words, 'Thy husband knew it all'; and by the choking indignation and desperate hope which we hear in her appeal when Iago comes in:

Disprove this villain, if thou be'st a man:
He says thou told'st him that his wife was false:
I know thou did'st not, thou'rt not such a villain:
Speak, for my heart is full.

(12) Even if Iago **had** betrayed much more of his true self to his wife than to others, it would make no difference to the contrast between his true self and the self he presented to the world in general. (13) But he never did so. (14) Only the feeble eyes of the poor gull Roderigo were allowed a glimpse into that pit.

*Bradley, *Shakespearean Tragedy,* pp. 215–16. I do not claim that Bradley *believed* himself to have offered an argument whose structure conforms to the explanatory hypothesis model; my claim rather is that his argument is most defensible if so viewed.

The explanatory hypothesis [which is the second premise of the deductive argument supporting Bradley's interpretation of Iago's character (Example 23-1)] is found in sentences 1, 5, and 8, though stated in different ways. The defense of this hypothesis rests heavily on its ability to explain two kinds of facts: Emilia's observed lack of suspicion in suspicious circumstances (mentioned in Bradley's sentences numbered 8, 9, and 10), and her apparently genuine expressions of strong emotion when the truth is presented (mentioned in Bradley's sentence numbered 11). About the relevance of the mention of Emilia's knowledge of certain of Iago's defects (sentences 3, 4, and 6), I speculate that Bradley was starting off by admitting some weak counter-evidence to his thesis.

To reach a full understanding of Bradley's argument, one must read all of his book, one must read *Othello* carefully a number of times—along with many other plays by Shakespeare, and one must read a number of other critical treatments of Shakespeare. Most of us have not done this. The point is that without such a background one is in no position to appraise—or even grasp fully—the total argument. This short quotation from Bradley's book only gives us a glimpse of the structure and complications of this argument. It is unavoidably presented out of context. All that most of us can hope to do here is to get a rough idea of what is going on.

The first fact that Bradley offers as explained by the hypothesis is Emilia's apparent failure to form "any suspicion of intrigue" (Sentence 9) even after seeing Othello's agitation about the absence of the handkerchief (which Othello had given to Desdemona, which Emilia on Iago's urging had stolen and given to Iago, and which Iago contended he had seen in Cassio's hands). The gap-filled explanation might go like this:

Example 23-3

Explanatory material:

1. Emilia did not doubt her husband. (the hypothesis)
2. If a woman does not doubt her husband, then she will not show suspicion of him in a suspicious situation.
3. The situation in which Othello showed agitation about the handkerchief was a suspicious situation.

Explicandum:

4. Emilia did not show suspicion of Iago in the situation in which Othello showed agitation about the handkerchief.

Statement 1 in the explanatory material of Example 23-3 is one version of the hypothesis; Statement 2 is a plausible gap-filler, which is perhaps a truism; and Statement 3 is a starting point on which, one assumes, most would agree—and is one of those borderline observation statements.

Note that another starting point here is the explicandum, which is the finishing point in the deductive argument providing the explanation. This fact illustrates well the two directions of reasoning in an argument in support of an explanatory hypothesis: the deduction goes in one direction, while the material inference goes in the other.

The next facts which are explained by Bradley's conclusion are mentioned in his Sentence 10: the tone of her speeches when it occurs to her that some scoundrel has poisoned Othello's mind, and the mention of the rogue who (she believes) had stirred up Iago's jealousy of her. First the tone of her speeches:

Example 23-4

Explanatory Material:

1. Emilia did not doubt her husband. (the hypothesis)
2. If a woman does not doubt her husband, then if it occurs to her that someone is a villain, it will probably not occur to her that her husband is a villain.
3. If it does not occur to a woman that her husband is a villain, then the tone of her speeches will not suggest that she thinks he is a villain.
4. It occurred to Emilia that someone is a villain.

Explicandum:

5. The tone of Emilia's speeches did not suggest that she thought that Iago was a villain.

The explicandum, Statement 5 in Example 23-4, is another borderline observation statement, which serves as a starting point in Bradley's argument. Any person who knows the play and is experienced in the use of the English language would probably say that this is an obvious statement—that anyone can see that her tone is as described in the statement. But we must admit that the thing observed is not a simple quality like a color or a length. Hence it is a borderline observation statement serving as a starting point.

The next thing is her mention of the rogue who (she believes) stirred up Iago's jealousy. The proposed hypothesis helps to explain an aspect of this situation as well. Actually the explanation is the same as the previous one, except that a different remark is referred to. In this case the remark is the following:

(After suggesting that some knave had poisoned the Moor Othello's mind)
O, fie upon him! Some such squire he was,
That turn'd your wit, the seamy side without,
And made you to suspect me with the Moor.

She is saying that the person who poisoned Othello's mind is like the (alleged) person who poisoned Iago's mind. Again the tone of the remarks does not suggest that she thought that Iago was a villain, and this tone is explained by Bradley's hypothesis. I shall not bother to depict this explanation, since it is the same as Example 23-4.

The next fact (Sentence 11) is her "thrice-repeated cry of astonishment and horror, 'My husband!', which follows Othello's words, 'Thy husband knew it all'." (Othello's words refer to Desdemona's alleged infidelity.

Emilia's husband, Iago, "knew" all about Desdemona's alleged infidelity and had given the information to Othello.)

Example 23-5

Explanatory Material:

1. Emilia did not doubt her husband. (the hypothesis)
2. If a woman does not doubt her husband, and is presented with clear proof that he is a villain, then she will probably show evidence of shock.
3. Othello (unwittingly) presented Emilia with clear proof that Iago was a villain.

Explicandum:

4. Emilia showed evidence of shock.

The explicandum is another borderline observation statement.

Note that the explanatory material here provided does not show why Emilia said "my husband" three times. It just explains why she showed evidence of being shocked. That we would come up with an explanation of her particular way of showing shock is unlikely and not necessary. The crucial thing is that this hypothesis explains why she appeared shocked:

OTHELLO: O, I were damn'd beneath all depth in hell,
But that I did proceed, upon just grounds,
To this extremity; thy husband knew it all.
EMILIA: My husband?
OTHELLO: Thy husband.
EMILIA: That she was false to wedlock?
OTHELLO: Ay, with Cassio: nay, had she been true,
If heaven would make me such another world,
Of one entire and perfect chrysolite,
I'd not have sold her for it.
EMILIA: My husband?
OTHELLO: Ay, 'twas he that told me first,
An honest man he is, and hates the slime
That sticks on filthy deeds.
EMILIA: My husband?
OTHELLO: What needs this iteration? woman, I say thy husband.
EMILIA: O mistress, villainy hath made mocks with love!
My husband say that she was false!
OTHELLO: He, woman;
I say thy husband: dost understand the word?
My friend, thy husband, honest, honest Iago.
EMILIA: If he say so, may his pernicious soul
Rot half a grain a day! he lies to the heart,
She was too fond of her most filthy bargain.

The last evidence to be explained is her "choking indignation and desperate hope which we hear in her appeal when Iago comes in". Note that Bradley says "which we hear" showing that he regards this as something like an observation. The explanation goes as follows:

Example 23-6

Explanatory Material:

1. Emilia did not doubt her husband. (the hypothesis)
2. If a woman does not doubt her husband, and is suddenly given strong proof that he is a villain, with apparent great emotion she will probably ask him about the alleged proof.
3. Othello had just given Emilia strong proof that her husband was a villain.

Explicandum:

4. With apparent great emotion Emilia asked Iago about the alleged proof.

Note again that the explicandum is not a description of the exact occurrence: the words used by Emilia are not deduced as the explicandum. But the generalized description of Emilia's action is explained. Again we have a borderline case of an observation. Like Bradley, I can "hear" the "choking indignation and desperate hope" of Emilia's speech in the passage quoted by Bradley at the end of the selection of his that I have quoted. So I am willing to treat his description as a starting point from which the actual explicandum of Example 23-6 can be derived.

Thus the ability of the hypothesis about Emilia to explain the facts Bradley cited constitutes support for this hypothesis. Furthermore, the hypothesis fits in with the rest of Bradley's interpretation of the characters in *Othello* although to my knowledge it is not **explained** by any system of knowledge. It is not, according to Bradley, inconsistent with any facts—although in a note he mentions two places where one might think there are inconsistencies with his hypothesis. I shall not go into his attempts to avoid these possible counter-examples, but will leave it to those of you who are interested enough to do so.*

Clearly, the tempting path of constructing a deductive argument, starting with Emilia's reaction and going to the thesis that she did not suspect Iago, will not work. Such an argument might look like this:

Example 23-7

Premises:

1. Emilia showed shock when she was presented with clear proof that her husband was a villain.
2. If a woman shows shock when presented with clear proof that her husband is a villain, then previous to that she did not think him to be a villain.

Conclusion:

3. Previous to that point, Emilia did not think Iago to be a villain.

* Bradley, *op. cit.*, pp. 439–40.

The trouble is with the second premise. There are too many possible exceptions, as the following competing hypotheses show: Perhaps Emilia knew all along that Iago was a villain, but did not know that he had gone this far. Or perhaps she even knew about the lies about Desdemona, but was feigning ignorance, feeling that Iago was about to be found out and that she had better disattach herself from him. The easy deductive path to the thesis (Sentence 3 in Example 23-7) fails because it uses a false premise.

The comparison of the simplicity of Bradley's hypothesis with competing hypotheses would require a full detailing of all the accompanying assumptions used in the argument for each, which is a task that would take up too much room for this book. The specialist in *Othello* would profit from such an undertaking, however. I have not gone into the question of inconsistency of other hypotheses with the data. This too must be left for the specialist in *Othello*, for my purpose cannot be to present all the evidence and come up with an authoritative evaluation of Bradley's interpretation of Shakespeare. Rather, mine is the more modest purpose of showing by example a way to look at a particular argument.

The choice of Bradley's analysis of *Othello* was not accidental. I wanted to show that the criteria of explanatory proof apply in a very different area from the physical sciences, which are the usual source of examples. The earlier illustrative use of the Hissarlik case was also a step in this direction. The explanatory approach to material inference is found in all fields using material inference, although some fields characteristically have general explanatory hypotheses (for example, physics, agriculture, and sociology), some fields characteristically have specific explanatory hypotheses (for example, history and literature), and some fields have both (for example, geology, astronomy, and anthropology).

If the whole discussion of *Othello* (and in particular of Emilia's beliefs about her husband Iago) appears to be characterized by an air of make-believe, it is by no means accidental. Although it is only a play, written presumably by Shakespeare, with no attempt to secure an accurate depiction of a particular set of real life persons, this *Othello* example was chosen with that aspect specifically in mind. The explanatory approach to justification **can** be used in such cases assuming that the author of the work of fiction has presented a possible set of human beings. Actually the argument can get much more complicated by taking into account the characteristics of the author and the likelihood of his presenting certain types of characters. In actual discussions of Shakespeare (including Bradley's) these complications do enter in. In order to keep things fairly simple, I have left them out, though they, along with many other parts of Bradley's analysis, could have been included.

Thus, I hope to have indicated—either by consideration or by noting my deliberate neglect—the structure of an attempted explanatory justification in a field in which some of you might be surprised to find explanatory justifications. The treatment was somewhat oversimplified, and is not an authoritative evaluation. But, hopefully, the structure of part of the argument is laid bare, with the places where it is subject to attack made clear. If these purposes have been achieved, then as a result of reading the previous discussion, a teacher who has developed facility at assumption-finding, probing, defining, deducing, and explaining will be better able to organize his discussion, presentations, and even units of instruction around the structure of an explanatory justification, and will be able to deal with those problems of explanatory justification that arise spontaneously.

Brown vs. Board of Education (1954)

The Brown decision, which declared racial segregation illegal in the public schools, is well known to all, and variously praised and condemned. As you read through the following selection from the opinion which is offered as a justification of the decision, ask yourself what kind of justification is being offered, what are the starting points, what is inferred from what, and what relevant factors are not mentioned (paragraphs are numbered for later reference and footnotes are omitted):

Example 23-8

(1) These cases come to us from the States of Kansas, South Carolina, Virginia, and Delaware. They are premised on different facts and different local conditions, but a common legal question justifies their consideration together in this consolidated opinion.

(2) In each of the cases, minors of the Negro race, through their legal representatives, seek the aid of the courts in obtaining admission to the public schools of their community on a nonsegregated basis. In each instance, they had been denied admission to schools attended by white children under laws requiring or permitting segregation according to race. This segregation was alleged to deprive the plaintiffs of the equal protection of the laws under the Fourteenth Amendment. In each of the cases other than the Delaware case, a three-judge federal district court denied relief to the plaintiffs on the so-called "separate but equal" doctrine announced by this Court in *Plessy* v. *Ferguson*, 163 U.S. 537. Under that doctrine, equality of treatment is accorded when the races are provided substantially equal facilities, even though these facilities be separate. . . .

(3) The plaintiffs contend that segregated public schools are not "equal" and cannot be made "equal", and that hence they are deprived of the equal protection of the laws. Because of the obvious importance of the question presented, the Court took jurisdiction. Argument was heard in the 1952 Term, and reargument was heard this Term on certain questions propounded by the Court.

(4) Reargument was largely devoted to the circumstances surrounding the adoption of the Fourteenth Amendment in 1868. It covered exhaustively consid-

eration of the Amendment in Congress, ratification by the states, then existing practices in racial segregation, and the views of proponents and opponents of the Amendment. This discussion and our own investigation convince us that, although these sources cast some light, it is not enough to resolve the problem with which we are faced. At best, they are inconclusive. The most avid proponents of the post-War Amendments undoubtedly intended them to remove all legal distinctions among "all persons born or naturalized in the United States". Their opponents, just as certainly, were antagonistic to both the letter and the spirit of the Amendments and wished them to have the most limited effect. What others in Congress and the state legislatures had in mind cannot be determined with any degree of certainty.

(5) An additional reason for the inconclusive nature of the Amendment's history, with respect to segregated schools, is the status of public education at that time. In the South, the movement toward free common schools, supported by general taxation, had not yet taken hold. Education of white children was largely in the hands of private groups. Education of Negroes was almost nonexistent, and practically all of the race were illiterate. In fact, any education of Negroes was forbidden by law in some states. Today, in contrast, many Negroes have achieved outstanding success in the arts and sciences as well as in the business and professional world. It is true that public school education at the time of the Amendment had advanced further in the North, but the effect of the Amendment on Northern States was generally ignored in the congressional debates. Even in the North, the conditions of public education did not approximate those existing today. The curriculum was usually rudimentary; ungraded schools were common in rural areas; the school term was but three months a year in many states; and compulsory school attendance was virtually unknown. As a consequence, it is not surprising that there should be so little in the history of the Fourteenth Amendment relating to its intended effect on public education.

(6) In the first cases in this Court construing the Fourteenth Amendment, decided shortly after its adoption, the Court interpreted it as proscribing all state-imposed discriminations against the Negro race. The doctrine of "separate but equal" did not make its appearance in this Court until 1896 in the case of *Plessy* v. *Ferguson*, . . . involving not education but transportation. American courts have since labored with the doctrine for over half a century. In this Court, there have been six cases involving the "separate but equal" doctrine in the field of public education. In *Cumming* v. *County Board of Education*, 175 U.S. 528, and *Gong Lum* v. *Rice*, 275 U.S. 78, the validity of the doctrine itself was not challenged. In more recent cases, all on the graduate school level, inequality was found in that specific benefits enjoyed by white students were denied to Negro students of the same educational qualifications. *Missouri ex rel. Gaines* v. *Canada*, 305 U.S. 337; *Sipuel* v. *Oklahoma*, 332 U.S. 631; *Sweatt* v. *Painter*, 339 U.S. 629; *McLaurin* v. *Oklahoma State Regents*, 339 U.S. 637. In none of these cases was it necessary to reexamine the doctrine to grant relief to the Negro plaintiff. And in *Sweatt* v. *Painter*, . . . the Court expressly reserved decision on the question whether *Plessy* v. *Ferguson* should be held inapplicable to public education.

(7) In the instant cases, that question is directly presented. Here, unlike *Sweatt* v. *Painter*, there are findings below that the Negro and white schools involved

have been equalized, or are being equalized, with respect to buildings, curricula, qualifications and salaries of teachers, and other "tangible" factors. Our decision, therefore, cannot turn on merely a comparison of these tangible factors in the Negro and white schools involved in each of the cases. We must look instead to the effect of segregation itself on public education.

(8) In approaching this problem, we cannot turn the clock back to 1868 when the Amendment was adopted, or even to 1896 when *Plessy* v. *Ferguson* was written. We must consider public education in the light of its full development and its present place in American life throughout the Nation. Only in this way can it be determined if segregation in public schools deprives these plaintiffs of the equal protection of the laws.

(9) Today, education is perhaps the most important function of state and local governments. Compulsory school attendance laws and the great expenditures for education both demonstrate our recognition of the importance of education to our democratic society. It is required in the performance of our most basic public responsibilities, even service in the armed forces. It is the very foundation of good citizenship. Today, it is a principal instrument in awakening the child to cultural values, in preparing him for later professional training, and in helping him to adjust normally to his environment. In these days, it is doubtful that any child may reasonably be expected to succeed in life if he is denied the opportunity of an education. Such an opportunity, where the state has undertaken to provide it, is a right which must be made available to all on equal terms.

(10) We come then to the question presented: Does segregation of children in public schools solely on the basis of race, even though the physical facilities and other "tangible" factors may be equal, deprive the children of the minority group of equal educational opportunities? We believe that it does.

(11) In *Sweatt* v. *Painter*, in finding that a segregated law school for Negroes could not provide them equal educational opportunities, this Court relied in large part on "those qualities which are incapable of objective measurement but which make for greatness in a law school". In *McLaurin* v. *Oklahoma State Regents*, the Court, in requiring that a Negro admitted to a white graduate school be treated like all other students, again resorted to intangible considerations: "his ability to study, to engage in discussions and exchange views with other students, and, in general, to learn his profession". Such considerations apply with added force to children in grade and high schools. To separate them from others of similar age and qualifications solely because of their race generates a feeling of inferiority as to their status in the community that may affect their hearts and minds in a way unlikely ever to be undone. The effect of this separation on their educational opportunities was well stated by a finding in the Kansas case by a court which nevertheless felt compelled to rule against the Negro plaintiffs:

> Segregation of white and colored children in public schools has a detrimental effect upon the colored children. The impact is greater when it has the sanction of the law; for the policy of separating the races is usually interpreted as denoting the inferiority of the Negro group. A sense of inferiority affects the motivation of a child to learn. Segregation with sanction of law, therefore, has a tendency to [retard] the educational and mental development of Negro children and to deprive them of some of the benefits they would receive in a racial[ly] integrated school system.

Whatever may have been the extent of psychological knowledge at the time of *Plessy* v. *Ferguson*, this finding is amply supported by modern authority.* Any language in *Plessy* v. *Ferguson* contrary to this finding is rejected.

(12) We conclude that in the field of public education the doctrine of "separate but equal" has no place. Separate educational facilities are inherently unequal. Therefore, we hold that the plaintiffs and others similarly situated for whom the actions have been brought are, by reason of the segregation complained of, deprived of the equal protection of the laws guaranteed by the Fourteenth Amendment. This disposition makes unnecessary any discussion whether such segregation also violates the Due Process Clause of the Fourteenth Amendment.

In analyzing this opinion, we must assume that the Court, even though it considered many more aspects of the case, referred primarily to those considerations that it feels support the decision. This opinion is rendered in a political context. The decision has been made. The opinion tries to put the decision in as strong a position as possible.

On the surface one might think that all that the judges had to do was to keep the Constitution in mind and see whether the facts do show that the practice of segregation was in conflict with what the clearly written Constitution dictates. It might be thought parallel to the case of the pilot who is given clearance to taxi at La Guardia Airport, but is told to hold short of Runway 22. A clear directive has been given. The facts determine whether he followed the directive. If he crossed the runway without further clearance, then he disobeyed the directive. But the segregation case is not clear like that at all. The judgment about whether the practice of segregation is in violation of the Constitution is not one that can be made mechanically like the pilot case. The phrase, "hold short of Runway 22", has a fairly clear, agreed-on interpretation if the plane proceeds across the runway. This is not so with the phrase in Paragraph 8, "deprives these plaintiffs of equal protection of the laws", as applied to the cases under consideration. There is doubt and controversy about the interpretation of this phrase.**

To put it another way, intelligent people who understand the English language and the system of labeling runways could not sincerely disagree that a pilot who crossed Runway 22, after being given that directive, was in conflict with the directive. But intelligent people who understand the English language did and do disagree about whether the practice of segregation is in conflict with the wording of the Constitution.

In effect, the Supreme Court was called upon to provide a programmatic definition of the phrase, "equal protection of the laws". There is an existing rule in the Constitution requiring equal protection of the laws. Since the

* Here the court cites works of a number of people, including Kenneth Clark, Theodore Brameld, and Gunnar Myrdal.

** For a fascinating discussion of the Court's role in interpreting law and setting precedents, see Edward H. Levi, *An Introduction to Legal Reasoning* (Chicago: The University of Chicago Press, 1948).

assumption is that the Constitution must be obeyed, arguments presented to the Court were attempts to capture the application of the phrase for each of the favored views: segregation and prohibition of segregation. An **equivalence-form** programmatic definition was neither required of nor supplied by the Court, but a **partial** programmatic definition was supplied—one that was put in terms of this one kind of case: segregation in public education. The Court ruled that segregation is a nonexample of equal protection of the laws, according to the programmatic notion developed by the Court.

The opinion notes the difficulty of determining just what the people who voted for the Fourteenth Amendment meant by its wording (Paragraph 4), but suggests that the current situation makes such a determination somewhat irrelevant anyway ("we cannot turn the clock back"). At the time of the passage of the Fourteenth Amendment, education, it is claimed, was not nearly as important as it is now (Paragraphs 5 and 9). The inference is that the people making the original decision about the Fourteenth Amendment could not have had a relevant intention in the area of education, because such an intention would have been formed on the basis of experience that is different from **today's experience**.

In considering the case, the Court assumed for itself the burden of programmatically defining "equal protection of the laws" for today's situation. The Court, therefore, was committed to making a value judgment in the light of today's facts. Once the Court agreed to rule on the segregation issue, it was committed to making such a value judgment, because it was committed to come up with a programmatic interpretation of "equal protection of the laws". Its interpretation might have made segregation (where tangible facilities are the same) an example of equal protection of the laws, or it might have made segregation a nonexample. In either case a value judgement was being made.

The first line of defense for the announced value judgment is the mention of the principle (the Fourteenth Amendment) which the judgment actually interprets. But the basic defense consists of a consideration of the consequences of the alternative courses of action that were up for endorsement. At the end of Paragraph 7, we find: "We must look instead to the effect of segregation itself on public education." The effects to which the Court gave the greatest weight apparently are the "generation of a feeling of inferiority as to their status in the community that may affect their hearts and minds in a way unlikely ever to be undone", the retardation of the "educational and mental development of Negro children", and the deprivation of some of the benefits they would receive in a racially integrated school system (Paragraph 11). A number of people regarded by the court as authorities are cited to back up these psychological claims.

The Court has thereby provided support for its value judgment. This support, since the guiding principle did not automatically generate an answer, basically depended upon a citation of believed effects. The Court made no attempt to present both sides with equal strength, for if it had, it would have tried to cite other effects as well, some of them being detrimental ones resulting from the judgment made by the Court (conflict, riots, death, loss of positions by Negro school teachers). These things were predictable and presumably were predicted by the Court. I infer that the members either thought that these consequences of the decision would have occurred anyway, or that they were worth undergoing when balanced against the benefits of eliminating segregation, or both.

Thus the opinion offered by the Court in defense of the Brown decision is basically a value argument, but one which, because of the political situation which faces any court, presented one side only. I chose this example not only because of the impact that it has had, but because it illustrates the fact that value issues pervade many aspects of life. Difficult as it is to justify value judgments, we cannot hide from them. Classroom teachers face them all the time, not only in their decisions about the use of the influence they wield but in their subject matter as well. An understanding of their structure, even when they are hidden in such places as Supreme Court opinions, helps us to handle them in the classroom.

Chapter Summary

In this chapter you have seen two examples of attempted justifications that might appear in the material studied by some class. The specific and unique nature of examples makes it impossible to exemplify all aspects of the processes of justification. Furthermore, examples inevitably raise problems not covered by a general discussion. For instance, in the cases considered in this chapter two things were taken into account that were not even mentioned in the general discussions in the previous three chapters: the development of an explanatory hypothesis about the belief of a **fictional** character, and the embedding of a value judgment in a **legal** decision. So it must be. I can suggest some general strategy and principles; and I can point out the importance of context in the application of the strategy and principles. The rest is up to you.

COMPREHENSION SELF-TEST

Application. Do the following for one or more of the indicated arguments:

a. State the conclusion.
b. Classify the argument (for example, value argument, material inference to a generalization, material inference to an explanatory conclusion, and so forth).

c. List the starting points in the argument.
d. Describe the relation between the starting points and the conclusion.
e. To the extent that you are in a position to do so, state whether the argument justifies the conclusion, and tell why you judge as you do.

23–1. Sinclair Lewis' criticism of the type of person represented by Babbitt in the book, *Babbitt.*

23–2. Arthur Miller's criticism of Mr. Keller's business ethics in *All My Sons.*

23–3. Some argument from Sir Philip Sidney's *An Apologie for Poetrie.*

23–4. William L. Shirer's criticism of Hitler's Germany in *Berlin Diary.*

23–5. Some section of Sir Francis Bacon's *Novum Organum.*

23–6. Some section of Galileo's *Dialogues Concerning Two New Sciences.*

23–7. The second version of Lavoisier's attack on the phlogiston theory as described in "The Overthrow of the Phlogiston Theory", edited by James B. Conant (Case 2 of *Harvard Case Histories in Experimental Science*).

23–8. Pasteur's argument against the theory of spontaneous generation, as found in "Pasteur's and Tyndall's Study of Spontaneous Generation", edited by James B. Conant (Case 7 of *Harvard Case Histories in Experimental Science*).

23–9. Gregor Mendel's defense of his hypothesis about the ratio in the offspring of hybrids, as presented in "Experiments in Plant Hybridization" (available from Harvard University Press, 1950).

23–10. Frederick Jackson Turner's argument for his frontier thesis, as presented in his "The Significance of the Frontier in American History", in American Historical Association, *Annual Report for 1893* (Washington, D.C.: The Association, 1894), pp. 199–227.

23–11. Upton Sinclair's views about the Chicago stockyards, as expressed in *The Jungle.*

23–12. Aldous Huxley's *Brave New World.*

23–13. A. C. Bradley's analysis of Hamlet in *Shakespearean Tragedy.*

23–14. Ptolemy's proof of the parallel postulate, as described in Morris Cohen and Ernest Nagel, *An Introduction to Logic and the Scientific Method,* pp. 413–15.

23–15. Arthur Schlesinger, Jr.'s view, defended in *The Age of Jackson,* to the effect that Western influence on the Jacksonian government is less than has generally been supposed, and that many of its controlling beliefs and motives come rather from the East and South. (You might want to raise a question about the [⁘] testability of this thesis as stated.)

23–16. One or more of Alfred Thayer Mahan's (1897) theses, defended in *The Interest of America in Sea Power,* to the effect that:

a. America needs protection of her chief harbors by fortifications and coast-defense ships;
b. America needs an offensive naval force; and
c. No foreign state should acquire a coaling position within 3,000 miles of San Francisco.

23–17. Herodotus' attempted justification of his hypothesis about the flooding of the Nile:*

19. So said the oracle. Now the Nile, when it overflows, floods not only the Delta, but also the tracts of country on both sides [of] the stream which are thought to belong to Libya and Arabia, in some places reaching to the extent of two days' journey from its banks, in some even exceeding that distance, but in others falling short of it.

    Concerning the nature of the river, I was not able to gain any information either from the priests or from others. I was particularly anxious to learn from them why the Nile, at the commencement of the summer solstice, begins to rise, and continues to increase for a hundred days—and why, as soon as that number is past, it forthwith retires and contracts its stream, continuing low during the whole of the winter until the summer solstice comes round again. On none of these points could I obtain any explanation from the inhabitants, though I made every inquiry, wishing to know what was commonly reported—they could neither tell me what special virtue the Nile has which makes it so opposite in its nature to all other streams, nor why, unlike every other river, it gives forth no breezes from its surface.

20. Some of the Greeks, however, wishing to get a reputation for cleverness, have offered explanations of the phenomena of the river, for which they have accounted in three different ways. Two of these I do not think it worth while to speak of, further than simply to mention what they are. One pretends that the Etesian winds cause the rise of the river by preventing the Nile-water from running off into the sea. But in the first place it has often happened, when the Etesian winds did not blow, that the Nile has risen according to its usual wont; and further, if the Etesian winds produced the effect, the other rivers which flow in a direction opposite to those winds ought to present the same phenomena as the Nile, and the more so as they are all smaller streams, and have a weaker current. But these rivers, of which there are many both in Syria and Libya, are entirely unlike the Nile in this respect.

21. The second opinion is even more unscientific than the one just mentioned, and also, if I may so say, more marvellous. It is that the Nile acts so strangely, because it flows from the ocean, and that the ocean flows all round the earth.

22. The third explanation, which is very much more plausible than either of

* Herodotus, *History* . . . , George Rawlinson, ed., Vol. II (London: J. Murray, 1858–60), pp. 28–36 (footnotes omitted).

This example was suggested to me by its appearance in a set of interesting examples collected by Russell Kahl in his *Studies in Explanation* (Englewood Cliffs, N. J.: Prentice-Hall, Inc., 1963). The analysis of any of this collection of examples, which are selected from physics, biology, psychology, sociology, and history, would be of value to you and might well be of use in your classes.

the others, is positively the furthest from the truth; for there is really nothing in what it says, any more than in the other theories. It is, that the inundation of the Nile is caused by the melting of snows. Now, as the Nile flows out of Libya, through Ethiopia, into Egypt, how is it possible that it can be formed of melted snow, running, as it does, from the hottest regions of the world into cooler countries? Many are the proofs whereby any one capable of reasoning on the subject may be convinced that it is most unlikely this should be the case. The first and strongest argument is furnished by the winds, which always blow hot from these regions. The second is, that rain and frost are unknown there. Now, whenever snow falls, it must of necessity rain within five days; so that, if there were snow, there must be rain also in those parts. Thirdly, it is certain that the natives of the country are black with the heat, that the kites and the swallows remain there the whole year, and that the cranes, when they fly from the rigours of a Scythian winter, flock thither to pass the cold season. If then, in the country whence the Nile has its source, or in that through which it flows, there fell ever so little snow, it is absolutely impossible that any of these circumstances could take place.

23. As for the writer who attributes the phenomenon to the ocean, his account is involved in such obscurity, that it is impossible to disprove it by argument. For my part I know of no river called Ocean, and I think that Homer, or one of the earlier poets, invented the name, and introduced it into his poetry.

24. Perhaps, after censuring all the opinions that have been put forward on this obscure subject, one ought to propose some theory of one's own. I will therefore proceed to explain what I think to be the reason of the Nile's swelling in the summer time. During the winter, the sun is driven out of his usual course by the storms, and removes to the upper parts of Libya. This is the whole secret in the fewest possible words; for it stands to reason that the country to which the Sun-god approaches the nearest, and which he passes most directly over, will be scantest of water, and that there the streams which feed the rivers will shrink the most.

25. To explain, however, more at length, the case is this. The sun, in his passage across the upper parts of Libya, affects them in the following way. As the air in those regions is constantly clear, and the country warm through the absence of cold winds, the sun in his passage across them acts upon them exactly as he is wont to act elsewhere in summer, when his path is in the middle of heaven—that is, he attracts the water. After attracting it, he again repels it into the upper regions, where the winds lay hold of it, scatter it, and reduce it to a vapour, whence it naturally enough comes to pass that the winds which blow from this quarter—the south and south-west—are of all winds the most rainy. And my opinion is that the sun does not get rid of all the water which he draws year by year from the Nile, but retains some about him. When the winter begins to soften, the sun goes back again to his old place in the middle of the heaven, and proceeds to attract water equally from all countries. Till

then the other rivers run big, from the quantity of rain-water which they bring down from countries where so much moisture falls that all the land is cut into gullies; but in summer, when the showers fail, and the sun attracts their water, they become low. The Nile, on the contrary, not deriving any of its bulk from rains, and being in winter subject to the attraction of the sun, naturally runs at that season, unlike all other streams, with a less burthen of water than in the summer time. For in summer it is exposed to attraction equally with all other rivers, but in winter it suffers alone. The sun, therefore, I regard as the sole cause of the phenomenon.

26. It is the sun, also, in my opinion, which, by heating the space through which it passes, makes the air in Egypt so dry. There is thus perpetual summer in the upper parts of Libya. Were the position of the heavenly regions reversed, so that the place where now the north wind and the winter have their dwelling became the station of the south wind and of the noonday, while, on the other hand, the station of the south wind became that of the north, the consequence would be that the sun, driven from the mid-heaven by the winter and the northern gales, would betake himself to the upper parts of Europe, as he now does to those of Libya, and then I believe his passage across Europe would affect the Ister exactly as the Nile is affected at the present day.
27. And with respect to the fact that no breeze blows from the Nile, I am of [the] opinion that no wind is likely to arise in very hot countries, for breezes love to blow from some cold quarter.

Suggested Further Reading about Justification

Observation

Black, Max. *Critical Thinking.* Englewood Cliffs, N.J.: Prentice-Hall, Inc., 1952, especially chap. xviii.

Cohen, Morris and Ernest Nagel. *An Introduction to Logic and Scientific Method.* New York: Harcourt Brace and Company, 1934, especially chap. *XI*, no. 5.

Gottschalk, Louis. *Understanding History.* New York: Alfred A. Knopf, 1951.

Hanson, Norwood Russell. "Observation and Interpretation," in Sidney Morgenbesser, ed., *Philosophy of Science Today.* New York: Basic Books, Inc., 1967, pp. 89–100.

Hume, David. *An Enquiry Concerning Human Understanding.* LaSalle, Illinois: The Open Court Publishing Company, 1907 (from a posthumous edition of 1777), especially Section II.

Lerner, Daniel. *Evidence and Inference.* New York: The Free Press of Glencoe, Inc., 1959.

Wigmore, John Henry. *A Students' Textbook of the Laws of Evidence.* Brooklyn: The Foundation Press, 1935.

Authority

Black, Max. *Critical Thinking*. Englewood Cliffs, N. J.: Prentice-Hall, Inc., 1952, especially chap. xiii, no.3.

Cohen, Morris and Ernest Nagel. *An Introduction to Logic and Scientific Method.* New York: Harcourt Brace and Company, 1934, especially chap. *X*.

Wigmore, John Henry. *A Students' Textbook of the Laws of Evidence.* Brooklyn: The Foundation Press, 1935.

Assumptions

Black, Max. *Critical Thinking*. Englewood Cliffs, N. J.: Prentice-Hall, Inc., 1952, various sections.

Ennis, Robert H. "Assumption-Finding," in B. O. Smith and Robert H. Ennis, eds., *Language and Concepts in Education.* Chicago: Rand McNally & Co., 1961, pp. 161–78.

Strawson, P. F. *Introduction to Logical Theory.* London: Methuen & Co. Ltd., 1952, especially chap. vi, no. 7.

Value judgments

Aristotle. *Nichomachaen Ethics.*

Brandt, Richard B., ed. *Value and Obligation: Systematic Readings in Ethics.* New York: Harcourt, Brace & World, Inc., 1961.

Hare, R. M. *The Language of Morals.* Oxford: At The Clarendon Press, 1952.

Melden, A. I., ed. *Ethical Theories: A Book of Readings.* Englewood Cliffs, N. J.: Prentice-Hall, Inc., 1950.

Moore, George Edward. *Principia Ethica.* Cambridge, England: The University Press, 1954 (original edition, 1903).

Stevenson, Charles L. *Ethics and Language.* New Haven: Yale University Press, 1944.

Sumner, William G. *Folkways.* Boston: Ginn and Company, 1940.

Westermarck, Edward. *The Origin and Development of the Moral Ideas.* London: Macmillan and Co., Ltd., 1906.

Material inference: broad introductory treatments

Beardsley, Monroe C. *Practical Logic.* New York: Prentice-Hall, Inc., 1950.

Black, Max. *Critical Thinking.* Englewood Cliffs, N. J.: Prentice-Hall, Inc., 1952.

Cohen, Morris R. and Ernest Nagel. *An Introduction to Logic and Scientific Method.* New York: Harcourt, Brace and Company, 1934.

Ennis, Robert H. "A Concept of Critical Thinking", *Harvard Educational Review,* Vol. XXXII, no. 1 (1962), pp. 81–111.

Hempel, Carl G. *Philosophy of Natural Science*. Englewood Cliffs, N. J.: Prentice-Hall, Inc., 1966.

Rudner, Richard S. *Philosophy of Social Science*. Englewood Cliffs, N. J.: Prentice-Hall, Inc., 1966.

Salmon, Wesley C. *Logic*. Englewood Cliffs, N. J.: Prentice-Hall, Inc., 1963.

Material inference: generalizations

Barker, S. F. *Induction and Hypothesis*. Ithaca, N.Y.: Cornell University Press, 1957.

Black, Max. "The Raison D'Etre of Inductive Argument," *British Journal for the Philosophy of Science*, Vol. XVII, no. 3 (1966), pp. 177–204.

Ennis, Robert H. "Enumerative Induction and Best Explanation," *Journal of Philosophy*, Vol. LXV, No. 18, pp. 523–29.

Harman, Gilbert H. "The Inference to the Best Explanation," *The Philosophical Review*, Vol. LXXIV, no. 1 (1965), pp. 88–95.

McCarthy, Philip J. *Sampling: Elementary Principles*, Bulletin No. 15. Ithaca, N.Y.: New York State School of Industrial and Labor Relations, Cornell Univ., 1951.

Salmon, Wesley C. *Foundations of Scientific Inference*. Pittsburgh: University of Pittsburgh Press, 1966.

Will, Frederick L. "Consequences and Confirmation," *The Philosophical Review*, Vol. LXXV, no. 1 (1966), pp. 34–58.

———. "Generalization and Evidence," in Max Black, ed., *Philosophical Analysis: A Collection of Essays*. Ithaca, N. Y.: Cornell University Press, 1950, pp. 384–413.

———. "Will the Future Be Like the Past?" in A. H. N. Flew, ed., *Logic and Language* (Second Series). New York: Philosophical Library, 1953, pp. 32–50.

Material inference: explanatory hypotheses

Black, Max. *Critical Thinking*. Englewood Cliffs, N. J.: Prentice-Hall, Inc., 1952.

Braithwaite, Richard Bevan. *Scientific Explanation*. Cambridge, Mass.: At the University Press, 1955.

Cohen, Morris R. and Ernest Nagel. *An Introduction to Logic and Scientific Method*. New York: Harcourt, Brace and Company, 1934.

Crane, Ronald S. *The Idea of the Humanities*. Chicago: University of Chicago Press, 1967.

Hempel, Carl G. *Aspects of Scientific Explanation*. New York: The Free Press of Glencoe, Inc., 1965.

Hirsch, Eric D., Jr. *Validity in Interpretation*. New Haven: Yale University Press, 1967.

Kaplan, Abraham. *The Conduct of Inquiry*. San Francisco: Chandler Publishing Company, 1964.

Nagel, Ernest. *The Structure of Science*. New York: Harcourt, Brace & World, Inc., 1961.

Toulmin, Stephen. *The Philosophy of Science*. London: Hutchinson University Library, 1953.

Conceptual statements

Donnellan, Keith S. "Necessity and Criteria," *The Journal of Philosophy*, Vol. LIX, no. 22 (October 1962), pp. 647–58.

Grice, H. P. "Utterer's Meaning and Intention," *The Philosophical Review*, Vol. 78, No. 2 (April, 1969), pp. 147-77.

Grice, H. P. and P. F. Strawson. "In Defense of a Dogma," *The Philosophical Review*, Vol. LXV, No. 2 (April 1956), pp. 141–58.

Hospers, John. *An Introduction to Philosophical Analysis*. Englewood Cliffs, N. J.: Prentice-Hall, Inc., 1967.

Putnam, Hilary. "The Analytic and the Synthetic," in Herbert Feigl and Grover Maxwell, eds., *Minnesota Studies in the Philosophy of Science*, Vol. III. Minneapolis: University of Minnesota Press, 1962, pp. 358–97.

Quine, Willard Van Orman. "Two Dogmas of Empiricism," in his *From a Logical Point of View*. Cambridge, Mass.: Harvard University Press, 1961, pp. 20–46.

Whorf, Benjamin Lee. *Language, Thought, and Reality*. Massachusetts: The Massachusetts Institute of Technology Press, 1956.

Causation

Gasking, Douglas. "Causation and Recipes," *Mind*, Vol. LXIV, No. 256 (October 1955), pp. 479–87.

Hart, H. L. A., and A. M. Honoré. *Causation in the Law*. Oxford: University Press, 1959, pp. 8–55 (Chapters 1 and 2).

Hume, David. *An Enquiry Concerning Human Understanding*. La Salle, Illinois: The Open Court Publishing Company, 1907 (from a posthumous edition of 1777), pp. 76–81.

Mill, John Stuart. *A System of Logic*, Vol. 1. London: Longmans, Green, and Co., 1879, 10th ed., pp. 376–86, 388–94.

Russell, Bertrand. "On the Notion of Cause," in his *Mysticism and Logic*. Garden City, N.Y.: Doubleday & Company, Inc., 1957 (first published in 1917), pp. 174–201.

APPENDIX A

Selected Reading about the Logical Aspects of Teaching

Anderson, Howard, ed. *Teaching Critical Thinking in the Social Studies,* Thirteenth Yearbook. Washington, D.C.:The National Council for the Social Studies, 1942.

Austin, Frances M. *The Art of Questioning in the Classroom.* London: University of London Press Ltd., 1963.

Bellack, Arno A., ed. *Theory and Research in Teaching.* New York: Bureau of Publications, Teachers College, Columbia University, 1963.

Black, Max, ed. *The Importance of Language.* Englewood Cliffs, N. J.: Prentice-Hall, Inc., 1962.

Broudy, Harry S. and John R. Palmer. *Exemplars of Teaching Method.* Chicago: Rand McNally & Co., 1965.

Broudy, Harry S., B. Othanel Smith, and Joe R. Burnett. *Democracy and Excellence in American Secondary Education.* Chicago: Rand McNally & Co., 1963.

Bruner, Jerome S. *The Process of Education.* New York: Random House Inc., 1960.

Cronbach, Lee J., ed. *Text Materials in Modern Education.* Urbana, Illinois: University of Illinois Press, 1955.

Dewey, John. *How We Think.* Boston: D. C. Heath and Company, 1933.

Dressel, Paul L. and Lewis B. Mayhew. *Science Reasoning and Understanding.* Dubuque, Iowa: Wm. C. Brown Company, 1954.

Elam, Stanley, ed. *Education and the Structure of Knowledge.* Chicago: Rand McNally and Co., 1964.

Feldman, Martin and Eli Seifman, eds., *The Social Studies: Structure, Models, and Strategies.* Englewood Cliffs, N. J.: Prentice-Hall, Inc., 1969.

Ford, G. W. and Lawrence Pugno, eds. *The Structure of Knowledge and the Curriculum.* Chicago: Rand McNally & Co., 1964.

Greene, Theodore M. "The Art of Responsible Conversation," *The Journal of General Education,* Vol. VIII, no. 1 (Oct. 1954), pp. 34–50.

Hamlyn, D. W. "The Logical and Psychological Aspects of Learning," in R. S. Peters, ed., *The Concept of Education.* New York: Humanities Press, Inc., 1967, pp. 24–43.

Henderson, Kenneth B. "A Logical Model for Conceptualizing and Other Related Activities," in B. Paul Komisar and C. J. B. Macmillan, eds., *Psychological Concepts in Education.* Chicago: Rand McNally & Co., 1967, pp. 96–105.

———. "Training in Linguistic Analysis in Teacher Education Curricula," in *The American Association of Colleges for Teacher Education,* Ninth Yearbook. Chicago, Illinois: The Assn., 1956, pp. 64–74.

———. "Unusual Departures in Teacher Education: A Course in Principles of Secondary Education," *Improving Instruction in Professional Education,* Thirty-Seventh Yearbook. Dubuque, Iowa: Wm. C. Brown Company, 1958, pp. 67–82.

———. "Uses of 'Subject Matter'," in B. Othanel Smith and Robert H. Ennis, eds., *Language and Concepts in Education.* Chicago: Rand McNally & Co., 1961, pp. 43–58.

Hirst, Paul H. "The Logical and Psychological Aspects of Teaching a Subject," in R. S. Peters, ed., *The Concept of Education.* New York: Humanities Press, Inc., 1967, pp. 44–60.

Hullfish, H. Gordon and Philip G. Smith. *Reflective Thinking: The Method of Education.* New York: Dodd, Mead & Company, 1961.

McClellan, James E. "The Logical and the Psychological: An Untenable Dualism?" in B. Othanel Smith and Robert H. Ennis, eds., *Language and Concepts in Education.* Chicago: Rand McNally & Co., 1961, pp. 144–60.

Martin, Harold C. and Richard M. Ohmann. *The Logic and Rhetoric of Exposition.* New York: Holt, Rinehart & Winston, Inc., 1964.

Meux, Milton and B. Othanel Smith. "Logical Dimensions of Teaching Behavior," in Bruce J. Biddle and William J. Ellena, eds., *Contemporary Research on Teacher Effectiveness.* New York: Holt, Rinehart & Winston, Inc., 1964, pp. 127–64.

Richards, I. A. *How to Read a Page.* Boston: Beacon Press, 1942.

———. *Interpretation in Teaching.* New York: Harcourt, Brace and Company, 1938.

Sanders, Norris M. *Classroom Questions: What Kinds?* New York: Harper and Row, 1966.

Smith, B. Othanel. "Logic, Thinking and Teaching," *Educational Theory,* Vol. VII, no. 4 (October 1957), pp. 225–33.

———. "New Approaches to Pedagogical Science," *Educational Theory,* Vol. I, no. 2 (August, 1951), pp. 79–86.

———. "The Logic of Teaching in the Arts," *Teachers College Record,* Vol. LXIII, no. 3 (1961), pp. 176–83.

———. "The Need for Logic in Method Courses," *Theory Into Practice,* Vol. III, no. 1 (1964), pp. 5–8.

Smith, B. Othanel and Milton O. Meux. *A Study of the Logic of Teaching.* [Cooperative Research Project No. 258 (7257)]. Urbana, Illinois: Bureau of Educational Research, College of Education, no date.

Smith, B. Othanel, *et al. A Study of the Strategies of Teaching.* Urbana, Illinois: Bureau of Educational Research, 1967.

Taylor, George Rogers. "Teaching the Art of Decision-Making," *The Journal of General Education,* Vol. VIII, no. 4 (July 1955), pp. 254–60.

APPENDIX B

Selected Texts from which Students Might Study about Clear and Critical Thinking

These books are arranged roughly in order of increasing difficulty.

Shanner, William. *A Guide to Logical Thinking.* Chicago: Science Research Associates, Inc., 1954.

Marriott, J. W. *Exercises in Thinking and Expressing.* New York: Harcourt, Brace and Company, 1925.

Emmet, E. R. *The Use of Reason.* London: Longmans, Green and Co. Ltd., 1960.

Organ, Troy Wilson. *The Art of Critical Thinking.* Boston: Houghton Mifflin Company, 1965.

Fearnside, W. Ward and William B. Holther. *Fallacy: The Counterfeit of Argument.* Englewood Cliffs, N. J.: Prentice-Hall, Inc., 1959.

Ennis, Robert H. *Ordinary Logic.* Englewood Cliffs, N. J.: Prentice-Hall, Inc., 1969.*

Little, Winston W., W. Harold Wilson, and W. Edgar Moore. *Applied Logic.* Boston: Houghton Mifflin Company, 1952.

*This book is essentially the first part of *Logic in Teaching.*

Carre, M. H. *Does It Follow?* London: Thomas Nelson and Sons Ltd., 1944.

Black, Max. *Critical Thinking.* Englewood Cliffs, N. J.: Prentice-Hall, Inc., 1952.

Beardsley, Monroe C. *Practical Logic.* New York: Prentice-Hall, Inc., 1950.

Stebbing, L. Susan. *Thinking to Some Purpose.* Great Britain: The Whitefriars Press Ltd., 1939.

Salmon, Wesley C. *Logic.* Englewood Cliffs, N. J.: Prentice-Hall, Inc., 1963.

Cohen, Morris R. and Ernest Nagel. *An Introduction to Logic and Scientific Method.* New York: Harcourt, Brace and Company, 1934.

Crawshay-Williams, Rupert. *Methods and Criteria of Reasoning.* London: Routledge & Kegan Paul, Ltd., 1957.

Answers

Assuming that you check the answers only after doing the exercises, the following set of answers can be helpful. Several qualifications and limitations to the use of these answers are in order:

1. Answers to the true-false questions are occasionally debatable. (Differences in the interpretation of some questions sometimes call for answers different from those given.) Make sure you understand whether your answer differs from the one I have suggested as a result of interpretation of the question, or for some other reason.
2. Although you are asked in the exercises to convert false statements into true ones by rewriting, I have not done so here because of the numerous ways of going about it. You can generally judge for yourself whether you have made the appropriate changes.
3. The particular method you use in solving logic problems might well differ from the one offered. Do not automatically abandon yours just because it is different from the method suggested. Yours may well be correct—there are frequently various routes to the solution of logic problems.
4. Since there is often room for differing interpretations of the sentences in the logic exercises, the fact that your judgment about validity differs from that given does not necessarily imply that yours is wrong. However, think very carefully about it before accepting a validity judgment that differs from the one suggested here.

Chapter 2: "Basic Ideas"

2–1. T **2–2.** F **2–3.** F

2–4. Valid argument, true premises, and false conclusion.

Chapter 3: "Sentence Reasoning"

3–1. If Mike is a dog, then Mike is an animal.

3–2. Mike is an animal, if Mike is a dog.

3–3. If Mary knows the rules of punctuation, then she did well on the test today.

3–4. If John is nearsighted, his eyes are defective.

3–5. John's eyes are defective, if he is nearsighted.

3–6. If in that sentence the word 'going' is a gerund, then it functions like a noun.

3–7. Mike, if he is a dog, is an animal.

3–8. The soil in your field is sweet, if Jones added the truckload of calcium carbonate to it.

3–9. If the President is not going to veto this bill, the Senate will not stand by him in his efforts to get his tax legislation passed.

3–10. Angles *A* and *B*, if they are alternate interior angles of parallel lines, are equal.

3–11. Joan's room has light-colored walls, if it is well lighted.

3–12. If the music room does not have light-colored walls, then it is not well lighted.

3–13. The livingroom, if Mrs. Smith likes it, is well lighted.

3–14. Denying the consequent. Valid.
3–15. Affirming the consequent. Invalid.
3–16. Affirming the antecedent. Valid.
3–17. Denying the consequent. Valid.
3–18. Affirming the consequent. Invalid.
3–19. Affirming the antecedent. Valid.
3–20. Denying the antecedent. Invalid.
3–21. Joan's room has light-colored walls. Affirming the antecedent (AA).
3–22. Nothing follows necessarily. DA.
3–23. It has light-colored walls. AA.
3–24. The sewing room does not have light-colored walls. DC.
3–25. The kitchen is not well lighted. AA.
3–26. My new office does not have dark-colored walls. DC.

3–27. The music room has light-colored walls. DC.

3–28. The livingroom does not have dark-colored walls. AA; then DC. (Note: An intermediate conclusion [The livingroom is well lighted.] is reached by AA. This conclusion is used as a premise to reach the final conclusion by DC.)

3–29. F **3–30.** T **3–31.** T **3–32.** F

3–33. Converse: If Mike is an animal, then Mike is a dog.
Contrapositive: If Mike is not an animal, then Mike is not a dog.

3–34. Same as 3–33.

3–35. Converse: If Mary did well on the test today, then she knows the rules of punctuation.
Contrapositive: If Mary did not do well on the test today, then she does not know the rules of punctuation.

3–36. Converse: If John's eyes are defective, then he is nearsighted.
Contrapositive: If John's eyes are not defective, then he is not nearsighted.

3–37. Same as 3–36.

3–38. Converse: If it functions like a noun, then the word 'going' in that sentence is a gerund.
Contrapositive: If it does not function like a noun, then the word 'going' in that sentence is not a gerund.

3–39. Same as 3–33.

3–40. Converse: If the soil in your field is sweet, then Jones added the truckload of calcium carbonate to it.
Contrapositive: If the soil in your field is not sweet, then Jones did not add the truckload of calcium carbonate to it.

3–41. Converse: If the Senate will not stand by him in his efforts to get his tax legislation passed, then the President is not going to veto the bill.
Contrapositive: If the Senate will stand by him in his efforts to get his tax legislation passed, then the President is going to veto the bill.

3–42. Converse: If angles A and B are equal, then they are alternate interior angles of parallel lines.
Contrapositive: If angles A and B are not equal, then they are not alternate interior angles of parallel lines.

3–43. Converse: If Joan's room has light-colored walls, then it is well lighted.
Contrapositive: If Joan's room does not have light-colored walls, then it is not well lighted.

3–44. Converse: If the music room is not well lighted, then it does not have light-colored walls.
Contrapositive: If the music room is well lighted, then it has light-colored walls.

3–45. Converse: If the livingroom is well lighted, then Mrs. Smith likes it.
Contrapositive: If the livingroom is not well lighted, then Mrs. Smith does not like it.

3–46. Valid. Contraposition.

3–47. Invalid. Conversion.

3–48. Valid. Double negation and AA. (Note: The principle of double negation is used to convert the second premise to an affirmed antecedent of the first premise.)

3–49. Invalid. AC.

3–50. Valid. DC.

3–51. Valid. AA.

3–52. Invalid. DA.

3–53. Valid. Contraposition.

3–54. Invalid. Conversion.

3–55. Valid. Contraposition.

3–56. Invalid. Conversion (of the contrapositive).

3–57. T **3–58.** F **3–59.** T **3–60.** T **3–61.** F

3–62. Worked as an example.

3–63. Let 'p' = 'Jones is President'
Let 'q' = 'Jones must be at least thirty-five years of age'
Premises:
$p \longrightarrow q$
p
Conclusion:
q
Valid. AA.

3–64. Let 'p' = 'This figure is an equilateral triangle'
Let 'q' = 'It has all sides equal'
Premises:
$p \longrightarrow q$
not q
Conclusion:
not p
Valid. DC.

3–65. Let 'p' = 'These two plants are not closely related'
Let 'q' = 'They can not be crossed'
Premises:
$p \longrightarrow q$
not p
Conclusion:
not q
Invalid. DA.

3–66. Let 'p' = 'There is no light reaching it'
Let 'q' = 'Photosynthesis can not occur in this plant'
Premises:
$p \longrightarrow q$
p

Conclusion:

q

Valid. AA.

3–67. Let 'p' = 'Great Birnam wood to high Dunsinane hill shall come against him'
Let 'q' = 'Macbeth shall be vanquished'
Premises:

not $p \longrightarrow$ not q
not p

Conclusion:

not q

Valid. AA.

3–68. Let 'p' = 'The beacon is lit'
Let 'q' = 'You may not fly'
Premises:

$p \longrightarrow q$
not p

Conclusion:

not q

Invalid. DA.

3–69. Let 'p' = 'Senator Franklin will oppose the tax legislation'
Let 'q' = 'Senator Inkling will vote in favor of it'
Let 'r' = 'My wife will be busy trying to . . . to help defeat him at the polls'
Let 's' = 'Dinners will not be very good around here for a while'

Part 1:

Premises:

p
$p \longrightarrow q$

Conclusion:

q

Valid. AA.

Part 2:

Premises:

q (from Part 1)
$q \longrightarrow r$

Conclusion:

r

Valid. AA.

Part 3:

Premises:

r (from Part 2)
$r \longrightarrow s$

Conclusion:

s

Valid. AA.

(I am willing to assume that 's' is essentially the same as the conclusion announced in the last sentence. Are you? If this is acceptable, the total argument is valid.)

3–70. Let 'p' = 'The Board of Education suspends young Brown from school'
Let 'q' = 'It will be punishing him for refusing to salute the flag on religious grounds'
Let 'r' = 'It will be acting unconstitutionally'
Part 1:
Premises:
not r
$q \longrightarrow r$
Conclusion:
not q
Valid DC.
Part 2:
Premises:
not q (from Part 1)
$p \longrightarrow q$
Conclusion:
not p
Valid. DC.
Hence the total argument is valid.

3–71. Antecedent.
3–72. $p \longrightarrow q$.
3–73. q.
3–74. Valid.
3–75. Consequent.
3–76. Not q.
3–77. Not p.
3–78. Affirming.
3–79. Consequent.
3–80. p.*
3–81. Invalid.
3–82. Denying.**
3–83. Antecedent.
3–84. Not p.
3–85. Nothing.
3–86. Invalid.

3–87. T **3–88.** T **3–89.** F **3–90.** T **3–91.** F
3–92. T **3–93.** F **3–94.** T **3–95.** T

3–96. Let 'p' = 'Your report is satisfactory'
Let 'q' = 'every word is spelled correctly'
Premises:
$p \longrightarrow q$
not p
Conclusion:
not q
Invalid. DA.

3–97. Let 'p' = 'triangles A and B are congruent'
Let 'q' = 'they have two angles and the included side equal'
Premises:
$p \longleftrightarrow q$
not p

* Note that as the question calls for argument forms, one must in answering give a conclusion, so that the argument can be properly termed invalid.

** The question asks for the **four** basic forms of conditional argument. As you have already given three of these forms, the fourth is called for.

Conclusion:

not q

Valid. Biconditional yields '$q \longrightarrow p$'. DC.

3–98. Let 'p' = 'the lighting in the livingroom is not indirect'
Let 'q' = 'it is not satisfactory'
Let 'r' = 'Mrs. Smith will not like it'

Premises:

$p \longrightarrow q$
$q \longrightarrow r$

Conclusion:

$p \longrightarrow r$

Valid. Conditional chain.

3–99. Let 'p' = 'Shakespeare had intended Polonius to be a comic figure'
Let 'q' = 'he would not have made Polonius the father of two tragic characters'

Premises:

$p \longrightarrow q$
not q

Conclusion:

not p

Valid. DC.

3–100. Let 'p' = 'Governor Jones signed the letter'
Let 'q' = 'serious damage to his chances for the Vice-Presidency was permitted by his advisers'
Let 'r' = 'they did not really want him to be candidate for the Vice-Presidency'

Premises:

$p \longrightarrow q$
$q \longrightarrow r$

Conclusion:

$p \longrightarrow r$

Valid. Conditional chain.

3–101. Let 'p' = 'the ceiling is not one thousand feet or above'
Let 'q' = 'you may not fly'
Let 'r' = 'the sequence report reads less than "10"'

Premises:

$p \longrightarrow q$
$r \longleftrightarrow p$
not r

Intermediate conclusion:

not p

Valid. Biconditional yields '$p \longrightarrow r$'. DC.

Final conclusion:

not q

Invalid. DA.

Note that 3–101 was broken up into parts in a different way from that used in 3–69 and 3–70. This variation illustrates the fact that various equally satisfactory ways can be used to analyze an argument, especially a complex one.

3–102. Let 'p' = 'he spells words as they sound to him'
Let 'q' = 'he spells "trough" as "troff"'
Let 'r' = 'he spells "didn't" as "ding"'
Premises:

$q \longrightarrow p$
$p \longrightarrow r$
not q
r

Conclusion:

p

Invalid. DA or AC.

3–103. Let 'p' = 'plants X and Y can be crossed'
Let 'q' = 'they are closely related'
Let 'r' = 'their immediate parents have produced hybrids in the past'
Premises:

$p \longrightarrow q$
$r \longrightarrow$ not p
not r

Conclusion:

q

Invalid. DA. (Note: The attempt to arrive at an intermediate conclusion, p, and then to try to derive the secondary conclusion, q, would not succeed, since the denial of r is the denial of an antecedent.)

3–104. p is sufficient for q. (or q is necessary for p) (3–96)

3–105. p is necessary and sufficient for q. (or q is necessary and sufficient for p) (3–97)

3–106. p is sufficient for q. (or q is necessary for p) (3–98)
q is sufficient for r. (or r is necessary for q)
p is sufficient for r. (or r is necessary for p)

3–107. p is sufficient for q. (or q is necessary for p) (3–99)

3–108. p is sufficient for q. (or q is necessary for p) (3–100)
q is sufficient for r. (or r is necessary for q)
p is sufficient for r. (or r is necessary for p)

3–109. p is sufficient for q. (or q is necessary for p) (3–101)
r is necessary and sufficient for p. (or p is necessary and sufficient for r)

3–110. q is sufficient for p. (or p is necessary for q) (3–102)
p is sufficient for r. (or r is necessary for p)

3–111. p is sufficient for q. (or q is necessary for p) (3–103)
r is sufficient for the falsity of p. (or the falsity of p is necessary for r)

3–112. T **3–113.** T **3–114.** T **3–115.** F **3–116.** T **3–117.** T

3–118. Let 'p' = 'this piece of cloth is warm'
Let 'q' = 'it is only 50 per cent wool'
p and q

3–119. Same symbolization as 3–118.
p and q

3–120. Let 'p' = 'Thomas Jefferson was a scholar'
Let 'q' = 'he was a gentleman'
Let 'r' = 'he was an astute politician'
p and q and r

3–121. Let 'p' = 'there will be rain within the week'
Let 'q' = 'the crops will be ruined'
p or q

3–122. Let 'p' = 'the two colors that you select will match'
Let 'q' = 'the room will be ugly'
p or q

3–123. Let 'p' = 'that figure is a square'
Let 'q' = 'it does not have four sides'
p or q (Even though the content justifies strong alternation. In some contexts 'p (or) q' would be an acceptable interpretation.)

3–124. Let 'p' = 'there is now a rainbow'
Let 'q' = 'there is now a completely overcast sky'
Not both p and q

3–125. Let 'p' = 'Abraham Lincoln thought that his Gettysburg Address was reverently received'
Let 'q' = 'he thought it was a failure'
p or q

3–126. Let 'p' = '*Alice in Wonderland* is a book for children'
Let 'q' = 'it is also a book for adults'
p and q

3–127. Let 'p' = 'Hamlet was in doubt of the guilt of his uncle'
Let 'q' = 'Hamlet was convinced that he had actually spoken to his father's ghost'
not both p and q

3–128. If there is not rain within the week, the crops will be ruined.

3–129. If the two colors that you select will not match, then the room will be ugly.

3–130. If that figure is not a square, it does not have four sides.

3–131. If Abraham Lincoln did not think that his Gettysburg Address was reverently received, then he thought it was a failure.

3–132. Let 'p' = 'this piece of cloth is warm'
Let 'q' = 'it is 50 per cent wool'
Let 'r' = 'the dog is shivering from cold'

Premises:

p and q

$r \longrightarrow$ not p

Conclusion:

not r

Valid. DC.

3–133. Let 'p' = 'the label on this piece of cloth reads "50 per cent" wool'
Let 'q' = 'it is 50 per cent wool'
Let 'r' = 'the piece of cloth is warm'
Premises:

r and q

$p \longrightarrow q$

Conclusion:

p

Invalid. AC.

3–134. Let 'p' = 'he was a scholar'
Let 'q' = 'he was a gentleman'
Let 'r' = 'he was an astute politician'
Let 's' = 'he made the mistake of which you are accusing him'
Premises:

$s \longrightarrow$ not r

p and q and r

Conclusion:

not s

Valid. DC.

3–135. Let 'p' = 'there will be rain within the week'
Let 'q' = 'the crops will be ruined'
Premises:

p or q

not p

Conclusion:

q

Valid. Denial of alternant.

3–136. Let 'p' = 'the two colors that you select will match'
Let 'q' = 'the room will be ugly'
Let 'r' = 'I help you select the colors'
Premises:

p or q

$r \longrightarrow p$

r

Intermediate conclusion:

p

Valid. Affirming the antecedent

Final conclusion:

not q

Invalid. Affirmation of an alternant.

3–137. Let 'p' = 'that figure is a square'
Let 'q' = 'it does not have four sides'
Premises:
p or q
not p
Conclusion:
q
Valid. Denial of alternant.

3–138. Let 'p' = 'there is now a rainbow'
Let 'q' = 'there is now a completely overcast sky'
Premises:
not both p and q
q
Conclusion:
not p
Valid. Affirmation of negajunct.

3–139. Let 'p' = 'Abraham Lincoln thought that his Gettysburg Address was reverently received'
Let 'q' = 'he thought it was a failure'
Premises:
p or q
not p
Conclusion:
q
Valid. Denial of alternant.

3–140. Let 'p' = 'Jones likes *Alice in Wonderland*'
Let 'q' = 'it is not a book for children'
Let 'r' = 'it is also a book for adults'
Premises:
$p \longrightarrow q$
not q
r
Conclusion:
p
Invalid. The valid conclusion is 'not p', by denial of consequent. Hence the conclusion given actually contradicts the validly drawn conclusion.

3–141. Let 'p' = 'Hamlet was in doubt about the guilt of his uncle'
Let 'q' = 'Hamlet was convinced that he had actually spoken to his father's ghost'
Premises:
not both p and q
q
Conclusion:
not p
Valid. Affirmation of negajunct.

3–142. F **3–143.** T **3–144.** T **3–145.** T.

3–146. (3–66), (using previous symbolization)

Statements:	Reasons:
1. $p \longrightarrow q$	1. Premise
2. p	2. Premise
3. q	3. 1, 2, AA

3–147. (3–67)

Statements:	Reasons:
1. not $p \longrightarrow$ not q	1. Premise
2. not p	2. Premise
3. not q	3. 1, 2, AA

3–148. (3–68)

Statements:	Reasons:
1. $p \longrightarrow q$	1. Premise
2. not p	2. Premise
3. ?	3. 1, 2, DA

3–149. (3–69)

Statements:	Reasons:
1. p	1. Premise
2. $p \longrightarrow q$	2. Premise
3. $q \longrightarrow r$	3. Premise
4. $r \longrightarrow s$	4. Premise
5. q	5. 1, 2, AA
6. r	6. 3, 5, AA
7. s	7. 4, 6, AA

(Note that this one can also be done just as easily with the conditional chain principle.)

3–150. (3–70)

Statements:	Reasons:
1. not r	1. Premise
2. $q \longrightarrow r$	2. Premise
3. $p \longrightarrow q$	3. Premise
4. not q	4. 1, 2, DC
5. not p	5. 3, 4, DC

3–151. (3–96)

Statements:	Reasons:
1. $p \longrightarrow q$	1. Premise
2. not p	2. Premise
3. ?	3. 1, 2, DA

3–152. (3–97)

Statements:	Reasons:
1. $p \longleftrightarrow q$	1. Premise
2. not p	2. Premise
3. $q \longrightarrow p$	3. 1, constituent of biconditional
4. not q	4. 2, 3, DC

3–153. (3–98)

Statements:	Reasons:
1. $p \longrightarrow q$	1. Premise
2. $q \longrightarrow r$	2. Premise
3. $p \longrightarrow r$	3. 1, 2, conditional chain

3–154. (3–99)

Statements:	Reasons:
1. $p \longrightarrow q$	1. Premise
2. not q	2. Premise
3. not p	3. 1, 2, DC

3–155. (3–100)

Statements:	Reasons:
1. $p \longrightarrow q$	1. Premise
2. $q \longrightarrow r$	2. Premise
3. $p \longrightarrow r$	3. 1, 2, conditional chain

3–156. (3–101)

Statements:	Reasons:
1. $p \longrightarrow q$	1. Premise
2. $r \longleftrightarrow p$	2. Premise
3. not r	3. Premise
4. $p \longrightarrow r$	4. 2, biconditional yields constituent
5. not p	5. 3, 4, DC
6. ?	6. 1, 5, DA

3–157. (3–102)

Statements:	Reasons:
1. $q \longrightarrow p$	1. Premise
2. $p \longrightarrow r$	2. Premise
3. not q	3. Premise
4. r	4. Premise
5. ?	5. 1, 3, DA or 2, 4, AC

3–158. (3–103)

Statements:	Reasons:
1. $p \longrightarrow q$	1. Premise
2. $r \longrightarrow$ not p	2. Premise
3. not r	3. Premise
4. ?	4. 2, 3, DA

3–159. (3–135)

Statements:	Reasons:
1. p or q	1. Premise
2. not p	2. Premise
3. q	3. 1, 2, denial of alternant

3–160. (3–136)

Statements:	Reasons:
1. p or q	1. Premise
2. $r \longrightarrow p$	2. Premise

3. r — 3. Premise
4. p — 4. 2, 3, AA
5. ? — 5. 1, 4, affirmation of alternant

3–161. (3–137)

Statements:	Reasons:
1. p or q	1. Premise
2. not p	2. Premise
3. q	3. 1, 2, denial of alternant

3–162. (3–138)

Statements:	Reasons:
1. not both p and q	1. Premise
2. q	2. Premise
3. not p	3. 1, 2, affirmation of negajunct.

3–163. (3–139)

Statements:	Reasons:
1. p or q	1. Premise
2. not p	2. Premise
3. q	3. 1, 2, denial of alternant

3–164. (3–140)

Statements:	Reasons:
1. $p \longrightarrow q$	1. Premise
2. not q	2. Premise
3. r	3. Premise
4. not p	4. 1, 2, DC

This statement at Step 4 contradicts the suggested conclusion, which therefore is not appropriate.

3–165. (3–141)

Statements:	Reasons:
1. not both p and q	1. Premise
2. q	2. Premise
3. not p	3. 1, 2, affirmation of negajunct

3–166.

Statements:	Reasons:
1. $p \longrightarrow q$	1. Premise
2. $q \longrightarrow r$	2. Premise
3. $r \longrightarrow s$	3. Premise
4. $s \longrightarrow t$	4. Premise
5. $t \longrightarrow v$	5. Premise
6. $p \longrightarrow r$	6. 1, 2, conditional chain
7. $p \longrightarrow s$	7. 3, 6, conditional chain
8. $p \longrightarrow t$	8. 4, 7, conditional chain
9. $p \longrightarrow v$	9. 5, 8, conditional chain

3–167. F **3–168.** T **3–169.** T **3–170.** F **3–171.** T.

3–172. and **3–181.**

Let 'p' = 'Governor Smith is actually planning to throw his hat in the ring'
Let 'q' = 'the reporters asked him to declare himself'
Let 'r' = 'he has refused to do so'

Statements:	Reasons:
1. $p \longrightarrow (q \longrightarrow r)$ (3–172)	1. Premise
2. p	2. Premise
3. not r	3. Premise
4. $q \longrightarrow r$	4. 1, 2, AA
5. not q	5. 3, 4, DC

3–173. (same symbolization assignment as 3–172)
$p \longrightarrow$ (not q or r)

3–174. (same assignment as 3–172)
(p and q) $\longrightarrow r$

3–175. and **3–182.**
Let 'p' = 'Iceland has ordered the fishing vessels of Great Britain to leave the area within ten miles of Iceland's shores'
Let 'q' = 'Iceland is sovereign in that ten-mile zone'
Let 'r' = 'the ships of Britain leave'

Statements:	Reasons:
1. $p \longrightarrow (q \longrightarrow r)$ (3–175)	1. Premise
2. p	2. Premise
3. r	3. Premise
4. $q \longrightarrow r$	4. 1, 2, AA
5. ?	5. 3, 4, AC

3–176. (same assignment as 3–175)
$p \longrightarrow (r \longrightarrow q)$

3–177 and **3–183.**
Let 'p' = 'Jones is given the *California Test of Mental Maturity* under standard conditions'
Let 'q' = 'his IQ is about 100'
Let 'r' = 'his score is about 100'
Let 's' = 'Jones knows calculus'

Statements:	Reasons:
1. $p \longrightarrow (q \longleftrightarrow r)$ (3–177)	1. Premise
2. not both s and q	2. Premise
3. s	3. Premise
4. r	4. Premise
5. not q	5. 2, 3, affirmation of negajunct
*6. p	6. Assumption
*7. $q \longleftrightarrow r$	7. 1, 6, AA
*8. $r \longrightarrow q$	8. 7, constituent of biconditional
*9. q	9. 4, 8, AA
*10. q and not q	10. 5, 9
11. not p	11. 10, indirect proof

Note that a separate step (number 10) was used to assert the contradiction. Example 3–36 in the text did not do so. Either way is all right.

3–178 and **3–184.**

Let 'p' = 'you put this mercury thermometer in the beaker of water'
Let 'q' = 'the thermometer read x'
Let 'r' = 'the temperature was x'

Statements:	Reasons:
1. $p \longrightarrow (q \longleftrightarrow r)$ (3–178)	1. Premise
2. p	2. Premise
3. q	3. Premise
4. $q \longleftrightarrow r$	4. 1, 2, AA
5. r	5. 3, 4, AA

3–179 and **3–185.**

Let 'p' = 'this small piece of dough is put in the warming pan'
Let 'q' = 'this small piece of dough will double in size in twenty minutes'
Let 'r' = 'the dough on the board will not rise sufficiently'
Let 's' = 'the dough is put in the oven'

Statements:	Reasons:
1. $p \longrightarrow (q$ or $(s \longrightarrow r))$ (3–179)	1. Premise
2. p	2. Premise
3. not q	3. Premise
4. s	4. Premise
5. q or $(s \longrightarrow r)$	5. 1, 2, AA
6. $s \longrightarrow r$	6. 3, 5, denial of alternant
7. r	7. 4, 6, AA

3–180 and **3–186.**

Let 'p' = 'lines AB and CD are not parallel to each other'
Let 'q' = 'a third line is drawn in the same plane'
Let 'r' = 'it will cross one and only one of them'
Let 's' = 'it will cross both of them'

Statements:	Reasons:
1. $p \longrightarrow (q \longrightarrow (r$ or $s))$ (3–180)	1. Premise
2. q	2. Premise
3. not r	3. Premise
4. not s	4. Premise
*5. p	5. Assumption
*6. $q \longrightarrow (r$ or $s)$	6. 1, 5, AA
*7. r or s	7. 2, 6, AA
*8. s	8. 3, 7, denial of alternant
*9. s and not s	9. 4, 8
10. not p	10. 9, indirect proof

3–187. Let 'p' = 'X was rubbed on Y'
Let 'q' = 'X is harder than Y'
Let 'r' = 'X scratched Y'
Let 's' = 'there are marks on Y'

Statements:	Reasons:
1. $p \longrightarrow (q \longleftrightarrow r)$	1. Premise
2. $r \longrightarrow s$	2. Premise

3. p	3. Premise
4. s	4. Premise
5. $q \leftrightarrow r$	5. 1, 3, AA
6. ?	6. 2, 4, AC

3–188. Let 'p' = 'this pronoun is the object of a preposition'
Let 'q' = 'it requires the objective form'
Let 'r' = 'it should appear as "him"'
Let 's' = 'It appears as "he"'
Let 't' = 'the sentence is in error'

Statements:	Reasons:
1. $p \longrightarrow q$	1. Premise
2. $q \longrightarrow r$	2. Premise
3. (s and r) $\longrightarrow t$	3. Premise
*4. s and p	4. Assumption
*5. q	5. 1, 4, AA
*6. r	6. 2, 5, AA
*7. t	7. 3, 4, 6, AA
8. (s and p) $\longrightarrow t$	8. 4, 7, conditional proof

3–189. Let 'p' = 'Communism is going to spread in Lower Slobbovia'
Let 'q' = 'the Prime Minister was defeated in the recent election'
Let 'r' = 'there has been an announcement of his defeat in the local newspaper'
Let 's' = 'the Lower Slobbovians are discontent'

Statements:	Reasons:
1. $p \longrightarrow q$	1. Premise
2. $q \longrightarrow r$	2. Premise
3. not r	3. Premise
4. s	4. Premise
5. not q	5. 2, 3, DC
6. not p	6. 1, 5, DC
*7. $s \longrightarrow p$	7. Assumption
*8. p	8. 4, 7, AA
*9. p and not p	9. 6, 8
10. not ($s \longrightarrow p$)	10. 9, indirect proof

3–190. Let 'p' = 'the wind is not from the east'
Let 'q' = 'the contour lines are close together'
Let 'r' = 'the hill is steep'
Let 's' = 'there is turbulence on the west side'
Let 't' = 'the wind is from the west'
Let 'u' = 'we will have a good race course close to the west shore'
Let 'v' = 'we must have our race on a triangular course with two buoys on the east shore'

Statements:	Reasons:
1. p	1. Premise
2. $q \leftrightarrow r$	2. Premise
3. $t \longrightarrow (r \longrightarrow s)$	3. Premise

4. not both s and u	4. Premise
5. not $u \longrightarrow v$	5. Premise
6. q	6. Premise
7. r	7. 2, 6, AA
*8. t	8. Assumption
*9. $r \longrightarrow s$	9. 3, 8, AA
*10. s	10. 7, 9, AA
*11. not u	11. 4, 10, affirmation of negajunct
*12. v	12. 5, 11, AA
13. $t \longrightarrow v$	13. 8, 12, conditional proof

Chapter 4: "Class Reasoning"

4–1. F **4–2.** F **4–3.** T

4–4. Parallelograms
Quadrilaterals

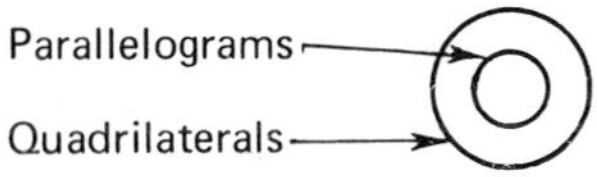

4–5. Quadrilaterals
Plane figures

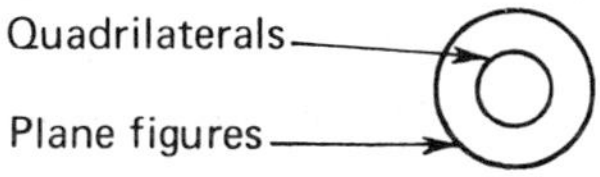

4–6. Books by Thomas Mann
Books on the top shelf

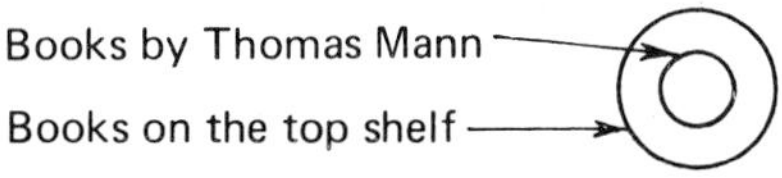

4–7. Chekhov's short stories
Stories that have fascinated me

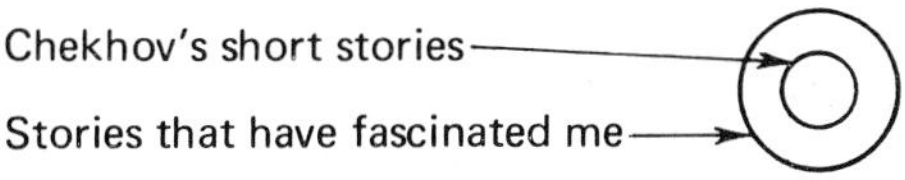

4–8. Acids
Compounds

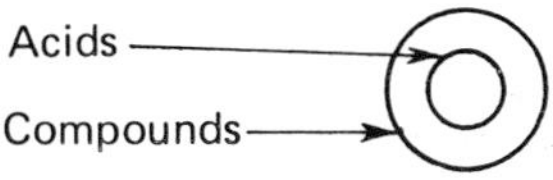

4–9. Stars in the Milky Way
Stars that are far away

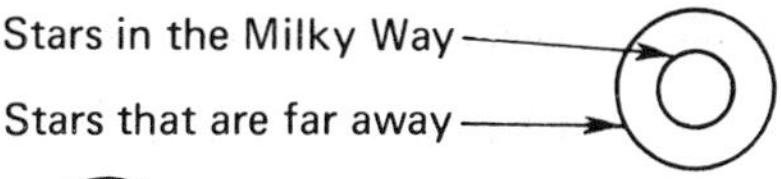

4–10. States
Things that have two senators

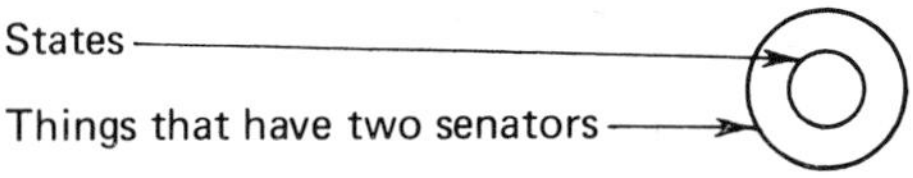

4–11. Unwanted plants
Woods

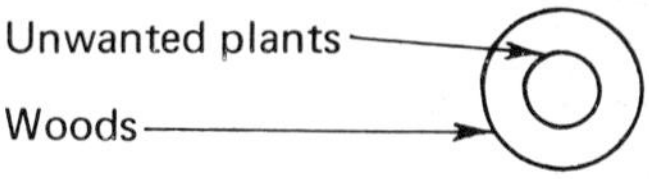

4–12. Parallelograms
Quadrilaterals
Plane figures

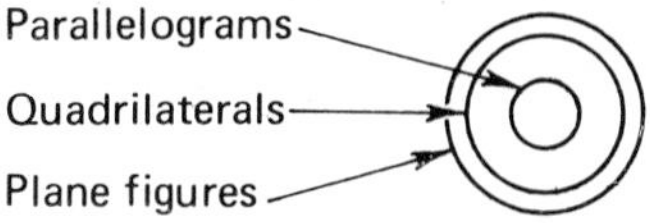

4–13. *Magic Mountain*
Books by Thomas Mann
Books on the top shelf
x

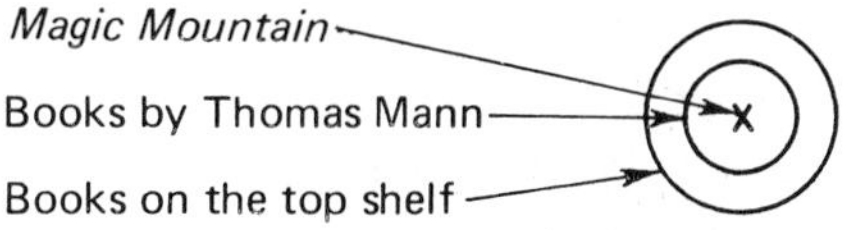

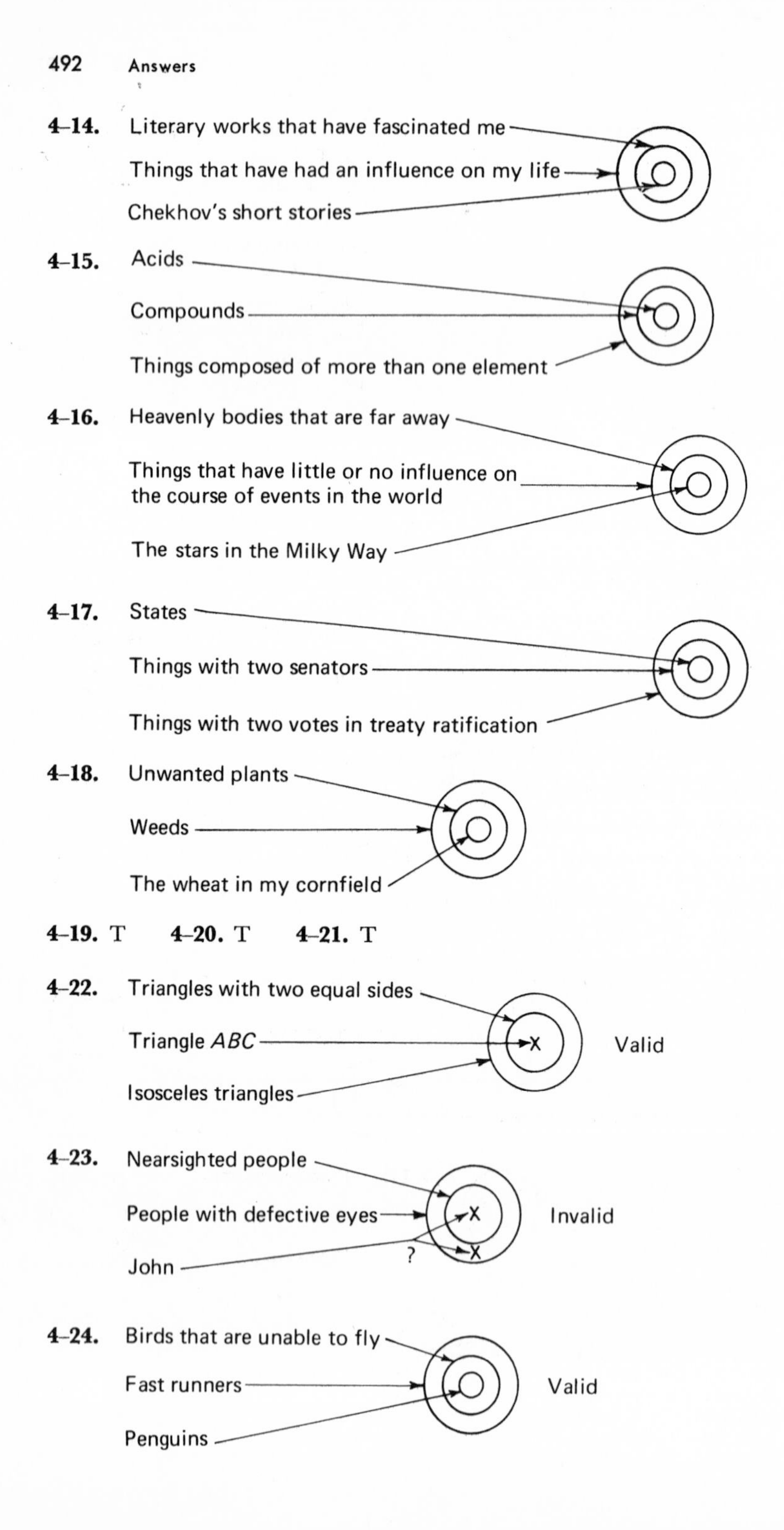
4–14.
Literary works that have fascinated me
Things that have had an influence on my life
Chekhov's short stories
4–15.
Acids
Compounds
Things composed of more than one element
4–16.
Heavenly bodies that are far away
Things that have little or no influence on the course of events in the world
The stars in the Milky Way
4–17.
States
Things with two senators
Things with two votes in treaty ratification
4–18.
Unwanted plants
Weeds
The wheat in my cornfield
4–19. T
4–20. T
4–21. T
4–22.
Triangles with two equal sides
Triangle ABC
X
Valid
Isosceles triangles
4–23.
Nearsighted people
People with defective eyes
X
Invalid
?
X
John
4–24.
Birds that are unable to fly
Fast runners
Valid
Penguins

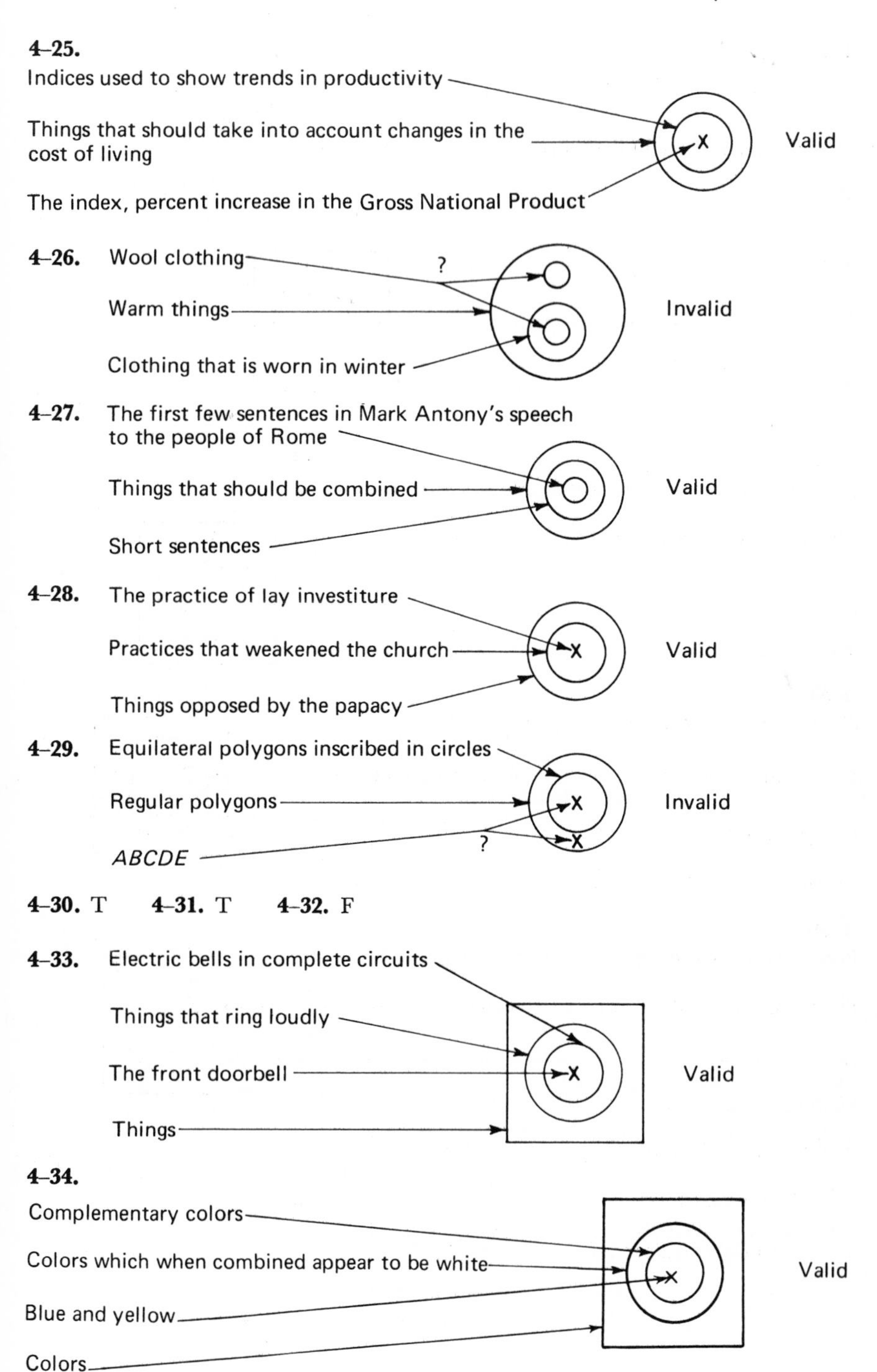
4–25.
Indices used to show trends in productivity
Things that should take into account changes in the cost of living
The index, percent increase in the Gross National Product
X
Valid
4–26.
Wool clothing
Warm things
Clothing that is worn in winter
?
Invalid
4–27.
The first few sentences in Mark Antony's speech to the people of Rome
Things that should be combined
Short sentences
Valid
4–28.
The practice of lay investiture
Practices that weakened the church
Things opposed by the papacy
X
Valid
4–29.
Equilateral polygons inscribed in circles
Regular polygons
ABCDE
?
X
X
Invalid
4–30. T
4–31. T
4–32. F
4–33.
Electric bells in complete circuits
Things that ring loudly
The front doorbell
Things
X
Valid
4–34.
Complementary colors
Colors which when combined appear to be white
Blue and yellow
Colors
X
Valid

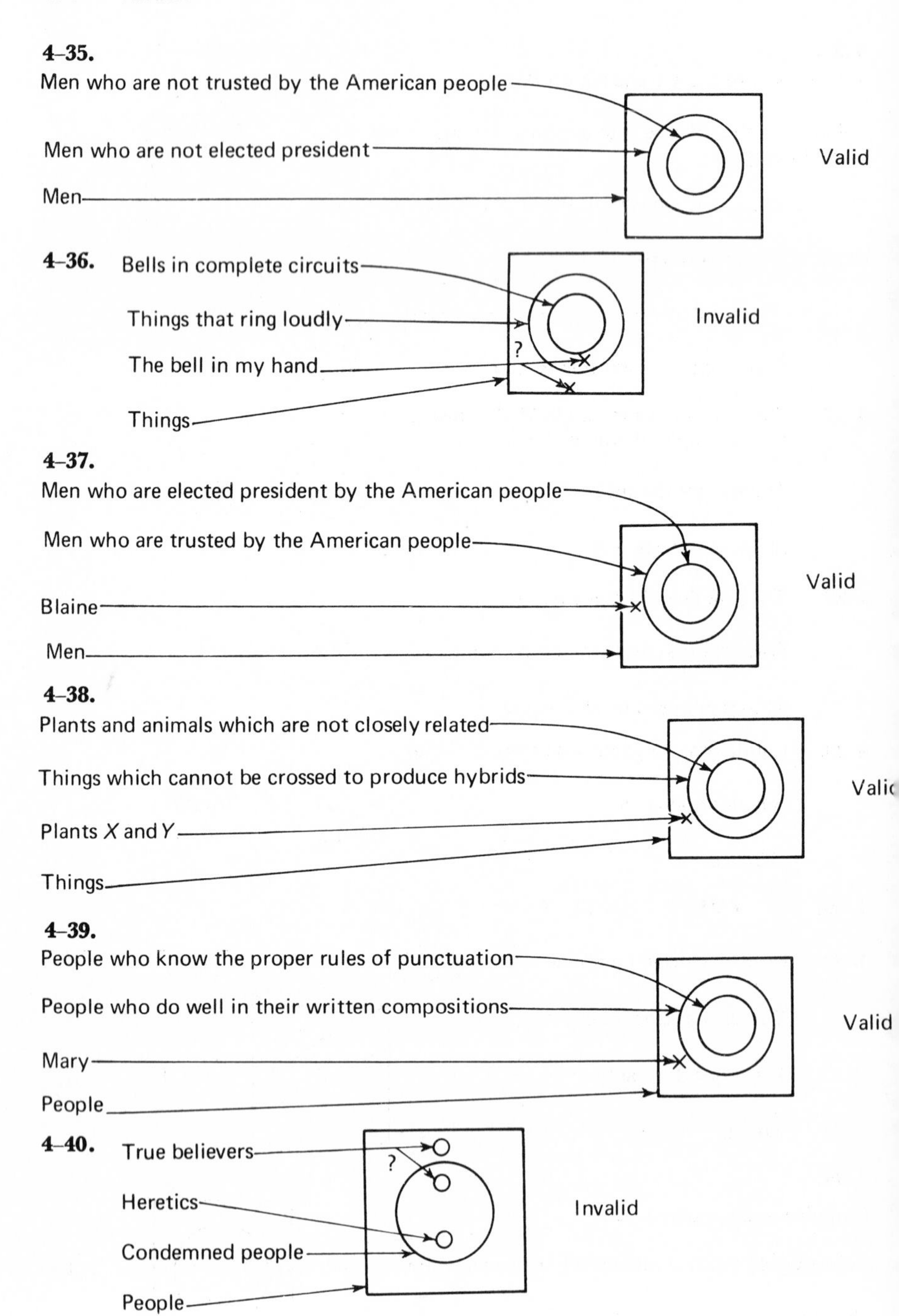
4–35.
Men who are not trusted by the American people
Men who are not elected president
Men
Valid
4–36.
Bells in complete circuits
Things that ring loudly
The bell in my hand
Things
?
Invalid
4–37.
Men who are elected president by the American people
Men who are trusted by the American people
Blaine
Men
Valid
4–38.
Plants and animals which are not closely related
Things which cannot be crossed to produce hybrids
Plants X and Y
Things
Valid
4–39.
People who know the proper rules of punctuation
People who do well in their written compositions
Mary
People
Valid
4–40.
True believers
Heretics
Condemned people
People
?
Invalid

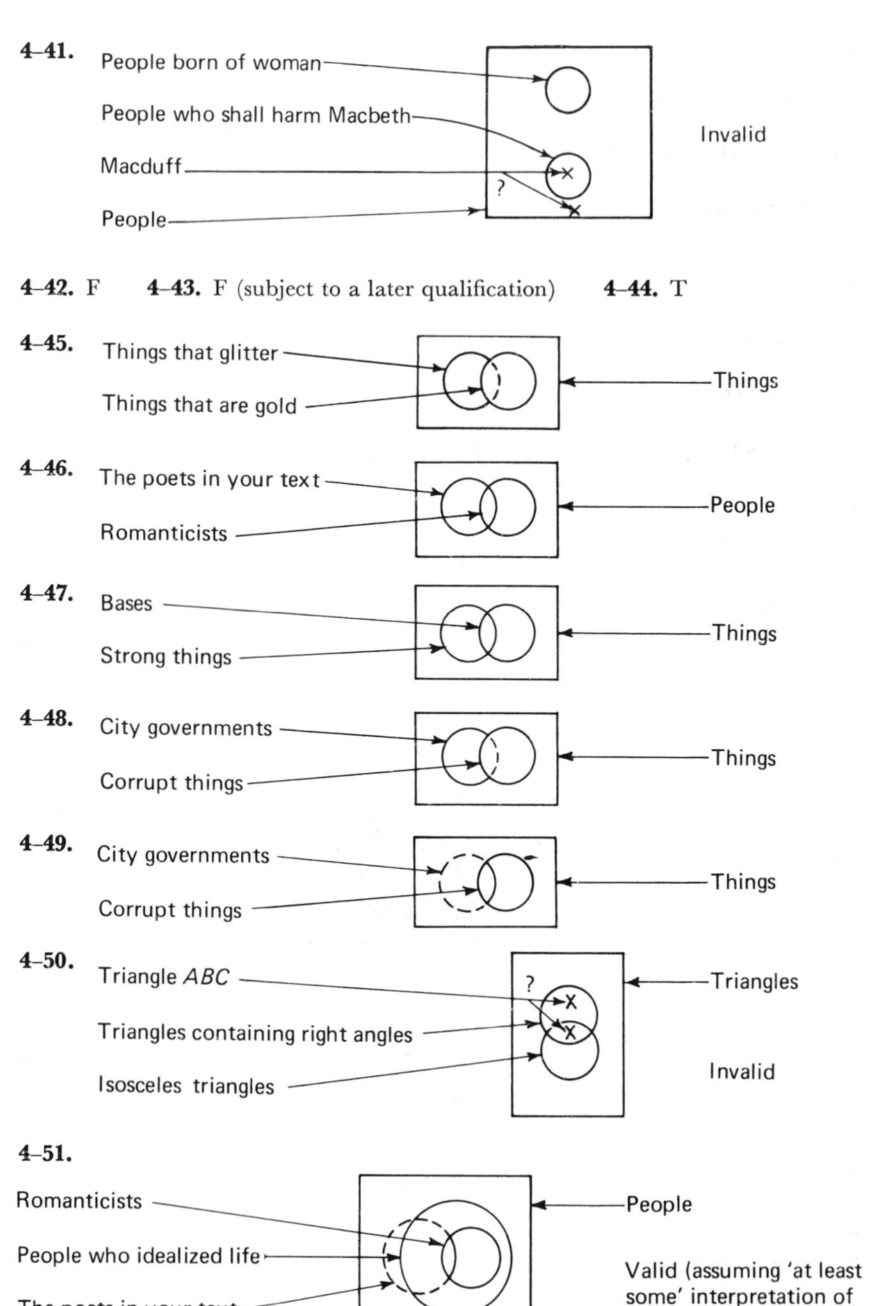
4–41.
People born of woman
People who shall harm Macbeth
Macduff
People
?
Invalid
4–42. F 4–43. F (subject to a later qualification) 4–44. T
4–45.
Things that glitter
Things that are gold
Things
4–46.
The poets in your text
Romanticists
People
4–47.
Bases
Strong things
Things
4–48.
City governments
Corrupt things
Things
4–49.
City governments
Corrupt things
Things
4–50.
Triangle ABC
Triangles containing right angles
Isosceles triangles
?
Triangles
Invalid
4–51.
Romanticists
People who idealized life
The poets in your text
People
Valid (assuming 'at least some' interpretation of conclusion)

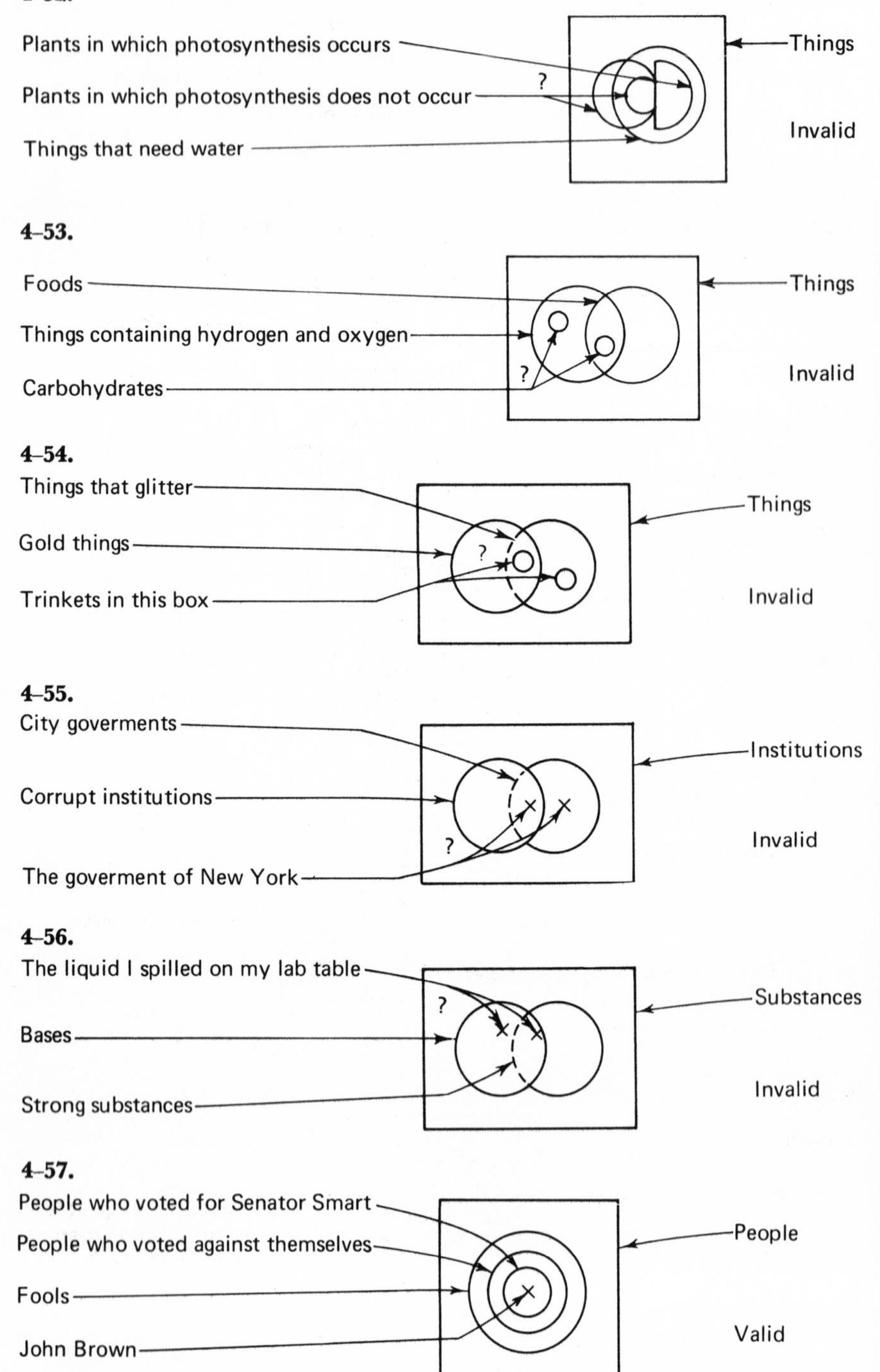
4–52.
Plants in which photosynthesis occurs
Plants in which photosynthesis does not occur
Things that need water
?
Things
Invalid
4–53.
Foods
Things containing hydrogen and oxygen
Carbohydrates
?
Things
Invalid
4–54.
Things that glitter
Gold things
Trinkets in this box
?
Things
Invalid
4–55.
City goverments
Corrupt institutions
The goverment of New York
?
Institutions
Invalid
4–56.
The liquid I spilled on my lab table
Bases
Strong substances
?
Substances
Invalid
4–57.
People who voted for Senator Smart
People who voted against themselves
Fools
John Brown
People
Valid

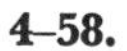

4–58.

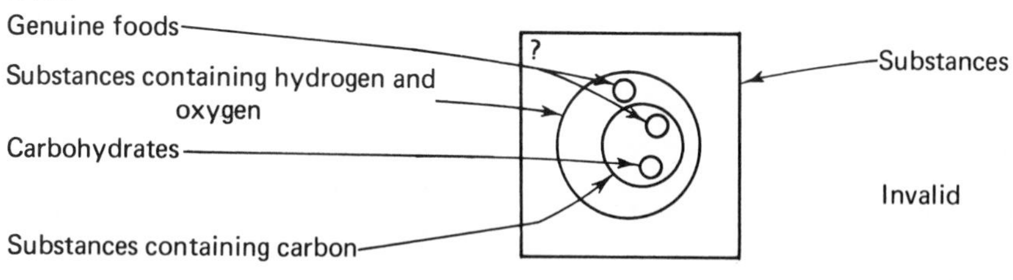

4–59.

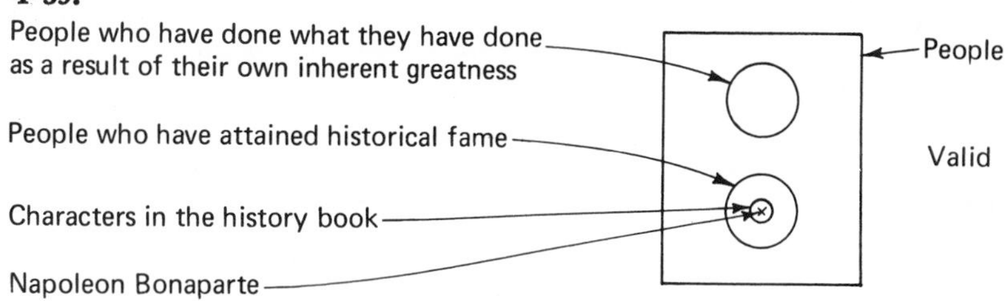

Note: Lewis Carroll's problems can be handled in a number of ways. One good strategy is to try to develop a series of concentric circles—at most two series of such circles.

4–60.

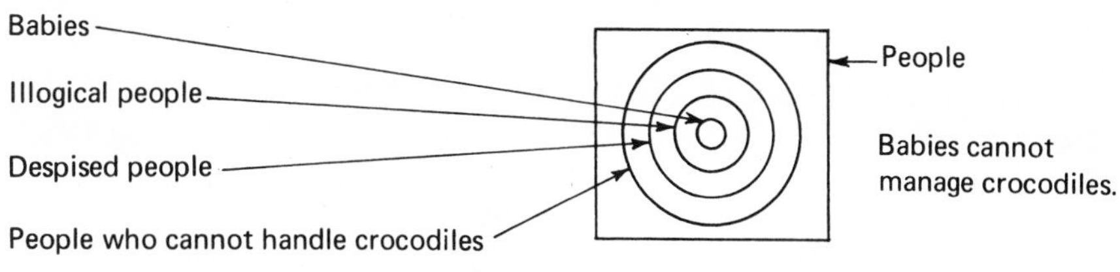

4–61.

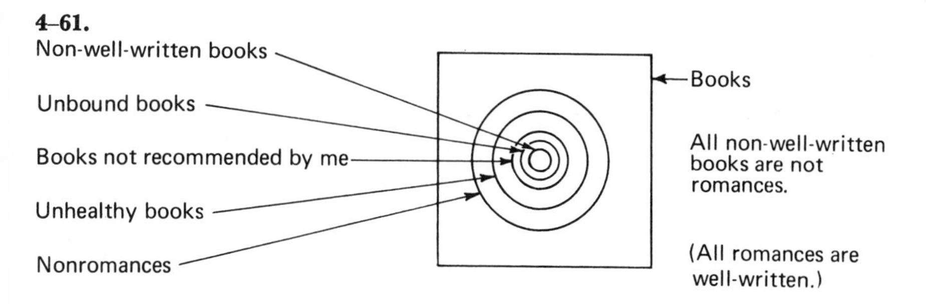

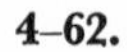

4–62.

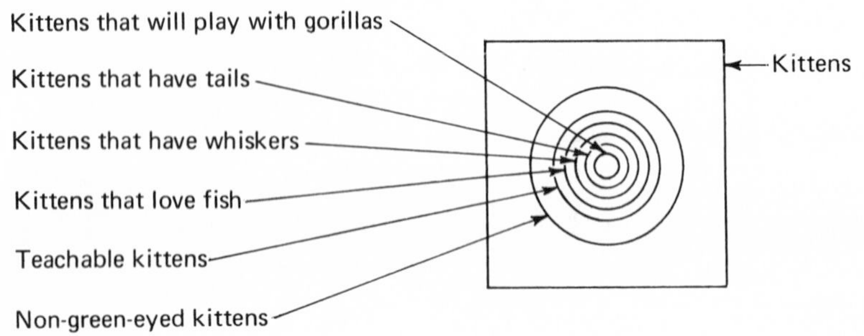

Kittens that will play with gorillas do not have green eyes.

4–63.

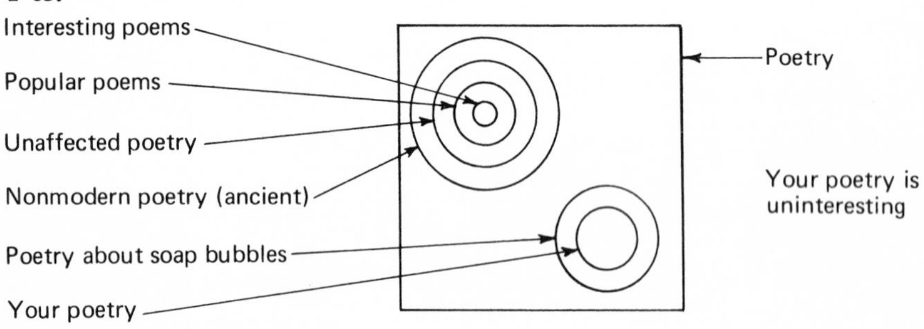

4–64. T **4–65.** F **4–66.** T

4–67.

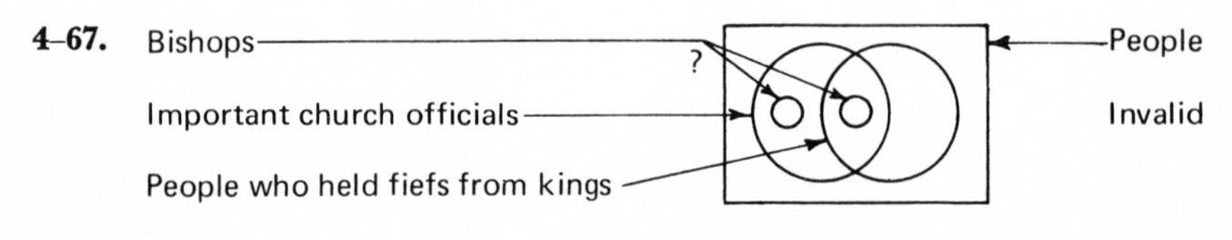

4–68.

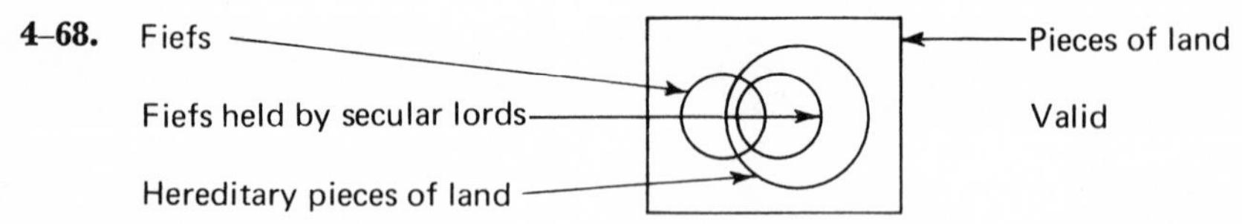

4–69.

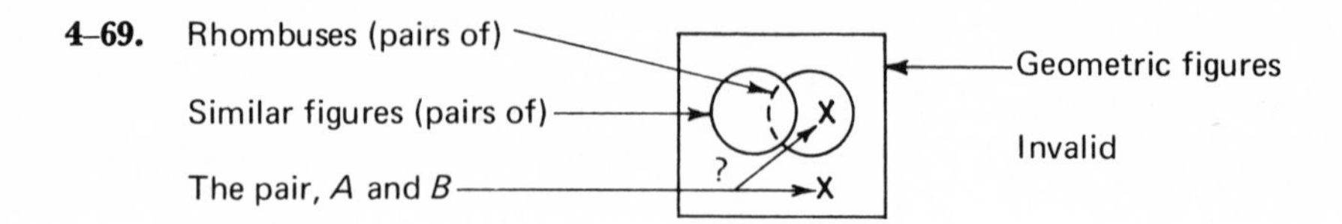

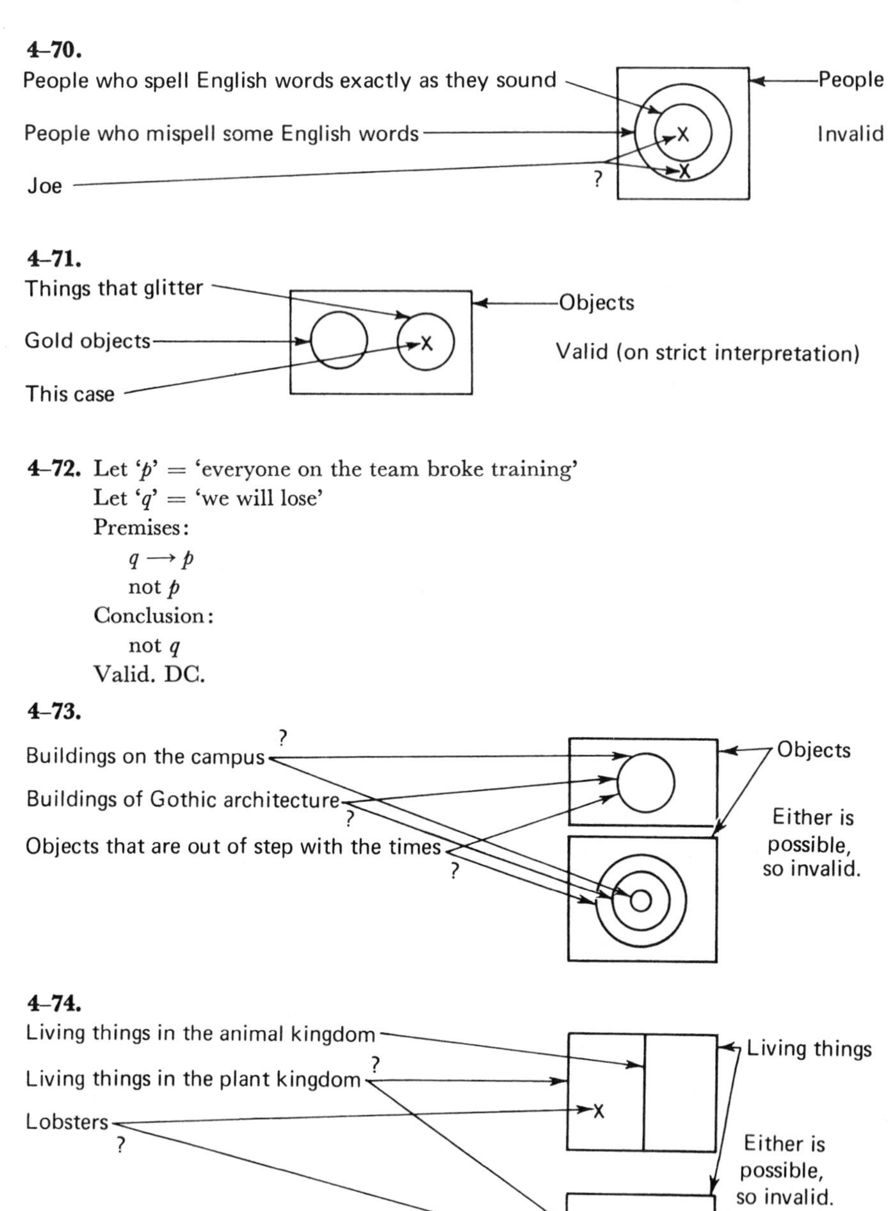

4–72. Let 'p' = 'everyone on the team broke training'
Let 'q' = 'we will lose'
Premises:
$q \longrightarrow p$
not p
Conclusion:
not q
Valid. DC.

4–75. Let 'p' = 'the present municipal airport should continue to be used for purposes of general aviation'
Let 'q' = 'it should be used to provide a site for a summer festival every year'
Let 'r' = 'the other airport is to be closed down'
Premises:

p (or) q
$p \longrightarrow r$
not r

Subconclusion (from the second and third premises):

not p

Valid. DC.
Conclusion:

q

Valid. Denial of alternant.

4–76. Let 'p' = 'Brown has a position on the Rules Committee'
Let 'q' = 'all the men on this list have declined to serve'
Let 'r' = 'Jones is on this list'
Let 's' = 'Jones has declined to serve'
Let 't' = 'Jones was appointed to the Appropriations Committee'
Premises:

$p \longrightarrow q$
r
$s \longrightarrow t$
not t

First subconclusion (using last two premises):

not s

Valid. DC.
Second subconclusion:

(q and r) $\longrightarrow s$

This conclusion must be accepted, since it represents a valid argument, as can be seen in the following diagram:

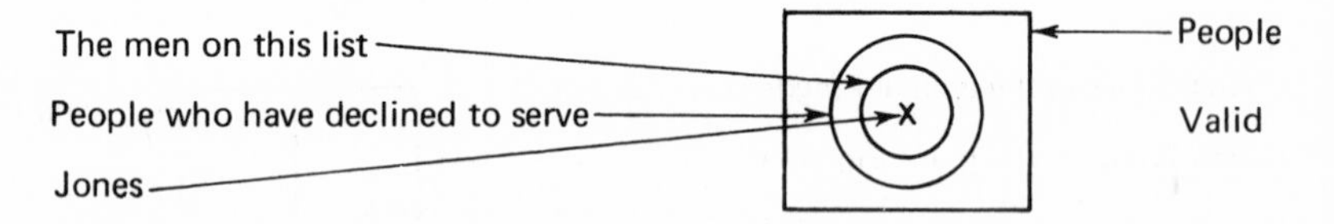

Third subconclusion (using first and second subconclusions):

not both q and r, which is the same as the following: not (q and r)

Valid. DC.
Fourth subconclusion (using third subconclusion and second premise):

not q

Valid. Affirmation of negajunct.
Final conclusion (using fourth subconclusion and first premise):

not p

Valid. DC.

Note: There are a number of ways this argument could have been handled. The important thing is to have an orderly step-by-step procedure. For an orderly sentence reasoning format see (❖) "Step-by-Step Organization of Arguments" in Chapter 3.

4–77. Let 'p' = 'the piece of wood sinks in the beaker of alcohol'
Let 'q' = 'its specific gravity is greater than one'
Let 'r' = 'anything with a specific gravity greater than one will sink in water'
Let 's' = 'it will sink in water'
Premises:
$q \longrightarrow p$
r
p
Conclusion:
s
Invalid because the first step, which combines premises 1 and 3, is invalid (AC).

4–78.

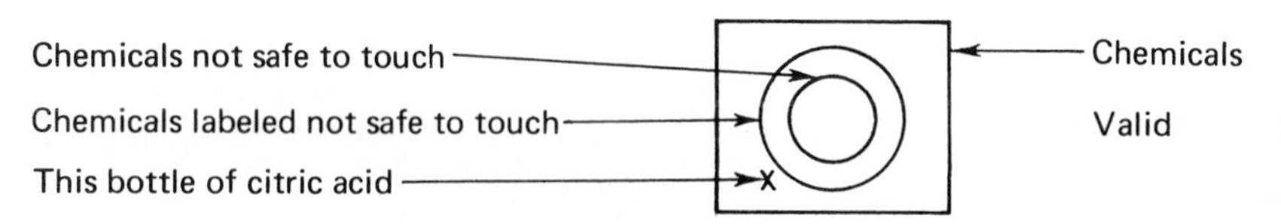

4–79. Let 'p' = 'he is really listening to this music'
Let 'q' = 'his eyes are closed'
Sentence reasoning premises:
$p \longrightarrow q$
not q
Sentence reasoning conclusion:
not p
Valid. DC. Hence we know that Frank is not really listening to this music. Next:

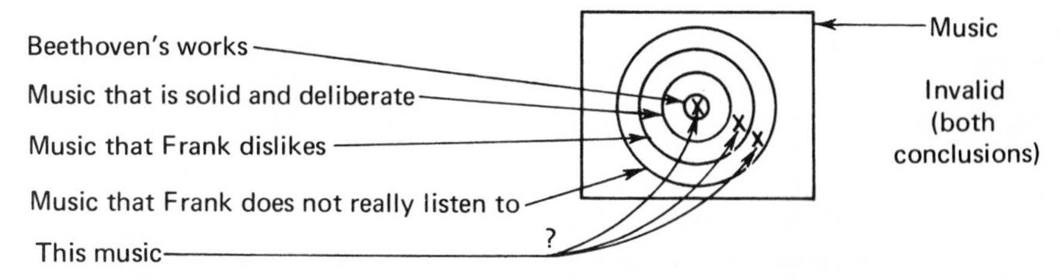

4–80. The strategy that I shall follow here is to reduce the alternation in the third sentence down to coverage of "my room" only, and then to eliminate the alternatives one by one. If the proposed conclusion is the only alternative left, then the argument is valid.

The rooms in Stone Hall

My room

Rooms that either have very dark-colored walls, or have no windows, or are large, or are well-lighted

Rooms

1. From the above the following is established: My room either has very dark-colored walls, or has no windows, or is large, or is well lighted. Next, to eliminate the last alternative:

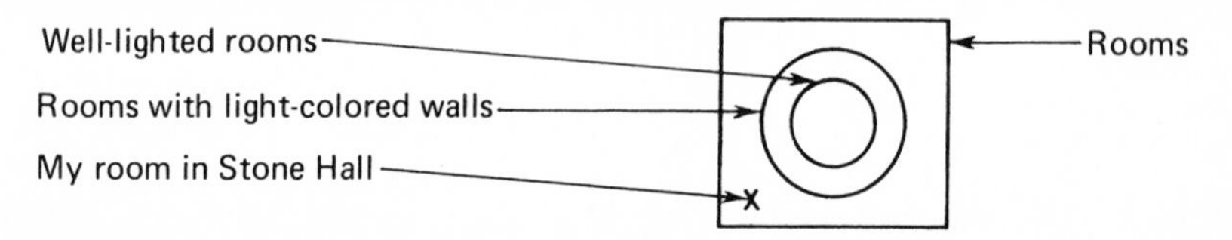

2. From this the following is established: My room in Stone Hall is not well lighted. Next, to eliminate the second alternative:

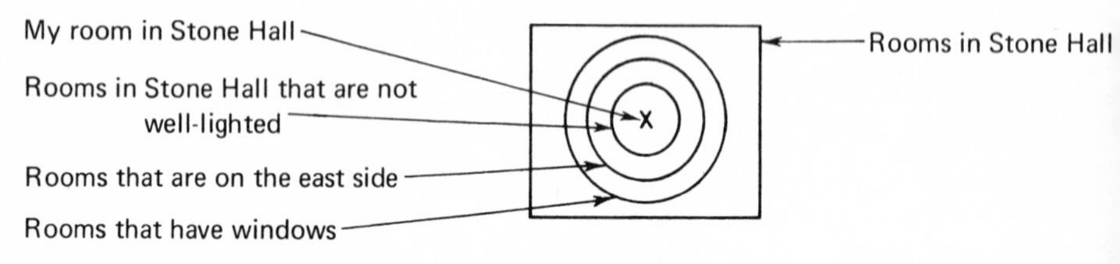

3. From this the following is established: My room in Stone Hall has windows. From here we can use only sentence reasoning:
   Let 'p' = 'my room has very dark-colored walls'
   Let 'q' = 'my room has no windows'
   Let 'r' = 'my room is large'
   Let 's' = 'my room is well lighted'
   Let 't' = 'some of the rooms in Stone Hall are small'
   Let 'u' = 'my room in Stone Hall is small'

Premises:	p or q or r or s	(This is number 1 above)
	not s	(This is number 2 above)
	not q	(This is number 3 above)
	t	
	$t \longrightarrow u$	

   First interim conclusion: u Valid. AA.

   Assuming that a small room is not large, we can on the basis of the first interim conclusion establish the second interim conclusion: not r

   Final conclusion: p Valid. Denial of alternants.

Chapter 5: "Practical Application of Deductive Logic"

5–1. T **5–2.** T **5–3.** F **5–4.** T **5–5.** F

*Chapter 6: "An Introduction to the Functions of Definitions"

6–1. F **6–2.** F **6–3.** T **6–4.** T

Chapter 7: "Stipulating a Meaning"

7–1. F **7–2.** T **7–3.** F **7–4.** T **7–5.** T

Chapter 8: "Reporting Usage"

8–1. T **8–2.** F **8–3.** F **8–4.** T
8–5. F **8–6.** F **8–7.** F **8–8.** F

8–12. c. the meaning
a. a meaning for someone
b. a meaning
___ meaningless

Chapter 9: "Shades of Definition"

9–1. F **9–2.** T **9–3.** T **9–4.** F **9–5.** T
9–6. F **9–7.** F **9–8.** T **9–9.** T

Chapter 10: "Equivalence Forms: Synonym and Classification Definition"

10–1. T **10–2.** F **10–3.** F **10–4.** T **10–5.** T
10–6. F **10–7.** T **10–8.** T **10–9.** F

10–14.

a 1a	e 6	i OK	m 1a
b 1b	f 2b	j 2a	n OK } Both are
c 2a (and b)	g 1a	k 2a (and b)	o OK } debatable
d 4	h 1b	l 2a	p 4

10–16. a. ", which . . . activities"
b. None
c. "which may be inscribed in a square and"
d. ", often used to solve algebraic problems"
e. None
f. ", and which most frequently . . . praise"

* From now on (Chapters 6–23) answers will be suggested only where there is a more or less standard answer.

g. "which can . . . sentence"
h. None
i. "the" and "that is commonly . . . countries"
j. "currently popular"
k. None
l. "which so many of us use"
m. None

Chapter 11: "Equivalence Forms: Equivalent-Expression Definition and Range Definition"

11–1. T **11–2.** T **11–3.** F **11–4.** F
11–5. T **11–6.** T **11–7.** F

Chapter 12: "Concrete Interpretation Forms"

12–1. F **12–2.** T **12–3.** F **12–4.** T **12–5.** F **12–6.** F

Chapter 14: "Basic Kinds of Explanation"

14–1. F **14–2.** F **14–3.** T **14–4.** T **14–5.** F
14–6. T **14–7.** F **14–17.** T **14–18.** T **14–19.** T

Chapter 15: "Gap-Filling"

15–1. F **15–2.** T **15–3.** F **15–4.** T **15–5.** T **15–6.** T

Chapter 16: "Introductory Evaluation and Probing of Reason-Giving Explanations"

16–1. T **16–2.** T **16–3.** F **16–19.** F
16–20. T **16–21.** T **16–26.** F **16–27.** F

Chapter 17: "Types of Explanation"

17–1. T **17–2.** T **17–3.** F **17–4.** T **17–5.** S **17–6.** A
17–7. S **17–8.** S **17–9.** A **17–10.** S **17–11.** S **17–12.** A
17–13. A **17–14.** S **17–15.** A **17–16.** S **17–17.** A **17–18.** S
17–19. S **17–20.** A **17–21.** S **17–22.** A **17–23.** A **17–24.** S

17–25. A **17–26.** A **17–27.** S **17–28.** A **17–30.** F **17–31.** T
17–32. F **17–33.** F **17–34.** T **17–35.** T **17–36.** F **17–37.** F
17–38. T **17–39.** F **17–42.** T **17–43.** F **17–44.** T **17–45.** F
17–50. F **17–51.** F **17–52.** T **17–53.** F **17–54.** F

Chapter 18 : "Testability/Applicability"

18–1. F **18–2.** F

Chapter 20 : "Early Stages of Justification Decisions"

20–1. F **20–2.** F **20–3.** T **20–4.** T **20–6.** F
20–7. F **20–8.** T **20–9.** T **20–12.** T **20–13.** T
20–14. F **20–15.** T **20–16.** F **20–17.** F **20–18.** T

Chapter 21 : "Value Statements"

21–1. E **21–2.** V **21–3.** V **21–4.** E **21–5.** V

Chapter 22 : "Material Inferences"

22–1. T **22–2.** F **22–3.** T **22–4.** F **22–5.** T
22–7. F **22–8.** T **22–9.** F **22–10.** T **22–11.** T
22–12. T **22–13.** T **22–14.** F

Index

Abrams, M. H., 135, 207
'Absolutism', clarification of, 417–19
Abstractness of subject matter, 287
Abstract terminology, 212, 220, 228–43
Accounting-for function of explanation, 292–96, 366–68, 370
Affirming the antecedent, 14, 27
  defined, 14
Affirming the consequent, 15, 27, 37
  defined, 15
Agreement with others:
  as a criterion for judging authorities, 393–94
  as a criterion for observation statements, 388
'All . . . are not. . . .', ambiguity of, 83–84
Alternation, 44–47, 54–55, 218
  defined, 44
  inclusive, 54–55
  relationship to conditional, 45–46, 54–55
  strong 'or':
    defined, 45–46
    symbolized, 46
  weak 'or', defined, 45–46
Ambiguity:
  of 'absolutism', 417–19
  of 'assumption', 396–97
  of 'authority', 392
Ambiguity (*cont.*)
  avoiding:
    between analytic and synthetic statements, 303–4
    consideration of cases, 137–39
    in explanation requests, 257–60
    making definitions explicit, 137
    in possible causal claims, 310–12
    through stipulation, 131, 139–40
    between testable and untestable doctrines, 339–53
  'need', meanings of, 141
  'role', meanings of, 140
  'some', meanings of, 76–79
American College Dictionary, 158–61
Analytic explanations, 306–8, 337, 344, 363, 366
Analytic statements:
  in analytic explanation, 306–8, 366
  defined, 300–301
  in reason-for-acting explanations, 324–25, 337
  and testability, 339–53
Analytic-synthetic distinction, 208–11, 300–304, 337, 339–53, 370–71, 382 fn., 468
  selected reading about, 370–71, 468
'And' (conjunction), 42–43
Anderson, Alan Ross, 119

Anderson, Howard, 469
'Antecedent' defined, 14 (*see also* Affirming the antecedent; Denying the antecedent)
Applicability, 263–64, 331, 337, 353–56
criterion stated, 353
defined, 355
Arbitrariness:
conveying arbitrariness of our language:
changes in meaning in our language, 133–36
different languages, existence of, 133
playing a game with words, 136
defined, 130
and 'good', 181–83
and value judgments, 420
Archimedes' Principle, practical application of, 113–16
'Argument' defined, 8
Aristotle, 4, 330, 406–7, 410, 466
Art, as defined by Tolstoy, 381
Assumption of order and intelligibility in nature, 399–401
Assumptions, 396–401, 466
defined, 396
explicit, 396–98
defined, 396
"for the sake of argument", 397
in indirect proof, 398
reasons for sometimes not defending, 397–98
implicit:
defined, 396
logical:
commitment to, 399–401
criteria for, 400–401
defined, 400
psychological:
defined, 398
explanatory power of, 399
pejorative force of 'assumption', 396
selected reading about, 466
(*see also* Gap fillers; Reason-giving explanation, completion of)
Auden, W. H., 146, 147
Austin, Frances M., 469
Austin, J. L., 252, 382
Authority, 392–96, 419, 466
accepted procedures, use of by, 393–94
agreement with other alleged authorities, 393–94
Authority (*cont.*)
ambiguity of, 392
cognitive, 392–96
disinterest of, 393
and the Establishment, 394–95
expertise of, 393
faculties, possession of, 393–94
power, 392
reputation of, 393
selected reading about, 466
study by, 393
trust in, 394–96
types of statements made by, 395–96
and value statements, 419

Beale, Howard K., 314
Beardsley, Monroe, 118, 466, 473
Bellack, Arno, 469
Belnap, Nuel D., Jr., 119
Benjamin, A. Cornelius, 251
Bennett, Jonathan F., 119
Biconditional, 35–37, 237–43
defined, 35
in operational and conditional definition, 237–43
symbolized, 36
Biddle, Bruce J., 470
Black, Max, 118, 223, 224, 251, 465, 466, 467, 469, 472
Borderline cases, 206–8, 385–87 (*see also* Range definition)
Bradley, A. C., 449–55
Braithwaite, Richard Bevan, 467
Brameld, Theodore, 459
Brandt, Richard, 414, 466
Bridgman, Percy W., 251
Brodbeck, May, 369
Broudy, Harry, 469
Brown, Robert, 369, 370
Brown *vs.* Board of Education (1954), 456–61
Bruner, Jerome S., 469
Bulk of evidence, as a criterion of justification of empirical statements, 426–28, 436–37
Burnett, Joe R., 469

Capitalization of letters in defined terms, 204
Carre, M. H., 472
Carroll, Lewis, 83, 154

Caton, Charles, 252
Causal explanation, 309–21, 337, 367, 444–45
- fields using, 320–21, 444–45
- requests for, 320
- singular *vs.* general, 315, 316–21
- (*see also* Causal language; Causality)

Causality, 32–33, 309–21, 337, 367–68, 441–45, 468
- alleged impossibility of proof of existence of, 311, 441, 445
- fields concerned with, 320–21, 444–45
- general causal claims, appraisal of, 443–44
- necessary and sufficient conditions, 32–33, 313–16
- selected reading about, 468
- singular causal claims, appraisal of, 442–43
- (*see also* Causal explanation; Causal language; 'Correlation' and causal claims)

Causal language:
- dual use of 'if . . . , then', 'whenever', 'is followed by', 'is correlated with', etc., 310–11
- eliminability, 310, 441, 445
- 'fundamental cause', 312–13
- generalizations, 315, 316–18, 367–68, 442–44
- 'immediate cause', 313
- meaning of 'cause', 441–42
- necessary and sufficient conditions, 32–33, 313–16
- 'partial cause', 312
- proximate cause, 313
- qualifications in, 444–45
- recipes, 441
- singular causal claims, 315, 316–18, 367, 442–44
  - difficulty of proving and disproving, 442–43
- synonyms, 310, 444–45
- 'the cause', 312
- 'the occasion', 313
- 'under normal conditions', 311–12

Census Bureau definition of 'rural', 142, 145, 147, 200
'*Ceteris paribus*', 95, 109, 110, 410
Circle representation of classes, 66–87
Circularity:
- defined, 201, 288
- in definition, 201–3
- in dictionaries, 155–57
- in explanation, 263–64, 288–91, 306–7, 309, 319, 325, 330, 337, 363

Clarification (*see* Probing; Meaning; Vagueness; Ambiguity; Examples and nonexamples; Counter-examples; Context, bearing of; Range definition; Classification definition; Equivalent-expression definition; 'Etc.' definition; Conditional definition; 'Why?'; Descriptive explanation; Reason-giving explanation; Testability; etc. Better still, read the whole book.)
Clark, Kenneth, 459
Classification definition, 194–214, 229
- advantages, 211
- and circularity, 201–3
- concrete interpretation, failure to provide, 229
- defined, 195
- difficulties, 212–13, 229
- equivalence rules, 197–99, 209–11
- negation in, 199–201
- parsimony, 208–9
- punctuation, 203–6
- rules for, 197–211
  - summarized, 213–14

Class reasoning, 11–12, 64–92
- combined with sentence reasoning, 87–90
- contrasted with sentence reasoning, 11–12
- described, 11–12

Class representation by circles, 66–87
Cluster concepts (*see* Range definition)
Cluster sample, 427, 431–32
Cohen, Morris, 119, 251, 465, 466, 467, 473
'Community', definition of, 230–35
Comparisons, possibility of, 378
Competitors' inconsistency with evidence, as a criterion of justification, 436, 439, 455
'Complete explanation', defined, 262 (*see also* Reason-giving explanation, completion of)
Complex sentences, 51–55

Conant, James B., 223, 357
Conceivability of counter-evidence, 301–2, 339–50
Conceivability of counter-examples, 301–2, 339–50
Concepts:
discovered or invented, 143
existence of, 143, 220
italics, use of, to indicate reference to, 204–5
(*see also* Loose concepts; Definition)
Conceptually-mistaken extra material in definitions, 209–11
Conceptual schemes, 380–82
Conceptual statements:
by alleged authorities, 395
defined, 381
evaluation of, 382
selected reading about, 468
truth of, 396
(*see also* Analytic-synthetic distinction)
Conclusions, distinguished from observation statements, 384–88
Concrete interpretation forms of definition, 228–43
conditional definition, 236–43
the 'etc.' definition, 232–33
examples and nonexamples, 234–36
the need for concrete interpretation, 229–34
operational definition, 237–43
'Concrete interpretation' interpreted, 233–34
Concreteness of terminology, 212, 228–43
Conditional chain, 37–40
defined, 38
Conditional definition, 236–43, 353
Conditional reasoning, 11–40
basic forms of, 14–16, 38
Conditionals:
and causal claims, 310–11
material implication interpretation, 59–62
in operational and conditional definition, 236–43
proving, 56–57
relationship to alternation, 45–46, 54–55
relationship to negajunction, 44, 60–62
symbolized, 25–28, 34, 36
Conjunction, 42–43
'Consequent' defined, 14 (*see also* Affirming the consequent; Denying the consequent)
Consistency with evidence, as a criterion of justification, 428, 436, 438–39, 454
Context, bearing of, 46, 98–100, 104–5, 107–8, 110–11, 112–13, 115–16, 184–86, 206–8, 220–21, 239–40, 257–60, 269–70, 271–73, 273–74, 274–76, 286–88, 288–91, 293–96, 318, 384–87, 394, 451, 460, 461
Contextual definition (*see* Equivalent-expression definition)
Contrapositive, 19–20
Controlled experiment, 439
Converse, 19
Copi, Irving, 119
Copleston, F. C., 399–401
'Correlation' and causal claims, 310, 444–45
Corroboration of observations statements, 388
Counter-examples, 167–70, 206–7, 284–86, 339–53, 378
conceivability of, 301–2, 339–50
defined, 167
Crane, Ronald S., 467
Crawshay-Williams, Rupert, 190, 470
Criteria, emphasis on, 11, 424, 448 (*see also* Criteria stated)
Criteria stated:
for assumptions:
logical, 400–401
psychological, 399, 436
for authorities, 393
for classification definition, 213–14
for conditional and operational definition, 236–38
for empirical generalizations, 426–27
for explanation:
descriptive, 256–57
reason-giving, 337
for explanatory conclusions, 436
for gap-filling explanations, 271
for observation statements, 388
for validity of deductions, 7, 16, 38, 43, 44, 46, 47, 68
Critical thinking, selected reading for study of, 472–73

Cronbach, Lee J., 252, 469
Crucial case, in gap-filling an explanation, 284–86, 363
Cues for different kinds of explanation, 257–60, 320, 326, 331–33
Cultural relativism (*see* Relativism, cultural)

Deductive model of explanation:
loosening of, 274–76, 311–12, 329–30
nondeductive justification explanation, 297, 335, 339, 364
presented, 261–63
selected reading about, 369–70
Deductive reasoning:
defined, 7
practical application steps:
conclusion, application of, 97–100, 104–5, 107–8, 112, 115–16
idealization of argument, 94–96, 103, 105–6, 109, 111, 113–14
presented, 7–119
selected reading about, 118–19
types of, 11–12, 100–102
used, 93–119, 168–69, 218, 236–43, 261–63, 267–76, 284–86, 324–25, 329–30, 336, 342, 344–52, 363, 364, 365, 366, 368, 369–70, 378–79, 398–401, 409–10, 436–39, 449, 451, 452, 453, 454–55
(*see also* Looseness of reasoning)
'Definiendum', defined, 191
'Definiens', defined, 191
Definition:
definition of, 124–26, 176–77
setting forth the meaning of a word, 125–26, 176–77
root meaning, to end or limit, 124, 177
and description, 125, 187–88 (*see also* Analytic-synthetic distinction; Analytic statements)
forms, 191–250
functions of, 125–90, 246–48, 250
interdependence with explanation and justification, 362, 456
as interpretive explanation, 255, 258
a loose concept, 125
looseness in, 206–8, 221–25
need for, 123–24
punctuation of, 203–6
selected reading about, 251–52
summary of form and function, 245–50
Definition by division (*see* Classification definition)
Definition *per genus et differentiam* (*see* Classification definition)
Denying the antecedent, 15, 27, 37
defined, 15
Denying the consequent, 15, 27, 449
defined, 15
Describing:
and defining, 125, 187–88 (*see also* Analytic-synthetic distinction; Analytic statements; Conceptual statements)
and observing (*see* Observation statements)
Descriptive explanation, 255–59
cues, 257–59
defined, 255–56
suggestions for, 256–57
Dewey, John, 178, 469
Dictionaries, 154–61
problems with, 155–61
circularity, 155–57
disagreement among dictionaries, 158–61
loss of nuances of meaning, 157–58
out-of-dateness, 158–61
recommended large dictionaries, 157
Dictionary of Anthropology, 158
A Dictionary of Contemporary American Usage, 157, 159–61, 162
Dictionary of Social Science, 158, 412
'Different', 183–86
Disinterest:
of alleged authority, 393
of observer and maker of observation statement, 388–89
Division, definition by (*see* Classification definition)
Donnellan, Keith, 371, 468
Double negation, 20
'Dough', controversy over meaning of, 245–50
Dray, William, 317, 369, 370
Dressel, Paul, 469

'Either-or' reasoning, 44–47 (*see also* Alternation)
Elam, Stanley, 470
Elementary cultural relativism (*see* Relativism, cultural)
Ellena, William J., 470

Emmet, E. R., 472
Empirical explanations, standard, 308–9, 337
Empirical relativism (*see* Relativism, cultural)
Empirical statements:
  agreement by impartial people—as an ideal, 380–81
  by alleged authorities, 395
  characteristics of, 380–81
  defined, 380
  inferring to (nondeductively), 423–45
  observation statements, 384–91
  relativism, empirical, 414
Ennis, Robert H., 141, 252, 267, 370, 466, 470, 472
Equivalence (in definition), 191–225, 460
  desirability of, 192–93
Equivalent-expression definition, 217–21
  categories, avoidance of, 221
  context, suggestion of, 220–21
  convenience, 219
  logical operators, in definition of, 218–19
  particles, in definition of, 218
  relational terms, in definition of, 218–19
Established usage, 153–54, 161–71
  '**an** established usage', 170–71
  determining that a usage is established, 170–71
  determining usage, 162–70
  and meaning, 153–54
  '**the** established usage', 170–71
'Etc.' definition, 282–83
Euler, Leonhard, 66
Euler circle system, 66–87, 168–69
  background, 66
  invalidity, use in exposure of, 70
  validity test, 68
Examples and nonexamples, 163–70, 207–8, 234–36, 353–55
  definition by, 234–36
Expertise:
  of alleged authorities, 393
  in causal claims, appraisal of, 442–44
  in counter-evidence, judging apparent bearing of, 438–39
  in deduction, the practical application of, 97–100, 107–8, 111, 112, 115, 116
  in explanatory conclusions, judging of, 439
Expertise (*cont.*)
  in inductive leap, making of, 432–34
  judging of in literary criticism, 451
'Explaining how' (*see* Descriptive explanation)
'Explaining the meaning of . . .' (*see* Definition; Interpretive explanation)
'Explaining why' (*see* Reason-giving explanation)
Explanation, 255–371 (*see* Descriptive explanation; Interpretive explanation; Reason-giving explanation)
  focus of, 269–70, 273–74
  frequency of in classroom, 362
  interdependence with definition and justification, 362, 456
  second order, 363
  selected reading about, 369–71
Explanatory conclusions:
  Bradley's interpretation of *Othello,* 452–56
  causal statements, 441–45 (*see also* Causality; Causal language)
  characterized, 423, 435
  fields in which they are inferred, 455
  justification of, 435–45, 449–56
  selected reading about, 467
  singular distinguished from general, 436
Explanatory power, as criterion of justification, 365–68, 436–45, 454
'Explicandum' defined, 261
'Explicans' defined, 261
Extent of the predicate class, 84–87

Fact-opinion distinction, 387–88
Facts:
  bearing on value judgments, 408–9
  (*see* Observation statements; Material inferences)
Faculties, possession of:
  by an alleged authority, 393–94
  by observer, 388–89
Faris, J. A., 119
Fearnside, W. Ward, 472
Feigl, Herbert, 369, 370, 371
Feldman, Martin, 470
Fisk, Milton, 119
Fitting in, as criterion of justification, 426, 428, 436–38, 454
Flew, Antony, 97, 240, 252, 329, 369

Focus of an explanation, 269–70, 273–74
'Follows necessarily' defined, 7
Ford, G. W., 470
Frank, Philipp, G., 382
'Freedom', 177–80
Frontier thesis of Frederick Jackson Turner, 95, 102–8
Functions of reason-giving explanation (*see* Reason-giving explanation)
Funk & Wagnall's New "Standard" Dictionary of the English Language, 157, 159–61

Gap-fillers, in explanation:
  alternate possibilities, 267–68, 349
  defined, 262
  (*see also* Reason-giving explanation, completion of)
Gardiner, Patrick, 317, 327, 369, 370
Gasking, Douglas, 441, 468
Geach, Peter, 205
Generalization, degree of in explanations, 274, 337, 339
Generalizations:
  distinguished from general statements, 424
  inferring to, 424–34
  prevalence, 425
  probabilistic, 424–26
  selected reading about, 467
  universal, 425–26
General semantics, 131
Generosity, in completing explanations, 271–73, 329, 344–45, 364
Genus et differentiam definition (*see* Classification definition)
'Good', 148–49, 180–83, 328–29, 405–8
Gottschalk, Louis, 465
Greater complexities, in sentence reasoning, 48–62
Greene, Theodore M., 470
Grice, H. P., 371, 468
Gross, Neal, 140

Hamlyn, D. W., 470
Hanson, Norwood Russell, 465
Hare, R. M., 466
Hart, H. L. A., 329, 468
Hawthorne studies, 443
Hayakawa, S. I., 131
Hempel, Carl, 152, 252, 317, 369, 370, 371, 382, 467
Henderson, Kenneth B., 470
Herodotus, 463–65
Hirsch, Eric D., Jr., 467
Hirst, Paul H., 470
Historical explanation:
  without empirical laws, 327
  generality of, 274, 317–18, 337
  reason-for-acting *vs.* causal and empirical, 326–27
  truisms as grounds for, 327
Holther, William B., 472
Honoré, A. M., 468
Hook, Sidney, 370
Hospers, John, 251, 369, 370, 468
Hullfish, H. Gordon, 470
Hume, David, 465, 468
Humpty Dumpty, 154
Hypothesis:
  criteria for, 436–41
  defined, 436
  specific and general distinguished, 436

Iago's character, 449–56
Identifying, 187
'If' (*see* Conditionals)
'If and only if', 35–37, 237–43
  in operational and conditional definition, 237–43
Implication (*see* Conditionals)
Implications, suggesting as way of probing, 284–86, 363, 378–79
Indirect proof, 55–56
Induction (*see* Material inferences)
Inductive leap, 427, 432–34
Instantiation, 89–90, 110, 114, 367
  definition, 90
Interpreting basic terms ('good', 'same', and 'different'), 183–86 (*see also* 'Good')
Interpretive explanation, 255–58
  cues, 258
  defined, 255
Italics, use of, to refer to concepts, 204–5

Justification, 93–116, 375–468
  aspect with which we are here concerned, 375–76
  assumption-finding claims, 396–401

Justification (*cont.*)
of empirical generalizations, 426–34
of explanatory conclusions, 435–45, 449–56
interdependence with definition and explanation, 362, 456
of observation statements, 384–90
of statements by alleged authorities, 392–96
and truth, 375–76
of value statements, 405–20
Justification function of explanation, 292–96, 297, 335, 364–68, 370

Kahl, Russell, 463
Kant, Immanuel, 330
Kaplan, Abraham, 467
Komisar, B. Paul, 141, 470

Lerner, Daniel, 465
Level of sophistication (*see* Sophistication, level of)
Levi, Edward H., 459
Lewis, C. I., 119
'Life Force' and testability, 342–53
Limiting, as type of defining, 186–87
Linsky, Leonard, 252, 371
'Literature', definition of, 358–69
Little, Winston W., 472
Logical aspects of teaching, selected reading about, 469–71
Logical operators:
definition of 'logical operators', 42
equivalent-expression definition for defining logical operators, 218–19
Loose concepts:
definition, 125
retaining looseness in definition, 223–25, 239–40
(*see also* Range definition)
Looseness in definition, 206–8 (*see also* Range definition; Conditional definition; Operational definition; 'Etc.' definition; Examples and nonexamples, definition by)
Looseness of criteria:
authorities, 392–96
for gap-filling explanations, 271–73
logical assumptions, 400–401
material inference, 426–27, 436
Looseness of criteria (*cont.*)
observation statements, 388–89
(*see also* Range definition; 'Etc.' definition; Conditional definition; Operational definition; Practical application of deductive logic; Loose concepts)
Looseness of reasoning:
in complete explanations, 274–76, 311–12, 329–30, 364
in handling inconsistent evidence, 438–39
in practical application of deduction, 93–100
Lyons, David, 94

McClellan, James E., 470
McEachern, Alexander W., 140
Macmillan, C. J. B., 470
'Manifest destiny', 341–42, 353
Mannheim, Karl, 376
Marriott, J. W., 472
Martin, Harold C., 470
Mason, Ward S., 140
Material implication, 44, 46, 51, 59–62, 119
selected reading about, 119
Material inferences, 423–45, 466–67
defined, 423
direction opposite from deduction, 452
to explanatory conclusions, 435–45
generalizing the evidence, 423, 424–34
and inductive inference, 423
selected reading about, 466–67
types of, 423
Maxwell, Grover, 370, 371
Mayhew, Lewis B., 469
Mead, Margaret, 417
Meaning:
'a meaning', 170–71
'a meaning **for him** (or **them**)', 170–71
and the biconditional, 238
and the definition of 'definition', 125–27
and established usage, 153, 170–71
meaninglessness, 340–44, 346, 349
relationships in operational and conditional definitions, 238
'**the** meaning', 170–71
vagueness, 376–79
(*see also* Definition)
Meehl, Paul E., 252

Melden, A. I., 466
Meux, Milton, 362, 370, 470, 471
Mill, John Stuart, 468
Moore, G. E., 149, 190, 252, 466
Moore, W. Edgar, 472
Multiple premises:
 in a complete reason-for-acting explanation, 324–25, 366
 conditional chain, 37–40
 Euler circle system, 81–82
 step-by-step organization of arguments, 49–51
Myrdal, Gunnar, 459

Nagel, Ernest, 119, 251, 465, 466, 467, 473
'Necessarily follows' defined, 7
Necessary conditions:
 causal, 32–33, 313–16
 in operational and conditional definitions, 237–39, 243
 truth conditions, 7, 30–32, 364–65, 400
 (*see also* Conditionals)
'Need', ambiguity of, 141
Negajunction, 43–44, 60–62
 affirming the negajunct, 43
 defined, 43
 denying the negajunct, 44
 relationship to conditional, 44, 60–62
Negation:
 in definition, 199–201
 double negation, 20
 Euler circle representation, 71–75
Newton's conceptual scheme, 380–81
Nonexamples and examples, 163–70, 207–8, 234–36, 353–55
'Not-both', 43–44 (*see also* Negajunction)

Obligation explanation, 328–34, 337, 339, 353–56, 363–65
 defined, 328
Obligation statements:
 indications of, 329
 value statements, merged with, 407–8
Observation, specification of in operational and conditional definition, 237–43
Observation statements:
 borderline between observation statements and conclusions, 384–88, 451–54
Observation statements (*cont.*)
 corroboration of, 388–89
 criteria for judging, 388–90
 direct *vs.* indirect, 384–87, 388
 indications of, 380
 and primary sources, 387
 selected reading about, 465
 (*see also* Observer)
Observer:
 access to the observed, 388–89
 condition of, 388–89
 disinterest of, 388–89
 preconceptions of, 388–89
 records, 388, 390
 reputation, 388–89
 sensory equipment, 388–89
 techniques, 388–89
 (*see also* Observation statements)
Ohmann, Richard M., 470
Omission of material (⁘) explained, 3–4
'Only if', 33–37, 237–43
 in operational and conditional definition, 237–43
Operational definition, 237–43, 353
 defined, 237
Oppenheim, Paul, 369
'Or' (*see* Alternation)
Order and intelligibility in nature, assumption of, 399–401
Order of premises, 18–19
Organ, Troy Wilson, 472
Orwell, George (*1984*), 358–68
'Other things being equal', 95, 109, 110, 410
The Oxford Book of Light Verse, 145, 146
Oxford English Dictionary, 157, 159–61
Oxford Universal English Dictionary, 124, 125

Palmer, John, 469
Parsimony:
 in definition, 208–11
  analytically-related extra material, 208–9, (defined) 210
  synthetically-related extra material, 209–11, (defined) 210
 (*see also* Simplicity; Testability)
Partial exclusion, 79–80 (*see also* 'Some')
Partial inclusion, 76–79 (*see also* 'Some')
Particles, definition of by use of equivalent-expression form, 218

Performative use of language, 382–83
Personal relativism, 416–17, 420
Persuasive definition (*see* Programmatic definition)
Peters, R. S., 470
Pike, Nelson, 330
Pitcher, George, 376
Possible implications, suggesting, 284–86, 363, 378–79
Post hoc fallacy, 441, 443
Potter, Simeon, 135
Practical application of deductive logic, 93–117 (*see also* Deductive reasoning, practical application steps; Deductive reasoning, used)
Pragmatic approach:
  conceptual statements, evaluation of, 381–82
  distinguishing observation statements from conclusions, 386–87
  same-different judgments, 183–86
  to stipulation, 397
  (*see also* Circularity; Context, bearing of; Looseness of reasoning; Practical application of deductive logic; Qualifications; Refinement, degree of, in subject matter; Sophistication, level of; Simplicity)
Predicate class, extent of, 84–87
Prediction generation:
  ability, and testability, 339, 351
  importance of, 351
Premises:
  defined, 8
  false premises, bearing of, 9–10, 99–100
  order of, 18–19
  putting an argument in shape, 22–25
  step-by-step organization of arguments, 49–51
  (*see also* Multiple premises)
Primary sources, 387
Probability, 425–26
'Probably', 97, 107, 108, 109, 111, 112, 115, 116, 239, 425–26, 444
Probing:
  for applicability, 353–55
  causal explanations, 318–20
  crucial cases in gap-filling explanations, 284–86, 363
  determining what the statement is, 376–79
Probing (*cont.*)
  explanations:
    for circularity, 288–91
    level of sophistication, 291
    truth, 283–86
  questions, 164–70, 195–97, 283–86, 288–91, 318–20, 323–27, 333
  reason-for-acting explanations, 323–27
  for statement meaning, 377–79
  for testability, 339–53
  value and obligation explanation, 333
  (*see also* 'Why?')
Programmatic definition, 177–80, 363–64, 459–61
  defined, 178, 179
  embodiment of a program, 178
  the value question, 179–80
'Propaganda':
  as a crucial term in a report, 125–27, 129–33, 136–40, 144, 153, 161–71, 192, 203, 303–4, 308, 376
  as defined by a variety of dictionaries, 158–61
Psychological aspects of logic in teaching, 1, 10–11, 229, 379
Pugno, Lawrence, 470
Punctuation conventions, 203–6
Putnam, Hilary, 371, 468
Putting an argument in shape, 22–25

Qualifications:
  in causal claims, 310, 444–45
  'ceteris paribus', 95, 109, 110, 410
  in explanatory conclusions, 438–39
  omission of at a given level of sophistication of subject matter, 287–88
  omission of in this book, 4
  in operational and conditional definition, 239–40
  'other things being equal', 95, 109, 110, 410
  in the practical application of deductive logic, 97, 107–8, 110, 112, 115, 116, 239–40, 274–76, 311–12, 329–30, 364, 438–39
  in prevalence generalizations, 425–26
  'under normal conditions', 110, 311–12
  (*see also* 'Probably')
Quine, Willard Van Orman, 119, 252, 371, 468
Quotes, use of, 203–4

Random sample, 427, 429–32
Range definition, 221–25, 364
Rationality, assumption of (in reason-for-acting explanations), 324–26
Reason-for-acting explanation, 322–27, 337, 344, 366
analytic gap-filler, 324–25
complexity of, 325
defined, 323
evaluation, 325–26
rationality, assumption of, 324–26
Reason-giving explanation:
completion of, 261–63, 267–77, 281, 283–86, 323–27, 363–67
causal explanation, special problem in, 318–20
loose deduction in, 274–76, 311–12, 329–30
proposing a gap-filler, 283–84
reason-for-acting explanation, special problem in, 323–27
reasons for not always doing so, 269–70
rules of thumb, 271–73
in sample classroom dialogue, 363–67
suggesting an implication of a gap-filler, 284–86
(*see also* Deductive model of explanation)
cues, 259–60, 320, 326, 331–33, 337
evaluation of:
function and type, 263–64, 292–97, 300–337
noncircularity, 263–64, 288–91, 306–7, 309, 319, 325, 330, 337
reason-for-acting explanation, special problem with, 323–27
sophistication, level of, 263–64, 286–88, 291, 307, 309, 319, 325, 330, 337
testability/applicability, 263–64, 309, 319, 325–26, 331, 337, 339–56
truth, 263–64, 281–86, 307–8, 309, 319, 325, 330, 337
functions:
accounting for and justifying, 292–96, 297, 337, 364–68, 370
of various types, 337
selected reading about, 369–71
subjunctive, use of in withholding complete endorsement, 282–83, 368
Reason-giving explanation (*cont.*)
tabulated and summarized, 337
types, 296–97, 300–337
listed, 304
tabulated and summarized, 337
Reasons:
need for securing, 384, 408
'**the** reason' distinguished from '**his** reason', 326
Records of observations, 388, 390
Refinement, degree of, in subject matter, 287–88
Relational terms, definition of by use of equivalent-expression form, 218–19
Relativism (*see* Relativism, cultural; Relativism, personal; Sociology of knowledge)
Relativism, cultural, 158, 412–16, 417–19
and 'absolutism', 417–19
as defined by two different dictionaries, 158
elementary type, 412–14
defined, 412
objections to, 413
empirical relativism:
defined, 414
relevance to other types of relativism, 414
sophisticated relativism:
defined, 414–15
objections to, 415–16
Relativism, personal, 416–17, 420
Reported definition, 153–73
advantages, 172
and conceptual statement, 381
definition, 153
disadvantages, 172–73
and established usage, 153–54
(*see also* Established usage; Meaning; Dictionaries)
Reporting usage, 153–75 (*see* Reported definition)
Reputation:
of alleged authority, 393
of observer, 388–89
Responsibility, personal:
inductive leap, 423
value judgments, 419–20
Retrodiction, 98, 104, 105, 108, 342
defined, 98

Richards, I. A., 470
Robinson, Richard, 145, 151, 152, 251
'Role', ambiguity of, 140
Romantic, 144, 147–48, 172, 224
Ross, W. D., 4, 330, 407, 413, 417
Rudner, Richard, 467
'Rural':
  ambiguity, 145
  defined:
    by Census Bureau, 142
    by *Webster's*, 142
  negation in definition of, 200
Russell, Bertrand, 119, 399–401, 468
Russell, L. J., 119
Ryle, Gilbert, 252

Salmon, Wesley, 118, 467, 473
'Same', 183–86
Sampling, 427–32
Sanders, Norris, 470
Scheffler, Israel, 178, 190, 251, 370
'Scientific method', definition of, 221–24
Scriven, Michael, 317, 327, 370
Second order explanation, 363
Seifman, Eli, 470
Sellars, Wilfred, 369
Sentence reasoning, 13–63, 87–90
  combined with class reasoning, 87–90
  contrasted with class reasoning, 11–12
Shades of definition, 176–88 (*see also* Programmatic definition; Interpreting basic terms; Limiting; Identifying; Describing)
Shakespeare's *Othello,* 449–55
Shanner, William J., 472
Shaw, George B., 342–53, 357
Simplicity:
  of Bradley's hypothesis, 455
  in completing explanations, 271–73, 364
  as a criterion for explanatory hypotheses, 436, 439–41
  as a criterion for implicit assumptions, 400–401
Smiley, T. J., 119
Smith, B. Othanel, 141, 267, 362, 370, 469, 470, 471
Smith, Philip G., 470
Sociology of knowledge, 376
'Some', 76–80
  ambiguity of, 76
'Some' (*cont.*)
  'at least some', 77–78
  partial inclusion and exclusion, 76–80
  'some, but not all', 78–79
Sophistication, level of, 4, 206–7, 263–64, 286–88, 291, 307, 309, 319, 325, 330, 337
  in this book, 4
Spencer, Herbert, 178
Starting points in arguments:
  assumptions, 396–401
  authorities, statements by, 392–96
  observation statements, 384–90
  (*see also* Premises)
Statement:
  as assertion, 301, 375–83
  determining what it actually is, 376–83
  types of, 379–83
    analytic, 209–11, 300–304
    causal, 304, 441–45
    conceptual, 209–11, 381–82
    empirical, 304, 380–81, 424
      universal, prevalence, and probabilistic generalization, 424
    general *vs.* singular, 274, 304, 315, 316–20, 325, 327, 330, 346, 348, 349, 380, 409–11, 424, 436, 442–44
    obligation, 304
    observation, 384–90
    synthetic, 209–11, 300–304
    theoretical, 380–81
    value, 304, 379–80, 405–6, 407–8
Stebbing, L. Susan, 473
Step-by-step organization of arguments, 49–51
Stevenson, C. L., 178, 190, 251, 466
Stipulated definition, 129–52, 381
  in conceptual statement, 381
  dangers and abuses of stipulation, 144–50
    inflexibility of people, 149
    invitation to ambiguity, 145
    loss of basic concepts, 148–49
    misleading one's audience, 145–47
    pretentiousness, 149–50
    verbiage, 149–50
  nature of stipulation, 129–31
    ambiguity, danger of, 131
    arbitrariness, a degree of, 130
    lack of truth and falsity, 132

Stipulated definition (*cont.*)
supposing a stipulation, 132–33
uses of stipulative definition, 140–44
ambiguity, elimination of, 140–41
concepts, introduction of, 143–44
meaning, avoiding fruitless arguments about, 144
meaning shifts in discussions, avoiding, 144
shorthand, 144
vagueness, reduction of, 141–43
Stratified sample, 427, 430–31
Strawson, P. F., 60, 119, 252, 301, 371, 466, 468
Structure of subject matter:
abstractness of subject matter, 287
assumptions, 396–401
basic terms, definition of:
'cause' (*see* Causal language)
'good', 'same', and 'different', 180–86
programmatic definition, 177–80
context, dependence on (*see* Context)
definition, 1, 123–250
concrete interpretation forms:
conditional and operational definition, 236–43
examples and nonexamples, 234–36
equivalence forms, 168–69, 191–225
classification definition, rules for, 197–209
equivalent-expression definition, 217–21
range definition, 221–25
form and function chart, 250
explanation, 1, 255–371
descriptive, 255–57, 258–59
interpretive (*see* Definition)
reason-giving, 259–371 (*see* Reason-giving explanation)
function and type, 292–97, 300–337, 361–69
(*see also* Deductive model of explanation)
summary chart, 337
interrelatedness of different aspects of structure, 361–69, 448–61
justification, 1, 7–116, 375–468
alleged authorities, statements by, 392–96
empirical generalizations, 426–34

Structure of subject matter (*cont.*)
explanatory conclusions, 435–45, 449–56
observation statements, 388–90
value statements and judgments, 405–20
level of sophistication (*see* Sophistication, level of)
literary criticism, structure of, an example of, 449–56
looseness *vs.* precision (*see* Loose concepts; Looseness of criteria; Looseness of reasoning)
models, 257
relationships between levels:
concrete interpretation, 228–34
conditional and operational definition, 236–43
empirical generalization and its evidence, 426–34
examples and nonexamples, 163–70, 207–8, 234–36, 353–55
explanatory hypothesis and its evidence, 435–45, 449–56
reason-giving explanation, 259–371
value judgments and consequences, 410–11
value judgments and general principles, 409–11
(*see also* Loose concepts; Looseness of criteria; Looseness of reasoning; Qualifications)
testability/applicability, 339–55
types of subject matter:
abstract, 287
analytic, 209–11, 300–304
causal, 304, 441–45
conceptual, 209–11, 381–82
empirical, 304, 380–81, 424
universal, prevalence, and probabilistic generalizations, 424
general *vs.* singular, 274, 304, 315, 316–20, 325, 327, 330, 346, 348, 349, 380, 409–11, 424, 436, 442–44
obligation statements, 304
observation statements, 384–90
synthetic, 209–11, 300–304
theoretical statements, 380–81
value statements, 304, 379–80, 405–6, 407–8

Subjunctive, in withholding complete endorsement of explanation, 282–83, 368
Substitutability (provided by some definitions), 192–93
Sufficient conditions, 30–33, 237–39, 313–16
  causal, 32–33, 313–16
  in operational and conditional definitions, 237–39
  truth conditions, 30–32 (*see also* Conditionals)
Sumner, William Graham, 357, 412, 466
Supply and demand, practical application of law of, 95, 108–11
Symbolization, 25–28, 36, 46, 52, 55, 79, 315
Synonym definition form, 193–94
'Synthetic statement' defined, 302
Systematic sample, 427, 430

Taylor, George Rogers, 471
Testability, 263–64, 309, 319, 325–26, 337, 339–53, 355
  'conceptual testability' defined, 355
  counter-examples:
    conceivability of, 301–2, 339–50
    use of, 350–53
  defined, 339–40
  practical, as distinguished from conceptual, 340
  selected reading about, 370–71
  strategy, 343–53
Theoretical statements:
  and frontier-of-knowledge, 381
  indications of, 380–81
Thorndike-Barnhart Comprehensive Desk Dictionary, 159–61
Tolstoy, Leo, 381
Toulmin, S., 97, 330, 467
Truth:
  alleged relativity of, 376
  in conceptual statements, 382, 396
  "for the most part" (of value statements), 407, 410
  and justification, 375–76
  necessary and sufficient conditions, 30–33, 364–65, 400 (*see also* Conditionals)
  tables, 61
  and validity, 9–10, 99–100, 423
Truth (*cont.*)
  of value statements, 382fn.
Turner, Frederick Jackson, 95, 102–8
Twain, Mark (*The Adventures of Huckleberry Finn*), 354–55, 359, 363

Unbiased sample, 427–32
'Under normal conditions', 110, 311–12
  in general causal claims, 311–12
Uniformity of nature, assumption of, 399–401
Universe of discourse:
  defined, 72–73
  negative and positive transformations, use in, 72–75
Urmson, J. O., 97, 252
Use-reference distinction, 203–4

Vagueness, 98, 110, 115, 376–79, 459–60
  of 'equal protection of the law', 459–60
  as problem in determining what is asserted, 376–79
  (*see also* Ambiguity; Testability; Range definition; Loose concepts)
Validity:
  defined (technical sense), 8
  Euler circle test, 68
  loosening of, 96, 104, 106–7, 110, 112, 114–15
  ordinary and technical sense, 8, 423
  and truth, 9–10, 99–100
Value explanation, 328–34, 337, 339, 353–56, 363–65
  defined, 328
  (*see also* Value judgments; Value statements)
Value judgments, 179–80, 328–34, 363–65, 409–11, 466
  consequences, examination of, 410–11
  embodied in a judicial decision, 459–61
  facts, bearing of, 408–9
  general principles, bearing of, 409–10, 411
  justification of, 405–20, 460
  selected reading about, 466
  (*see also* Value statements)
Value statements:
  by alleged cognitive authorities, 395, 419

Value statements (*cont.*)
and commitment to action, 407
controversy about, 407
defined, 379–80
indications of, 329, 379–80, 405–8
justification of, 405–20, 460
and obligation statements, 407–8
principles as rules of thumb, 410
truth of, 382fn., 406–7
(*see also* Value judgments)
Variety of evidence, as a criterion of justification, 426, 428–34, 436–37

Waismann, Friedrich, 240, 252, 329
Warner, Bruce, 449
Warner, W. Lloyd, 431
Warren, Austin, 364, 381, 395, 401
Webster's Collegiate Dictionary, 124
Webster's New Collegiate Dictionary, 135, 142, 159–61, 207
Webster's Seventh New Collegiate Dictionary, 159–61
Webster's Third New International Dictionary, 157, 159–61
Wellek, René, 364, 381, 395, 401
Westermarck, Edward, 466
White, Morton, 371
Whitehead, Alfred North, 119
Whorf, Benjamin Lee, 382, 468
'Why?':
as a cue for reason-giving explanation, 259–60, 337
in determining the meaning of a statement, 378–79
examples and nonexamples, used together with, 164–70
frequency of, 362
in securing reasons for a statement, 384
as a thought-provoker, 362
(*see* Reason-giving explanation)
Wigmore, John Henry, 390, 465, 466
Will, Frederick L., 467
Wilson, W. Harold, 472
Wright, G. H. von, 101, 119